Data Science in Psychology

Nataša Kovač • Marko Simeunović •
Hojjatollah Farahani
Editors

Data Science in Psychology

Using Python in Psychological Research

Springer

Editors

Nataša Kovač
University of Donja Gorica
Podgorica, Montenegro

Marko Simeunović
University of Donja Gorica
Podgorica, Montenegro

Hojjatollah Farahani
Tarbiat Modares University
Tehran, Iran

ISBN 978-3-032-18311-8 ISBN 978-3-032-18312-5 (eBook)
https://doi.org/10.1007/978-3-032-18312-5

This Springer imprint is published by the registered company Springer Nature Switzerland AG
The registered company address is: Gewerbestrasse 11, 6330 Cham, Switzerland

Preface

Over the last decade, psychology has experienced a profound transformation driven by the growing influence of data science and computational methods. Research questions that once relied solely on traditional statistics and experimental datasets now demand large-scale data integration, advanced modeling, and automation. This book, *Data Science in Psychology: Using Python in Psychological Research*, has been written in response to that transformation.

Psychological science, at its core, seeks to understand the complexities of human thought, emotion, and behavior through evidence-based reasoning. Data are central to this pursuit, from careful collection and preprocessing to rigorous statistical and computational analysis. Yet, as research questions become more complex, the tools and methods used by psychologists must also evolve. Python, with its readability, open-source nature, and extensive libraries for scientific computing, provides an ideal platform for bridging traditional psychological methods with the capabilities of modern data science.

This book introduces readers to the use of Python as a powerful analytical language for psychological research. It is designed for students, researchers, and educators who wish to integrate data-driven techniques into their scientific practice without requiring an advanced mathematical background. The focus is on conceptual understanding, practical coding skills, and direct application to real-world psychological data.

The content unfolds through four major parts that mirror the natural process of research, from understanding foundations to applying advanced methods and interpreting results. The opening chapters establish the context, introducing Python programming in relation to psychological science and tracing the evolution of the discipline into a data-rich field. The narrative then moves to the crucial preparatory phase, discussing methods of data collection, cleaning, and preparation, as essential steps to ensure that datasets are valid, consistent, and ready for meaningful analysis. The central section of the book, and by far the most comprehensive, explores a range of statistical and computational techniques for testing hypotheses and modeling complex psychological phenomena. It brings together classical inferential methods with modern data science approaches such as Bayesian modeling, shrinkage regression, clustering, and machine learning algorithms, including Support Vector Machines and neural networks. Finally, the concluding chapters focus on the interpretation, visualization, and communication of results, emphasizing the importance of clarity, reproducibility, and critical reflection in psychological reporting.

Throughout the book, each chapter provides Python examples, code explanations, and case studies from applied psychology. Topics include classical and contemporary techniques such as Confirmatory Factor Analysis, Item Response Theory, Latent Class and Profile Analysis, Bayesian inference, clustering, shrinkage regression, Support Vector Machines, and deep learning models. Additional chapters explore innovative approaches like Bootstrap Exploratory Graph Analysis, simulations, and metaheuristics, demonstrating how these methods can uncover hidden structures in psychological data.

This book also emphasizes the interpretive and ethical dimensions of data science in psychology, understanding not only how to compute results but also how to make meaningful and responsible inferences from them.

Our collective experience as authors, spanning psychology, mathematics, computer science, and engineering, has shown that the most significant progress in psychological research often emerges at the intersection of disciplines. The dialogue between theory and computation, between statistical reasoning and algorithmic modeling, has become indispensable for understanding complex human behavior. By combining diverse expertise, we have witnessed how mathematical precision can illuminate psychological constructs, how algorithms can reveal hidden behavioral patterns, and how technological innovation can enhance the rigor and reproducibility of psychological inquiry.

This book is not only a guide to methods but also a reflection of a shared vision, one that values interdisciplinary thinking as a foundation of modern science. We believe that the integration of data science and psychology opens new horizons for discovery, empowering researchers to ask more nuanced questions and to uncover deeper layers of meaning within data. It is our hope that readers will approach the techniques presented here not merely as computational tools, but as a mindset, a way of thinking that embraces curiosity, analytical integrity, and creativity. By doing so, they join a growing community of scholars who view data not just as numbers but as narratives of the human mind waiting to be understood.

Podgorica, Montenegro — Nataša Kovač
Podgorica, Montenegro — Marko Simeunović
Tehran, Iran — Hojjatollah Farahani
Autumn, 2025

Contents

Part I Python and Psychological Sciences Background

Introduction to Python Programming 3
Nataša Kovač, Kruna Ratković, Marko Simeunović, Lisa-Christina Winter Done, Stevan Kordić, and Hojjatollah Farahani

Introduction to Psychological Sciences 33
Nataša Kovač, Hojjatollah Farahani, Peter Watson, Lisa-Christina Winter Done, and Kruna Ratković

Datasets for Psychological Sciences 61
Nataša Kovač, Lisa-Christina Winter Done, Kruna Ratković, Hojjatollah Farahani, and Peter Watson

Part II Data Preparation

Collecting the Data in Psychological Sciences 87
Nataša Kovač, Marija Blagojević, Peter Watson, Hojjatollah Farahani, Lisa-Christina Winter Done, and Kruna Ratković

Datasets Preparation 103
Nataša Kovač, Marija Blagojević, Kruna Ratković, Marko Simeunović, Lisa-Christina Winter Done, Zhiyong Johnny Zhang, Hojjatollah Farahani, and Peter Watson

Data Preprocessing 127
Nataša Kovač, Kruna Ratković, Marko Simeunović, Lisa-Christina Winter Done, Peter Watson, Hojjatollah Farahani, and Zhiyong Johnny Zhang

Part III Data Processing

The Difference Between Data Science, Statistics, Machine Learning, and Artificial Intelligence 153
Nataša Kovač, Marko Simeunović, Kruna Ratković, Marija Blagojević, Ulfeta Marovac, Hojjatollah Farahani, and Lisa-Christina Winter Done

Data Modelling 173
Nataša Kovač, Kruna Ratković, Marko Simeunović, Marija Blagojević, Ulfeta Marovac, and Hojjatollah Farahani

Confirmatory Factor Analysis 203
Nataša Kovač, Marija Blagojevič, Kruna Ratković, Peter Watson, Zhiyong Johnny Zhang, and Hojjatollah Farahani

Graded Item Response Theory: Developing and Validating a Psychological Scale 227
Nataša Kovač, Marija Blagojević, Kruna Ratković, Peter Watson, and Hojjatollah Farahani

Bootstrap Exploratory Graph Analysis 247
Nataša Kovač, Kruna Ratković, Marko Simeunović, and Hojjatollah Farahani

Clustering Methods 269
Nataša Kovač, Kruna Ratković, Marko Simeunović, Hojjatollah Farahani, and Liang Zhao

Latent Class Analysis and Latent Profile Analysis 295
Nataša Kovač, Marija Blagojević, Kruna Ratković, Hojjatollah Farahani, and Peter Watson

Time-Dependent Modelling in Psychological Data 323
Nataša Kovač, Marija Blagojević, Zhiyong Johnny Zhang, Kruna Ratković, Peter Watson, and Hojjatollah Farahani

Shrinkage Regression: Ridge Regression, LASSO, and Elastic Net Regression 351
Nataša Kovač, Kruna Ratković, Marko Simeunović, and Hojjatollah Farahani

Bayesian Data Analysis 371
Nataša Kovač, Kruna Ratković, Marko Simeunović, Ulfeta Marovac, Hojjatollah Farahani, Stevan Kordić, and Zhiyong Johnny Zhang

Support Vector Machine Algorithm 387
Nataša Kovač, Kruna Ratković, Marko Simeunović, Ulfeta Marovac, and Hojjatollah Farahani

Classification in Psychological Research 409
Nataša Kovač, Kruna Ratković, Marko Simeunović, Ulfeta Marovac, Hojjatollah Farahani, and Liang Zhao

Natural Language Processing and Psychological Sciences 447
Nataša Kovač, Kruna Ratković, Ulfeta Marovac, Hojjatollah Farahani, Marija Blagojević, and Peter Watson

Metaheuristics in Psychological Data Analysis 473
Nataša Kovač, Kruna Ratković, Hojjatollah Farahani, and Stevan Kordić

Simulations in Psychological Research 503
Nataša Kovač, Kruna Ratković, Hojjatollah Farahani, Stevan Kordić, and Peter Watson

Part IV Interpretation of Results

Interpreting Statistical Results 529
Nataša Kovač, Kruna Ratković, Marko Simeunović, Hojjatollah Farahani, Stevan Kordić, Peter Watson, and Zhiyong Johnny Zhang

Advanced Data Interpretation Strategies 547
Nataša Kovač, Kruna Ratković, Marko Simeunović, Hojjatollah Farahani, Stevan Kordić, and Peter Watson

Reporting and Discussing Findings 573
Nataša Kovač, Kruna Ratković, Marko Simeunović, Hojjatollah Farahani, and Peter Watson

Index 599

Contributors

Nataša Kovač Faculty of Applied Sciences, University of Donja Gorica, Podgorica, Montenegro

Marko Simeunović Faculty of Applied Sciences, University of Donja Gorica, Podgorica, Montenegro

Hojjatollah Farahani Department of Psychology, Faculty of Humanities, Tarbiat Modares University, Tehran, Iran

Kruna Ratković Faculty of Applied Sciences, University of Donja Gorica, Podgorica, Montenegro

Marija Blagojević Faculty of Technical Sciences, University of Kragujevac, Čačak, Serbia

Lisa-Christina Winter Done OpenPsai (Two Kermis), Zug, Switzerland

Stevan Kordić Faculty of Maritime Studies, University of Montenegro, Kotor, Dobrota, Montenegro

Ulfeta Marovac Department of Technical and Technological Sciences, State University in Novi Pazar, Novi Pazar, Serbia

Peter Watson MRC Cognition and Brain Sciences Unit, University of Cambridge, Cambridge, UK

Zhiyong Johnny Zhang Department of Psychology, University of Notre Dame, Notre Dame, IN, USA

Liang Zhao Faculty of Philosophy, Science and Letters at Ribeirão Preto, University of São Paulo, Ribeirão Preto - SP, Brazil

Part I
Python and Psychological Sciences Background

The opening part of this book introduces the conceptual and technical foundations upon which the rest of the volume is built. It brings together two worlds that increasingly overlap—the rigorous study of human behavior and the computational power of modern programming. By examining both the evolution of psychological science and the rise of Python as a leading language for data analysis, this section establishes the rationale for integrating data science into psychological research.

Readers are first introduced to the basic principles of Python programming and its advantages for scientific computation, emphasizing simplicity, flexibility, and reproducibility. The discussion then turns to the nature of psychological inquiry—its history, methodologies, and the growing influence of data-driven perspectives. Finally, the section highlights the role of datasets in shaping modern research, explaining how data collection, validation, and representation form the starting point for any meaningful analysis.

Together, these chapters lay the groundwork for the rest of the book: They equip readers with the essential tools, both conceptual and practical, to understand how computational methods can enrich psychological exploration and make evidence-based research more transparent, replicable, and impactful.

Introduction to Python Programming

Nataša Kovač, Kruna Ratković, Marko Simeunović, Lisa-Christina Winter Done, Stevan Kordić, and Hojjatollah Farahani

1 Brief History of Python

Python is one of the most widely used programming languages today, known for its simplicity, readability, and versatility. The language was first conceptualised in the late 1980s and officially introduced in 1991 by Guido van Rossum at the Centrum Wiskunde & Informatica in the Netherlands [1]. Inspired by the ABC programming language [2], van Rossum sought to create a language that was both powerful and easy to learn, reducing the complexity associated with many existing programming languages of the time.

Python's design philosophy focuses on readability and simplicity, making it accessible to both beginners and experienced developers. A core feature of the language is its use of indentation to define code blocks, which enforces a clear and uniform structure. Guido van Rossum adopted this approach deliberately to improve clarity and to steer programmers away from the syntactic complexity often found in languages like C and Perl [3].

The development of Python is summarised in Table 1. From its inception, the language was shaped by multiple programming paradigms, supporting procedural, object-oriented, and functional approaches. The first official public release, Python

N. Kovač · K. Ratković · M. Simeunović (✉)
Faculty of Applied Sciences, University of Donja Gorica, Podgorica, Montenegro
e-mail: natasa.kovac@udg.edu.me; kruna.ratkovic@udg.edu.me; marko.simeunovic@udg.edu.me

L.-C. W. Done
OpenPsai (Two Kermis), Zug, Switzerland

S. Kordić
Faculty of Maritime Studies, University of Montenegro, Dobrota, Montenegro

H. Farahani
Department of Psychology, Faculty of Humanities, Tarbiat Modares University, Tehran, Iran

N. Kovač et al. (eds.), *Data Science in Psychology*,
https://doi.org/10.1007/978-3-032-18312-5_1

Table 1 Python development timeline

Year	Version	Main features and contextual significance
1991	Python 0.9	First public release. Included fundamental programming constructs such as classes, functions, exception handling, and built-in data types (strings, lists, dictionaries). Established Python's guiding principles of readability and simplicity
1994	Python 1.0	Expanded language expressiveness with functional programming tools (`lambda`, `map`, `filter`, `reduce`). Signified Python's shift from a research project to a versatile scripting language, gaining attention in both academia and industry
2000	Python 2.0	Introduced list comprehensions, reference counting with cycle-detecting garbage collection, and early Unicode support, enhancing usability for international applications. The Python Software Foundation (PSF) was founded to ensure independent governance and long-term sustainability
2008	Python 3.0	Represented a major redesign focused on removing inconsistencies and legacy constructs. Key changes included redefining `print` as a function, adopting Unicode as the default text representation, and distinguishing true division (/) from floor division (//). Although not backward compatible, this release modernised the language for future growth
2020	–	Official end of Python 2 support after two decades of use. Marked the completion of the community's transition to Python 3, unifying development efforts and standardising the ecosystem
2023	Python 3.11	Added structural pattern matching (`match/case`) and dictionary merge operators (|, |=), alongside significant performance optimisations (up to 60% faster). Demonstrated Python's evolution towards both expressiveness and computational efficiency, ensuring continued relevance in fields such as data science, AI, and Web development

1.0, appeared in January 1994 and introduced essential features such as exception handling, functions, and modular programming. This release established the groundwork for Python's evolution into one of the most versatile and influential programming languages in contemporary computing.

During the late 1990s and early 2000s, Python underwent significant improvements, leading to the release of Python 2.0 in 2000. This version introduced key enhancements such as list comprehensions and garbage collection based on reference counting. One of the challenges of Python 2.x was its long-term compatibility issues, as certain design choices created obstacles for future upgrades. To address these concerns, the Python Software Foundation (PSF) announced Python 3.0 in 2008, marking a major shift in the language's development.

Python 3.0 introduced several important changes aimed at improving consistency and eliminating legacy design flaws. Key modifications included improved Unicode support, changes in integer division, and the standardisation of print statements as functions [4]. While Python 3 provided a more streamlined experience, the transition from Python 2 to Python 3 was slow due to backward compatibility issues, leading to the continued use of Python 2.x in many projects for over a decade. Eventually, official support for Python 2 was discontinued on January 1, 2020 [5].

One of the reasons behind Python's widespread adoption is its strong community support and extensive ecosystem of libraries. Over the years, Python has evolved from a general-purpose programming language into a dominant force in areas such as data science, artificial intelligence, web development, and automation. The introduction of libraries like `NumPy` [6], `pandas` [7], and `TensorFlow` [8] has positioned Python as a leading language in scientific computing and machine learning. Python's simplicity and vast standard library have made it a preferred choice for scripting and automation tasks across various industries.

The widespread adoption of Python has been reinforced by its close alignment with contemporary software engineering practices. Its comprehensive support for frameworks such as Django and Flask has established the language as a cornerstone of modern Web development, while its seamless compatibility with cloud computing environments has strengthened its position in enterprise-level applications [9]. In addition, Python's open source model, coupled with an active and collaborative developer community, ensures continued refinement and innovation, allowing the language to remain adaptable to rapidly evolving technological landscapes.

At present, Python continues to advance through successive releases that prioritise both performance and usability. Notable enhancements in versions 3.9 and 3.10 include more efficient dictionary operations, the introduction of structural pattern matching, and targeted performance optimisations [10]. The path of Python development is systematically shaped by Python Enhancement Proposals (PEPs), which provide a formal mechanism through which the global developer community can participate in defining and directing the future evolution of the language [11].

As one of the most versatile and widely adopted programming languages, Python has firmly established itself as an essential tool for software development, research, and automation. Its ease of use, combined with a robust ecosystem, ensures that Python will remain a dominant force in programming for years to come.

2 Python vs Other Programming Languages

When undertaking psychological research, choosing the appropriate programming language is crucial, given the direct impact this choice has on productivity, ease of data manipulation, and analysis. Among various programming languages such as R, MATLAB, Java, and C++, Python emerges as a prominent choice due to several distinct characteristics that specifically cater to the requirements of psychological research.

Python stands out due to its simplicity and readability, crucial for researchers who may not have a formal background in computer science [3]. Unlike languages like Java and C++, which require a deeper understanding of syntax and memory management, Python's syntax closely resembles English, facilitating a gentle learning curve. This ease of use significantly lowers the barrier to entry, enabling psychologists to swiftly transition from learning basics to performing complex analyses and visualisations [6].

Another pivotal advantage of Python is its robust ecosystem, enriched by a wealth of libraries tailored specifically for data science, statistical analysis, and machine learning. Libraries such as `NumPy`, `pandas`, and `scikit-learn` provide ready-to-use functions for sophisticated data manipulation and analysis, functionalities that are fundamental in psychological studies involving large datasets [7]. In contrast, while MATLAB and R also boast substantial data analysis capabilities, Python's general-purpose nature allows researchers to seamlessly integrate data analysis with other computational tasks such as Web scraping, text processing, or automating workflows, tasks that are cumbersome or less intuitive in specialised languages.

Python offers superior flexibility through extensive compatibility and interoperability. Python can easily interface with other languages such as C, Java, and R, a feature particularly advantageous in interdisciplinary psychological research. For instance, integrating statistical methods initially developed in R into Python workflows is feasible and straightforward, enhancing collaborative research efforts where multiple languages and tools are used simultaneously [12].

One of Python's most distinguishing strengths in psychological sciences is its powerful visualisation capabilities. Visualisation libraries such as `Matplotlib` and `Seaborn` allow researchers not only to efficiently visualise statistical relationships and patterns but also to generate publication-quality figures effortlessly [13, 14]. These visualisation tools exceed those commonly available in Java or C++, where graphical capabilities typically require extensive additional programming effort and third-party libraries.

Python's open-source nature, coupled with a vibrant and supportive community, also positions it favourably among researchers. The continuous development and maintenance by an active community guarantee regular updates and support, contrasting sharply with MATLAB, a proprietary platform with substantial licensing costs. Accessibility due to Python's free distribution significantly broadens its appeal among educational institutions and individual researchers, especially in settings with limited resources [15].

The scalability and efficiency of Python further set it apart from other programming languages used in psychological research. While languages like Java and C++ are well regarded for their speed and computational efficiency, they typically demand more intricate code structures and extensive debugging. Python balances performance with simplicity effectively, particularly with implementations such as PyPy or Cython that optimise computationally intensive tasks without significant overhead or complexity [16].

From an employability perspective, Python consistently ranks as one of the most desirable and widely used languages across diverse industries, including academia, industry research, and the private sector [17]. Its versatility ensures that knowledge gained through psychological research can be directly transferable to other sectors, enhancing career prospects for students and professionals alike.

Table 2 Comparative analysis of Python and other programming languages

Properties	Python	R	MATLAB	Java	C++
Easy to learn	✓	✓	✓	✗	✗
Free and open source	✓	✓	✗	✓	✓
Extensive libraries for data analysis	✓	✓	✓	✗	✗
Strong data visualisation capabilities	✓	✓	✓	✗	✗
Widely used in academia	✓	✓	✓	✓	✓
Great community support	✓	✓	✓	✓	✓
Versatility (general-purpose)	✓	✗	✗	✓	✓
Simple syntax	✓	✓	✗	✗	✗
Integration capability	✓	✓	✓	✓	✗
Scalability and efficiency	✓	✗	✗	✓	✓
Strong AI and ML frameworks	✓	✓	✓	✗	✗
Popularity and employability	✓	✓	✓	✓	✓

Considering these critical factors, a comparative summary highlighting Python's relative strengths across several criteria is provided in Table 2. Table 2 illustrates Python's advantages in various aspects relevant to psychological research. Its intuitive syntax, extensive libraries for data analysis [18], strong visualisation tools, and powerful machine learning frameworks contribute significantly to its popularity among researchers, making Python an ideal choice compared to other programming languages such as R, MATLAB, Java, and C++.

Despite Python's evident advantages, it is essential to acknowledge that other programming languages also have unique strengths. R, for example, remains exceptionally popular in statistical communities for its sophisticated statistical modelling capabilities and its extensive library of statistical tools [19]. MATLAB also has an importance in certain subfields of psychology, such as neuroscience, due to the use of specialised toolboxes and the historically widespread use in experimental psychology [20]. Java's strength lies primarily in applications that require platform-independent solutions, such as large-scale psychological experiments conducted over the Internet or complex cognitive simulations [21].

3 Setting Up a Development Environment

Establishing a development environment is the first step for psychologists who want to integrate Python programming into their research workflow. This process involves the following steps:

1. Setting up Python environment
2. Selecting appropriate Integrated Development Environment (tool for coding)
3. Learning where to access resources for troubleshooting and expanding one's knowledge

A properly configured environment ensures smooth and efficient workflows, allowing researchers to focus on exploring psychological phenomena rather than struggling with technical barriers.

A Python environment is defined as a computational setup that comprises the Python interpreter, the necessary libraries, and the configuration of environment variables, system paths, and dependencies, all of which collectively ensure the successful execution of code. It can be broadly categorised into several types depending on its scope and purpose. *The system or global environment* refers to the default Python installation available across the operating system, but it often leads to dependency conflicts when multiple projects are maintained simultaneously [22]. To address this, *virtual environments* such as those created with `venv` or `virtualenv` provide lightweight, project-specific isolation of the interpreter and libraries, thereby ensuring reproducibility and consistency across projects [23]. *Conda environments*, offered through the Anaconda or Miniconda distributions, extend this concept by managing not only Python packages but also external dependencies such as compilers or non-Python libraries, which makes them especially valuable in scientific computing and data science workflows [24]. More recently, *containerised environments* using platforms such as Docker have gained prominence by encapsulating the interpreter, dependencies, and operating system components into portable units, enabling complete reproducibility and facilitating deployment across heterogeneous infrastructures [25].

Regardless of whether one works with the global installation or within a virtual environment, the installation of the Python interpreter constitutes the essential first step. The interpreter serves as the core component of the Python environment, as it executes code and provides access to the standard library. Virtual environments, in turn, are built upon this system-level installation by creating isolated workspaces that replicate the interpreter and manage project-specific dependencies. Consequently, without the prior installation of Python, neither the global environment nor any form of virtual environment can be properly configured or utilised.

The Python interpreter is open-source software, which implies that it can be freely downloaded and utilised without cost. The official Python website (https://www.python.org/) provides installation binaries for multiple operating systems, including Windows, macOS, Linux, and Android, accompanied by comprehensive installation guides. The installation process itself is user-friendly and is carried out through an installation wizard, as illustrated in Fig. 1. To facilitate smoother execution of Python scripts from the command line (using CMD on Windows or Terminal on macOS/Linux), it is advisable to add the Python interpreter to the system PATH variable. This can be accomplished automatically during the installation process by selecting the option **Add Python.exe to PATH** (Fig. 1), or it may be configured manually after the installation is complete.

For handling packages in Python, the `pip` (Python Package Installer) manager constitutes the standard mechanism for installing, updating, and managing third-party libraries. By default, `pip` is bundled with the official Python installation from version 3.4 onwards, thereby granting users immediate access to the Python Package

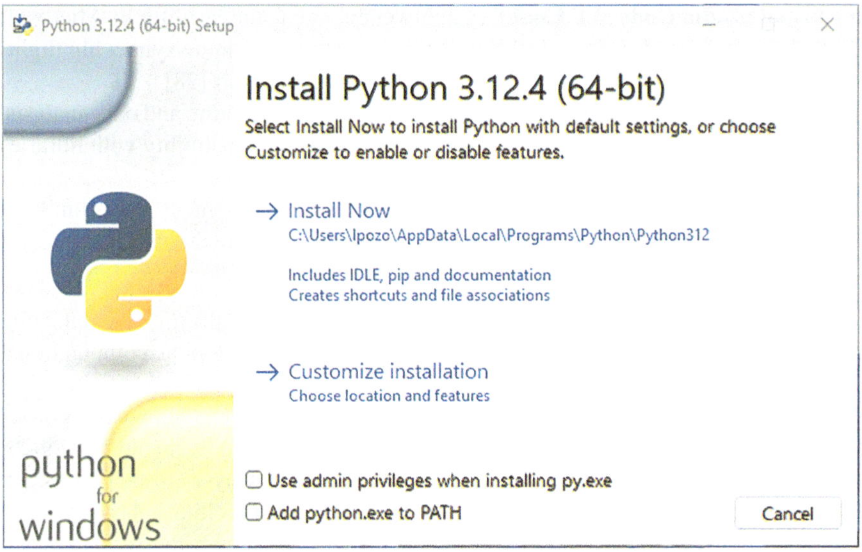

Fig. 1 Illustration of Python interpreter installation wizard

Index (PyPI), which serves as the principal repository of open-source Python software [26]. The inclusion of `pip` within the default installation significantly streamlines dependency management, promotes reproducibility across computing environments, and facilitates its adoption in both academic research and industrial practice. In addition, the availability of a command-line interface enables the automation of tasks and integration into development pipelines, further reinforcing pip's role as an indispensable element of the contemporary Python ecosystem.

With the Python interpreter and the `pip` package manager in place, a functional environment is established that provides all the essential components required to begin coding. The interpreter ensures the execution of Python scripts, while pip enables the installation and management of third-party libraries, thereby extending the core functionality of Python to meet the needs of diverse applications. From this point onwards, any text editor can be employed to write Python code, since the interpreter is capable of executing scripts independently of the development interface. However, Integrated Development Environments (IDEs) are often preferred because they provide advanced functionalities including syntax highlighting, code completion, debugging tools, and project management features, which collectively enhance productivity and support best practices in software development. Popular Python IDEs include:

- **PyCharm**: A professional IDE developed by JetBrains, offering advanced features such as code completion, debugging, testing, and version control integration, and widely adopted for large-scale development projects [27]

- **Visual Studio Code (VS Code)**: A lightweight, open-source editor by Microsoft that can be extended into a full IDE through plugins, providing syntax highlighting, debugging, Git integration, and multi-language support [28]
- **Spyder**: An IDE specifically designed for scientific computing and data analysis, featuring a variable explorer, integrated plotting, and compatibility with libraries such as `NumPy`, `SciPy`, and `Matplotlib` [29]
- **Jupyter Notebook**: A browser-based interactive environment that combines code, narrative text, and visualisations in the form of notebooks, making it a standard tool in data science, machine learning, and education [30]

For psychologists, **Jupyter Notebook** offers a practical platform for conducting statistical analyses, processing experimental data, and developing computational models within a transparent and reproducible workflow. Its capacity to integrate code execution with explanatory text and visual outputs supports rigorous documentation of research procedures, making it particularly valuable for collaborative projects and open science practices. By enabling analyses to be performed, annotated, and shared within a single environment, Jupyter facilitates both methodological clarity and efficient communication of findings across the psychological research community [18].

Beginning work in Jupyter Notebook requires several preparatory and procedural steps that together establish an interactive and reproducible computational environment. First, Python must be installed on the system, accompanied by the pip package manager, through which Jupyter itself can be installed using the command `pip install notebook`. Once installed, the notebook server is initiated by opening a command-line interface and executing the command `jupyter notebook`. This action launches a local server and automatically opens the Jupyter interface in the default Web browser. Within the interface, users may navigate to their preferred working directory and create a new notebook file `(.ipynb)` by selecting the Python kernel, which defines the interpreter responsible for executing the code. The notebook environment is structured into discrete cells, within which users may write and execute code using the keyboard shortcut `Shift+Enter`, thereby displaying outputs immediately below the corresponding cell (Fig. 2). Alongside code cells, Markdown cells may be added to include explanatory text, structured documentation, or mathematical notation written in `LaTeX`, which allows for precise integration of theoretical commentary with computational steps. Notebooks may be saved, reopened, and shared in their native format, ensuring that both the code and its explanatory context are preserved. This workflow—from installation, server initiation, and kernel selection to interactive coding and documentation—provides psychologists and other researchers with a transparent and systematic framework for conducting and communicating computational analyses.

In addition to the browser-based interface, Jupyter Notebooks can also be created and edited directly within integrated development environments such as PyCharm (Professional Edition) and Visual Studio Code. These IDEs provide native support for `(.ipynb)` files, enabling researchers to work with notebooks inside a familiar coding environment while taking advantage of advanced features such

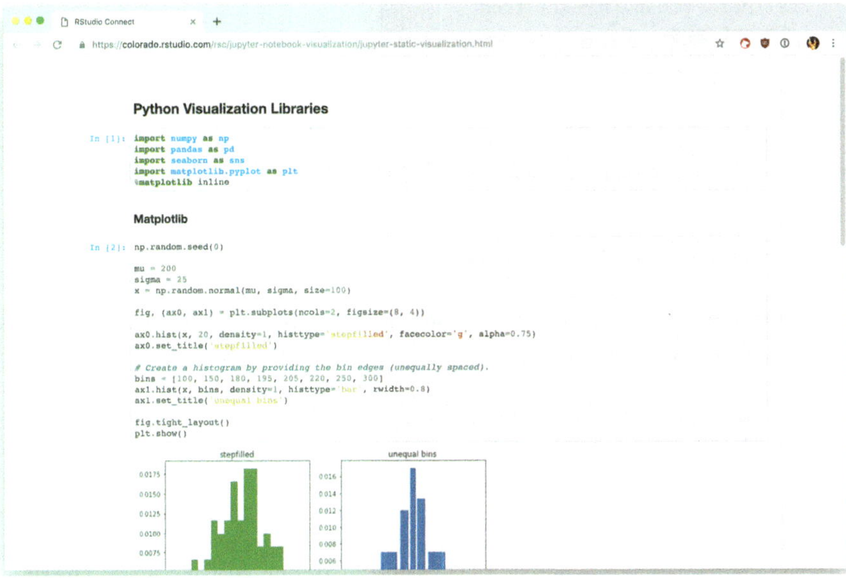

Fig. 2 Representation of Python code within a Jupyter Notebook

as debugging, version control integration, and project management. This flexibility allows users to select either the lightweight browser interface of Jupyter or the extended functionalities of full-featured IDEs, depending on the requirements of their research workflows.

Psychological researchers frequently work on multiple projects that require distinct sets of libraries or even different versions of Python. Virtual environments provide a solution by creating isolated workspaces for each project, thereby preventing conflicts between dependencies and ensuring reproducibility of results. A new virtual environment can be created from the terminal using the command `python -m venv myenv`, which generates a folder named `myenv` containing all necessary interpreter files. Activation differs by operating system: on macOS/Linux the command `source myenv/bin/activate` is used, whereas on Windows, the equivalent command is `myenv\Scripts\activate`. Once activated, the terminal prompt displays the environment's name (e.g. myenv), signalling that any subsequently installed libraries will be contained within that environment alone. This practice not only avoids version mismatches when collaborating with colleagues but also ensures compatibility with older scripts, making virtual environments an essential tool for managing psychological research workflows.

After the environment has been configured, it is important to verify that the Python interpreter and essential tools are functioning as expected. This can be achieved by executing a short diagnostic script designed to confirm the installation and to test the successful import of commonly used libraries:

```
# Test Python installation
import sys
print(f"Python version: {sys.version}")

# Test library imports
try:
    import numpy, pandas, matplotlib, seaborn, scipy, sklearn
    print("All libraries are imported successfully.")
except ImportError as e:
    print(f"Error importing libraries: {e}")
```

Executing this script verifies that Python and its associated libraries have been installed correctly, thereby providing a reliable foundation for subsequent programming tasks.

The Python programming language is supported by a vibrant global community that contributes to its continuous development, documentation, and dissemination. This community-driven model ensures not only the rapid improvement of the language but also the availability of extensive educational resources for learners at all levels. The official Python website provides comprehensive documentation, tutorials, and reference materials [31], while platforms such as Stack Overflow [32], GitHub [33], and Reddit [34] facilitate collaborative problem-solving and knowledge exchange. In addition, Massive Open Online Courses (MOOCs) offered by providers such as Coursera [35], edX [36], and Udemy [37], together with specialised educational platforms like Real Python [38] and DataCamp [39], make structured learning widely accessible. The abundance of openly available resources, combined with an active and inclusive user community, makes Python particularly suitable for adoption in both academic and professional contexts, where ongoing support and shared expertise are essential for sustained skill development.

4 Basic Program Structures: Variables, Sequences, Selections, Loops, and Functions

Understanding the fundamental programming structures represented in Fig. 3 is essential for effective data analysis and application of computational tools in psychological sciences. Python, renowned for its readability and simplicity, provides powerful yet straightforward structures for managing data, executing logical flows, and structuring computational tasks. Familiarity with these structures empowers psychologists to automate repetitive tasks, analyse complex data efficiently, and build reproducible experiments with ease [40, 41].

In Python, as in other programming languages, the basic structures revolve around variables, sequences, selections (conditionals), loops, and functions. Mastering these elements is the cornerstone for constructing robust computational workflows within psychological research [42].

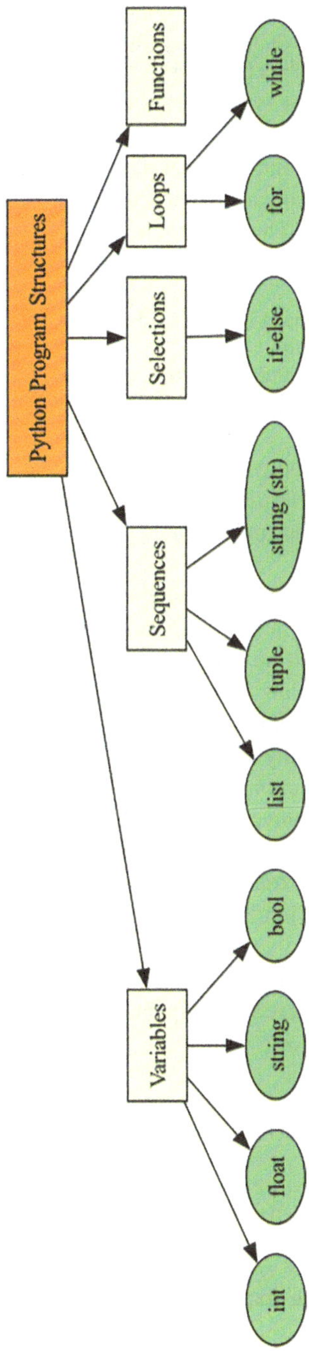

Fig. 3 Taxonomy of basic Python structures

Variables are fundamental units of programming that allow users to store, manage, and manipulate data. Python variables serve as labels for data stored in memory, and their strength lies in their dynamic typing, meaning they do not require explicit declaration of data types [43]. Unlike languages like Java or C++, Python dynamically infers data types during execution, simplifying development and reducing errors.

Python provides a range of fundamental data types—such as integers, floating-point numbers, strings, and booleans—that are especially relevant for applications in psychological research [44]. The example below demonstrates how variables can be assigned across these different data types.

```
participant_id = 101
age = 25
reaction_time = 2.45
is_valid = True
```

In this example, variables represent meaningful concepts such as a participant's identifier, demographic attributes, or experimental metrics. Such intuitive variable labelling promotes readable and maintainable code, which is crucial for collaborative research contexts [45].

In Python, sequences constitute a category of data structures that include lists, tuples, and strings, each designed to store ordered collections of elements. They provide researchers with an efficient means of organising, accessing, and manipulating multiple data points within a single variable. Among these, lists are particularly prominent because they are mutable, allowing elements to be added, removed, or modified dynamically. Tuples, by contrast, are immutable, making them suitable for storing fixed collections of values such as demographic attributes that should not be altered during analysis. Strings also belong to the sequence category, but they specifically represent ordered sequences of characters and are commonly used to store and manipulate textual data, such as participant names or open-ended survey responses. This distinction in mutability and data type specialisation allows researchers to select the most appropriate sequence structure for different aspects of their work. For instance, a psychologist conducting a survey study can store participant responses in a list, fixed participant details in a tuple, and text responses as strings, as demonstrated below:

```
# List: mutable collection of participant responses
responses = [5, 4, 3, 5, 2]   # Likert-scale survey responses

# Tuple: immutable demographic data
demographics = ("Participant_01", 25, "Female")

# String: textual data from open-ended response
comment = "I found the experiment very engaging."
```

Python also facilitates operations on sequences, including indexing, slicing, appending, and sorting. For example, selecting a subset of responses can be simply done with slicing:

```
subset_responses = responses[1:4]
```

This provides intuitive and powerful mechanisms for working with large datasets common in psychology [46]. Python's tuple type, being immutable, offers an excellent way to store data that must remain constant, enhancing data integrity in psychological research.

Selections, implemented using conditional statements (`if`, `elif`, and `else`), enable execution of specific code block based on logical condition. For psychological research, conditional logic is invaluable for data validation, categorisation, or adaptive experiments [47]. For example, researchers may employ selection structures to categorise a participant's score:

```
score = 75
if score >= 90:
    category = "Excellent"
elif score >= 70:
    category = "Good"
else:
    category = "Needs Improvement"
```

The readability and clarity of Python's conditional statements are advantageous for both novice programmers and experienced researchers alike, minimising cognitive overhead and reducing errors in implementation [40, 42].

Loops provide mechanisms for executing repetitive tasks efficiently, significantly reducing the manual labour involved in data processing and analysis. Python offers two primary loop structures: `for` loops and `while` loops. The `for` loop, widely used in psychology research, iterates over items within a collection such as a list, tuple, or range:

```
participants = ['Anna', 'Tom', 'Jack', 'Mia']
for participant in participants:
    print(f"Analyzing data for {participant}")
```

Alternatively, the `while` loop executes repeatedly until a specified condition is no longer met, which is ideal for dynamic and conditional repetitions:

```
trials_completed = 0
max_trials = 100
while trials_completed < max_trials:
    perform_trial()
    trials_completed += 1
```

Loops empower psychologists to automate tasks such as repeated data entry, experimental trials, or iterative statistical computations efficiently [48].

Functions in Python allow sequences of commands or algorithms to be encapsulated into reusable units. By promoting modularity, clarity, and reusability, functions support effective collaboration and ensure reproducibility of research outcomes [40]. Within psychological sciences, functions are frequently employed for tasks such as data preprocessing, scoring of psychological instruments, or performing statistical analyses. Their practical utility can be illustrated through a function that calculates basic descriptive statistics, such as the mean and standard deviation of a dataset:

```
import numpy as np

def calculate_stats(data):
    mean_val = np.mean(data)
    std_dev = np.std(data)
    return mean_val, std_dev

reaction_times = [0.35, 0.42, 0.38, 0.46]
mean_rt, std_rt = calculate_stats(reaction_times)
```

Functions also support parameters and arguments, enabling flexibility and customisation, which are highly beneficial in complex psychological experiments involving varied experimental conditions [41].

When these basic programming structures, including variables, sequences, selections, loops, and functions, are used effectively, Python becomes a highly powerful tool for psychological research. For example, combining loops with conditional selections and sequences provides an effective pipeline for analysing psychometric data, administering adaptive assessments, or processing EEG and reaction-time data [49].

Through Python, psychologists can not only automate tedious tasks but also ensure precise data handling and reproducibility, ultimately increasing the reliability and efficiency of psychological research workflows. Learning these fundamental structures lays a robust foundation for adopting advanced computational techniques, including machine learning and natural language processing, which are increasingly prevalent in psychological research contexts [50].

Mastery of Python's basic programming structures significantly empowers psychologists, providing capabilities far exceeding traditional manual analysis or spreadsheet-based procedures. By equipping researchers with foundational programming skills, psychology as a discipline can more effectively utilise computational advances, thus enriching its analytical depth and expanding research possibilities.

5 Manipulation with Structures and Classes

Data structures and object-oriented concepts are at the core of Python's flexibility and power. They facilitate the organisation of complex data, promote code reusability, and provide the tools to model your experiments. For psychological research, these techniques can streamline data collection, automate coding of participant attributes and responses, and manage experimental procedures with greater clarity and efficiency [40, 48]. Python provides several built-in data structures, namely lists, tuples, sets, and dictionaries, that are integral to efficient data handling and manipulation.

A list is a mutable sequence of elements, making it one of the most versatile data structures for iterative tasks and dynamic data collection (e.g. storing response times or survey answers). For example, you can store reaction times from a memory task in a list:

```
reaction_times = [2.15, 2.38, 1.94, 2.01]
```

You can then perform operations such as inserting, removing, and sorting:

```
reaction_times.append(2.22)    # Add a new data point
reaction_times.remove(1.94)    # Remove an outlier
reaction_times.sort()          # Sort in ascending order
print(reaction_times)
```

These operations allow researchers to dynamically update or preprocess data, which is useful for dealing with changing experimental conditions or incomplete datasets.

A tuple is similar to a list but immutable; once created, its contents cannot be altered. Tuples work well for data that should remain constant after declaration. For instance, if you are working with a fixed set of experimental groups:

```
experimental_groups = ("control", "treatment1", "treatment2")
```

Because tuples cannot be modified in-place, they help ensure the integrity of data structures when the values must remain the same throughout an analysis [43].

A set is an unordered collection of unique elements. Sets are helpful for quickly determining membership or uniqueness in a dataset. For example, if you want to track the unique responses participants give to an open-ended question, you can store them in a set:

```
unique_answers = set()
unique_answers.add("Cognitive overload")
unique_answers.add("Stress")
unique_answers.add("Cognitive overload")  # Duplicate is ignored
print(unique_answers)  # {'Stress', 'Cognitive overload'}
```

Sets provide efficient membership testing (e.g. checking if a specific response is in the set) and can simplify data-cleaning tasks by filtering out duplicates.

A dictionary (`dict`) stores data in key-value pairs. It is one of Python's most powerful built-in data structures due to its speed and intuitive syntax [3]. In psychological experiments, dictionaries can map participant identifiers to attributes (like age, group, or condition):

```
participant_info = {
  "P101": {"age": 28, "condition": "control"},
  "P102": {"age": 32, "condition": "treatment1"},
  "P103": {"age": 24, "condition": "treatment2"}
}
```

Dictionaries make it easy to update and retrieve data by key, supporting complex or nested experimental designs, as shown in the nested structure above (each participant is mapped to another dictionary containing detailed attributes).

Tables 3 and 4 summarise frequently used list and dictionary operations, particularly relevant for data manipulation in psychological research.

While Python's built-in data structures are invaluable for many tasks, certain problems benefit from more structured, extensible solutions. Object-Oriented Programming (OOP) addresses this by allowing you to create classes, blueprints for objects that encapsulate both data (attributes) and behaviours (methods) [51].

Research workflows in psychology often involve repeating patterns: participants, trials, stimuli, and procedures. By creating classes, you can define a consistent interface to handle such entities. Classes support modularity, reusability, and clarity. For instance, a study tracking multiple participants might benefit from a `Participant` class managing attributes like identifiers, demographic data, or aggregated test results. This approach not only keeps code organised but also simplifies collaboration [45].

A minimal Python class can be created using the `class` keyword:

Table 3 Common list operations

Operation	Example
Append an item	`my_list.append(x)`
Insert at index	`my_list.insert(index, x)`
Remove by value	`my_list.remove(x)`
Pop from end (or index)	`my_list.pop()` / `my_list.pop(index)`
Sort	`my_list.sort()`
Reverse	`my_list.reverse()`

Table 4 Common dictionary operations

Operation	Example
Access value by key	`my_dict[key]`
Add or update value	`my_dict[key] = value`
Remove key	`del my_dict[key]`
Check for key existence	`if key in my_dict:`
Get all keys	`my_dict.keys()`
Get all values	`my_dict.values()`

```
class Participant:
  def __init__(self, pid, age, condition):
      self.pid = pid
      self.age = age
      self.condition = condition
      self.responses = []

  def add_response(self, response):
      self.responses.append(response)

  def average_response(self):
      if len(self.responses) == 0:
          return None
      return sum(self.responses) / len(self.responses)
```

- The `__init__` method is the *constructor*, automatically called when you instantiate (create) the class. It initialises attributes like participant ID, age, condition, etc.
- `self` refers to the instance being created, providing access to attributes (`pid`, `age`, `condition`, `responses`);
- `add_response` and `average_response` are *methods* that define the behaviours associated with each participant object.

To create and use objects (instances of a class), you call the class as if it were a function:

```
# Create Participant objects
p1 = Participant(pid="P101", age=28, condition="control")
p2 = Participant(pid="P102", age=32, condition="treatment1")

# Add responses and compute statistics
p1.add_response(3.5)
p1.add_response(4.0)
p2.add_response(2.8)

print(f"Average response for {p1.pid}: {p1.average_response()}")
print(f"Average response for {p2.pid}: {p2.average_response()}")
```

Through this interface, you manage each participant's data more systematically than using parallel lists or nested dictionaries.

One of the powerful features of OOP is inheritance, where new classes (subclasses) can reuse and extend the functionality of existing classes (superclasses). In psychological research, for instance, you might create a specialised participant type for a specific experiment:

```
class ClinicalParticipant(Participant):
    def __init__(self, pid, age, condition, diagnosis):
        super().__init__(pid, age, condition)
        self.diagnosis = diagnosis
```

Now, a `ClinicalParticipant` inherits attributes and methods from `Participant` but also adds a `diagnosis` attribute. This is beneficial when working with various participant types that share core functionality but have additional attributes or behaviours.

Practical considerations and best practices are:

- **Modular Design**: Keep classes and data structures in separate files (modules) to promote clarity and reusability [15].
- **Readability**: Use self-descriptive variable and method names. For instance, `add_response` is clearer than `ar()`.
- **Encapsulation**: Classes should ideally expose a concise interface and hide irrelevant implementation details (i.e. keep internal attributes private when appropriate).
- **Avoid Overengineering**: Use classes when they add clarity or reduce repetition. For simpler tasks or one-off analyses, Python's built-in data structures might be sufficient.
- **Testing and Validation**: As with any code, ensure that class methods (e.g. `average_response`) behave correctly by testing with sample data.

The following snippet illustrates a mini-workflow in which classes and data structures come together to manage participants in a reaction-time experiment.

```
class Experiment:
  def __init__(self, name):
      self.name = name
      self.participants = []

  def add_participant(self, participant):
      self.participants.append(participant)

  def average_rt(self):
      # Returns the overall average reaction time across all participants
      all_rts = []
      for p in self.participants:
          all_rts.extend(p.responses)
      return sum(all_rts)/len(all_rts) if all_rts else None

# Using our previously defined Participant class
p1 = Participant("P101", 28, "control")
p1.add_response(2.15)
p1.add_response(2.38)

p2 = Participant("P102", 32, "treatment")
p2.add_response(1.94)
p2.add_response(2.01)

# Create an Experiment and add participants
experiment = Experiment("Memory Task")
experiment.add_participant(p1)
experiment.add_participant(p2)

print(f"Overall average RT: {experiment.average_rt()} s")
```

The `Experiment` class stores multiple participants and aggregates their data. This structure is scalable to handle more complex designs, including multiple tasks, sessions, or experimental groups, demonstrating how classes can orchestrate data management within psychological research workflows.

6 Python Modules

In Python, both *modules* and *libraries* play a crucial role in organising and reusing code, but they serve slightly different purposes. A *module* refers to a single Python file that contains functions, classes, or variables that can be reused in different parts of your code. On the other hand, a *library* is typically a collection of modules bundled together to provide a wide range of functionalities. For example, `math` is a module that provides mathematical functions, while `numpy` is a library that offers a suite of tools for numerical computing, built using multiple modules.

The primary distinction lies in their scale and structure. A module is the fundamental building block in Python's organisational hierarchy, while libraries are larger frameworks often containing multiple modules. For instance, when you import the `random` module, you're accessing a single file that includes functions for random number generation. In contrast, when you import a library like `pandas`, you gain access to a collection of modules designed for data manipulation and analysis.

Despite these differences, both modules and libraries share similarities in their purpose: enabling code reusability, simplifying complex tasks, and enhancing productivity. In Python, modules are particularly versatile as they allow researchers to create custom functionalities tailored to their specific needs, extending the language's capabilities beyond its standard features.

Modules in Python are an essential feature, enabling users to break down large programs into smaller, manageable components. Every Python file ending with the `.py` extension is considered a module. Modules can be either *built-in* (provided by Python) or *user-defined* (created by the user).

Python includes a rich set of built-in modules that provide a wide range of functionalities out of the box. These modules are part of the *Python Standard Library* and do not require installation. Examples include:

- **math**: Provides mathematical functions such as `sqrt`, `sin`, and `cos`
- **os**: Offers functionalities for interacting with the operating system, such as file and directory management
- **random**: Enables generation of random numbers, shuffling sequences, and selecting random items

For instance, the `math` module can be used as follows:

```
import math
result = math.sqrt(16)
print(f"The square root of 16 is {result}")
```

Researchers can create their own modules to encapsulate specific functionality. For example, a psychologist analysing reaction times might create a custom module `reaction_analysis.py` with functions to calculate averages, identify outliers, and generate visualisations. To use this module, it can be imported like any standard Python module:

```
import reaction_analysis
reaction_analysis.process_data('data.csv')
```

This modular approach makes code reusable, easier to debug, and shareable with collaborators.

Modules can be imported in various ways depending on the scope and specificity required. The standard import syntax is:

```
import module_name
```

For accessing specific components, the `from ...import ...` syntax is used:

```
from math import sqrt, pi
print(sqrt(25), pi)
```

To avoid importing the entire module, this method improves efficiency and readability.

Beyond Python's built-in modules, researchers often rely on third-party libraries to extend functionality (see Fig. 4) and streamline tasks. These libraries are created and maintained by the Python community and can be installed using the `pip` package manager. For example, `pip install scipy`.

Popular third-party libraries widely used in psychological research include:

- **numpy**: Facilitates numerical computations, array manipulations, and mathematical operations
- **pandas**: Provides tools for data manipulation and analysis, including handling large datasets and performing data cleaning
- **matplotlib** and **seaborn**: Enable data visualisation through plots, charts, and statistical graphics
- **scikit-learn**: Offers machine learning algorithms for classification, regression, clustering, and more
- **scipy**: Supports scientific computing, including optimisation, integration, and statistical analysis
- **nltk**: Provides tools for natural language processing, including text tokenisation, sentiment analysis, and linguistic feature extraction

To explore these and many other libraries, comprehensive resources such as curated lists and documentation hubs are available. For an overview of Python libraries and their functionalities, the following resources are highly recommended:

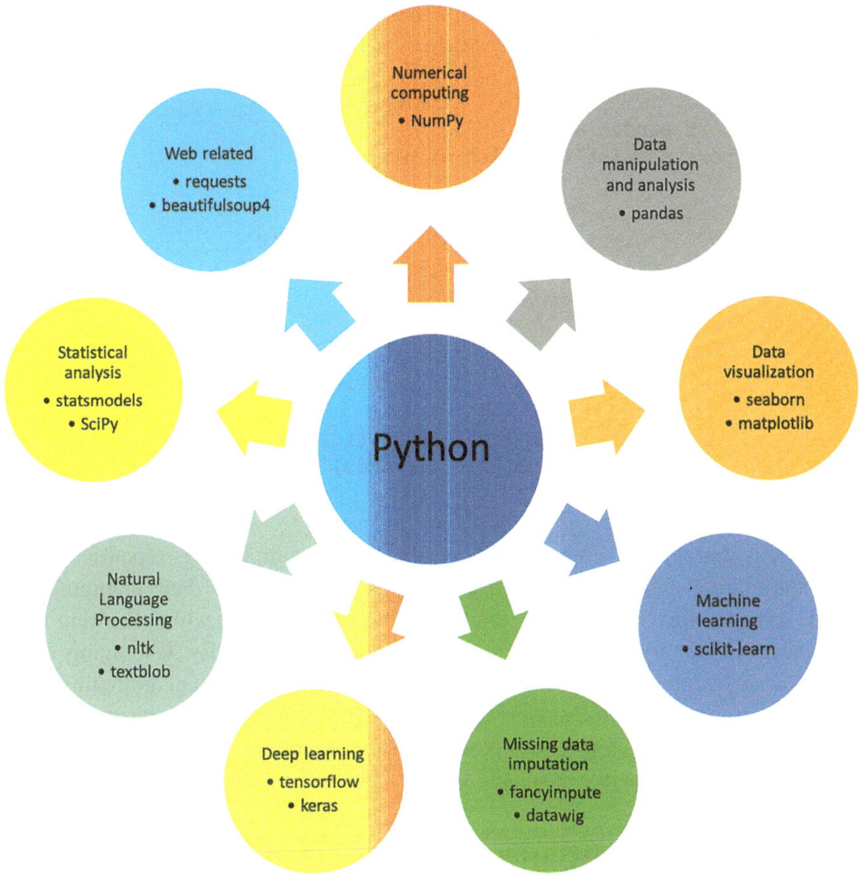

Fig. 4 Core Python libraries for psychological data science applications

- **Python Awesome**: A platform showcasing categorised Python libraries across various domains, including data science, machine learning, and psychology [52]
- **Awesome Python**: A GitHub repository containing a curated list of Python frameworks, libraries, and resources [53]
- **PyPI (Python Package Index)**: The official repository for Python packages, where you can search for libraries by keywords and read descriptions and usage details [54]

By consulting these resources, psychologists can discover new tools tailored to their specific needs. For example, a researcher analysing text data may explore `nltk` for linguistic processing or `textblob` for sentiment analysis. Similarly, those performing machine learning tasks may find specialised libraries like `xgboost` or `tensorflow` useful for predictive modelling.

To test the capabilities of some common libraries, consider the following example, which demonstrates the use of `pandas` for loading data and `matplotlib` for visualising it:

```
import pandas as pd
import matplotlib.pyplot as plt

# Create a sample dataset
data = {'Participant': ['A', 'B', 'C', 'D'],
        'ReactionTime': [1.5, 2.3, 1.8, 2.0]}
df = pd.DataFrame(data)

# Plot the data
df.plot(x='Participant', y='ReactionTime', kind='bar',
 ↪  legend=False)
plt.title('Reaction Times of Participants')
plt.ylabel('Reaction Time (seconds)')
plt.show()
```

For psychologists, modules are invaluable in simplifying repetitive tasks and automating processes. Modules such as `pandas` for data manipulation, `matplotlib` for visualisation, and `scikit-learn` for machine learning have become essential tools in modern psychological research. By leveraging these modules, researchers can focus on deriving insights rather than grappling with technical complexities. Consider the `statistics` module, part of *Python's Standard Library*, which provides basic statistical functions. Psychologists can use it to compute measures like mean and standard deviation without relying on external tools:

```
import statistics

data = [1.2, 3.5, 2.8, 4.0, 3.3]
mean = statistics.mean(data)
stdev = statistics.stdev(data)

print(f"Mean: {mean}, Standard Deviation: {stdev}")
```

7 Data Visualisation

Data visualisation refers to the graphical representation of information and data using visual elements such as charts, graphs, and maps. This powerful approach is an essential aspect of modern psychological research, offering researchers a way to quickly understand complex data, reveal underlying patterns, and communicate findings effectively to both scientific and general audiences [55]. Good visualisation transforms numerical and textual data into visual representations, making insights readily understandable and actionable. As psychology increasingly relies on large-scale datasets, effective visualisation techniques become indispensable to bridge the gap between data complexity and human comprehension [56].

In psychology, visualisation not only clarifies statistical relationships but also illuminates psychological processes that may not be readily apparent through numerical analysis alone [57]. For instance, visual methods can reveal subtle changes in emotional states, cognitive processes, or behavioural patterns over time, providing intuitive clarity and interpretive power beyond raw statistical outputs [58]. Given psychology's focus on abstract and often intangible constructs, visualisation provides tangible representations that aid both researchers and practitioners in understanding psychological phenomena.

Python offers numerous visualisation libraries tailored for various research needs and complexities, making it particularly well-suited to psychological research. Among the most influential libraries are `Matplotlib`, `Seaborn`, `Plotly`, and `Bokeh`, each catering to specific visualisation needs and complexities. `Matplotlib` is foundational, providing the flexibility to produce detailed, publication-quality figures suitable for a variety of psychological research contexts [13]. `Seaborn`, built on top of `Matplotlib`, streamlines statistical visualisation by incorporating predefined themes and styles that enhance readability and interpretability, particularly suited to exploratory data analysis in psychology [14]. The following Python example illustrates visualisation of mean questionnaire scores obtained from participants assigned to two experimental conditions: a control group and a treatment group:

```
import matplotlib.pyplot as plt
import numpy as np

# Example: Questionnaire scores for two groups in a psychology experiment
group_labels = ["Control", "Treatment"]
mean_scores = [65, 78]          # average questionnaire scores
std_devs = [8, 6]               # standard deviations

x = np.arange(len(group_labels))

# Create bar chart with error bars
plt.bar(x, mean_scores, yerr=std_devs, capsize=5, color=['skyblue', 'salmon'])
plt.xticks(x, group_labels)
plt.ylabel("Mean Questionnaire Score")
plt.title("Effect of Treatment on Questionnaire Scores")

plt.show()
```

`Plotly` and `Bokeh`, on the other hand, are specifically designed for interactive data visualisation, enabling researchers to engage dynamically with data. Interactive visualisations allow psychologists to explore data layers interactively, manipulate variables, and understand multivariate interactions and nuances in real time. `Plotly`, for instance, supports interactive plots, graphs, and dashboards directly embedded within Web applications or `Jupyter notebooks`, significantly improving the ease of sharing interactive research outputs [59]. Likewise,

Bokeh facilitates detailed and interactive graphical representations, enabling psychologists to produce dynamic visualisations that enhance comprehension and facilitate collaborative interpretation of complex psychological datasets [60].

To illustrate the use of interactive visualisation in psychological research, consider a dataset derived from an experiment measuring participants' reaction times across multiple trials. Reaction time is a fundamental measure in cognitive psychology, frequently used to assess attention, learning, and processing speed. In this example, data are simulated for two groups—a control group and a treatment group—over five consecutive trials. An interactive line graph generated with Plotly allows researchers to examine group differences in performance and to visualise how reaction times evolve across trials, thereby providing insights into potential learning effects or treatment efficacy.

```
import plotly.express as px
import pandas as pd

# Example dataset: Reaction times (ms) across trials for two groups
data = {
    "Trial": [1, 2, 3, 4, 5, 1, 2, 3, 4, 5],
    "ReactionTime": [520, 510, 495, 490, 485, 515, 500, 480, 470, 465],
    "Group": ["Control"]*5 + ["Treatment"]*5
}

df = pd.DataFrame(data)

# Line chart with Plotly
fig = px.line(df,
              x="Trial",
              y="ReactionTime",
             color="Group",
             markers=True,
             title="Reaction Time Across Trials by Group",
             labels={"ReactionTime": "Reaction Time (ms)", "Trial": "Trial Number"})

fig.show()
```

Beyond these libraries, advanced Python-based visualisation tools such as NetworkX and Gephi provide capabilities for analysing and visualising relational data, essential for psychological research involving social networks, cognitive networks, or complex inter-individual dynamics. NetworkX supports the visualisation and analysis of complex networks, enabling researchers to capture and visually represent interactions such as friendship networks, collaboration patterns, and cognitive associations [61]. Gephi, although not exclusively Python-based, can easily integrate with Python workflows and offers specialised visualisation capabilities for large-scale network data, providing insights into structural properties and relationships within psychological networks [62].

Visualisation in psychological research is not merely about creating visually appealing graphics; it is deeply connected to the interpretability and reproducibility of scientific findings. An essential component of visualisation involves communicating the uncertainty and variability inherent in psychological data. Researchers often use confidence intervals, error bars, or shading to indicate uncertainty visually, thus fostering transparency in statistical inference and interpretation. This emphasis on uncertainty visualisation aligns with current practices promoting open science and reproducibility in psychology [63].

Visualisation plays a crucial role in communicating findings to non-specialist audiences, including policymakers, educational practitioners, and the general public. Clear, intuitive visualisations are instrumental in disseminating complex psychological insights effectively, bridging the communication gap between researchers and broader audiences [64]. For instance, visualisations depicting mental health trends over time, changes in public sentiment regarding psychological interventions, or the distribution of behavioural traits in populations facilitate evidence-based decision-making, shaping educational and health policies and interventions [65].

In psychological practice, visualisation also supports diagnostic and therapeutic processes. Tools designed to visualise psychological data in real time, such as dashboards displaying therapeutic progress or emotional state changes, provide clinicians with actionable insights to optimise interventions. For instance, visualisation dashboards summarising patient self-reports and behavioural metrics can help therapists adjust treatment plans dynamically, improving therapeutic outcomes and patient engagement [66].

In recent years, the integration of artificial intelligence and machine learning into data visualisation, known as *intelligent visualisation*, has further enriched visualisation practices in psychology. Intelligent visualisation systems adapt dynamically to user interactions and dataset changes, providing personalised views and revealing hidden psychological patterns through sophisticated computational techniques. For instance, AI-driven visual analytics systems can automatically highlight anomalous behavioural patterns or cognitive declines, alerting researchers and practitioners to subtle but meaningful changes that might otherwise remain unnoticed [67].

Ethical considerations in psychological data visualisation are becoming increasingly prominent. Ethical visualisation practices demand accuracy, transparency, and sensitivity to avoid misrepresenting or distorting psychological data, potentially leading to misinterpretations or stigmatisation. Careful visual representation ensures ethical integrity, supports valid interpretations, and maintains public trust in psychological research [68].

Given the myriad of benefits associated with effective visualisation, psychologists are encouraged to adopt and enhance their proficiency with visualisation tools. Incorporating these tools within standard research workflows not only enhances scientific rigour but also significantly enriches the analytical and communicative capabilities of psychological researchers.

Table 5 summarises and compares the primary visualisation libraries and tools available in Python, illustrating their specific advantages, recommended applications, and suitability for various types of psychological datasets and research questions. This table acts as a concise reference for researchers and practitioners seeking the most appropriate visualisation solution for their particular research objectives and data characteristics.

Data visualisation constitutes a fundamental pillar of modern psychological research, significantly advancing our ability to interpret complex phenomena and

Table 5 Python visualisation libraries and their characteristics relevant to psychological research

Library features	Matplotlib	Seaborn	Plotly	Bokeh	NetworkX
Publication-quality graphics	✓	✓	✓	✓	
Ease of use (simple syntax)		✓	✓	✓	
Interactive visualisations			✓	✓	
Statistical plotting support		✓	✓		
Customisation flexibility	✓	✓	✓	✓	
Real-time data visualisation			✓	✓	
Integration with Web applications			✓	✓	
Network/relational data visualisation					✓
Scalable to large datasets			✓	✓	✓
Support for uncertainty visualisation	✓	✓	✓		
Open source	✓	✓	✓	✓	✓

communicate findings effectively. Python, through its rich ecosystem of visualisation tools and libraries, empowers psychologists to create detailed, dynamic, and insightful visual representations, supporting a deeper and detailed understanding of human cognition, emotion, and behaviour.

References

1. G. van Rossum, Python: a high-level programming language. Technical Report. CWI Report, Centrum Wiskunde & Informatica (CWI), Amsterdam (1991)
2. L. Geurts, L. Meertens, S. Pemberton, *The ABC Programmer's Handbook* (Prentice-Hall International, Englewood Cliffs, 1987)
3. M. Lutz, *Learning Python*, 5th edn. (O'Reilly Media, Sebastopol, 2013)
4. D. Beazley, *Python Essential Reference*, 4th edn. (Addison-Wesley, Boston, 2009)
5. Sunsetting Python 2. Python 2 official end-of-life announcement. https://www.python.org/doc/sunset-python-2/ (2020). Accessed 08 Mar 2025
6. T.E. Oliphant, Python for scientific computing. Comput. Sci. Eng. **9**(3), 10 (2007)
7. W. McKinney, pandas: A foundational Python library for data analysis, in *Proceedings of the Python for Scientific Computing Conference* (2010)
8. A. Martín, A. Ashish, B. Paul, B. Eugene, C. Zhifeng, C. Craig, S.C. Greg, D. Andy, D. Jeffrey, D. Matthieu, et al. TensorFlow: Large-Scale Machine Learning on Heterogeneous Systems. arXiv preprint. arXiv:1603.04467 (2016). Software available from https://www.tensorflow.org
9. M. Grinberg, *Flask Web Development*, 2nd edn. (O'Reilly Media, Sebastopol, 2018)
10. Python 3.13. Python 3.13 release notes. https://docs.python.org/release/3.13.1/ (2021). Accessed 08 Mar 2025
11. Python PEPs. Python enhancement proposals (PEPs). https://peps.python.org/ (2021). Accessed 08 Mar 2025
12. G. Van Rossum, F.L. Drake Jr, *The Python Language Reference* (Python Software Foundation, Wilmington, 2014)
13. J.D. Hunter, Matplotlib: A 2D graphics environment, Comput. Sci. Eng. **9**(03), 90 (2007)
14. M.L. Waskom, Seaborn: statistical data visualization. J. Open Source Softw. **6**(60), 3021 (2021)
15. G. Van Rossum, F.L. Drake Jr, Python tutorial. History **42**(4), 1 (2010)

16. S. Behnel, R. Bradshaw, C. Citro, L. Dalcin, D.S. Seljebotn, K. Smith, Cython: the best of both worlds. Comput. Sci. Eng. **13**(2), 31 (2010)
17. S. Overflow, Stack Overflow developer survey. https://stackoverflow.com/ (2024). Accessed 22 Mar 2025
18. N. Kovač, K. Ratković, H. Farahani, P. Watson, A practical applications guide to machine learning regression models in psychology with python. Methods Psychol. **11**, 100156 (2024)
19. R. R Core Team, et al. R: A language and environment for statistical computing. https://www.r-project.org/ (2025). Accessed 22 Mar 2025
20. MathWorks. MATLAB documentation. https://www.mathworks.com (2025). Accessed 22 Mar 2023
21. C.S. Horstmann, G. Cornell, C. Java, *Core Java, Volume I: Fundamentals* (Pearson Education, London, 2024)
22. G. van Rossum, F.L. Drake, *Python Reference Manual* (Centrum voor Wiskunde en Informatica (CWI), Amsterdam, 1995). https://www.python.org/doc/
23. A. Martelli, A. Ravenscroft, S. Holden, D. Ascher, *Python in a Nutshell*, 3rd edn. (O'Reilly Media, Sebastopol, 2017)
24. Anaconda, Inc., Anaconda distribution. https://www.anaconda.com/ (2022). Accessed 22 Aug 2025
25. D. Merkel, Docker: lightweight linux containers for consistent development and deployment. Linux J. **2014**(239), 2 (2014). https://www.linuxjournal.com/content/docker-lightweight-linux-containers-consistent-development-and-deployment
26. P.S. Foundation, Python 3 documentation (2025). https://docs.python.org/3/. Accessed 18 Feb 2025
27. JetBrains, PyCharm documentation. https://www.jetbrains.com/pycharm/documentation/ (2023). Accessed 23 Jan 2023
28. Microsoft, Visual Studio code documentation. https://code.visualstudio.com/docs (2023). Accessed 23 Jan 2023
29. Spyder Project Contributors, Spyder: The scientific python development environment. https://www.spyder-ide.org/ (2023). Accessed 22 Aug 2025
30. P. Jupyter, Jupyter Notebook documentation. https://jupyter.org/documentation (2023). Accessed 23 Jan 2023
31. Python Software Foundation, Python official website. https://www.python.org/ (2025). Accessed 22 Aug 2025
32. Stack Overflow, Stack Overflow: where developers learn, share, & build careers. https://stackoverflow.com/ (2023). Accessed 23 Jan 2023
33. GitHub, Inc., Github: where the world builds software. https://github.com/ (2025). Accessed 22 Aug 2025
34. Reddit, Inc., Reddit: the front page of the internet. https://www.reddit.com/ (2025). Accessed 22 Aug 2025
35. Coursera, Inc., Coursera: Online courses & certificates. https://www.coursera.org/ (2025). Accessed 22 Aug 2025
36. edX Inc., edx: Access 2500+ online courses from 140 institutions. https://www.edx.org/ (2025). Accessed 22 Aug 2025
37. Udemy, Inc., Udemy: Online courses anytime, anywhere. https://www.udemy.com/ (2025). Accessed 22 Aug 2025
38. RealPython, Beginner Python tutorials. https://realpython.com/start-here/ (2023). Accessed: 23 Jan 2023
39. DataCamp, Inc., Datacamp: Learn data science online. https://www.datacamp.com/ (2025). Accessed 22 Aug 2025
40. A. Downey, *Think Python: How to Think Like a Computer Scientist* (O'Reilly Media, Inc., Sebastopol, 2012)
41. A. Sweigart, *Automate the Boring Stuff with Python: Practical Programming for Total Beginners* (No Starch Press, San Francisco, 2019)

42. T. Halswanter, *An Introduction to Statistics with Python: With Applications in the Life Sciences*, 2nd edn. (Springer, Berlin, 2012)
43. J.M. Zelle, *Python Programming: An Introduction to Computer Science*, 4th edn. (Franklin, Beedle & Associates, Inc., Portland, 2024)
44. J. Yuan, C. Chen, W. Yang, M. Liu, J. Xia, S. Liu, A survey of visual analytics techniques for machine learning. Comput. Vis. Media **7**, 3 (2021)
45. T. Gaddis, *Starting Out with Python (No REVEL or MyLab Programming)*, 6th edn. (Pearson Education, Inc., London, 2023)
46. E. Matthes, *Python Crash Course: A Hands-On, Project-Based Introduction to Programming* (No Starch Press, San Francisco, 2023)
47. S.D. Edwin, *Python for Experimental Psychologists: A Fun Way of Learning How to Code Your Experiments and Analyses* (Routledge, Milton Park, 2024)
48. W.F. Punch, R. Enbody, *Practice of Computing Using Python* (The Addison-Wesley Publishing Company, Boston, 2012)
49. K.J. Millman, M. Aivazis, Python for scientists and engineers. Comput. Sci. Eng. **13**(2), 9 (2011)
50. D. Jurafsky, J.H. Martin, *Speech and Language Processing: An Introduction to Natural Language Processing, Computational Linguistics, and Speech Recognition with Language Models*, 3rd edn. (Stanford University, Stanford, 2025). https://web.stanford.edu/~jurafsky/slp3/. Online manuscript released January 12, 2025
51. D. Phillips, *Python Object-Oriented Programming*, 4th edn. (Packt Publishing, Birmingham, 2021). https://www.packtpub.com/product/python-object-oriented-programming-fourth-edition/9781801077262
52. Python Awesome, Explore Python libraries. https://pythonawesome.com (2023). Accessed 23 Jan 2023
53. V. Chen, Awesome Python: A curated list of awesome Python frameworks, libraries, and software. https://github.com/vinta/awesome-python (2023). Accessed 23 Jan 2023
54. P.P.I. (PyPI), The official repository of Python libraries. https://pypi.org (2023). Accessed 23 Jan 2023
55. K. Healy, *Data Visualization: A Practical Introduction* (Princeton University Press, Princeton, 2024)
56. T. Munzner, *Visualization Analysis and Design* (CRC Press, Boca Raton, 2014)
57. E. Loken, A. Gelman, Measurement error and the replication crisis. Science **355**(6325), 584 (2017). https://doi.org/10.1126/science.aal3618
58. L. Tay, V. Ng, A. Malik, J. Zhang, J. Chae, D.S. Ebert, Y. Ding, J. Zhao, M. Kern, Big data visualizations in organizational science. Organ. Res. Methods **21**(3), 660 (2018)
59. C. Sievert, *Interactive Web-Based Data Visualization with R, Plotly, and Shiny* (Chapman and Hall/CRC, Boca Raton, 2020)
60. C. Bokeh Development Team, Bokeh: Python library for interactive visualization, GitHub (2018)
61. A. Hagberg, P.J. Swart, D.A. Schult, Exploring network structure, dynamics, and function using NetworkX. Technical report. Los Alamos National Laboratory (LANL), Los Alamos, NM (2008)
62. M. Bastian, S. Heymann, M. Jacomy, Gephi: an open source software for exploring and manipulating networks, in *Proceedings of the International AAAI Conference on Web and Social Media*, vol. 3.1 (2009), pp. 361–362
63. L. Wilkinson, in *Handbook of Computational Statistics: Concepts and Methods* (Springer, Berlin, 2011), pp. 375–414
64. S.D. Evergreen, *Effective Data Visualization: The Right Chart for the Right Data* (SAGE Publications, Thousand Oaks, 2019)
65. A. Cairo, *The Truthful Art: Data, Charts, and Maps for Communication* (New Riders, Indianapolis, 2016)

66. Y. Lu, C. Wang, FAVis: visual analytics of factor analysis for psychological research, in *2024 IEEE Visualization and Visual Analytics (VIS)* (IEEE, Piscataway, 2024), pp. 51–55
67. X. Wang, Z. Wu, W. Huang, Y. Wei, Z. Huang, M. Xu, W. Chen, VIS+ AI: integrating visualization with artificial intelligence for efficient data analysis. Front. Comput. Sci. **17**(6), 176709 (2023)
68. M. Correll, Ethical dimensions of visualization research, in *Proceedings of the 2019 CHI Conference on Human Factors in Computing Systems* (2019), pp. 1–13

Introduction to Psychological Sciences

Nataša Kovač, Hojjatollah Farahani, Peter Watson, Lisa-Christina Winter Done, and Kruna Ratković

1 Brief History of Psychological Science

The origins of psychology trace back to ancient Greece, where philosophers such as Plato and Aristotle explored the nature of the psyche and cognitive processes. Plato's introspective dialogues posited that knowledge is innate within the psyche, accessible through self-reflection, whereas Aristotle's empirical observations established a framework for analysing behaviour as a function of sensory input [1]. These foundational inquiries framed the mind as a complex system, initiating a discourse that persisted across centuries.

During the seventeenth and eighteenth centuries, Enlightenment philosophers René Descartes and John Locke advanced these concepts. Descartes' dualistic theory, which distinguished the mind and body as separate entities, introduced a mechanistic model of mental function, while Locke's empiricism underscored experience as the primary source of knowledge [2]. These philosophical developments facilitated psychology's divergence from metaphysics, prompting scholars to prioritise observable and quantifiable phenomena to elucidate cognitive and behavioural processes.

N. Kovač (✉) · K. Ratković
Faculty of Applied Sciences, University of Donja Gorica, Podgorica, Montenegro
e-mail: natasa.kovac@udg.edu.me; kruna.ratkovic@udg.edu.me

H. Farahani
Department of Psychology, Faculty of Humanities, Tarbiat Modares University, Tehran, Iran
e-mail: h.farahani@modares.ac.ir

P. Watson
MRC Cognition and Brain Sciences Unit, University of Cambridge, Cambridge, UK
e-mail: Peter.Watson@mrc-cbu.cam.ac.uk

L.-C. W. Done
OpenPsai (Two Kermis), Zug, Switzerland

N. Kovač et al. (eds.), *Data Science in Psychology*,
https://doi.org/10.1007/978-3-032-18312-5_2

The late nineteenth century marked psychology's transition into a scientific discipline. In 1879, Wilhelm Wundt established the first experimental psychology laboratory at the University of Leipzig, Germany, an event widely regarded as the inception of experimental psychology [3]. Wundt's methodology of introspection, involving systematic analysis of sensory experiences, aimed to identify the fundamental components of consciousness. This structuralist approach, further developed by Edward B. Titchener, sought to deconstruct mental processes into their elemental units [4].

Concurrently, William James at Harvard University pursued an alternative perspective. Rejecting structuralism's constraints, James advocated for functionalism, which examined how mental processes facilitate adaptation to environmental demands [5]. His seminal text, *Principles of Psychology*, integrated philosophical inquiry with empirical data, highlighting the dynamic interactions among mind, body, and environment. James's functionalist framework aligned with the pragmatic ethos of the United States, where psychology was gaining traction.

G. Stanley Hall, a disciple of James, significantly contributed to the institutionalisation of psychology in the United States. In 1883, Hall established the first American psychological laboratory at Johns Hopkins University and founded the American Psychological Association (APA) in 1892 [6]. His initiatives to professionalise the discipline, alongside his research on child development and education, expanded psychology's scope and societal impact.

The early twentieth century saw the emergence of diverse theoretical frameworks, each offering distinct perspectives on human behaviour. Sigmund Freud's psychoanalysis, introduced in the 1890s, emphasised the role of the unconscious mind in shaping behaviour through latent drives and conflicts [7]. Freud's therapeutic methods, including free association and dream analysis, provided novel approaches to addressing psychological distress. Despite ongoing debates regarding its empirical validity, psychoanalysis significantly influenced clinical practice and cultural discourse.

In contrast, behaviourism rejected introspective and psychoanalytic methods, advocating for an objective focus on observable behaviour. John B. Watson, drawing on Ivan Pavlov's research on conditioned reflexes, posited that environmental stimuli shape behaviour [8]. B.F. Skinner further developed behaviourism through operant conditioning, demonstrating how reinforcement and punishment modulate behaviour [9]. Behaviourism's emphasis on measurable outcomes dominated American psychology for decades, influencing fields such as education and behavioural therapy.

By the mid-twentieth century, the limitations of behaviourism's focus on external stimuli spurred the cognitive revolution. Advances in computer science and linguistics inspired researchers like George A. Miller and Noam Chomsky to investigate mental processes such as memory, perception, and language [10, 11]. The cognitive paradigm conceptualised the mind as an information-processing system, reinvigorating research on internal mental states and establishing cognitive psychology as a core discipline.

Humanistic psychology, championed by Carl Rogers and Abraham Maslow, emerged as an alternative to behaviourism and psychoanalysis, emphasising individual potential and self-actualisation [12, 13]. This approach prioritised personal growth and meaning, influencing fields such as counselling, education, and organisational psychology. Its holistic perspective resonated with the cultural transformations of the 1960s, addressing societal concerns about identity and purpose.

The latter half of the twentieth century witnessed psychology's diversification into specialised subfields, driven by scientific advancements and societal needs. Clinical psychology, formalised at the 1949 Boulder Conference, integrated scientific rigour with practical application to address post—World War II mental health demands [14]. Neuropsychology, supported by technologies such as electroencephalography and functional magnetic resonance imaging, elucidated the neural underpinnings of behaviour, with Donald Hebb's work on learning providing a foundational framework [15].

Social psychology, advanced by Kurt Lewin and others, investigated how social contexts influence behaviour, addressing phenomena such as conformity, prejudice, and group dynamics [16]. Developmental psychology, building on Jean Piaget's theories of cognitive development, explored lifespan psychological changes [17]. Cross-cultural psychology challenged Western-centric assumptions, demonstrating the influence of cultural contexts on psychological processes [18].

Initiatives aimed at promoting diversity and inclusion have played a significant role in shaping the trajectory of psychology. Landmark contributions were made by figures such as Margaret Floy Washburn, the first woman to receive a doctoral degree in psychology, and Francis Cecil Sumner, the first African American to achieve this distinction, thereby broadening the discipline's inclusivity [19]. Contemporary historiographical scholarship, including special issues of the *History of Psychology* journal published by the APA, highlights the critical importance of integrating marginalised voices—encompassing women, people of color, and non-Western perspectives—into the discipline's historical narrative [20, 21].

Analyses of psychological research from 1995 to 2015 indicate evolving priorities within the discipline. Neuroscience-related topics, including brain imaging and psychopharmacology, have gained prominence, reflecting technological advancements and an increased focus on biological mechanisms [22]. Conversely, humanistic and psychoanalytic approaches have declined in academic research, as the field prioritises empirical rigour and quantifiable outcomes. Methodological innovations, such as meta-analyses and big data analytics, have enhanced the generalisability of findings across diverse populations [23].

Despite its empirical orientation, psychology remains a multifaceted discipline. While neuroscience dominates high-impact journals, social and humanistic approaches thrive in applied contexts, addressing issues such as mental health equity and workplace diversity [24]. The APA's commitment to equity, diversity, and inclusion reinforces efforts to amplify underrepresented perspectives, ensuring that psychology encompasses the breadth of human experience [23].

The historical development of psychology reflects a sustained endeavour to understand human cognition and behaviour. From Wundt's laboratory to contemporary research, psychologists have navigated philosophical, scientific, and societal shifts to construct a discipline that balances rigour with humanistic inquiry. Each theoretical paradigm, such as structuralism, functionalism, behaviourism, cognitivism, humanism, and others, has contributed to a comprehensive understanding of the mind and behaviour. As psychology continues to advance, it upholds a legacy of scientific curiosity and societal relevance, fostering ongoing exploration of the complexities of human experience.

2 Psychology as a Cross-Cutting Discipline

Psychology, as a dynamic and ever-evolving field, has transcended its traditional boundaries to become a cornerstone of cross-disciplinary, multidisciplinary, and transdisciplinary research (Table 1). By weaving together insights from diverse domains, psychology not only deepens our understanding of the human mind and behaviour but also addresses complex societal challenges with empathy, rigour, and innovation. This exploration highlights recent advancements in psychology's role as a cross-cutting discipline, drawing on seminal studies to illustrate its transformative potential. Through collaboration with fields like neuroscience, education, and technology, psychology fosters holistic solutions that resonate with the lived experiences of individuals and communities, blending scientific precision with a profound commitment to human well-being.

Table 1 Psychology as a cross-cutting discipline: comparative approaches

Approach	Definition	Characteristics
Cross-disciplinary	Viewing one discipline through the lens of another, integrating insights to enrich perspectives	– Focus on conceptual transfer
		– Often theoretical in nature
		– Provides new interpretive frameworks
Multidisciplinary	Collaboration among several disciplines, each contributing specialised expertise while maintaining boundaries	– Parallel contributions from multiple fields
		– Problem-focused but discipline-specific methods retained
		– Broader understanding emerges from combination
Transdisciplinary	Synthesis of disciplinary knowledge into new frameworks or fields, often involving non-academic stakeholders	– Blurs or transcends disciplinary boundaries
		– Co-creation with practitioners and communities
		– Generates innovative and socially impactful solutions

At its core, cross-disciplinary psychology involves integrating perspectives from multiple fields to tackle multifaceted problems, often viewing one discipline through the lens of another. Multidisciplinary approaches, by contrast, bring together experts from different domains, each contributing specialised knowledge while maintaining disciplinary boundaries. For instance, Schilcher et al. [25] exemplified this in their FALKE project, which united 14 disciplines, including psychology, education, and linguistics, to study how teachers explain complex concepts. By combining cognitive psychology with educational theory and linguistic analysis, the study revealed ways to enhance teaching effectiveness, offering practical tools for educators while advancing theoretical insights into learning processes. Such collaborations demonstrate how multidisciplinary psychology can create a broader and deeper understanding of human behaviour by leveraging diverse expertise.

Transdisciplinary psychology pushes these boundaries further, synthesising disciplinary insights to forge new frameworks or even novel fields of inquiry. This approach often involves non-academic stakeholders, ensuring that research is both scientifically robust and socially impactful. A prime example is the emergence of the learning sciences, as traced by Pea and Linn [26]. This transdisciplinary field integrates psychology, computer science, and education to explore learning as a contextual, interactive process. By blending psychological theories of cognition with computational models, researchers have developed adaptive technologies that personalise education, transforming how we teach and learn. This work highlights psychology's ability to transcend traditional silos, creating innovative solutions that address real-world needs.

Psychology's cross-cutting role also shines in applied settings, where it collaborates with fields like technology and health to tackle pressing challenges. Article [27] explored how psychology intersects with computer science to advance clinical practice, using tools like virtual reality to treat anxiety and artificial intelligence to improve diagnostic precision. Similarly, Aliman et al. [28] proposed a transdisciplinary AI observatory, merging psychological insights into human cognition with technical analyses of AI risks. Their framework examines the ethical and social implications of AI, illustrating psychology's critical role in shaping responsible technological development. These examples underscore how psychology's cross-disciplinary nature enables it to address global issues with both scientific depth and ethical sensitivity.

Another compelling application is the transdisciplinary study of animal-assisted interventions by Trevathan-Minnis et al. [29]. By integrating psychology, ethology, and clinical social work, this research developed evidence-based guidelines for mental health professionals incorporating animals into therapy. The resulting standards enhance therapeutic outcomes and ethical practices, benefiting both humans and animals. This work exemplifies how psychology can bridge academic and practical domains, fostering collaborations that amplify its impact on well-being.

What makes these approaches uniquely powerful is their ability to balance rigorous science with a human-centred perspective. Psychology's commitment to inclusivity and ethical practice ensures that its research resonates with diverse communities. The APA Publication Manual [23] emphasises accessible, bias-free communication, a principle reflected in studies [30] on spirituality in therapy, which explore how personal beliefs shape therapeutic relationships. By prioritising cultural sensitivity, psychology creates interventions that are both effective and deeply respectful of individual experiences. In transdisciplinary projects, such as those in the learning sciences, engaging educators and students as co-creators of knowledge further democratises research, empowering communities to shape their futures.

Despite its promise, cross-disciplinary and transdisciplinary psychology faces challenges, including coordinating diverse methodologies and navigating institutional barriers. Authors in [31] note that logistical hurdles can derail collaborative projects, but strategies like shared vocabularies and structured problem-solving can mitigate these issues. Looking ahead, psychology is poised to explore new frontiers, such as climate psychology, where it collaborates with environmental science to address climate-related stress, or neuroethics, where it joins philosophy and neuroscience to tackle ethical dilemmas in brain research. These emerging areas highlight psychology's potential to remain a vital force in addressing humanity's most pressing questions.

Psychology's role as a cross-cutting, multidisciplinary, and transdisciplinary discipline reflects its unique ability to blend scientific inquiry with a deep understanding of the human condition. From revolutionising education to advancing mental health and guiding ethical technology, psychology's collaborative spirit drives innovation while staying grounded in empathy. As it continues to evolve, psychology will undoubtedly inspire new ways of thinking, offering hope and insight in a complex and ever-changing world.

3 Place of Modern Technology in Psychological Science

The development of psychological science has been significantly influenced by the incorporation of advanced data science methodologies, producing a dynamic intersection between computational innovation and the systematic investigation of the human mind. A foundational milestone was the introduction of *electroencephalography* (EEG) in the early twentieth century, which enabled the measurement of brain activity with millisecond precision, thereby providing an immediate window into neural processes [32]. By recording electrical signals via scalp electrodes, EEG facilitated the extraction of features associated with cognition, although its restricted spatial resolution highlighted the need for complementary techniques. The subsequent emergence of *functional magnetic resonance imaging* (fMRI) addressed this limitation by employing blood-oxygen-level-dependent contrasts to capture brain activity with high spatial resolution, thereby advancing the capacity to examine functional connectivity in detail [33]. In tandem, EEG and fMRI have produced multimodal datasets that integrate temporal sensitivity with spatial accuracy, laying the foundation for data-driven insights into the neural basis of cognition.

The narrative expanded with eye-tracking technology, which quantifies gaze patterns to decode attentional and perceptual processes. By tracking fixations and saccades, eye-tracking systems produced high-dimensional data that illuminated behaviours like reading and decision-making [34]. Integrating eye-tracking data with EEG enabled the computation of fixation-related potentials, providing a multimodal dataset to model neural responses during naturalistic tasks [35]. *Quantitative EEG* (qEEG) further enriched this landscape, employing spectral analysis and network modelling to quantify brain states, supporting applications like neurofeedback for mental health interventions [36].

A transformative chapter unfolded with the rise of artificial intelligence (AI) and machine learning (ML), which revolutionised the analysis of psychological data. Supervised and unsupervised algorithms, applied to EEG, fMRI, and eye-tracking datasets, identified latent patterns predictive of cognitive workload, emotional states, or early neurological disorders [37]. Deep learning models advanced *brain-computer interfaces* (BCIS), using neural networks to decode imagined speech from EEG signals, enabling communication for individuals with motor impairments [38]. AI also facilitated cross-modal integration, combining EEG's temporal precision with fMRI's spatial resolution to reconstruct mental imagery through generative models, pushing the boundaries of cognitive data science [39].

This data-driven revolution faces significant challenges. EEG data are prone to artefacts from motion or environmental noise and require robust preprocessing pipelines, including filtering and independent component analysis [40]. In the case of fMRI, it has a temporal lag and high computational cost, demanding efficient algorithms for real-time analysis, while its expense limits dataset scalability [41]. Eye-tracking data, though rich, capture only overt attention, necessitating fusion with other modalities to model subjective states [42]. AI models, particularly deep neural networks, often lack interpretability, posing challenges for validation and ethical deployment in domains like clinical diagnostics or neuromarketing [43].

Despite these hurdles, the synergy of these technologies has redefined psychological data science, fostering interdisciplinary pipelines that integrate neuroscience, psychology, and computational methods. In neuromarketing, EEG and eye-tracking data feed predictive models to optimise advertising strategies [44]. In education, AI-driven BCIS leverage real-time cognitive data to personalise learning environments, enhancing outcomes through adaptive algorithms [45]. Clinically, qEEG and fMRI datasets inform ML models for precision diagnostics and therapeutic planning in conditions like depression, epilepsy, and autism [46].

This era of psychological data science reflects a relentless pursuit of knowledge, where each technological advance generates new datasets and analytical challenges, driven by the goal of decoding human cognition. As EEG streams capture neural dynamics, fMRI datasets map functional networks, eye-tracking records attentional patterns, and AI models synthesise these into predictive insights, the field stands at the forefront of discovery. These elements, grounded in computational rigour and inspired by the human mind, underscore a core principle of data science: when technology and data are harnessed with precision and purpose, they illuminate the intricate patterns of human experience, advancing our understanding of what it means to think, feel, and be.

4 Common Approaches in the Application of Modern Technologies

Contemporary psychological research is increasingly underpinned by technological innovations that facilitate novel forms of data collection, analysis, and intervention. This section outlines several of the most prevalent approaches through which modern technologies are integrated into psychological science.

A widely adopted application is the utilisation of online platforms for participant recruitment and data acquisition. Services such as Amazon Mechanical Turk, Prolific, and other specialised research portals enable researchers to access large and diverse samples with relative efficiency [47, 48]. Web-based studies can incorporate a range of instruments—including self-report questionnaires, cognitive tasks, and multimedia stimuli—thereby extending the reach of traditional laboratory-based methodologies.

Wearable devices, including smartwatches and fitness trackers, represent another powerful tool for psychological research. These technologies provide continuous and unobtrusive monitoring of physiological and behavioural parameters, such as heart rate, physical activity, sleep quality, and stress indicators derived from galvanic skin responses. When combined with Ecological Momentary Assessment (EMA), wearables enable the simultaneous collection of subjective self-reports and objective physiological data, offering a fine-grained understanding of mood, stress, and engagement in naturalistic contexts [49].

Neuroimaging and neurophysiological methods, including fMRI, EEG, and functional near-infrared spectroscopy (fNIRS), have transformed investigations of brain-behaviour relationships. These techniques provide insights into the neural substrates of cognition, emotion, and social interaction. Supported by advanced computational and statistical approaches, high-dimensional imaging data can be analysed to identify neural patterns associated with complex psychological constructs.

Digital interventions, delivered through mobile applications, Web-based platforms, or immersive virtual environments, have also become increasingly prominent in applied psychology. Interventions such as cognitive behavioural therapy (CBT) modules, mindfulness-based training, and structured self-help programmes can be delivered remotely, enabling real-time monitoring and adaptive feedback. Moreover, the digital format produces detailed behavioural traces—such as response times, adherence patterns, and symptom trajectories—that can be leveraged to refine and personalise therapeutic approaches.

While these technological advances offer considerable opportunities for innovation, they also introduce important ethical and methodological challenges. Issues of data privacy, informed consent, and digital equity require careful attention, particularly given the sensitive nature of wearable and neuroimaging data. Secure data storage, anonymisation protocols, and safeguards against sampling biases are essential to ensure that the integration of technology into psychological science proceeds responsibly and inclusively.

5 Pipeline: From Data Collection Towards Conclusions

In psychological research, the process of inquiry may be conceptualised as a methodological pipeline extending from study design through to final interpretation, with each stage building upon and refining the preceding one. The integration of data science methodologies and Python-based automated workflows within this pipeline offers substantial benefits in terms of methodological rigour, analytical efficiency, and reproducibility of empirical findings. The following section delineates the principal components of this research pipeline and identifies Python tools and practices that can be effectively employed at each stage.

Any empirical investigation in psychology commences with the formulation of precise research questions or hypotheses. Within data-science-oriented workflows, this initial planning stage encompasses several critical components:

- *Conceptual model*: Specification of the central psychological constructs, their operational definitions, and the hypothesised relationships among them.
- *Study design*: Selection of an appropriate methodological framework—experimental, quasi-experimental, or observational. At this stage, researchers frequently conduct power analyses (e.g. using `statsmodels` in Python) to determine the sample size required to detect expected effects with adequate statistical power [50].

```
from statsmodels.stats.power import TTestIndPower

# Example power analysis for a two-sample t-test
analysis = TTestIndPower()

# Suppose we hypothesize an effect size (Cohen's d) of
↪ 0.5
# We want alpha=0.05 and power=0.8
sample_size = analysis.solve_power(effect_size=0.5,
↪ alpha=0.05, power=0.8)
print(f"Recommended sample size per group:
↪ {sample_size:.2f}")
```

- *Ethical and logistical considerations*: Obtaining approval from relevant ethics committees, establishing robust data privacy and security procedures, and defining recruitment strategies for participants.

A well-conceived design not only provides a coherent framework for addressing the research questions but also mitigates potential data quality challenges that may emerge during subsequent stages of the research pipeline.

As outlined in Sect. 4, recent technological developments have significantly expanded the range of data sources accessible to psychological research:

- *Survey platforms and online experiments*: Python can interact with online platforms (e.g. through APIs) to facilitate automated data retrieval. Experimental frameworks such as `PsychoPy` enable the design of both laboratory-based tasks and online experiments incorporating customised stimuli [51].
- *Wearables and sensors*: Physiological measures—including heart rate, electrodermal activity, and movement—can be continuously recorded and processed using Python libraries for Bluetooth or serial communication (e.g. `pyserial`, `bleak`).
- *Social media and digital trace data*: Large-scale behavioural datasets may be collected through Web scraping techniques and RESTful APIs, with tools such as `requests` or `tweepy` (for Twitter) providing efficient interfaces for data acquisition.

Once data are obtained, rigorous documentation of collection procedures—including the timing of assessments, participant demographics, and instructions provided—is essential to ensure transparency, reproducibility, and interpretability of results.

Following acquisition, researchers typically initiate preprocessing using Python libraries such as `pandas`, which facilitate the detection of duplicate entries, management of missing values, and conversion of variables to appropriate data types:

```python
import pandas as pd

#Example of basic data cleaning

df = pd.read_csv("raw_data.csv")
df.drop_duplicates(inplace=True)

#Simple imputation

df.fillna(value={"age": df["age"].mean()}, inplace=True)
```

Data preprocessing frequently extends beyond these initial steps to include:

- *Feature selection and engineering*: Constructing composite variables (e.g. deriving a stress index from multiple physiological indicators)
- *Normalisation and scaling*: Essential for advanced modelling approaches such as neural networks
- *Outlier treatment*: Applying statistical thresholds or domain-specific knowledge to manage extreme values

A thorough preprocessing stage reduces error variance and enhances the robustness of subsequent statistical analyses [52].

Before engaging in formal hypothesis testing, researchers generally conduct exploratory data analysis (EDA) to evaluate distributions, detect anomalies, and examine preliminary relationships:

- *Descriptive statistics*: Functions such as `df.describe()` provide concise numerical summaries.
- *Visualisation*: Libraries including `matplotlib`, `seaborn`, and `plotly` allow for the creation of histograms, boxplots, and scatterplots to highlight distributions and potential outliers.
- *Correlations*: Pairwise correlation matrices (e.g. via `df.corr()`) reveal bivariate associations among variables of interest.

Robust EDA can identify potential confounders, distributional skewness, or violations of assumptions that may shape subsequent modelling choices.

At the inferential stage, both classical statistical tests and modern computational methods are employed, depending on the research questions and data structure:

- *Inferential statistics*: Libraries such as `scipy.stats` or `pingouin` support hypothesis tests including t-tests and ANOVAs [53].
- *Regression analysis*: `statsmodels` and `scikit-learn` enable the estimation of linear and logistic regression models to examine predictive relationships.
- *Bayesian approaches*: Packages such as `PyMC` facilitate the integration of prior information and provide posterior distributions, offering richer interpretive frameworks than traditional point estimates.
- *ML methods*: Libraries including `scikit-learn`, `TensorFlow`, and `PyTorch` can be applied to classification (e.g. identifying clinical or psychological symptoms with decision trees, random forests, support vector machines) [54] or clustering (e.g. grouping participants by psychometric profiles).

To ensure that models capture substantive rather than artefactual patterns, diagnostic procedures are indispensable:

- *Residual analysis*: Assessing predicted versus observed values to detect heteroscedasticity or nonlinearity.
- *Cross-validation*: Techniques such as K-fold validation in `scikit-learn` provide reliable estimates of generalisability while mitigating overfitting.
- *Model comparison*: Evaluating alternative models using information criteria (AIC, BIC) or predictive performance metrics (e.g. RMSE, accuracy, F1-score).

Interpretation extends beyond statistical significance. Researchers are increasingly encouraged to consider:

- *Effect sizes*: Metrics such as Cohen's d, partial η^2, or Bayes factors provide information on practical significance.

- *Confidence and credible intervals*: Critical for assessing the precision of estimates.
- *Theoretical integration*: Situating results within broader psychological theories and empirical literatures.
- *Limitations*: Explicit recognition of potential confounds, assumptions, and representativeness issues affecting generalisability.

Finally, transparency and reproducibility are essential components of contemporary data science practice. Python's ecosystem offers extensive support for open science:

- *Notebooks and scripts*: Platforms such as `Jupyter` and `Google Colab` integrate code, output, and narrative text into reproducible workflows [55, 56].
- *Version control*: Tools like GitHub and GitLab track modifications to scripts and datasets, enhancing collaboration and accountability [57].
- *Open data and code sharing*: Increasingly encouraged by journals, repositories such as OSF and Zenodo enable the dissemination of datasets and analysis pipelines, promoting independent verification and meta-analytic synthesis [58, 59].

6 Statistical Analysis in Psychology

In psychological sciences, statistical analysis represents far more than a methodological add-on. Statistical analysis is the foundational structure upon which empirical inference is built. Psychological constructs are often abstract, latent, and complex, making statistics indispensable in transforming observational or experimental data into interpretable and valid conclusions. From the earliest stages of hypothesis testing to the final interpretation of research results, statistical techniques allow psychologists to uncover patterns, quantify behaviours, and make evidence-based decisions that extend beyond anecdotal observations. Typical steps in research are shown in Fig. 1.

The roots of statistical application in psychology can be traced back to the discipline's effort to differentiate itself from speculative philosophy. The pioneering works of Galton, Pearson, and Fisher introduced statistical reasoning into behavioural research, gradually replacing narrative speculation with quantitative rigour [60]. In contemporary practice, statistical methods are inseparable from every aspect of psychological research, whether it involves designing controlled experi-

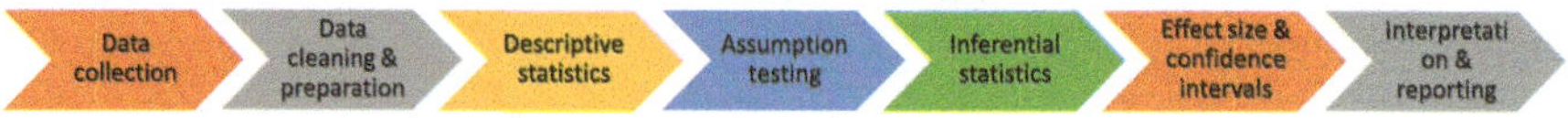

Fig. 1 Flowchart of statistical analysis pipeline in research

Fig. 2 Conceptual diagram of variable types and statistical tests

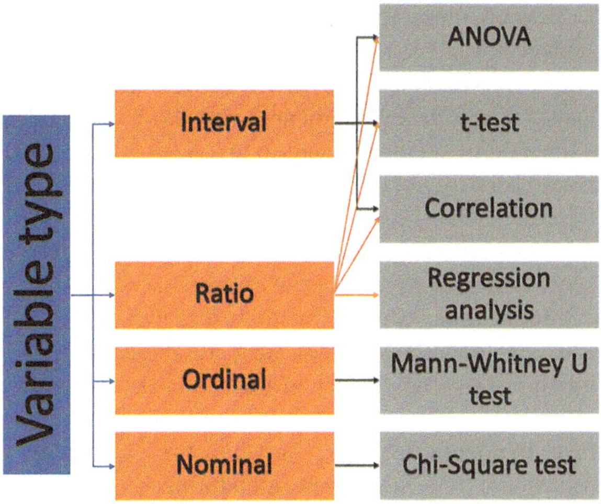

ments, assessing psychometric properties of instruments, or evaluating intervention effectiveness.

At the heart of most psychological research lies the inferential statistics framework. This approach allows researchers to generalise findings from a sample to a broader population while accounting for random variation. Techniques such as t-tests, χ^2 tests, and analysis of variance (ANOVA) are routinely applied to determine whether observed differences between groups are statistically significant or merely products of chance [53]. For example, a clinical psychologist investigating the impact of cognitive behavioural therapy on anxiety scores may rely on ANOVA to compare outcomes across different treatment groups. Which methodology and type of test will be used in the research largely depends on the type of variable being observed, as shown in Fig. 2.

Statistical analysis also facilitates the estimation of the effect sizes, providing a clearer picture of the magnitude of observed differences. While significance testing tells us whether an effect exists, effect size quantification tells us how meaningful that effect is. This is an essential consideration in applied psychology, where practical implications matter more than statistical significance [50].

Correlational analysis serves another crucial function in psychology by identifying relationships between variables [61]. Pearson's correlation coefficient r and Spearman's rank correlation are among the most widely used measures for understanding associations in both experimental and observational data. These analyses are central to psychological models that seek to map connections between traits, symptoms, attitudes, and behaviours. The interpretive caution that *correlation does not imply causation* remains essential, as latent confounders or reverse causality may obscure causal pathways [62].

Beyond these foundational tools, regression analysis offers a more flexible statistical framework. Linear regression is commonly used to predict psychological outcomes based on a set of predictor variables. Whether predicting academic performance from self-regulation and stress levels, or modelling depressive symptoms as a function of socioeconomic status and social support, regression techniques allow researchers to isolate the unique contribution of each variable while controlling for others [52]. Logistic regression, meanwhile, is suited to categorical outcomes, such as predicting whether an individual will relapse after therapy based on a constellation of psychological markers.

Multivariate statistical methods such as MANOVA, factor analysis, and structural equation modelling (SEM) are particularly relevant when dealing with multidimensional psychological constructs. For instance, in personality psychology, factor analysis has been instrumental in developing trait-based models such as the Big Five, by identifying latent variables that account for covariation among observed behaviours [63]. SEM goes a step further by allowing researchers to test theoretical models involving multiple variables, direct and indirect effects, and mediating paths within a single statistical framework [64].

In psychometrics, statistical analysis plays a central role in test construction and validation. Item Response Theory (IRT) and Classical Test Theory (CTT) are used to assess item-level performance, reliability, and validity of psychological scales [65]. Cronbach's alpha, a measure of internal consistency, remains a staple in evaluating the reliability of psychological instruments, although newer approaches like McDonald's Omega are gaining attention for their more robust assumptions [66].

Another domain where statistical analysis proves critical is in the use of longitudinal and time-series data. Psychological processes often unfold over time, necessitating methods like repeated measures ANOVA, growth curve modelling, and cross-lagged panel models to capture temporal dynamics [67]. These methods are essential in developmental psychology and clinical trials, where understanding change trajectories offers richer insights than cross-sectional snapshots.

With the rise of computational psychology and digital data sources, the scope of statistical methods has further expanded. ML algorithms and Bayesian inference are increasingly being used for predictive modelling and uncertainty quantification in psychological research [68]. Bayesian approaches are particularly attractive in psychology due to their capacity to integrate prior knowledge into the statistical inference process and provide more intuitive probabilistic interpretations [69].

Importantly, the integrity of statistical analysis depends not only on the methods themselves but also on the transparency and reproducibility of the analytical process. The replication crisis in psychology has underscored the need for rigorous statistical practices, preregistration of hypotheses, and full disclosure of analytical decisions [70]. The APA now strongly encourages researchers to go beyond mere p-values and provide comprehensive statistical reporting that includes confidence intervals, effect sizes, and model diagnostics [23].

7 Data Validation Tests and Performance Measures

Data validation tests and performance measures ensure the accuracy and interpretability of psychological research. This section outlines various validation strategies ranging from fundamental data integrity checks to sophisticated psychometric and ML performance measures and illustrates how they can be implemented within a Python workflow [54, 71].

Data integrity checks form the bedrock of any empirical study. They aim to confirm that the dataset is internally consistent, complete, and free from errors.

- *Data type consistency*: Ensuring variables are stored in appropriate formats (e.g. numeric vs. categorical). In Python, `df.dtypes` (pandas) helps confirm or convert variable types.
- *Range and domain checks*: Verifying that numeric variables fall within logical ranges (e.g. age in years, Likert-scale responses from 1 to 5). One can easily flag anomalies using Boolean indexing:

```python
import pandas as pd

# Example: Flag unrealistic ages (< 10 or > 100)
df_invalid_ages = df[(df["age"] < 10) | (df["age"] > 100)]
```

- *Missingness patterns*: Determining if missing data are Missing Completely At Random (MCAR), Missing At Random (MAR), or Not Missing At Random (NMAR) [52]. Simple checks using `df.isna().sum()` can highlight patterns. Multiple imputation techniques (`statsmodels.imputation.mice.MICEData`) can handle MAR data effectively;
- *Duplicate detection*: Identifying duplicate participants, rows, or IDs. In Python, `df.duplicated()` checks for repeated entries, which can then be examined or dropped as warranted by the study design.

Many statistical techniques used in psychology (e.g. t-tests, ANOVAs) assume normality or homogeneity of variances.

- *Visual inspection*: Histograms, Q-Q plots, and box plots (`seaborn` or `matplotlib`) remain an effective first glance at distribution shapes.
- *Statistical tests*: The Shapiro-Wilk and Kolmogorov-Smirnov tests (`scipy.stats`) can formally check if data deviate from normality. For homogeneity of variance, Levene's test or Bartlett's test are commonly applied [53].
- *Non-parametric alternatives*: If data violate normality or homoscedasticity, researchers can employ non-parametric tests (e.g. Mann-Whitney U, Kruskal-Wallis) or transform data (e.g. log, square root) to better satisfy assumptions.

In psychological assessment, reliability refers to the consistency of a measure, while validity addresses whether the measure accurately captures the intended construct. Python libraries like `pingouin` simplify common reliability metrics:

- *Internal consistency*: Cronbach's alpha or McDonald's omega can be computed to evaluate consistency across items in a questionnaire. For instance:

```
import pingouin as pg

# Suppose 'df_items' has columns for each questionnaire item
cronbach_alpha = pg.cronbach_alpha(data=df_items)
print(cronbach_alpha)
```

- *Test-retest reliability*: Repeated measures of the same participants over time can be correlated to assess stability.
- *Validity checks*: Construct validity (factor analysis, correlations with theoretically related constructs), convergent/discriminant validity, and criterion validity (predictive power) are integral to confirming a measure's robustness.

Outliers can significantly skew parameter estimates and inflate error rates in psychological studies [52]. They may represent genuine extreme cases or data entry mistakes. Common techniques include:

- *Statistical approaches*: Z-scores ($\pm$ 3) or Interquartile Range (IQR) methods.
- *Model-based approaches*: Fitting a regression model or clustering algorithm (`scikit-learn`) to detect unusual points in multidimensional space.
- *Decision strategies*: Once identified, outliers can be retained (if theoretically justifiable), winsorised, or removed, depending on the study's analytic goals.

When psychological research ventures into predictive frameworks, such as classifying clinical diagnoses, forecasting behaviour, or clustering personality types, the question of model performance becomes critical:

- *Classification metrics*: Accuracy, precision, recall, F_1-score, and the confusion matrix (`sklearn.metrics.confusion_matrix`) are particularly relevant when detecting phenomena such as clinically significant symptoms.
- *Regression metrics*: Mean Squared Error (MSE), Mean Absolute Error (MAE), and R^2 gauge the predictive accuracy for continuous psychological outcomes (e.g. stress or mood scores).
- *Receiver Operating Characteristic-Area Under the Curve (ROC-AUC) and Precision-Recall Area Under the Curve (PR-AUC)*: These provide insight into a classifier's performance across different thresholds, which can be crucial when balancing false positives and false negatives (e.g. identifying at-risk individuals).

```
from sklearn.metrics import roc_auc_score, precision_score

# Example usage for binary classification predictions
auc = roc_auc_score(y_true, y_pred_probs)
precision = precision_score(y_true, y_pred_classes)
```

- *Cross-validation and resampling*: K-fold cross-validation, bootstrapping, or Monte Carlo resampling (`sklearn.model_selection`) help assess generalisability by repeatedly training on subsets of the data and testing on held-out folds.

In applying data science techniques to psychological data, interpretability and fairness take on special importance:

- *Interpretability tools*: Methods such as permutation importance, partial dependence plots, or SHAP (SHapley Additive exPlanations) can elucidate how features (e.g. demographic or psychometric variables) influence model predictions.
- *Fairness considerations*: Ensuring that predictive models do not inadvertently discriminate against specific groups (e.g. based on gender, race, age) is both an ethical and methodological priority, requiring careful checks and potential use of debiasing techniques.

Finally, clear documentation of validation steps and performance measures is essential for research transparency and reproducibility. Researchers should:

- Provide explicit criteria for data inclusion/exclusion (e.g. participant dropout, outlier thresholds).
- Report data quality metrics (e.g. proportion of missing data, reliability coefficients).
- Specify performance metrics (e.g. accuracy, AUC), rationale for the chosen metrics, and the results of cross-validation procedures.

Sharing code (e.g. via GitHub) and annotated Jupyter notebooks can further strengthen confidence in the robustness of findings.

8 Visualising Psychological Data Using Seaborn

Data visualisation constitutes a central component of both exploratory data analysis and the dissemination of findings within psychological science. Well-designed graphical representations can reveal underlying patterns, highlight anomalies, and convey complex results more effectively than tabular displays [72]. Within the Python ecosystem, the `seaborn` library—built on top of `matplotlib`—provides a concise and versatile framework particularly suited to the visualisation of psychological datasets. The present section outlines several commonly employed `seaborn` plotting techniques and illustrates their application through practical code examples that demonstrate how to generate clear and informative visualisations.

Psychological research often involves continuous variables such as test scores, reaction times, or scale responses. Visualising these distributions helps researchers assess normality, detect skew, and identify potential outliers [52].

A simple starting point for distribution visualisation is given in the following:

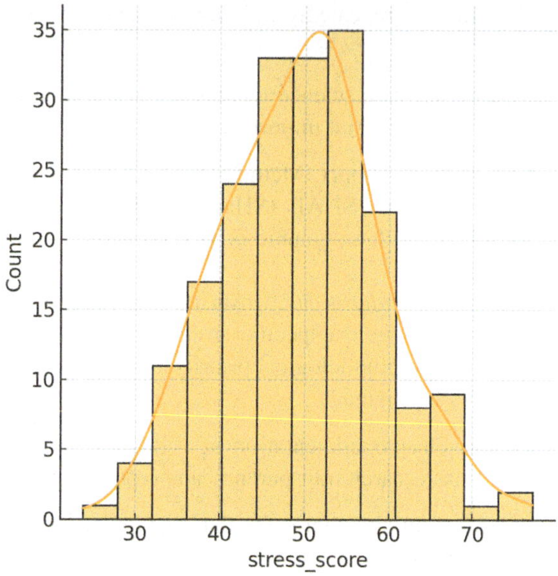

Fig. 3 Distribution of `Stress Scores` (histogram with KDE)

```
import seaborn as sns
import matplotlib.pyplot as plt
# 'df' is a pandas DataFrame, 'stress_score' is a continuous
↪ variable
sns.displot(data=df, x="stress_score", kde=True)
↪ plt.title("Distribution of Stress Scores") plt.show()
```

By default, `displot` creates a histogram. Setting `kde=True` overlays a kernel density estimate, providing a smooth approximation of the distribution. An example of this type of visualisation, illustrating the distribution of psychological stress scores, is shown in Fig. 3.

Boxplots and *violin plots* can reveal the central tendency and spread of data, as well as potential outliers. These visualisations are particularly useful when comparing distributions across different experimental conditions. For example, if `group` refers to an experimental condition (e.g. control vs. treatment) and `reaction_time` is a continuous outcome measure, then a boxplot (Fig. 4) and a violin plot (Fig. 5) can provide complementary views of the data distribution:

```
sns.boxplot(data=df, x="group", y="reaction_time")
plt.title("Reaction Times by Group")
plt.show()

sns.violinplot(data=df, x="group", y="reaction_time")
plt.title("Violin Plot of Reaction Times by Group")
plt.show()
```

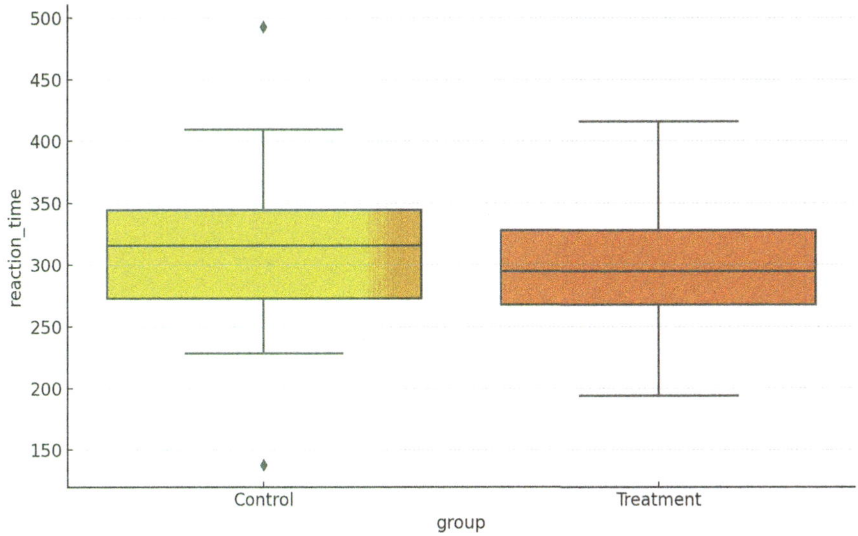

Fig. 4 `Reaction Times` by group (boxplot)

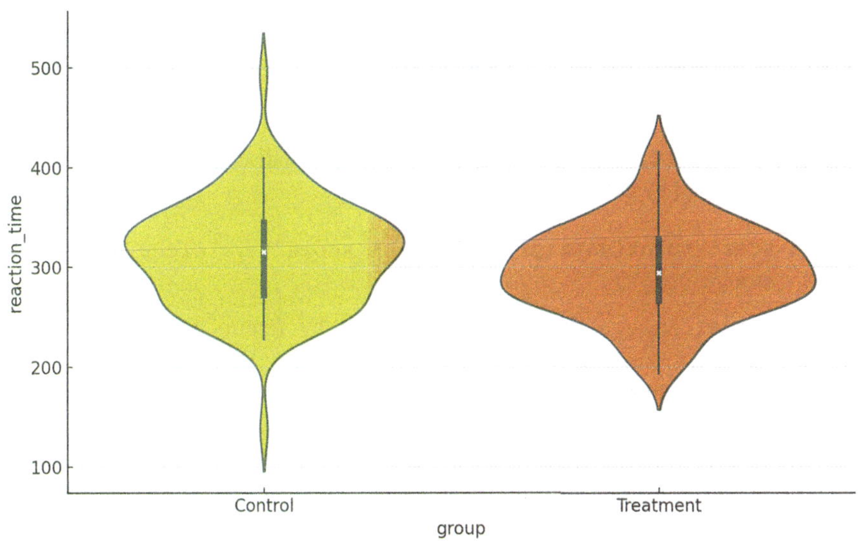

Fig. 5 Violin plot of `Reaction Times` by group

In psychological research, understanding relationships between variables, such as correlations among questionnaires or associations between predictors and outcomes, is crucial. We have two common methods to do that using `seaborn`.

Scatterplots are a straightforward and effective way to visualise the relationship between two continuous variables. In psychological research, they are often used

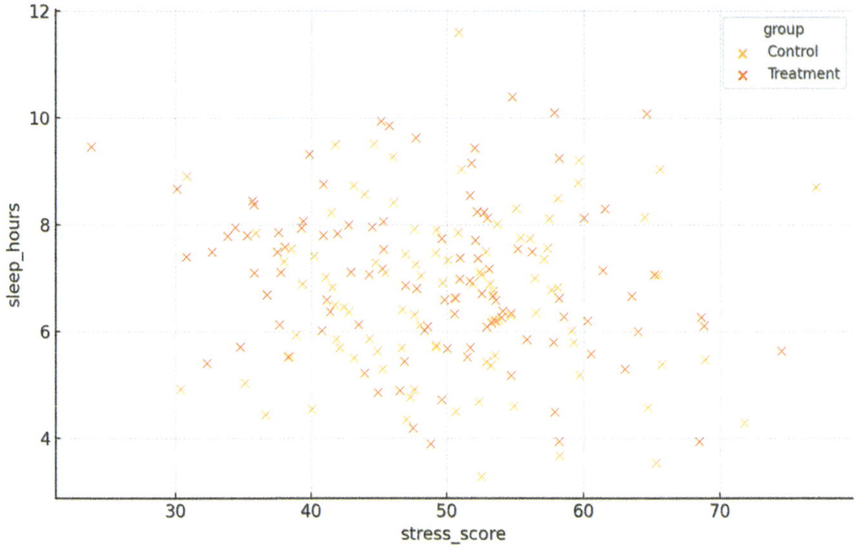

Fig. 6 `Stress` vs `Sleep`, coloured by group (scatterplot)

to explore associations between behavioural or self-reported measures. Optional arguments such as `hue` or `style` can be used to encode additional grouping variables, enabling a multi-dimensional view of the data. For instance, in the plot below, `stress_score` and `sleep_hours` are visualised with group membership distinguished by colour (Fig. 6):

```
sns.scatterplot(data=df, x="stress_score", y="sleep_hours",
↪ hue="group")
plt.title("Stress vs. Sleep, Colored by Group") plt.show()
```

The `seaborn` library provides convenient functions to add regression lines to scatterplots, allowing for quick visual assessment of potential linear relationships between two continuous variables. This is particularly useful during exploratory analysis or early hypothesis generation. In the example below, we visualise the association between self-reported anxiety scores and cortisol levels, a biological stress marker. The fitted regression line (in red) provides an immediate visual cue about the direction and strength of the relationship (Fig. 7):

```
sns.regplot(data=df, x="anxiety_score", y="cortisol_level",
↪ line_kws={"color":"red"})
plt.title("Association between Anxiety and Cortisol")
plt.show()
```

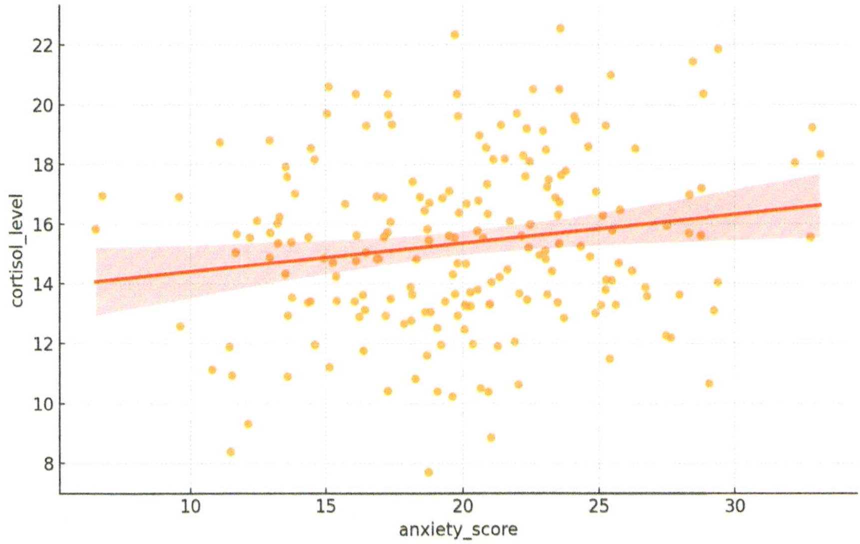

Fig. 7 Association between `Anxiety` and `Cortisol` (regression plot)

When analysing datasets with several continuous variables, it is often useful to explore their pairwise relationships simultaneously. The `pairplot` function from the `seaborn` library provides a quick and effective way to generate a grid of scatterplots, histograms, and density plots for each pair of variables. This visualisation helps identify potential correlations, outliers, or distributional patterns. In the example below, we explore the relationships among anxiety scores, stress scores, and hours of sleep (Fig. 8).

```
sns.pairplot(df[["anxiety_score", "stress_score",
↪  "sleep_hours"]])
plt.suptitle("Pairwise Relationships", y=1.02)
plt.show()
```

Many psychological studies involve categorical or ordinal data, such as diagnostic categories, intervention groups, or Likert-scale responses. One of the most effective ways to visualise the frequency of categorical variables is through a *count plot*. This type of visualisation is useful for summarising sample characteristics, such as the distribution of diagnoses in a clinical study or the number of participants per experimental condition. The following Python example uses `seaborn`'s `countplot` to display the frequency of different diagnostic categories in a dataset, as shown in Fig. 9:

```
sns.countplot(data=df, x="diagnosis_type")
plt.title("Count of Each Diagnosis")
plt.show()
```

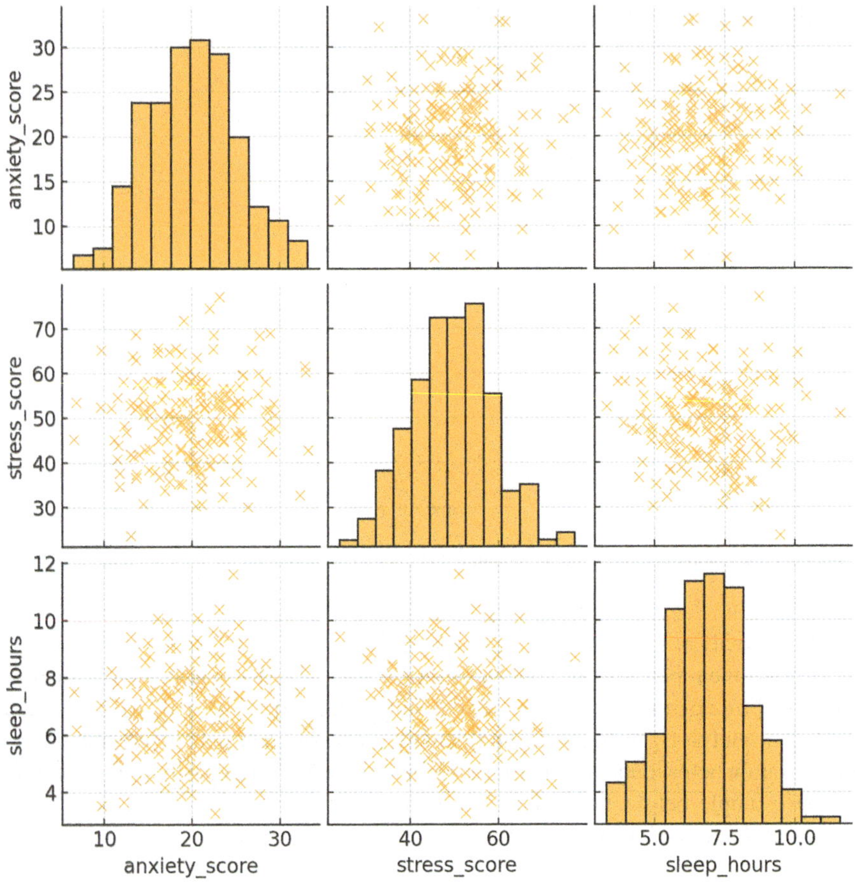

Fig. 8 Pairwise relationships (pairplot)

For group comparisons on a specific variable, such as evaluating the mean stress score across different therapy modalities, a *bar plot* with error bars is a useful visualisation technique. This type of plot communicates not only central tendency (e.g. the mean) but also variability, typically represented by standard deviation or confidence intervals. The example below demonstrates how to create such a plot using `seaborn`'s `barplot` function, where stress scores are compared across therapy types. The resulting output is shown in Fig. 10:

```
sns.barplot(data=df, x="therapy_type", y="stress_score",
↪ ci="sd")
plt.title("Mean Stress Score by Therapy Type")
plt.show()
```

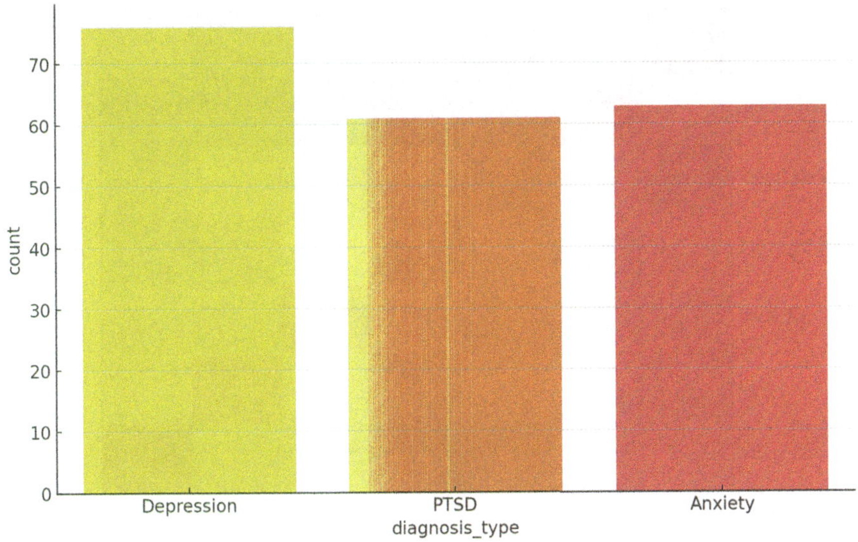

Fig. 9 Count of each diagnosis

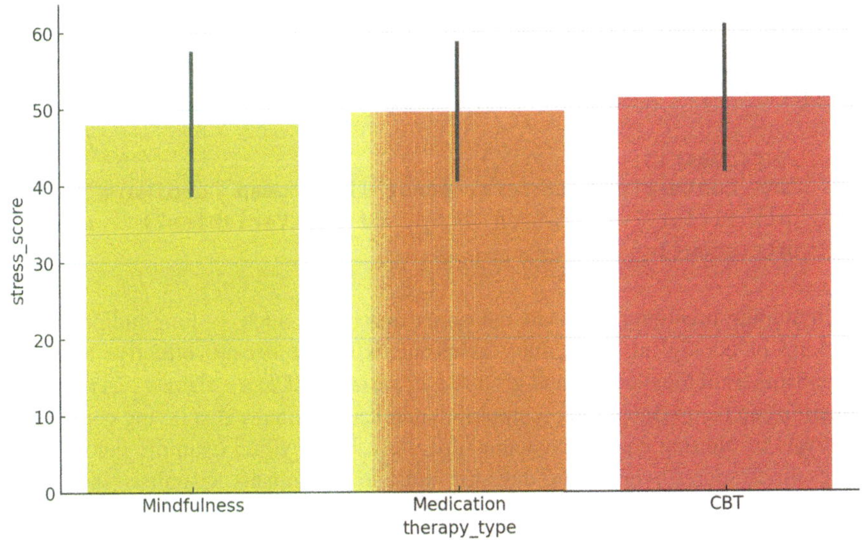

Fig. 10 Mean `Stress Score` by `Therapy Type`

Heatmaps are particularly useful for visualising correlation matrices or confusion matrices in classification tasks. In psychological data analysis, they allow researchers to quickly identify strong associations or potential multicollinearity among variables. The example below demonstrates how to compute and visualise a correlation matrix using `seaborn`'s `heatmap` function. The resulting figure

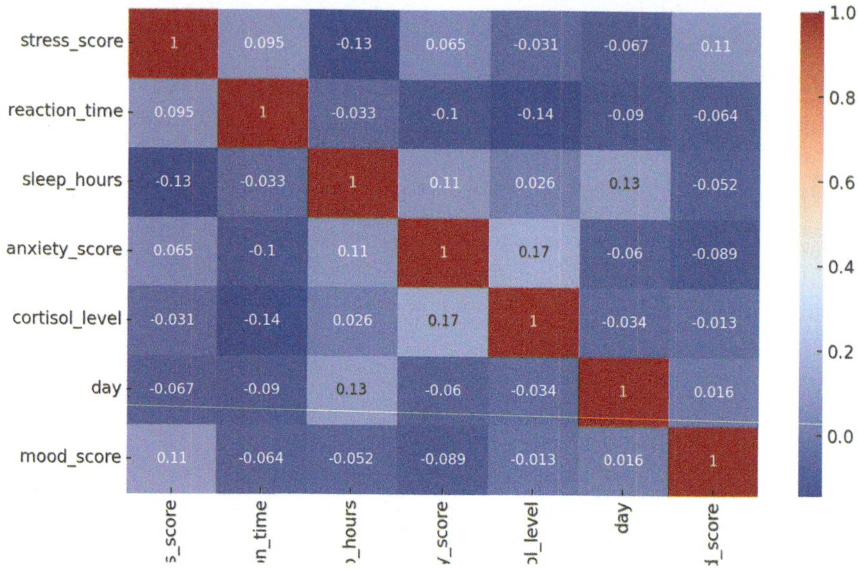

Fig. 11 Heatmap showing correlation of key variables

highlights pairwise relationships between key psychological variables and is shown in Fig. 11.

```
corr_matrix = df.corr()
sns.heatmap(corr_matrix, annot=True, cmap="coolwarm")
plt.title("Correlation Matrix of Key Variables")
plt.show()
```

In studies involving repeated measures over time, such as longitudinal mood tracking or ecological momentary assessments, *line plots* are effective tools for visualising individual trends and group-level variation. The `seaborn.lineplot` function can be used to depict temporal dynamics, optionally displaying confidence intervals or plotting each participant separately. The Python example below illustrates mood scores over several days for multiple participants, visualised in Fig. 12:

```
sns.lineplot(data=df, x="day", y="mood_score",
↪ hue="participant_id", estimator=None)
plt.title("Mood Score over Time by Participant")
plt.show()
```

Best practices can be summarised as follows:

- *Use clear labels and titles*: Axis labels should precisely describe the psychological construct or scale, and figure titles should concisely state the main message.

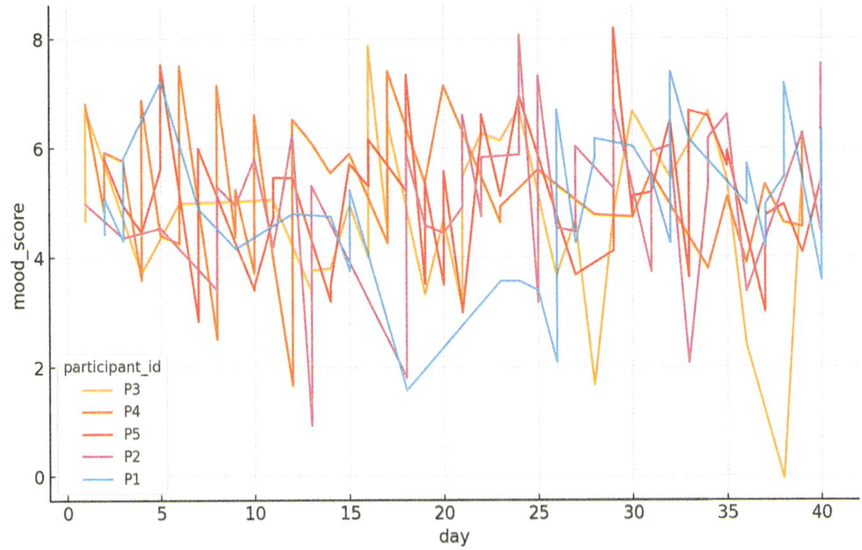

Fig. 12 Timeseries of `Mood Score` over `Time` by `Participant`

- *Color palettes*: `seaborn` provides themed palettes (e.g. `deep`, `pastel`, `muted`). Use contrasting colours for clarity, particularly when distinguishing multiple categories.
- *Annotations*: Adding annotations or reference lines can highlight critical thresholds (e.g. clinical cutoffs) or expected patterns.
- *Subplots and faceting*: `FacetGrid` and `sns.catplot` can produce multi-panel plots, enabling a more systematic comparison across groups or conditions.

References

1. C.D. Green, *Early Psychological Thought: Ancient Accounts of Mind and Soul*, ed. by P. R. Groff (Praeger, Westport, 2003)
2. C.J. Goodwin, *A History of Modern Psychology* (John Wiley & Sons, Hoboken, 2022)
3. W. Wundt, in *Readings in the History of Psychology*, ed. by W. Dennis (Appleton-Century-Crofts, New York, 1948), pp. 248–250
4. E.B. Titchener, The postulates of a structural psychology. Philos. Rev. **7**(5), 449 (1898)
5. W. James, *The Principles of Psychology Volume II by William James (1890)* (Henry Holt and Company, New York, 1890)
6. G.S. Hall, *Life and Confessions of a Psychologist* (D. Appleton, New York City,1924)
7. S. Freud, *The interpretation of dreams*. (Leipzig & Vienna, Franz Deuticke,1900)
8. J.B. Watson, Psychology as the behaviorist views it. Psychol. Rev. **20**(2), 158 (1913)
9. B.F. Skinner, *The Behavior of Organisms: An Experimental Analysis* (BF Skinner Foundation, Cambridge, 2019)

10. G.A. Miller, The magical number seven, plus or minus two: some limits on our capacity for processing information. Psychol. Re. **63**(2), 81 (1956)
11. N. Chomsky, Logical structure in language. J. Am. Soc. Inf. Sci. **8**(4), 284 (1957)
12. C.R. Rogers, in *Psychotherapist's Casebook: Theory and Technique in Practice*, ed. by I.L. Kutash, A. Wolf (Jossey-Bass, San Francisco, 1986), pp. 197–208
13. A.H. Maslow, A theory of human motivation. Psychol. Rev. **50**(4), 370 (1943)
14. D. Shakow, Seventeen years later: clinical psychology in light of the 1947 Committee on Training in Clinical Psychology Report. Am. Psychol. **20**(5), 353 (1965)
15. D.O. Hebb, *The Organization of Behavior: A Neuropsychological Theory* (Psychology Press, Milton Park, 2005)
16. K. Lewin, Frontiers in group dynamics: concept, method and reality in social science; social equilibria and social change. Hum. Relat. **1**(1), 5 (1947)
17. J. Piaget, M. Cook, et al., *The Origins of Intelligence in Children*, vol. 8.5 (International Universities Press, New York, 1952)
18. H.C. Triandis, et al., *Culture and Social Behavior*, vol. 330 (McGraw-Hill New York, 1994)
19. M.F. Washburn, *The Animal Mind: A Text-Book of Comparative Psychology*, vol. 2 (Macmillan, New York, 1926)
20. A. Rutherford, M. Pettit, Feminism and/in/as psychology: the public sciences of sex and gender. Hist. Psychol. **18**(3), 223 (2015)
21. A.C. Brock, The future of the history of psychology revisited. Hist. Psychol. **19**(3), 175 (2016)
22. O. Wieczorek, S. Unger, J. Riebling, L. Erhard, C. Koß, R. Heiberger, Mapping the field of psychology: trends in research topics 1995–2015. Scientometrics **126**(12), 9699 (2021)
23. A.P. Association, et al., *Publication Manual of the American Psychological Association* (American Psychological Association Washington, 2020)
24. J. Henrich, S.J. Heine, A. Norenzayan, The weirdest people in the world? Behav. Brain Sci. **33**(2–3), 61 (2010)
25. A. Schilcher, S. Krauss, P. Kirchhoff, A. Lindl, S. Hilbert, K. Asen-Molz, C. Ehras, M. Elmer, M. Frei, L. Gaier, et al., FALKE: experiences from transdisciplinary educational research by fourteen disciplines, in *Frontiers in Education*, vol. 5 (Frontiers Media SA, Lausanne, 2021), p. 579982
26. R. Pea, M.C. Linn, Personal perspectives on the emergence of the learning sciences: 1970s–2005, in *Frontiers in Education*, vol. 5 (Frontiers Media SA, Lausanne, 2020), p. 130
27. G. Riva, Virtual reality in clinical psychology. Compr. Clin. Psychol. 91–105 (2022). https://10.1016/B978-0-12-818697-8.00006-6. Epub 2022 Apr 12. PMCID: PMC7500920
28. N.M. Aliman, L. Kester, R. Yampolskiy, Transdisciplinary AI observatory—retrospective analyses and future-oriented contradistinctions. Philosophies **6**(1), 6 (2021)
29. M. Trevathan-Minnis, A. Johnson, A.R. Howie, Recommendations for transdisciplinary professional competencies and ethics for animal-assisted therapies and interventions. Vet. Sci. **8**(12), 303 (2021)
30. L. Mangione, T.G. Plante, Spirituality in clinical practice: integrating who we are with what we do. Spiritual. Clin. Pract. **11**(1), 1 (2024)
31. N. Heitzmann, A. Opitz, M. Stadler, D. Sommerhoff, M.C. Fink, A. Obersteiner, R. Schmidmaier, B.J. Neuhaus, S. Ufer, T. Seidel, et al., Cross-disciplinary research on learning and instruction–coming to terms. Front. Psychol. **11**, 562658 (2021)
32. H. Berger, Über das Elektrenkephalogramm des Menschen. Archiv für Psychiatrie und Nervenkrankheiten **87**(1), 527 (1929). https://doi.org/10.1007/BF01797193
33. S. Ogawa, T.M. Lee, A.R. Kay, D.W. Tank, Brain magnetic resonance imaging with contrast dependent on blood oxygenation. Proc. Natl. Acad. Sci. **87**(24), 9868 (1990)
34. K. Rayner, Eye movements in reading and information processing: 20 years of research. Psychol. Bull. **124**(3), 372 (1998)
35. O. Dimigen, W. Sommer, A. Hohlfeld, A.M. Jacobs, R. Kliegl, Coregistration of eye movements and EEG in natural reading: analyses and review. J. Exp. Psychol. Gen. **140**(4), 552 (2011)

36. R.W. Thatcher, Validity and reliability of quantitative electroencephalography. J. Neurotherapy **14**(2), 122 (2010)
37. F. Lotte, L. Bougrain, A. Cichocki, M. Clerc, M. Congedo, A. Rakotomamonjy, F. Yger, A review of classification algorithms for EEG-based brain–computer interfaces: a 10 year update. J. Neural Eng. **15**(3), 031005 (2018)
38. D. Lopez-Bernal, D. Balderas, P. Ponce, A. Molina, A state-of-the-art review of EEG-based imagined speech decoding. Front. Hum. Neurosci. **16**, 867281 (2022)
39. G. Shen, K. Dwivedi, K. Majima, T. Horikawa, Y. Kamitani, End-to-end deep image reconstruction from human brain activity. Front. Comput. Neurosci. **13**, 21 (2019)
40. J.A. Urigüen, B. Garcia-Zapirain, EEG artifact removal—state-of-the-art and guidelines. J. Neural Eng. **12**(3), 031001 (2015)
41. R. Poldrack, *The New Mind Readers: What Neuroimaging Can and Cannot Reveal About Our Thoughts* (Princeton University Press, Princeton, 2018)
42. K. Holmqvist, M. Nyström, R. Andersson, R. Dewhurst, H. Jarodzka, J. Van de Weijer, *Eye Tracking: A Comprehensive Guide to Methods and Measures* (oup Oxford, Oxford, 2011)
43. A. Adadi, M. Berrada, Peeking inside the black-box: a survey on explainable artificial intelligence (XAI). IEEE Access **6**, 52138 (2018)
44. A. Hakim, D.J. Levy, A gateway to consumers' minds: achievements, caveats, and prospects of electroencephalography-based prediction in neuromarketing. Wiley Interdiscip. Rev. Cogn. Sci. **10**(2), e1485 (2019)
45. M. Spüler, W. Rosenstiel, M. Bogdan, Adaptive SVM-based classification increases performance of a MEG-based Brain-Computer Interface (BCI), in *Artificial Neural Networks and Machine Learning–ICANN 2012: 22nd International Conference on Artificial Neural Networks, Lausanne, September 11–14, 2012, Proceedings, Part I 22* (Springer, Berlin, 2012), pp. 669–676
46. R.E. Frye, S. Vassall, G. Kaur, C. Lewis, M. Karim, D. Rossignol, Emerging biomarkers in autism spectrum disorder: a systematic review. Ann. Transl. Med. **7**(23), 792 (2019)
47. Amazon mechanical turk, https://www.mturk.com (2005). Accessed 25 Aug 2025
48. Prolific, https://www.prolific.com (2014). Accessed 25 Aug 2025. First released 2014; location: London, UK
49. S. Shiffman, A.A. Stone, M.R. Hufford, Ecological momentary assessment. Ann. Rev. Clin. Psychol. **4**(1), 1 (2008)
50. J. Cohen, *Statistical Power Analysis for the Behavioral Sciences* (Routledge, Milton Park, 2013)
51. J.W. Peirce, J.R. Gray, S. Simpson, M. MacAskill, R. Höchenberger, H. Sogo, E. Kastman, J.K. Lindeløv, PsychoPy2: experiments in behavior made easy. Behav. Res. Methods **51**(1), 195 (2019). https://doi.org/10.3758/s13428-018-01193-y
52. B.G. Tabachnick, L.S. Fidell, *Using Multivariate Statistics*, 7th edn. (Pearson, London, 2021)
53. F.J. Gravetter, L.B. Wallnau, *Essentials of Statistics for the Behavioral Sciences* (Wadsworth Cengage Learning, Boston, 2011)
54. N. Kovač, K. Ratković, H. Farahani, P. Watson, A practical applications guide to machine learning regression models in psychology with python. Methods Psychol. **11**, 100156 (2024)
55. P. Jupyter, Jupyter Notebook documentation. https://jupyter.org/documentation (2023). Accessed 23 Jan 2023
56. Google, Google colaboratory. https://colab.research.google.com/ (2024). Accessed 25 Aug 2025
57. GitHub, Inc., Github: where the world builds software. https://github.com/ (2025). Accessed 22 Aug 2025
58. Center for Open Science, Open science framework (OSF). https://osf.io/ (2011). Accessed 25 Aug 2025
59. CERN, OpenAIRE. Zenodo. https://zenodo.org/ (2013). Accessed 25 Aug 2025
60. G. Gigerenzer, in *The Probabilistic Revolution, Vol. 1: Ideas in History; Vol. 2: Ideas in the Sciences*, ed. by L. Kruger, L.J. Daston, M. Heidelberger (The MIT Press, Cambridge, 1987), pp. 11–33

61. J. Cohen, P. Cohen, S.G. West, L.S. Aiken, *Applied Multiple Regression/Correlation Analysis for the Behavioral Sciences* (Routledge, Milton Park, 2013)
62. J.E. Hunter, F.L. Schmidt, *Methods of Meta-Analysis: Correcting Error and Bias in Research Findings* (Sage, Thousand Oaks, 2004)
63. R.R. McCrae, P.T. Costa Jr, Personality trait structure as a human universal. Am. Psychol. **52**(5), 509 (1997)
64. R.B. Kline, *Principles and Practice of Structural Equation Modeling* (Guilford Publications, New York City, 2023)
65. S.E. Embretson, S.P. Reise, *Item Response Theory for Psychologists* (Psychology Press, Milton Park, 2013)
66. R.P. McDonald, *Test Theory: A Unified Treatment* (Lawrence Erlbaum Associates, Mahwah, 1999)
67. J.D. Singer, J.B. Willett, *Applied Longitudinal Data Analysis: Modeling Change and Event Occurrence* (Oxford University Press, Oxford, 2003)
68. T. Yarkoni, J. Westfall, Choosing prediction over explanation in psychology: lessons from machine learning. Perspect. Psychol. Sci. **12**(6), 1100 (2017)
69. J.K. Kruschke, *Doing Bayesian Data Analysis*, 2nd edn. (Academic Press, Boston, 2015). https://doi.org/10.1016/B978-0-12-405888-0.00025-8. https://www.sciencedirect.com/science/article/pii/B9780124058880000258
70. B.A. Nosek, G. Alter, G.C. Banks, D. Borsboom, S.D. Bowman, S.J. Breckler, S. Buck, C.D. Chambers, G. Chin, G. Christensen, et al., Promoting an open research culture. Science **348**(6242), 1422 (2015)
71. N. Kovač, K. Ratković, P. Watson, H. Farahani, F. Bagheri Sheykhangafshe, Machine learning classification models for predicting chronic pain. Curr. Psychol. **44**(18), 15409–15422 (2025)
72. E.R. Tufte, *Envisioning Information* (Graphics Press, Cheshire, 1990)

Datasets for Psychological Sciences

Nataša Kovač, Lisa-Christina Winter Done, Kruna Ratković, Hojjatollah Farahani, and Peter Watson

1 The Problem Statements

The formulation of a problem statement in psychological research is far more than an administrative or rhetorical step. A problem statement is the conceptual anchor that defines the scope, purpose, and methodological pathway of the study. In psychological sciences, crafting a meaningful problem statement involves not only articulating a theoretical gap but also translating this into measurable constructs that can be operationalised through data. According to Creswell and Poth [1], a strong problem statement is characterised by its clarity, relevance to the discipline, and its capacity to direct hypotheses and research questions through methodological precision.

One of the enduring challenges in defining problem statements within psychology lies in the inherently *multidimensional nature* of psychological phenomena. Emotions, cognition, behaviour, and social context are often intertwined, making it difficult to isolate variables without oversimplifying the human experience. As Toomela [2] emphasises, psychological inquiry must navigate the tension between

N. Kovač (✉) · K. Ratković
Faculty of Applied Sciences, University of Donja Gorica, Podgorica, Montenegro
e-mail: natasa.kovac@udg.edu.me

L.-C. W. Done
OpenPsai (Two Kermis), Zug, Switzerland

H. Farahani
Department of Psychology, Faculty of Humanities, Tarbiat Modares University, Jalal AleAhmad Nasr, Tehran, Iran
e-mail: h.farahani@modares.ac.ir

P. Watson
MRC Cognition and Brain Sciences Unit, University of Cambridge, Cambridge, England
e-mail: Peter.Watson@mrc-cbu.cam.ac.uk

N. Kovač et al. (eds.), *Data Science in Psychology*,
https://doi.org/10.1007/978-3-032-18312-5_3

reductionist modelling and the complexity of real-world behaviour. For example, exploring the relationship between anxiety and decision-making must consider not only neurobiological responses but also personal history, social pressure, and environmental stimuli.

The operationalisation of psychological constructs into measurable variables frequently introduces *epistemological and methodological dilemmas*. Unlike fields where direct measurement is possible (e.g. physics), psychological data often rely on proxy measures, such as Likert scales, behavioural tasks, or self-report inventories, each with varying degrees of reliability and validity. Borsboom [3] argues that construct validity becomes the central epistemic concern in psychology: The problem is not whether data are precise, but whether they genuinely reflect the phenomenon of interest.

In recent years, another layer of complexity has emerged through the *replication crisis*, which has pushed researchers to rethink how problem statements are framed concerning generalisability and statistical inference. As Open Science Collaboration [4] famously demonstrated, a significant number of findings in psychological science fail to replicate, often because the problem statements lacked ecological validity or the original sample was not representative. This crisis has led to a shift in how psychologists now approach the initial stages of research design, with greater emphasis on *pre-registration*, *power analysis*, and *multi-site collaboration* [5].

Problem statements in psychology are also influenced by *interdisciplinary pressures*, especially from neuroscience, data science, and social epidemiology. Researchers today are expected to contextualise their problems within broader theoretical frameworks, such as developmental systems theory [6], biopsychosocial models [7], or social determinants of mental health [8], which calls for integrating variables across levels of analysis. For instance, a study investigating depression may include genetic markers, cortisol levels, questionnaire responses, and socio-economic indices, requiring the problem statement to reconcile vastly different data modalities.

The *temporal dimension* of psychological phenomena adds another complication. Some research problems unfold over time and require longitudinal modelling or repeated measures designs to capture their dynamics [9]. In such cases, the problem statement must anticipate issues like attrition, developmental change, and time-varying confounders. When designing a study on adolescent identity formation, for instance, researchers must define the problem not just in static terms (e.g. identity scores) but also in dynamic trajectories (e.g. identity exploration and commitment over time).

Ethical and cultural considerations must shape the articulation of psychological problem statements. Constructs like *well-being*, *intelligence*, or *resilience* may not be universally understood or valued in the same way across different cultures [10]. Failure to culturally calibrate the problem statement can result in biased research that reinforces stereotypes or ignores indigenous conceptualisations of mental health. Increasingly, there is a push for *culturally responsive research design* that includes stakeholders from the target population during the problem formulation phase [11].

Beyond theoretical clarity, psychological problem statements must also grapple with dynamic system interactions that evolve over time and across contexts. Lerner [6] argues that human development must be seen through a developmental systems lens, while person-context relations are observed rather than seeing them as isolated variables. This perspective challenges the conventional assumption that psychological constructs can be universally defined and measured, instead highlighting the bidirectional, co-constitutive nature of mental and behavioural outcomes.

This shift towards systems-oriented inquiry brings to light several epistemological tensions. For instance, the need for reductionist control in experimental paradigms often conflicts with the open-ended, emergent qualities of human behaviour in real-world contexts. As Overton [12] notes, such tensions are not merely methodological but philosophical, rooted in the competing worldviews of mechanistic versus relational science. In applied research, this tension manifests when studies aim to isolate the *effect* of cognitive reappraisal on stress while ignoring situational affordances, cultural beliefs, and ecological validity.

Another vital consideration in modern psychological problem formulation is the integration of qualitative complexity. As Creswell and Poth [1] explain, qualitative frameworks are essential for uncovering lived experiences, narratives, and contextual factors that statistical modelling might obscure. For example, thematic analyses of coping strategies among refugees can yield culturally embedded insights that would be invisible through psychometric scaling alone. Hence, mixed-methods designs are increasingly favoured in psychological science to enhance problem definition through methodological triangulation [13].

Digital psychology and the rise of big data from mobile apps, social media, and digital phenotyping introduce novel problem spaces. Researchers must now articulate problems that are meaningful within digital contexts while being vigilant about data provenance, ethical usage, and algorithmic bias [14]. For example, a study on sleep disruption using wearable technology must account for both sensor accuracy and the sociotechnical context in which data are generated.

Cultural diversity and epistemic justice also demand more careful articulation of problem statements. As Sue [15] critiques, mainstream psychological problem framing often marginalises non-Western knowledge systems and frames deviation from Western norms as dysfunction. Contemporary frameworks such as cultural-clinical psychology [16] encourage researchers to frame questions that accommodate plural conceptions of mental health, healing, and identity.

The emergence of ecological momentary assessment (EMA) tools and longitudinal smartphone-based sampling is expanding how time and environment are encoded into psychological problems. Rather than static snapshots, researchers can now frame dynamic, moment-by-moment problems that reflect lived reality, such as *how do affective fluctuations over 24 hours predict goal disengagement among adolescents under exam stress?* [17]. Such temporal granularity enhances ecological validity while demanding more sophisticated analytical frameworks like multilevel modelling or time-series clustering.

Ethical imperatives have become central to framing psychological problems, particularly in vulnerable or marginalised populations. Questions must be co-developed with stakeholders to ensure cultural safety, autonomy, and reciprocal benefit. Participatory action research (PAR) and community-based approaches are increasingly adopted to shift from *subjects* to *partners*, ensuring that problem statements reflect community needs rather than academic convenience [18].

2 Available Data Inputs

This section presents a systematic overview of prevalent data input formats employed in psychological research and demonstrates, through illustrative `Python` code examples, how such data can be efficiently imported, processed, and managed within analytical workflows.

Table 1 provides an overview of common data formats in psychology and their typical applications. Online survey platforms like `Qualtrics`, `SurveyMonkey`,

Table 1 Common data sources and file formats in psychology with their applications

Source	Format(s)	Use in psychological research
Online survey platforms (Qualtrics, SurveyMonkey, Google Forms)	`.csv`, `.xlsx`	Store questionnaire responses, Likert-scale items, demographics; easy import into Python (`pandas`)
Experimental software (PsychoPy, E-Prime, OpenSesame, Presentation)	`.csv`, `.tsv`, `.txt`	Trial-by-trial logs with reaction times, accuracy, and event markers
Structured/nested data (web services, repositories)	`.json`	Hierarchical data, often retrieved via APIs; may need flattening before analysis
Electroencephalography (EEG) devices	`.edf`, `.set`	Raw EEG signals and metadata; processed with libraries like `MNE-Python`
Neuroimaging (MRI, fMRI, MEG)	`.nii` (NIfTI)	Volumetric brain imaging data for structural and functional analyses
Wearable sensors (heart rate monitors, skin conductance devices, smartwatches)	`.csv`, proprietary binary	Physiological measures such as heart rate variability, stress, and activity monitoring
Open repositories (OpenNeuro, ICPSR, Zenodo)	API outputs: `.json`, `.csv`	Direct programmatic access to datasets; supports reproducibility and large-scale analyses
Relational databases (MySQL, PostgreSQL, SQLite)	Database tables	Structured data storage with integrity and concurrency for large or collaborative projects
Qualitative data (interviews, open-ended surveys)	`.txt`, `.csv`	Transcripts and narrative responses; analysed with NLP methods for sentiment, topics, or discourse

and Google Forms are popular means to collect psychological data [19–21]. Such platforms typically export responses as .csv or .xlsx files, which can be easily imported into Python using the pandas library.

```
import pandas as pd

# Reading from a CSV file
survey_df = pd.read_csv("my_survey_responses.csv")

# Reading from an Excel file
survey_df_xlsx = pd.read_excel("my_survey_responses.xlsx",
↪ sheet_name=0)

# Display the first few rows
print(survey_df.head())
```

Data obtained from Likert-type questionnaires (e.g. measuring stress, anxiety, or depression) often appear in such files as numeric or categorical codes, requiring thorough documentation. Researchers should ensure that the meaning of each scale point and variable is clearly described in a data dictionary, typically included in the same folder or project repository.

Many psychologists use specialised programs to run behavioural experiments such as PsychoPy (Python-based), E-Prime, OpenSesame, and Presentation [22–25]. These platforms typically output trial-by-trial data logs in .csv, .tsv, or .txt formats containing reaction times, accuracy scores, and other task-relevant measures. The standard pandas functions can handle these files:

```
# Reading tab-separated values
rt_data = pd.read_csv("reaction_times.tsv", sep='\t')

# Display summary statistics
print(rt_data.describe())
```

Some software exports more complex or nested structures (e.g. JSON [26]). In such cases, pandas provides dedicated methods like pd.read_json(), but additional pre-processing might be necessary to flatten nested data.

Wearable devices (e.g. heart rate monitors, electroencephalography (EEG) caps, and smartwatches) and neuroimaging equipment (e.g. magnetic resonance imaging (MRI), functional MRI (fMRI), and magnetoencephalography (MEG)) can generate large datasets in specialised formats:

- **EEG data**: commonly stored in .edf or .set files. Researchers often use libraries such as MNE-Python to handle and pre-process EEG signals.

```python
import mne

raw_eeg_data = mne.io.read_raw_edf("participant_01.edf",
    preload=True)
print(raw_eeg_data.info)
```

- **fMRI / neuroimaging data**: commonly distributed in `NIfTI` (`.nii`) files. Libraries like `nibabel` help read and manipulate these files, and `NiPy` or `fMRIPrep` can process them for statistical analysis.

```python
import nibabel as nib

fmri_img = nib.load("subj01_bold.nii")
fmri_data = fmri_img.get_fdata()
print(fmri_data.shape)
```

Physiological data (e.g. heart rate variability and galvanic skin response) can also be recorded via specialised hardware and exported as `.csv` or proprietary binary formats. In many cases, open-source tools and scripts exist to convert these formats to more convenient tabular structures for `pandas`.

An increasing number of psychological and sociological databases offer *application programming interfaces* (`APIs`) for direct data retrieval [27]. For example, large-scale repositories or open data portals (e.g. `OpenNeuro`, `ICPSR`, or `Zenodo`) allow programmatic access to large sample data, meta-analyses, or data from published studies [28]. In Python, the `requests` library is frequently used to interact with RESTful APIs, while `pandas` can parse data in JSON or CSV formats returned by the API.

```python
import requests
import pandas as pd

api_url = "https://some_psych_data_portal.org/api/endpoint"
response = requests.get(api_url)

if response.status_code == 200:
    data_json = response.json()
    api_df = pd.json_normalize(data_json['records'])
    print(api_df.head())
else:
    print(f"API request failed with status
    {response.status_code}")
```

Such programmatic access encourages reproducible workflows, as the script can fetch the latest data automatically, reducing manual steps and potential errors.

When study data are stored in relational databases (MySQL, PostgreSQL, SQLite, etc.) [29], `pandas` and Python's `sqlalchemy` or `sqlite3` libraries can help query and load relevant tables. This approach may be preferable for larger datasets or multi-team collaborations, where data integrity and concurrency are essential.

```
from sqlalchemy import create_engine

engine = create_engine("sqlite:///psych_study.db")
query = "SELECT * FROM participants;"
participants_df = pd.read_sql_query(query, con=engine)

print(participants_df.head())
```

In qualitative research, psychologists often gather transcripts from interviews or open-ended survey responses. These can be stored in `.txt` or `.csv` files with columns containing responses. Python's built-in file handling and libraries like `NLTK`, `spaCy`, or `gensim` enable textual analyses ranging from basic frequency counts to advanced topic modelling or sentiment analysis.

```
import pandas as pd

qual_data = pd.read_csv("open_ended_responses.csv")
print(qual_data["response_text"].head())

# Sample basic text preprocessing with NLTK
import nltk
nltk.download('stopwords')
from nltk.corpus import stopwords

def preprocess_text(text):
    words = nltk.word_tokenize(text.lower())
    words = [w for w in words if w.isalpha() and w not in
     ↪  stopwords.words('english')]
    return words

qual_data["processed_text"] =
 ↪  qual_data["response_text"].apply(preprocess_text)
print(qual_data["processed_text"].head())
```

In many cases, textual data are combined with numeric or categorical information about the participants (e.g. group membership and demographic characteristics). Merging such data by participant IDs allows for mixed-methods analyses, bridging quantitative and qualitative insights.

Psychological datasets often span multiple files or sources: one file for participant demographics, another for post-test outcomes, and a third for psychophysiological measures. To create a unified dataset, pandas offers merging capabilities:

```
demo_df = pd.read_csv("participants_demographics.csv")
outcomes_df = pd.read_csv("post_test_scores.csv")

merged_df = pd.merge(demo_df, outcomes_df,
 ↪  on="participant_id", how="inner")
print(merged_df.columns)
```

This ensures a single DataFrame containing all relevant variables, ready for subsequent cleaning, exploration, or modelling.

When preparing psychological datasets for analysis, several practical considerations can help ensure data quality and consistency from the outset. Careful pre-processing not only reduces errors but also sets a strong foundation for replicable and transparent research. These practices are particularly important when working with complex or longitudinal datasets:

- **Maintain consistent coding schemes**: For example, if gender is coded as M/F in one file and 1/2 in another, harmonise these representations immediately upon data import.
- **Document variable names and encoding**: Create a data dictionary describing each variable's meaning, range, and coding (especially for Likert scales, clinical cut-offs, or specialised indexes).
- **Adhere to best practices for data structure**: Long-format (tidy) data are often preferable for analyses in Python, especially when dealing with repeated measures or multi-level data.
- **Perform initial validation checks**: Confirm that participant IDs match across files, and ensure there are no unintentional duplicates or missing merges before further analyses.
- **Automate data retrieval when possible**: APIs and database queries allow code-based (re)loading of data, reducing manual errors and facilitating reproducible pipelines.

Establishing these routines early in the data analysis process can significantly enhance the efficiency and reliability of psychological research workflows.

3 Means of Data Validation

Data validation encompasses a range of checks and procedures designed to confirm that the variables, measurements, and observations accurately reflect what they purport to measure. An overview of common data validation strategies in psychological research is given in Table 2. In practice, validation can range from

Table 2 Overview of common data validation strategies in psychological research

Validation type	Description and purpose
Data type consistency	Ensure declared and actual types match (e.g. categorical variables not stored as floats and numeric scores not stored as strings). Prevents misinterpretation and calculation errors
Duplicate detection	Identify repeated rows from survey resubmissions or double entry. Removal avoids bias from inflated sample sizes
Range checks	Verify values fall within valid scale limits (e.g. questionnaire minimum and maximum). Flags transcription errors and implausible responses
Missing data handling	Assess extent and pattern of missingness. Approaches include listwise deletion (MCAR assumption), mean/median imputation (simple but variance reducing), or multiple imputation (robust pooled estimates)
Outlier detection	Detect extreme values via ± 3 SD or interquartile range (IQR) rule. Evaluate whether values are true clinical phenomena or input errors; apply robust statistics or transformations when appropriate
Psychometric validation	Assess reliability and validity of scales. Cronbach's α (internal consistency), exploratory/confirmatory factor analysis (construct validity). Ensures items measure intended latent constructs
Logical consistency checks	Verify internal study logic (e.g. start date before end date, control participants not attending therapy, age above eligibility threshold). Detects structural inconsistencies in datasets
Automation of validation	Implement scripts or continuous integration (CI) pipelines to run checks automatically. Enhances reproducibility, transparency, and scalability of research workflows

simple, rule-based checks (e.g. verifying valid score ranges) to more advanced psychometric approaches (e.g. internal consistency or factor analysis). This section reviews common data validation strategies and provides illustrative `Python` code examples.

Many psychological variables are categorical (e.g. group labels), while others are numeric (e.g. questionnaire scores). Ensuring consistency between the declared type and actual data is essential:

- A categorical variable stored as `float` or `int` can cause misinterpretations (e.g. `1.0` vs. `1`).
- A numeric variable stored as `object` or `string` can impede statistical calculations.

In Python, you can quickly inspect data types using `pandas`:

```
import pandas as pd

df = pd.read_csv("psychological_data.csv")
print(df.dtypes)
```

If data types are incorrectly specified, they should be systematically converted to the appropriate formats to ensure consistency and validity of subsequent analyses:

```
# Convert a column to categorical
df["group"] = df["group"].astype("category")

# Convert a column to numeric
df["anxiety_score"] = pd.to_numeric(df["anxiety_score"],
↪ errors="coerce")
```

Duplicate rows can arise from repeated submissions of online surveys or double data entry. These may bias analysis by inflating the sample size or weighting certain responses more than others. Identifying duplicates is straightforward:

```
# Find duplicates based on a unique identifier, e.g.
↪ participant_id
duplicates = df[df.duplicated(subset=["participant_id"],
↪ keep=False)]
if not duplicates.empty:
    print("Found duplicates:")
    print(duplicates)
```

After reviewing, duplicates can be removed with `df.drop_duplicates` if they are genuinely unintended repeats.

In psychological studies, scales and indices (e.g. Beck Depression Inventory and perceived stress scores) often have defined minimum and maximum values. Checking for out-of-range values is a simple yet critical procedure:

```
# Suppose the valid range is 0-63 for a measure
invalid_mask = (df["depression_score"] < 0) |
↪ (df["depression_score"] > 63)
invalid_entries = df[invalid_mask]
print("Invalid depression scores found:")
print(invalid_entries)
```

If invalid entries exist, researchers must determine if they are a result of transcription errors, outliers, or genuine anomalies requiring additional scrutiny.

Real-world psychological datasets frequently contain missing values, often arising from participant non-responses or technical malfunctions. Addressing missingness is a critical step, as the chosen method of treatment can substantially influence the reliability and validity of subsequent analyses [30]. The first task is to quantify the extent of missing data and evaluate whether its occurrence is systematically associated with specific variables or participant subgroups.

```
missing_summary = df.isnull().sum()
print(missing_summary)
```

Once identified, researchers must determine an appropriate strategy for managing incomplete data. The principal options include:

- **Listwise deletion (complete-case analysis)** removes participants with any missing values on the variables of interest. Although straightforward, this method reduces statistical power and introduces bias unless the data are *missing completely at random* (MCAR).
- **Mean or median imputation** replaces missing values with a central tendency measure of the variable. This method is simple to implement but can distort variance estimates.
- **Multiple imputation** generates several plausible versions of the dataset by predicting missing values from available information. Analyses are conducted on each dataset, and results are pooled to yield robust estimates.

In Python, multiple imputation and simpler approaches can be performed using libraries such as `statsmodels.imputation` or `scikit-learn`:

```
from sklearn.impute import SimpleImputer

# Example: median imputation for numeric columns
num_cols = ["anxiety_score", "stress_level"]
imputer = SimpleImputer(strategy="median")
df[num_cols] = imputer.fit_transform(df[num_cols])
```

Beyond missing data, psychological datasets often contain extreme values. These may reflect either genuine phenomena (e.g. clinically elevated distress scores) or simple entry errors. A conventional approach is to flag values more than ± 3 standard deviations from the mean:

```
import numpy as np

score = "stress_level"
mean_val = df[score].mean()
std_val = df[score].std()

outliers_mask = (df[score] < mean_val - 3*std_val) | \
                (df[score] > mean_val + 3*std_val)
outliers = df[outliers_mask]
print(outliers)
```

Alternatively, the interquartile range (IQR) method, which identifies observations outside $[Q1 - 1.5 \times IQR, Q3 + 1.5 \times IQR]$, is particularly appropriate for skewed or non-normal distributions. When extreme values are genuine, robust estimation procedures or transformations (e.g. logarithmic or square root) may be employed to mitigate their influence [31].

Psychological measurement also necessitates psychometric validation to ensure that scales are both internally consistent and construct valid. Cronbach's alpha remains the most widely used reliability index for multi-item scales, indicating the degree to which items measure a common latent construct [32]:

```
import numpy as np
def cronbach_alpha(df_items):
    df_items = df_items.dropna()
    item_scores = df_items.values
    n_items = item_scores.shape[1]
    var_sum = np.sum(item_scores.var(axis=0, ddof=1))
    total_var = np.var(item_scores.sum(axis=1), ddof=1)
    alpha = (n_items / (n_items - 1)) * (1 - var_sum /
     ↪  total_var)
    return alpha

# Example with multiple items measuring anxiety
anxiety_items = df[["anx_item1", "anx_item2", "anx_item3",
 ↪  "anx_item4"]]
alpha_value = cronbach_alpha(anxiety_items)
print(f"Cronbach's alpha for anxiety scale =
 ↪  {alpha_value:.3f}")
```

A value between 0.70 and 0.80 is often regarded as acceptable in early stage research, whereas more established instruments typically require coefficients of 0.80 or higher. Beyond alpha, confirmatory and exploratory factor analysis (CFA and EFA) help to establish dimensional validity, with Python packages such as `factor_analyzer` or `pingouin` supporting these procedures.

Finally, even structurally sound datasets may exhibit logical inconsistencies. For instance:

- A participant's `start_date` must precede their `end_date`.
- Individuals assigned to an untreated control group should not display nonzero therapy attendance.
- Demographic attributes should conform to study constraints (e.g. minimum age in adult-only trials).

Such inconsistencies can be identified with tailored logic checks:

```
invalid_order = df[df["start_date"] > df["end_date"]]
if not invalid_order.empty:
    print("Inconsistent date ordering found:")
    print(invalid_order)

# Example: Untreated group with non-zero therapy sessions
mask = (df["treatment_group"] == 0) &
 ↪  (df["therapy_sessions_attended"] > 0)
print("Participants who are 'untreated' yet attended
 ↪  sessions:")
print(df[mask])
```

Together, these procedures—handling missing values, managing outliers, validating psychometric properties, and enforcing logical consistency—form the foundation of rigorous data pre-processing in psychological science.

To prevent manual repetition of checks and ensure reproducibility, researchers can automate data validation in Python. A simple approach is to create a validation script or *notebook* that reads the raw data, performs all checks, and exports a summary report (e.g. as `.csv` or `.pdf`). More advanced users may adopt *continuous integration* (`CI`) pipelines (for instance with `GitHub Actions`) that run validation automatically whenever new data are pushed to a repository.

Automating validation procedures in psychological data processing brings several key benefits that enhance both efficiency and reliability:

- *Consistency*: All checks execute identically each time, reducing human error.
- *Transparency*: Each validation step is documented in code, aiding peer review.
- *Scalability*: As the project or dataset grows, the same validation routine applies with minimal modifications.

By carefully validating data before proceeding to statistical modelling or hypothesis testing, researchers can prevent spurious findings and misinterpretations. Python provides an extensive ecosystem of libraries (`pandas`, `numpy`, `scipy`, `pingouin`, `factor_analyzer`, etc.) that support these validation steps at scale, reinforcing the rigour and reproducibility of psychological research.

4 Exploring Datasets with Visualisations

The exploration of psychological datasets through visualisation is a required step in the research process, serving as a bridge between raw data and meaningful interpretation. While previous sections of this chapter have focused on conceptualising problem statements, understanding available data inputs, and ensuring data integrity through validation techniques, this section turns towards making sense of data through visual representation. Visualisation is not merely an aesthetic enhancement to data reporting. It is a powerful methodological tool that allows researchers to uncover latent patterns, detect anomalies, and comprehend complex relationships among variables that might otherwise remain obscure through numerical summaries alone [33, 34].

In psychological sciences, where datasets often include a variety of categorical, ordinal, and continuous variables, which range from psychometric scores and behavioural assessments to demographic and contextual attributes, visualisation techniques enable a more intuitive grasp of structure and distribution [35]. Effective visualisations can illuminate variation across participant groups, highlight central tendencies and dispersion, and reveal associations that may further guide statistical modelling decisions [36].

Visual analytics play a key role in the early stages of data analysis, known as exploratory data analysis (EDA), where the primary goal is not hypothesis

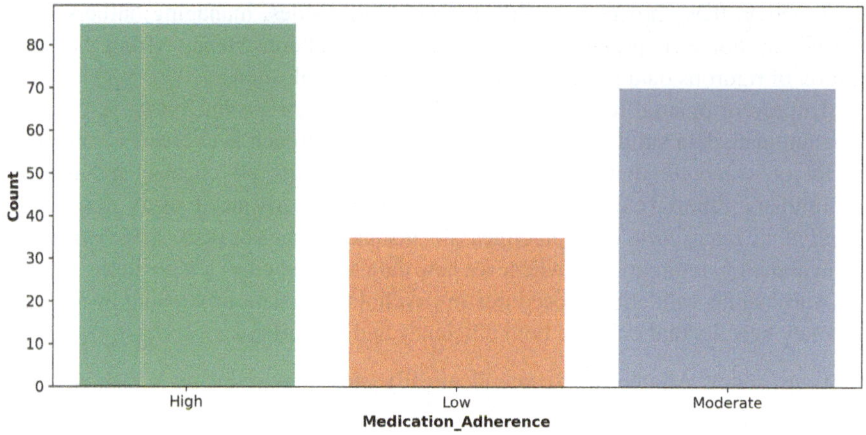

Fig. 1 Distribution of medication adherence levels among participants

testing but rather understanding the shape and nature of the data [37]. This stage allows researchers to evaluate assumptions, check for missing data and outliers, and prepare the dataset for more sophisticated analyses. In the context of psychological research, where differences in human behaviour and cognitive states can be subtle, visualisation supports a data-driven approach to interpretation that is grounded in clarity and transparency [38].

This section introduces different graphical techniques used to explore psychological datasets, including categorical plots, distribution histograms, violin and box plots, swarm plots, correlation heatmaps, and group comparison visualisations. Each method is tailored to address specific analytical needs, whether it be examining distributional properties, comparing subgroups, or identifying potential multicollinearity among variables. The goal is not only to demonstrate the possibilities that offer Python but also to emphasise how visualisations contribute substantively to the scientific reasoning process in psychology [39–41].

The count plot in Fig. 1 for `Medication Adherence` provides a compelling visualisation of participants' behavioural compliance within the studied sample. This categorical variable reflects individuals' engagement with prescribed medical or therapeutic regimens. As illustrated, the distribution is not uniform. The majority of participants report *high adherence*, while a considerable proportion indicates *moderate adherence*, and a smaller yet notable group falls into the *low adherence* category. This asymmetric distribution suggests a predominantly health-conscious sample, yet highlights a non-negligible subgroup exhibiting behavioural disengagement. Such patterns are predominant when analysing treatment outcomes or designing tailored interventions [42, 43]. Stratifying this distribution across experimental conditions or psychological scores in subsequent visualisations may help uncover deeper relationships between adherence behaviours and cognitive-emotional variables.

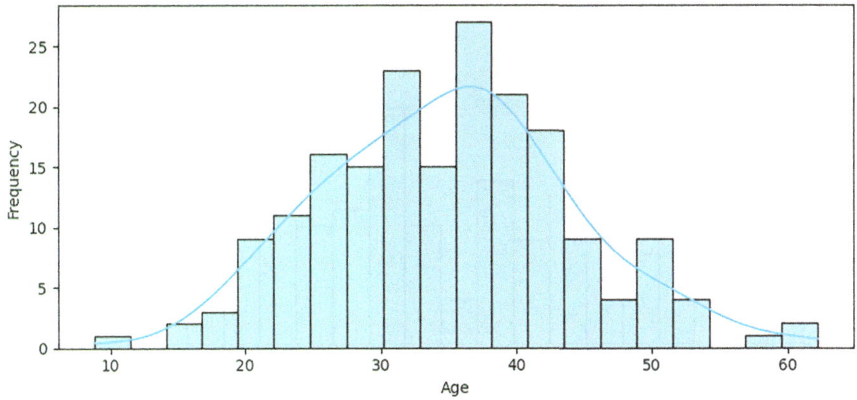

Fig. 2 Age distribution of psychological study participants

Understanding the distribution of numerical variables plays a foundational role in psychological research. Distributions offer crucial information about the tendencies, variability, and potential anomalies within a dataset. In the context of psychological sciences, these patterns often hint at deeper behavioural, clinical, or cognitive implications. Visualising such distributions through histograms with overlaid kernel density estimation (KDE) curves helps researchers comprehend whether their variables approximate normality or exhibit skewness, kurtosis, or multimodality, all of which can affect statistical modelling and inferential validity [36, 44].

The distribution of `Age` in the observed dataset (see Fig. 2) presents a relatively symmetric bell-shaped curve, roughly resembling a normal distribution. Such patterns are desirable in many statistical applications, especially when parametric tests are applied. The histogram shows that most participants are concentrated around the mean age, with a narrowing towards younger and older extremes. This configuration suggests a balanced sampling across adult age groups, a key strength in psychological research aiming to generalise findings across developmental stages [45].

The KDE curve reinforces this visual interpretation by tracing a smooth contour over the bar plot, indicating where participant density is the highest. The moderate spread and symmetry suggest homogeneity in the age-related sampling strategy and support the use of parametric procedures such as *t-tests* or ANOVA for subsequent analysis [46].

Unlike `Age`, variable `Therapy Sessions Attended` (see Fig. 3) displays a more discrete, multimodal pattern with no clear bell shape. Peaks are visible at both ends of the distribution, particularly around 0 and 20 sessions, which may reflect underlying behavioural or treatment adherence subgroups within the sample. For instance, a subset of participants might have dropped out early or never started therapy, while others may have completed a full therapy regimen.

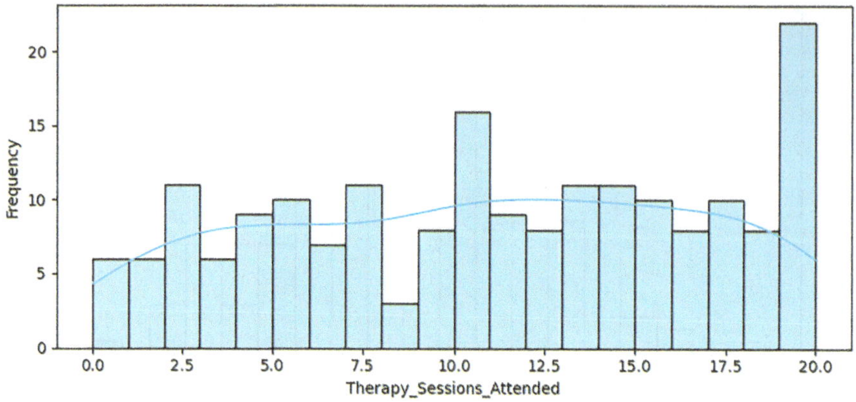

Fig. 3 Distribution of therapy sessions attended by participants

This type of bimodal or irregular distribution is not uncommon in clinical psychology, especially in real-world intervention data where motivational, financial, or contextual factors impact attendance rates [42, 47]. Such characteristics caution researchers against assuming normality and instead suggest the application of non-parametric statistics such as the *Kruskal-Wallis* or *Mann-Whitney U* test when comparing groups based on this variable [48].

The contrast between these two distributions underscores a critical lesson for psychological researchers: *Not all variables behave in the same statistical space*. While `Age` is often amenable to linear models and classical assumptions of normality, variables like `Therapy Sessions Attended` defy such assumptions and call for careful methodological tailoring. The visual exploration of distributions acts as an early diagnostic tool, helping to anticipate which transformations or statistical paths may be needed downstream. Researchers can thus use these plots as a guide not only for descriptive understanding but also for shaping the appropriate inferential framework.

The box plot in Fig. 4 presents a compelling visualisation that encapsulates key distribution characteristics across the Clinical, Control, and Experimental groups. Box plots serve as a standard method for visualising the spread and central tendency of a variable, allowing researchers to assess group differences, detect skewness, and identify *potential outliers*, which are known as values that behave differently than the rest of the data.

In Fig. 4, each group displays a median value (horizontal line within the box), an interquartile range (IQR shown as a box), and whiskers that represent data points within 1.5 times the IQR [49]. Several outliers outside the whiskers are visible in the Clinical and Experimental groups. These points reflect individuals with exceptionally high frequencies of social interaction, potentially indicating participants with atypical behaviour patterns or unique lifestyle characteristics. While such cases are valuable from a behavioural science perspective, they pose methodological challenges. Outliers can disproportionately influence statistical

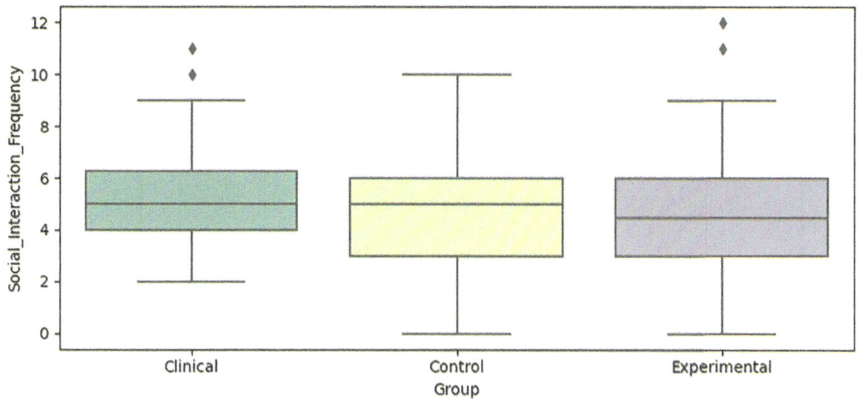

Fig. 4 Box plot of social interaction frequency by group

measures, including means and standard deviations, and potentially skew hypothesis testing results [31].

In psychological data analysis, retaining or removing outliers must be a thoughtful decision. Outliers might indicate:

- Measurement errors or data entry mistakes
- True behavioural variability, reflecting subpopulations with distinct psychosocial profiles
- Or instances of non-normally distributed behaviour, common in naturally occurring social interaction patterns [36]

If retained, appropriate robust statistical techniques should be applied, such as *median-based analyses*, *bootstrapping*, or *non-parametric tests*, to ensure valid conclusions. Alternatively, sensitivity analysis can help compare results with and without outliers, offering transparency in data interpretation. Comparing the three groups, one observes relatively similar medians but slight differences in spread and outlier density, which may point to structural variability in social engagement levels across the psychological conditions or interventions assigned. This insight becomes particularly critical when such behavioural indicators serve as predictors or outcomes in psychological models.

Violin plots offer a powerful combination of box plots and kernel density plots, making them ideal for visualising the distribution and density of psychological variables across categorical groups [50]. Unlike traditional box plots, violin plots additionally reveal the full distribution shape, identifying skewness, bimodality, and outliers in a more detailed way. To illustrate their utility, we focus first on `Stress Level` across Clinical, Control, and Experimental groups shown in Fig. 5. The visualisation reveals not only differences in central tendency, where the Clinical group displays a higher median stress level, but also wider dispersion in stress responses within this group. The density contours further suggest a *possible multimodal distribution*, particularly in the Clinical and Experimental groups,

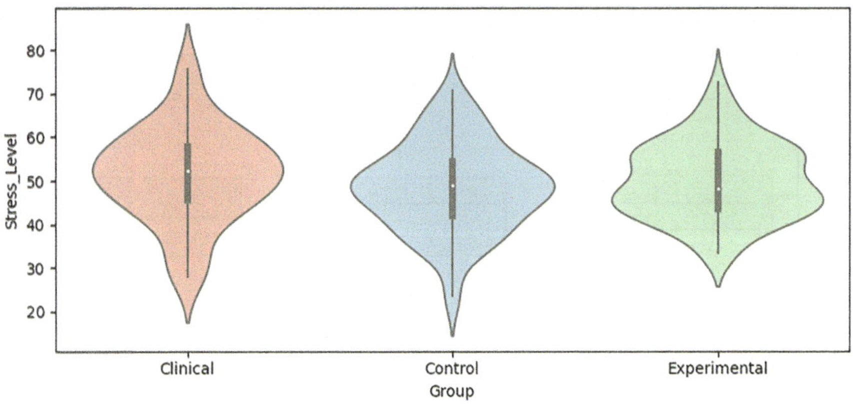

Fig. 5 Violin plot of stress level distribution across participant groups

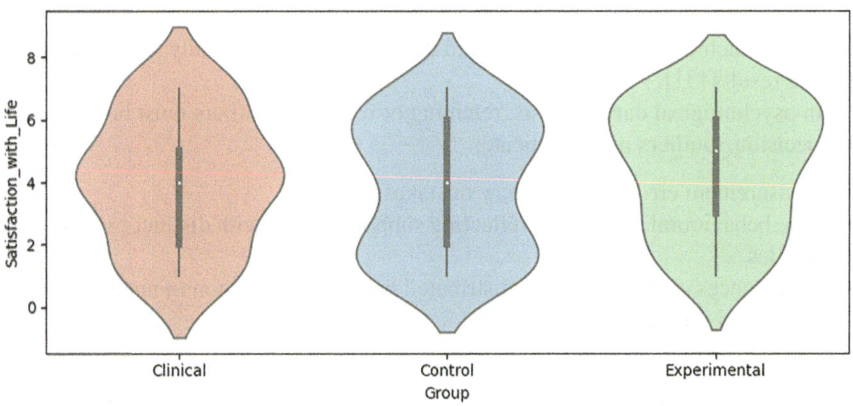

Fig. 6 Violin plot of Satisfaction with Life distribution across participant groups

which might indicate subgroups with differing psychological stress responses. Such patterns may point towards clinical heterogeneity and varying psychological resilience mechanisms [51, 52].

The violin plot in Fig. 6 for `Satisfaction with Life` displays some different behaviour. Although the medians vary slightly across groups, the distribution is relatively symmetric for all three. The Experimental group displays a slightly *right-skewed distribution*, indicating a subset of individuals reporting particularly high life satisfaction. This may suggest a therapeutic or psychological enhancement effect for participants in experimental interventions [53, 54]. The compact shape in the Control group suggests lower variation in reported satisfaction, potentially reflecting less dynamic intervention exposure.

Violin plots can expose not only differences between groups in psychological variables but also the shape and dispersion of underlying participant responses,

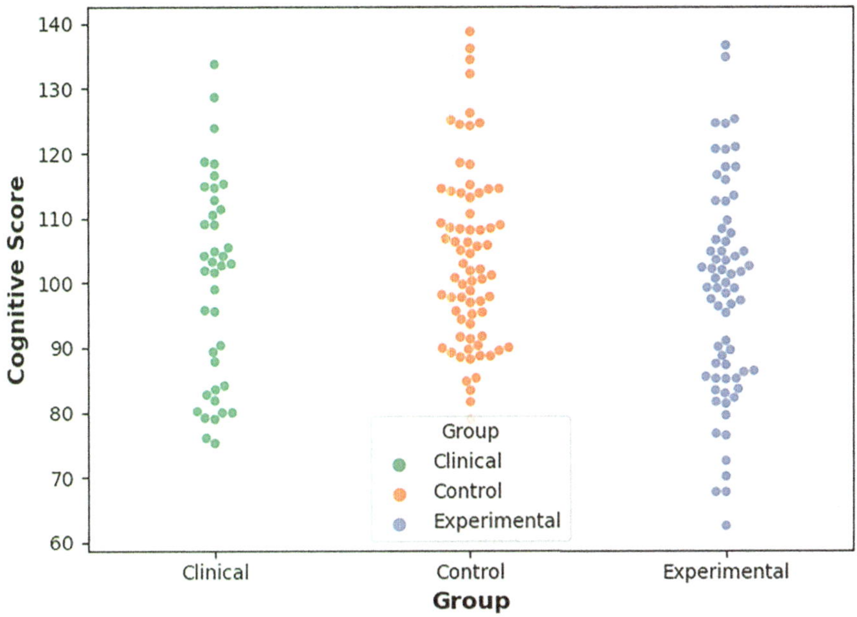

Fig. 7 Swarm plot of cognitive scores across participant groups

providing rich analytical insights that could inform both clinical interpretation and intervention development.

The swarm plot of `Cognitive Score` (see Fig. 7) offers a detailed perspective on how cognitive functioning is distributed across three distinct psychological categories. Unlike aggregate plots such as bar graphs or boxplots, swarm plots provide a *point-by-point visualisation*, highlighting individual variability and density within each group [55]. What makes this plot particularly valuable is its ability to show both the distributional spread and potential clustering of cognitive scores:

- The Control group exhibits a tight, dense cluster around the 100–110 range, suggesting a fairly homogeneous cognitive performance profile. This is consistent with expectations in psychological research, where control groups often consist of individuals with average or normative profiles [46].
- The Clinical group, in contrast, displays greater dispersion, with some participants scoring well below 80 and a few above 120. This heterogeneity could be indicative of divergent cognitive profiles common in clinical populations, possibly driven by underlying psychopathologies, neurodevelopmental conditions, or comorbidities [56].
- The Experimental group shows a bimodal distribution tendency, with clusters around both lower and higher ranges. This might suggest differential cognitive effects of an experimental intervention or diverse participant characteristics in this group of participants.

This swarm plot thus becomes a powerful visual tool not only to compare central tendencies across groups but also to reveal patterns such as:

- Skewness or multimodality
- Outliers or extreme performers
- Distribution overlap across groups or group separation based on performance

These insights are critical for refining hypotheses about cognitive functioning and identifying subgroup dynamics that might otherwise remain obscured in summary statistics alone [36]. Given the visible variation in cognitive scores across groups, the swarm plot highlights opportunities for more advanced statistical exploration to uncover meaningful patterns. To further deepen our understanding, several methods could be applied:

- *Post hoc ANOVA* or *Kruskal-Wallis test*: These are statistical tests used to determine whether the differences in cognitive scores between groups are statistically significant or just due to chance. While the plot shows visual differences, these tests help quantify and validate whether those differences truly matter in a scientific sense. If the scores differ across groups, such tests can tell us which groups are most distinct from one another in terms of cognitive performance.
- *Correlation analysis with other variables*: By examining how Cognitive Score relates to other psychological measures, we can better understand what might be influencing cognitive function. For instance, if individuals with higher depression scores consistently show lower cognitive scores, this might point to a broader pattern worthy of psychological or clinical attention.
- *Multivariate clustering*: This is a technique that groups individuals who have similar patterns across multiple variables, not just the Cognitive Score. For example, participants with similar levels of anxiety, sleep hours, and cognitive performance might form distinct psychological profiles or subgroups. These insights can be incredibly valuable for tailoring interventions or understanding underlying conditions.

These methods are suggested not to complicate the analysis, but rather to enhance the interpretability and depth of understanding beyond what can be seen in visual plots alone. Visualisation sparks the questions, while the statistical analysis provides the answers. By integrating these techniques, even researchers new to statistics can move from *what we see* to *what we know*, building more robust conclusions about group differences and psychological constructs.

The pair plot (see Fig. 8) is a powerful visualisation tool that provides a comprehensive view of the relationships between several variables simultaneously. It is particularly useful in psychological research where multiple behavioural, cognitive, and emotional dimensions are parallelly analysed.

In the matrix of scatterplots in Fig. 8, each cell displays a comparison between two variables:

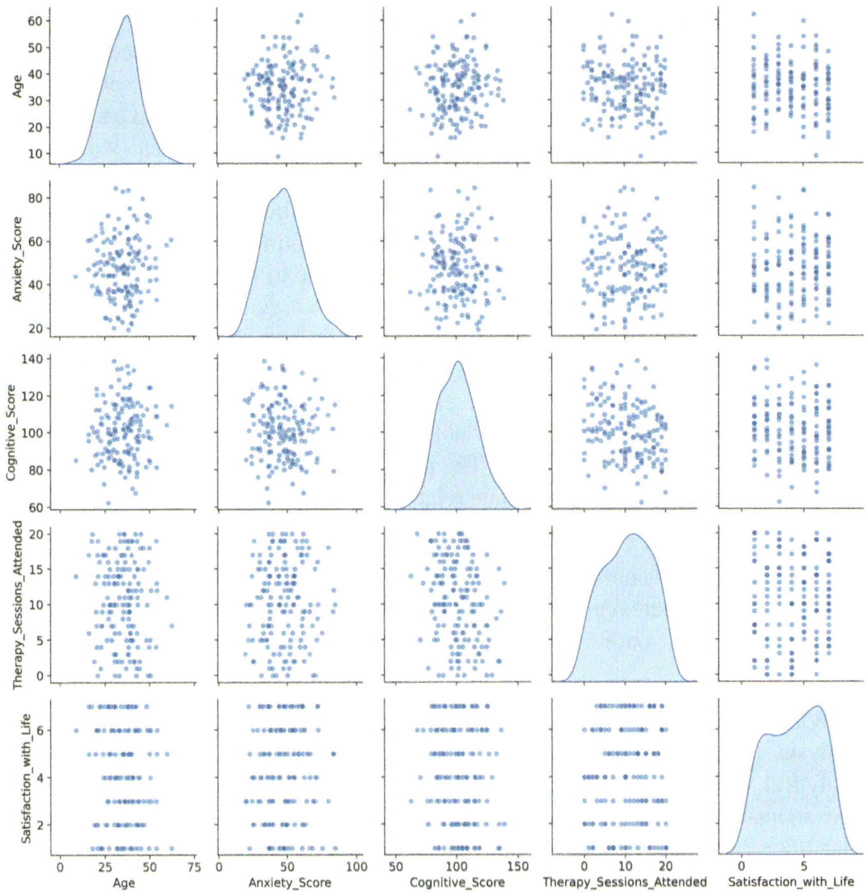

Fig. 8 Pair plot of psychological variables—distribution and inter-variable patterns

- The diagonal cells contain univariate kernel density plots (smooth histograms) that show the distribution of each variable. These plots help identify the shape of the data distribution, whether it is normal, skewed, or multimodal.
- The remaining cells display scatterplots that illustrate bivariate relationships, i.e. how two variables change together across all observations. These plots allow us to visually inspect trends, potential correlations, clustering, or outliers.

Figure 8 can give some important patterns and insights in data structure. `Age`, `Anxiety Score`, and `Cognitive Score` exhibit near-normal or slightly skewed distributions, indicating a broad and fairly balanced range of participant responses. `Therapy Sessions Attended` shows a uniform or slightly right-skewed distribution, suggesting many participants attended fewer sessions, while some had high engagement. `Satisfaction with Life` appears discretised, likely due to it being measured on a *Likert-type scale*, creating peaks at whole number response categories. The scatterplot between `Age` and `Cognitive Score` does not indicate a strong linear relationship, implying cognitive performance remains relatively stable across age groups in this sample. Although subtle, there appears to be an inverse spread between `Anxiety Score` and `Satisfaction with Life`, suggesting that higher anxiety levels might correlate with lower satisfaction in some cases. This is a well-documented phenomenon in psychological literature [57, 58]. Surprisingly, no strong pattern emerges between `Therapy Sessions` and `Satisfaction with Life`, hinting that therapy frequency alone may not predict life satisfaction, potentially due to other moderating factors such as therapy quality or personal context [59]. No evident linear relationship is visible between `Anxiety Score` and `Cognitive Score`, indicating that cognitive abilities and anxiety might be independently distributed in this dataset.

Even for readers unfamiliar with complex statistics, pair plots serve as an intuitive gateway to understanding variable interplay, acting as a bridge between raw numbers and structured hypotheses. The pair plot visual tool enhances exploratory data analysis by revealing multivariate relationships before statistical testing begins. Researchers can use these insights to:

- Identify potential confounding variables.
- Choose appropriate regression predictors or control variables.
- Detect clusters, outliers, or unexpected interactions between psychological dimensions.

While visualisations serve as an effective complement to textual and statistical analysis, they are far more than decorative additions. They represent powerful analytical tools that allow researchers to uncover underlying patterns, trends, and anomalies within psychological data. Visual plots provide intuitive insights that often precede or guide formal statistical testing, making them essential in formulating and answering research questions. Psychological researchers must become well-versed in a diverse set of visualisation techniques, not only to enhance communication but also to ensure accurate interpretation of complex datasets and to select the most appropriate plots for each analytical goal.

References

1. J.W. Creswell, C.N. Poth, *Qualitative Inquiry and Research Design: Choosing Among Five Approaches*, 5th edn. (SAGE Publications, New York, 2024)
2. A. Toomela, in *Experimental Psychology: Ambitions and Possibilities* (Springer, Berlin, 2022), pp. 113–151
3. D. Borsboom, *Measuring the Mind: Conceptual Issues in Contemporary Psychometrics* (Cambridge University, Cambridge, 2005)
4. O.S. Collaboration, Estimating the reproducibility of psychological science. Science **349**(6251), aac4716 (2015)
5. B.A. Nosek, C.R. Ebersole, A.C. DeHaven, D.T. Mellor, The preregistration revolution. Proc. Natl. Acad. Sci. **115**(11), 2600 (2018)

6. R.M. Lerner, in *Handbook of Child Psychology*, vol. 1, ed. by R.M. Lerner (Wiley, New York, 2006), pp. 1–17
7. G.L. Engel, The need for a new medical model: a challenge for biomedicine. Science **196**(4286), 129 (1977)
8. V. Patel, S. Saxena, C. Lund, G. Thornicroft, F. Baingana, P. Bolton, D. Chisholm, P.Y. Collins, J.L. Cooper, J. Eaton, et al., The Lancet Commission on global mental health and sustainable development. The Lancet **392**(10157), 1553 (2018)
9. J.D. Singer, J.B. Willett, *Applied Longitudinal Data Analysis: Modeling Change and Event Occurrence* (Oxford University, Oxford, 2003)
10. J. Henrich, S.J. Heine, A. Norenzayan, The weirdest people in the world? Behav. Brain Sci. **33**(2–3), 61 (2010)
11. J.P. Gone, Redressing first nations historical trauma: theorizing mechanisms for indigenous culture as mental health treatment. Transcult. Psychiatry **50**(5), 683 (2013)
12. W.F. Overton, The process-relational paradigm and relational-developmental-systems meta-model as context. Res. Hum. Dev. **11**(4), 323 (2014)
13. A. Tashakkori, *SAGE Handbook of Mixed Methods in Social & Behavioral Research* (SAGE, New York, 2010)
14. K. Huckvale, S. Venkatesh, H. Christensen, Toward clinical digital phenotyping: a timely opportunity to consider purpose, quality, and safety. NPJ Digital Med. **2**(1), 88 (2019)
15. S. Sue, Science, ethnicity, and bias: where have we gone wrong?. Am. Psychol. **54**(12), 1070 (1999)
16. Y.E. Chentsova-Dutton, A.G. Ryder, Cultural-clinical psychology, in *Handbook of Cultural Psychology* (2019), pp. 365–394
17. I. Myin-Germeys, Z. Kasanova, T. Vaessen, H. Vachon, O. Kirtley, W. Viechtbauer, U. Reininghaus, Experience sampling methodology in mental health research: new insights and technical developments. World Psychiatry **17**(2), 123 (2018)
18. M. Cargo, S.L. Mercer, The value and challenges of participatory research: strengthening its practice. Annu. Rev. Public Health **29**(1), 325 (2008)
19. Qualtrics International Inc. Qualtrics [computer software] (2025). https://www.qualtrics.com
20. SurveyMonkey Inc. Surveymonkey [online survey platform] (2025). https://www.surveymonkey.com
21. Google LLC. Google forms [web application] (2025). https://forms.google.com
22. J.W. Peirce, J.R. Gray, S. Simpson, M. MacAskill, R. Höochenberger, H. Sogo, E. Kastman, J.K. Lindeløv, PsychoPy2: experiments in behavior made easy. Behav. Res. Methods **51**(1), 195 (2019). https://doi.org/10.3758/s13428-018-01193-y
23. Psychology Software Tools, Inc., *E-Prime 2.0: Psychology Software Tools*. Pittsburgh, PA (2012). https://pstnet.com/products/e-prime/
24. S. Mathôt, D. Schreij, J. Theeuwes, OpenSesame: an open-source, graphical experiment builder for the social sciences. Behav. Res. Methods **44**(2), 314 (2012). https://doi.org/10.3758/s13428-011-0168-7
25. Neurobehavioral Systems, Inc., *Presentation Software*. Albany, CA (2023). https://www.neurobs.com/presentation
26. ECMA International, The JSON data interchange syntax, standard ECMA-404. Tech. rep., ECMA International (2017). https://www.ecma-international.org/publications-and-standards/standards/ecma-404/
27. E. Gamma, R. Helm, R. Johnson, J. Vlissides, *Design Patterns: Elements of Reusable Object-Oriented Software* (Addison-Wesley, Boston, 1995)
28. CERN, OpenAIRE. Zenodo. https://zenodo.org/ (2013). Accessed: 2025-08-25
29. E.F. Codd, A relational model of data for large shared data banks. Commun. ACM **13**(6), 377 (1970). https://doi.org/10.1145/362384.362685
30. C.K. Enders, *Applied Missing Data Analysis* (Guilford Press, New York, 2010)
31. R.R. Wilcox, *Introduction to Robust Estimation and Hypothesis Testing* (Academic Press, New York, 2011)

32. L.J. Cronbach, Coefficient alpha and the internal structure of tests. Psychometrika **16**(3), 297 (1951). https://doi.org/10.1007/BF02310555
33. W.S. Cleveland, *Visualizing Data* (Hobart Press, New York, 1993)
34. E.R. Tufte, P.R. Graves-Morris, *The Visual Display of Quantitative Information*, vol. 2.9 (Graphics Press, Cheshire, 1983)
35. R. McElreath, *Statistical Rethinking: A Bayesian Course with Examples in R and Stan* (Chapman and Hall/CRC, New York, 2018)
36. A. Field, *Discovering Statistics Using IBM SPSS Statistics* (SAGE Publications Limited, New York, 2024)
37. J.W. Tukey, et al., *Exploratory Data Analysis*, vol. 2 (Springer, Berlin, 1977)
38. H. Wickham, G. Grolemund, *R for Data Science: Import, Tidy, Transform, Visualize, and Model Data*, vol. 1 (2017)
39. F. Pedregosa, G. Varoquaux, A. Gramfort, V. Michel, B. Thirion, O. Grisel, M. Blondel, P. Prettenhofer, R. Weiss, V. Dubourg, et al., Scikit-learn: machine learning in Python. J. Mach. Learn. Res. **12**, 2825 (2011)
40. J.D. Hunter, Matplotlib: A 2D graphics environment. Comput. Sci. Eng. **9**(03), 90 (2007)
41. W. McKinney, et al., Data structures for statistical computing in Python. SciPy **445**(1), 51 (2010)
42. M.R. DiMatteo, Variations in patients' adherence to medical recommendations: a quantitative review of 50 years of research. Med. Care **42**(3), 200 (2004)
43. L. Osterberg, T. Blaschke, Adherence to medication. N. Engl. J. Med. **353**(5), 487 (2005)
44. F.J. Gravetter, L.B. Wallnau, *Essentials of Statistics for the Behavioral Sciences* (Wadsworth Cengage Learning, Boston, 2011)
45. R.J. Cohen, M.E. Swerdlik, S.M. Phillips, *Psychological Testing and Assessment: An Introduction to Tests and Measurement*, 10th edn. (Mayfield Publishing Co, California, 2021)
46. B.G. Tabachnick, L.S. Fidell, *Using Multivariate Statistics*, 7th edn. (Pearson, London, 2021)
47. A.E. Kazdin, Evidence-based treatment and practice: new opportunities to bridge clinical research and practice, enhance the knowledge base, and improve patient care. Am. Psychol. **63**(3), 146 (2008)
48. S. Siegel, N.J. Castellan Jr, *Nonparametric Statistics for the Behavioral Sciences*, 2nd edn. (Mcgraw-Hill Book Company, New York, 1988)
49. R. McGill, J.W. Tukey, W.A. Larsen, Variations of box plots. Am. Stat. **32**(1), 12 (1978)
50. J.L. Hintze, R.D. Nelson, Violin plots: a box plot-density trace synergism. Am. Stat. **52**(2), 181 (1998)
51. S. Cohen, T. Kamarck, R. Mermelstein, A global measure of perceived stress. J. Health Soc. Behav., 385–396 (1983)
52. W.R. Lovallo, *Stress and Health: Biological and Psychological Interactions* (SAGE Publications, New York, 2015)
53. E. Diener, R.A. Emmons, R.J. Larsen, S. Griffin, The satisfaction with life scale. J. Pers. Assess. **49**(1), 71 (1985)
54. S. Lyubomirsky, K. Layous, How do simple positive activities increase well-being? Curr. Dir. Psychol. Sci. **22**(1), 57 (2013)
55. M.L. Waskom, Seaborn: statistical data visualization. J. Open Source Soft. **6**(60), 3021 (2021)
56. M.D. Lezak, *Neuropsychological Assessment* (Oxford University, Oxford, 2004)
57. C.D. Ryff, Happiness is everything, or is it? Explorations on the meaning of psychological well-being. J. Pers. Soc. Psychol. **57**(6), 1069 (1989)
58. E. Diener, E.M. Suh, R.E. Lucas, H.L. Smith, Subjective well-being: three decades of progress. Psychol. Bull. **125**(2), 276 (1999)
59. B.E. Wampold, *The Great Psychotherapy Debate: Models, Methods, and Findings* (Routledge, England, 2013)

Part II
Data Preparation

The second part of the book is devoted to one of the most critical yet often underestimated stages of any scientific investigation—preparing data for analysis. In psychological research, where data can originate from experiments, surveys, observations, or digital traces of behavior, ensuring their quality, consistency, and validity are essential. Without well-prepared data, even the most sophisticated analytical methods lose their meaning.

This part guides readers through the key stages of data preparation, from collection and representation to cleaning, transformation, and validation. It explains how different data collection methodologies shape the structure and interpretability of datasets, and how thoughtful preprocessing safeguards against errors, missing values, or distortions that could bias results. The chapters emphasize not only technical implementation in Python, but also the logic behind each step—helping researchers to understand why certain methods are chosen and how they affect the conclusions drawn from data.

Readers will appreciate that data preparation is not a mechanical prelude to analysis but an integral part of scientific reasoning. It is here, in the meticulous organization and refinement of data, that the foundation for credible, reproducible, and insightful psychological research is truly established.

Collecting the Data in Psychological Sciences

Nataša Kovač, Marija Blagojević, Peter Watson, Hojjatollah Farahani, Lisa-Christina Winter Done, and Kruna Ratković

1 Properties of Data

Psychological science, concerned with the systematic study of human behaviour, cognitive processes, and their biological underpinnings, is fundamentally dependent on data. Empirical data constitute the foundation for theory construction, hypothesis testing, and the elucidation of psychological phenomena. Within the discipline, data may take the form of qualitative evidence, such as interview transcripts and narrative analyses, or quantitative measures derived from psychometric instruments, experimental designs, and statistical modelling. The characteristics of these data—including their structure, scope, type, accuracy, and validity—are pivotal in shaping the interpretation of findings and their subsequent application in psychological research.

Data generated in psychological research are commonly distinguished into two principal categories: *qualitative* and *quantitative*. Each category may be further

N. Kovač (✉) · K. Ratković
Faculty of Applied Sciences, University of Donja Gorica, Podgorica, Montenegro
e-mail: natasa.kovac@udg.edu.me; kruna.ratkovic@udg.edu.me

M. Blagojević
Faculty of Technical Sciences, University of Kragujevac, Cacak, Serbia
e-mail: marija.blagojevic@uni.kg.ac.rs

P. Watson
MRC Cognition and Brain Sciences Unit, University of Cambridge, Cambridge, England
e-mail: Peter.Watson@mrc-cbu.cam.ac.uk

H. Farahani
Department of Psychology, Faculty of Humanities, Tarbiat Modares University, Tehran, Iran
e-mail: h.farahani@modares.ac.ir

L.-C. W. Done
OpenPsai (Two Kermis), Zug, Switzerland

N. Kovač et al. (eds.), *Data Science in Psychology*,
https://doi.org/10.1007/978-3-032-18312-5_4

subdivided according to the nature of the data and the methodological approaches employed for their acquisition. A schematic overview of the hierarchical organisation of data types and their associated collection methods is presented in Fig. 1.

Qualitative data include information typically collected through methods such as interviews, open-ended questionnaires, ethnographic observation, or discourse and content analyses. These data are primarily descriptive and often subjective, as they reflect the interpretations of both participants and researchers. Their analysis requires interpretive approaches, including coding procedures, thematic analysis, grounded theory, or phenomenological methods. Qualitative research thereby facilitates an in-depth understanding of individual experiences, meanings, and the underlying motivations of human behaviour [1].

Quantitative data consist of numerical measurements obtained through standardised procedures such as psychometric tests, closed-ended questionnaires, controlled experiments, or structured observational tools. Such data enable the application of a wide range of statistical techniques, including descriptive analyses, correlation, regression, and hypothesis testing, which support the identification of patterns and the testing of theoretical propositions. Compared to qualitative approaches, quantitative research is characterised by its emphasis on objectivity, precision, and replicability in the study of psychological phenomena [2].

In addition to this basic classification, data in psychological science can also be examined with respect to different levels of measurement, as conceptualised by Stevens [3]. These include nominal, ordinal, interval, and ratio scales. For instance, the nominal scale involves categorising data without inherent order (e.g. participant gender), whereas the interval scale is characterised by equal intervals between values but lacks a true zero point (e.g. temperature in Celsius).

To ensure accurate interpretation and effective application of data in psychological research, it is essential to consider their fundamental properties. An overview of several key properties is presented in Fig. 2.

Validity concerns the extent to which an instrument or research procedure accurately measures the construct it is intended to assess. Within psychological research, several distinct forms of validity are recognised, each addressing different aspects of measurement accuracy and appropriateness:

- *Construct validity* refers to the degree to which an instrument accurately measures the theoretical construct it purports to assess (e.g. whether a self-report questionnaire on anxiety truly captures the construct of anxiety rather than related phenomena such as depression).
- *Criterion validity* concerns the extent to which the obtained data are related to an external criterion or outcome measure (e.g. whether high scores on an intelligence test reliably predict academic achievement or job performance).
- *Ecological validity* denotes the extent to which research findings can be generalised to real-world settings and everyday life contexts.

Reliability refers to the consistency of results, meaning the ability to obtain similar results if the research is repeated. Reliability is often measured using the test-retest method, internal consistency (e.g. through Cronbach's alpha), or interrater reliability.

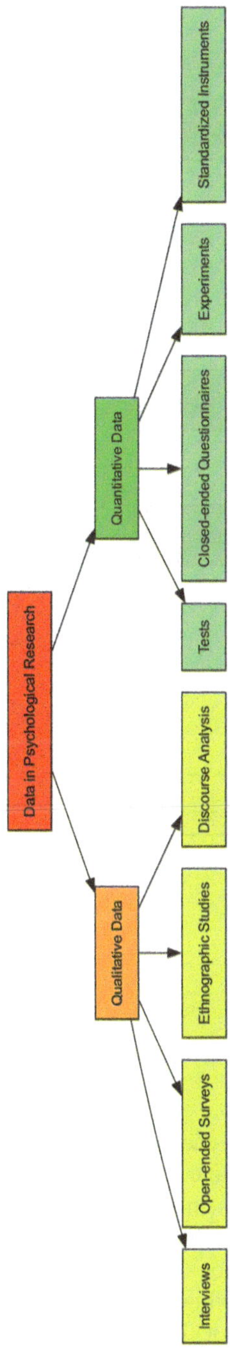

Fig. 1 Taxonomy of data types in psychological research

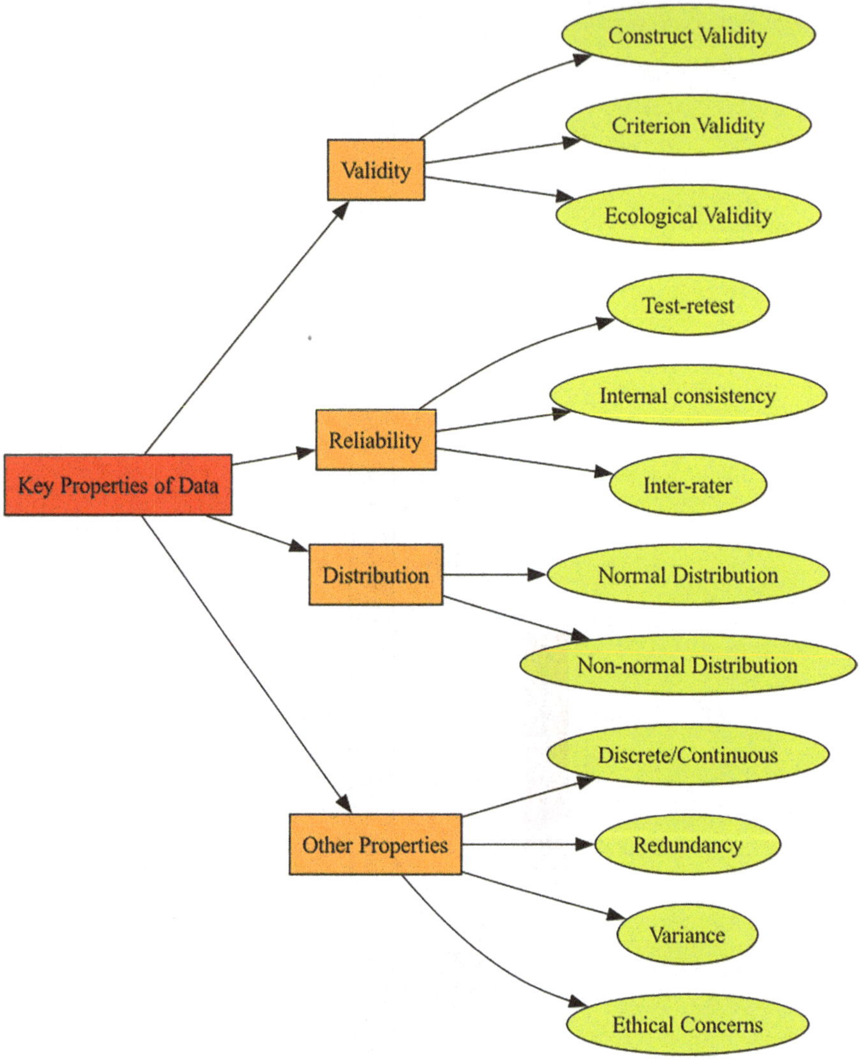

Fig. 2 Overview of key data properties in psychological research

Data in psychological research can be categorised as either *discrete* or *continuous*. Discrete data represent countable values (e.g. the number of children in a family or the number of correct responses on a test), whereas continuous data may assume any value within a given range (e.g. height, weight, or reaction time).

Another important consideration is the *distribution of data*. Many statistical procedures assume normality, making the assessment of data distribution a critical step prior to analysis. When data deviate from the normal distribution, researchers may employ non-parametric methods, which are less restrictive in their assumptions [4].

Issues such as *redundancy* and *variance* further influence the quality of data. Redundancy arises when identical or overlapping information is collected multiple times or in varying formats, which can reduce efficiency and complicate analysis. Conversely, variance reflects the degree of diversity in the dataset; higher variance often indicates greater heterogeneity, which, when coupled with adequate sample size, can strengthen the robustness of statistical inferences.

Psychological research frequently involves the collection of sensitive information, including data on personal experiences, attitudes, emotions, and mental health. Consequently, adherence to *ethical standards* for privacy and confidentiality is of paramount importance. Researchers are typically required to obtain informed consent, comply with relevant data protection regulations (e.g. GDPR in the European Union), and ensure that data are anonymised or pseudonymised to safeguard participants from potential misuse.

A comprehensive understanding of data properties—encompassing data types, validity, reliability, and ethical considerations—is indispensable for the sound conduct, analysis, and interpretation of psychological research. Careful selection of appropriate data collection methods and analytic strategies ensures that findings are accurate, meaningful, and applicable in real-world contexts. Illustrative examples of diverse data types, pre-processing procedures, and transformation methods are provided in previous studies [5–11].

2 Main Sources of Data

Psychological science draws upon a wide range of data sources to explore the complexity of human cognition, affect, and behaviour. These include textual and numerical data, biological measures such as neuroimaging and electrophysiological recordings, as well as oculomotor data obtained through eye-tracking methodologies. Each of these sources offers distinct methodological strengths, enabling researchers to investigate psychological processes from qualitative, quantitative, neurobiological, and perceptual perspectives. The integration of diverse data modalities enhances the comprehensiveness of psychological inquiry, allowing for more rigorous and multidimensional accounts of mental phenomena. This section outlines the principal data sources employed in psychological research, their applications and limitations, and the benefits of combining them through contemporary analytical and computational techniques. A schematic overview of these sources and their associated methods of acquisition across research contexts is provided in Fig. 3 [12].

Textual data, obtained from interviews, surveys, diaries, or digital platforms, capture subjective human experiences in qualitative form. This data type preserves detailed accounts of emotions, beliefs, and personal narratives, enabling in-depth exploration of psychological states. For instance, qualitative analysis of diary entries can elucidate coping mechanisms for grief, while natural language processing (NLP) of social media content can identify mental health trends across populations [13]. Recent developments in NLP have improved the detection of psychological

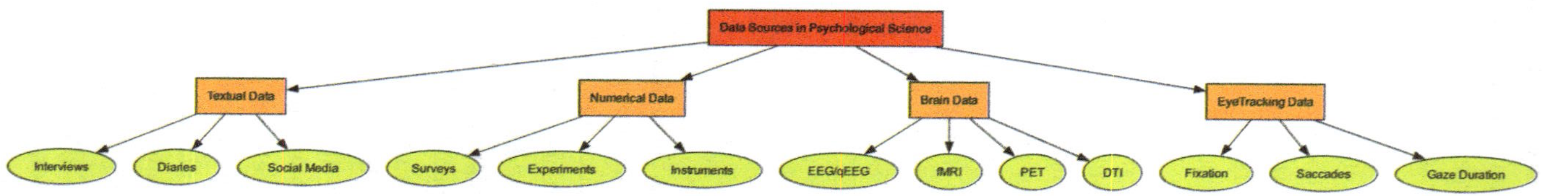

Fig. 3 Classification of major data sources in psychological science

markers, such as indicators of stress or loneliness, in large-scale digital datasets [14]. The subjective nature of textual data necessitates rigorous analytical frameworks to mitigate bias, and large-scale processing requires advanced computational infrastructure. Textual data's strength lies in its ability to anchor research in authentic human experiences, providing context to quantitative findings.

Numerical data, derived from structured surveys, experimental paradigms, or psychometric instruments, provide a quantitative foundation for psychological research. Represented as scores, response times, or statistical aggregates, numerical data support hypothesis testing with high precision and replicability. For example, the Beck Depression Inventory quantifies depressive symptom severity, enabling standardised comparisons across cohorts [15]. Numerical data facilitate the identification of statistical relationships, such as correlations between cognitive abilities and academic performance, and support predictive modelling for clinical applications. Recent machine learning (ML) applications have enhanced the predictive power of numerical data, improving treatment outcome forecasts [16]. Its focus on measurable variables may overlook contextual nuances, necessitating integration with qualitative data to achieve a balanced perspective.

Brain-derived data, collected via neuroimaging and electrophysiological methods, provide direct insights into the neural correlates of psychological processes. Electroencephalography (EEG) and quantitative EEG (qEEG) measure cortical electrical activity with high temporal resolution, suitable for studying dynamic processes like attention or decision-making [17]. qEEG processes EEG signals into frequency-based metrics, aiding in the identification of biomarkers for conditions such as ADHD or epilepsy. Functional magnetic resonance imaging (fMRI) maps brain activity through blood oxygen level-dependent signals, offering precise spatial localisation of cognitive and emotional processes [18]. Positron emission tomography (PET) assesses metabolic and neurochemical activity, contributing to research on disorders like addiction [19]. Structural magnetic resonance imaging (MRI) and diffusion tensor imaging (DTI) provide detailed visualisations of brain anatomy and connectivity, supporting investigations into neurological disorders [20]. Each method not only presents unique strengths, including EEG's temporal precision, fMRI's spatial resolution, and PET's metabolic insights, but also faces challenges such as high costs, complex data processing, and participant constraints. Recent innovations, such as portable EEG systems, have expanded the feasibility of real-world neural data collection [21].

Eye-tracking data, acquired through specialised devices that monitor gaze patterns, fixations, and saccades, offer valuable insights into visual attention and cognitive processing in psychological research. This data type quantifies where and how long individuals focus their gaze, revealing attentional biases, decision-making processes, and emotional responses. For example, eye-tracking studies have demonstrated that individuals with anxiety disorders exhibit hypervigilance toward threat-related stimuli, as evidenced by prolonged fixations on negative images [22]. Eye-tracking is particularly useful in studying implicit processes, such as reading comprehension, social cognition, and developmental disorders like autism, where atypical gaze patterns may indicate altered social attention [23]. Its noninvasive nature and high temporal resolution make it suitable for both laboratory and naturalistic settings, though challenges include calibration requirements and sensitivity to environmental factors. Recent advancements in mobile eye-tracking technology have broadened its applicability, enabling studies in dynamic contexts like virtual reality or real-world interactions [24].

The integration of textual, numerical, brain-derived, and eye-tracking data enhances the validity and scope of psychological research. Multimodal approaches, such as simultaneous EEG-fMRI or combining eye-tracking with fMRI, combine temporal and spatial precision to elucidate brain-behaviour relationships [25]. For example, EEG-fMRI studies have correlated neural oscillations with functional connectivity, advancing understanding of disorders like depression [26], while eye-tracking paired with fMRI has revealed how visual attention modulates neural activity in emotional processing [27]. Similarly, integrating textual narratives with psychometric scores, qEEG, and eye-tracking data enables comprehensive profiling of mental health conditions, informing personalised interventions. These integrative methods address the limitations of individual data types, fostering robust conclusions.

Advancements in computational methodologies, particularly ML, have amplified the utility of these data sources. ML algorithms applied to EEG data enable accurate classification of psychiatric conditions, while fMRI-based models predict treatment efficacy [28]. NLP of textual data facilitates the identification of psychological distress indicators in large datasets. Eye-tracking data, when processed with ML, can classify attentional patterns associated with disorders like schizophrenia [29]. These tools enhance the scalability and accessibility of psychological research, addressing complex challenges such as mental health disparities and cognitive decline. Ethical considerations, including transparency and fairness in algorithmic applications, have been emphasised in recent literature [30].

Psychological science leverages textual, numerical, brain-derived, and eye-tracking data to construct a rigorous and multifaceted understanding of mental processes. Textual data provide qualitative depth, numerical data ensure quantitative precision, brain-derived data reveal biological mechanisms, and eye-tracking data elucidate visual and attentional processes. The integration of these sources, supported by advanced computational tools, enables researchers to address both theoretical and applied questions with enhanced accuracy and relevance. As methodological and technological innovations progress, the continued synthesis of these data types will advance the field's capacity to elucidate the intricacies of human psychology.

3 Overview of Data Collection Methodologies

Data collection is a fundamental step in psychological research, as the validity and reliability of any study depend on the quality of the data gathered. Selecting an appropriate data collection methodology is crucial because it determines how well the collected data represent psychological constructs and influences the accuracy of subsequent analyses [2]. The diversity of data collection techniques available in psychology reflects the range of research questions, from experimental approaches that isolate causal relationships to observational methods that capture natural behaviours. The choice of a data collection method depends on multiple factors, including the nature of the research question, the population being studied, and the practical constraints of time and resources [31].

In psychological sciences, data collection methodologies can be broadly categorised into self-report methods, observational techniques, experimental designs, and physiological and neuroscientific measures. The overview of these methodologies is shown in Fig. 4. Each method has its advantages and limitations, and the decision to use one over another should be guided by the theoretical framework of the study and the specific hypotheses being tested [32]. Understanding these methodologies is essential for designing studies that are not only methodologically sound but also ethically responsible and replicable.

Figure 5 presents a more detailed version, offering a visual taxonomy that highlights both hierarchical and categorical organisation among methods. Primary categories (orange boxes) are linked to their respective techniques (yellow ellipses), emphasising structural organisation and methodological grouping.

One of the most commonly used data collection strategies in psychology is self-reporting, in which participants provide information about their thoughts, emotions, or behaviours through structured or semi-structured instruments. Self-report methods, such as surveys and questionnaires, are widely used due to their efficiency in gathering large amounts of data from diverse populations [33]. These methods allow researchers to assess subjective experiences that may not be directly observable, such as anxiety, personality traits, or cognitive biases.

Surveys can be administered in various ways, including paper-based forms, online surveys, or structured interviews. Technological advancements have enabled the widespread use of web-based survey platforms, increasing accessibility and reducing response biases associated with face-to-face interactions [34]. The effectiveness of surveys depends largely on the design of the questions, the response format, and the degree of social desirability bias that may influence how participants respond. For example, Likert-scale surveys are commonly used to measure attitudes and emotions, providing quantitative data that can be analysed statistically [35]. Self-report methods have been criticised for their reliance on introspection and potential biases, such as memory distortions and response tendencies, that can affect data accuracy.

Interviews offer a more in-depth alternative to surveys, allowing researchers to explore psychological constructs in greater detail [36]. Structured interviews follow a fixed set of questions, ensuring consistency across participants, whereas semi-structured and unstructured interviews provide flexibility to explore unexpected themes. In clinical psychology, interviews are a primary method for diagnosing mental health conditions, with standardised tools such as the Structured Clinical Interview for DSM-5 (SCID-5) ensuring diagnostic reliability [37]. Although interviews can provide rich qualitative data, they are time-consuming and require trained interviewers to minimise bias.

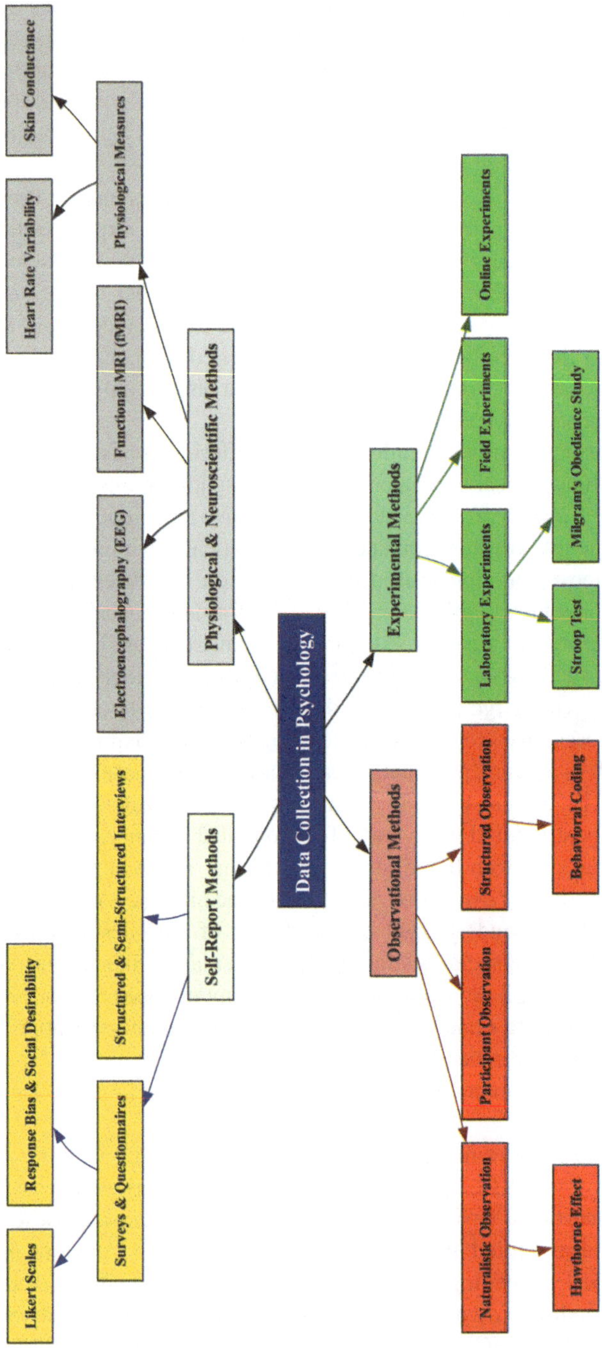

Fig. 4 Classification of data collection methodologies in psychological research

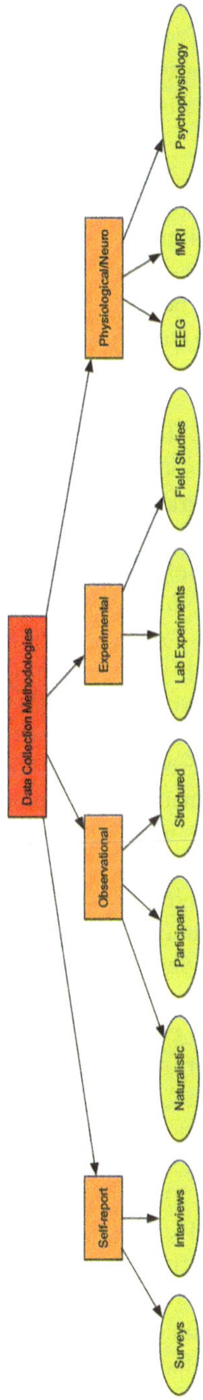

Fig. 5 Hierarchical representation of data collection methodologies

Psychological research widely uses observational techniques to record behaviour in natural or controlled environments. Unlike self-report methods, observational research allows researchers to collect data without relying on participants' subjective interpretations, reducing biases related to self-perception [38]. Observational methods can be classified into naturalistic observation, participant observation, and structured observation.

Naturalistic observation involves studying behaviour in real-world settings without intervention, making it valuable for understanding social interactions, developmental processes, and non-verbal communication [39]. For example, developmental psychologists frequently use naturalistic observation to study how children interact in playgrounds, capturing authentic behaviours that may not emerge in laboratory settings. The major challenge of this method is maintaining objectivity and ensuring that the presence of an observer does not influence behaviour, a phenomenon known as the Hawthorne effect [40].

Participant observation differs from naturalistic observation in that the researcher actively engages in the social setting while collecting data [41]. This method is commonly used in ethnographic research to study cultural influences on behaviour, as seen in cross-cultural psychology. Although participant observation provides rich qualitative insights, it introduces challenges related to researcher bias and ethical considerations regarding informed consent.

Structured observation involves systematically recording specific behaviours using predefined coding schemes [42]. This approach enhances reliability and allows for statistical comparisons between individuals or groups. For instance, in studies of parent-child interactions, researchers may use structured observation to quantify instances of positive reinforcement or disciplinary behaviours. Advances in technology have facilitated automated observational data collection, with video analysis software and ML algorithms increasingly used to enhance coding accuracy [43].

Experimental research is considered the gold standard for establishing causal relationships in psychology. Experiments involve manipulating independent variables to assess their effect on dependent variables while controlling for extraneous factors [44]. Laboratory experiments offer high internal validity, ensuring that observed effects are attributable to experimental manipulations rather than confounding variables. They often suffer from low external validity, as artificial settings may not reflect real-world conditions.

A well-known example of experimental research in psychology is the *Stroop test*, where individuals are required to state the colour of a printed word while disregarding the actual word's meaning [45]. This task has been widely utilised in cognitive psychology to investigate attentional control and interference processing. Similarly, experiments in social psychology, such as Milgram's studies on obedience, illustrate how carefully designed manipulations can provide insight into key aspects of human behaviour, particularly in understanding authority and compliance [46].

In recent years, field experiments have gained popularity as a means of increasing ecological validity while maintaining experimental control. These studies take place in real-world settings, such as schools or workplaces, allowing researchers to exam-

Table 1 Mapping of methods to data types and uses

Method	Qual	Quant	BrainB	AttentionB	Use case
Interview	✓				Clinical diagnostics, narrative data
Survey		✓			Attitude measurement
EEG/qEEG			✓	✓	Real-time cognition, neurofeedback
Eye-tracking				✓	Gaze behaviour, attentional shifts
fMRI			✓		Brain localisation of emotional tasks

ine behaviour under natural conditions. Advances in computational psychology have also led to the rise of online experiments, which facilitate large-scale data collection with diverse participant samples [47]. Advancements in technology have allowed psychologists to integrate physiological and neuroscientific techniques into data collection. These methods offer objective measurements of brain activity, physiological arousal, and bodily responses that are not accessible through self-report or behavioural observation [12].

EEG and fMRI have become essential tools in investigating the neural mechanisms underlying cognition and emotion [48]. EEG is particularly valuable due to its high temporal resolution, allowing researchers to track rapid cognitive processes such as shifts in attention. In contrast, fMRI excels in providing detailed spatial resolution, making it useful for pinpointing specific brain regions activated during different tasks. Psychophysiological indicators, including heart rate variability, skin conductance, and pupil dilation, offer valuable insights into autonomic nervous system activity [49]. These physiological measures are frequently employed in studies on stress, anxiety, and emotional processing, providing a more objective assessment of bodily responses than self-reported data.

To summarise how different methods relate to data types and applications in psychology, Table 1 presents a comprehensive mapping that supports method selection in empirical research. Each row represents a methodological approach, while the columns reflect abbreviated data classifications: *Qual* refers to qualitative data, *Quant* to quantitative data, *BrainB* to brain-based data, and *AttentionB* to attention-based data. The final column, *Use Case*, outlines the most common applications of each method within psychological research. This compact matrix format allows for a direct comparison of methods, supporting decisions about which technique aligns best with a given research objective.

References

1. J.W. Creswell, C.N. Poth, *Qualitative Inquiry and Research Design: Choosing Among Five Approaches*, 5th edn. (SAGE Publications, New York, 2024)
2. G.M. Breakwell, J. Barnett, D.B. Wright, *Research Methods in Psychology* (SAGE Publications Ltd, New York, 2020)
3. S.S. Stevens, On the theory of scales of measurement. Science **103**(2684), 677 (1946)

4. A. Field, *Discovering Statistics Using IBM SPSS Statistics* (SAGE Publications, New York, 2013)
5. M. Blagojević, M. Blagojević, V. Ličina, Web-based intelligent system for predicting apricot yields using artificial neural networks. Sci. Hortic. **213**, 125 (2016)
6. M. Blagojević, Ž. Micić, A web-based intelligent report e-learning system using data mining techniques. Comput. Electr. Eng. **39**(2), 465 (2013)
7. M. Blagojević, Ž. Micić, The use of artificial neural networks in supporting education and curriculum planning. Int. J. Eng. Educ. **36**(6), 1752 (2020)
8. Ž. Jovanović, M. Blagojević, D. Janković, A. Peulić, Patient comfort level prediction during transport using artificial neural network. Turk. J. Electr. Eng. Comput. Sci. **27**(4), 2817 (2019)
9. M. Blagojević, M. Papić, M. Vujičić, M. Šućurović, Artificial neural network model for predicting air pollution: case study of the Moravica district, Serbia. Environ. Prot. Eng. **44**(1), 129 (2018)
10. N. Stanković, M. Blagojević, M. Papić, D. Karuović, Artificial neural network model for prediction of students' success in learning programming. J. Sci. Ind. Res. **80**, 249 (2021)
11. D. Knežević, M. Blagojević, A. Ranković, Electricity consumption prediction model for improving energy efficiency based on artificial neural networks. Stud. Inform. Control **32**(1), 69 (2023)
12. J.T. Cacioppo, L.G. Tassinary, G. Berntson, *Handbook of Psychophysiology* (Cambridge University, Cambridge, 2007)
13. J.W. Pennebaker, M.R. Mehl, K.G. Niederhoffer, Psychological aspects of natural language use: Our words, our selves. Annu. Rev. Psychol. **54**(1), 547 (2003)
14. J.C. Eichstaedt, M.L. Kern, D.B. Yaden, H.A. Schwartz, S. Giorgi, G. Park, C.A. Hagan, V.A. Tobolsky, L.K. Smith, A. Buffone, J. Iwry, M.E.P. Seligman, L.H. Ungar, Closed- and open-vocabulary approaches to text analysis: A review, quantitative comparison, and recommendations. Psychol. Methods **26**(4), 398 (2021). https://doi.org/10.1037/met0000349
15. A.T. Beck, R.A. Steer, G. Brown, Beck depression inventory–II (BDI-II) [database record] (1996). https://doi.org/10.1037/t00742-000. APA PsycTests
16. A.M. Chekroud, M. Hawrilenko, H. Loho, J. Bondar, R. Gueorguieva, A. Hasan, J. Kambeitz, P.R. Corlett, N. Koutsouleris, H.M. Krumholz, J.H. Krystal, M. Paulus, Illusory generalizability of clinical prediction models. Science **383**(6679), 164 (2024). https://doi.org/10.1126/science.adg8538
17. M.X. Cohen, *Analyzing Neural Time Series Data: Theory and Practice* (MIT Press, New York, 2014). https://doi.org/10.7551/mitpress/9609.001.0001
18. R. Poldrack, *The New Mind Readers: What Neuroimaging Can and Cannot Reveal about our Thoughts* (Princeton University, Princeton, 2018)
19. N.D. Volkow, G.J. Wang, J.S. Fowler, D. Tomasi, Addiction circuitry in the human brain. Annu. Rev. Pharmacol. Toxicol. **52**, 321 (2011). https://doi.org/10.1146/annurev-pharmtox-010611-134625
20. S. Mori, J. Zhang, Principles of diffusion tensor imaging and its applications to basic neuroscience research. Neuron **51**(5), 527 (2006). https://doi.org/10.1016/j.neuron.2006.08.012
21. S. Debener, R. Emkes, M. De Vos, Unobtrusive ambulatory EEG using a smartphone and flexible printed electrodes around the ear. Sci. Rep. **5**, 16743 (2015). https://doi.org/10.1038/srep16743
22. T. Armstrong, B.O. Olatunji, Eye tracking of attention in the affective disorders: a meta-analytic review and synthesis. Clin. Psychol. Rev. **32**(8), 704 (2012). https://doi.org/10.1016/j.cpr.2012.09.004
23. T.W. Frazier, M.E. Strauss, E.W. Klingemier, E.E. Zetzer, S.N. Parikh, E.A. Youngstrom, A meta-analysis of gaze differences to social and nonsocial information between individuals with and without autism. J. Am. Acad. Child Adolesc. Psychiatry **56**(7), 546 (2017). https://doi.org/10.1016/j.jaac.2017.05.005
24. V. Clay, P. König, S. König, Eye tracking in virtual reality. J. Eye Mov. Res. **12**(1), 1 (2019). https://doi.org/10.16910/jemr.12.1.3

25. J. Jorge, W. van der Zwaag, P. Figueiredo, EEG-fMRI integration for the study of human brain function. NeuroImage **102**, 24 (2014). https://doi.org/10.1016/j.neuroimage.2013.05.114
26. M. McVoy, M.E. Aebi, K. Loparo, S. Lytle, A. Morris, N. Woods, M. Sajatovic, Resting-state quantitative electroencephalography demonstrates differential connectivity in adolescents with major depressive disorder. J. Child Adolesc. Psychopharmacol. **29**(5), 370 (2019). https://doi.org/10.1089/cap.2018.0166
27. M. Mulckhuyse, E.S. Dalmaijer, Distracted by danger: temporal and spatial dynamics of visual selection in the presence of threat. Cogn. Affect. Behav. Neurosci. **16**(2), 315 (2016). https://doi.org/10.3758/s13415-015-0391-2
28. C.W. Woo, L.J. Chang, M.A. Lindquist, T.D. Wager, Building better biomarkers: brain models in translational neuroimaging. Nat. Neurosci. **20**(3), 365 (2017). https://doi.org/10.1038/nn.4478
29. P.J. Benson, S.A. Beedie, E. Shephard, I. Giegling, D. Rujescu, D. St Clair, Simple viewing tests can detect eye movement abnormalities that distinguish schizophrenia cases from controls with exceptional accuracy. Biol. Psychiatry **88**(10), 716 (2012). https://doi.org/10.1016/j.biopsych.2012.04.019
30. N. Martinez-Martin, T.R. Insel, P. Dagum, H.T. Greely, M.K. Cho, Data mining for health: staking out the ethical territory of digital phenotyping. NPJ Digital Med. **1**, 68 (2018). https://doi.org/10.1038/s41746-018-0075-8
31. H. Coolican, *Research Methods and Statistics in Psychology* (Psychology Press, Milton Park, 2017)
32. K.A. Goodwin, C.J. Goodwin, *Research in Psychology: Methods and Design* (Wiley, New York, 2016)
33. J.P. Robinson, P.R. Shaver, L.S. Wrightsman, *Measures of Personality and Social Psychological Attitudes: Measures of Social Psychological Attitudes*, vol. 1 (Academic Press, New York, 2013)
34. S.D. Gosling, S. Vazire, S. Srivastava, O.P. John, Should we trust web-based studies? A comparative analysis of six preconceptions about internet questionnaires. Am. Psychol. **59**(2), 93 (2004)
35. R. Likert, A technique for the measurement of attitudes. Arch. Psychol. **22**(140), 55 (1932)
36. J. Vaivio, *Interviews–Learning the Craft of Qualitative Research Interviewing* (Taylor & Francis, New York, 2012)
37. M.B. First, Structured clinical interview for the DSM (SCID), in *The Encyclopedia of Clinical Psychology* (2014), pp. 1–6
38. R.F. Baumeister, *Encyclopedia of Social Psychology*, vol. 1 (SAGE, New York, 2007)
39. A.D. Pellegrini, F. Symons, J. Hoch, *Observing Children in Their Natural Worlds: A Methodological Primer* (Psychology Press, Milton Park, 2012)
40. J. McCambridge, J. Witton, D.R. Elbourne, Systematic review of the Hawthorne effect: new concepts are needed to study research participation effects. J. Clin. Epidemiol. **67**(3), 267 (2014)
41. J.P. Spradley, *Participant Observation* (Waveland Press, Long Grove, 2016)
42. R. Bakeman, J.M. Gottman, *Observing Interaction: An Introduction to Sequential Analysis* (Cambridge University, Cambridge, 1997)
43. T. Yarkoni, Psychoinformatics: new horizons at the interface of the psychological and computing sciences. Curr. Dir. Psychol. Sci. **21**(6), 391 (2012)
44. A. Field, G.J. Hole, *How to Design and Report Experiments* (SAGE Publications Ltd, New York, 2002)
45. J.R. Stroop, Studies of interference in serial verbal reactions. J. Exp. Psychol. **18**(6), 643 (1935)
46. S. Milgram, Behavioral study of obedience. J. Abnorm. Soc. Psychol. **67**(4), 371 (1963)
47. U.D. Reips, Standards for Internet-based experimenting. Exp. Psychol. **49**(4), 243 (2002)
48. S.J. Luck, *An Introduction to the Event-Related Potential Technique* (MIT Press, New York, 2014)
49. M.E. Dawson, A.M. Schell, D.L. Filion, et al., The electrodermal system. Handb. Psychophysiol. **2**, 200 (2007)

Datasets Preparation

Nataša Kovač, Marija Blagojević, Kruna Ratković, Marko Simeunović, Lisa-Christina Winter Done, Zhiyong Johnny Zhang, Hojjatollah Farahani, and Peter Watson

1 Datasets and Their Representation in Python

A dataset constitutes a collection of related data points, typically represented in tabular form, where rows signify individual cases or observations, and columns represent variables or attributes pertinent to these cases. Datasets play a crucial role in translating theoretical constructs into empirical analysis. These collections might comprise observational data, survey responses, experimental measurements, or psychometric evaluations [1]. Understanding datasets and their proper representation is essential for reliable research outcomes and valid statistical inferences.

N. Kovač · K. Ratković · M. Simeunović (✉)
Faculty of Applied Sciences, University of Donja Gorica, Podgorica, Montenegro
e-mail: natasa.kovac@udg.edu.me; kruna.ratkovic@udg.edu.me; marko.simeunovic@udg.edu.me

M. Blagojević
Faculty of Technical Sciences, University of Kragujevac, Čačak, Serbia
e-mail: marija.blagojevic@uni.kg.ac.rs

L.-C. W. Done
OpenPsai (Two Kermis), Zug, Switzerland

Z. J. Zhang
Department of Psychology, University of Notre Dame, Notre Dame, IN, USA
e-mail: zhiyongzhang@nd.edu

H. Farahani
Department of Psychology, Faculty of Humanities, Tarbiat Modares University, Jalal AleAhmad Nasr, Tehran, Iran
e-mail: h.farahani@modares.ac.ir

P. Watson
MRC Cognition and Brain Sciences Unit, University of Cambridge, Cambridge, England
e-mail: Peter.Watson@mrc-cbu.cam.ac.uk

N. Kovač et al. (eds.), *Data Science in Psychology*,
https://doi.org/10.1007/978-3-032-18312-5_5

The nature of datasets can vary widely depending on the research question, ranging from simple observational data to complex multidimensional arrays collected through surveys, experiments, or psychometric assessments [2]. A common structure for datasets, especially in psychological research, involves participants as rows and their recorded variables or measurements as columns. Variables within a dataset may represent different types of data, such as categorical or nominal data (e.g. gender or experimental condition), ordinal data (e.g. Likert scale responses), interval data (e.g. temperature in degrees Celsius), or ratio data (e.g. response times in milliseconds) [3]. This categorisation of data types is critical because it determines appropriate methods for statistical analysis and visualisation.

Representing datasets in Python involves the utilisation of powerful and flexible data structures designed to accommodate different types and sizes of data. Python offers several built-in and external libraries, each tailored to efficiently handle datasets for various analytical tasks. Among the reasons for Python's popularity in data science is its ability to manage and process large datasets efficiently, supported by libraries specifically designed for data manipulation, such as `pandas`, `numpy`, and `scipy` [4].

`pandas` is one of Python's most essential data analysis libraries that introduces intuitive and powerful data structures, such as `series` and `DataFrame`. A `series` represents a one-dimensional labelled array capable of holding data of any type. Each element in a `series` is associated with an index, allowing intuitive data access. For instance, a `series` can store a single psychological measure, such as anxiety scores across multiple participants. A DataFrame constitutes a two-dimensional labelled structure similar to a table or spreadsheet, supporting heterogeneous data types within columns [5]. A typical psychological dataset might be stored in a `DataFrame` with each participant as a row and each psychological measure as a column, facilitating quick and intuitive access to individual records or subsets of variables. The versatility and ease of use provided by `pandas` have made it valuable for data cleaning, preparation, and analysis tasks in psychology research.

Python supports multiple dataset formats, each tailored to specific types of research and analysis methods. Files known as Comma-Separated Values (CSVs, `.csv`) are perhaps the simplest and most common format that represents datasets as plain text, making them universally readable across different software and platforms. For more complex and structured data storage needs, Python offers support for other formats like *JavaScript Object Notation* (JSON, `.json`), Excel files (XLSX, `.xlsx/.xls`), and specialised scientific formats such as *Hierarchical Data Format version 5* (HDF5, `.hdf5`) and *Network Common Data Form* (NETCDF, `.netCDF`).

Reading these various dataset formats into usable structures is facilitated by simple, intuitive syntax in Python. `pandas` allows researchers to load CSV files with a single function call (`read_csv()`), immediately converting them into DataFrames. Similarly, JSON data can be imported directly into Python dictionaries or DataFrames with equal simplicity (`read_json()`), demonstrating Python's accessibility even to researchers with limited programming experience.

Recent advancements in data science emphasise the representation of large datasets through efficient storage solutions. Formats like HDF5 are introduced to handle larger and more complex datasets. Python's `h5py` library offers a user-friendly interface to handle HDF5 files. HDF5 enables researchers to store vast amounts of data in a hierarchical and compressed structure, significantly enhancing storage efficiency and data retrieval speed [6]. *Apache Parquet*, supported by Python's `pyarrow` library, provides another efficient method for handling large datasets, especially beneficial when working within big data environments or when real-time data analytics is required [7]. Such formats are essential in neuropsychological studies, where large imaging datasets such as functional magnetic resonance imaging generate massive quantities of data requiring specialised storage solutions.

Beyond basic storage and retrieval, Python supports advanced data manipulation techniques important for psychological research. Operations such as filtering, sorting, grouping, and aggregating data can be effortlessly executed using Pandas' built-in methods. Such capabilities empower researchers to conduct preliminary data inspections, identify trends or outliers, and prepare datasets rigorously for subsequent statistical or machine learning analyses [8].

Python's compatibility with numerical and scientific libraries like `numpy` and `scipy` extends its utility beyond simple tabular data. `numpy` arrays allow researchers to handle numerical datasets efficiently, especially useful in quantitative psychology research involving psychometric testing or signal processing [9]. `scipy` extends these capabilities by providing statistical functions, integration routines, and optimisation algorithms, essential for complex psychological modelling and hypothesis testing.

Data representation extends beyond tabular or numerical data. Psychological datasets may also include textual data, audio clips, or visual information, often processed through specialised libraries. For example, textual data from open-ended survey questions or interview transcripts can be structured and analysed using libraries such as `NLTK` or `spaCy`, designed specifically for natural language processing [10, 11]. These libraries facilitate the representation of textual data by enabling pre-processing steps such as tokenisation, stemming, and sentiment analysis, converting qualitative insights into quantitative data that can be integrated into a structured dataset.

Another critical aspect of dataset representation in Python is managing metadata that includes descriptive information about datasets, such as collection methods, variable definitions, and measurement scales. Effective metadata management ensures dataset clarity, facilitating data sharing, reproducibility, and collaborative research efforts [12]. Python libraries like `pandas-profiling` (recently renamed to `ydata-profiling`) automatically generate comprehensive metadata summaries, including data types, missing values, descriptive statistics, and correlations, significantly improving the understanding of researchers about their datasets before analysis [13].

Psychological datasets frequently require integration from multiple sources or formats, highlighting Python's versatility. Data might originate from electronic data capture systems, online survey platforms like Qualtrics, physiological monitoring equipment, or cognitive testing software. Python simplifies data integration by providing seamless interfaces for reading and combining various file formats, including CSV, Excel, JSON, and relational databases [4]. Libraries such as `openpyxl` and `xlrd` specialise in handling Excel files with multiple sheets or advanced formatting, common in longitudinal or large-scale psychological research.

Understanding the variety of dataset structures is also important for identifying the most effective representation in Python. Datasets may be structured as cross-sectional, longitudinal, hierarchical, or relational [14]. Cross-sectional datasets capture data at a single point in time, whereas longitudinal datasets track changes across multiple time points, essential for developmental psychology or intervention studies. Hierarchical datasets account for data structured across nested levels, such as individual participants within groups or schools, requiring specific analytic and representational strategies such as hierarchical linear modelling or multilevel modelling. Python supports these complex structures with specialised data-handling capabilities, ensuring robust analytical accuracy.

Dataset representation in Python is significantly enhanced through interactive environments such as *Jupyter Notebooks*, which combine code, visualisations, and narrative descriptions in one accessible document. This integration provides transparency and reproducibility, essential in psychological science [15]. Using these interactive notebooks, researchers can document their data representation choices, analytic procedures, and reasoning transparently, fostering open science practices and collaborative research.

2 Manipulating with Datasets in Python: Reading, Writing, and Modifying

Manipulation of datasets is a cornerstone of data preparation in Python. This process includes reading data from various sources, writing it back after processing, and modifying it to fit the requirements of subsequent analyses. Effective data manipulation is critical for ensuring the validity of results. From survey responses and experimental logs to large-scale longitudinal data, researchers are constantly faced with the challenge of integrating, cleaning, and transforming raw data into an analysable format. Python's comprehensive ecosystem of libraries makes it a powerful tool for this task. In psychological research, datasets often originate from multiple formats, spreadsheets, databases, or experimental data logs, making Python's versatility and its comprehensive library ecosystem essential for handling diverse data types. Python's rich functionality allows researchers to clean, reshape, and modify data efficiently, ensuring it is ready for meaningful analysis.

The primary tool for dataset manipulation in Python is the `pandas` library, which provides two primary data structures: the `DataFrame`, which resembles a table with rows and columns, and the `Series`, which represents a single column of data. These data structures enable researchers to organise and manipulate datasets with minimal effort. Unlike traditional spreadsheet software, Python can handle much larger datasets and perform operations on them in seconds, making it particularly useful in fields requiring big data analysis. The `DataFrame` is the backbone of most data manipulation tasks, offering intuitive and powerful methods for reading, writing, and transforming data. Python's popularity in the data science community is largely due to its combination of ease of use and advanced data-handling capabilities [4].

The strength of Python is its flexibility in reading datasets from various formats. The first step in any data manipulation workflow is loading data into Python. This involves reading datasets from various file formats such as CSV, Excel, JSON, SQL databases, and even web APIs. The diversity of supported formats ensures that researchers can integrate data from multiple sources seamlessly. For instance, psychological studies often combine self-reported questionnaire data stored in spreadsheets with physiological measures stored in specialised formats. Python's ability to read such diverse files without extensive conversion processes saves both time and effort. The `pandas` library simplifies these tasks with dedicated functions such as `read_csv()`, `read_excel()`, and `read_json()`. For instance, loading a CSV file into a `DataFrame` is as straightforward as

```python
import pandas as pd
df = pd.read_csv("data.csv")
```

Once loaded, the dataset can be inspected with commands like `df.head()`, which displays the first few rows, or `df.info()`, which summarises its structure. These functions allow researchers to gain an immediate understanding of the dataset's composition, such as the number of columns, data types, and the presence of missing values, enabling quick and informed decisions about further processing steps. In psychological studies, this is crucial for verifying data integrity, checking for missing values, and ensuring that all variables are correctly formatted before further analysis. In addition to basic exploration, Python supports conditional reading of data, allowing researchers to load only relevant parts of large datasets. This is particularly useful when dealing with high-frequency experimental data where only a specific time window or a subset of participants is needed. The following example demonstrates basic manipulation with dataset:

```
import pandas as pd

# Load dataset (e.g., responses from a psychological survey)
df = pd.read_csv("psychology_survey.csv")

# Inspect first few rows
print(df.head())

# Summarize dataset structure
print(df.info())

# Check for missing values in each column
print(df.isnull().sum())

# Example: load only selected columns (e.g., participant_id and anxiety_score)
cols = ["participant_id", "anxiety_score"]
df_subset = pd.read_csv("psychology_survey.csv", usecols=cols)

# Example: load only rows that meet a condition (e.g., participants over 30 years old)
df_conditional = pd.read_csv("psychology_survey.csv")
df_conditional = df_conditional[df_conditional["age"] > 30]

print(df_conditional.head())
```

In some cases, datasets are stored in SQL databases, requiring different methods for reading the data. Python's integration with SQL allows for efficient querying and retrieval of data directly into a `DataFrame`. Python's `pandas` library integrates seamlessly with SQL, allowing researchers to execute SQL queries and import the results directly into a `DataFrame` using `read_sql()`. This integration is especially useful for large-scale projects involving multiple data sources, such as studies combining survey responses with physiological measurements stored in relational databases [16]. Using the `read_sql()` function, researchers can filter and retrieve only the necessary data from large databases, improving both speed and memory usage:

```
import pandas as pd
import sqlite3

# Example: connect to an SQLite database (could also be MySQL, PostgreSQL, etc.)
conn = sqlite3.connect("psychology_study.db")

# Define an SQL query (e.g., select anxiety scores and heart rate for participants over 30)
query = """
SELECT participant_id, age, anxiety_score, heart_rate
FROM study_data
WHERE age > 30
"""

# Load the query results directly into a DataFrame
df = pd.read_sql(query, conn)

# Inspect the data
print(df.head())
print(df.info())

# Close the connection
conn.close()
```

Writing datasets back to files after processing is another key aspect of data manipulation. After cleaning and transforming data, researchers often need to save the processed dataset for future use or share it with collaborators. The `pandas` library provides various functions to write data to files. The most commonly used formats are CSV and Excel, although more advanced formats such as HDF5 and SQL are also supported. The typical command for writing data to files is

```
df.to_csv("processed_data.csv", index=False)
```

This command saves the dataset in CSV format, making it easy to share with colleagues or use in future analyses. The `index=False` parameter ensures that row indices are not included in the saved file, maintaining a clean format. Excel files can be written similarly using `to_excel()`, which supports multiple sheets and custom formatting. For large-scale studies or projects with high-frequency data collection, storing datasets in HDF5 format offers significant advantages over traditional file formats. HDF5 supports hierarchical data storage, allowing researchers to store multiple related datasets in a single file while ensuring faster read and write speeds [6]. This is particularly relevant in experiments where high-frequency data collection results in large datasets that cannot be efficiently managed with plain text files.

In collaborative research environments, saving datasets in a widely accepted format ensures reproducibility and transparency. The growing emphasis on open science in psychology has made dataset sharing a critical aspect of research, and Python's flexibility supports this initiative by facilitating data export in various formats [17].

Modifying datasets involves a range of operations, from filtering and selecting subsets of data to reshaping and merging multiple datasets. One of the most powerful aspects of Python is its ability to perform these operations with concise code. Unlike traditional point-and-click software, Python allows for automation and reproducibility. Once a set of data cleaning steps is defined, they can be executed repeatedly with minimal effort, ensuring consistency across analyses.

One of the most common operations in dataset manipulation is filtering rows based on specific conditions. For example, to extract participants older than 50 from a dataset, the following command can be used:

```
df_filtered = df[df["Age"] > 50]
```

This command creates a new `DataFrame` containing only rows where the `Age` column is greater than 50. Such filtering is invaluable for segmenting data into subgroups, such as different age categories or experimental conditions.

Missing values are a common issue in real-world datasets [18]. In PsAIchology-style predictive pipelines, careful data cleaning is paired with algorithm spot-checking and cross-validation before model selection [19]. In psychological research, incomplete responses in surveys or missing measurements in experiments can pose significant challenges. Python offers several strategies for dealing with missing values. The `fillna()` method replaces missing values with a specified value, while `dropna()` removes rows or columns with missing data. For more advanced handling of missing data, techniques such as multiple imputation are available through specialised libraries like `fancyimpute` and `scikit-learn` [20]. Multiple imputation ensures that missing values are replaced with plausible estimates, preserving the dataset's statistical properties and avoiding biases that can arise from the simple deletion of incomplete cases [21]. Recent ML tutorials in psychology emphasise pairing rigorous data cleaning with cross-validated model comparisons to ensure robust downstream performance [22].

Complex datasets often require reshaping or merging multiple datasets. The `pivot_table()` function in `pandas` allows researchers to create summary tables, while `merge()` facilitates the combination of datasets based on shared columns. These operations are essential for preparing data for modelling and visualisation. For instance, combining demographic data with experimental results enables a more comprehensive analysis of behavioural patterns across different groups.

While `pandas` is the primary tool for data manipulation, other libraries enhance its capabilities. The `numpy` library [23] is essential for numerical computations, providing efficient array operations. For more specialised tasks, `scipy` offers statistical functions, while `pyjanitor` simplifies data cleaning by extending `pandas` with additional functions for common cleaning tasks.

Interactive computing environments like Jupyter Notebooks [24] have further transformed the data manipulation process. By combining code, text, and visualisations in a single document, Jupyter Notebooks ensure that every step of the data manipulation process is transparent and reproducible [22]. This is particularly valuable in psychological research, where reproducibility and transparency are essential for maintaining scientific integrity.

3 Dataset Visualisation and Interpretation

Visualisation is a cornerstone of psychological research, as it transforms abstract numerical data into concrete graphical forms and can reveal structure that summary statistics can miss [25]. This process enables the identification of patterns, relationships, and anomalies that may otherwise remain obscured in tabular formats. Visual methods thus serve both as exploratory tools and as powerful means of communicating findings. Table 1 summarises the most commonly used visualisation techniques and their primary purposes [26]. PsAIchology highlights EDA as a gateway to model comparison (e.g. boosting, random forest, and MLP) and to rigorous performance assessment [19].

During *Exploratory Data Analysis (EDA)*, visualisation is particularly valuable for examining the structure of data before formal modelling [27]. Graphical techniques help detect missing values, inspect distributions, and explore associations that are more perceptible visually than in numerical summaries [28]. Patterns such as

Table 1 Summary of visualisation techniques and their purposes in psychological research

Graph type	Purpose in psychological research
Histogram	Displays the frequency distribution of a single continuous variable; useful for examining variable distributions and detecting skewness or outliers
Scatter plot	Examines the relationship between two continuous variables; enables detection of linear or non-linear trends, clusters, heteroscedasticity, and outliers
Pair plot	Provides a matrix of scatter plots and histograms across several variables; supports multivariate exploration and identification of potential associations
Heatmap	Encodes the strength and direction of pairwise relationships between variables; useful for quickly identifying correlated constructs and potential redundancies
Boxplot	Highlights the presence of outliers and summarises the spread of a variable; particularly valuable for detecting anomalies and comparing groups

clustering, linear relationships, or heteroscedasticity become evident through plots, allowing researchers to refine hypotheses and guide subsequent analyses.

Outlier detection is another crucial function [29]. Techniques such as boxplots and histograms reveal cases that diverge from the majority of observations. These may represent genuine but rare psychological phenomena or errors that must be corrected prior to analysis. Visualisation is equally vital for communication: histograms, scatter plots, pair plots, and heatmaps distil complex statistical findings into accessible representations for both experts and non-specialists, supporting applications in policy, clinical practice, and further research.

Histograms are commonly used to display the frequency distribution of continuous variables. In Fig. 1, a histogram illustrates the distribution of depression scores among participants.

```
import matplotlib.pyplot as plt
import seaborn as sns

# Generate a simple histogram
plt.hist(data['Depression'], bins=10, color='skyblue',
 ↪  edgecolor='black')
plt.title('Histogram of Depression Scores')
plt.xlabel('Depression Score')
plt.ylabel('Frequency')
plt.show()
```

Scatter plots are effective for examining relationships between two continuous variables, making it possible to detect linear or non-linear associations, clusters, and potential outliers and to guide hypothesis generation [30]. Figure 2 shows the relationship between anxiety and stress levels.

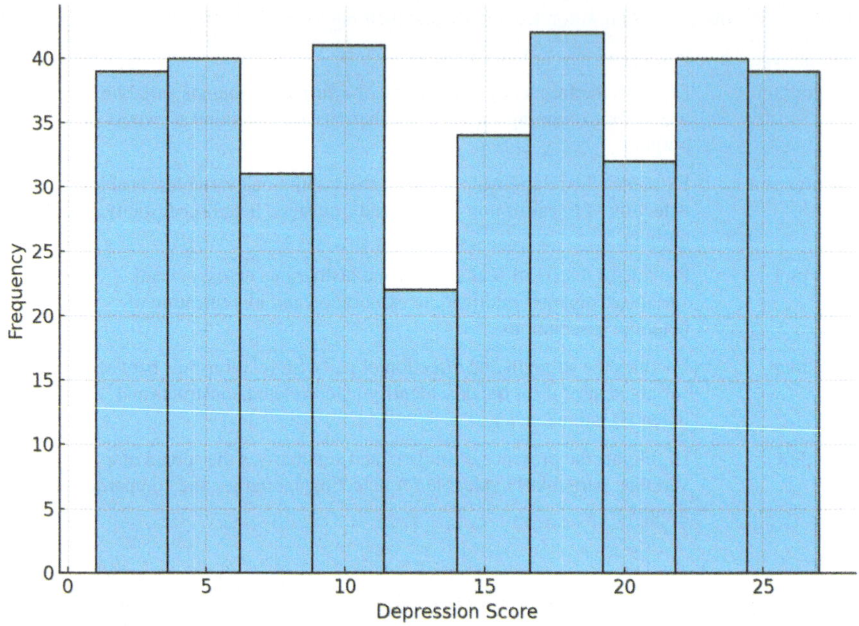

Fig. 1 Histogram of *Depression Scores*

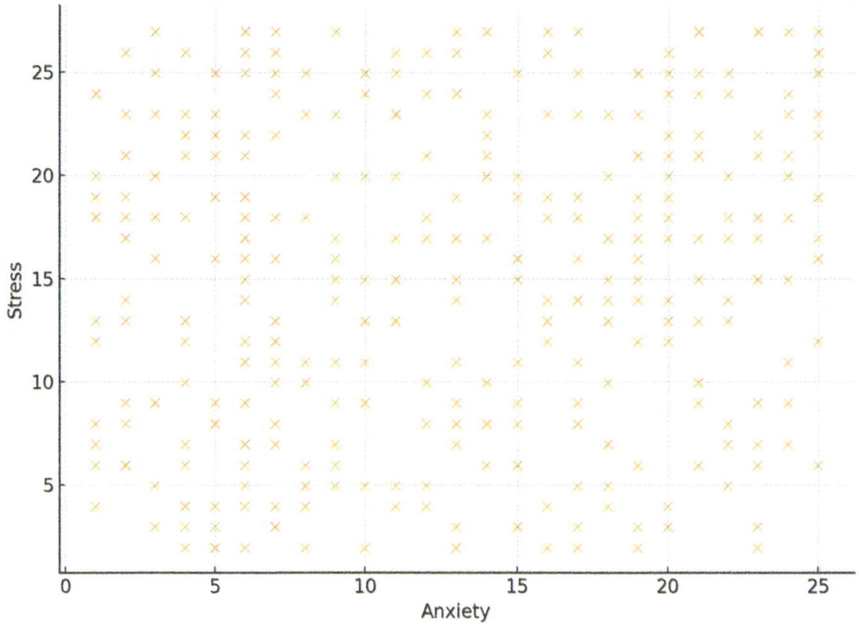

Fig. 2 Scatter plot of *Anxiety* vs. *Stress*

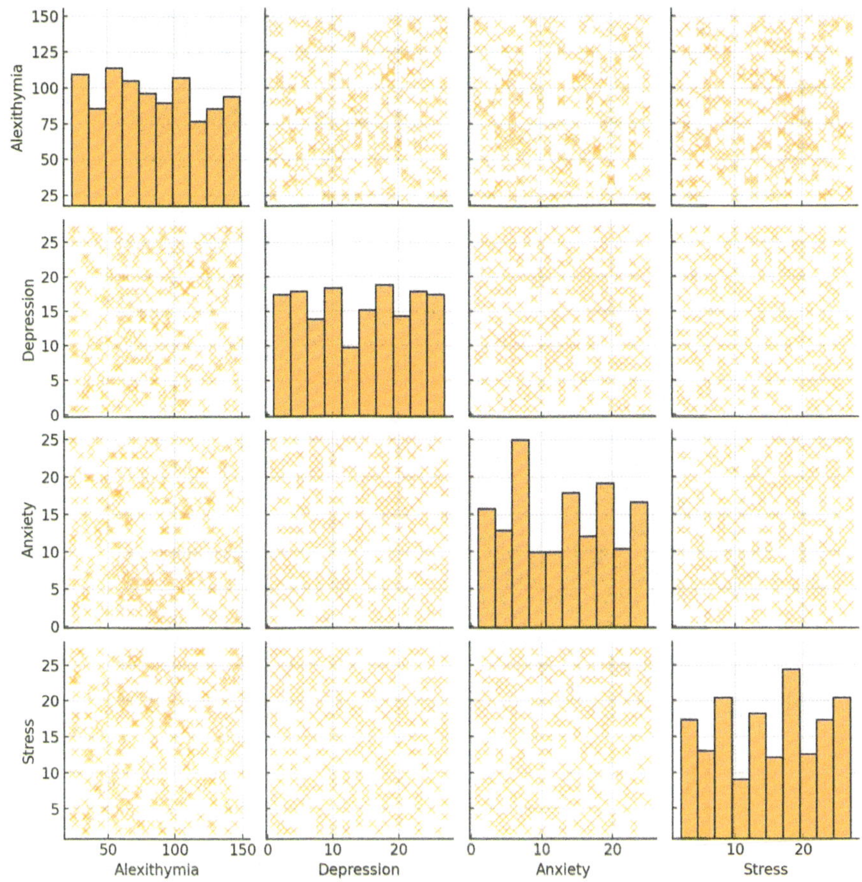

Fig. 3 Pair plot of psychological variables

```
# Scatter plot between Anxiety and Stress
sns.scatterplot(x='Anxiety', y='Stress', data=data)
plt.title('Scatter Plot of Anxiety vs Stress')
plt.xlabel('Anxiety')
plt.ylabel('Stress')
plt.show()
```

Pair plots provide an overview of multiple variables simultaneously, combining scatter plots and histograms to facilitate the detection of interrelations. Figure 3 illustrates the relationships among alexithymia, depression, anxiety, and stress.

```
sns.pairplot(data[['Alexithymia', 'Depression', 'Anxiety',
↪ 'Stress']])
plt.show()
```

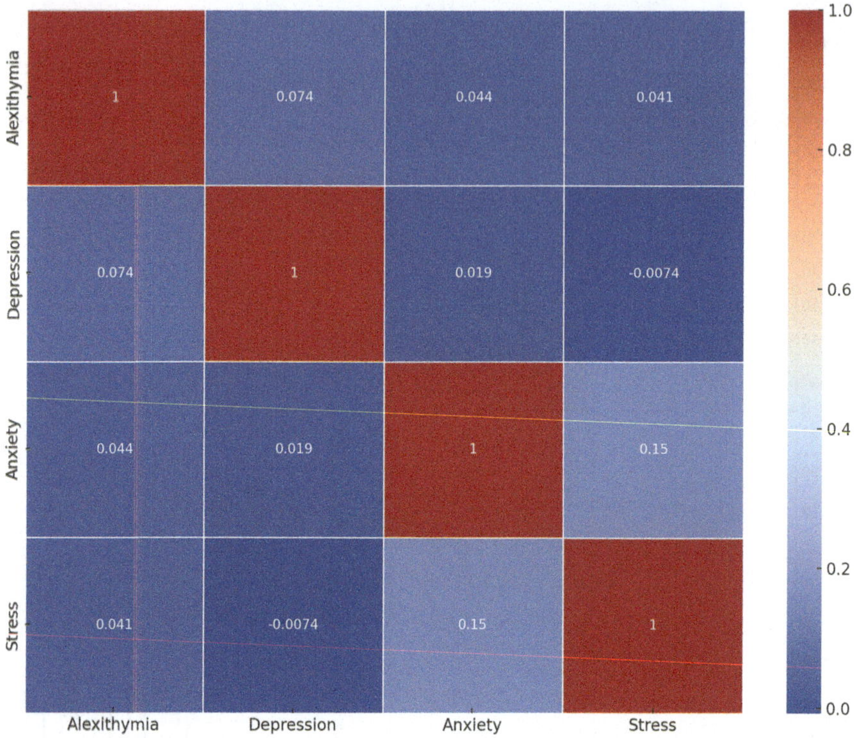

Fig. 4 Correlation heatmap among psychological variables

Heatmaps are useful for visualising correlation matrices, encoding both the strength and direction of associations [31]. Figure 4 presents correlations among several psychological variables.

```
correlation_matrix = data.corr()
sns.heatmap(correlation_matrix, annot=True, cmap='coolwarm')
plt.title('Correlation Heatmap')
plt.show()
```

Interpreting visualisations requires awareness of the dataset's origin, the constructs being measured, and the assumptions of the instruments. Visual patterns, while informative, must not be mistaken for causal relationships [32]. Patterns do not imply causality and may reflect confounding or measurement artefacts [33]. For example, a positive correlation between anxiety and stress may reflect shared underlying factors rather than a direct effect. Similarly, scatter plots may conceal curvilinear dynamics or subgroup-specific trajectories, as seen in resilience research where visual inspection revealed distinct adaptive patterns overlooked by correlations.

Visualisation also aids in identifying anomalies such as clusters, gaps, or measurement errors. In studies of emotion recognition, scatter plots revealed distinctive eye-tracking patterns in individuals with autism spectrum conditions—insights that emerged from exploration rather than hypothesis testing. However, design choices strongly influence interpretation: poor bin widths, misleading colour schemes, or cluttered plots can obscure true patterns.

Effective visualisation must therefore balance clarity and accuracy, grounding interpretations in theory and empirical evidence. Graphs are best regarded as hypothesis-generating tools that inspire further testing. When thoughtfully designed, they function as both mirrors of established knowledge and lenses that magnify subtle phenomena, stimulating new research directions [34].

The integration of visualisation and interpretation is essential to psychological science. Visual methods reveal structure, foster creativity, and enhance communication, while careful interpretation ensures rigor and guards against bias. Together, they enable researchers to navigate complex psychological data with precision and insight. The following section demonstrates these principles in practice through a case study of dataset preparation, visualisation, and interpretation.

4 Case Study

The dataset used in this case study is derived from a psychological investigation focused on assessing the effectiveness of mindfulness training in reducing stress among adult participants. It comprises demographic details, including participant identifiers, age, gender, educational background, and employment status, as well as psychological variables, such as stress levels measured before and after the mindfulness intervention. Additional measures include the number of hours participants spent practising mindfulness and follow-up periods to monitor the sustained impacts of the training.

Effective psychological research strongly relies on careful and systematic dataset preparation. The initial phase involves importing the data into Python, commonly done using `panda`'s library due to its robustness and flexibility in handling diverse formats. Once loaded, researchers typically examine the dataset structure using commands like `df.head()` and `df.info()`, providing an immediate overview of the variables, data types, and the initial integrity of the dataset, resulting in:

```
ID  Age Gen  PreStr PostStr MindHr Group         FUM
0   45  M    59.41  43.80   25.69  Control       3
1   38  F    51.47  34.95   17.18  Control       3
2   47  M    53.30  46.99   40.15  Control       3
3   58  NaN  58.02  45.43   41.55  Control       6
4   37  F    53.00  34.02   16.95  Experimental  3

<class 'pandas.core.frame.DataFrame'>
RangeIndex: 200 entries, 0 to 199
Data columns (total 8 columns):
```

```
 #      Column        Non-Null Count      Dtype
---     ------        --------------      -----
0       ID            200     non-null    int64
1       Age           200     non-null    int64
2       Gen           200     non-null    object
3       PreStr        190     non-null    float64
4       PostStr       185     non-null    float64
5       MindHr        200     non-null    float64
6       Group         200     non-null    object
7       FUM           200     non-null    int64
dtypes: float64(3), int64(3), object(2)
memory usage: 12.6+ KB
None
```

A crucial step in dataset preparation is identifying missing values (Fig. 5), as incomplete data can significantly bias analyses and lead to inaccurate conclusions. Visual methods, such as heatmaps, provide an intuitive representation of missing data, clearly revealing which variables contain gaps. Addressing missing data requires thoughtful strategies; numerical variables often benefit from median or mean imputation, chosen for their ability to preserve the central tendency of the data. In psychological research, it is preferable to use group-specific medians or means when dealing with subpopulations (e.g. control vs. experimental groups), as this maintains the integrity of comparative analyses. Categorical variables, such as gender, require explicit handling, commonly replacing missing entries with a category like `Not Disclosed`, ensuring that analyses accurately reflect participant demographics without artificially skewing categorical distributions.

Starting with the visualisation of missing values, readers can observe significant differences before and after cleaning. Initially, several variables such as `Gender`, `PreStressScore`, and `PostStressScore` contained missing values, represented by distinct yellow markers. After preparation, these values have been systematically addressed, resulting in a fully complete dataset. This highlights the importance of carefully managing missing data, as unaddressed gaps can significantly reduce the reliability of subsequent statistical analyses. Researchers should consider that not all missing data can or should be filled with simple imputation strategies; sometimes, more advanced methods like multiple imputation might be necessary, especially when data is missing systematically or when the proportion of missing data is substantial.

Another critical phase involves detecting and managing outliers, as psychological datasets frequently contain atypical observations. Outliers, if left unmanaged, can distort statistical tests, skew mean values, and impair the overall validity of conclusions drawn from the analysis [35]. Researchers employ visualisations like boxplots (see Fig. 6) to easily identify anomalous values. Once identified, outliers are often addressed through quantile-based capping, where extreme values are limited within upper and lower bounds derived statistically. This approach maintains the original shape of the data distribution while reducing distortion from extreme data points.

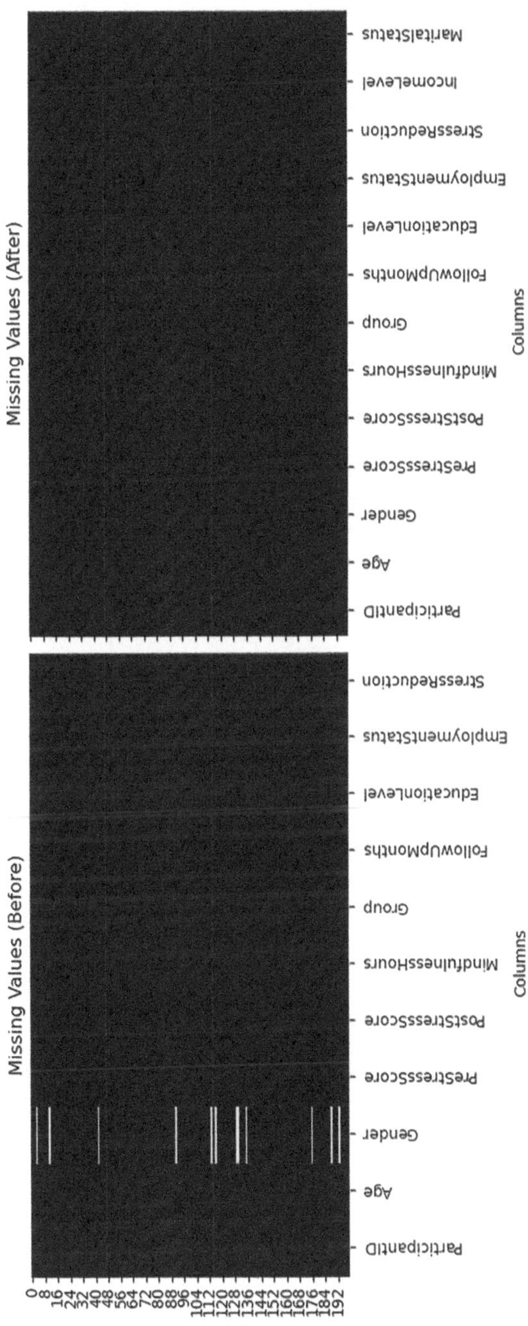

Fig. 5 Missing values

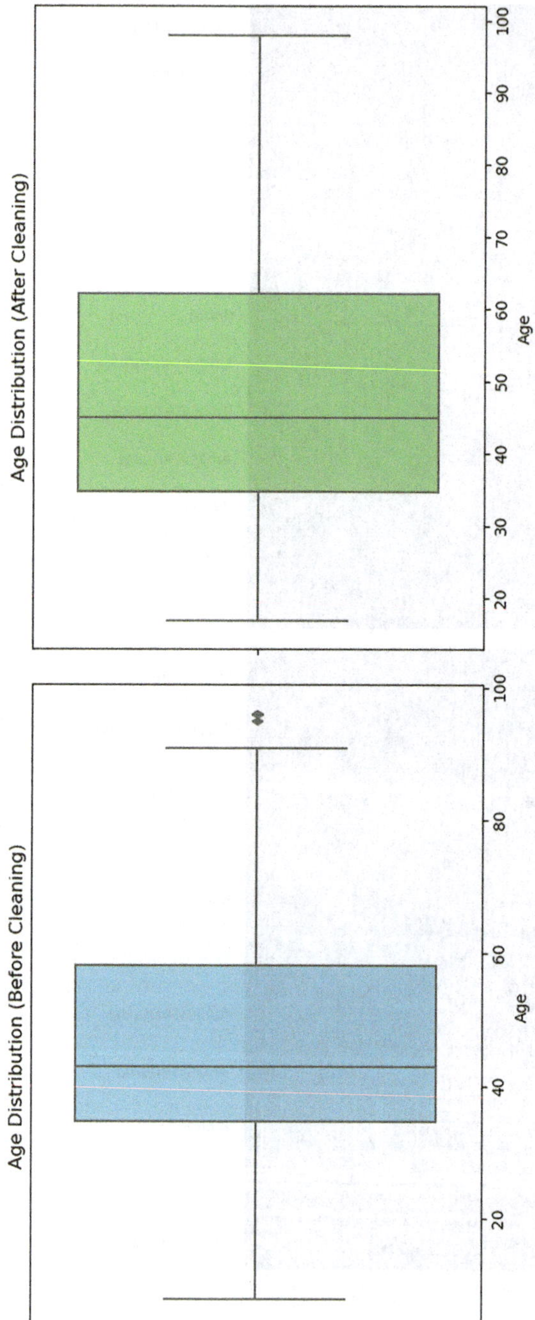

Fig. 6 Outliers detection

Figure 6 depicts outliers in variables like age and mindfulness training hours through boxplots, clearly showing the distribution of values before and after cleaning. Initially, several outliers are apparent, indicating that a subset of participants presented with significantly higher age values or disproportionately high mindfulness practice hours compared to the general group. After dataset cleaning, these extreme values are effectively managed by capping, significantly reducing their influence while retaining the authenticity of the original data distribution. The reader should recognise that while controlling outliers is often necessary to stabilise analyses, it is crucial to assess whether extreme values genuinely represent anomalies or meaningful variations in real-world data. Occasionally, these outliers might offer critical insights into subgroup behaviours or atypical participant profiles, warranting further investigation.

Filtering datasets based on research-specific conditions is also important, as it allows researchers to hone in on subgroups of particular interest. For instance, identifying participants who demonstrated significant stress reduction (such as a reduction exceeding ten points) provides valuable insights into the effectiveness of the mindfulness intervention. This targeted filtering enables researchers to derive meaningful conclusions relevant to the specific hypotheses and research questions posed by the study. This filtering can be achieved by the following commands:

```
# #Step 6: Filtering Data Based on Conditions
# Filtering: Participants who reduced stress significantly (>
↪  10 points)
df['StressReduction'] = df['PreStressScore'] -
↪  df['PostStressScore']
significant_reduction_df = df[df['StressReduction'] > 10]

print(f"Participants with significant stress reduction (>10):
↪  {len(significant_reduction_df)}")
```

Data merging and reshaping further enrich the dataset by combining information from multiple sources [36]. This aligns with PsAIchology's emphasis on integrating diverse psychological and behavioural data sources for ML modelling [19]. Integrating additional demographic data, such as income level and marital status, provides a broader context, supporting detailed analyses of how social and economic factors might interact with psychological interventions. A step-by-step regression workflow shows how pre-processing choices (encoding, scaling, and outlier handling) flow into model training and evaluation [22].

```
# Load additional demographic data
additional_df = pd.read_csv("new_data.csv")

# Merge the datasets on 'ParticipantID'
df_merged = pd.merge(df, additional_df, on='ParticipantID',
↪  how='left')

# Preview merged data
print(df_merged.head())
```

Pivot tables become essential at this stage, summarising complex interactions and highlighting differences between groups, such as comparing stress reduction across gender and experimental conditions. Such reshaping and summarisation enhance interpretability and clarify underlying patterns, making the dataset ready for further sophisticated analyses.

```
pivot_summary = pd.pivot_table(
    df,
    values='StressReduction',
    index='Group',
    columns='Gender',
    aggfunc='mean'
)

print(pivot_summary)
```

```
Gender           Female       Male  Not Disclosed      Other
Group
Control       15.064988  12.895389      11.778177  12.856572
Experimental  13.466929  12.382973      12.081533  15.590009
```

Visualisation techniques offer powerful tools for researchers to understand, verify, and communicate the impacts of their data preparation decisions. Histograms, scatter plots, and comparative visualisations (before and after cleaning) clearly illustrate how manipulations have influenced the dataset, whether through reducing data variability, clarifying relationships, or enhancing data quality. Visual comparisons vividly demonstrate the necessity and impact of rigorous data preparation, reinforcing trust in subsequent analyses and conclusions.

The histograms in Fig. 7 depicting stress reduction scores illustrate distributions before and after data preparation. Initially, the stress reduction scores show a distribution with noticeable irregularities, including some negative values (indicating increases in stress after intervention, possibly errors or anomalies). After preparation, the distribution appears smoother and more consistent, with reduced irregularities and a clearer central tendency. This visualisation demonstrates the effectiveness of careful data cleaning in enhancing the interpretability and accuracy of psychological measures. Researchers should remain cautious, as aggressive data cleaning might inadvertently eliminate meaningful variability or important subgroups; thus, each data transformation must be justified by theoretical and methodological considerations.

The scatter plots in Fig. 8 comparing mindfulness hours against stress reduction scores offer additional insights. Before data preparation, a higher degree of noise and variability is visible, including outlier points significantly deviating from the general pattern. After data cleaning, a clearer relationship between mindfulness practice and stress reduction emerges, potentially revealing underlying patterns obscured by data irregularities. It is advisable for researchers to critically evaluate such visual patterns; if the relationship remains weak even after cleaning, additional variables

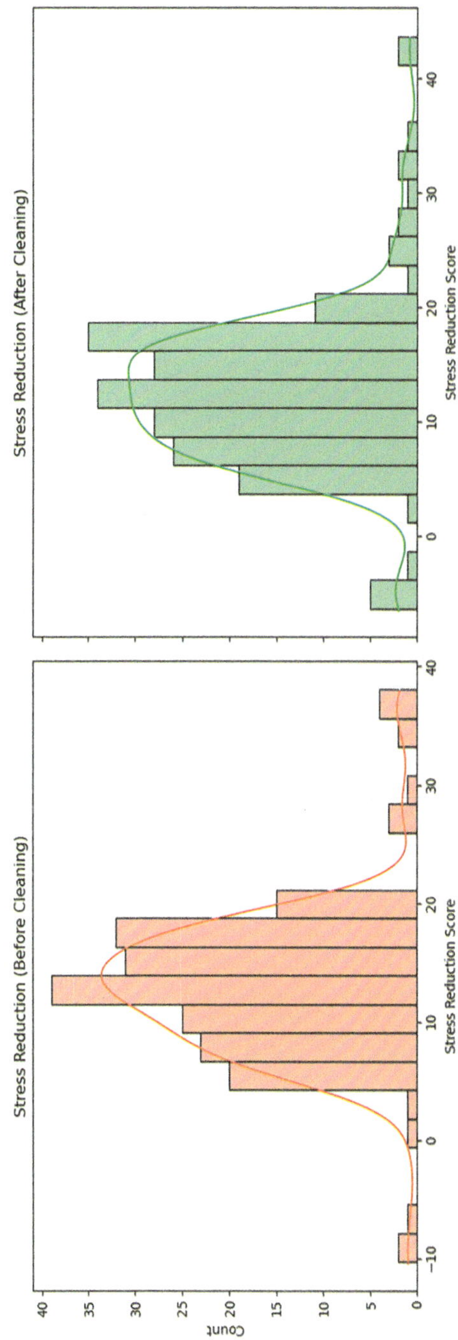

Fig. 7 Distribution comparison (histograms)

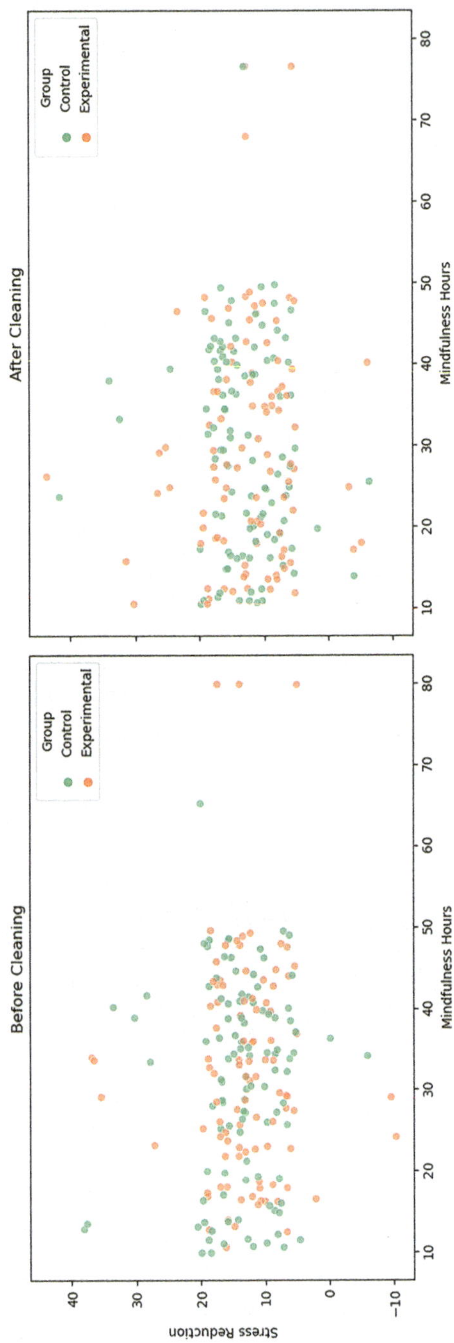

Fig. 8 Distribution comparison (scatter plot)

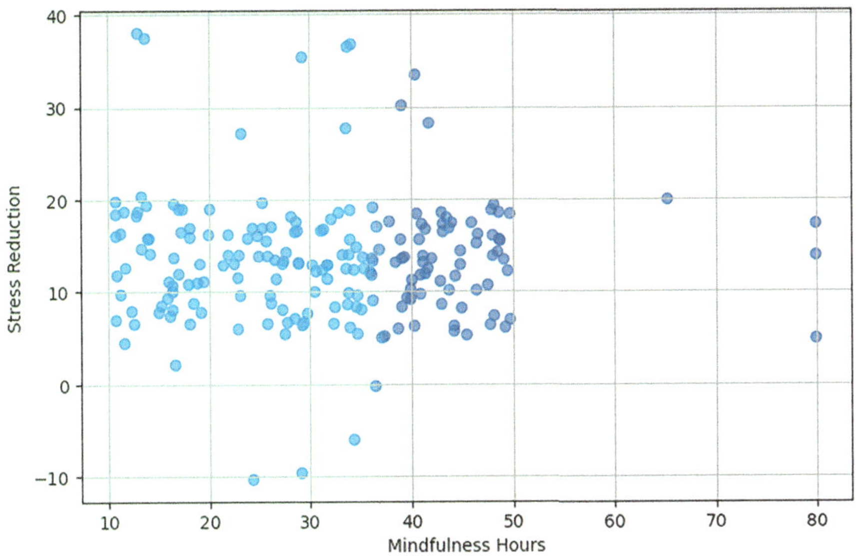

Fig. 9 *Mindfulness training hours* vs. *stress reduction*

or moderating factors might be influencing outcomes, suggesting the need for more complex modelling or further data collection.

The distribution in Fig. 9 further emphasises that most participants cluster within a reasonable range of practice hours and stress reduction. Notable outliers persist despite cleaning, indicating genuinely high levels of commitment or unusual responses to mindfulness practice. Researchers should carefully investigate these cases individually, as they may highlight either methodological anomalies or genuine psychological phenomena worth further qualitative or quantitative exploration.

Finally, after thorough preparation, the cleaned and processed dataset is saved for subsequent analysis or archival purposes, supporting reproducibility, transparency, and open science practices [37]. By documenting each step clearly and saving the prepared data explicitly, researchers facilitate collaborative verification, secondary analyses, and future explorations, all central tenets of high-quality psychological research.

```
df_merged.to_csv('final_psychology_dataset.csv', index=False)
print("The final dataset was saved successfully.")
```

References

1. P. Rosenbaum, *Observation and Experiment: An Introduction to Causal Inference* (Harvard University, Harvard, 2017)
2. K.A. Goodwin, C.J. Goodwin, *Research in Psychology: Methods and Design* (Wiley, New York, 2016)

3. A. Field, G.J. Hole, *How to Design and Report Experiments* (SAGE Publications Ltd, New York, 2002)
4. J. VanderPlas, *Python Data Science Handbook: Essential Tools for Working with Data* (O'Reilly Media, Inc., New York, 2016)
5. W. McKinney, *Python for Data Analysis: Data Wrangling with Pandas, NumPy, and IPython* (O'Reilly Media, Inc., New York, 2017)
6. A. Collette, *Python and HDF5: Unlocking Scientific Data* (O'Reilly Media, Inc., New York, 2013)
7. T. Sarkar, in *Productive and Efficient Data Science with Python: With Modularizing, Memory profiles, and Parallel/GPU Processing* (Springer, Berlin, 2022), pp. 47–84
8. A.C. Müller, S. Guido, *Introduction to Machine Learning with Python: A Guide for Data Scientists* (O'Reilly Media, Inc., New York, 2016)
9. C.R. Harris, K.J. Millman, S.J. Van Der Walt, R. Gommers, P. Virtanen, D. Cournapeau, E. Wieser, J. Taylor, S. Berg, N.J. Smith, et al., Array programming with NumPy. Nature **585**(7825), 357 (2020)
10. S. Bird, E. Klein, E. Loper, *Natural Language Processing with Python: Analyzing Text with the Natural Language Toolkit* (O'Reilly Media, Inc., New York, 2009)
11. M. Honnibal, I. Montani, spacy 2: Natural language understanding with Bloom embeddings, convolutional neural networks and incremental parsing (2020). https://spacy.io
12. C.L. Borgman, *Big Data, Little Data, no Data: Scholarship in the Networked World* (MIT Press, New York, 2017)
13. S. Brugman, pandas-profiling: Exploratory Data Analysis for Python (2019). https://github.com/ydataai/ydata-profiling. Accessed April 2025
14. J.B. Nezlek, *Diary Methods for Social and Personality Psychology* (SAGE Publications Ltd, New York, 2012). https://doi.org/10.4135/9781446287903
15. F. Perez, B.E. Granger, Project Jupyter: computational narratives as the engine of collaborative data science. Retrieved September **11**(207), 108 (2015)
16. P. Harrington, *Machine Learning in Action* (Manning Publications, New York, 2012)
17. C. Gandrud, *Reproducible Research with R and R Studio* (Chapman and Hall/CRC, New York, 2018)
18. R.J. Little, Missing data analysis. Annu. Rev. Clin. Psychol. **20**, 149–173 (2024)
19. H. Farahani, P. Watson, T. Bezan, N. Kovač, L.C. Winter, M. Blagojević, P. Azadfallah, A. Allahyari, S. Masoumian, P. Jiménez, PsAIchology: an intelligent direction in psychological sciences, in *10th International Scientific Conference Technics, Informatics and Education-TIE 2024* (Faculty of Technical Sciences Čačak, University of Kragujevac, Kragujevac, 2024)
20. F. Pedregosa, G. Varoquaux, A. Gramfort, V. Michel, B. Thirion, O. Grisel, M. Blondel, P. Prettenhofer, R. Weiss, V. Dubourg, et al., Scikit-learn: machine learning in Python, J. Mach. Learn. Res. **12**, 2825 (2011)
21. A. Mirzaei, S.R. Carter, A.E. Patanwala, C.R. Schneider, Missing data in surveys: key concepts, approaches, and applications. Res. Soc. Adm. Pharm. **18**(2), 2308 (2022)
22. N. Kovač, K. Ratković, H. Farahani, P. Watson, A practical applications guide to machine learning regression models in psychology with python. Methods Psychol. **11**, 100156 (2024)
23. S. Van Der Walt, S.C. Colbert, G. Varoquaux, The NumPy array: a structure for efficient numerical computation. Comput. Sci. Eng. **13**(2), 22 (2011)
24. T. Kluyver, B. Ragan-Kelley, F. Pérez, B. Granger, M. Bussonnier, J. Frederic, K. Kelley, J. Hamrick, J. Grout, S. Corlay, et al., in *Positioning and Power in Academic Publishing: Players, Agents and Agendas* (IOS Press, New York, 2016), pp. 87–90
25. D. Amoah-Oppong, B. Acheampong, J.Y. Bio, J. Arhin, L.A. Donkor, J.O. Dansowa, *Effective Data Visualisation for Researchers: Principles, Tools and Applications* (Deep Science Publishing, Turkey, 2025)
26. D. Srivastava, An introduction to data visualization tools and techniques in various domains. Int. J. Comput. Trends Technol. **71**(4), 125 (2023)
27. J.W. Tukey, et al., *Exploratory Data Analysis*, vol. 2 (Springer, Berlin, 1977)

28. S. Few, *Show Me the Numbers: Designing Tables and Graphs to Enlighten* (Analytics Press, New York, 2012)
29. Z. Li, Y. Zhao, X. Hu, N. Botta, C. Ionescu, G.H. Chen, ECOD: unsupervised outlier detection using empirical cumulative distribution functions. IEEE Trans. Knowl. Data Eng. **35**(12), 12181 (2022)
30. A. Filipowicz, Data visualization and statistical analysis in behavioral research, J. Appl. Stat. **50**(4), 123–135 (2023)
31. Z. Gu, R. Eils, M. Schlesner, Complex heatmaps reveal patterns and correlations in multidimensional genomic data. Bioinformatics **32**(18), 2847 (2016)
32. C.C. Aggarwal, A. Hinneburg, D.A. Keim, On the surprising behavior of distance metrics in high dimensional space, in *International Conference on Database Theory* (2001), pp. 420–434
33. J. Chishtie, I.A. Bielska, A. Barrera, J.S. Marchand, M. Imran, S.F.A. Tirmizi, L.A. Turcotte, S. Munce, J. Shepherd, A. Senthinathan, et al., Interactive visualization applications in population health and health services research: systematic scoping review. J. Med. Internet Res. **24**(2), e27534 (2022)
34. L. Breiman, *Random Forests* (Springer, Berlin, 2006)
35. Y. Shimizu, Multiple desirable methods in outlier detection of univariate data with r source codes. Front. Psychol. **12**, 819854 (2022)
36. C. Cheng, L. Messerschmidt, I. Bravo, M. Waldbauer, R. Bhavikatti, C. Schenk, V. Grujic, T. Model, R. Kubinec, J. Barceló, A general primer for data harmonization. Sci. Data **11**(1), 152 (2024)
37. F. Pargent, R. Schoedel, C. Stachl, Best practices in supervised machine learning: a tutorial for psychologists. Adv. Methods Pract. Psychol. Sci. **6**(3), 25152459231162559 (2023)

Data Preprocessing

Nataša Kovač, Kruna Ratković, Marko Simeunović, Lisa-Christina Winter Done, Peter Watson, Hojjatollah Farahani, and Zhiyong Johnny Zhang

1 Outliers and Missing Data Identification

Data pre-processing plays a critical role in ensuring the accuracy and reliability of analyses in psychological research [1]. Among the most common issues that arise during this process are outliers and missing data. Addressing these challenges effectively is essential to produce valid results, as outliers can distort statistical models and missing data can reduce the overall quality of the analysis [2]. In psychological research, where datasets are often collected from human participants through surveys, experiments, or observational studies, data inconsistencies can introduce substantial bias if not handled properly. Recognising outliers and missing values is thus a fundamental step in preparing data for analysis.

Outliers are extreme data points that differ significantly from other observations in a dataset [3]. They may result from various causes, including data entry errors, measurement inaccuracies, or genuine rare events [4]. In psychological experiments,

N. Kovač · K. Ratković · M. Simeunović (✉)
Faculty of Applied Sciences, University of Donja Gorica, Podgorica, Montenegro
e-mail: natasa.kovac@udg.edu.me; kruna.ratkovic@udg.edu.me; marko.simeunovic@udg.edu.me

L.-C. W. Done
OpenPsai (Two Kermis), Zug, Switzerland

P. Watson
MRC Cognition and Brain Sciences Unit, University of Cambridge, Cambridge, UK
e-mail: Peter.Watson@mrc-cbu.cam.ac.uk

H. Farahani
Department of Psychology, Faculty of Humanities, Tarbiat Modares University, Tehran, Iran
e-mail: h.farahani@modares.ac.ir

Z. J. Zhang
Department of Psychology, University of Notre Dame, Notre Dame, IN, USA
e-mail: zhiyongzhang@nd.edu

N. Kovač et al. (eds.), *Data Science in Psychology*,
https://doi.org/10.1007/978-3-032-18312-5_6

reaction time data, questionnaire responses, and physiological measurements often contain outliers that may indicate errors or meaningful but unusual behaviour. For example, in cognitive performance studies, an extremely fast reaction time could indicate that a participant guessed instead of carefully considering their response, whereas an unusually slow reaction time might suggest distraction. Understanding whether an outlier represents an error or a meaningful observation is critical in deciding how to handle it.

There are several ways to detect outliers [5], ranging from visual inspection to advanced statistical methods. Visual techniques, such as histograms and density plots, allow researchers to assess the distribution of data and spot anomalies that may warrant further investigation. Box plots and scatter plots offer a quick and intuitive way to identify outliers. In psychological datasets, scatter plots can be particularly useful for detecting outliers in multivariate data. For example, a study analysing stress levels and heart rate might show unexpected values where stress is high but heart rate remains low, suggesting data entry errors or physiological anomalies. A box plot highlights data points that fall outside the interquartile range (IQR) as potential outliers. Consider the following Python code that generates a box plot for visualising reaction times:

```python
import pandas as pd
import matplotlib.pyplot as plt
# Load dataset
df = pd.read_csv("reaction_time_data.csv")

# Create a box plot for the ReactionTime column
plt.boxplot(df["ReactionTime"].dropna())
plt.title("Box Plot of Reaction Times")
plt.ylabel("Reaction Time (ms)")
plt.show()
```

Box plots are effective for identifying extreme values, but they do not indicate whether an outlier is due to measurement errors, data recording issues, or meaningful variability. In addition to visual methods, statistical techniques provide a more rigorous approach. The z-score is one of the simplest ways to detect univariate outliers. A z-score greater than 3 or less than -3 is often considered an outlier [4]. Here is how to calculate z-scores for identifying outliers:

```python
from scipy.stats import zscore

# Calculate z-scores for the ReactionTime column
df["z_score"] = zscore(df["ReactionTime"])

# Identify outliers with z-scores greater than 3 or less than -3
outliers = df[(df["z_score"] > 3) | (df["z_score"] < -3)]
print(f"Number of outliers: {len(outliers)}")
```

While z-scores help identify univariate outliers [6], psychological research often involves complex datasets where relationships between multiple variables must be considered. In such cases, Mahalanobis distance provides a more sophisticated method for detecting multivariate outliers by considering the overall covariance structure of the data. This technique is especially useful in studies involving personality traits, where an unusual combination of scores across multiple dimensions may signal an error or an exceptional case [7].

Missing data is another significant challenge that researchers face. It can result from incomplete responses, technical failures, or participant dropout in longitudinal studies. For instance, in a mental health survey, participants might skip questions about sensitive topics, leading to systematic missingness. Similarly, in neuroimaging studies, data loss may occur due to movement artefacts or equipment malfunctions. The impact of missing data on analysis depends on its pattern and mechanism [8, 9]. Missing data mechanisms can be classified into three categories: *missing completely at random* (MCAR), *missing at random* (MAR), and *missing not at random* (MNAR) [10].

For instance, if missing values are entirely independent of both observed and unobserved data, they are considered MCAR [11] and do not introduce systematic bias. MAR occurs when missingness is related to observed variables [12]. In a survey study, participants with higher anxiety levels might be more likely to skip questions about mental health, resulting in data that are not missing completely at random. MNAR arises when missingness depends on unobserved data [13], such as participants refusing to report their income due to privacy concerns. Python provides various tools for identifying and visualising missing data. The `pandas` library makes it easy to count and summarise missing values:

```
# Count missing values in each column
missing_counts = df.isnull().sum()
print(missing_counts)
```

For more comprehensive visualisation, the `missingno` library offers visual tools such as heatmaps to identify patterns of missingness:

```
import missingno as msno
# Visualize missing data as a heatmap
msno.matrix(df)
plt.show()
```

These visualisations can reveal clusters of missing data, helping researchers determine whether the missingness follows a specific pattern [14]. For example, in a longitudinal study on sleep patterns, a heatmap could show that missing values are concentrated on weekends, suggesting a nonrandom pattern [12].

Addressing outliers and missing data is essential for preserving the validity of psychological research [5]. In ML-first PsAIchology workflows, these steps are prerequisites for fair train/validation evaluation and hyperparameter tuning [15]. In an applied tutorial, these steps precede model fitting and are inspected via error metrics and SHAP explanations to verify impact [1]. While outliers may represent rare but important cases, they can also distort the results of statistical models if not handled appropriately. Decisions regarding whether to remove, transform, or retain outliers should be guided by domain knowledge and research objectives. Missing data, on the other hand, can reduce statistical power and introduce bias if left unaddressed [13]. Researchers must carefully consider the most suitable strategy for each dataset, balancing accurate representation with statistical demands and aligning choices with current benchmarking evidence [16].

In subsequent sections, we will explore various data interpolation strategies and advanced handling methods to address these challenges effectively. The growing use of machine learning (ML) in psychological data processing [1] has also introduced new techniques for detecting and handling outliers, including robust regression methods and anomaly detection algorithms [17]. These approaches, alongside traditional statistical techniques, help ensure that psychological research is conducted with the highest level of methodological rigour [18].

2 Common Data Interpolation Strategies

Data interpolation strategies enable researchers to estimate and replace missing values, preserving the integrity of datasets while minimising bias. Selecting an appropriate interpolation method depends on the nature of the missing data, the structure of the dataset, and the research objectives. This section explores widely used interpolation techniques and their applications in psychological studies.

Table 1 summarises the interpolation and imputation methods to handle missing data. One of the simplest approaches to address missing values is *mean imputation*, where missing values in a variable are replaced by the mean of observed values. This method maintains the overall distribution, but reduces variability, potentially underestimating standard errors and distorting relationships among variables [19]. *Median imputation* provides a robust alternative, particularly in datasets with skewed distributions, as it is less sensitive to extreme values [20]. In Python, mean and median imputation can be performed using the `SimpleImputer` module from the `sklearn.impute` library:

```
from sklearn.impute import SimpleImputer
import numpy as np

# Example dataset with missing values
data = np.array([[1, 2, np.nan], [4, np.nan, 6], [7, 8, 9]])

# Mean imputation
mean_imputer = SimpleImputer(strategy='mean')
data_mean = mean_imputer.fit_transform(data)

# Median imputation
median_imputer = SimpleImputer(strategy='median')
data_median = median_imputer.fit_transform(data)

print("Mean Imputation:\n", data_mean)
print("Median Imputation:\n", data_median)
```

Table 1 Summary of interpolation and imputation methods for handling missing data

Method	Primary goal/data scope	Strengths/limitations
Mean imputation	Single variable (univariate) in cross-sectional data	+ Simple, fast; preserves mean
		– Underestimates variance; attenuates correlations; biases SEs
Median imputation	Single variable (univariate); robust to skew/outliers	+ Robust to outliers and skewed distributions
		– Still reduces variability; may distort parametric relations
Linear interpolation	Time-ordered or index-based series (univariate)	+ Preserves local trend; easy to explain
		– Poor for non-linear dynamics; ignores uncertainty
Polynomial interpolation	Ordered data (univariate); captures curvature	+ Flexibly models non-linearity
		– Overfitting/oscillation at higher degrees; unstable extrapolation
Spline interpolation (cubic)	Ordered data (univariate); locally adaptive smoothness	+ Smooth, stable local fit; less oscillation than high-degree polynomials
		– Choice of knots/boundaries affects results
Multiple imputation (MICE)	Multivariate (cross-sectional/longitudinal datasets)	+ Preserves relationships among variables; valid inference with pooled estimates
		– Computationally more complex; requires diagnostics

A more advanced approach is *linear interpolation*, which estimates missing values by fitting a straight line between adjacent known data points [21]. The formula for linear interpolation is given by Eq. 1:

$$y = y_1 + \frac{(y_2 - y_1)(x - x_1)}{x_2 - x_1}, \tag{1}$$

where y represents the interpolated value at the missing data point x. The values x_1 and x_2 are the closest observed data points surrounding x, while y_1 and y_2 are their respective function values. This method assumes a constant rate of change between observed points, making it suitable for datasets where trends are approximately linear [22]. Python `pandas` library contains `interpolate` method that implements linear interpolation:

```
import pandas as pd
import numpy as np

# Creating a dataset with missing values
data = pd.Series([1, 2, np.nan, 4, 5, np.nan, 7, 8])

# Linear interpolation
data_interpolated = data.interpolate(method='linear')

print("Interpolated Data:\n", data_interpolated)
```

Polynomial interpolation extends this approach by fitting a higher-order polynomial function to the surrounding data points [23]. Unlike linear interpolation, polynomial interpolation can capture more complex patterns in data fluctuations [24]. The polynomial interpolation can be described by the following relation:

$$P_n(x) = \sum_{i=0}^{n} a_i x^i, \tag{2}$$

where $P_n(x)$ is the polynomial function of degree n, and $a_i, i = 0, \ldots, n$ are the coefficients determined based on the available data. The variable x represents the point where interpolation is performed. By increasing the polynomial degree, the function can fit more complex curves; however, higher-degree polynomials may lead to overfitting [25], making the estimated values unstable in some cases. Polynomial interpolation is implemented in Python numpy library:

```
import numpy as np
from scipy.interpolate import interp1d

# Sample data with missing values
x = np.array([0, 1, 2, 4, 5])
y = np.array([1, 2, 3, 5, 6])

# Creating a polynomial interpolator (cubic)
poly_interp = interp1d(x, y, kind='cubic',
 ↪ fill_value="extrapolate")

# Estimating a missing value at x=3
y_missing = poly_interp(3)

print("Interpolated Value at x=3:", y_missing)
```

Another widely used method is *spline interpolation*, which fits piecewise polynomials between known data points to create a smooth curve. Unlike polynomial interpolation, which fits a single equation to the entire dataset, spline interpolation ensures local adaptability by using lower-degree polynomials within segmented intervals. The most common form of spline interpolation is the *cubic spline interpolation*, defined as [26]

$$S_i(x) = a_i + b_i(x - x_i) + c_i(x - x_i)^2 + d_i(x - x_i)^3, \tag{3}$$

where $S_i(x)$ represents the spline function within a given interval i. The variable x is the point at which interpolation is performed, while x_i is the starting point of the interval. The coefficients a_i, b_i, c_i, and d_i define the cubic polynomial for each segment, ensuring a smooth approximation across multiple intervals. This method is particularly useful for datasets with nonlinear patterns, as it balances flexibility with stability in interpolation. Spline interpolation can be implemented using the `scipy.interpolate` module:

```
from scipy.interpolate import CubicSpline

# Known data points
x = np.array([0, 1, 2, 4, 5])
y = np.array([1, 2, 3, 5, 6])

# Cubic spline interpolation
spline_interp = CubicSpline(x, y)

# Estimating missing value at x=3

y_spline = spline_interp(3)

print("Spline Interpolated Value at x=3:", y_spline)
```

For datasets with missing values in multiple variables, *multivariate imputation techniques*, such as multiple imputation by chained equations (MICE), provide a robust solution [27]. PsAIchology recommends pairing imputation with algorithmic spot-checking to benchmark models under identical resampling schemes [15]. MICE generates multiple plausible values for missing entries by iteratively modelling each variable based on the observed data [10]. This method can be implemented using the `IterativeImputer` module in `sklearn`:

```
from sklearn.experimental import enable_iterative_imputer
from sklearn.impute import IterativeImputer

# Example dataset with missing values
data = np.array([[1, 2, np.nan], [4, np.nan, 6], [7, 8, 9]])

# Multiple Imputation (MICE)
mice_imputer = IterativeImputer()
data_mice = mice_imputer.fit_transform(data)

print("MICE Imputed Data:\n", data_mice)
```

Choosing the appropriate interpolation method depends on several factors, including the amount of missing data, the structure of the dataset, and the assumptions underlying each method [16]. While simple imputation techniques such as mean and median substitution are computationally efficient, they may introduce biases that affect subsequent analyses. More advanced methods, such as spline interpolation and ML-based approaches, provide greater accuracy but require careful parameter selection to avoid overfitting.

3 Handling Data Inconsistency in Psychological Sciences

Data inconsistency represents a methodological concern in psychological research, primarily due to the different nature of data collection involving human participants. Such inconsistencies typically emerge through variations in measurement procedures, inconsistent respondent behaviours, or errors in data entry, and can profoundly affect the accuracy of statistical analyses and subsequent interpretations [28] because psychological data frequently encompasses diverse data collection methods, such as questionnaires, behavioural tests, and neurophysiological measures, ensuring consistency becomes especially complex.

One of the predominant sources of data inconsistency in psychological research arises from measurement instruments themselves [29]. Researchers often utilise established questionnaires or psychometric scales, but subtle variations between different versions of these instruments can introduce inconsistencies. This issue is exacerbated in cross-cultural research, where translated versions of standardised instruments may differ in interpretation and meaning, leading to variable participant responses across different linguistic or cultural groups [30]. Consequently, researchers must implement careful calibration procedures, including cognitive interviewing and pilot testing, to ensure conceptual equivalence across versions of measurement tools.

Beyond measurement instruments, inconsistencies also frequently result from procedural variations during data collection. For example, studies employing multiple sites or research teams may inadvertently introduce methodological differences, such as varying participant instructions, inconsistent measurement time intervals, or differing laboratory equipment calibrations. These procedural inconsistencies, although seemingly minor, can significantly distort data distributions and correlations. Researchers should thus establish rigorous protocols at the onset of data collection, supplemented by regular training and monitoring of research personnel. Such proactive strategies minimise procedural deviations and thus enhance data consistency [31].

Human error constitutes another significant cause of inconsistency in psychological datasets. Despite technological advancements, much psychological research still relies on manual data entry from surveys or observational records, increasing the probability of transcription errors or misinterpretation of handwritten responses. While manual verification methods remain effective, integrating automated validation procedures can substantially reduce such inconsistencies. For instance, predefined rules within data collection software or automated error detection scripts using languages like Python can rapidly identify and rectify improbable or inconsistent data points, such as implausible age ranges or inconsistent demographic responses [13].

Another subtle but prevalent source of data inconsistency arises from participant-related factors, including contradictory responses or response biases, which are commonplace in psychological assessments. Participants may intentionally or unintentionally provide conflicting information across different items or measurements due to fatigue, misunderstanding instructions, social desirability biases, or malingering. Psychological scales designed with built-in validation checks, such as reverse-scored items or parallel forms of measurement, enable researchers to detect these inconsistent response patterns. Statistical analyses such as item response theory (IRT) further facilitate identification of inconsistent responses by assessing response patterns at an individual participant level, thus enabling precise intervention through targeted participant re-assessment or exclusion when justified [32].

To effectively resolve detected inconsistencies, researchers often employ statistical corrections or data imputation methods tailored to the specific nature of the inconsistency. Statistical corrections can involve re-coding data based on known errors or logical impossibilities, informed by careful cross-checking against original data sources. In more complex cases, multivariate imputation methods like MICE have emerged as particularly robust solutions for dealing with inconsistent or incomplete psychological data [33]. These methods estimate plausible values for inconsistent or missing data points by iteratively modelling each problematic variable based on other observed variables within the dataset, thus preserving the overall relationships and distributional characteristics inherent in the original data.

Visualising inconsistencies through graphical methods can also substantially enhance their identification and subsequent handling. Visualisation techniques such as correlation matrices, scatter plots, and heatmaps facilitate intuitive detection of irregular patterns or outlier clusters indicative of underlying inconsistencies. For instance, heatmaps depicting correlations among theoretically related psychological measures, such as anxiety, stress, and depressive symptoms, can reveal unusual discrepancies or negative correlations that are conceptually implausible, signalling potential data inconsistencies. These visual approaches allow researchers not only to pinpoint problematic areas quickly but also to communicate the nature and scope of data quality issues clearly in publications and presentations [34, 35].

In longitudinal psychological studies, inconsistencies often appear as irregularities in repeated measurements, typically arising from changing measurement contexts or participant attrition. Handling such inconsistencies requires sophisticated statistical modelling approaches, including mixed-effects models and growth curve analyses, which inherently account for inconsistent timing or missing data points. These approaches enable researchers to preserve and accurately interpret longitudinal data integrity despite inevitable inconsistencies encountered over extended periods of participant observation [12].

Data integration from multiple sources, such as combining self-report measures with physiological or observational data, can further complicate consistency management. Integrative approaches must ensure that different measurement modalities align correctly regarding timing, measurement units, and conceptual definitions. For example, integrating questionnaire-based anxiety measures with physiological stress markers (e.g. cortisol levels or heart rate variability) demands rigorous data alignment and synchronisation protocols to ensure accurate interpretation and consistency across diverse data streams [36].

Preventative measures remain paramount in reducing future occurrences of data inconsistency. Rigorous initial training of research personnel, standardisation of measurement procedures, and precise operational definitions significantly mitigate potential inconsistencies. Researchers should maintain meticulous data management logs documenting all procedures, alterations, and resolutions applied throughout the study. Such transparent record-keeping supports reproducibility and provides critical context for interpreting statistical outcomes, ultimately enhancing the robustness of psychological findings [37].

Data inconsistency remains an unavoidable challenge within psychological sciences due to the inherently complex nature of human-based data collection methods and measurement tools. Through proactive methodological rigour, systematic detection processes, thoughtful statistical correction strategies, and preventative practices, researchers can effectively mitigate the impact of inconsistencies. Ensuring consistency within psychological datasets fundamentally improves data quality, thereby bolstering the credibility, replicability, and validity of psychological research findings.

4 Univariate and Multivariate Normality: From the Kolmogorov-Smirnov Test to Mardia's Test

Normality refers to the assumption that a variable follows a normal distribution (Gaussian distribution) [38]. The probability density function (PDF) of a normal distribution with mean (μ) and variance (σ^2) is given by

$$f(x) = \frac{1}{\sqrt{2\pi\sigma^2}} \exp\left(-\frac{(x-\mu)^2}{2\sigma^2}\right). \tag{4}$$

A normal distribution has a symmetric, bell-shaped curve centred at the mean. Many statistical methods, such as t-tests, ANOVA, and linear regression, assume that the data are normally distributed. Therefore, it is essential to assess normality before applying these methods.

Two statistics that are commonly used to assess normality are *skewness* and *kurtosis*. Skewness measures the asymmetry of the distribution of a variable:

$$\text{Skewness} = \frac{\frac{1}{n}\sum_{i=1}^{n}(x_i - \bar{x})^3}{\left(\frac{1}{n}\sum_{i=1}^{n}(x_i - \bar{x})^2\right)^{3/2}}, \tag{5}$$

where x_i, $i = 1, \ldots, n$, are the data points, $\bar{x}$ is the mean of the data, and n is the number of observations. A skewness value of zero indicates a symmetric distribution, while positive skewness indicates a longer tail on the right and negative skewness indicates a longer tail on the left.

Kurtosis measures *tailedness* of a distribution:

$$\text{Kurtosis} = \frac{\frac{1}{n}\sum_{i=1}^{n}(x_i - \bar{x})^4}{\left(\frac{1}{n}\sum_{i=1}^{n}(x_i - \bar{x})^2\right)^2}. \tag{6}$$

Higher kurtosis indicates heavier tails, while lower kurtosis suggests lighter tails. The kurtosis of a normal distribution is 3. Therefore, kurtosis can measure the deviation from a normal distribution.

There are multiple approaches for assessing univariate normality, which can be broadly divided into *graphical methods* and *statistical tests*. Graphical techniques provide an intuitive, visual impression of the data distribution, while statistical tests offer a more formal evaluation. Among the most commonly employed graphical methods are histograms, box plots, and quantile–quantile (Q-Q) plots. A histogram displaying a bell-shaped curve, or a symmetric box plot without extreme outliers, is indicative of normality. The Q–Q plot compares the observed quantiles of the dataset with the theoretical quantiles of a normal distribution; alignment of points along a straight diagonal line supports the assumption of normality.

In addition to graphical inspection, a range of statistical tests has been developed to formally evaluate data normality. These include the Shapiro–Wilk test, Kolmogorov–Smirnov test, Anderson–Darling test, Lilliefors test, Jarque–Bera test, and the D'Agostino–Pearson test, each differing in their sensitivity to aspects such as sample size, skewness, and kurtosis [39, 40]. Particular attention is given here to the Kolmogorov–Smirnov test, a non-parametric procedure designed to assess the degree of agreement between an empirical distribution and a specified theoretical distribution. When applied to normality testing, the method compares the empirical cumulative distribution function (ECDF) of the sample with the cumulative distribution function (CDF) of the normal distribution. Significant deviations between the two functions provide evidence against the null hypothesis of normality.

The Kolmogorov-Smirnov statistic measures the maximum absolute difference D_n between the ECDF of the sample and the CDF of the reference normal distribution:

$$D_n = \sup_x |F_n(x) - F(x)|, \tag{7}$$

where $F_n(x)$ is the ECDF of the sample and $F(x)$ is the cumulative distribution function (CDF) of the normal distribution. A Python implementation of this test is given in the following:

```
import numpy as np
import scipy.stats as stats
import matplotlib.pyplot as plt

# Generate normal data
data = np.random.normal(loc=0, scale=1, size=100)

# Histogram
plt.hist(data, bins=20, color="lightblue", edgecolor="black")
plt.title("Histogram")
plt.show()

# Q-Q Plot
stats.probplot(data, dist="norm", plot=plt)
plt.title("Q-Q Plot")
plt.show()

# Kolmogorov-Smirnov test
ks_test = stats.kstest(data, 'norm')
print("Kolmogorov-Smirnov test:", ks_test)
```

Multivariate normality refers to the assumption that multiple variables follow a multivariate normal distribution. The Mardia's test is a widely used method to assess multivariate normality. It is based on the skewness and kurtosis of the data. Multivariate skewness measures the asymmetry of a multivariate distribution and is defined as

$$b_1^p = \frac{1}{n^2} \sum_{i=1}^{n} \sum_{j=1}^{n} \left((\mathbf{x}_i - \bar{\mathbf{x}})^T \mathbf{S}^{-1} (\mathbf{x}_j - \bar{\mathbf{x}}) \right)^3, \tag{8}$$

where n is the sample size, $\mathbf{x}_i$ and $\mathbf{x}_j$ are p-dimensional observations, $\bar{\mathbf{x}}$ is the mean vector, and $\mathbf{S}$ is the sample covariance matrix. For a multivariate normal distribution, the expected value of b_1^p is zero. Multivariate kurtosis measures the extent to which a multivariate distribution has heavy tails compared to the normal distribution:

$$b_2^p = \frac{1}{n} \sum_{i=1}^{n} \left((\mathbf{x}_i - \bar{\mathbf{x}})^T \mathbf{S}^{-1} (\mathbf{x}_i - \bar{\mathbf{x}}) \right)^2. \tag{9}$$

For a multivariate normal distribution, the expected value of b_2^p is $p(p+2)$, where p is the number of variables. Under the null hypothesis of multivariate normality, Mardia's multivariate skewness follows an asymptotic χ^2 distribution as it is shown by

$$nb_1^p \sim \chi^2_{p(p+1)(p+2)/6}, \tag{10}$$

where the degrees of freedom are given by $p(p+1)(p+2)/6$. If nb_1^p exceeds the critical value from the χ^2 distribution at a given significance level α, we reject H_0, suggesting that the data is not multivariate normal.

Under the null hypothesis of multivariate normality, a standardised kurtosis statistic can be computed as

$$z_{b_2} = \frac{b_2^p - p(p+2)}{\sqrt{\frac{8p(p+2)}{n}}}, \tag{11}$$

which approximately follows a standard normal distribution. If $|z_{b_2}|$ exceeds the critical value from the standard normal distribution at a given significance level α, we reject H_0, suggesting that the data is not multivariate normal.

A Python implementation of this test is given in the following:

```
import numpy as np
import pingouin as pg

# Generate multivariate normal data
data = np.random.multivariate_normal(mean=[0, 0], cov=[[1,
↪  0.5], [0.5, 1]], size=100)

# Generate sample data (multivariate normal)
np.random.seed(42)
data = np.random.multivariate_normal(mean=[0, 0, 0],
↪  cov=np.eye(3), size=100)

# Perform Mardia's test
mardia_test = pg.multivariate_normality(data, alpha=0.05)
print(mardia_test)
```

5 Case Study—Available Datasets and Their Properties

Psychological datasets frequently present unique analytical challenges, such as missing values, outliers, and inconsistencies, arising naturally from complex human behaviours and measurement imperfections. Addressing these issues effectively requires careful preliminary examination of dataset characteristics. In this case study, we methodically explore these characteristics through clear Python code and detailed explanations to support researchers in understanding their data. We focus on understanding the characteristics of real-world psychological datasets through systematic *exploratory data analysis* (EDA). If not properly understood, dataset features can distort downstream analyses and lead to misleading conclusions.

The dataset used in this case study includes 10,000 participants and simulates data collected from psychological assessments and experimental conditions. Each row represents one individual and includes the following variables:

- `Age`, `Gender`: Basic demographic attributes
- `PersonalityTrait`, `CognitiveTestScore`, `StressLevel`, `AnxietyScore`, `DepressionScore`: Continuous psychological measures
- `SocialInteractionLevel`, `EmotionRecognition`: Performance-based or behavioural scores
- `ExperimentalCondition`: A categorical variable (Control, TherapyA, TherapyB)
- `BehavioralOutcome`: A binary target variable indicating behavioural deviation (0 = no issue, 1 = at-risk)

These variables are common psychological constructs such as Big Five traits, anxiety inventories, and affect recognition metrics. Before performing statistical modelling, we must first explore the dataset's structure, types, and general statistics. We begin by confirming the fundamental structure of our dataset, ensuring it has loaded correctly and that all variables are of the expected type:

```python
import pandas as pd

# Load the dataset
df = pd.read_csv("Psychological_CaseStudyDataset.csv")

# Dataset dimensions and types
print(f"Dataset dimensions: {df.shape}")
print("\nColumn data types:\n", df.dtypes)

# Display first 5 rows neatly
print("\nFirst 5 rows:")
print(df.head().to_string(index=False))
```

```
Dataset dimensions: (10000, 12)

Column data types:
ID                int64
Age               float64
Gen               object
Trait             float64
CogS     float64
Strs              float64
Anx               float64
Dep               float64
SocI              float64
EmR               float64
Cnd      object
Out               int64
```

```
First 5 rows:
ID     Age  Gen   Trait CogS   Strs  Anx   Dep   SocI  EmR   Cnd Out
2021   35.6 O     49.09 110.16 70.78 43.28  37.23 41.71 79.22  C   1
1161   10.0 M     52.29  89.89 55.42 53.36  42.27 83.91 75.37  B   0
  36   22.8 F     41.51  71.89 71.37 46.26  48.19 60.12 66.32  A   0
   3   41.5 NaN   55.02 115.61  NaN  47.99  36.99 77.40 82.24  C   1
3168   36.6 F     41.72    NaN 63.09 51.25  20.83 86.64 89.52  B   0
```

The resulting output confirms we have a dataset with 10,000 observations and 12 variables, each capturing demographic, cognitive, and behavioural dimensions relevant to psychological analysis. A quick inspection of the first rows immediately reveals the nature of the data and any initial irregularities, such as missing entries (marked as NaN).

To gain deeper insights, descriptive statistics are computed for continuous variables. These measures include mean, standard deviation, minimum, maximum, and quartiles, revealing the central tendencies and spread of the data.

```
summary_stats = df.describe().round(2).T

# Display clearly formatted statistics
print("\nSummary Statistics:")
print(summary_stats.to_string())
```

This kind of formatted output neatly organises key information. It helps identify potential issues, such as variables with unrealistic ranges (e.g. negative ages) or unusually high standard deviations, suggesting significant variability that requires further investigation.

Exploring the distribution of categorical variables is equally essential. Detects class imbalance or unusual distributions, which can critically influence subsequent analyses, particularly in classification problems:

```
categorical_vars = ["Gender", "ExperimentalCondition",
↪ "BehavioralOutcome"]

for var in categorical_vars:
    print(f"\n{var} distribution:")
    counts = df[var].value_counts(dropna=False)
    percentages = df[var].value_counts(normalize=True,
    ↪ dropna=False) * 100
    cat_summary = pd.DataFrame({"Count": counts, "Percentage
    ↪ (%)": percentages.round(2)})
    print(cat_summary.to_string())
```

```
Gender distribution:
        Count  Percentage (%)
Gender
Female   4368           43.68
Male     4144           41.44
Other     988            9.88
NaN       500            5.00

ExperimentalCondition distribution:
                       Count  Percentage (%)
ExperimentalCondition
Control                 4046           40.46
TherapyB                3021           30.21
TherapyA                2933           29.33

BehavioralOutcome distribution:
                   Count  Percentage (%)
BehavioralOutcome
0                   5010            50.1
1                   4990            49.9
```

For example, the gender distribution reveals a small percentage of missing data, and the experimental conditions reflect the designed proportions. Such insights are crucial for decisions about data imputation or stratified sampling.

Missing data is common, but problematic, in psychological research. Identifying the volume and pattern of missingness enables informed decisions regarding imputation or exclusion strategies:

```
# Missing values count and percentage
missing_counts = df.isnull().sum()
missing_percentages = (missing_counts / len(df) * 100).round(2)

missing_report = pd.DataFrame({
    'Missing Values': missing_counts,
    'Percentage (%)': missing_percentages
}).sort_values('Missing Values', ascending=False)

print("\nMissing Data Report:")
print(missing_report.to_string())
```

```
Missing Data Report:
                        Missing Values  Percentage (%)
Age                                500             5.0
Gender                             500             5.0
PersonalityTrait                   500             5.0
CognitiveTestScore                 500             5.0
StressLevel                        500             5.0
AnxietyScore                       500             5.0
DepressionScore                    500             5.0
SocialInteractionLevel             500             5.0
EmotionRecognition                 500             5.0
ParticipantID                        0             0.0
ExperimentalCondition                0             0.0
BehavioralOutcome                    0             0.0
```

This concise table indicates that several variables exhibit an identical 5% missingness, suggesting systematic or random missing data mechanisms that must be carefully managed to avoid bias in analyses.

Outliers can dramatically distort statistical analyses. The z-score method, a standardised measure of deviation from the mean, efficiently identifies these problematic points:

```
from scipy.stats import zscore
import numpy as np

# Identify numeric columns and calculate z-scores
numeric_cols =
↪  df.select_dtypes(include=np.number).columns.tolist()
z_scores = df[numeric_cols].apply(zscore, nan_policy='omit')

# Count significant outliers (|Z| > 3)
outliers = (np.abs(z_scores) > 3).sum()
outlier_report = outliers[outliers >
↪  0].sort_values(ascending=False)

print("\nOutlier Detection (z-score method):")
print(outlier_report.to_string())
```

```
Outlier Detection (z-score method):
AnxietyScore              177
DepressionScore           107
CognitiveTestScore         28
Age                        26
PersonalityTrait           25
SocialInteractionLevel     12
EmotionRecognition          9
StressLevel                 6
```

Results from this test provide immediate clarity, indicating that variables such as AnxietyScore and DepressionScore have notable numbers of outliers. Identifying these cases early allows researchers to decide whether these points represent genuine phenomena, measurement errors, or data entry issues.

Correlation analysis identifies relationships between individual predictors and the target outcome, helping prioritise features in modelling. Strong correlations suggest direct predictive potential, while weak correlations may justify feature reduction:

```
# Correlation analysis with the target variable
correlations =
↪ df.corr(numeric_only=True)['BehavioralOutcome'].drop('Beha
↪ vioralOutcome').sort_values(ascending=False).round(3)

print("\nCorrelations with BehavioralOutcome:")
print(correlations.to_string())
```

```
Correlations with BehavioralOutcome:
StressLevel                0.131
AnxietyScore               0.118
DepressionScore            0.081
ParticipantID              0.000
PersonalityTrait          -0.003
Age                       -0.003
CognitiveTestScore        -0.018
SocialInteractionLevel    -0.073
EmotionRecognition        -0.088
```

The presented results highlight variables with the strongest positive (e.g. StressLevel) and negative (e.g. EmotionRecognition) correlations with behavioural outcomes. These correlations direct researchers towards relevant psychological constructs for deeper analysis or intervention planning.

Examining group-level means across experimental conditions uncovers the potential effects of experimental manipulations. Differences suggest successful interventions or group-based sampling effects:

```
# Group-wise means by experimental condition
group_means = df.groupby('ExperimentalCondition').mean(numeric
↪ _only=True).round(2).T

print("\nGroup-wise Means by Experimental Condition:")
print(group_means.to_string())
```

```
Group-wise Means by Experimental Condition:
ExperimentalCondition   Control  TherapyA  TherapyB
ParticipantID           5005.07   5039.69   4956.33
Age                       35.01     34.97     34.88
PersonalityTrait          49.90     50.17     50.02
CognitiveTestScore        99.83     99.29     99.76
StressLevel               61.03     61.16     61.42
AnxietyScore              51.06     51.16     51.17
DepressionScore           40.85     41.06     41.46
SocialInteractionLevel    69.73     70.06     69.56
EmotionRecognition        75.02     75.01     75.17
BehavioralOutcome          0.49      0.51      0.50
```

This neatly organised output compares control and therapy groups, quickly highlighting whether interventions (e.g. `TherapyA` and `TherapyB`) significantly affected psychological measures such as stress or depression.

Through systematic data examination, we identified essential dataset characteristics, including distributions, missing data patterns, outlier presence, and critical variable correlations. This scrutiny provides a robust foundation, ensuring all subsequent analyses, such as modelling, hypothesis testing, or inferential statistics, are grounded on accurate assumptions about data quality and structure. Understanding dataset properties early prevents potential analytical pitfalls, safeguarding the integrity and interpretability of psychological research.

In Sect. 6, these findings will be further enriched through visual explorations, helping researchers interpret complex patterns intuitively and effectively.

6 Visualising Pre-processed Data

A concise inspection of data *after* outliers have been addressed, missing values have been imputed or removed, and any transformations (e.g. normalisation or scaling) have been applied is crucial. At this stage, plots can help verify that data cleaning was effective and reveal any lingering anomalies before proceeding to formal analyses.

Since this book already contains a comprehensive overview of `seaborn` visualisations, this section will highlight only the relevant approaches for confirming preprocessing outcomes.

Sometimes, a simple table of descriptive statistics can confirm that the mean, standard deviation, and observed ranges are in expected bounds for each variable. For example:

```python
summary_table = df_preprocessed.describe()
print(summary_table)
```

The data below presents the output of a Python-based summary, generated using the `describe()` function from the `pandas` library. It provides key descriptive statistics that characterise the cleaned dataset across five psychological variables.

```
       RT       Anxiety      DepressImp      CogLoad      MemPerf
count  300.00   300.00          300.00       300.00        300.00
mean   549.39    44.77           22.88         3.51         74.85
std     77.94     9.56            6.08         0.69          8.05
min    300.00    20.28            4.62         1.50         55.78
25%    495.34    37.96           19.06         3.01         69.61
50%    554.74    44.81           23.18         3.51         75.25
75%    600.13    51.16           26.95         3.98         80.81
max    800.00    70.00           37.16         5.36         95.00
```

When extreme outliers were present in `df` before cleaning, verifying that `df_preprocessed` exhibits plausible minimum and maximum values helps confirm the effectiveness of your filtering or transformation procedures. Similarly, it is good practice to check that the summary statistics are consistent and that relationships between key variables have not meaningfully changed.

If the preprocessing involved removing outliers or applying transformations for normality, re-plotting histograms or box plots can reveal whether the distribution has improved. For instance:

```
import seaborn as sns
import matplotlib.pyplot as plt

sns.histplot(df_preprocessed["ReactionTime"], kde=True)
plt.title("Distribution After Outlier Handling")
plt.xlabel("Reaction Time (ms)")
plt.show()
```

This quick histogram (with an optional KDE) shows whether the distribution is more symmetric or if problematic tails persist.

Use box plots (or violin plots) to confirm whether high-leverage points or extreme values still exist in each group or condition, especially if your dataset is structured by participant group:

```
sns.boxplot(data=df_preprocessed, x="Condition",
 ↪ y="AnxietyScore")
plt.title("Post-Cleaning Anxiety Scores by Condition")
plt.show()
```

If many data points still appear as outliers, consider revisiting your outlier detection rules.

Pairplots or scatter plots of your *cleaned* variables can verify that odd clusters or unusual pairwise relationships have not gone uncorrected. For instance:

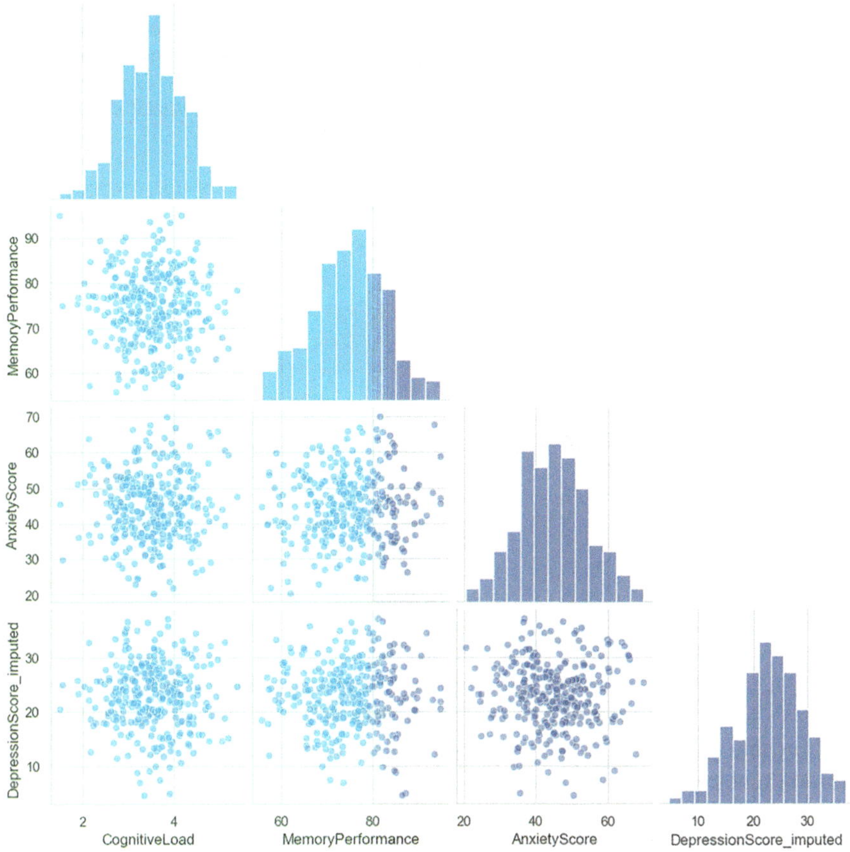

Fig. 1 Pairwise scatter plots of key psychological variables

```
sns.pairplot(df_preprocessed[["StressScore","SleepHours","Mo
↪ odScore"]])
plt.suptitle("Pairwise Relationships After Preprocessing",
↪ y=1.02)
plt.show()
```

Any unexpected patterns here indicate inconsistent data entry or incomplete cleaning (e.g. missed outliers in one variable). Figure 1 displays pairwise scatter plots among key variables after preprocessing. The visual absence of clustering or outlier artefacts supports the assumption of well-processed and structurally consistent data.

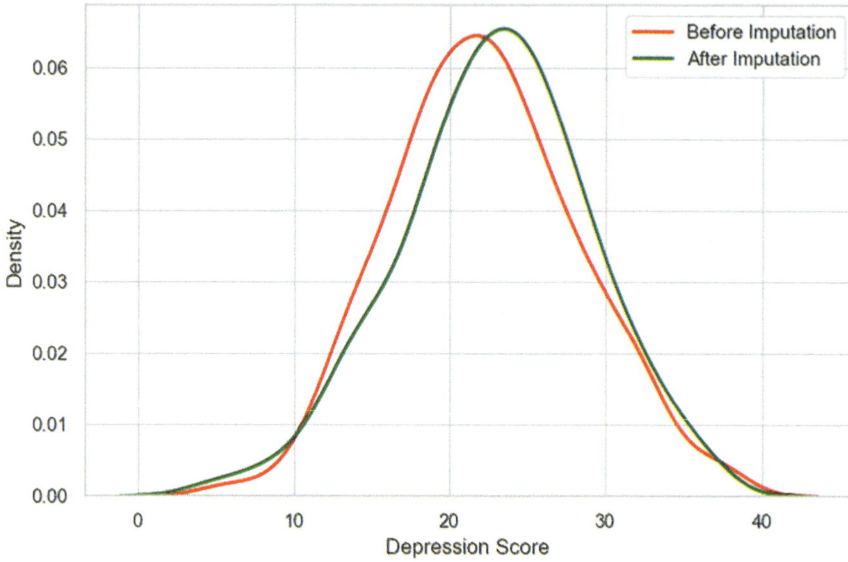

Fig. 2 Pairwise scatter plots of key psychological variables

If you used imputation for missing data, comparing distributions of imputed values (e.g. via a histogram or a box plot) with original, non-missing values can confirm that your imputation process introduced neither unrealistic nor overly uniform replacements:

```
# Compare original vs. imputed
sns.kdeplot(df_preprocessed["DepressionScore"],
↪  label="Post-Imputation")
sns.kdeplot(df_original["DepressionScore"].dropna(),
↪  label="Original Non-missing")
plt.title("Depression Score Distribution Before and After
↪  Imputation")
plt.legend()
plt.show()
```

Figure 2 compares the distribution of depression scores before and after imputation. The close alignment between the two distributions supports the conclusion that imputed values are statistically plausible.

References

1. N. Kovač, K. Ratković, H. Farahani, P. Watson, A practical applications guide to machine learning regression models in psychology with python. Methods Psychol **11**, 100156 (2024)

2. H. Aguinis, R.K. Gottfredson, H. Joo, Best-practice recommendations for defining, identifying, and handling outliers. Organiz Res Methods **16**(2), 270 (2013)
3. B. Iglewicz, D.C. Hoaglin, *Volume 16: How to Detect and Handle Outliers* (Quality Press, Welshpool, 1993)
4. V. Barnett, T. Lewis, et al., *Outliers in Statistical Data*, vol. 3.1 (Wiley, New York, 1994)
5. M. Olteanu, F. Rossi, F. Yger, Meta-survey on outlier and anomaly detection. Neurocomputing **555**, 126634 (2023)
6. J. Oguamalam, U. Radojičić, P. Filzmoser, Minimum regularized covariance trace estimator and outlier detection for functional data. Technometrics **66**(4), 588 (2024)
7. B.G. Tabachnick, *Using Multivariate Statistics*. Alyn and Bacon, Boston (2007)
8. P.D. Allison, Missing data. SAGE Handbook Quant Methods Psychol **23**, 72 (2009)
9. W. Ren, Z. Liu, Y. Wu, Z. Zhang, S. Hong, H. Liu, M.D. in Electronic health Records (MINDER) Group, Moving beyond medical statistics: a systematic review on missing data handling in electronic health records. Health Data Sci. **4**, 0176 (2024)
10. D.B. Rubin, *Flexible Imputation of Missing Data*, 2nd edn. (Chapman and Hall/CRC, Boca Raton, 2018), pp. 29–62
11. J.L. Schafer, J.W. Graham, Missing data: our view of the state of the art. Psychol. Methods **7**(2), 147 (2002)
12. C.K. Enders, *Applied Missing Data Analysis* (Guilford Publications, New York, 2022)
13. R.J. Little, D.B. Rubin, *Statistical Analysis with Missing Data*, vol. 793 (Wiley, Hoboken, 2019)
14. C. Bruch, Imputation of missing values in survey data (version 1.0), Social Science Open Access Repository (2023)
15. H. Farahani, P. Watson, T. Bezan, N. Kovač, L.C. Winter, M. Blagojević, P. Azadfallah, A. Allahyari, S. Masoumian, P. Jiménez, PsAIchology: An intelligent direction in psychological sciences, in *10th International Scientific Conference Technics, Informatics and Education-TIE 2024*, Faculty of Technical Sciences Čačak, University of Kragujevac (2024)
16. M. Afkanpour, E. Hosseinzadeh, H. Tabesh, Identify the most appropriate imputation method for handling missing values in clinical structured datasets: a systematic review. BMC Med. Res. Methodol. **24**(1), 188 (2024)
17. A. Blázquez-García, A. Conde, U. Mori, J.A. Lozano, Water leak detection using self-supervised time series classification. Inf. Sci. **574**, 528 (2021)
18. F. Pedregosa, G. Varoquaux, A. Gramfort, V. Michel, B. Thirion, O. Grisel, M. Blondel, P. Prettenhofer, R. Weiss, V. Dubourg, et al., Scikit-learn: machine learning in Python. J. Mach. Learn. Res. **12**, 2825 (2011)
19. P.D. Allison, *Missing Data* (SAGE Publications, Thousand Oaks, 2002)
20. C.K. Enders, *Applied Missing Data Analysis* (Guilford Press, New York, 2010)
21. B.G. Tabachnick, L.S. Fidell, *Using Multivariate Statistics*, 7th edn. (Pearson, London, 2019)
22. M. Kazijevs, M.D. Samad, Deep imputation of missing values in time series health data: a review with benchmarking. J. Biomed. Inf. **144**, 104440 (2023)
23. D.B. Rubin, *Multiple Imputation for Nonresponse in Surveys* (Wiley, Hobken, 1987)
24. L. He, Y. Zhu, Z. Lu, A cubic spline interpolation based numerical method for fractional differential equations. J. Ind. Manag. Optim. **20**(8), 2770 (2024)
25. S. Rostyslav, V. Olena, K. Anastasiia, Leveraging quadratic polynomials in python for advanced data analysis. F1000Research **13**, 490 (2024)
26. R.T. Trevor Hastie, J. Friedman, *The Elements of Statistical Learning: Data Mining, Inference, and Prediction*, 2nd edn. (Springer, Berlin, 2009)
27. S. Chaput-Langlois, Z.L. Stickley, T.D. Little, C. Rioux, Multiple imputation when variables exceed observations: an overview of challenges and solutions. Collabra Psychol. **10**(1), 92993 (2024)
28. J.E. Hunter, F.L. Schmidt, *Methods of Meta-Analysis: Correcting Error and Bias in Research Findings* (Sage, Thousand Oaks, 2004)

29. E. Maassen, E.D. D'Urso, M.A. Van Assen, M.B. Nuijten, K. De Roover, J.M. Wicherts, The dire disregard of measurement invariance testing in psychological science. Psychol. Methods **30**, 966–979 (2023)
30. F. Van de Vijver, K. Leung, Methods and data analysis of comparative research. Handbook Cross-Cultural Psychol. **1**, 257 (1997)
31. A.E. Kazdin, *Research Design in Clinical Psychology* (Cambridge University Press, Cambridge, 2021)
32. S.E. Embretson, S.P. Reise, *Item Response Theory for Psychologists* (Psychology Press, Milton Park, 2013)
33. M.J. Azur, E.A. Stuart, C. Frangakis, P.J. Leaf, Multiple imputation by chained equations: what is it and how does it work? Int. J. Methods Psychiatric Res. **20**(1), 40 (2011)
34. W.G. Jacoby, *Statistical Graphics for Visualizing Multivariate Data* (Sage, Thousand Oaks, 1998)
35. W.W.Y. Chan, A survey on multivariate data visualization, Department of Computer Science and Engineering. Hong Kong University of Science and Technology **8**(6), 1 (2006)
36. J.T. Cacioppo, L.G. Tassinary, G. Berntson, *Handbook of Psychophysiology* (Cambridge University Press, Cambridge, 2007)
37. A.P. Association, et al., *Publication Manual of the American Psychological Association* (American Psychological Association, Washington, DC, 2020)
38. A. Field, *Discovering Statistics Using IBM SPSS Statistics* (Sage Publications, Thousand Oaks, 2013)
39. N.M. Razali, Y.B. Wah, Power comparisons of Shapiro–Wilk, Kolmogorov–Smirnov, Lilliefors and Anderson–Darling tests. J. Stat. Model. Analyt. **2**(1), 21 (2011)
40. H.C. Thode, *Testing for Normality* (Dekker, New York, 2002)

Part III
Data Processing

The third part of this book represents the analytical core of the journey—where data are transformed into insight. After establishing the conceptual and practical foundations in the previous chapters, this part explores the methods, models, and algorithms that allow researchers to examine hypotheses, uncover patterns, and build predictive frameworks within psychological science.

Readers are introduced to both classical and modern approaches to data analysis. The chapters begin by clarifying the relationship between data science, statistics, machine learning, and artificial intelligence—disciplines that share common goals but differ in their methods and assumptions. From there, the discussion progresses toward practical applications of modeling, factor analysis, clustering, and classification techniques, demonstrating how these tools can be implemented in Python to answer complex psychological questions.

This part also introduces more advanced analytical strategies, such as Bayesian inference, shrinkage regression, and time-dependent modeling, illustrating how these approaches expand the range of phenomena that can be studied in psychology. Whether estimating latent structures, identifying behavioral subgroups, or modeling change over time, readers will learn how computational methods provide new perspectives on enduring psychological theories.

It bridges quantitative rigor with conceptual understanding. It shows that the value of data processing lies not only in the accuracy of models but also in their ability to reveal meaning—to connect numbers, patterns, and probabilities back to the rich complexity of human thought and behavior.

The Difference Between Data Science, Statistics, Machine Learning, and Artificial Intelligence

Nataša Kovač, Marko Simeunović, Kruna Ratković, Marija Blagojević, Ulfeta Marovac, Hojjatollah Farahani, and Lisa-Christina Winter Done

1 Data Science and Statistics Fundamentals

Data science has increasingly emerged as a transformative discipline in psychological research, integrating statistical methodologies, computational tools, and theoretical frameworks to derive insights from data. At its essence, data science combines diverse approaches, including exploratory analysis, statistical inference, and predictive modelling, to understand complex behavioural phenomena. The advent of powerful computational resources and open-source software tools such as Python has further democratised access to sophisticated statistical methods, enabling researchers to handle large-scale datasets effectively and rigorously [1].

Fundamental to data science in psychological research is the effective utilisation of statistics. Statistics provides the foundation necessary for drawing meaningful conclusions from empirical data, offering methodologies for collecting, analysing, interpreting, and presenting data. This statistical foundation supports researchers in

N. Kovač · M. Simeunović (✉) · K. Ratković
Faculty of Applied Sciences, University of Donja Gorica, Podgorica, Montenegro
e-mail: natasa.kovac@udg.edu.me; marko.simeunovic@udg.edu.me; kruna.ratkovic@udg.edu.me

M. Blagojević
Faculty of Technical Sciences, University of Kragujevac, Čačak, Serbia
e-mail: marija.blagojevic@uni.kg.ac.rs

U. Marovac
Department of Technical and Technological Sciences, State University in Novi Pazar, Novi Pazar, Serbia

H. Farahani
Department of Psychology, Faculty of Humanities, Tarbiat Modares University, Tehran, Iran
e-mail: h.farahani@modares.ac.ir

L.-C. W. Done
OpenPsai (Two Kermis), Zug, Switzerland

N. Kovač et al. (eds.), *Data Science in Psychology*,
https://doi.org/10.1007/978-3-032-18312-5_7

distinguishing true psychological effects from random variability inherent in measurement processes [2]. Essential statistical concepts, such as descriptive statistics, inferential testing, and regression analysis, form the backbone of psychological research, guiding both hypothesis testing and data-driven exploration.

Descriptive statistics constitute the first step in understanding psychological data. Measures such as means, medians, variances, standard deviations, and correlation coefficients offer concise summaries of data characteristics, allowing researchers to quickly grasp data distributions and inter-variable relationships. For instance, skewness and kurtosis indicators describe the degree of asymmetry and the sharpness of psychological measures like anxiety scores or reaction times, thereby informing appropriate choices for subsequent inferential procedures [3]. Visualising these descriptive measures through graphical methods further facilitates intuitive comprehension of underlying patterns and potential anomalies within datasets [4].

Beyond mere description, inferential statistics allow psychological researchers to generalise findings from sampled data to broader populations. Central to inferential methods is hypothesis testing, wherein researchers assess the validity of theoretical predictions by analysing sample data. The choice of appropriate statistical tests, such as *t-tests*, *ANOVA*, χ^2 tests, or *non-parametric tests*, depends on the data structure, measurement scales, and specific research hypotheses [5]. An important consideration in applying these inferential methods is ensuring adherence to underlying statistical assumptions, including assumptions like normality, equality of variances, and independence of observations, since violations of these conditions can affect the validity of the analysis [6].

Increasingly, psychological research has turned towards predictive and explanatory modelling techniques, such as regression analysis, to unravel complex relationships among multiple variables. Regression models range from simple linear regression to sophisticated multilevel or hierarchical models. They allow researchers not only to predict outcomes but also to understand the underlying mechanisms driving psychological phenomena. For example, *hierarchical linear modelling* (HLM) is particularly valuable for analysing nested data structures common in psychological studies, such as repeated measurements within individuals or individuals within treatment groups [7]. Similarly, logistic regression and generalised linear models extend traditional linear approaches to binary, categorical, or count data frequently encountered in psychological assessments.

The *Bayesian statistical paradigm* has gained traction within psychology, complementing traditional frequentist approaches. Bayesian statistics provide a coherent framework for updating prior beliefs based on observed data, allowing for probabilistic interpretations of psychological phenomena. This approach is especially valuable in small-sample research, where traditional frequentist methods might lack sufficient power, or in studies involving complex hierarchical models, where Bayesian methods can flexibly incorporate prior knowledge [8]. Bayesian analysis, made possible by modern computational approaches such as *Markov Chain Monte Carlo* (MCMC) simulations, is now widely accessible through software like *Stan* or *PyMC3*, providing powerful tools for psychological data analysis [9, 10].

The integration of statistical methodologies with computational data science tools has significantly expanded the analytical capabilities available to psychologists. Modern programming languages such as Python have become indispensable for psychological data analysis, offering powerful libraries and frameworks for statistical modelling, data visualisation, and machine learning (ML) [11]. Libraries such as `pandas`, `NumPy`, and `SciPy` in Python allow researchers to manage, transform, and analyse complex psychological datasets efficiently [12, 13]. These tools have streamlined the implementation of statistical methods and enhanced reproducibility in psychological science by facilitating transparent, code-based analyses.

One crucial aspect of contemporary data science in psychology is data preprocessing, involving rigorous cleaning and normalisation procedures to ensure data quality before analysis. Issues such as missing data, outliers, and inconsistent responses are common in psychological research and require careful handling to preserve the integrity of analyses. Techniques such as multiple imputation, robust estimation, and data transformation (e.g. logarithmic or Box-Cox transformations) significantly enhance data quality, thus improving the reliability of statistical conclusions [14]. Proper preprocessing not only improves analytic accuracy but also ensures reproducibility and interpretability of psychological research outcomes.

Reproducibility and transparency have emerged as critical considerations in psychological statistics and data science. Concerns about replicability crises in psychology have led to increased emphasis on open science practices, such as data sharing, pre-registration, and publication of analytic code. Open-source platforms like *GitHub* and tools such as *Jupyter Notebooks* facilitate these practices, enabling researchers to document their analytical procedures thoroughly and transparently [15]. The adoption of these practices enhances scientific rigour, facilitates peer verification of results, and fosters collaborative research endeavours across the psychological sciences.

Ethical considerations permeate all aspects of statistical practice in psychology. Researchers must remain vigilant against common pitfalls such as p-hacking, selective reporting of significant results, and misinterpretation of statistical significance. Ethical statistical practice demands honest reporting of findings, clear delineation between exploratory and confirmatory analyses, and careful attention to statistical power and effect sizes [16]. Upholding these standards not only strengthens the validity of psychological research but also maintains public trust in psychological science as a discipline.

Data science and statistical fundamentals form the methodological backbone of contemporary psychological research. By integrating robust statistical techniques, computational tools, and ethical best practices, researchers can reliably interpret complex psychological data, ensuring that conclusions drawn from empirical research are both scientifically valid and broadly meaningful.

2 Machine Learning and Artificial Intelligence

ML and artificial intelligence (AI) have become fundamental to modern computing, driving automation, decision-making, and complex problem-solving across various industries. AI refers to the broader field of simulating human intelligence using computational systems, while ML focuses on developing algorithms capable of learning from data without explicit programming [17]. The rapid advancement of ML and AI has been facilitated by increasing computational power, the availability of large datasets, and improvements in mathematical modelling. These technologies now power applications such as autonomous vehicles, medical diagnostic systems, fraud detection, personalised recommendation engines, and language translation.

A core aspect of ML is its ability to generalise from observed data, allowing models to make accurate predictions or decisions when exposed to new, unseen examples. This generalisation is achieved by training models on datasets that capture underlying relationships between variables. The performance of ML models is influenced by factors such as the quality of data, the choice of features, model complexity, and the amount of labelled information available. In general, ML methods are grouped into three core types: *supervised*, *unsupervised*, and *reinforcement* learning [18]. Figure 1 illustrates a structured overview of these three primary categories and their associated techniques.

Supervised learning represents the most commonly applied type of ML, in which models are trained using labelled datasets—each input instance corresponds to a predefined output. The goal is for the algorithm to capture the mapping between inputs and outputs, allowing it to generate accurate predictions on unseen data. Supervised learning is categorised into *classification* and *regression* tasks [19]. Classification problems involve assigning data points to predefined categories, such as detecting spam emails, recognising handwritten digits, or diagnosing medical conditions. In health psychology, recent work used psychological scales to classify chronic pain severity with multiple algorithms and standard metrics [20]. Widely used classification algorithms encompass logistic regression, decision trees, random forests, support vector machines (SVMs), and deep neural networks [21]. Conversely, regression models aim to predict continuous numerical outcomes, for instance, estimating housing values based on factors like location, square footage, and the number of bedrooms. Algorithms commonly used for regression include linear regression, ridge regression, and gradient boosting machines [22].

One of the key challenges in supervised learning is overfitting, which occurs when a model memorises training data instead of learning underlying patterns. Overfitting results in poor generalisation, meaning the model performs well on training data but poorly on new, unseen data. Regularisation techniques such as Lasso and Ridge regression help prevent overfitting by penalising large coefficient values, reducing model complexity [23]. Methods such as cross-validation, dropout in neural networks, and early stopping are used to ensure the model does not learn noise instead of meaningful structures in the data. Despite these challenges, supervised learning remains a dominant approach in fields where labelled data is

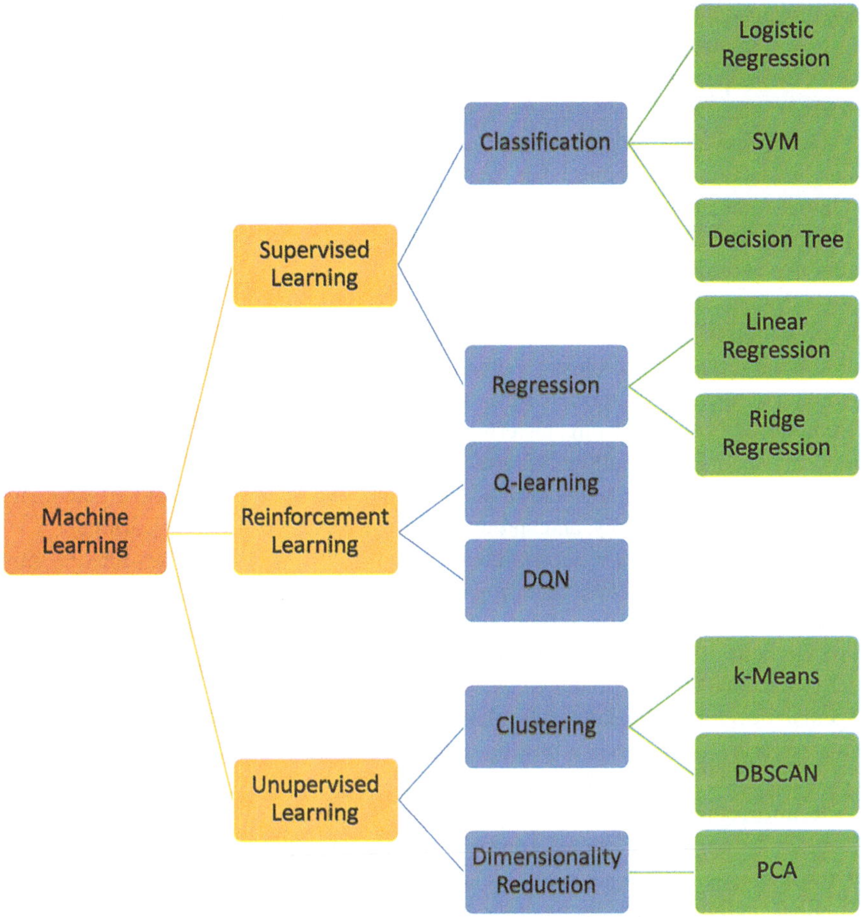

Fig. 1 Machine learning taxonomy diagram

available, making it essential in applications such as speech recognition, disease diagnosis, and fraud detection.

Unsupervised learning, in contrast to supervised approaches, operates without labelled data. Its purpose is to uncover underlying structures and latent patterns within datasets that lack predefined target values. This technique is widely used for clustering, dimensionality reduction, and anomaly detection [19]. Clustering methods, including k-means, hierarchical clustering, and density-based spatial clustering of applications with noise (DBSCAN), organise data points into groups based on feature similarity. These methods are extensively used in customer segmentation, market research, and medical image analysis, where similar groups need to be identified based on shared characteristics [21]. Another important unsupervised learning method is principal component analysis (PCA), which is used for dimensionality reduction by transforming high-dimensional data into a lower-dimensional space while preserving its variance. PCA is widely applied in areas such as image compression, financial risk analysis, and gene expression studies [22].

One of the main strengths of unsupervised learning lies in its capacity to analyse vast amounts of unstructured data, including text, images, and social media content, without requiring expensive manual labelling. One of the main challenges is the difficulty in evaluating model performance. Complementary supervised studies on affective and interpersonal features illustrate prediction of relational-risk outcomes [24]. Unlike supervised learning, where accuracy can be directly measured against labelled outputs, unsupervised models require alternative evaluation metrics, such as silhouette scores and cluster validation techniques, to assess their effectiveness. Another challenge is interpretability; while supervised models provide clear output predictions, the results from clustering or dimensionality reduction algorithms often require expert interpretation. Nevertheless, unsupervised learning continues to gain traction, particularly in fields such as natural language processing (NLP), anomaly detection in cybersecurity, and automatic feature extraction in deep learning.

Reinforcement learning constitutes a separate branch of ML that aims to train agents to make sequential decisions through continuous interaction with their environment. Rather than relying on labelled data, these agents learn through a process of trial and error, guided by feedback in the form of rewards or penalties [25]. The objective is to maximise cumulative rewards over time, enabling the agent to develop optimal decision-making strategies. This technique has been highly successful in applications requiring adaptive and autonomous behaviour, such as robotics, game playing, and autonomous vehicles.

Reinforcement learning operates through key components: an agent, an environment, a set of possible actions, a reward function, and a policy that guides the agent's behaviour. Algorithms such as Q-learning, deep Q-networks (DQNs), and policy gradient methods have significantly advanced reinforcement learning applications [26]. A notable breakthrough was the development of AlphaGo, an AI system created by DeepMind that defeated human world champions in the board game Go. By combining deep reinforcement learning with Monte Carlo tree search, AlphaGo demonstrated the ability to make strategic decisions with superhuman performance. Similar reinforcement learning techniques are now being applied in self-driving cars, where vehicles learn to navigate roads safely by optimising driving strategies through real-world interactions.

One of the main challenges in reinforcement learning is the need for large amounts of computational resources and training time. Unlike supervised learning, which learns from static datasets, reinforcement learning requires continuous interaction with an environment, often leading to high computational costs. Reinforcement learning models can be unstable and difficult to tune, as small changes in hyperparameters can lead to drastically different behaviours. Despite these challenges, reinforcement learning remains a promising field, particularly in applications requiring real-time decision-making and long-term strategy optimisation.

AI extends beyond ML by incorporating various methodologies, including symbolic reasoning, rule-based systems, and expert systems. The origins of AI can be traced back to the mid-twentieth century, when pioneers such as Alan Turing proposed the idea of intelligent machines capable of reasoning and problem-solving. The foundational work of John McCarthy, Marvin Minsky, and others in the 1950s and 1960s established AI as a field of study, focusing on symbolic reasoning and logic-based systems. Early AI models were largely rule-based, relying on explicitly programmed sets of logical statements to perform tasks such as theorem proving and game playing [17]. These early systems struggled with scalability, as encoding human-like reasoning into rigid rules became increasingly complex for real-world applications.

The 1980s and 1990s saw a shift in AI research towards expert systems, which attempted to capture domain-specific human expertise in structured knowledge bases. Systems such as MYCIN and DENDRAL demonstrated the potential of AI in medical diagnosis and chemical analysis, but they remained constrained by their reliance on manually curated knowledge [27]. As computational power increased, researchers began exploring probabilistic models and statistical learning methods, leading to the development of Bayesian networks and Markov decision processes that could handle uncertainty more effectively [18]. These advancements laid the foundation for modern AI systems capable of learning from data rather than relying solely on predefined rules.

A significant turning point in AI came with the emergence of deep learning, a subset of ML inspired by the structure and functioning of the human brain. Unlike traditional AI models that depended on explicit rules, deep learning leverages artificial neural networks to learn hierarchical representations of data automatically [28]. One of the earliest breakthroughs in deep learning was the success of convolutional neural networks (CNNs) in image recognition tasks, demonstrated by the AlexNet model in the 2012 ImageNet competition [29]. CNNs revolutionised computer vision by enabling machines to recognise objects, faces, and handwriting with unprecedented accuracy. Similarly, recurrent neural networks (RNNs) and transformer-based architectures like generative pre-trained transformer (GPT) have transformed natural language processing (NLP), allowing AI systems to generate human-like text, translate languages, and analyse sentiment in textual data [30].

Beyond deep learning, AI research continues to evolve with the introduction of reinforcement learning, generative AI, and neuromorphic computing. Reinforcement learning has enabled AI systems to achieve superhuman performance in strategic decision-making tasks, as demonstrated by AlphaGo, which defeated world champions in the board game Go by learning optimal strategies through self-play [26]. Generative AI, particularly generative adversarial networks (GANs), has made significant contributions to creative fields, enabling the synthesis of realistic images, music, and even deepfake videos [31]. Meanwhile, neuromorphic computing aims to mimic the structure of the human brain at a hardware level, developing AI chips that process information more efficiently and powerfully than traditional processors [32].

Despite its advancements, AI still faces challenges related to interpretability, ethics, and computational efficiency. One of the primary concerns in AI deployment is the *black box* nature of deep learning models, making it difficult to understand how decisions are made. This lack of transparency has led to increased research in explainable AI (XAI), with techniques such as SHAP (Shapley Additive Explanations) and LIME (Local Interpretable Model-Agnostic Explanations) being developed to provide insights into model behaviour [33]. Ethical concerns also arise from biased datasets, where AI systems can inadvertently reinforce societal prejudices, affecting decisions in hiring, law enforcement, and financial lending [34]. Addressing these issues requires interdisciplinary collaboration, regulatory oversight, and fairness-aware AI model development.

As AI continues to evolve, its integration into everyday life is becoming increasingly seamless. From virtual assistants and autonomous vehicles to medical diagnosis and personalised education, AI-driven technologies are shaping the future of human-computer interaction. The convergence of AI with fields such as neuroscience, quantum computing, and robotics holds promise for the development of more adaptive, efficient, and ethically aligned intelligent systems. The continuous advancement of AI algorithms, coupled with responsible AI governance, will be crucial in ensuring that these technologies remain beneficial, transparent, and aligned with human values.

3 Choosing the Optimal Data Processing Approach: Costs vs. Time vs. Accuracy

The process of data processing is inherently complex and encompasses multiple stages, including collection, validation, transformation, storage, analysis, and visualisation. Each stage requires distinct resources and tools, yet all are directed towards the common objective of generating meaningful information that can effectively support decision-making. Data processing requires careful balancing between several key factors:

- *Size and structure of data*: As the volume of data grows, the challenge of handling it efficiently increases. Unstructured data (such as text or images) adds additional complexity to the process compared to structured data (like tables).
- *Computational resources*: Each stage of data processing requires a certain level of computational resources, including processing power, memory, and storage. These resources affect the speed and capacity of processing.
- *Algorithm complexity*: The algorithms used for data processing, whether simple transformations or complex analyses (such as ML), impact both efficiency and outcomes.
- *User intervention and automation*: In some stages of data processing, significant expert intervention is necessary, while in others, automation can accelerate processes and reduce errors.

All these components together contribute to successful data processing, but they also pose challenges related to processing time, resource costs, and the accuracy of the results. Due to the complexity of this process, optimising data processing becomes crucial. It involves improving processing efficiency to achieve a balance between the following factors:

- Cost: The resources used, including computational capacity, memory, energy, and human resources, and their associated costs
- Time: The speed of data processing, or how long it takes to prepare, transform, and analyse the data
- Accuracy: The quality of the results obtained from data processing, or the degree to which the data accurately addresses the hypotheses or solves the problems posed

The goal of optimisation is to balance efficiency, resource savings, and data quality. The PsAIchology framework operationalises this via algorithm spot-checking and cross-validation for model selection in psychological ML pipelines [35]. Effective data optimisation is crucial for enhancing the quality and efficiency of data processing. The selection of an optimal data processing algorithm largely depends on the type of data and the problem being addressed. For numerical and categorical data, learning is typically conducted using classical ML methods or deep learning techniques. The choice of method depends on the target variable: if the target variable is numerical, regression algorithms are commonly used; if the target variable is categorical, classification algorithms are more appropriate. In cases of unsupervised learning, clustering algorithms are often applied, independent of the target variable [21]. For text data, methods such as Naive Bayes, SVM, and large language models (like BERT and GPT) are often applied, depending on the task [36]. These models are widely used in tasks like sentiment analysis, text classification, and natural language understanding. Naive Bayes and SVM are effective for simpler tasks, while large language models are more suited for complex tasks requiring deeper context and language comprehension. In image processing, convolutional neural networks (CNNs) are typically used for their ability to efficiently recognise patterns [28]. The key to choosing the optimal algorithm lies in understanding the data type, whether it involves classification, regression, or clustering, and selecting the most suitable approach for the task at hand. Evaluating processing time is a crucial aspect when choosing algorithms, as some algorithms train quickly but have slower predictions, and vice versa. Instance-based learning algorithms, such as k-nearest neighbours (k-NN), operate by storing the entire training set and making predictions by comparing each new instance with the entire set. Although k-NN's training process is simple and fast because it only involves storing data, the prediction process becomes very slow with large datasets. This is because the algorithm needs to search through the entire dataset for each new instance to find the nearest neighbours.

In small datasets, k-NN is efficient and simple, but as the dataset size grows, the prediction time increases significantly due to the higher number of comparison operations and similarity calculations. Therefore, k-NN is not suitable for large datasets as it slows down predictions, even though the training remains relatively fast.

In contrast, pre-trained models, such as logistic regression (LR), support vector machines (SVMs), and neural networks, train a model based on data and create an abstract representation that allows faster predictions on new data. These algorithms are generally more efficient for predictions, especially with large datasets, although training can be more time-consuming, particularly for complex models like convolutional neural networks (CNNs) and recurrent neural networks (RNNs). Model accuracy is a significant performance factor when choosing an algorithm. Accuracy is evaluated using metrics such as accuracy, precision, recall, and F1 score for classification tasks, or MSE and R2 for regression. Testing various models, like random forest, SVM, and naive Bayes, on a validation dataset helps in selecting the algorithm that delivers the best results.

Cost estimation is equally important, as different algorithms have varying resource demands. For instance, algorithms such as k-NN and logistic regression are less resource-intensive, while more complex models, like deep neural networks and random forest, require higher computational resources, including more memory and processing power.

To evaluate the performance and processing time of different algorithms, Python libraries like time and `cProfile` can be used for profiling and analysis. The time library in Python is commonly used for measuring the total processing time of specific code blocks, such as model training and prediction. `cProfile` is a more advanced profiling tool in Python that allows you to obtain detailed insights into the performance of your code [37].

These techniques allow users to determine which algorithms best balance processing time and accuracy, depending on the dataset size and task specifics. In the following code, we present a comparison of the performance of two ML models: k-NN and LR. The comparison is conducted on a balanced version of the balance scale dataset. The balance scale dataset represents psychological experimental results, where the goal is to predict the direction of a balance scale based on various attributes like weight and distance. From the original dataset, we have selected two classes, left and right, and ensured that the number of instances for each class is equal, thus balancing the dataset. The balanced dataset allows for a more accurate comparison of model performance. For both models, we evaluate their performance in terms of execution time and accuracy. Specifically, we compare the training and testing times, as well as precision, recall, and F1 score, to provide a comprehensive overview of their efficiency and accuracy in handling this dataset.

```
# Importing required libraries
import pandas as pd
from sklearn.model_selection import train_test_split
from sklearn.preprocessing import StandardScaler
from sklearn.linear_model import LogisticRegression
from sklearn.neighbors import KNeighborsClassifier
from sklearn.metrics import accuracy_score, precision_score
from sklearn.metrics import recall_score, f1_score
import time as time_module
import cProfile

# Loading ARFF file
data, meta = arff.loadarff('data.arff')

# Convert to Pandas DataFrame
df = pd.DataFrame(data)

# Data preparation
X = df.drop(columns=['class'])
y = df['class']

# Splitting data into training and testing sets
X_train, X_test, y_train, y_test =
train_test_split(X, y, test_size=0.3, random_state=42)

# Data standardization
scaler = StandardScaler()
X_train = scaler.fit_transform(X_train)
X_test = scaler.transform(X_test)

# Function for training and measuring the performance of k-NN
def train_knn():
    start_time = time_module.time()
    knn_model = KNeighborsClassifier(n_neighbors=5)
    knn_model.fit(X_train, y_train)
    duration_fit = time_module.time() - start_time

    start_time = time_module.time()
```

```
        knn_predictions = knn_model.predict(X_test)
        knn_accuracy = accuracy_score(y_test, knn_predictions)
        knn_precision = precision_score(y_test, knn_predictions)
        knn_recall = recall_score(y_test, knn_predictions)
        knn_f1 = f1_score(y_test, knn_predictions)
        duration_pred = time_module.time() - start_time

        print(f"KNN Model Performance:")
        print(f"Accuracy: {knn_accuracy:.4f}")
        print(f"Precision: {knn_precision:.4f}")
        print(f"Recall: {knn_recall:.4f}")
        print(f"F1-Score: {knn_f1:.4f}")
        print(f"Execution Time (Fit):{duration_fit:.4f} seconds")
        print(f"Execution Time (Predict):{duration_pred:.4f} seconds")

    # Function for training and measuring the performance of LR
    def train_logreg():
        start_time = time_module.time()
        logreg_model = LogisticRegression(max_iter=1000)
        logreg_model.fit(X_train, y_train)
        duration_fit = time_module.time() - start_time

        start_time = time_module.time()
        logreg_predictions = logreg_model.predict(X_test)
        logreg_accuracy = accuracy_score(y_test, logreg_predictions)
        logreg_precision = precision_score(y_test, logreg_predictions)
        logreg_recall = recall_score(y_test, logreg_predictions)
        logreg_f1 = f1_score(y_test, logreg_predictions)
        duration_pred = time_module.time() - start_time

        print(f"Logistic Regression Model Performance:")
        print(f"Accuracy: {logreg_accuracy:.4f}")
        print(f"Precision: {logreg_precision:.4f}")
        print(f"Recall: {logreg_recall:.4f}")
        print(f"F1-Score: {logreg_f1:.4f}")
        print(f"Execution Time (Fit):{duration_fit:.4f} seconds")
        print(f"Execution Time (Predict):{duration_pred:.4f} seconds")


    # Running both functions to compare the
    # performance of KNN and Logistic Regression
    # models on the balanced dataset
    train_knn()
    train_logreg()
```

For the dataset used in this analysis, the performance evaluation of the models provided the following results:

```
KNN Model Performance:
Accuracy: 0.9769
Precision: 0.9753
Recall: 0.9753
F1-Score: 0.9753
Execution Time (Fit):0.0020 seconds
Execution Time (Predict):0.0100 seconds

Logistic Regression Model Performance:
Accuracy: 0.9653
Precision: 0.9518
Recall: 0.9753
F1-Score: 0.9634
Execution Time (Fit):0.0208 seconds
Execution Time (Predict):0.0073 seconds
```

The results show that the KNN model outperforms the logistic regression model in several key areas. It achieved higher accuracy (97.69% compared to 96.53% for LR), indicating that it classifies data more accurately. The k-NN model performed better in terms of precision and F1 score, demonstrating a stronger ability to predict classes with fewer errors. Training time for the k-NN model was significantly faster (0.0020 seconds), making it more efficient in scenarios where training time is a critical factor. Logistic regression showed slightly faster prediction times, which could be advantageous when predictions on a large number of instances are frequently required.

If we want to examine the performance of the LR model in more detail, we can use `cProfile.run('train_logreg()')`, which provides a comprehensive breakdown of execution time and resource usage during both the training and prediction processes.

```
# Profiling the performance and execution time of LR
print("\nProfiling Logistic Regression model:")
cProfile.run('train_logreg()')
```

The output gives detailed information about function calls, including:

- Total number of function calls: 18,586 calls (18,480 of which are primitive calls)
- Total execution time: 0.027 seconds
- For each function, we can see:
  - `ncalls`: the number of times each function is called
  - `tottime`: the total time spent in that function, excluding time spent in sub-functions
  - `percall`: the average time per function call
  - `cumtime`: the cumulative time spent in the function, including time spent in all functions it calls

This output helps identify bottlenecks in the code and which functions are consuming the most time during execution.

4 Visualising Model Performance

Model performance visualisation is a crucial step in the data processing and ML development process. It allows for a better understanding of how the model works, helps identify potential problems, and provides insight into areas where improvements can be made.

Various graphs are commonly used to evaluate model performance. One of the most widely applied is the ROC curve (receiver operating characteristic curve), which graphically represents the relationship between the true positive rate (TPR) and the false positive rate (FPR). This visualisation is particularly useful for assessing binary classification models.

A Python implementation for generating the ROC curve, along with its corresponding output displayed in Fig. 2, is presented below. This approach enables researchers to evaluate the trade-off between sensitivity and specificity across various classification thresholds.

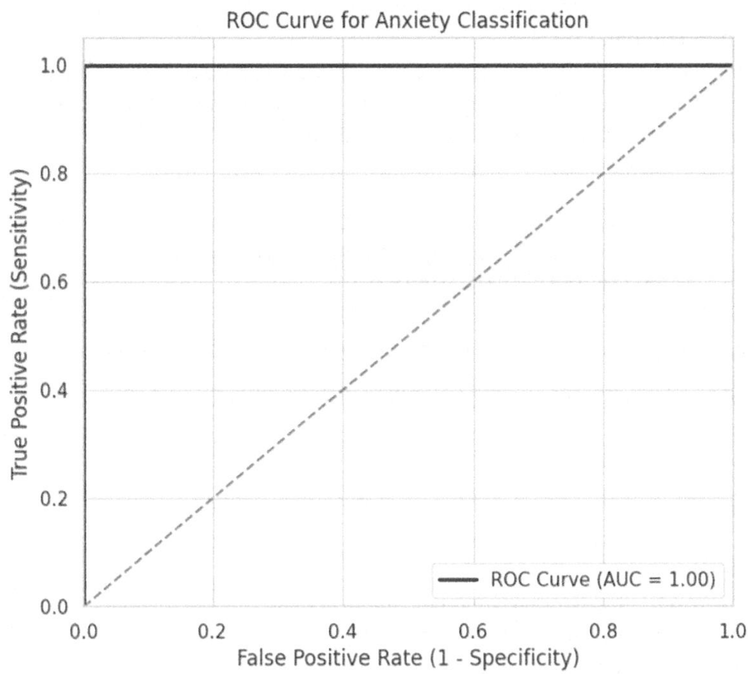

Fig. 2 Example of an ROC curve

```
import pandas as pd
import numpy as np
import matplotlib.pyplot as plt
from sklearn.metrics import roc_curve, auc
from sklearn.model_selection import train_test_split
from sklearn.linear_model import LogisticRegression

# Load dataset from CSV file (assumed to contain 'anxiety_score' and 'label'
↪ columns)
df = pd.read_csv("anxiety_dataset.csv")

# Extract feature and label
anxiety_scores = df['anxiety_score'].values
true_labels = df['label'].values  # 1 = High Anxiety, 0 = Low Anxiety

# Train-test split
X_train, X_test, y_train, y_test = train_test_split(
    anxiety_scores.reshape(-1, 1), true_labels, test_size=0.3,
    ↪ random_state=42)

# Train logistic regression classifier
model = LogisticRegression()
model.fit(X_train, y_train)

# Predict probabilities for the positive class
y_probs = model.predict_proba(X_test)[:, 1]

# Compute ROC curve
fpr, tpr, thresholds = roc_curve(y_test, y_probs)
roc_auc = auc(fpr, tpr)

# Plot the ROC curve
plt.figure(figsize=(7, 6))
plt.plot(fpr, tpr, color='blue', lw=2, label=f'ROC Curve (AUC =
↪ {roc_auc:.2f})')
plt.plot([0, 1], [0, 1], color='grey', linestyle='--')
plt.xlim([0.0, 1.0])
plt.ylim([0.0, 1.05])
plt.xlabel('False Positive Rate (1 - Specificity)')
plt.ylabel('True Positive Rate (Sensitivity)')
plt.title('ROC Curve for Anxiety Classification')
plt.legend(loc="lower right")
plt.show()
```

In this example, the test scores are used to train a logistic regression classifier. Individuals with scores above the mean are labelled as having high anxiety. The classifier is evaluated using the ROC curve, where a larger area under the curve (AUC) indicates better performance. The higher the AUC, the better the model is at distinguishing between the classes. AUC values close to 1.0 imply near-perfect classification, whereas a value near 0.5 suggests no discriminative ability, equivalent to random guessing.

An equally valuable diagnostic tool is the loss curve, which tracks the value of the loss function during model training and validation. A typical use case is visualising

Table 1 Confusion matrix structure

Predicted \Actual	Positive (P)	Negative (N)
Positive (P)	TP (true positive)	FP (false positive)
Negative (N)	FN (false negative)	TN (true negative)

how training and validation loss evolve over epochs. This can indicate whether the model is overfitting (validation loss increases, while training loss decreases) or underfitting (both remain high).

Another essential visual tool is the confusion matrix, which provides a tabular representation of classification outcomes. For a binary classification problem, the confusion matrix is structured as shown in Table 1:

From the confusion matrix, several key performance metrics are computed. These include accuracy (Eq. 1), precision (Eq. 2), recall or sensitivity (Eq. 3), specificity (Eq. 4), F1 score (Eq. 5), and the false positive rate (Eq. 6).

Accuracy quantifies the overall proportion of correctly classified instances among all predictions:

$$\text{Accuracy} = \frac{TP + TN}{TP + TN + FP + FN}. \tag{1}$$

Precision measures the proportion of true positive predictions among all instances classified as positive:

$$\text{Precision} = \frac{TP}{TP + FP}. \tag{2}$$

Recall, also known as sensitivity or the true positive rate, reflects the proportion of actual positives correctly identified:

$$\text{Recall (TPR)} = \frac{TP}{TP + FN}. \tag{3}$$

Specificity, or the true negative rate, captures the proportion of correctly identified negative cases:

$$\text{Specificity (TNR)} = \frac{TN}{TN + FP}. \tag{4}$$

The F1 score balances precision and recall by computing their harmonic mean:

$$\text{F1} = 2 \cdot \frac{\text{Precision} \cdot \text{Recall}}{\text{Precision} + \text{Recall}}. \tag{5}$$

False positive rate (FPR) indicates the proportion of negative instances that are incorrectly classified as positive:

Fig. 3 Confusion matrix representation of binary classification outcomes

	Prediction	
Actual	P	N
P	50	10
N	5	35

$$\text{False Positive Rate (FPR)} = \frac{FP}{FP + TN}. \tag{6}$$

These metrics provide a deeper understanding of model performance and are especially useful in scenarios with class imbalance or high costs associated with misclassification.

In practical applications such as mental health screening or behavioural assessment, ROC curves and confusion matrices support evidence-based decision-making. They help determine optimal thresholds, evaluate the trade-offs between sensitivity and specificity, and validate the clinical relevance of automated models.

An intuitive way to evaluate classification performance is through a confusion matrix. This matrix visually summarises the correct and incorrect predictions made by the model across the actual class labels. It provides a structured view of true positives, true negatives, false positives, and false negatives, allowing for rapid identification of performance strengths and weaknesses. A typical example is shown in Fig. 3.

The example above shows a confusion matrix with values such as 50 true positives (TP), 5 false positives (FP), 10 false negatives (FN), and 35 true negatives (TN). Based on these values, key performance metrics can be calculated, providing deeper insights into the model's effectiveness. Such visualisations make error analysis more straightforward and help identify areas for improvement. When analysing real data, additional visualisation techniques are often employed. Scatter plots, for instance, allow data to be examined in a 2D space, offering a visual overview of how the model distinguishes between different classes [19]. Heatmaps, on the other hand, illustrate data density and highlight areas where the model places the most focus. They are especially valuable in fields such as image analysis, where visualising the model's focus can provide crucial interpretability insights.

To create these visualisations, a variety of tools and libraries are commonly used. `Matplotlib` serves as a fundamental library for generating basic graphics [38], while `Seaborn` enhances visualisations with aesthetically refined designs [39]. For interactive visualisations, `Plotly` offers dynamic and engaging graphical representations. These tools simplify the process of generating insightful visualisations that aid in both model evaluation and development.

References

1. F. Provost, T. Fawcett, *Data Science for Business: What You Need to Know About Data Mining and Data-Analytic Thinking* (O'Reilly Media, Santa Rosa, 2013)
2. J. Cohen, P. Cohen, S.G. West, L.S. Aiken, *Applied Multiple Regression/Correlation Analysis for the Behavioral Sciences* (Routledge, New York, 2013)
3. A. Field, *Discovering Statistics Using IBM SPSS Statistics* (Sage Publications Limited, Thousand Oaks, 2024)
4. E.R. Tufte, *The Visual Display of Quantitative Information* (Graphics Press, Cheshire, 2001)
5. R.B. Kline, *Principles and Practice of Structural Equation Modeling* (Guilford Publications, New York, 2023)
6. D.C. Howell, *Fundamental Statistics for the Behavioral Sciences.* (Thomson & Wadsworth Publishing, London, 2010)
7. S.W. Raudenbush, A.S. Bryk, *Hierarchical Linear Models: Applications and Data Analysis Methods* (Sage Publications, Thousand Oaks, 2002)
8. J.K. Kruschke, T.M. Liddell, Bayesian data analysis for newcomers. Psychon. Bull. Rev. **25**(1), 155 (2018)
9. B. Carpenter, A. Gelman, M.D. Hoffman, D. Lee, B. Goodrich, M. Betancourt, M. Brubaker, J. Guo, P. Li, A. Riddell, Stan: a probabilistic programming language. J. Stat. Softw. **76**(1), 1 (2017). https://doi.org/10.18637/jss.v076.i01
10. J. Salvatier, T.V. Wiecki, C. Fonnesbeck, Probabilistic programming in python using PyMC3. PeerJ Comput. Sci. **2**, e55 (2016). https://doi.org/10.7717/peerj-cs.55
11. N. Kovač, K. Ratković, H. Farahani, P. Watson, A practical applications guide to machine learning regression models in psychology with python. Methods Psychol. **11**, 100156 (2024)
12. W. McKinney, *Python for Data Analysis: Data Wrangling with Pandas, NumPy, and IPython* (O'Reilly Media, Santa Rosa, 2017)
13. H. Wickham, G. Grolemund, *R for Data Science: Import, Tidy, Transform, Visualize, and Model Data*, vol. 1 (O'Reilly Media, Santa Rosa, 2017)
14. R.J. Little, D.B. Rubin, *Statistical Analysis with Missing Data*, vol. 793 (Wiley, Hoboken, 2019)
15. B.A. Nosek, G. Alter, G.C. Banks, D. Borsboom, S.D. Bowman, S.J. Breckler, S. Buck, C.D. Chambers, G. Chin, G. Christensen, et al., Promoting an open research culture. Science **348**(6242), 1422 (2015)
16. D. Lakens, F.G. Adolfi, C.J. Albers, F. Anvari, M.A. Apps, S.E. Argamon, T. Baguley, R.B. Becker, S.D. Benning, D.E. Bradford, et al., Justify your alpha. Nat. Human Behav. **2**(3), 168 (2018)
17. S. Russell, P. Norvig, *Artificial Intelligence: A Modern Approach*, 3rd edn. (Prentice Hall, Upper Saddle River, 2010)
18. K.P. Murphy, *Machine Learning: A Probabilistic Perspective* (MIT Press, Cambridge, 2012)
19. R.T. Trevor Hastie, J. Friedman, *The Elements of Statistical Learning: Data Mining, Inference, and Prediction*, 2nd edn. (Springer, Berlin, 2009)
20. N. Kovač, K. Ratković, P. Watson, H. Farahani, F. Bagheri Sheykhangafshe, Machine learning classification models for predicting chronic pain. Current Psychol. **44**, 1–14 (2025)
21. C.M. Bishop, N.M. Nasrabadi, *Pattern Recognition and Machine Learning*, vol. 4 (Springer, Berlin, 2006)
22. G. James, D. Witten, T. Hastie, R. Tibshirani, *An Introduction to Statistical Learning* (Springer, Berlin, 2013)
23. J.H. Friedman, Greedy function approximation: a gradient boosting machine. Ann. Stat. **29**(5), 1189 (2001)
24. H. Farahani, P. Watson, N. Kovač, F.B. Sheykhangafshe, P. Azadfallah, A. Allahyari, F. Esrafilian, R.R. Chesli, *International Handbook of Love: Transcultural and Transdisciplinary Perspectives* (Springer, Berlin, 2025), pp. 1–22

25. R.S. Sutton, A.G. Barto, *Reinforcement Learning: An Introduction*, 2nd edn. (MIT Press, Cambridge, 2018)
26. D. Silver, A. Huang, C.J. Maddison, A. Guez, L. Sifre, G. Van Den Driessche, J. Schrittwieser, I. Antonoglou, V. Panneershelvam, M. Lanctot, et al., Mastering the game of go with deep neural networks and tree search. Nature **529**, 484 (2016)
27. N.J. Nilsson, *Artificial Intelligence: A New Synthesis* (Morgan Kaufmann, San Francisco, 1998)
28. I. Goodfellow, Y. Bengio, A. Courville, *Deep Learning* (MIT Press, Cambridge, 2016). http://www.deeplearningbook.org
29. A. Krizhevsky, I. Sutskever, G. Hinton, ImageNet classification with deep convolutional neural networks, in *Advances in Neural Information Processing Systems (NeurIPS)*, 25 (2012)
30. A. Vaswani, N. Shazeer, N. Parmar, J. Uszkoreit, L. Jones, A.N. Gomez, L. Kaiser, I. Polosukhin, Attention is all you need, in *Advances in Neural Information Processing Systems (NeurIPS)*, 30 (2017)
31. A. Radford, J. Wu, R. Child, D. Luan, D. Amodei, I. Sutskever, Language models are few-shot learners (2019). arXiv preprint arXiv:2005.14165
32. R.M. Giacomo Indiveri, B. Linares-Barranco, Neuromorphic computing with emerging memory technologies. Proc. IEEE **99**(10), 1550 (2011)
33. C. Molnar, *Interpretable Machine Learning* (Leanpub, Victoria, 2019)
34. S. Barocas, A.D. Selbst, Big data's disparate impact. California Law Rev. **104**, 671 (2016)
35. H. Farahani, P. Watson, T. Bezan, N. Kovač, L.C. Winter, M. Blagojević, P. Azadfallah, A. Allahyari, S. Masoumian, P. Jiménez, PsAIchology: An intelligent direction in psychological sciences, in *10th International Scientific Conference Technics, Informatics and Education-TIE 2024* (Faculty of Technical Sciences Čačak, University of Kragujevac, 2024)
36. D. Jurafsky, J.H. Martin, *Speech and Language Processing: An Introduction to Natural Language Processing, Computational Linguistics, and Speech Recognition with Language Models*, 3rd edn. (Stanford University, Redwood City, 2025). https://web.stanford.edu/~jurafsky/slp3/. Online manuscript released January 12, 2025
37. P.S. Foundation, Python 3 documentation (2025). https://docs.python.org/3/. Accessed 18 Feb 2025
38. J.D. Hunter, Matplotlib: A 2D graphics environment. Comput. Sci. Eng. **9**(03), 90 (2007)
39. M.L. Waskom, Seaborn: statistical data visualization. J. Open Source Softw. **6**(60), 3021 (2021)

Data Modelling

Nataša Kovač, Kruna Ratković, Marko Simeunović, Marija Blagojević, Ulfeta Marovac, and Hojjatollah Farahani

1 Optimal Data Model and Modelling in Psychological Sciences

In the preceding chapters, emphasis was placed on data collection, visualisation, and processing as prerequisites for ensuring data quality in psychological research. The next critical step is *data modelling*, which encompasses two fundamental objectives: prediction and description. Predictive modelling constructs representations of a system capable of forecasting outcomes, while descriptive modelling extracts non-trivial insights from available data. In essence, data models provide a formal framework for organising and analysing information, enabling the derivation of meaningful conclusions. In practice, models are often implemented as executable code, facilitating tasks such as classification, prediction, and estimation. Within psychological sciences, appropriately selected models allow researchers to identify patterns, predict behaviour, and empirically test hypotheses [1].

An optimal model balances complexity with performance, seeking accuracy, interpretability, and efficiency while avoiding overfitting. The goal is not neces-

N. Kovač · K. Ratković · M. Simeunović (✉)
Faculty of Applied Sciences, University of Donja Gorica, Podgorica, Montenegro
e-mail: natasa.kovac@udg.edu.me; kruna.ratkovic@udg.edu.me; marko.simeunovic@udg.edu.me

M. Blagojević
Faculty of Technical Sciences, University of Kragujevac, Čačak, Serbia
e-mail: marija.blagojevic@uni.kg.ac.rs

U. Marovac
Department of Technical and Technological Sciences, State University in Novi Pazar, Novi Pazar, Serbia

H. Farahani
Department of Psychology, Faculty of Humanities, Tarbiat Modares University, Tehran, Iran
e-mail: h.farahani@modares.ac.ir

N. Kovač et al. (eds.), *Data Science in Psychology*,
https://doi.org/10.1007/978-3-032-18312-5_8

sarily to achieve maximal accuracy on training data, but rather to ensure robust generalisation to unseen cases. Model performance evaluation quantifies predictive ability and guides the selection of models that yield reliable results under real-world conditions [2]. Despite its conceptual simplicity, this process is prone to error, often due to misapplication of evaluation techniques or insufficient understanding of their assumptions.

Evaluation employs both techniques and metrics. Techniques, such as *K-fold cross-validation*, divide the dataset into K folds, each serving as a test set once; *bootstrapping* generates resampled subsets, making it particularly useful for small datasets; and *leave-one-out cross-validation (LOO-CV)* tests the model on each observation individually, providing high accuracy at considerable computational cost [3].

Metrics complement these techniques by quantifying predictive performance. Common measures include: accuracy, the overall proportion of correct predictions (sensitive to class imbalance); precision, the proportion of true positives among all positive predictions (relevant when false positives are costly); recall, the proportion of actual positives correctly identified (critical when false negatives are unacceptable); the F1 score, a harmonic mean of precision and recall, balancing their trade-offs; and the ROC curve with its associated AUC, which summarises the trade-off between sensitivity and specificity, offering an aggregate indicator of discriminative ability [4–6].

The selection of appropriate evaluation methods depends on the research question, data characteristics, and intended application. By integrating robust techniques with context-specific metrics, researchers can identify models that not only perform well statistically but also provide valid, interpretable, and generalisable insights in psychological research.

In clinical psychology, machine learning (ML) offers significant potential to improve patient outcomes by providing accurate predictions and decision support. For ML models to be effective in this field, several factors need to be carefully considered, including generalisability, the handling of high-dimensional data, and the balance between model accuracy and execution speed.

Generalisability and Cross-Validation To ensure that ML models in clinical psychology perform well across different patient populations, generalisability is key. Models should be tested on new, unseen data to avoid overfitting to the training dataset. Techniques like K-fold cross-validation and bootstrapping help estimate how well the model will perform in real-world clinical settings, where patient characteristics can vary widely. These methods provide more stable and reliable estimates of model performance by repeatedly training and testing on different subsets of the data.

Quantitative Data and Multivariate Analysis Psychological research often involves complex datasets, with numerous variables such as patient demographics, clinical measurements, and biomarkers. ML models are particularly well-suited for analysing high-dimensional data and uncovering patterns that may not be immediately obvious through traditional statistical methods. For example, predicting a patient's response to treatment or identifying mental health risk factors can be more accurately achieved by considering multiple variables simultaneously, leading to more robust and personalised treatment recommendations.

Balancing Speed and Accuracy In clinical environments, particularly in real-time monitoring or decision support systems, there is often a trade-off between model accuracy and the time it takes for the model to generate predictions. For instance, in mental health assessments or therapy decision-making, clinicians may require quick feedback while ensuring that the model's predictions are accurate enough to inform decisions. Optimising for both speed and accuracy is essential to ensure that the model is both practical and reliable in a clinical context. This balance can be achieved by setting specific performance thresholds for speed (e.g. ensuring execution time remains under a certain limit) while prioritising accuracy for critical decisions.

Clinical Decision Support ML's primary goal in clinical psychology is to assist in decision-making, particularly in diagnosing, predicting treatment outcomes, and monitoring patient progress. These models should provide clinically relevant insights, such as determining whether a patient is likely to respond well to a particular therapy or predicting future psychological conditions. To be useful in a clinical setting, models must be interpretable, enabling clinicians to understand and trust the model's recommendations. Furthermore, ML should be integrated seamlessly into clinical workflows, supporting healthcare providers without replacing human.

Net Benefit Analysis for Clinical Relevance In psychological research, net benefit analysis can be used to evaluate the overall effectiveness of a model by balancing true positives (correct diagnoses) and false positives (incorrect diagnoses). False positives can lead to unnecessary interventions, while false negatives may result in missed opportunities for treatment. By focusing on the net benefit of a model, which takes into account both the positive and negative consequences of predictions, researchers can ensure that the model offers practical value in real-world settings. This approach is especially important in clinical psychology, where timely and accurate interventions are critical for improving patient outcomes [7].

As noted by [8], within the context of model optimisation, the use of both *satisficing* and *optimising* criteria provides a structured way to address competing evaluation parameters. This dual approach enables researchers to balance multiple requirements simultaneously, a consideration of particular importance in applications involving psychological data.

For instance, in Alzheimer's disease cognitive function research, a model predicting the rate of cognitive decline might have the following criteria: Accuracy of predicting the rate of decline (optimising metric) should be as high as possible, while the time for predictions per patient should be under 1 second (satisficing criterion). In this way, although the data processing speed must be fast enough for clinical applications (satisficing criterion), the model is then optimised to provide the most accurate predictions regarding cognitive decline.

Similarly, when developing a model to analyse physical parameters of users, such as heart rate or respiratory frequency in psychological studies, you might prioritise the false negative rate (optimising metric, i.e. minimising missed critical changes in physical state) while limiting the maximum error in predicting physical parameters to a certain threshold, such as 5% (satisficing criterion).

Defining these metrics helps the team focus on achieving quick and accurate results, which is crucial in clinical and psychological applications, where data accuracy and response speed are essential for decision-making.

2 Performance of Data Models: Systematic Approach vs. Experience

The performance of a data model is crucial to the success of all data-driven applications and systems. In addition to the importance of model design, attention must also be paid to the choice of approach for performance optimisation. The two main strategies in this context are the *systematic approach* and the *experiential approach*. The systematic approach is based on formal methods and theories, while the experiential approach relies on prior knowledge and established practices. This subsection will present the differences between these two approaches, along with their advantages and disadvantages in the context of data model performance (Table 1).

Systematic approach involves applying formal methods and theoretical principles to design and optimise data models. This approach is based on using mathematical and computational theories, such as database theory, normalisation, complexity theory, and algorithm analysis. According to this approach, data model performance can be predicted and predetermined through rigorous analyses. For example, when using the relational data model, the systematic approach includes applying normalisation rules to reduce data redundancy, thereby improving query efficiency and reducing database complexity [9].

One of the key elements of the systematic approach is query optimisation. Complexity analysis helps identify the most efficient ways to access data [10]. The systematic approach enables precise modelling and assessment of resources such as response time, memory consumption, and system load. This further allows for an objective comparison of different data models.

Although the systematic approach is theoretically highly effective, it can be limited in practice when applied to complex real-world systems due to unpredictable factors. These factors include variations in queries, user behaviour, and infrastructure. Data modelling must also take into account the real needs of applications.

Advanced methods of the systematic approach include automatic indexing and data partitioning, which enable better organisation of large volumes of information. Techniques such as denormalisation, in cases where data retrieval is more frequent than data entry, can improve performance.

Table 1 Comparison of systematic and experiential approaches to data model optimisation

Dimension	Systematic approach	Experiential approach
Basis	Formal methods, mathematical and computational theories (e.g. normalisation, complexity analysis, algorithm theory)	Empirical knowledge, best practices, prior project experience, and iterative testing
Techniques	Query optimisation, automatic indexing, partitioning, denormalisation when appropriate	Trial-and-error, performance tuning, use of distributed systems (e.g. Hadoop, NoSQL)
Strengths	Predictable, precise modelling of performance; objective comparison of models; resource optimisation	Flexible and adaptive; effective in unpredictable, dynamic, or complex environments; leverages real-world feedback
Limitations	May not capture real-world variability (e.g. diverse queries, user behaviour, infrastructure changes)	Relies on subjective expertise; outcomes may be inconsistent across domains; harder to generalise
Application context	Foundational design, ensuring structural integrity, and efficiency	Performance fine-tuning under real conditions; adapting to evolving business and technical requirements
Extensions	Advanced indexing and partitioning; theoretical scalability	Integration with AI/ML for adaptive optimisation; automated adjustments based on usage patterns
Integration	Serves as baseline framework	Provides empirical adjustments; best results often achieved by combining both approaches

Experiential approach to data modelling is based on applying best practices, expert knowledge, and learning from previous projects. This approach often relies on empirical data and iterative testing. In practice, database designers frequently draw on past implementation experience to optimise performance. Throughout this process, they identify patterns and conditions that can either enhance or hinder model efficiency. For example, in cases involving large volumes of data, an experiential approach may suggest using distributed systems such as Hadoop or NoSQL databases, which scale more effectively with large datasets [11]. This is something that could not be achieved through a purely theoretical approach.

The experiential approach also relies on the *trial-and-error* methodology. Data model designers apply various techniques and methodologies and then test performance under real-world conditions. Based on feedback, optimisations continue until a satisfactory balance between performance and resource usage is achieved. This approach is highly effective when dealing with unpredictable data and complex business requirements. It enables flexibility and adaptability in response to dynamic changes in the environment.

This approach also has its weaknesses. It may be prone to errors stemming from subjective opinions and a lack of objective criteria. Experience is often difficult to generalise across different systems or domains, which can make it challenging to apply acquired knowledge in new situations.

In modern environments, the experiential approach is often combined with artificial intelligence and ML methods to further enhance data model performance. For example, automated database optimisation based on usage pattern analysis can improve performance without requiring human intervention.

Although systematic and experiential approaches to data modelling are often seen as opposing methods, they are frequently combined in practice. For example, the systematic approach can serve as the foundation for data design and structure, while the experiential approach is used for fine-tuning performance under specific conditions. In many cases, the best results come from integrating both approaches. The theoretical approach is applied first, and then, through experiments in real conditions, the model is adjusted and optimised.

Furthermore, a hybrid approach that incorporates elements of both systematic and experiential methods is becoming increasingly popular in modern systems. For example, large tech companies use data analytics to model theoretical performance while also applying adaptive optimisation strategies based on real-world user interaction data.

3 Data Modelling Process Steps

The data modelling process is a crucial phase in data analysis, used to identify patterns, predict future events, and make informed decisions. In this process, data, typically stored in files such as CSV, Excel, or JSON formats, undergoes a series of careful steps to create a model that can efficiently process the data and provide valuable insights. Essentially, the process involves defining goals, collecting and preparing data, selecting and training models, and evaluating their performance to ensure high-quality results. An important part of the process is the continuous improvement of the model to adapt to new data and changes in the environment. The following steps represent the key stages in the data modelling process [1]:

1. **Defining goals and problem**: This step involves setting the goals of the model and defining the problems to be solved, such as predicting outcomes, classifying data, or regression tasks.
2. **Data collection and preprocessing**: In this phase, relevant data is collected, missing values are handled, and data is prepared for further analysis through cleaning, transformation, and formatting.
3. **Exploratory Data Analysis (EDA)**: EDA is performed to explore data distributions, correlations, and potential issues such as data imbalance or variable dependencies.
4. **Feature selection and engineering**: This step involves selecting relevant features and engineering new features to improve the model's performance.

5. **Model selection and training**: Based on the problem type and data characteristics, the appropriate model is selected (e.g. regression, classification, deep learning), and it is trained using the prepared data.
6. **Model evaluation and optimisation**: The model's performance is evaluated using metrics such as accuracy, recall, or F1 score, and optimisation techniques like hyperparameter tuning and cross-validation are applied to improve results.

The problems in psychology that can be addressed with ML encompass key aspects of clinical practice, such as diagnosis, prognosis, treatment prediction, and biomarker monitoring [7]. ML enables the identification of mental disorders based on symptoms and patient behaviour, as well as predicting the development of mental conditions over time. It can also assist in selecting the optimal therapeutic approach based on patient characteristics and their response to treatment. The detection and monitoring of biomarkers, such as biological parameters associated with mental disorders, allow for better tracking and understanding of mental health. All these applications of ML contribute to improving diagnosis, prognosis, and treatment in psychology.

In this context, defining goals for data modelling in psychology is crucial. Set goals, such as diagnosis, prognosis, treatment prediction, and biomarker monitoring, directly influence how data will be collected, prepared, and analysed. For example, goals like predicting therapy response or identifying specific biomarkers shape the choice of modelling methodologies, such as classification, regression, or clustering. These goals guide the selection of relevant features in the data, enabling efficient and precise modelling aligned with the specific needs of psychological and psychiatric practice.

The second step involves collecting relevant data, handling missing values, eliminating outliers, and standardising data formats. Different types of data, such as structured data (e.g. numerical values from tests or measurements), unstructured data (e.g. patient interviews or clinical notes), and time-series data (e.g. changes in mental state over time), require specific preprocessing techniques [12–14]. For example, numerical data may require normalisation or scaling [15], while unstructured text data may need tokenisation, stemming, or lemmatisation [16]. Time-series data may require smoothing or transformations to account for temporal changes, and pattern recognition techniques such as n-gram analysis or anomaly detection can be applied to identify recurring trends or outliers in the data [17]. Transformations such as scaling and normalisation help adjust the data for the model to achieve better results. Preprocessing is a crucial step in preparing the data for further analysis. This process involves cleaning, transforming, and formatting data to ensure consistency, reliability, and readiness for modelling. Proper handling of missing values, outliers, and inconsistencies is critical in this phase, as it ensures that the data used for ML is of high quality, which is essential for obtaining accurate and meaningful results [1]. Here is an example of data normalisation in Python using methods from the `sklearn` preprocessing library, which is used for standardising and scaling data to improve the performance of ML models. The `StandardScaler` method standardises the data to have a mean of 0 and a standard deviation of 1, while the `MinMaxScaler` scales the data to a specified range, typically [0, 1].

```
from sklearn.preprocessing import StandardScaler, MinMaxScaler
import numpy as np

data = np.array([[100, 0.1, 300], [200, 0.2, 400],
[300, 0.3, 500], [400, 0.4, 600]])

scaler_standard = StandardScaler()
data_standardized = scaler_standard.fit_transform(data)

scaler_minmax = MinMaxScaler()
data_normalized = scaler_minmax.fit_transform(data)
```

In this example, the `StandardScaler` standardises each feature of the data, and the `MinMaxScaler` normalises the values to a range of 0 to 1, which is particularly useful for algorithms that are sensitive to the scale of input features, such as neural networks and distance-based models like KNN. EDA is a key step in understanding the dataset before applying any ML models. It involves examining data distributions, correlations, and potential issues such as missing values, outliers, or class imbalances. EDA helps in identifying patterns, trends, and relationships among variables, allowing data scientists to refine their models accordingly. An example of performing EDA using Python, where we visualise the distribution of features and check for correlations between them using the pandas, `matplotlib`, and `seaborn` libraries, is given in the following:

```
import pandas as pd
import matplotlib.pyplot as plt
import seaborn as sns

# Load example dataset
data = pd.read_csv('dataset.csv')

# Summary statistics and data types
# Gives mean, std, min, 25th percentile, median, max
print(data.describe())
# Provides info on missing values, data types
print(data.info())

# Visualizing distributions of numerical features
data.hist(figsize=(10, 8), bins=30)
plt.suptitle('Feature Distributions')
plt.show()

# Checking for correlations between variables
correlation_matrix = data.corr()
sns.heatmap(correlation_matrix, annot=True, cmap='coolwarm',
 ↪ linewidths=0.5)
plt.title('Correlation Heatmap')
plt.show()
```

Function `describe()` gives an overview of the data's statistical properties, while `hist()` visualises the distribution of numerical features. The `corr()` function calculates correlations between features, and `sns.heatmap()` creates a heatmap to visually inspect these correlations. EDA also allows you to check for issues like skewed distributions, missing values, or strong correlations between features, which may require preprocessing or feature engineering. Feature selection and engineering is a crucial step in building ML models, as it involves selecting the most relevant features and potentially creating new ones to enhance the model's performance. After conducting an EDA, it is essential to define key characteristics (feature engineering). This process includes selecting or creating significant features that can improve model accuracy. It may involve techniques such as dimensionality reduction, feature extraction, or using methods like principal component analysis (PCA) to simplify the feature space.

For example, after performing EDA to understand the data distributions and correlations, you can use PCA to reduce the dimensionality of your data, making it easier for your model to process and learn from the essential patterns:

```
from sklearn.decomposition import PCA

# Assuming 'data' is your dataset and 'target' is the target
↪ variable
# Perform PCA for dimensionality reduction
pca = PCA(n_components=5)
X_reduced = pca.fit_transform(data.drop('target', axis=1))

# Check the explained variance ratio for the selected
↪ components
print(pca.explained_variance_ratio_)
```

In this code, PCA reduces the dataset's dimensionality by selecting the top 5 components, which retain the most variance from the original features. This can help improve model performance by focusing on the most important patterns in the data while discarding less relevant features.

By combining EDA insights with feature engineering techniques like PCA, one can ensure that the model is working with the most valuable information, thereby enhancing its predictive power.

Based on the problem type (regression, classification, etc.) and data characteristics, the appropriate model is selected and trained using the prepared dataset. For instance, if the problem is related to predicting a continuous variable, a regression model like linear regression may be used:

```
from sklearn.linear_model import LinearRegression

# Model selection and training (Linear Regression)
model = LinearRegression()
model.fit(X_train, y_train)
```

In this example, a linear regression model is created and trained on the training data (`X_train, y_train`). After training the model, it is essential to evaluate its performance to ensure it generalises well to new data. Cross-validation and performance metrics like accuracy, recall, and F1 score are commonly used for this purpose [18]. Model optimisation techniques like hyperparameter tuning using `GridSearchCV` or `RandomSearchCV` can be applied to improve performance.

```
from sklearn.model_selection import cross_val_score

# Model evaluation using cross-validation
scores = cross_val_score(model, X, y, cv=5)
print(f'Cross-validation scores: {scores}')
```

Here, cross-validation is applied to evaluate the model on different data splits, providing a more reliable measure of performance. For model optimisation, techniques like `GridSearchCV` allow fine-tuning hyperparameters to find the best-performing model:

```
from sklearn.model_selection import GridSearchCV

# Model optimisation using GridSearchCV
param_grid = {'alpha': [0.1, 1, 10]}
grid_search = GridSearchCV(model, param_grid, cv=5)
grid_search.fit(X_train, y_train)
```

In this case, `GridSearchCV` is used to find the optimal value of the hyperparameter alpha for the model.

4 Modelling Methodologies

The choice of a modelling methodology depends on the nature of the data, the research objectives, and the trade-off between model interpretability and predictive performance. Data modelling methodologies can be categorised into three main approaches: statistical models, ML models, and hybrid techniques that integrate elements of both.

Statistical models have long been the foundation of data analysis, providing interpretable frameworks based on mathematical relationships. These models are particularly valuable in psychology, where hypothesis-driven research requires a clear understanding of relationships between variables. Linear regression is one of the most widely used statistical models, assuming a linear relationship between an independent variable and a dependent variable:

$$Y = \beta_0 + \beta_1 X + \varepsilon, \tag{1}$$

where Y represents the dependent variable, X is the independent variable, β_0 is the intercept, β_1 is the regression coefficient, and ε represents the error term. Linear regression is useful for explaining relationships between psychological constructs, such as the effect of stress levels on cognitive performance [3]. When assumptions such as normality and homoscedasticity are violated, alternative techniques such as logistic regression, generalised linear models (GLMs), or non-parametric regression methods may be preferred.

Beyond traditional statistical models, *ML methodologies* offer more flexible approaches for handling complex, high-dimensional datasets. Unlike statistical models that rely on predefined assumptions, ML algorithms learn patterns from data, making them suitable for non-linear relationships and large datasets. Decision trees, support vector machines, and artificial neural networks are commonly employed ML techniques. Among these, tree-based models, such as random forests and gradient boosting machines, have gained popularity due to their ability to handle missing data, interactions between variables, and high-dimensional feature spaces [2]. A decision tree model recursively splits the data into homogeneous subsets, with each node representing a decision rule. An example of a decision tree applied in Python using the `sklearn` library is shown below:

```
from sklearn.tree import DecisionTreeClassifier
from sklearn.model_selection import train_test_split
from sklearn.datasets import load_iris

# Load dataset
iris = load_iris()

X_train, X_test, y_train, y_test =
 ↪  train_test_split\\(iris.data, iris.target, test_size=0.2,
 ↪  random_state=42)

# Train decision tree model
clf = DecisionTreeClassifier(max_depth=3)
clf.fit(X_train, y_train)

# Predict on test data
y_pred = clf.predict(X_test)
```

In addition to decision trees, neural networks have demonstrated remarkable performance in modelling complex relationships within data. Deep learning models, such as convolutional neural networks (CNNs) and recurrent neural networks (RNNs), are particularly effective for structured and sequential data. One of the major challenges of ML models is their interpretability. In psychological research, where explainability is often crucial, models such as SHAP (Shapley Additive Explanations) and LIME (Local Interpretable Model-Agnostic Explanations) are used to enhance model transparency [19].

Another emerging trend in data modelling is the use of *hybrid approaches* that combine statistical and ML techniques. Hybrid models aim to leverage the strengths of both methodologies, improving predictive accuracy while maintaining interpretability. For instance, generalised additive models (GAMs) extend traditional linear models by allowing for non-linear relationships between predictors and outcomes, while still being interpretable [20]. Similarly, ensemble techniques such as stacking integrate multiple models, combining linear regression with tree-based models or neural networks to enhance performance.

Model selection and evaluation remain crucial steps in the data modelling process. Performance metrics such as mean squared error (MSE), root mean squared error (RMSE), and R-squared (R^2) are commonly used to assess regression models, while classification models are evaluated using accuracy, precision, recall, and F1 score. Cross-validation techniques, such as k-fold cross-validation, help ensure model robustness by preventing overfitting [3]. An example of cross-validation applied in Python using `scikit-learn` is demonstrated below:

```
from sklearn.model_selection import cross_val_score
from sklearn.ensemble import RandomForestClassifier

# Train a Random Forest model with cross-validation
rf = RandomForestClassifier(n_estimators=100, random_state=42)
cv_scores = cross_val_score(rf, X_train, y_train, cv=5)

# Print average performance
print(f"Mean CV Accuracy: {cv_scores.mean():.3f}")
```

Ultimately, the choice of a modelling methodology depends on the research question and data characteristics. While statistical models remain the preferred approach in hypothesis-driven research, ML techniques provide powerful alternatives for handling large and complex datasets. The integration of hybrid models offers promising directions for balancing predictive power and interpretability, making data modelling a continuously evolving field.

5 Imputation Techniques

Imputation techniques are a cornerstone of data preprocessing, particularly in psychological research, where datasets often suffer from incomplete or missing entries. These gaps in data arise due to various factors, such as participant dropout, unanswered survey questions, or errors during data collection. Missing data, if not handled properly, can compromise the validity of research findings, leading to biased results and diminished statistical power. Imputation techniques aim to address this issue by estimating and replacing missing values, thereby preserving the integrity of the dataset and ensuring robust analyses.

In psychological research, imputing missing data comes with ethical responsibilities. Researchers must carefully weigh the potential consequences of filling in sensitive or personal data, such as mental health scores or socioeconomic indicators, especially when these variables are highly individualised. For instance, imputing missing responses in a survey on depression levels might obscure true underlying patterns if the imputation does not account for the context of the missingness. Failing to disclose the imputation method used can lead to a lack of transparency in research findings, which is a critical ethical concern in psychological studies [21].

One important ethical principle is to ensure that imputed values do not introduce biases or misrepresent the population under study. Imputation methods that oversimplify complex data relationships can result in findings that lack generalisability or validity. Transparency is essential, and researchers should document the type of imputation method used, the assumptions made, and the potential limitations of the chosen approach. Ethical guidelines from organisations such as the *American Psychological Association* (APA) emphasise the importance of full disclosure when handling and reporting imputed data [22].

Before applying any imputation techniques, it is vital to examine the characteristics of the dataset, as this informs the choice of method. Visualising missing data patterns can reveal whether the missingness is systematic or random. Tools such as the `missingno` library in Python allow researchers to graphically inspect the extent and distribution of missing values. For example, this visualisation can help identify clusters of missingness and determine whether certain variables or groups of participants are more affected:

```
import missingno as msno
import pandas as pd

df = pd.read_csv('data.csv')
msno.matrix(df)
```

Visualisations such as heatmaps and dendrograms generated by tools like `missingno` can help guide the selection of appropriate imputation techniques based on the extent and structure of missing data [23].

Statistical checks can also aid in understanding the nature of the missing data. For instance, researchers might test for correlations between missingness and observed variables to identify potential cases of missing at random [16]. Summary statistics, such as the proportion of missing values for each variable, provide additional insight into the feasibility of certain imputation techniques. When a large percentage of data is missing, simple methods like mean or median imputation may oversimplify the data and fail to preserve underlying relationships. Advanced methods like multiple imputation or ML algorithms are more suitable for handling extensive missingness [24].

The effectiveness of imputation techniques must be evaluated to ensure they do not distort the dataset. One approach is to compare the imputed values against known data points in cases where partial information is available. For numerical data, metrics such as *mean absolute error* (MAE) or *root mean squared error* (RMSE) can quantify the accuracy of imputed values. For categorical data, accuracy and precision scores can be used to assess the performance of methods like mode or random forest imputation. Researchers should evaluate how imputation affects downstream analyses, such as regression models or hypothesis tests, to ensure that the imputed data does not introduce bias [25].

In longitudinal studies, where repeated measurements are collected over time, missing data poses unique challenges. Techniques such as *last observation carried forward* (LOCF) and linear interpolation can be effective for filling in gaps between time points. More sophisticated approaches, such as mixed-effects models or ML methods like recurrent neural networks (RNNs), can capture temporal dependencies and provide more accurate imputations for longitudinal datasets [26]. For example, in a study tracking changes in anxiety levels over six months, a mixed-effects model could account for both individual variability and group-level trends, providing more accurate imputations than simpler methods.

The choice of an imputation method must also consider computational efficiency, particularly for large datasets. Parallelised imputation algorithms, such as those implemented in `fancyimpute` or `scikit-learn`, allow for efficient processing of big data while maintaining accuracy. Researchers are encouraged to validate their imputation results through sensitivity analyses and comparison with original data distributions to ensure that imputed values align with the dataset's overall structure [27].

To apply appropriate imputation techniques, it is essential first to understand the types of missing data. Missing data can be classified into three categories: *missing completely at random* (MCAR), *missing at random* (MAR), and *missing not at random* (MNAR) [24, 28]. MCAR occurs when the missingness is entirely independent of any variables in the dataset. For example, a participant accidentally skips a survey question. MAR, on the other hand, means the missingness depends on observed data but not on the missing values themselves. For instance, younger participants may be more likely to skip a specific question, creating a pattern linked to age. MNAR occurs when the missingness depends on unobserved values, such as when individuals with higher stress levels deliberately avoid answering a question about mental health. Identifying the type of missing data helps researchers select the most appropriate imputation method [28].

Imputation techniques vary in complexity, from simple methods that make broad assumptions to advanced algorithms that incorporate multiple variables and ML. *Mean imputation*, one of the simplest methods, involves replacing missing values with the mean of the observed data for that variable [28]. Although easy to implement, this approach can distort variability and relationships among variables, potentially biasing analyses [28].

Median imputation is often used as a more robust alternative, particularly when dealing with skewed data. Replacing missing values with the median instead of the mean reduces the influence of outliers, making it suitable for psychological datasets where extreme responses are common. For categorical data, *mode imputation* replaces missing entries with the most frequently occurring category, a straightforward approach that maintains consistency within the dataset [24].

A more sophisticated method is *k-nearest neighbours (k-NN) imputation*, which estimates missing values based on the nearest neighbours in the dataset [29]. This technique considers the similarity between observations, using distances in feature space to infer plausible values. For example, in a study on anxiety levels, k-NN imputation could estimate missing scores by examining participants with similar demographic and psychological profiles. However, k-NN can be computationally intensive, especially for large datasets, and requires careful parameter tuning to avoid overfitting [25].

In psychological research, *multiple imputation* (MI) has gained popularity due to its ability to account for uncertainty in the imputed values. MI generates several complete datasets by sampling from a distribution of plausible values for the missing entries. Each dataset is then analysed separately, and the results are pooled to provide more accurate estimates and confidence intervals. By incorporating variability in the imputed data, MI reduces the risk of underestimating standard errors, making it a powerful tool for hypothesis testing [28, 30].

As datasets grow larger and more complex, traditional imputation methods may fall short in capturing complex patterns. *Regression-based imputation* uses regression models to predict missing values based on observed variables. For example, if a participant's income data is missing, a regression model could estimate it using age, education level, and occupation as predictors. This approach is particularly useful in psychological studies where variables often exhibit strong interdependencies [28].

ML techniques, such as *random forest imputation*, have also emerged as powerful alternatives. Random forests can handle non-linear relationships and interactions between variables, making them ideal for psychological datasets with complex structures [31]. In this approach, missing values are iteratively estimated by training decision trees on the observed data. Similarly, *deep learning methods* are being explored for imputation, leveraging neural networks to model high-dimensional data with intricate dependencies [32].

When selecting an imputation technique, researchers must consider the nature of their dataset, the underlying assumptions of the method, and the impact on subsequent analyses. Simpler methods like mean or median imputation may suffice for exploratory analyses, but advanced techniques such as multiple imputation or ML are preferred for hypothesis-driven research. It is crucial to assess the imputation method's performance through validation techniques, such as comparing imputed values with known data or evaluating the impact on predictive accuracy [30].

In Python, several libraries facilitate the implementation of imputation techniques. For example, the `SimpleImputer` class from the `scikit-learn` library supports basic methods such as mean, median, and mode imputation [25]. More advanced approaches, such as multiple imputation, can be implemented using the `IterativeImputer` from `scikit-learn` or the `mice` package available in R, which integrates seamlessly with Python through tools like `rpy2`. Open-source tools such as `fancyimpute` and `datawig` further expand the range of imputation methods, including matrix factorisation and deep learning [32].

Imputation techniques are indispensable in psychological research, ensuring that incomplete datasets do not undermine the validity of findings. From basic methods like mean and median imputation to advanced algorithms incorporating ML, researchers have a wide array of tools at their disposal. By carefully selecting and validating imputation methods, psychologists can preserve the integrity of their data, enabling more reliable and insightful analyses.

6 Case Study

The dataset `data.csv` contains information collected from 100 participants, designed to capture demographic, behavioural, and group-related data. Each row in the dataset corresponds to an individual participant, while the columns represent specific attributes or variables measured during the study.

This column `Participant` serves as the unique identifier for each individual in the dataset. The values in this column are alphanumeric, such as *P1*, *P2*, and so on, where *P* stands for *Participant* followed by a sequential number. This identifier does not carry intrinsic information about the participant but ensures that each entry can be uniquely referenced.

The `Age` column represents each participant's age in years. The data is numerical and spans a wide range to capture participants from different stages of adulthood. Missing values in this column may indicate that certain participants did not record or provide age data. The distribution of `Age` can provide insights into the demographic diversity of the study sample.

The column `ReactionTime` measures the time each participant takes to respond to a specific stimulus during an experiment. The data is numerical and recorded in seconds, with precision to several decimal places. It is a key behavioural measure often used in psychological and cognitive studies to assess processing speed, attentional focus, or decision-making efficiency. Missing values may result from participants not completing the task or technical issues during data collection.

The `Group` column categorises participants into one of two groups: *control* or *experimental*. These groups typically represent different conditions in the study,

	Participant	Age	ReactionTime	Score	Group
0	P1	56.0	NaN	74.0	Control
1	P2	46.0	2.233737	NaN	Experimental
2	P3	NaN	1.419443	72.0	Control
3	P4	25.0	NaN	80.0	Control
4	P5	38.0	2.738335	79.0	Control

Fig. 1 First five rows of the dataset displaying participants' attributes, including missing values represented as `NaN`

such as participants who received a particular intervention (Experimental) versus those who did not (control). This categorical variable is crucial for comparing outcomes between groups and understanding the effects of the experimental condition.

The `Score` column represents a numerical performance metric obtained during the study, such as a test result, task accuracy, or survey rating. The values range from 50 to 100, indicating varying performance levels among participants. Missing values in this column might indicate participants who did not complete the task or who provided incomplete responses.

This dataset is a blend of demographic (Age), behavioural (ReactionTime), categorical (Group), and performance (Score) data. While most columns contain numerical data, the `Group` column is categorical, and the `Participant` column serves as an identifier. Missing values in key columns, such as `Age`, `ReactionTime`, and `Score`, highlight the need for appropriate preprocessing and imputation techniques to ensure the integrity of analyses.

In Fig. 1, the first five rows of the dataset are displayed, generated by calling the `df.head()` function. Each row represents an individual participant, identified by the unique *Participant* ID. In the table, the data values for each column (`Age`, `ReactionTime`, `Score`, etc.) are presented. Missing data is indicated as `NaN` (Not a Number) in some columns. For example, certain entries in the `Age`, `ReactionTime`, and `Score` columns may appear as `NaN`, signifying that no value was recorded or available for those specific participants.

The following code is designed to explore and summarise a dataset while providing visual insights into its structure. It begins by loading the dataset from a file named `data.csv` into a `pandas` *DataFrame*. The code then calculates basic statistics for all columns, such as averages, ranges, and the number of unique values, and it includes information about missing values and data types for each column. This summary is saved as a new file named `columnStats.csv`, which can be reviewed later.

```
import pandas as pd
import matplotlib.pyplot as plt
import seaborn as sns
import missingno as msno

# Load the dataset
file_path = "data.csv"  # Replace with your actual file path
df = pd.read_csv(file_path)

# Basic statistics for each column
column_stats = df.describe(include='all').transpose()

# Add missing value statistics
column_stats['Missing Values'] = df.isnull().sum()
column_stats['Unique Values'] = df.nunique()
column_stats['Data Type'] = df.dtypes

# Save the column stats to a CSV for review
column_stats.to_csv("columnStats.csv")
print("Column characteristics saved to 'columnStats.csv'.")

# Visualize each column
for column in df.columns:
    if column == 'Participant':
        continue  # Skip visualization for the Participant
         ↪ column

    plt.figure(figsize=(8, 4))
    if df[column].dtype == 'object':
        # Categorical data: Bar plot of value counts
        sns.countplot(data=df, x=column, palette='Set2')
        plt.title(f"Value Counts for {column}")
        plt.ylabel("Frequency")
    else:
        # Numeric data: Histogram with KDE
        sns.histplot(df[column], kde=True, bins=20,
         ↪ color='blue',
        ^^I^^I^^Iedgecolor='black')
        plt.title(f"Distribution of {column}")
        plt.xlabel(column)
        plt.ylabel("Frequency")
```

```
        plt.tight_layout()
        plt.show()

    # Calculate counts of existing and missing values for each
    ↪ column
    missing_stats = pd.DataFrame({
        'Existing': df.notnull().sum(),
        'Missing': df.isnull().sum()
    })

    # Plot missing vs. existing values for each column
    plt.figure(figsize=(10, 6))
    missing_stats.plot(kind='bar', stacked=True, figsize=(10, 6),
    ^^I^^Icolor=["skyblue", "salmon"], edgecolor="black")
    plt.title("Counts of Existing and Missing Values by Column")
    plt.xlabel("Columns", fontsize=12)
    plt.ylabel("Count", fontsize=12)
    plt.xticks(rotation=0, ha="right", fontsize=10)
    plt.legend(["Existing Values", "Missing Values"], fontsize=10)
    plt.grid(axis="y", linestyle="--", alpha=0.7)
    plt.tight_layout()

    # Show the plot
    plt.show()

    # Generate the missing data matrix
    msno.matrix(df)
    plt.xticks(rotation=0)
    plt.show()
```

To make the data more understandable, the code includes visualisations for each column in the dataset, except for the `Participant` column, as it is shown in Fig. 2. For columns containing categorical data (e.g. group labels or categories), bar plots are created to display the frequency of each category. For numerical columns, histograms and smooth density curves are generated to illustrate how the data is distributed.

In addition to individual column visualisations, the code creates a summary plot (Fig. 3) showing the number of missing and existing values for each column. This stacked bar chart highlights the completeness of the dataset, making it easy to identify which columns have significant amounts of missing data and which are fully observed. The charts use clear colour coding, with blue representing existing values and red representing missing ones, and include labels and titles for better readability.

The visualisation part of the code ends with the missing data matrix creation and its visualisation. Each column in the plot corresponds to a feature in the dataset, such as `Participant`, `Age`, `ReactionTime`, `Score`, and `Group`. The rows represent individual observations or participants, allowing a detailed examination of missingness across both features and participants. This matrix is shown in Fig. 4.

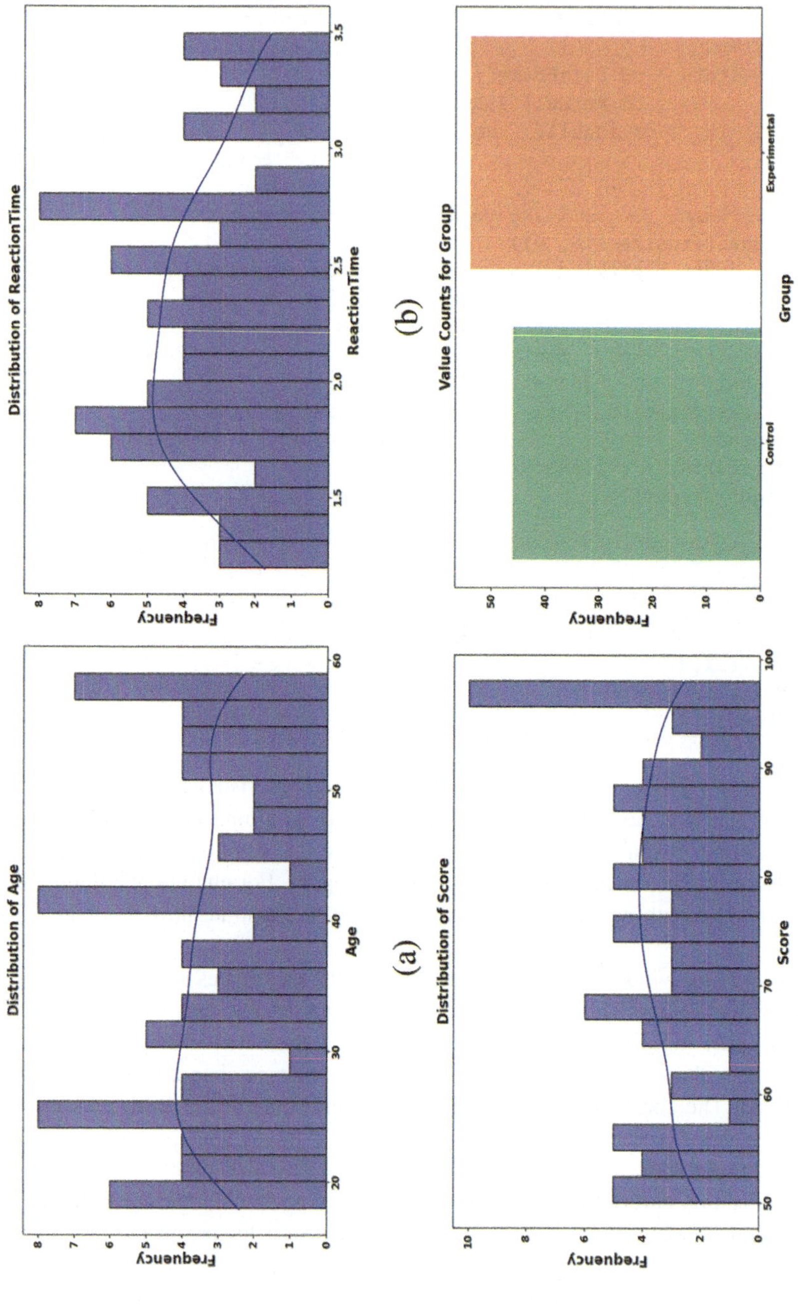

Fig. 2 Matrix of four plots showing the distribution of **(a)** `Age`, **(b)** `ReactionTime`, **(c)** `Score`, and **(d)** the value counts for `Group`

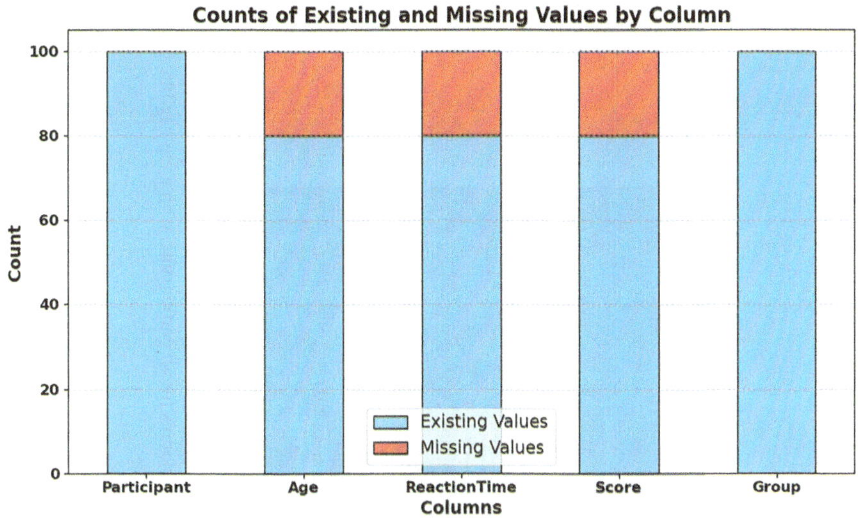

Fig. 3 Bar chart showing the counts of existing and missing values for each column in the dataset

In this plot, the black bars indicate observed or non-missing data, while white spaces signify missing values. For instance, the features `Age`, `ReactionTime`, and `Score` show significant gaps, reflecting missing entries. On the other hand, the columns `Participant` and `Group` are filled with black, indicating that these features are fully observed and contain no missing data. This visual distinction makes it easy to identify which variables in the dataset are incomplete and require attention during preprocessing.

One of the critical features of this visualisation is the zig-zag line displayed on the right side of the matrix. This line represents the total count of non-missing values for each participant. The height of the line reflects the completeness of the data for that specific participant. A higher position of the line suggests that most features are observed, whereas a drop in the line indicates participants with multiple missing values. The zig-zag nature of the line reveals variability in the completeness of data across participants, highlighting that some have complete records, while others are missing significant portions of their information.

From the plot, it is apparent that missing values are not uniformly distributed across the dataset. For example, the `ReactionTime` feature exhibits a noticeable clustering of missing values in the middle rows, suggesting a possible systematic pattern in how this data was collected or lost. Such patterns could result from specific experimental conditions, data entry errors, or participant-related factors. Understanding these patterns is crucial, as they provide insights into whether the missingness might be completely at random, related to other observed variables, or tied to unobserved factors.

The implications of this visualisation for data analysis are substantial. Variables such as `Score` with considerable missing entries may require careful handling to

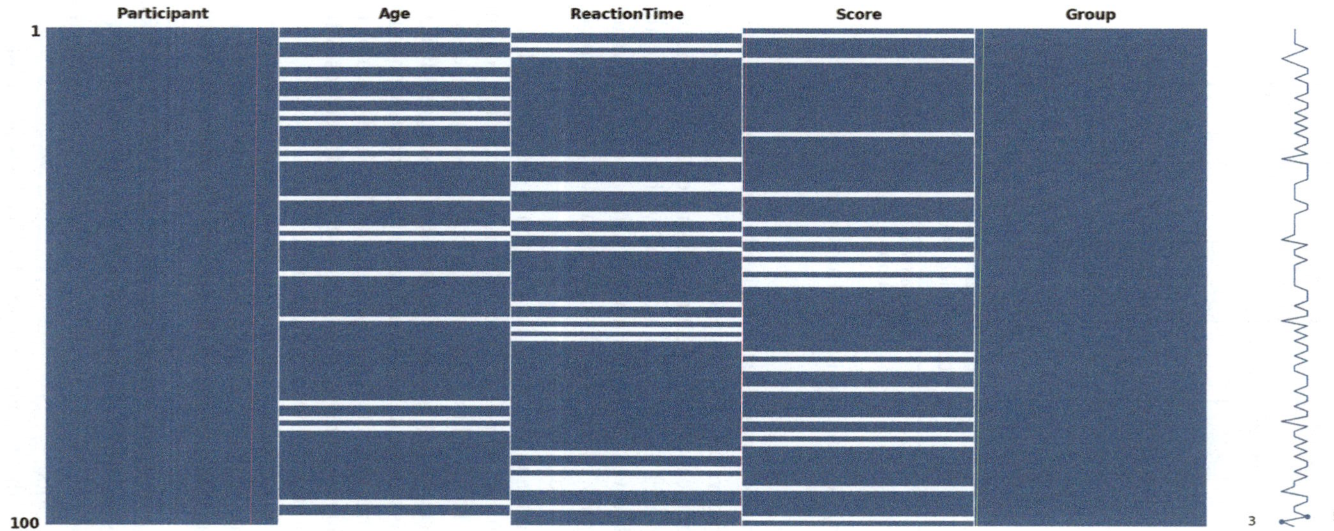

Fig. 4 Missing data matrix illustrating the presence (dark bars) and absence (white gaps) of data across columns for all participants, with a zig-zag line on the right indicating the total non-missing values per row

ensure that subsequent analyses are not biased. Columns like `Participant` and `Group`, which are fully complete, can serve as reliable anchors for the dataset, potentially aiding in grouping or identifying specific subsets of the data.

The next steps for addressing these issues would typically involve applying imputation techniques to fill in the gaps, particularly in features like `Age`, `ReactionTime`, and `Score`. Before proceeding with any imputation, it is essential to investigate the nature of the missingness further. Identifying whether the data is missing completely at random (MCAR), missing at random (MAR), or missing not at random (MNAR) will guide the choice of imputation strategy and ensure that the integrity of the dataset is preserved. Here is a Python implementation to investigate the nature of missingness in the dataset:

```
import pandas as pd
import numpy as np
import seaborn as sns
import matplotlib.pyplot as plt
from scipy.stats import chi2_contingency, ttest_ind

# Load the dataset
file_path = "data.csv"  # Replace with your actual file path
df = pd.read_csv(file_path)

# Function to test MCAR using randomness of missingness
↪ patterns
def test_mcar(data):
    missing_indicator = data.isnull().astype(int)
    missing_patterns = missing_indicator.sum(axis=1)
    groups = [data.loc[missing_patterns == i].dropna(axis=1)
    ^^Ifor i in set(missing_patterns)
^^I^^Iif (missing_patterns == i).sum() > 1]

    p_values = []
    for col in data.columns:
        if data[col].dtype != "object" and
        ↪ data[col].isnull().any():
            observed = [group[col] for group in groups
            ^^Iif col in group.columns]
            if len(observed) > 1:
                try:
                    t_stat, p_value = ttest_ind(observed[0],
                    ↪ observed[1],
                    ^^I^^I^^Inan_policy="omit")
                    p_values.append((col, p_value))
                except ValueError:
                    p_values.append((col, np.nan))  # Handle
                    ↪ edge cases
    return p_values

# Function to test MAR using chi-square test
```

```
def test_mar(data, target_col):
    results = {}
    for col in data.columns:
        if col != target_col and data[col].dtype == "object":
            try:
                contingency_table = pd.crosstab(data[col],
                ^^I^^Idata[target_col].isnull())
                chi2, p_value, _, _ =
                ↪ chi2_contingency(contingency_table)
                results[col] = p_value
            except ValueError:
                results[col] = np.nan  # Handle edge cases
    return results

# Analyze missingness
def analyze_missingness(data):

    print("\nTesting for MCAR...")
    mcar_results = test_mcar(data)
    if mcar_results:
        print("MCAR Test Results:")
        for col, p_value in mcar_results:
            print(f"{col}: p-value = {p_value:.4f}")
        if any(p_value > 0.05 for _, p_value in mcar_results):
            print("\nData might be Missing Completely at
             ↪ Random.")
    else:
        print("No valid groups found for MCAR testing.")

    print("\nTesting for MAR...")
    mar_results = {}
    for col in data.columns:
        if data[col].isnull().any():
            mar_results[col] = test_mar(data, col)
    for target, dependencies in mar_results.items():
        print(f"\nTesting dependency of missingness in
         ↪ {target}...")
        for col, p_value in dependencies.items():
            if not np.isnan(p_value):
                print(f"Dependency on {col}: p-value =
                 ↪ {p_value:.4f}")
    if any(p_value < 0.05 for _,
    ^^Idependencies in mar_results.items() for _,
    ^^Ip_value in dependencies.items() if not
    ↪ np.isnan(p_value)):
        print("\nData might be Missing at Random.")
```

```
    print("\nTesting for MNAR...")
    for col in data.columns:
        if data[col].isnull().any():
            observed = data[~data[col].isnull()][col].dropna()
            missing = data[data[col].isnull()][col]
            if len(observed) > 0 and len(missing) > 0:
                try:
                    t_stat, p_value = ttest_ind(observed,
                     ↪ missing,
                    ^^Inan_policy="omit")
                    print(f"{col}: MNAR p-value =
                     ↪ {p_value:.4f}")
                    if p_value < 0.05:
                        print(f"Data in {col} might be MNAR.")
                except ValueError:
                    print(f"{col}: MNAR test could not be
                     ↪ performed.")
            else:
                print(f"{col}: MNAR test skipped (insufficient
                 ↪ data).")

# Run the analysis
analyze_missingness(df)
```

For the dataset used in this case study, the analysis yielded the following results:

```
Testing for MCAR...
No valid groups found for MCAR testing.

Testing for MAR...
Testing dependency of missingness in Age...
Dependency on Participant: p-value = 0.4530
Dependency on Group: p-value = 0.8804

Testing dependency of missingness in ReactionTime...
Dependency on Participant: p-value = 0.4530
Dependency on Group: p-value = 0.7255

Testing dependency of missingness in Score...
Dependency on Participant: p-value = 0.4530
Dependency on Group: p-value = 0.3938

Testing for MNAR...
Age: MNAR p-value = nan
ReactionTime: MNAR p-value = nan
Score: MNAR p-value = nan
```

For MCAR, the analysis indicates that no valid groups were found for testing. This result often occurs when there is insufficient variability in the patterns of missing data across rows or when the dataset does not provide enough distinct missingness combinations to compare groups. Consequently, it is not possible to determine whether the data is missing completely at random using this test.

For MAR, the results explore whether the missingness in specific columns, such as `Age`, `ReactionTime`, and `Score`, is dependent on other variables like `Participant` or `Group`. The p-values for these tests are all quite high (above 0.05), suggesting no statistically significant relationship between the missingness in these columns and the tested variables. This implies that the missingness in `Age`, `ReactionTime`, and `Score` does not appear to depend on the values of `Participant` or `Group`. This does not completely rule out MAR as a possibility; it only indicates no dependency on the variables tested in this dataset.

For MNAR, the results are inconclusive because the p-values are returned as `nan`. This outcome typically arises when there are insufficient observed or missing data points in the tested columns to perform a valid statistical comparison. Without enough data to compare the distributions of observed and missing values, the test cannot assess whether the missingness is dependent on unobserved factors within the column itself. As a result, the MNAR hypothesis remains unresolved for this dataset.

These findings suggest that while MCAR and MNAR cannot be definitively confirmed or ruled out, the high p-values for MAR indicate that missingness in this dataset is unlikely to be explained by relationships with the tested variables. Given the results, using methods designed for MAR, such as multiple imputation or regression-based imputation, appears to be the most practical approach for this dataset. Implementation of this imputation technique is shown in the following code:

```
import pandas as pd
import numpy as np
import seaborn as sns
import matplotlib.pyplot as plt
from sklearn.experimental import enable_iterative_imputer
from sklearn.impute import IterativeImputer

# Load the dataset
file_path = "data.csv"  # Replace with your actual file path
df = pd.read_csv(file_path)

# Create a copy for visualisation
df_original = df.copy()

# Imputation
imputer = IterativeImputer(max_iter=10, random_state=42)
df_imputed = pd.DataFrame(imputer.fit_transform(
^^Idf.select_dtypes(include=[np.number])),
^^Icolumns=df.select_dtypes(include=[np.number]).columns)
```

```
# Combine imputed numerical columns back with original
↪  non-numeric columns
df_imputed_combined = df.copy()
df_imputed_combined[df_imputed.columns] = df_imputed

# Visualise distributions of imputed vs original data for
↪  numerical columns
for col in df_imputed.columns:
    plt.figure(figsize=(10, 5))
    sns.kdeplot(df_original[col], label="Original (with NaN)",
    ↪  color="red",
    ^^Ifill=True)
    sns.kdeplot(df_imputed[col], label="Imputed", color="blue",
    ↪  fill=True)
    plt.title(f"Distribution of {col} Before and After
    ↪  Imputation")
    plt.xlabel(col)
    plt.ylabel("Density")
    plt.legend()
    plt.tight_layout()
    plt.show()
```

The plots shown in Fig. 5 represent the results of running the imputation code applied to the dataset. The code used regression-based imputation (via iterative imputation) to estimate missing values in the `Age`, `ReactionTime`, and `Score` columns. The visualisations compare the original data, including missing values, with the imputed data, allowing for an examination of the effects of imputation on the distributions of these variables.

In Fig. 5, we observe that the original data, indicated by the red shaded area, contains gaps due to missing values, while the imputed data, shown in blue, provides complete distributions. The overlap of the red and blue regions demonstrates how well the imputed values align with the observed data. For each variable, the imputed data fills in missing sections, while preserving the overall structure and spread of the original distributions, indicating that the imputation process successfully maintains the integrity of the dataset.

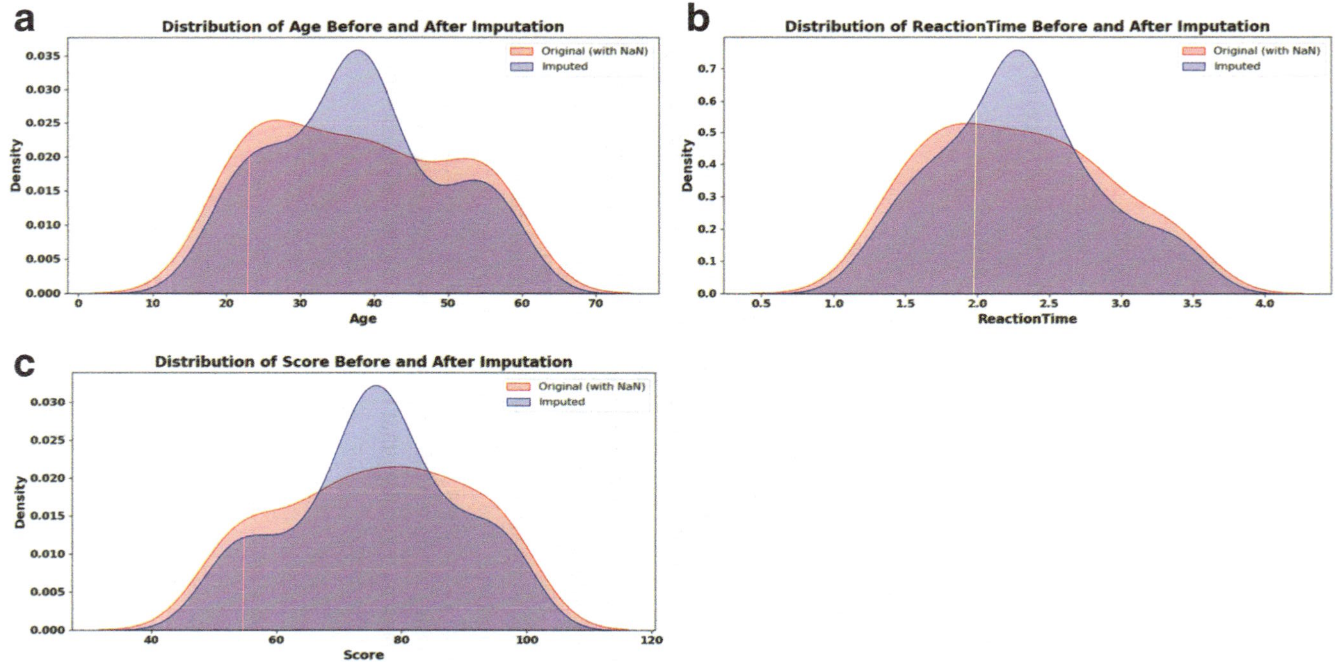

Fig. 5 Matrix of three plots showing distribution of (**a**) `Age`, (**b**) `ReactionTime`, and (**c**) `Score`, before and after imputation

References

1. M. Kantardzic, *Data Mining: Concepts, Models, Methods, and Algorithms* (Wiley, Hoboken, 2011)
2. R.T. Trevor Hastie, J. Friedman, *The Elements of Statistical Learning: Data Mining, Inference, and Prediction*, 2nd edn. (Springer, Berlin, 2009)
3. G. James, D. Witten, T. Hastie, R. Tibshirani, *An Introduction to Statistical Learning* (Springer, Berlin, 2013)
4. A. Mishra, Metrics to evaluate your machine learning algorithm, Towards Data Sci. 2018. [Online]. Available: https://towardsdatascience.com/top-machine-learning-algorithms-for-classification-2197870ff501/
5. Ž. Vujović, et al., Classification model evaluation metrics. Int. J. Adv. Comput. Sci. Appl. **12**(6), 599 (2021)
6. N. Kovač, K. Ratković, P. Watson, H. Farahani, F. Bagheri Sheykhangafshe, Machine learning classification models for predicting chronic pain. Current Psychol. **44**, 1–14 (2025)
7. D.B. Dwyer, P. Falkai, N. Koutsouleris, Machine learning approaches for clinical psychology and psychiatry. Ann. Rev. Clin. Psychol. **14**(1), 91 (2018)
8. A. Ng, *Machine Learning Yearning: Technical Strategy for AI Engineers, in the Era of Deep Learning* (Self-Publishing, 2018)
9. R. Elmasri, S.B. Navathe, *Fundamentals of Database Systems*, 7th edn. (Pearson, London, 2015)
10. J.D. Ullman, *Principles of Database and Knowledge-Base Systems* (Computer Science Press, New York, 1988)
11. T. White, *Hadoop: The Definitive Guide*, 4th edn. (O'Reilly Media, Santa Rosa, 2015)
12. I.R. Galatzer-Levy, J.P. Onnela, Machine learning and the digital measurement of psychological health. Ann. Rev. Clin. Psychol. **19**(1), 133 (2023)
13. A. Le Glaz, Y. Haralambous, D.H. Kim-Dufor, P. Lenca, R. Billot, T.C. Ryan, J. Marsh, J. Devylder, M. Walter, S. Berrouiguet, et al., Machine learning and natural language processing in mental health: systematic review. J. Med. Int. Res. **23**(5), e15708 (2021)
14. A. Avdic, U. Marovac, D. Jankovic, Automated labeling of terms in medical reports in Serbian. Turkish J. Electr. Eng. Comput. Sci. **28**(6), 3285 (2020)
15. B. Dou, Z. Zhu, E. Merkurjev, L. Ke, L. Chen, J. Jiang, Y. Zhu, J. Liu, B. Zhang, G.W. Wei, Machine learning methods for small data challenges in molecular science. Chem. Rev. **123**(13), 8736 (2023)
16. R.J. Little, A test of missing completely at random for multivariate data with missing values. J. Am. Stat. Assoc. **83**(404), 1198 (1988)
17. U.A. Marovac, N. Mitić, N-gram analysis of COG categorized protein sequences. Commun. Math. Comput. Chem. **74**, 575 (2015)
18. N. Kovač, K. Ratković, H. Farahani, P. Watson, A practical applications guide to machine learning regression models in psychology with python. Methods Psychol. **11**, 100156 (2024)
19. C. Molnar, *Interpretable Machine Learning* (Leanpub, Victoria, 2019)
20. T. Hastie, R. Tibshirani, Generalized additive models. Stat. Sci. **1**(3), 297 (1990)
21. L. Wilkinson, Statistical methods in psychology journals: guidelines and explanations. Am. Psychol. **54**(8), 594 (1999)
22. A.P. Association, et al., *Publication Manual of the American Psychological Association* (American Psychological Association, Washington, DC, 2020)
23. S. Alsufyani, M. Forshaw, S.J. Fernstad, Visualization of missing data: a state-of-the-art survey (2024). arXiv preprint arXiv:2410.03712
24. S. Van Buuren, *Flexible Imputation of Missing Data*, 2nd edn. (CRC Press, Boca Raton, 2018)
25. F. Pedregosa, G. Varoquaux, A. Gramfort, V. Michel, B. Thirion, O. Grisel, M. Blondel, P. Prettenhofer, R. Weiss, V. Dubourg, et al., Scikit-learn: machine learning in Python. J. Mach. Learn. Res. **12**, 2825 (2011)

26. Z. Ghahramani, An introduction to hidden Markov models and Bayesian networks. Int. J. Pattern Recogn. Artif. Intell. **15**(01), 9 (2001)
27. I.R. White, P. Royston, A.M. Wood, Multiple imputation using chained equations: issues and guidance for practice. Stat. Med. **30**(4), 377 (2011)
28. R.J. Little, D.B. Rubin, *Statistical Analysis with Missing Data*, vol. 793 (Wiley, Hoboken, 2019)
29. M. Syahrizal, S. Aripin, D.P. Utomo, M. Mesran, S. Sarwandi, N.A. Hasibuan, The application of the K-NN imputation method for handling missing values in a dataset, in *AIP Conference Proceedings*, vol. 3048 (AIP Publishing, 2024)
30. D.B. Rubin, *Multiple Imputation for Nonresponse in Surveys*, vol. 81 (Wiley, Hoboken, 2004)
31. S. Jäger, A. Allhorn, F. Bießmann, A benchmark for data imputation methods. Front. Big Data **4**(1), 1 (2021)
32. P.S. Foundation, Scikit-learn documentation. https://scikit-learn.org/ (2023). Accessed: 23 Jan 2023

Confirmatory Factor Analysis

Nataša Kovač, Marija Blagojevič, Kruna Ratković, Peter Watson, Zhiyong Johnny Zhang, and Hojjatollah Farahani

1 Basics of the CFA: Definition, Use, and Key Concepts

Confirmatory Factor Analysis (CFA) is a hypothesis-driven methodology which tests whether the relationships between observed variables and their underlying latent constructs are consistent with what theory anticipates. Rooted in the broader family of structural equation modelling (SEM), CFA allows researchers to evaluate how well a specified factor model fits empirical data, thus providing evidence for construct validity and theoretical robustness [1, 2]. To better situate CFA within the wider methodological landscape, Fig. 1 presents a visual taxonomy of factor analysis techniques and their extensions. This hierarchical diagram illustrates the position of CFA relative to Exploratory Factor Analysis (EFA) and Structural Equation Modelling (SEM), while also highlighting key methodological branches that

N. Kovač (✉) · K. Ratković
Faculty of Applied Sciences, University of Donja Gorica, Podgorica, Montenegro
e-mail: natasa.kovac@udg.edu.me; kruna.ratkovic@udg.edu.me

M. Blagojevič
Faculty of Technical Sciences, University of Kragujevac, Čačak, Serbia
e-mail: marija.blagojevic@uni.kg.ac.rs

P. Watson
MRC Cognition and Brain Sciences Unit, University of Cambridge, Cambridge, England
e-mail: Peter.Watson@mrc-cbu.cam.ac.uk

Z. J. Zhang
Department of Psychology, University of Notre Dame, Notre Dame, IN, USA
e-mail: zhiyongzhang@nd.edu

H. Farahani
Department of Psychology, Faculty of Humanities, Tarbiat Modares University, Tehran, Iran
e-mail: h.farahani@modares.ac.ir

N. Kovač et al. (eds.), *Data Science in Psychology*,
https://doi.org/10.1007/978-3-032-18312-5_9

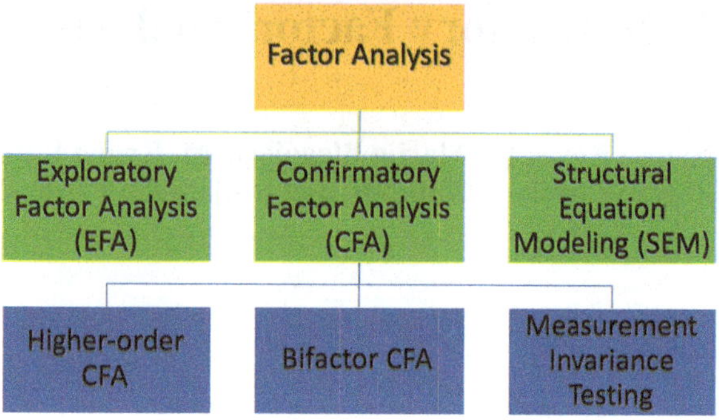

Fig. 1 Taxonomy of factor analysis and its methodological extensions

stem from CFA, such as higher order CFA, bifactor modelling, and measurement invariance testing [3].

CFA is built on the notion that psychological phenomena are not directly observable but can be inferred from patterns of responses to items or indicators. These latent constructs are statistically represented through factors, while individual questionnaire items or behavioural measures are treated as manifest variables. The model posits that one or more latent factors influence each observed variable and contains an element of measurement error [4]. This framework thus allows researchers to not only explore the structure of psychological constructs but also quantify the degree to which observed indicators reflect their intended latent domains [4].

The application of CFA is particularly prevalent in scale development and validation studies, where the goal is to examine whether a proposed factor structure appropriately captures the construct being measured. For example, in developing a measure of emotional intelligence, a researcher may hypothesise that it comprises distinct yet related dimensions such as self-awareness, self-regulation, motivation, empathy, and social skills [5]. CFA provides a formal statistical framework to evaluate whether this multidimensional model aligns with the empirical covariance structure of the data [6].

CFA plays a role in assessing the reliability and coherence of measurement models. CFA allows for estimating the strength of the relationship (factor loading) between each observed variable and its respective latent factor [1]. This enables researchers to identify underperforming items, revise instruments, and build more precise and psychometrically sound measures. CFA accounts for measurement error, improving the reliability of constructs by isolating the true variance associated with each factor [7].

One of the fundamental assumptions underlying CFA is unidimensionality, which posits that a set of items designed to measure a specific factor should load primarily on that factor and not on others. When cross-loadings are constrained to zero, the model can assess whether items are uniquely associated with their designated latent variables. This specificity enhances the interpretability of psychological instruments and ensures that each factor represents a distinct dimension of the broader construct being studied [8].

The logic of CFA is also central to the theory of construct validation proposed by Cronbach and Meehl [9], who emphasised the importance of testing theoretical relationships among constructs rather than relying solely on face validity. Through CFA, researchers can evaluate convergent and discriminant validity. Convergent validity is assessed when items presumed to measure the same construct demonstrate high factor loadings, while discriminant validity is examined by testing whether factors intended to be distinct are indeed statistically separate. This dual assessment strengthens the theoretical coherence of psychological models and reinforces the validity of instruments in empirical research [10]. When those validated constructs are used as predictors, psychology-focused Maximum Likelihood (ML) tutorials provide transparent preprocessing-to-evaluation templates for regression modelling [11].

Another significant strength of CFA lies in its flexibility. Researchers can test simple one-factor models or develop more complex multidimensional structures with correlated or hierarchical latent constructs. For example, in personality psychology, the five-factor model has been extensively evaluated using CFA to test whether items cluster around the domains of openness, conscientiousness, extraversion, agreeableness, and neuroticism. In educational psychology, cognitive ability tests are routinely modelled using CFA to assess general intelligence (g-factor) and domain-specific aptitudes [12].

While the core application of CFA is to evaluate measurement models, it is also applicable in cross-cultural and longitudinal research. Measurement invariance testing is often integrated within the CFA framework because it helps determine whether a construct is perceived and measured equivalently across different populations, time points, or conditions. This capability ensures that group comparisons or pre-post assessments reflect real differences in the latent trait, not measurement error or some kind of bias [13].

One of the most important CFA's technical parameters is the *factor loading*, which indicates the strength and direction of the relationship between an observed variable and its latent factor. Higher loadings suggest a stronger alignment with the construct. Error variances are modelled explicitly, representing measurement error not captured by the latent factor. This structural separation enhances model accuracy and allows for a better understanding of the measurement properties of psychological instruments [1].

Researchers often visualise CFA models using path diagrams (see Fig. 2), where latent factors are typically shown as ovals and observed variables as rectangles, and arrows represent the directional relationships. These diagrams serve as tools in model specification, allowing visualisation of hypothesised relations before estimation. Such visual modelling contributes to transparency, especially when complex hierarchical or bifactor structures are involved [8].

Application of CFA requires thoughtful theoretical grounding and careful methodological considerations. A model with a good statistical fit is not necessarily a theoretically sound one. Theory should guide model specification, and empirical evidence should serve as a means of refining conceptual clarity. This philosophical stance aligns with current trends in psychological methodology, where transparency,

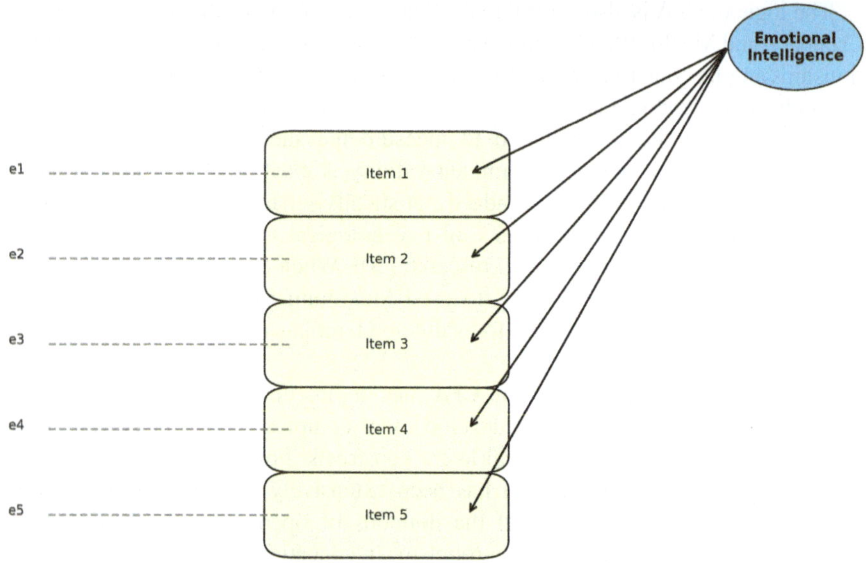

Fig. 2 Standard path diagram of CFA

replicability, and theory-driven analysis are required [14] and are echoed in recent Python-based workflows for reproducible modelling in psychology [11].

2 Technical Aspects: Sample Size, Estimation Methods, and Item Loadings

CFA model estimation methods include ML, which assumes multivariate normality and estimates parameters by maximising the likelihood function, making it the most commonly used approach [15]. Generalised Least Squares (GLS) minimises weighted differences between observed and model-implied covariance matrices, providing efficient estimates under normality. Weighted Least Squares (WLS) is suitable for categorical or non-normally distributed data, often used in large samples [16]. Bayesian estimation incorporates prior distributions and uses Markov Chain Monte Carlo (MCMC) sampling for parameter estimation, making it flexible for complex models [17]. The choice of method depends on data distribution, sample size, and model complexity.

The ML method is the most widely used estimation technique in CFA due to its desirable statistical properties, such as asymptotic efficiency, consistency, and unbiasedness under multivariate normality. The ML estimator works by finding the set of model parameters (factor loadings, variances, covariances, and error terms) that maximise the likelihood function, given the observed data or covariance matrix.

Given a sample covariance matrix **S** and a model-implied covariance matrix $\Sigma(\theta)$ (where θ represents the set of model parameters), ML estimation seeks to minimise the **discrepancy function**:

$$F_{ML} = \log|\Sigma(\theta)| + \mathrm{tr}(\mathbf{S}\Sigma(\theta)^{-1}) - \log|\mathbf{S}| - p, \tag{1}$$

where p is the number of observed variables, $|\Sigma(\theta)|$ and $|\mathbf{S}|$ denote the determinants of the model-implied and sample covariance matrices, respectively, and $\mathrm{tr}(\cdot)$ represents the trace operator. If raw data are provided, the sample covariance matrix can be calculated. The minimisation of F_{ML} ensures that the model-implied covariance structure best fits the observed data, which leads to the ML estimation of the model parameters.

ML estimation in CFA relies on several key assumptions. First, the observed variables should follow a multivariate normal distribution. Violation of this assumption can lead to biased standard errors and incorrect model fit assessments. Second, ML estimation is asymptotically efficient, meaning it performs well in large samples (typically $n > 200$). Small sample sizes may lead to convergence issues or inaccurate parameter estimates [18]. Third, it assumes the model is correctly specified, and if the factor model is incorrectly specified, ML estimates may be biased or misleading [19].

When the assumptions hold, the ML estimation provides statistically efficient and consistent parameter estimates, allows for hypothesis testing through likelihood ratio tests and χ^2 goodness-of-fit tests, and can easily extend to full-information ML (FIML) for handling missing data directly. ML is sensitive to violations of multivariate normality. In such cases, robust ML estimators (e.g. Satorra-Bentler correction) or alternative methods like WLS are recommended.

WLS is an alternative estimation method for CFA, particularly useful when data deviate from the assumption of multivariate normality. The WLS estimator minimises the following discrepancy function:

$$F_{WLS} = (\mathbf{s} - \boldsymbol{\sigma}(\theta))'\mathbf{W}(\mathbf{s} - \boldsymbol{\sigma}(\theta)), \tag{2}$$

where **s** is the vectorised sample covariance matrix (which can also be polychoric/tetrachoric correlation matrix for categorical data), $\sigma(\theta)$ is the vectorised model-implied covariance matrix, and **W** is a *weighting matrix*, often the inverse of the asymptotic covariance matrix of **s**, ensuring that parameter estimates are efficient.

The choice of W is critical, and it determines the specific variant of WLS used. For example, in the Full Weighted Least Squares (Full WLS), the full asymptotic covariance matrix of the sample covariance structure is used as W. In the Diagonally Weighted Least Squares (DWLS), only the *diagonal* elements of the asymptotic covariance matrix as weights are used.

Unlike ML, which assumes multivariate normality, WLS provides valid estimates even when this assumption is violated. It is particularly useful for Likert-scale responses and binary data. WLS requires larger sample sizes than ML to ensure stability and accuracy of estimation.

3 Model Development and Validation: Modifications, Fit Assessment, and Validity

CFA serves as a cornerstone of psychometric validation, intertwining theoretical and empirical processes to ensure the measurement instruments accurately represent psychological constructs [1]. The process of model development and validation in CFA extends far beyond the initial specification, embracing iterative cycles of hypothesis testing, modification, and rigorous fit assessments to align closely with theoretical expectations and empirical realities.

The initial phase in CFA is explicit model specification, which is guided fundamentally by theory [4]. This phase involves the precise delineation of latent constructs and their corresponding indicators. During model specification, researchers explicitly define the hypothesised factor structure, specifying which items load onto which latent factors, based on existing theoretical frameworks. At this stage, latent constructs and their observed variables must be carefully chosen to ensure conceptual clarity and empirical viability [10]. Misspecification at this stage can lead to significant interpretation problems in later analysis stages, emphasising the necessity of robust theoretical grounding and careful selection of measurement items [20].

Once the initial model is specified and estimated, it is evaluated through model fit indices, which quantify the adequacy of the theoretical assumptions. Absolute fit indices, such as the χ^2 statistic and Root Mean Square Error of Approximation (RMSEA), directly gauge how well the hypothesised model reproduces observed covariance matrices. χ^2 statistics are notably sensitive to sample size, often indicating significant misfit even in practically acceptable models [21]. Consequently, researchers frequently rely on alternative indices such as RMSEA, where values below 0.08 indicate acceptable fit and values below 0.05 represent excellent fit [22, 23]. Incremental fit indices, including the Comparative Fit Index (CFI) and Tucker-Lewis Index (TLI), further complement the evaluation by comparing the hypothesised model to a baseline independence model, with CFI and TLI values exceeding 0.90 indicating acceptable fit and values over 0.95 denoting excellent model adequacy [24].

Practically, initial CFA models rarely achieve optimal fit without iterative modifications. Modification indices (MIs), which suggest potential improvements in model fit if specific parameters are relaxed, provide valuable guidance for model refinement [8]. Typical modifications include permitting cross-loadings or introducing correlated residuals between items that theoretically share specific sources of variance [6]. Importantly, modifications should always be theoretically justifiable to prevent models from becoming empirically driven rather than theory-based. MacCallum et al. [25] caution explicitly against *capitalising on chance*, a practice of arbitrarily relaxing constraints based purely on statistical indices rather than theoretical justification.

Another important aspect of CFA validation is assessing reliability and item quality through factor loadings and residual analysis [26]. Standardised factor loadings ideally should exceed 0.70 to indicate strong convergent validity; signifying a substantial proportion of item variance is accounted for by the factor [27]. Conversely, items with consistently low loadings across iterations should be reviewed critically or possibly removed to enhance the precision and theoretical integrity of the measurement model [28].

Beyond statistical fit, CFA inherently involves comprehensive validity assessments that encompass convergent, discriminant, and criterion-related validity [10]. Convergent validity evaluates whether observed variables truly reflect their respective latent constructs, typically confirmed through high standardised loadings and average variance extracted (AVE) exceeding 0.50. Discriminant validity assesses whether latent constructs represent distinct theoretical entities, evidenced by AVE values surpassing squared inter-factor correlations [29, 30]. Criterion-related validity further extends the evaluation by examining the association between latent factors and external variables theoretically anticipated to correlate with these constructs. This process often involves integrating CFA within Structural Equation Modelling frameworks to examine predictive pathways to external criteria, strengthening the interpretative value and practical utility of latent constructs [4, 6].

Advanced validation practices, such as cross-validation and factorial invariance, offer additional robustness checks that ensure the generalisability and consistency of the measurement models across different samples and contexts [31]. Cross-validation methods, including split-sample techniques and independent replication studies, help establish the external validity of the model, demonstrating that measurement structures remain stable beyond the initial sample [32], mirroring best-practice ML workflows [33]. Factorial invariance testing ensures that constructs maintain consistent measurement properties across different groups or longitudinal studies. Sequential invariance testing, progressing from configural to metric, scalar, and strict invariance, provides robust evidence of measurement consistency and supports meaningful group comparisons and longitudinal research [34].

The role of theoretical guidance throughout model validation cannot be overstated. Each iteration, modification, and assessment must remain theoretically coherent to ensure the empirical representations align accurately with the underlying psychological constructs. This theory-driven approach mitigates the risk of overfitting and enhances both the scientific rigour and interpretive clarity of the final measurement models [14].

The iterative cycle of CFA model development and validation, which includes theoretical specification, empirical refinement, rigorous fit assessment, and validity evaluations, ensures that psychological constructs are represented with accuracy, reliability, and validity. Through a careful blend of theory and empirical evidence, CFA provides psychologists with a powerful methodological tool capable of addressing complex measurement challenges inherent in psychological research.

4 Advanced Applications: Higher Order CFA and Factorial Invariance

Higher order CFA is an extension of standard CFA used to model hierarchical structures where latent variables are influenced by more abstract, higher order latent constructs. It is particularly useful in psychology, social sciences, and educational measurement when constructs are assumed to have multiple dimensions that can be grouped under broader conceptual categories.

In a standard CFA model, observed variables $X_{ij}, i = 1, \ldots, n, j = 1, \ldots, p$, are modelled as being influenced by a set of q first-order latent factors $F_k, k = 1, \ldots, q$:

$$X_{ij} = \sum_{k=1}^{q} \lambda_{jk} F_{ik} + \epsilon_{ij}, \tag{3}$$

where X_{ij} is the observed data for participant i on the observed variable j, λ_{ij} is the factor loading of the j-th observed variable on the k-th latent factor, F_{ik} is the factor score for participant i on the k-th latent factor, and ϵ_{ij} is the error term or uniqueness factor score.

In higher order CFA, these first-order latent factors F_{ik} represented by Eq. 4 are themselves influenced by a set of higher order latent factors $H_l, l = 1, \ldots, r$, such that

$$F_{ik} = \sum_{l=1}^{r} \gamma_{kl} H_{il} + \delta_{ik}, \tag{4}$$

where H_{il} is the higher order latent factor score for participant i, γ_{kl} is the factor loading of the k-th first-order factor on the l-th higher order factor, and δ_{ik} is the unique term for the k-th first-order factor.

Thus, the higher order model captures the covariance among first-order factors through the presence of an overarching higher order latent construct. Estimation of higher order CFA models typically follows standard CFA estimation techniques discussed above. Higher order CFA is commonly used in psychological research, e.g. general intelligence influencing multiple cognitive abilities, and educational assessment, e.g. overall academic ability, influences subdomains like math, reading, and science. It can provide a more parsimonious representation of complex constructs and help in understanding hierarchical relationships among latent constructs.

Factorial invariance, also known as measurement invariance, is a fundamental concept in CFA that assesses whether the same latent construct is measured equivalently across different groups or over time. Establishing factorial invariance ensures that observed differences in factor scores reflect true differences in the latent construct rather than variations in measurement properties. This is particularly important in psychological and social sciences, where constructs such as intelligence, personality, and attitudes must be measured consistently across diverse populations (e.g. cultures, genders, and age groups). Without factorial invariance, group comparisons may be biased, leading to inaccurate conclusions.

Factorial invariance is tested by fitting a series of nested CFA models and comparing their fit. Typically, a multi-group CFA approach is used hierarchically, progressing from less restrictive to more restrictive models. Different types of factorial invariance have been defined in the literature. Configural invariance is the least restrictive form, requiring that the same factor structure (i.e. the same number of factors and pattern of factor loadings) holds across groups. The metric or weak invariance requires that factor loadings are equal across groups, ensuring that the latent construct has the same meaning across groups. The scalar or *strong invariance* requires that item intercepts are also equal across groups, in addition to equal factor loadings. Strict invariance further requires that residual variances (measurement errors) are equal across groups. This ensures that the reliability of measurement is consistent across groups. By systematically testing configural, metric, scalar, and strict invariance, researchers can confirm that observed differences in latent variables reflect true differences rather than measurement artefacts.

Factorial invariance testing can be summarised by the following steps:

Step 1: *Configural invariance*—estimate a multi-group CFA model without constraining any parameters across groups. If the model fits well, proceed to metric invariance.

Step 2: *Metric invariance (weak invariance)*—In the multi-group CFA model, constrain factor loadings to be equal across groups. Compare model fit to the configural invariance model using fit indices (e.g. ΔCFI < 0.01, ΔRMSEA < 0.015) or a χ^2 difference test. If metric invariance holds, latent factor scores can be meaningfully compared in terms of relative standing within each group.

Step 3: *Scalar invariance (strong Invariance)*—constrain both factor loadings and item intercepts to be equal across groups. Compare the model fit to the metric invariance model. If scalar invariance holds, latent means can be meaningfully compared across groups.

Step 4: *Residual invariance (strict invariance)*—constrain item residual variances to be equal across groups.

5 Latent vs. Observed Variables

One of the central concepts in Confirmatory Factor Analysis (CFA) is the distinction between *latent* and *observed variables*, which provides the foundation for modelling theoretical constructs and their empirical manifestations. Latent variables, also referred to as hidden or unobserved factors, represent abstract traits or concepts that cannot be measured directly. Instead, they are inferred from a set of observed variables. For instance, in psychological research, a latent construct such as *stress* cannot be directly quantified, but its influence can be observed through indicators such as *anxiety levels* or *physical health* outcomes [35]. CFA enables researchers to evaluate how such latent variables explain variation in observed measures, thereby testing theoretical expectations and providing a structured account of abstract phenomena.

Defining latent variables involves operationalising constructs that capture complex, multidimensional aspects of behaviour, cognition, or social interaction. These constructs may include traits, attitudes, or skills, and CFA is particularly powerful in modelling their effects on observed outcomes. By linking latent factors with observed indicators, researchers gain insight into the underlying processes that drive measurable behaviour and can test hypotheses regarding their causal relationships.

In contrast, *observed variables* are the directly measured data collected through instruments such as surveys, tests, interviews, or physiological assessments. Within CFA, they function as indicators of latent constructs. For example, intelligence tests provide observed scores that act as indicators for the latent factor of *intelligence*. The statistical relationship between latent and observed variables is typically modelled through regression, whereby shared variance among observed indicators is attributed to the underlying latent factor [1]. Observed variables thus serve as the empirical basis for testing theoretical constructs, while also allowing for the identification of measurement error.

CFA models assume that each observed variable reflects one or more latent variables, in addition to unique variance associated with measurement error. Sources of error may include inconsistencies in data collection, participant biases, or limitations of the instruments themselves. By explicitly modelling these errors, CFA improves the reliability and validity of conclusions. Furthermore, the technique enables researchers to evaluate model fit using indicators such as the χ^2 statistic, CFI, or RMSEA, ensuring that the data support theoretical assumptions.

Despite its strengths, latent variable modelling presents challenges. Accurate specification of constructs and their indicators is critical; misspecification can lead to biased estimates and misleading conclusions. Multicollinearity among observed variables may also complicate estimation by obscuring the unique contributions of latent factors. These limitations underscore the need for careful variable selection and rigorous evaluation of model assumptions.

The distinction between latent and observed variables is thus essential for applying CFA in psychological and social sciences research. Latent variables provide a framework for representing abstract constructs such as intelligence, personality traits, or motivation, while observed variables supply the measurable data needed for empirical testing. By modelling their interplay, CFA facilitates theory-driven analysis, accounts for measurement error, and yields deeper insights into complex psychological and social processes. When carefully specified and validated, CFA represents a robust methodological tool for advancing research across disciplines.

6 Evaluating and Comparing Factor Structures

In CFA, the evaluation of the factor structure focuses on determining how well the hypothesised model represents the observed data and whether the associations between observed indicators and latent factors align with theoretical assumptions. This process entails examining model fit indices, factor loadings, residuals, and modification indices, as well as assessing the convergent and discriminant validity of the constructs.

To assess whether the overall model adequately reproduces the observed covariance or correlation matrix, we can use various fit statistics and fit indices. First, the χ^2 test can be used to evaluate the overall fit of the hypothesised model to the observed data. The χ^2 test statistic based on maximum likelihood estimation is typically computed as

$$\chi^2 = (N - 1) \cdot F_{\mathrm{ML}}, \tag{5}$$

where N is the sample size, and F_{ML} is the discrepancy function under Maximum Likelihood estimation. The χ^2 statistic follows a χ^2 distribution with degrees of freedom $df = \frac{p(p+1)}{2} - q$, where p is the number of observed variables and q is the number of estimated parameters. A non-significant χ^2 statistic (i.e. $p > 0.05$) indicates a good model fit, and a significant result (i.e. $p < 0.05$) suggests that the model does not adequately fit the data. The χ^2 test is sensitive to sample size, and large samples can lead to significant results even for trivial model misfit [36]. In contrast, small samples may not provide enough power to detect significant misfit. Therefore, it is important to interpret the χ^2 test in conjunction with other fit indices and consider the practical significance of the results rather than relying solely on statistical significance. The commonly used fit indices include the RMSEA, the CFI, the TLI, and the Standardised Root Mean Square Residual (SRMR). For CFI, values >0.90 indicate acceptable fit and >0.95 indicate good fit [37]. For TLI, values >0.90 are acceptable and >0.95 are good. For RMSEA, values <0.08 indicate acceptable fit and <0.05 indicate good fit. For SRMR, values <0.08 are acceptable and <0.05 are good.

In CFA, factor loadings represent the strength of the relationship between observed indicators and their corresponding latent constructs. Evaluating individual factor loadings is useful for assessing the quality and validity of the factor structure. The standardised factor loadings can be interpreted as the correlation between the observed variable and the latent factor. High factor loadings suggest that the observed variable is a good indicator of the latent construct, while low factor loadings may indicate that the observed variable does not adequately represent the latent construct. Generally speaking, standardised loadings should typically be at least 0.30. A value greater than 0.7 is considered strong loading, while a value between 0.3 and 0.7 is considered moderate loading. Values below 0.3 are considered weak loadings and may indicate that the item should be removed or revised. In addition, the significance of a loading can usually be tested using a z-statistic. Ideally, each indicator should load significantly on only one factor, indicating a simple factor structure. Large cross-loadings suggest poor discriminant validity and may warrant model modification.

When a model does not fit the data well, researchers may consider modifying the model to improve fit. Model modification provides a systematic way to improve model fit when the initial model does not adequately fit the data, while ensuring changes remain theoretically justified. A common approach involves examining MIs, which estimate how much the model χ^2 would decrease if a fixed parameter were freely estimated. High MIs may indicate useful modifications, such as adding correlated error terms or cross-loadings. Another diagnostic is standardised residuals, which highlight discrepancies between observed and model-implied covariances; large residuals suggest areas needing refinement. Based on these diagnostics, researchers may add or remove parameters such as factor loadings or covariances. All modifications should be guided by theory to avoid overfitting. An iterative approach is typically used, with model fit evaluated after each change using fit indices like RMSEA, CFI, TLI, and SRMR. Finally, to ensure the modified model generalises well, validation on an independent dataset or through split-sample cross-validation is recommended.

For non-nested models, the χ^2 difference test is not appropriate, as the models do not have a hierarchical relationship. In such cases, one common approach is to use information criteria, such as the Akaike Information Criterion (AIC) or the Bayesian Information Criterion (BIC). These criteria provide a measure of model fit while penalising for model complexity. A lower AIC or BIC value indicates a better-fitting model. BIC is more stringent than AIC in penalising model complexity and is often favoured in large-sample contexts.

7 Bifactor CFA

The bifactor model within CFA represents an advanced approach to modelling complex structural relationships between latent variables and observed indicators. This model is particularly useful when researchers aim to analyse situations where a variable or scale can be considered the result of multiple latent factors acting simultaneously, but not entirely independently. The bifactor CFA model allows for the analysis and understanding of how specific factors and a common factor influence the manifestations that are measured through observed variables. Given its versatility, the bifactor model is applied across various disciplines, especially in psychometrics, educational research, and psychological studies [38]. Through a deeper understanding of the relationships between variables, the bifactor CFA enables better interpretation and validation of theories in complex research settings.

The bifactor model in CFA is based on two types of latent factors: the general factor and specific factors. Each observed variable in this model is connected to both types of factors. The general factor, often referred to as the *g-factor*, explains the shared variation among all indicators and is considered the core factor present in all observations. On the other hand, specific factors (also known as *s-factors*) account for additional variation in each indicator that is not explained by the general factor. These specific factors represent variations unique to certain dimensions or subscales, while the general factor encompasses all common variations.

The bifactor model allows researchers to distinguish between variations that appear across all indicators and those that occur only in specific indicators [39]. For example, in a model used to analyse different dimensions of personality, the general factor might encompass the overall personality factor, while the specific factors might capture traits such as openness to experience, emotional stability, or social engagement. By using the bifactor model, researchers can separate the factors influencing all indicators from those that influence only specific variables, allowing for more precise data analysis and interpretation.

One of the primary advantages of the bifactor model is its ability to clarify and accurately model the relationships between the general factor and specific factors in situations where there is evident overlap between them. In many cases, factors used in traditional factor analyses may be overly correlated, which complicates the interpretation of their contributions. By using the bifactor model, researchers can more clearly differentiate between the common variations that affect all indicators and those that are unique to certain variables.

The bifactor model also provides a better understanding of the relationships between the general and specific factors, enabling a more detailed examination of different components within the model. This becomes particularly significant in studies dealing with complex and multidimensional constructs, such as personality traits, academic achievement, and even mental health. Traditional models may struggle to precisely separate the general variation common to all indicators from the specific variations present in certain subscales. The bifactor model provides a way to clearly distinguish these variations, thus improving the validity and accuracy of the results.

The bifactor model helps in better interpretation and validation in situations where factors are not entirely independent. In standard models with correlations between factors, confusion may arise regarding the specific influences of each factor, as their variations overlap. By adopting the bifactor approach, researchers can clearly distinguish the role of the general factor while simultaneously considering the specific influences of each factor on the observed variables.

The bifactor model is used across a wide range of research fields, from psychometric testing to educational studies and health assessments. For example, in educational research, the bifactor model can be useful for analysing how different academic skills, such as reading, writing, and mathematical abilities, contribute to overall academic achievement, while also considering the specific variations associated with each of these skills. By using the bifactor model in educational tests, researchers can better understand how various aspects of academic abilities combine to form a general level of achievement, while simultaneously clarifying which specific skills are most significant for particular academic outcomes.

In psychological research, the bifactor model can be used to understand how different personality traits (such as extraversion, neuroticism, and openness to experience) contribute to the overall personality, as well as how specific dimensions of these traits influence behaviour or emotional responses in individuals. The model can also be useful in studies examining various aspects of mental health, such as depression, anxiety, or stress, as it enables an analysis of how general factors influence these components while accounting for specific variations in symptoms.

The bifactor model is particularly useful in psychometric tests where it is crucial to clarify the relationships between general and specific factors. For instance, in intelligence tests, the general factor may encompass overall problem-solving ability, while specific factors might include verbal, numerical, or visual reasoning abilities. By using the bifactor model, researchers can precisely determine which abilities contribute to the general factor while accurately identifying the specific abilities that affect the overall score.

As with all CFA models, assessing the bifactor model requires careful testing through various goodness-of-fit indices [40]. The most commonly used indices in evaluating CFA models include the χ^2 test, which examines the overall fit of the model to the data, and indices such as RMSEA (Root Mean Square Error of Approximation), CFI (Comparative Fit Index), and TLI (Tucker-Lewis Index), which help assess the accuracy and quality of the model. Using these indices allows researchers to ensure that the model accurately reflects the data structure and aligns well with theoretical assumptions.

In addition to basic goodness-of-fit tests, the assessment of the bifactor model also involves analysing the specific relationships between the general and specific factors. It is important to evaluate whether the specific factors are significantly different from the general factor, as excessive correlation may indicate a problem with the model that may reduce its precision and validity. Analysing residuals and measurement errors can also uncover potential issues in the model, such as imperfections in data collection or inaccuracies in measurement instruments.

For the validation of the bifactor model, researchers often use methods such as cross-validation, which allows for testing the stability and generalisability of the model on an independent dataset. This can help assess the robustness of the model and determine whether the results remain consistent across different datasets.

Bifactor CFA represents a powerful tool for researchers who want to model complex relationships between general and specific latent variables. This model enables a more detailed and accurate analysis of structural relationships between variables, which is of great significance in psychological, educational, and other social science research. Although it requires careful selection of the number of factors and rigorous model testing, bifactor CFA offers a wealth of information that can aid in better understanding data and theoretical constructs.

The bifactor model is particularly useful in situations where researchers want to clarify the relationships between general and specific factors, especially when factor overlap complicates data interpretation. As such, bifactor CFA provides researchers with the opportunity to more accurately assess complex relationships between latent variables and gain deeper insights into the nature of the data.

8 Applications and Case Studies

CFA is widely used in various fields to test the validity of latent constructs and ensure measurement reliability. In psychology, CFA is frequently applied to validate psychological constructs such as intelligence, personality traits, and mental health conditions. For example, the Big Five Personality Traits (Openness, Conscientiousness, Extraversion, Agreeableness, and Neuroticism) are often assessed using CFA to confirm that questionnaire items load onto their respective factors. CFA has also been used to validate depression or anxiety scales like the Beck Depression Inventory (BDI).

In education, CFA is employed to assess the validity of educational assessments and testing instruments. For instance, the SAT or GRE can be evaluated using CFA to ensure that the test items accurately measure verbal and quantitative reasoning. In student engagement research, CFA has been used to verify whether survey questions measure dimensions such as behavioural, emotional, and cognitive engagement.

In marketing, CFA is applied to validate constructs related to consumer behaviour, brand loyalty, and customer satisfaction. For example, a company may use CFA to confirm that items in a customer satisfaction survey accurately represent dimensions like service quality and product reliability.

In health and medical research, CFA is used to validate health-related quality of life (HRQoL) measures and clinical scales. For instance, the SF-36 health survey can be evaluated using CFA to confirm that its dimensions (e.g. physical functioning and mental health) are distinct yet related constructs. Validated psychometric constructs are also used as inputs to modern predictive pipelines in health psychology. For instance, ML models have used PTSD, alexithymia, anxiety, depression, and related scales to predict chronic pain severity [41].

In organisational research, CFA is used to assess constructs such as leadership styles, employee engagement, and organisational commitment. For example, the Multifactor Leadership Questionnaire (MLQ) can be validated using CFA to ensure that different leadership styles (e.g. transformational and transactional) are accurately represented.

Table 1 Description of test scores

Variable	Description
visual	Scores on visual perception test, test 1
cubes	Scores on cubes test, test 2
paper	Scores on paper form board test, test 3
lozenge	Scores on lozenges test, test 4
general	Scores on general information test, test 5
paragrap	Scores on paragraph comprehension test, test 6
sentence	Scores on sentence completion test, test 7
wordc	Scores on word classification test, test 8
wordm	Scores on word meaning test, test 9
add	Scores on add test, test 10
code	Scores on code test, test 11
counting	Scores on counting groups of dots test, test 12
straight	Scores on straight and curved capitals test, test 13
wordr	Scores on word recognition test, test 14
numberr	Scores on number recognition test, test 15
figurer	Scores on figure recognition test, test 16
object	Scores on object-number test, test 17
numberf	Scores on number-figure test, test 18
figurew	Scores on figure-word test, test 19

CFA is a powerful statistical tool with broad applications across psychology, education, marketing, healthcare, and business. It ensures that measurement instruments are valid, reliable, and applicable across different populations and research settings. PsAIchology frames these validated constructs as inputs to predictive ML models, comparing algorithms under cross-validated settings [42].

We illustrate how to conduct confirmatory factor analysis using the data from the classic 1939 study by Karl J. Holzinger and Frances Swineford [43]. In the study, 26 tests intended to measure a general factor and five specific factors were administered to seventh and eighth grade students in two schools, the Grant-White School ($n = 145$) and Pasteur School ($n = 156$). Data used in this example include 19 tests intended to measure four domains: spatial ability, verbal ability, speed, and memory. In addition, only data from the 145 students in the Grant-White School are used. The 19 tests used in the example are described in Table 1.

The path diagram for the model is given in Fig. 3. Note that there are four factors in the model: verbal, spatial, reasoning, and speed. And the indicators of each factor are also known.

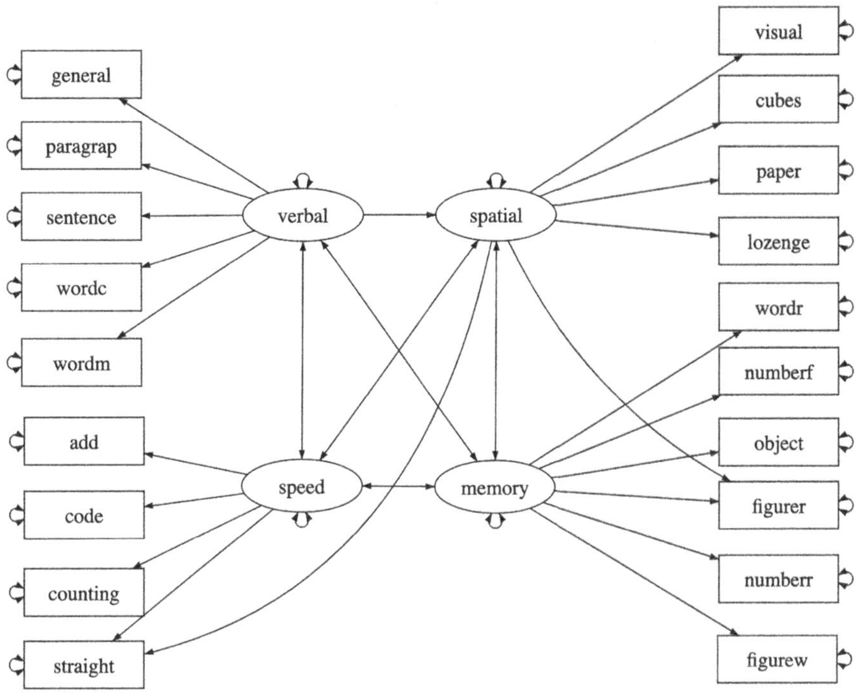

Fig. 3 Confirmatory factor analysis model

To estimate a confirmatory factor model, the Python package `semopy` can be used. A confirmatory factor model cannot be identified without proper constraints, that is, by fixing some parameters to be known values in the model. The reason is that factors are unmeasured and thus have no scales. To identify a model, the factors have to be given specific scales. There are two ways to do this. First, we can fix the variance of a factor to be 1. This is to standardise the factor. Second, we can fix the loading of one observed variable or indicator to be 1. This is essentially to make the factor have the same scale as the observed variables. Fixing a factor loading or a factor variance is the minimum requirement to identify a factor model.

To use `semopy`, we need to first specify the factor model. A factor model takes the format $factor =\sim y1 + y2 + y3$. Note that we use the symbol $=\sim$ to define a factor. The factor is on the left of the symbol, and the indicators are on the right of it. The covariance is specified using $\sim\sim$. The Python code for the example is given below:

```
import pandas as pd
import semopy as sem

Pasteur = pd.read_csv('https://advstats.psychstat.org/data/Pas
↪ teur.csv')
Pasteur.head()

# Define the factor model
cfa_model = '''
spatial =~ visual+cubes+paper+lozenge+straight+figurer
verbal =~ general+paragrap+sentence+wordc+wordm
speed =~ add+code+counting+straight
memory =~ wordr+numberr+figurer+object+numberf+figurew
spatial ~~ verbal + speed + memory
verbal ~~ speed + memory
speed ~~ memory
'''

# Create the SEM model
model = sem.Model(cfa_model)

# Fit the model to the data
model.fit(Pasteur)

# Get parameter estimates and model fit statistics
params = model.inspect()
print(params)

# Check model fit
fit_stats = sem.calc_stats(model)
print(fit_stats.T)
```

The parameter estimates and model fit statistics are printed. The output includes the estimated factor loadings, variances, and covariances, as well as fit indices such as χ^2, RMSEA, and CFI. The χ^2 statistic is 243.78 with the degrees of freedom 144 and a p-value close to 0. Therefore, one would reject the hypothesis that the model fits the data simply based on it. CFI is 0.899, which is smaller than the cut-off value of 0.95. It also suggests a bad fit. The RMSEA = 0.067, which lies within the range of a reasonable fit model.

```
lval   op    rval       Estimate  Std.Err   z-value  p-value
0      ~     spatial      1.00      -         -        -
1      ~     spatial      0.40     0.09      4.52     0.00
2      ~     spatial      0.23     0.05      4.57     0.00
3      ~     spatial      1.08     0.18      6.01     0.00
4      ~     spatial      1.64     0.56      2.90     0.00
5      ~     speed        1.13     0.23      4.89     0.00
```

```
6     ~    spatial     0.53     0.14     3.82    0.00
7     ~    memory      0.48     0.11     4.53    0.00
8     ~    verbal      1.00     -        -       -
9     ~    verbal      0.28     0.02    11.89    0.00
10    ~    verbal      0.46     0.03    13.36    0.00
11    ~    verbal      0.39     0.04    10.21    0.00
12    ~    verbal      0.59     0.05    12.64    0.00
13    ~    speed       1.00     -        -       -
14    ~    speed       0.74     0.12     6.22    0.00
15    ~    speed       0.70     0.13     5.30    0.00
16    ~    memory      1.00     -        -       -
17    ~    memory      0.54     0.11     5.06    0.00
18    ~    memory      0.38     0.07     5.38    0.00
19    ~    memory      0.28     0.06     4.66    0.00
20    ~    memory      0.24     0.05     4.44    0.00
21    ~~   verbal     22.27     5.82     3.82    0.00
22    ~~   speed      26.91    10.15     2.65    0.01
23    ~~   memory     10.88     5.05     2.15    0.03
24    ~~   spatial    29.30     6.45     4.54    0.00
25    ~~   speed      71.24    18.18     3.92    0.00
26    ~~   memory     11.75     7.83     1.50    0.13
27    ~~   verbal     97.29    15.46     6.29    0.00
28    ~~   memory     49.32    15.72     3.14    0.00
29    ~~   speed     236.68    64.67     3.66    0.00
30    ~~   memory     61.50    16.02     3.84    0.00
31    ~~   add       399.09    55.54     7.19    0.00
32    ~~   code       88.81    18.42     4.82    0.00
33    ~~   counting  258.41    34.01     7.60    0.00
34    ~~   cubes      19.50     2.40     8.14    0.00
35    ~~   figurer    40.98     5.65     7.25    0.00
36    ~~   figurew    14.02     1.75     7.99    0.00
37    ~~   general    41.61     6.01     6.93    0.00
38    ~~   lozenge    52.87     7.76     6.81    0.00
39    ~~   numberf    15.56     1.98     7.86    0.00
40    ~~   numberr    43.52     5.79     7.52    0.00
41    ~~   object     16.61     2.33     7.12    0.00
42    ~~   paper       6.49     0.80     8.12    0.00
43    ~~   paragrap    4.18     0.57     7.32    0.00
44    ~~   sentence    6.63     1.06     6.25    0.00
45    ~~   straight  667.01    90.48     7.37    0.00
46    ~~   visual     21.32     4.52     4.72    0.00
47    ~~   wordc      13.24     1.67     7.94    0.00
48    ~~   wordm      14.16     2.06     6.87    0.00
49    ~~   wordr      81.98    12.85     6.38    0.00

Model Fit Summary:
DoF               144.00
DoF Baseline      171.00
Chi$^2$              243.79
Chi$^2$ p-value        0.00
Chi$^2$ Baseline  1158.45
CFI                  0.90
GFI                  0.79
AGFI                 0.75
```

```
NFI              0.79
TLI              0.88
RMSEA            0.07
AIC             88.87
BIC            229.17
LogLik           1.56
```

9 Visualising CFA Results

Visualising CFA results can help interpret relationships between observed variables and latent constructs. In a path diagram, observed and latent variables, along with their relationships, are represented graphically. Specifically, a path diagram consists of two types of graphical components: variables and arrows.

Three types of variables are allowed in a SEM path diagram: observed, latent, and constant variables. A rectangle or square is used to represent an observed variable, and an ellipse or oval is used to denote a latent variable. Optionally, a triangle can be used to indicate a constant of 1.

Two types of arrows, a directed one and an undirected one, are allowed to define the relationship of the variables in a diagram. A directed arrow, represented by a one-way arrow, is used to indicate that one variable can predict another variable. It typically means a regression relationship. A directed arrow points from the predicting variable towards the outcome variable. A directed arrow from an ellipse (a latent variable) to a rectangle (an observed variable) represents a factor loading; otherwise, it indicates a regression coefficient.

An undirected arrow is represented by a two-way arrow. If an undirected arrow connects two variables, it is the covariance between the two variables. But if an undirected arrow starts from one variable and ends on the same variable, it represents a variance or a residual variance. Both shapes and arrows can be labelled. The label of a variable is the name of the variable, and the label of an arrow is the value of the parameter.

Figure 3 shows such a path diagram. After the CFA, the path diagram can be generated with the estimated parameters. Continuing the example from the previous section, we can visualise the CFA results using the `sem.semplot` function. The following code generates a path diagram of the CFA model with the estimated parameters.

```
    sem.semplot(model, 'cfa.svg',
...                  plot_covs=True,
...                  plot_ests=True)
```

In the code above, the `sem.semplot` function generates a path diagram of the CFA model and saves it as an SVG file named `cfa.svg`. The `plot_covs` argument is set to `True`, which means that the covariance between the observed

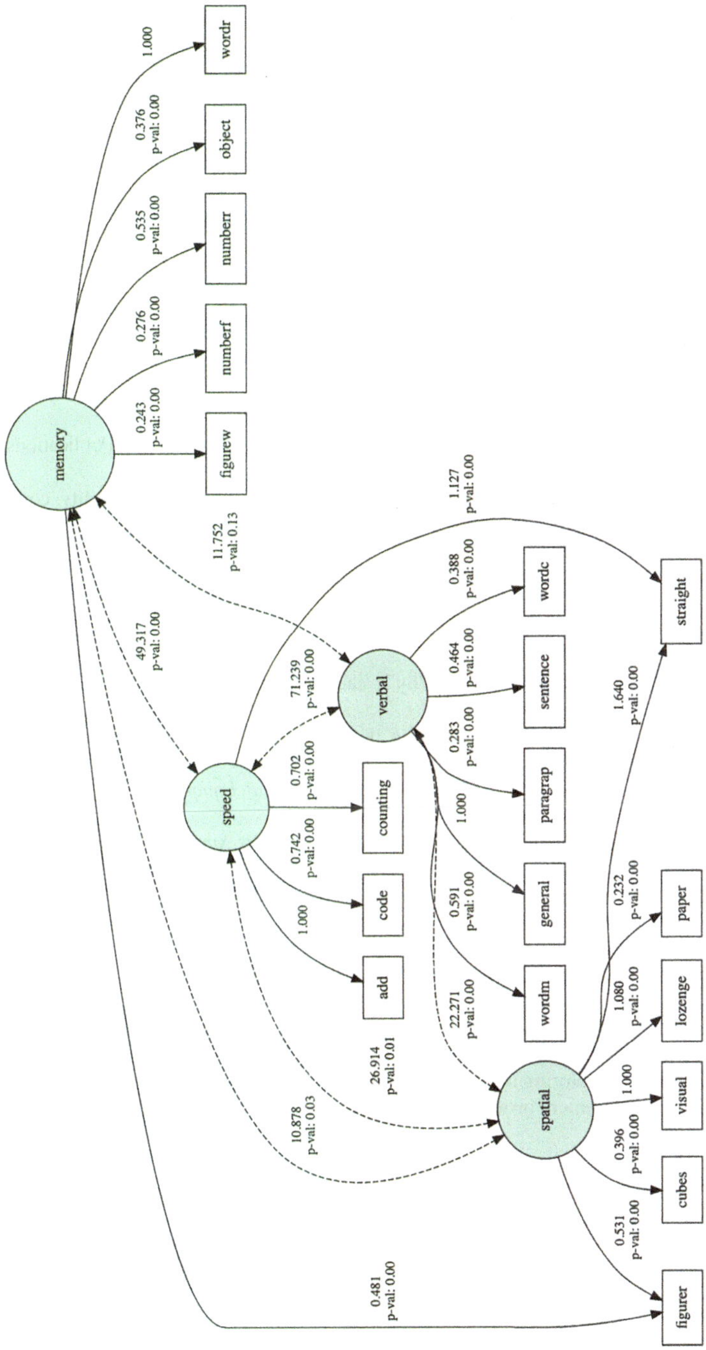

Fig. 4 Path diagram with the estimated parameters

variables will be plotted. The `plot_ests` argument is also set to `True`, which means that the estimated parameters will be plotted.

The resulting path diagram is shown in Fig. 4. The observed variables are represented by rectangles, and the latent factors are represented by ellipses. The directed arrows represent the factor loadings. The estimated parameters are shown next to the arrows. The undirected arrows represent the covariance between the observed variables. In addition, the p-value of each parameter is shown below the estimated parameter. If the p-value is less than 0.05, the parameter is considered statistically significant. Note that some of the factor loadings are fixed at 1, and therefore, no associated p-value is shown.

References

1. T.A. Brown, *Confirmatory Factor Analysis for Applied Research* (Guilford Publications, New York, 2015)
2. G.W. Cheung, H.D. Cooper-Thomas, R.S. Lau, L.C. Wang, Reporting reliability, convergent and discriminant validity with structural equation modeling: a review and best-practice recommendations. Asia Pac. J. Manag. **41**(2), 745 (2024)
3. A. Gegenfurtner, Bifactor exploratory structural equation modeling: a meta-analytic review of model fit. Front. Psychol. **13**, 1037111 (2022)
4. R.B. Kline, *Principles and Practice of Structural Equation Modeling* (Guilford Publications, New York, 2023)
5. D. Goleman, Emotional intelligence. Why it can matter more than IQ. Learning **24**(6), 49 (1996)
6. B.M. Byrne, *Structural Equation modeling With Mplus: Basic Concepts, Applications, and Programming* (Routledge, England, 2013)
7. T. Raykov, G.A. Marcoulides, *A First Course in Structural Equation Modeling* (Routledge, England, 2012)
8. T.A. Whittaker, R.E. Schumacker, *A Beginner's Guide to Structural Equation Modeling* (Routledge, England, 2022)
9. L.J. Cronbach, P.E. Meehl, Construct validity in psychological tests. Psychol. Bull. **52**(4), 281 (1955)
10. J.F. Hair, W.C. Black, B.J. Babin, R.E. Anderson, *Multivariate Data Analysis*, 8th edn. (Cengage Learning, Boston, 2019)
11. N. Kovač, K. Ratković, H. Farahani, P. Watson, A practical applications guide to machine learning regression models in psychology with python. Methods in Psychol. **11**, 100156 (2024)
12. S.P. Reise, K.F. Widaman, R.H. Pugh, Confirmatory factor analysis and item response theory: two approaches for exploring measurement invariance. Psychol. Bull. **114**(3), 552 (1993)
13. W. Meredith, Measurement invariance, factor analysis and factorial invariance. Psychometrika **58**(4), 525 (1993)
14. J.K. Flake, E.I. Fried, Measurement schmeasurement: Questionable measurement practices and how to avoid them. Adv. Methods Pract. Psychol. Sci. **3**(4), 456 (2020)
15. P.W. Lei, L.K. Shiverdecker, Performance of estimators for confirmatory factor analysis of ordinal variables with missing data. Struct. Equ. Model. Multidiscip. J. **27**(4), 584 (2020)
16. C.G. Park, Implementing alternative estimation methods to test the construct validity of Likert-scale instruments. Korean J. Women Health Nurs. **29**(2), 85 (2023)
17. R. Chandra, J. Simmons, Bayesian neural networks via MCMC: a python-based tutorial. IEEE Access **12**, 70519 (2024)

18. M. Yildirim, Sample size in confirmatory factor analysis: Monte Carlo simulation study, in *Proceedings of the V. International Applied Statistics Congress (UYIK 2024)* (Istanbul, Türkiye, 2024). Conference Presentation, May 21–23, 2024
19. T. Zhang, *Relative Performance of MLR, WLSMV, and Bayes Estimators: An Investigation Using Confirmatory Factor Analysis with Ordinal Data*. Ph.D. thesis (University of South Carolina, South Carolina, 2024)
20. S.B. MacKenzie, P.M. Podsakoff, N.P. Podsakoff, Construct measurement and validation procedures in MIS and behavioral research: integrating new and existing techniques, in *MIS Quarterly* (2011), pp. 293–334
21. H.W. Marsh, K.T. Hau, Z. Wen, In search of golden rules: comment on hypothesis-testing approaches to setting cutoff values for fit indexes and dangers in overgeneralizing Hu and Bentler's (1999) findings. Struct. Equ. Model. **11**(3), 320 (2004)
22. L.t. Hu, P.M. Bentler, Cutoff criteria for fit indexes in covariance structure analysis: conventional criteria versus new alternatives. Struct. Equ. Model. Multidiscip. J. **6**(1), 1 (1999)
23. D.A. Kenny, B. Kaniskan, D.B. McCoach, The performance of RMSEA in models with small degrees of freedom. Sociol. Methods Res. **44**(3), 486 (2015)
24. P.M. Bentler, Comparative fit indexes in structural models. Psychol. Bull. **107**(2), 238 (1990)
25. R.C. MacCallum, M. Roznowski, L.B. Necowitz, Model modifications in covariance structure analysis: the problem of capitalization on chance. Psychol. Bull. **111**(3), 490 (1992)
26. S.M. Bell, R.P. Chalmers, D.B. Flora, The impact of measurement model misspecification on coefficient omega estimates of composite reliability. Educ. Psychol. Meas. **84**(1), 5 (2024)
27. C. Fornell, D.F. Larcker, Evaluating structural equation models with unobservable variables and measurement error. J. Mark. Res. **18**(1), 39 (1981)
28. R.L. Worthington, T.A. Whittaker, Scale development research: a content analysis and recommendations for best practices. Couns. Psychol. **34**(6), 806 (2006)
29. A.M. Farrell, Insufficient discriminant validity: a comment on Bove, Pervan, Beatty, and Shiu (2009). J. Bus. Res. **63**(3), 324 (2010)
30. M. Rönkkö, E. Cho, An updated guideline for assessing discriminant validity. Organ. Res. Methods **25**(1), 6 (2022)
31. R. Cudeck, M.W. Browne, Cross-validation of covariance structures. Multivar. Behav. Res. **18**(2), 147 (1983)
32. J.W. Osborne, D.C. Fitzpatrick, Replication analysis in exploratory factor analysis: what it is and why it makes your analysis better. Pract. Assess. Res. Eval. **17**(15), n15 (2012)
33. K. Ratković, N. Kovač, M. Simeunović, Hybrid LSTM model to predict the level of air pollution in Montenegro. Appl. Sci. **13**(18), 10152 (2023)
34. R. Van De Schoot, P. Schmidt, A. De Beuckelaer, K. Lek, M. Zondervan-Zwijnenburg, *Measurement Invariance* (2015)
35. J.C. Anderson, D.W. Gerbing, Structural equation modeling in practice: a review and recommended two-step approach. Psychol. Bull. **103**(3), 411 (1988)
36. D. Goretzko, K. Siemund, P. Sterner, Evaluating model fit of measurement models in confirmatory factor analysis. Educ. Psychol. Meas. **84**(1), 123 (2024)
37. D. McNeish, M.G. Wolf, Dynamic fit index cutoffs for one-factor models. Behav. Res. Methods **55**(3), 1157 (2023)
38. H. Marsh, A. Alamer, When and how to use set-exploratory structural equation modelling to test structural models: a tutorial using the R package lavaan. Br. J. Math. Stat. Psychol. **77**(3), 459 (2024)
39. S.A. Neufeld, M. St Clair, J. Brodbeck, P.O. Wilkinson, I.M. Goodyer, P.B. Jones, Measurement invariance in longitudinal bifactor models: review and application based on the P factor. Assessment **31**(4), 774 (2024)
40. W. Revelle, *Psych: Procedures for Personality and Psychological Research*. Software, vol. 2024 (2024)
41. N. Kovač, K. Ratković, P. Watson, H. Farahani, F. Bagheri Sheykhangafshe, Machine learning classification models for predicting chronic pain, in *Current Psychology*, pp. 1–14 (2025)

42. H. Farahani, P. Watson, T. Bezan, N. Kovač, L.C. Winter, M. Blagojević, P. Azadfallah, A. Allahyari, S. Masoumian, P. Jiménez, PsAIchology: an intelligent direction in psychological sciences, in *10th International Scientific Conference Technics, Informatics and Education-TIE 2024* (Faculty of Technical Sciences Čačak, University of Kragujevac, Kragujevac, 2024)
43. K.J. Holzinger, F. Swineford, *A Study in Factor Analysis: The Stability of a Bifactor Solution*. Supplementary Educational Monographs, vol. 48 (University of Chicago Press, Chicago, 1939)

Graded Item Response Theory: Developing and Validating a Psychological Scale

Nataša Kovač, Marija Blagojević, Kruna Ratković, Peter Watson, and Hojjatollah Farahani

1 Overview of Graded Item Response Theory

Graded item response theory (GIRT) is an extension of the broader item response theory framework designed to analyse ordinal response data, where individuals respond to items on a graded scale. Unlike traditional measurement models that assume equal intervals between response categories, graded item response theory provides a more flexible framework that accounts for varying distances between different levels of a latent trait. This characteristic is particularly important in psychological assessments where ordinal data is frequently used, such as Likert-type scales, rating scales, and multi-level response categories. Classical test theory and linear models often assume that moving from one response category to the next represents an equal step in the underlying construct, which may not always reflect the psychological reality of how individuals perceive and respond to assessment items. In contrast, graded item response theory models these transitions probabilistically, allowing for a more accurate representation of how respondents progress through ordered categories based on their latent trait level [1–3]. This flexibility

N. Kovač (✉) · K. Ratković
Faculty of Applied Sciences, University of Donja Gorica, Podgorica, Montenegro
e-mail: natasa.kovac@udg.edu.me; kruna.ratkovic@udg.edu.me

M. Blagojević
Faculty of Technical Sciences, University of Kragujevac, Čačak, Serbia
e-mail: marija.blagojevic@uni.kg.ac.rs

P. Watson
MRC Cognition and Brain Sciences Unit, University of Cambridge, Cambridge, England
e-mail: Peter.Watson@mrc-cbu.cam.ac.uk

H. Farahani
Department of Psychology, Faculty of Humanities, Tarbiat Modares University, Tehran, Iran
e-mail: h.farahani@modares.ac.ir

N. Kovač et al. (eds.), *Data Science in Psychology*,
https://doi.org/10.1007/978-3-032-18312-5_10

enhances the precision of measurement, particularly in domains such as personality assessment, clinical psychology, and educational testing, where individual differences in response behaviour can introduce variability in how response thresholds should be interpreted. By incorporating item-specific threshold parameters, graded item response theory ensures that each transition between categories is estimated separately, improving the ability to capture meaningful distinctions in respondents' psychological attributes. This capability makes it a powerful tool for developing and refining scales that seek to measure latent constructs in a more psychometrically robust manner.

At its core, graded item response theory is based on the graded response model, originally developed to model polytomous item responses [1]. The fundamental principle behind the graded response model is that an individual's probability of selecting a particular response category depends on their latent trait level, often referred to as θ. This trait represents an unobserved psychological construct, such as intelligence, depression, or personality, which is inferred from observed responses. Each item in a psychological scale is characterised by a set of threshold parameters that define the points along the latent continuum where the probability of endorsing one response category surpasses the probability of endorsing a lower category.

The graded response model assumes that the probability of a respondent choosing a particular category follows a cumulative logistic function. The probability of selecting category k or higher for item i is defined by

$$P(Y_i \geq k|\theta) = \frac{1}{1 + e^{-a_i(\theta - b_{ik})}}, \tag{1}$$

where $P(Y_i \geq k|\theta)$ represents the probability that an individual with latent trait level θ selects response category k or higher, a_i is the item discrimination parameter, and b_{ik} represents the threshold parameters for response category k. The discrimination parameter a_i determines how strongly an item differentiates individuals at different levels of the latent trait, with higher values indicating greater differentiation. The threshold parameters b_{ik} define the points along the latent continuum where an individual is equally likely to select category k or the preceding category.

The function described in Eq. (1) is cumulative, meaning it models the probability of selecting a category at least as high as k. To obtain the probability of selecting a specific category, the cumulative probabilities are computed as

$$P(Y_i = k|\theta) = P(Y_i \geq k|\theta) - P(Y_i \geq k + 1|\theta), \tag{2}$$

where $P(Y_i = k|\theta)$ is the probability of selecting category k exactly. This formulation ensures that the probabilities for all possible categories sum to one [4, 5].

An essential feature of graded item response theory is its ability to model item characteristics such as discrimination and category thresholds. Discrimination parameters determine how sharply an item distinguishes between individuals with different trait levels, while threshold parameters indicate where along the latent trait continuum individuals transition between response categories. Well-constructed items exhibit high discrimination and logically ordered thresholds, ensuring that higher response categories are associated with increasing levels of the latent trait [2, 6].

The estimation of graded item response theory parameters is typically performed using maximum likelihood estimation or Bayesian estimation techniques [7]. Maximum likelihood methods involve optimising the likelihood function to obtain parameter estimates that maximise the probability of the observed data. Bayesian approaches, on the other hand, incorporate prior distributions for model parameters, allowing for more robust estimates, particularly when sample sizes are small or when item parameters exhibit large variability [8].

Graded item response theory is widely applied in psychological scale development due to its flexibility in handling ordered categorical responses. Traditional psychometric methods, such as classical test theory, assume that observed scores are linear representations of the latent trait, which may not always hold in practice. By explicitly modelling the relationship between responses and the latent construct, graded item response theory provides a deeper understanding of how individual items contribute to the overall measurement. This advantage is particularly evident in personality assessments, clinical diagnostic tools, and educational testing, where response categories often follow an ordinal structure rather than an interval scale [5, 6].

One of the key advantages of graded item response theory over simpler measurement approaches is its ability to assess item functioning across different populations. By estimating item characteristic curves, researchers can evaluate whether certain items function differently for distinct demographic groups, a phenomenon known as differential item functioning [9]. This ensures that the scale measures the intended construct equitably across diverse respondent groups.

Despite its strengths, implementing GIRT requires careful consideration of model assumptions, data quality, and interpretability of item parameters. The assumption of monotonicity, which states that the probability of endorsing a higher response category increases with the latent trait, must hold for the model to be valid. Local independence is required, meaning that item responses should only be related through the latent trait and not through external factors such as response styles or test-taking strategies [8].

2 Assumptions of Graded Item Response Theory

GIRT provides an advanced psychometric approach for analysing responses on ordered categorical scales, which are extensively used in psychological and behavioural sciences. Despite its powerful flexibility and analytical precision, the successful application of GIRT is predicated upon several fundamental assumptions. These assumptions, if adequately satisfied, enable GIRT models to provide meaningful, precise, and valid inferences about latent psychological constructs [2].

A primary assumption underlying GIRT, as in all item response theory models, is the unidimensionality of the construct being measured. Unidimensionality implies that respondents' item responses are governed by a single underlying latent trait or dimension [10]. In psychological contexts, this means that scales designed to measure constructs such as anxiety, depression, or self-esteem should predominantly reflect one overarching latent factor. Although perfect unidimensionality is rarely attainable in practice, scales should exhibit a dominant latent dimension, with secondary factors having minimal influence. The presence of strong secondary dimensions or factors can distort item parameter estimates, leading to inaccuracies in interpreting the latent construct [11].

Assessing the assumption of unidimensionality typically involves exploratory and confirmatory factor analyses. Exploratory factor analysis (EFA) is employed to initially evaluate the structure of a scale, ensuring items primarily load onto a single factor. Subsequently, confirmatory factor analysis (CFA) explicitly tests this hypothesised structure against empirical data, providing statistical evidence of unidimensionality [12]. Researchers can apply bifactor models as a contemporary solution when mild multidimensionality exists, allowing for a general factor with additional specific factors that capture minor variations without substantially violating the assumption of unidimensionality [13].

A second key assumption in GIRT is local independence, which states that, conditional on the latent trait level, item responses should be independent of each other. In practical terms, after accounting for the primary latent trait (such as psychological distress), responses to individual items should not be systematically related. Violations of this assumption, often termed local dependence, occur when responses to one item systematically influence responses to another as a result of shared wording, overlapping item content, or response bias [14]. Local dependence can inflate item discrimination parameters, producing misleading interpretations of item performance and latent trait estimation.

Methods to detect violations of local independence include inspecting residual correlations from factor analyses and item response theory residual analyses. High residual correlations between items indicate potential local dependence, suggesting modifications such as rephrasing or eliminating redundant items [15]. In some cases, modelling approaches like multidimensional IRT models or testlet models can be adopted to handle clusters of locally dependent items, preserving the accuracy and validity of latent trait estimates [16].

Another pivotal assumption underlying GIRT is monotonicity. This assumption posits that the probability of endorsing a higher response category should increase monotonically as the latent trait increases. For instance, in an anxiety scale, as a respondent's latent anxiety increases, the likelihood of selecting higher response categories (e.g. *often anxious* or *always anxious*) should rise correspondingly. Non-monotonic response patterns, in which probabilities decrease at certain levels of the latent trait, indicate problematic items. These patterns may result from ambiguous item wording, reversed scoring that confuses respondents, or inconsistencies in scale responses [17].

Monotonicity can be evaluated visually through item characteristic curves (ICCs) or statistically through methods such as Mokken scaling, which specifically tests for violations of monotonicity. Items demonstrating non-monotonic response functions require revision or removal, ensuring the integrity and accuracy of the measurement instrument [18].

GIRT also assumes the existence of ordered response categories that accurately reflect incremental increases in the underlying trait. Each response category should represent a distinct and progressively higher position on the latent trait continuum. In psychological assessments, this ordering reflects the theoretical assumption that respondents perceive and respond consistently with increasing psychological intensity or frequency. Respondents may sometimes perceive categories differently, creating inconsistencies or category disordering [19]. Disordered thresholds indicate that adjacent response categories do not correspond neatly to increasing levels of the latent trait, thus complicating interpretation.

Methods such as *Rasch analysis* or *threshold order evaluation* within polytomous IRT models are frequently employed to detect and rectify category disordering issues. When disordering occurs, researchers can combine or restructure problematic categories, thus restoring theoretical coherence to the scale's response continuum [20].

In addition to these core assumptions, GIRT models depend on the accurate estimation of item parameters, including discrimination, which reflects how sharply an item differentiates individuals at various levels of the latent trait, and thresholds, which represent points along the latent trait continuum that separate response categories. Accurate parameter estimation assumes sufficient sample sizes and adequate item coverage across the latent trait spectrum. Small sample sizes or limited item distribution along the trait continuum can result in imprecise estimates, undermining the model's reliability and interpretive power. Simulation studies and guidelines generally recommend sample sizes of several hundred participants to ensure robust parameter estimation, particularly when employing more complex models or when the trait distribution is unevenly represented by the items [21].

The assumption of measurement invariance, closely related to differential item functioning (DIF), is critical. Measurement invariance assumes that the scale's items function equivalently across different subgroups of respondents, such as gender, age, or cultural groups. Violations of invariance, identified via DIF analysis, imply that the latent construct may be measured differently across groups, potentially leading to biased conclusions. Techniques including logistic regression methods, likelihood ratio tests, and item response theory-based DIF analyses systematically evaluate this assumption, ensuring fairness and comparability across diverse respondent populations [9].

Lastly, it is essential to emphasise the assumption regarding the suitability of the logistic cumulative function in modelling graded responses. The logistic function is commonly employed due to its mathematical tractability and interpretability, yet its appropriateness relies on empirical verification through model fit assessments.

Researchers should regularly examine model fit indices, such as *comparative fit indices* (CFI), *Tucker-Lewis Index* (TLI), and *Root Mean Square Error of Approximation* (RMSEA), ensuring that the logistic model provides an adequate representation of the underlying response patterns [2].

Understanding and rigorously testing these assumptions underpinning GIRT are paramount for ensuring the reliability, validity, and interpretability of psychological measurement scales. By systematically verifying assumptions such as unidimensionality, local independence, monotonicity, ordered thresholds, adequate item parameter estimation, measurement invariance, and logistic function suitability, psychological researchers can confidently employ GIRT to achieve precise and meaningful insights into latent psychological constructs.

3 Item Characteristics

In GIRT, the psychometric properties of items, collectively known as item characteristics, significantly influence how effectively psychological scales measure underlying latent traits. Item characteristics encompass several essential parameters, notably item discrimination, item thresholds, and category response functions, each critically determining the item's utility in psychological measurement [1, 22].

The first crucial item characteristic in GIRT is *item discrimination*, typically denoted by the parameter a. This parameter captures the extent to which an item can differentiate between individuals possessing varying levels of a latent psychological trait [23]. Items with higher discrimination values provide greater sensitivity, meaning they more clearly distinguish between respondents at adjacent trait levels. Discrimination parameters directly influence the precision of latent trait estimates, as items with low discrimination contribute minimally to distinguishing individual differences, thereby weakening the overall scale quality [24].

In psychological practice, item discrimination is interpreted using item characteristic curves (ICCs), where a steep slope signifies high discrimination. Such items are particularly valuable in clinical assessments and diagnostic scales, as they reliably separate respondents with different degrees of severity or intensity of a psychological trait, such as anxiety, depression, or personality traits [25]. Conversely, items with flatter slopes reflect poor discrimination, indicating that respondents across a broad range of latent trait levels respond similarly. These low-discrimination items usually require revision or removal from the scale to maintain measurement accuracy [19].

Evaluating and optimising discrimination parameters involves iterative testing and refinement processes. Statistical tools, such as the item information function (IIF), quantify precisely how much information an item provides across the trait continuum. The IIF peaks at trait levels where discrimination is maximal, highlighting the most informative items for particular segments of the latent trait distribution [10]. This analysis informs psychometricians about areas where item refinement might be necessary, ensuring that the scale reliably covers the entire latent trait range of interest.

Another fundamental characteristic in GIRT models pertains to *item thresholds*, denoted as b_{ik}, which define the boundaries between response categories. Threshold parameters represent the points along the latent trait continuum at which respondents transition from one response category to another. For instance, in a depression scale employing Likert-type responses (*never*, *sometimes*, *often*, *always*), each threshold parameter delineates the precise latent trait level at which a respondent is equally likely to select two adjacent response categories [26].

Ideally, thresholds should be ordered logically, increasing progressively along the latent trait continuum. Disordered thresholds, where higher response categories are not consistently associated with increasing levels of the trait, suggest issues related to item clarity, the wording of response options, or conceptual ambiguity. Disordered thresholds undermine interpretability, leading to inaccurate conclusions about respondents' trait levels. Resolving these issues typically involves either collapsing problematic categories or rephrasing response options to ensure respondents perceive a clear incremental progression consistent with theory [20].

In the graded response model, threshold parameters are visually inspected using category response functions (CRFs). CRFs explicitly represent the probability of selecting each response category as a function of the latent trait. These graphical representations enable psychologists to diagnose potential problems with category ordering visually. Effective CRFs should demonstrate clear peaks at distinct points along the trait continuum, smoothly transitioning between categories without excessive overlap or ambiguity [27].

An additional consideration related to item characteristics in GIRT involves understanding the *category spacing* within items. Unlike traditional psychometric assumptions, which presume equal spacing between response options (as in classical Likert scales), GIRT explicitly models varying psychological distances between adjacent categories. For instance, respondents might perceive a significant psychological gap between *rarely* and *sometimes*, but relatively minor distinctions between *sometimes* and *often*. This modelling ensures a more realistic representation of respondents' internal psychological scales, enhancing measurement precision [28].

To assess category spacing empirically, researchers frequently use advanced item analysis tools, such as Rasch partial credit models and generalised partial credit models [29]. These methods allow detailed exploration of how respondents perceive category distances, providing valuable diagnostic information for item refinement. Correcting issues with unequal or illogical category spacing enhances respondents' interpretive clarity and ensures the instrument faithfully represents the theoretical construct it seeks to measure [19].

Psychometric research in recent years has emphasised the importance of item characteristics related to *measurement invariance* and *item bias detection* (also known as differential item functioning, DIF). Measurement invariance ensures that item characteristics, such as discrimination and thresholds, remain consistent across diverse groups, including gender, ethnicity, or age. Items that demonstrate significant DIF indicate that individuals from different groups, despite having the same level of the latent trait, respond differently due to influences unrelated to the trait itself, potentially introducing bias [9].

Item characteristic analysis via DIF detection employs statistical techniques, including logistic regression and multiple-group IRT modelling, to test the equivalence of item parameters across groups. Items exhibiting substantial DIF require scrutiny to determine the underlying cause, whether linguistic complexity, cultural nuances, or context-specific interpretations. Resolving these issues often involves culturally sensitive revisions, ensuring fairness and equitable measurement across populations [30].

Recent advancements in computational methodologies have substantially enhanced the robustness of estimating item characteristics. Bayesian estimation approaches, such as *Markov Chain Monte Carlo* (MCMC) techniques, increasingly complement traditional maximum likelihood estimation in GIRT. Bayesian methods incorporate prior information about item parameters, resulting in more stable and accurate estimates, particularly in small or sparse data conditions common in psychological research [8]. The ability to integrate expert knowledge or previous psychometric results through Bayesian priors enriches the quality and interpretability of item characteristic estimates, particularly in complex psychological scales involving multidimensional constructs or small sample studies [31].

Detailed exploration and precise estimation of item characteristics are fundamental to successful GIRT application in psychological research. Through careful management of item discrimination, threshold parameters, category spacing, measurement invariance, and leveraging contemporary computational techniques, psychometricians can create highly sensitive, accurate, and equitable psychological measurement instruments.

4 Item and Model Fit

In the development and validation of psychological scales within GIRT, the evaluation of how individual items and the entire model fit the data is of paramount importance. The assessment of item and model fit plays a crucial role in verifying the accuracy and reliability of the scale. This process is also essential for making informed decisions about potential modifications to the scale to improve its psychometric properties. Ensuring that the scale is not only valid but also appropriate for measuring the latent traits it is designed to assess requires a thorough analysis of both individual items and the overall model.

In GIRT, the fit assessment process involves several layers of analysis, starting with the evaluation of individual items and then the evaluation of the entire model. Through this, researchers ensure that scale not only measures the intended constructs but also functions effectively in practice, not just in theory. This process is dynamic and requires careful monitoring throughout the entire scale development cycle.

Item fit refers to the ability of each item to adequately model the responses of participants according to the theoretical framework of the model. Each item should align with the assumptions of the model to ensure that it is properly contributing to the scale's overall measurement of the latent trait. The fit of an item is evaluated by assessing whether it meets expectations regarding both the difficulty and the discrimination of the item.

In GIRT, the evaluation of item fit is typically done through statistical tests. These tests determine whether specific items satisfy the model's assumptions, specifically the ability of an item to discriminate between respondents at various levels of the latent trait. The most commonly used tests for assessing item fit are the infit and outfit statistics, which help quantify discrepancies between expected and observed responses at the item level. According to [32], the infit statistic is sensitive to responses that are *too predictable* or *too irregular*, suggesting that they may not conform to the expected response pattern. The outfit statistic, on the other hand, identifies items that deviate from the model's predictions more severely, indicating that they may not function properly within the scale as a whole.

An important aspect of item fit evaluation is the analysis of response patterns. When evaluating an item's fit, it is essential to consider the distribution of responses. For a scale to be effective, each item must generate a diverse range of responses across all levels of the latent trait. If all responses for a particular item are concentrated within a narrow range or skewed toward one end of the scale, this may indicate that the item lacks sufficient discrimination to differentiate respondents with varying levels of the latent trait [33]. This could point to a poorly designed item, one that might need to be revised or removed. For example, if an item fails to distinguish between respondents with different levels of the latent trait, it will not provide useful data and may introduce bias into the overall measurement.

After assessing the fit of individual items and making the necessary modifications, the next step is the evaluation of the overall model. Model fit refers to how well the entire scale (i.e. all items together) aligns with the data and whether the model as a whole provides an adequate measurement of the latent traits it is intended to assess. Evaluating model fit requires considering the scale as an integrated entity, taking into account not only the fit of individual items but also how they function together to produce a meaningful and accurate measurement of the latent trait.

Several methods are used to assess model fit in GIRT, with one of the most important being the χ^2 test or likelihood ratio test. These statistical tests compare observed data with predicted data, allowing researchers to determine whether the model adequately explains the relationships among the items. If the model fits well, the observed and predicted data will be closely aligned, indicating that the model accurately represents the data. If the χ^2 value is significantly high, it suggests that the model does not fit the data adequately and that modifications may be necessary [23].

In addition to these statistical tests, other indices are commonly used to assess model fit, such as the Root Mean Square Error of Approximation (RMSEA) and the Comparative Fit Index (CFI). RMSEA evaluates how well the model fits the data by comparing differences between observed and predicted data, with lower values indicating a better fit. CFI, on the other hand, compares the fit of the target model to a baseline model, where values closer to 1.0 indicate a better fit [34]. Both of these indices help assess the overall adequacy of the model and assist researchers in determining whether modifications are necessary.

Graphical analysis provides an additional method for evaluating model fit, complementing statistical tests. One of the most commonly used graphical tools for visualising model fit in GIRT is Item Characteristic Curves (ICCs), which illustrate the relationship between the level of the latent trait and the probability of correct responses for each item [35]. By visually inspecting ICCs, researchers can identify items that may not function as expected within the model. For instance, if an ICC deviates from the expected pattern, it may indicate that the item does not appropriately measure the latent trait. These visual tools help pinpoint areas of the model that need improvement.

If the evaluation of the item and model fit indicates that the scale is not functioning optimally, several steps can be taken to improve its precision and effectiveness. Items that exhibit poor fit may be either removed or modified. This could involve rewording an item, adjusting its response options, or modifying the scoring system. If the scale lacks sufficient discrimination between respondents at different levels of the latent trait, new items may be added to increase the range of the scale and improve its measurement capabilities.

Refining the model itself is another key strategy for improving fit. This process may involve revisiting the theoretical framework underlying the scale and adjusting the model to better reflect the observed relationships. For instance, if the initial model includes parameters that do not meaningfully contribute to explaining the data, they can be removed or replaced with more appropriate parameters. In some cases, researchers may find it necessary to reassess the fundamental assumptions of the model to ensure their validity and applicability in the given context.

These steps are crucial not only for achieving a good model fit but also for ensuring that the scale accurately measures the intended latent traits. Continuous refinement of items and models contributes to the development of precise, reliable, and valid instruments for measuring latent constructs.

It is important to note that the evaluation of items and model fit is not a one-time process but an ongoing aspect of scale development. As new data are collected, the scale may require further adjustments to maintain its accuracy and reliability. This continuous evaluation is essential to ensure that the scale remains relevant and effective in measuring the intended latent traits. When the scale is applied to different populations or contexts, the model's fit may need to be reassessed. For example, a scale that performs well in one population may not function as effectively in another. Researchers must carefully evaluate model fit across different groups and ensure that the scale remains valid and reliable across diverse settings and contexts.

The evaluation of item and model fit is a crucial aspect of the development and validation of psychological scales. The application of GIRT methodologies enables researchers to evaluate the accuracy and validity of individual items and the overall model. This process not only helps in identifying problematic items but also leads to the continuous refinement of the scale to ensure that it accurately measures the latent traits it was designed to assess. Ongoing evaluation and improvement of model fit are essential for maintaining high psychometric standards and ensuring the reliability and validity of the scale across diverse populations and contexts.

5 Differential Item Functioning Analysis

DIF analysis is a critical step in ensuring that psychological assessments measure constructs equivalently across different groups. It identifies items that function differently for subgroups of respondents who possess the same level of the underlying latent trait. DIF detection is essential in maintaining fairness, validity, and interpretability of test scores, particularly in contexts involving cross-cultural research, clinical diagnostics, or demographic comparisons [9].

At its core, DIF refers to a violation of measurement invariance, where individuals from different groups (e.g. gender, age, or cultural background) with the same latent trait level respond differently to an item. Such differences may arise due to item wording, cultural interpretation, or response styles. DIF is generally classified into two types: uniform DIF, where the difference is constant across trait levels, and non-uniform DIF, where the magnitude or direction of difference varies with the trait level [2].

To test for DIF in Graded Item Response Theory, researchers often rely on nested model comparisons that evaluate whether item parameters differ significantly across predefined groups, such as gender or ethnicity. One commonly used method is the likelihood ratio test, which compares two hierarchically related models: a constrained model where item discrimination and threshold parameters are held equal across groups and an unconstrained model where these parameters are freely estimated. The difference in model fit, typically assessed via a χ^2 test, serves as an indicator of DIF. A statistically significant result implies that at least one item behaves differently across groups, suggesting potential bias in the measurement [36].

While the likelihood ratio test provides a flexible parametric framework, another widely used approach involves logistic regression-based DIF analysis. In this method, each item response is regressed on the latent trait (often proxied by total score or factor score), group membership, and an interaction term between the two. A significant group term indicates the presence of uniform DIF, while non-uniform DIF arises when the interaction between group and latent ability is statistically significant. This approach is advantageous due to its interpretability and ability to accommodate both binary and polytomous items under ordinal logistic regression models [9, 37]. Logistic regression is computationally efficient and can be extended to account for covariates or nested data structures, making it an appealing option for large-scale psychological assessments.

The choice between likelihood-based and regression-based methods depends on the modelling context and research question. While the likelihood ratio test is preferred when working within IRT parameter estimation software, logistic regression is often more accessible and transparent for exploratory DIF screening or initial psychometric validation. Regardless of the method, it is crucial to interpret DIF findings in light of both statistical and practical significance. A statistically significant DIF effect may not necessarily imply meaningful impact on test scores or decisions; hence, effect size measures such as McFadden's pseudo R^2 or odds ratio comparisons are often recommended as complementary indices [30].

Modern computational tools allow for the implementation of DIF analysis within IRT frameworks using either classical or Bayesian estimation. The following Python example demonstrates a basic approach to DIF detection using simulated data and logistic regression:

```
import pandas as pd
import numpy as np
import statsmodels.api as sm

# Simulated data
np.random.seed(42)
theta = np.random.normal(0, 1, 500)
group = np.random.binomial(1, 0.5, 500)  # 0: Group A, 1: Group
↪  B
item_response = (theta + 0.5 * group + np.random.normal(0, 1,
↪  500)) > 0.5

# Logistic regression to test DIF
df = pd.DataFrame({'Response': item_response.astype(int),
                   'Theta': theta,
                   'Group': group,
                   'Interaction': theta * group})

X = sm.add_constant(df[['Theta', 'Group', 'Interaction']])
model = sm.Logit(df['Response'], X).fit()
print(model.summary())
```

This example fits a logistic regression model to test both uniform and non-uniform DIF. The coefficients for `Group` and `Interaction` provide evidence for DIF: A significant group effect indicates uniform DIF, while a significant interaction implies non-uniform DIF. Although simplified, this method highlights the core logic behind DIF detection in Item Response Theory.

Graphical methods are also useful for visualising DIF. Item characteristic curves can be plotted separately for each group, showing how the probability of item endorsement changes across levels of the latent trait. Significant deviations between the curves may indicate DIF. Figure 1 displays an illustrative comparison of item characteristic curves for two groups.

The solid line represents the reference group (Group A), while the dashed line represents the focal group (Group B) exhibiting uniform DIF. At equivalent levels

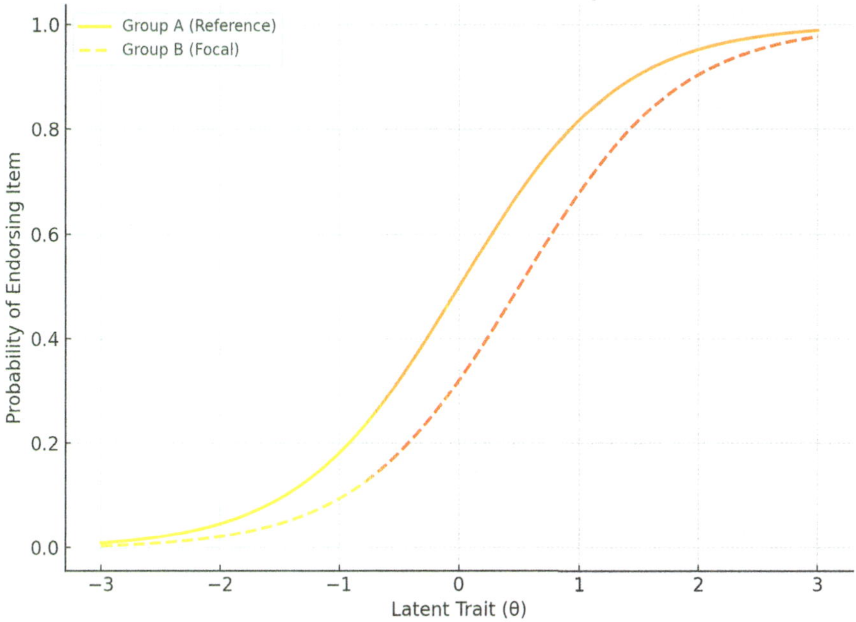

Fig. 1 Item characteristic curves for two groups showing uniform DIF

of the latent trait, individuals from Group B consistently show a higher probability of endorsing the item, suggesting the item favours that group and does not function equivalently across groups.

DIF detection is not only a statistical requirement but also an ethical obligation when developing psychological tests. Ignoring DIF can lead to biased inferences, misclassification, and unfair decisions, especially in high-stakes assessments such as clinical diagnosis or educational selection. Therefore, DIF analysis must be a routine component of scale validation pipelines, ensuring measurement equivalence and enhancing the generalisability of psychological research findings.

6 Applications and Case Studies

In this case study, we explored how university students experience internal shame by analysing their responses to a short questionnaire with four items, using IRT. A total of 561 (362 females and 199 males) students took part, each rating items on a 5-point scale. A Two-Parameter Logistic Model is employed to estimate both the discrimination (a) and difficulty (b) parameters of each binary-scored item, based on individuals' latent traits (θ), thereby modelling the probability of endorsing an item as a logistic function of ability.

```python
import numpy as np
import pandas as pd
import matplotlib.pyplot as plt
from scipy.optimize import minimize
from scipy.special import expit  # sigmoid function

# Simulated data: 10 students x 4 items on a 1-5 Likert scale
# Converted to binary (1 if >=3, else 0)
data = pd.DataFrame({
    "Item1": [1, 2, 3, 4, 5, 2, 3, 1, 4, 5],
    "Item2": [2, 1, 4, 5, 5, 3, 2, 1, 3, 4],
    "Item3": [3, 3, 2, 4, 5, 3, 4, 2, 4, 5],
    "Item4": [2, 1, 3, 4, 5, 2, 3, 1, 4, 5]
})
binary_data = (data >= 3).astype(int)

# Step 1: Estimate person ability (theta) using sum score
theta_est = binary_data.sum(axis=1).apply(lambda x: (x - 2)/2)

# Step 2: Define the 2PL likelihood for a single item
def neg_log_likelihood(params, theta, responses):
    a, b = params
    prob = expit(a * (theta - b))
    likelihood = responses * np.log(prob + 1e-9) + (1 -
     ↪ responses) * np.log(1 - prob + 1e-9)
    return -np.sum(likelihood)

# Step 3: Estimate a, b for each item
item_params = {}
for item in binary_data.columns:
    responses = binary_data[item].values
    result = minimize(neg_log_likelihood, x0=[1.0, 0.0],
     ↪ args=(theta_est.values, responses), bounds=[(0.01, 5),
     ↪ (-4, 4)])
    a_hat, b_hat = result.x
    item_params[item] = {'a': a_hat, 'b': b_hat}

# Step 4: Print estimated parameters
print("Estimated 2PL Parameters:")
for item, params in item_params.items():
    print(f"{item}: a (discrimination) = {params['a']:.2f}, b
     ↪ (difficulty) = {params['b']:.2f}")
```

```
# Step 5: Plot Item Characteristic Curves
theta_range = np.linspace(-3, 3, 100)
plt.figure(figsize=(10, 6))
for item, params in item_params.items():
    a, b = params['a'], params['b']
    prob = expit(a * (theta_range - b))
    plt.plot(theta_range, prob, label=item)

plt.title("2PL Model - Item Characteristic Curves")
plt.xlabel("Latent Trait (Theta)")
plt.ylabel("Probability of Endorsing Item")
plt.grid(True)
plt.legend()
plt.show()
```

Results:

```
Estimated 2PL Parameters:
Item1: a (discrimination) = 5.00, b (difficulty) = 0.17
Item2: a (discrimination) = 3.55, b (difficulty) = 0.13
Item3: a (discrimination) = 1.38, b (difficulty) = -0.91
Item4: a (discrimination) = 5.00, b (difficulty) = 0.17
```

A 2PL IRT analysis was conducted on a 4-item Likert scale designed to measure shame, focusing on discrimination parameters to assess how effectively each item distinguishes individuals across the shame variable continuum. Items 1 and 4 (discrimination, $a = 5.0$) and Item 2 ($a = 3.55$) demonstrated strong discriminative power, indicating they are highly effective at differentiating respondents with varying shame levels. These items are likely central to the scale's ability to capture nuanced differences in shame, making them valuable for precise measurement. In contrast, Item 3 ($a = 1.38$) showed weaker discrimination, suggesting it contributes less to the scale's overall precision and may benefit from revision.

Difficulty parameters ($b = 0.17$ for Items 1 and 4, 0.13 for Item 2, and -0.91 for Item 3) were less interpretable for shame but revealed potential redundancy, as Items 1 and 4 shared identical values. This overlap suggests they may measure similar aspects of shame, warranting a content review to ensure they capture distinct facets. The scale appears most informative for individuals with average shame levels, but Item 3's lower discrimination and the possible redundancy of Items 1 and 4 highlight opportunities to enhance the scale's efficiency. Future steps include evaluating model fit and exploring item information to optimise the scale's reliability and validity for shame measurement.

Figure 2 shows how the 4-item Likert scale measures shame, plotting the chance of endorsing each item as shame increases. Steeper curves mean better differentiation between people with different shame levels. Items 1 and 4 have identical curves (discrimination, $a = 5.0$; difficulty, $b = 0.17$), so we describe Item 1 under Item 4. Their sharp curves spike around average shame ($\theta = 0.17$), making them great at picking out differences but hinting they might overlap too

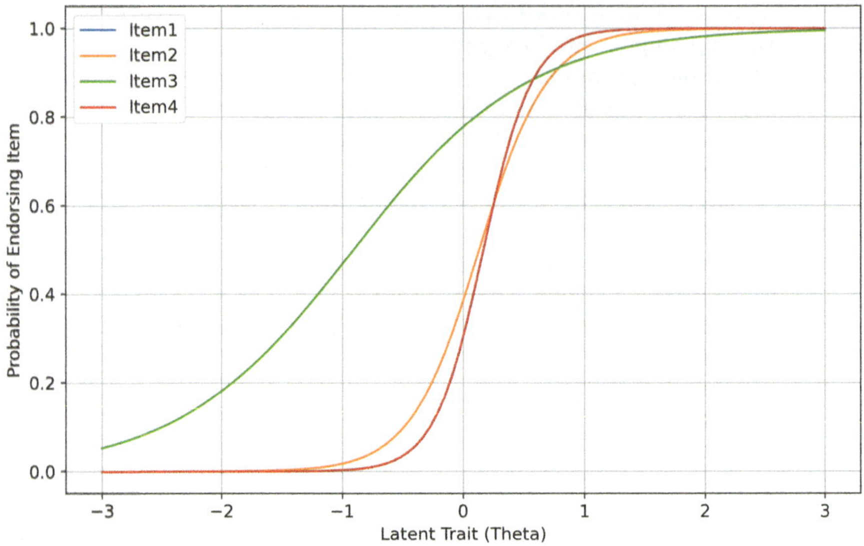

Fig. 2 Item characteristic curves from the 2PL IRT model

much. Item 2's curve ($a = 3.55$, $b = 0.13$) is also steep, rising near average shame ($\theta = 0.13$), so it is solid at distinguishing shame levels. Item 3 ($a = 1.38$, $b = -0.91$), though, has a flatter curve, centred lower ($\theta = -0.91$), meaning it is less helpful for pinpointing shame differences, especially for those with higher shame. The ICCs show the scale works best around average shame, but Item 3 could use a tweak, and Items 1 and 4 need checking to avoid doubling up on the same aspect of shame.

7 Visualising Item Response Theory Results

Visualisation of results allows researchers to intuitively and efficiently interpret how individual items and the overall instrument function. Visual displays facilitate the interpretation of complex statistical results and enable quick identification of potential problems in the instrument. Probability visualisation can be particularly useful for understanding how different levels of a latent construct are reflected in respondents' answers [2].

One of the most commonly used graphical representations in analysis is the ICC. ICCs illustrate the probability that a respondent selects a particular response to an item depending on their level of the latent construct. For each item, the ICC shows how the probability of selecting a specific response category changes as a function of the latent trait. Key aspects of ICC are:

- *Item Discrimination:* The slope of the curve indicates how discriminative an item is, i.e. how sensitive it is to changes in the latent construct. A steeper slope signifies higher discrimination, meaning the item more effectively differentiates respondents with different levels of the latent trait [38];
- *Response Thresholds:* For multiple-choice items, there are thresholds between response categories (e.g. between *agree* and *strongly agree*). The ICC curve can display these thresholds as points where the probability of selecting a response shifts. For example, if the threshold is high, it means that a higher level of the latent construct is needed to select the response *agree* instead of *disagree* [2].

ICC visualisations are instrumental in evaluating how effectively individual items operate within the context of the measured construct. These curves provide insights into whether an item functions as intended, specifically, whether its slope appropriately reflects its discriminative power. A steep slope in an ICC typically indicates that the item is sensitive to differences in the latent trait, effectively distinguishing between respondents with varying levels of the construct. ICCs can reveal whether the response thresholds between categories are logically positioned, ensuring that transitions between response levels align with theoretical expectations and the conceptual structure of the scale [2].

Visualisation of the results can also include graphical comparisons of items based on their discrimination and response thresholds. This approach allows researchers to group items with similar characteristics while easily identifying those that differ in discrimination or thresholds. Such visualisations are valuable for scale optimisation, as items with very low discrimination can be modified or removed [38].

Item discrimination can be visualised using a graph that displays discrimination coefficients for each item. Items with high discrimination parameters typically provide clearer distinctions between respondents with different levels of the latent trait [39].

Response thresholds can be represented using histograms or dot plots that illustrate the values at which changes in response probabilities occur. Visualisation of these parameters allows researchers to assess how different items function and identify those that do not provide sufficient information to measure the latent trait [5] accurately.

Result visualisation can also play a crucial role in comparative analyses with established psychological instruments. By juxtaposing the outcomes of a newly developed scale against those from validated, widely used measures, researchers can gain valuable insights into the psychometric properties of their instrument. This type of analysis is especially informative when assessing aspects such as convergent validity, how well a new scale correlates with theoretically related constructs measured by existing tools [2].

One common approach to such comparisons is the use of scatterplots. These plots illustrate the relationship between total or factor scores derived from the new scale and those from established measures. When a clear linear relationship is observed, this suggests a strong association and reinforces the conceptual overlap between the constructs being measured. Scatterplots can also reveal outliers, potential ceiling or floor effects, or non-linear patterns that might indicate measurement discrepancies or subgroup-specific differences [5].

Beyond visual inspection, researchers can compute correlation coefficients between the new and existing scales and represent them graphically. For instance, bar plots or heatmaps displaying correlation strengths across multiple subscales offer an intuitive way to examine how well different dimensions align. This graphical representation allows for a quick visual synthesis of the degree of convergent or discriminant validity across components of the scale.

These comparative visualisations not only support psychometric evaluation but also contribute to the refinement of new instruments. By identifying items or dimensions that show weak or inconsistent alignment with validated constructs, researchers can make informed decisions about item revisions, scale restructuring, or theoretical re-specification. This iterative process, supported by both statistical and visual evidence, enhances the robustness and interpretability of newly developed psychological measurement tools.

Another valuable visualisation in IRT analysis is the *Person-Item Map*, sometimes referred to as the *Wright Map*. This graphical representation plots both respondents and items along the same latent trait continuum, typically on a vertical axis. Items are positioned based on their estimated difficulty, while individuals are located according to their latent trait levels (e.g. ability, depression severity, or self-efficacy). This dual-axis alignment provides a holistic view of how well the scale items cover the range of respondent abilities [2].

One of the primary advantages of the Person-Item Map is its ability to reveal mismatches between item difficulty and respondent distribution. For instance, if a large proportion of respondents cluster in areas where no items are present, it may indicate that the instrument lacks sensitivity for that segment of the trait spectrum. This insight is critical for refining item pools and improving measurement precision. The map highlights which items are most informative for distinguishing between individuals with different levels of the latent trait. Items positioned in regions with dense respondent clustering are particularly useful, as they maximise the scale's discriminative power in those ranges [38]. Thus, the Person-Item Map not only facilitates diagnostic evaluation of a test's structure but also informs targeted revisions and scale optimisation.

Visual representations play a crucial role in modern IRT analysis, offering several distinct advantages in both interpretation and communication. One of the primary benefits is the rapid identification of potential issues within the model. Through graphical displays, researchers can quickly detect items that deviate from theoretical expectations, such as those with low discrimination, misaligned response thresholds, or unusual response patterns. These visual cues help pinpoint areas where the model may require refinement.

Visualisation tools, such as ICCs, Person-Item Maps, and posterior distribution plots, facilitate a deeper understanding of the model's complex outputs. These tools allow researchers to interpret latent structures and individual item behaviour with greater clarity, helping them draw more informed conclusions about measurement quality and construct validity [2].

In addition to aiding internal analysis, visualisations also serve as powerful tools for communicating findings. By translating complex statistical results into intuitive graphics, researchers can more effectively convey their results to diverse audiences, including collaborators, reviewers, and practitioners. This enhances the transparency and accessibility of psychometric research, making advanced IRT techniques more approachable to non-specialists [5].

References

1. F. Samejima, Estimation of latent ability using a response pattern of graded scores. Psychometrika **34**, 1 (1969)
2. S.E. Embretson, S.P. Reise, *Item Response Theory for Psychologists* (Lawrence Erlbaum Associates, Mahwah, 2000)
3. W.J. van der Linden, *Handbook of Item Response Theory* (Chapman and Hall/CRC, New York, 2016)
4. E. Muraki, A generalized partial credit model: application of an EM algorithm. Appl. Psychol. Meas. **17**(2), 159 (1993)
5. R. de Ayala, *The Theory and Practice of Item Response Theory* (Guilford Press, New York, 2009)
6. S.P. Reise, D.P. Morizot, R.H. Hays, The role of the item response theory in clinical assessment. Psychol. Assess. **17**(3), 447 (2005)
7. F.B. Baker, S.H. Kim, *Item Response Theory: Parameter Estimation Techniques* (CRC Press, New York, 2004)
8. J.P. Fox, *Bayesian Item Response Modeling: Theory and Applications* (Springer, New York, 2010)
9. B.D. Zumbo, Three generations of DIF analyses: considering where it has been, where it is now, and where it is going. Lang. Assess. Q. **4**(2), 223 (2007)
10. F.M. Lord, M.R. Novick, *Statistical Theories of Mental Test Scores* (IAP, New York, 2008)
11. C. Mars, *Item Response Theory: Understanding Statistics Measurement* (2010)
12. T.A. Brown, *Confirmatory Factor Analysis for Applied Research* (Guilford Publications, New York, 2015)
13. A. Rodriguez, S.P. Reise, M.G. Haviland, Evaluating bifactor models: calculating and interpreting statistical indices. Psychol. Methods **21**(2), 137 (2016)
14. W.M. Yen, Scaling performance assessments: strategies for managing local item dependence. J. Educ. Meas. **30**(3), 187 (1993)
15. W.H. Chen, D. Thissen, Local dependence indexes for item pairs using item response theory. J. Educ. Behav. Stat. **22**(3), 265 (1997)
16. H. Wainer, E.T. Bradlow, X. Wang, *Testlet Response Theory and Its Applications* (Cambridge University, Cambridge, 2007)
17. K. Sijtsma, I.W. Molenaar, *Introduction to Nonparametric Item Response Theory*, vol. 5 (SAGE, New York, 2002)
18. W.H. Van Schuur, Mokken scale analysis: between the Guttman scale and parametric item response theory. Polit. Anal. **11**(2), 139 (2003)
19. G.N. Masters, in *Handbook of Item Response Theory* (Chapman and Hall/CRC, New York, 2016), pp. 109–126
20. T.G. Bond, C.M. Fox, *Applying the Rasch Model: Fundamental Measurement in the Human Sciences* (Psychology Press, Hove, 2013)
21. M.O. Edelen, B.B. Reeve, Applying item response theory (IRT) modeling to questionnaire development, evaluation, and refinement. Qual. Life Res. **16**, 5 (2007)

22. S.P. Reise, N.G. Waller, Item response theory and clinical measurement. Annu. Rev. Clin. Psychol. **5**(1), 27 (2009)
23. S.E. Embretson, S.P. Reise, *Item Response Theory for Psychologists* (Psychology Press, Hove, 2013)
24. F.B. Baker, S.H. Kim, et al., *The Basics of Item Response Theory Using R*, vol. 10 (Springer, Berlin, 2017)
25. R.P. Chalmers, mirt: A multidimensional item response theory package for the R environment. J. Stat. Softw. **48**, 1 (2012)
26. M.D. Reckase, 18 multidimensional item response theory. Handbook Statist. **26**, 607 (2006)
27. R. Ostini, M.L. Nering, *Polytomous Item Response Theory Models*, vol. 144 (SAGE, New York, 2006)
28. D. Andrich, A rating formulation for ordered response categories. Psychometrika **43**(4), 561 (1978)
29. E. Muraki, A generalized partial credit model: application of an EM algorithm. Appl. Psychol. Meas. **16**(2), 159 (1992)
30. R.D. Penfield, A framework for evaluating the consequences of differential item functioning in polytomous items. Appl. Meas. Educ. **18**(1), 61 (2005)
31. A. Gelman, J.B. Carlin, H.S. Stern, D.B. Dunson, A. Vehtari, D.B. Rubin, *Bayesian Data Analysis* (Chapman and Hall/CRC, New York, 2014)
32. T.G. Bond, C.M. Fox, *Applying the Rasch Model: Fundamental Measurement in the Human Sciences* (Lawrence Erlbaum Associates, Mahwah, 2007)
33. B.D. Wright, J.M. Linacre, Reasonable mean-square fit values. Rasch Meas. Trans. **8**(3), 370 (1994)
34. M.W. Browne, R. Cudeck, in *Testing Structural Equation Models*, ed. by K.A. Bollen, J.S. Long (SAGE, New York, 1993), pp. 136–162
35. R.K. Hambleton, R.W. Jones, Comparison of classical test theory and item response theory and their applications to test development. Educ. Meas. Issues Pract. **12**(3), 38 (1993)
36. D. Thissen, L. Steinberg, H. Wainer, in *Test Equating, Scaling, and Linking: Methods and Practices*, ed. by M.J. Kolen, R.L. Brennan (Springer, Berlin, 2001), pp. 119–138
37. H. Swaminathan, F.M. Rogers, Detecting differential item functioning using logistic regression procedures. J. Educ. Meas. **30**(4), 315 (1993)
38. F.B. Baker, *The Basics of Item Response Theory* (ERIC Clearinghouse on Assessment and Evaluation, College Park, 2001)
39. R. Bock, M. Aitkin, Marginal maximum likelihood estimation of item parameters: application of an EM algorithm. Psychometrika **46**(4), 443 (1981)

Bootstrap Exploratory Graph Analysis

Nataša Kovač, Kruna Ratković, Marko Simeunović, and Hojjatollah Farahani

1 Overview of Exploratory Graph Analysis

Exploratory Graph Analysis (EGA) is an innovative psychometric approach that utilises concepts from network analysis and graph theory to uncover latent structures in psychological data [1, 2]. As traditional factor-analytic approaches, such as exploratory factor analysis (EFA) or principal component analysis (PCA), have limitations, especially when dealing with complex, interrelated psychological constructs, EGA has gained attention due to its intuitive graphical interpretation and flexibility in handling complex dimensional structures.

EGA conceptualises psychological constructs as networks composed of interconnected items, where nodes represent variables or items, and edges denote relationships such as correlations or partial correlations [3]. Unlike conventional factor analysis, which explicitly assumes latent variables drive item responses, EGA adopts a data-driven approach to directly identify cohesive clusters within the correlation structure of psychological variables. By focusing on the relational dynamics among observed items, EGA offers a complementary perspective to traditional latent variable modelling [4].

One of the primary motivations behind using EGA in psychological research lies in its capacity to effectively handle complex or overlapping constructs. Psychological phenomena often consist of closely interwoven dimensions that traditional factor analysis methods sometimes inadequately separate, especially when latent factors overlap significantly or when constructs share multiple items [5]. EGA

N. Kovač · K. Ratković · M. Simeunović (✉)
Faculty of Applied Sciences, University of Donja Gorica, Podgorica, Montenegro
e-mail: natasa.kovac@udg.edu.me; kruna.ratkovic@udg.edu.me; marko.simeunovic@udg.edu.me

H. Farahani
Department of Psychology, Faculty of Humanities, Tarbiat Modares University, Tehran, Iran
e-mail: h.farahani@modares.ac.ir

N. Kovač et al. (eds.), *Data Science in Psychology*,
https://doi.org/10.1007/978-3-032-18312-5_11

addresses these complexities by applying network community detection algorithms, providing an empirically grounded partitioning of items into coherent groups, or communities, without requiring strong assumptions about item independence or factor orthogonality.

In EGA, community detection algorithms, such as the Walktrap or Louvain methods, are frequently employed to identify cohesive clusters of items based on their relational structure [6]. Walktrap, for instance, simulates random walks across network structures to find densely interconnected communities, making it particularly suited for psychological data where items within a construct exhibit strong mutual dependencies [7]. Louvain is another popular method that iteratively optimises modularity, which measures the strength of division into clusters, effectively capturing item groupings that maximise internal coherence while minimising external connections [8].

The choice between these algorithms can influence results, making careful algorithm selection an essential consideration in EGA applications [9]. Studies have demonstrated that the Walktrap algorithm typically excels with datasets of moderate complexity, offering reliable identification of latent constructs, especially in psychological scales characterised by moderate sample sizes [10]. Louvain is more computationally efficient and is often preferred in larger datasets, making it a viable alternative for extensive psychological assessments.

Beyond cluster identification, EGA provides robust visualisation tools that offer intuitive and immediate insights into the data structure. Graphical representations, known as network plots, visually communicate the strength of relationships among items through edge thickness and the centrality or importance of items via node size. These visual representations enhance interpretability, aiding researchers in clearly identifying central items that substantially contribute to latent constructs, as well as peripheral items that might be candidates for removal or revision [11].

Another substantial benefit of EGA is its inherent emphasis on exploratory data analysis. While confirmatory methods require predefined hypotheses about factor structures, EGA enables researchers to explore the data structure without imposing restrictive theoretical constraints initially. This exploratory capability makes EGA particularly valuable in initial stages of scale development, exploratory studies, or scenarios where theoretical foundations are still being developed or tested empirically [12].

A significant conceptual advancement provided by EGA is its treatment of dimensionality estimation. Traditional methods often depend on eigenvalue-based criteria (such as Kaiser's rule or parallel analysis) to determine the number of latent dimensions, potentially yielding unstable or inflated dimensional solutions, especially in smaller or noisier datasets. EGA empirically derives dimensionality by directly identifying the optimal community structure through network-based clustering algorithms, thus providing a more robust and theoretically meaningful determination of dimensions [13].

EGA explicitly addresses issues related to scale dimensionality and stability. Network-based dimensionality estimation is complemented by methods for quantifying dimension stability, such as bootEGA, which employs repeated resampling procedures to ensure robustness and replicability of dimensional findings [14]. Such stability assessments significantly enhance confidence in psychological measures, addressing growing concerns about replicability and robustness in psychological sciences.

In terms of limitations, EGA, like any other statistical approach, requires careful consideration of methodological nuances. The accuracy of identified networks heavily depends on sample size, item characteristics, and choice of correlation estimators (e.g. Pearson correlations, polychoric correlations, or partial correlation estimates such as graphical lasso). Researchers must ensure adequate sample sizes to avoid instability in community detection and dimensionality estimation, particularly when applying EGA in datasets with high dimensionality and complexity [15].

Network interpretations must consider potential confounding due to measurement artefacts, response biases, or item wording effects that may produce spurious network structures. Complementing EGA with traditional psychometric evaluations, such as classical item analysis and measurement invariance testing, remains essential to ensure validity and reliability of psychological scales derived from network analysis [12].

EGA represents a significant methodological innovation in psychological measurement, offering researchers robust tools for uncovering latent structures in psychological data. By leveraging advances in network analysis and computational methods, EGA enables precise, interpretable, and empirically grounded insights into the dimensional architecture of psychological constructs, addressing limitations inherent in traditional psychometric methods and enhancing the reliability, validity, and interpretability of psychological research findings.

2 Comparing EGA with Factor Analytic Methods

In this section, we discuss EGA with traditional factor analytic methods such as EFA, Confirmatory Factor Analysis (CFA), and PCA that have long served as the backbone of psychometric evaluations (Table 1). EGA offers a novel approach that can overcome some inherent limitations of these classical techniques. This section aims to delineate the critical conceptual and methodological differences between EGA and factor analytic methods, highlighting specific scenarios in psychological research where EGA may provide superior interpretability and validity.

Traditional factor analytic methods operate on the fundamental assumption of latent variables that drive the variance in observed data [2]. EFA, for example, identifies underlying latent factors by examining patterns of covariance among observed variables, using factor extraction and rotation procedures to simplify factor structure [16]. CFA extends this approach by testing explicit theoretical models of how latent constructs cause responses to manifest variables, applying strict a priori structural constraints to validate hypothesised factor structures [17].

In contrast, EGA reframes psychological data as interconnected networks where items (variables) are nodes and relationships among items, typically estimated

Table 1 Comparison of EGA and traditional factor analytic methods

Aspect	Factor analysis	EGA
Conceptual basis	Latent variables explain covariance among items	Items form networks; edges represent relationships
Methodology	Factor extraction, rotations, and model constraints	Community detection algorithms identify clusters
Data assumptions	Linear, additive relations from latent constructs	Captures interdependencies and nonlinear interactions
Dimensionality	Estimated via eigenvalues, scree plots, or parallel analysis	Estimated directly through network clustering
Interpretability	Factor loadings or path diagrams; less intuitive in large models	Clear graphical representation of clusters and centrality
Robustness	Sensitive to extraction, rotation, and model specification	Sensitive to choice of detection algorithms and correlations
Strengths	Best for theory-driven testing and validation	Best for exploratory analysis, scale development, and complex constructs
Complementarity	Provides confirmatory rigor	Provides exploratory insight; complements factor analysis

as partial correlations, constitute edges [1, 14]. Rather than presuming a causal latent structure, EGA empirically detects cohesive item clusters or communities through network community detection algorithms like Walktrap or Louvain. These algorithms dynamically partition the network, highlighting structural cohesion within clusters while minimising connections across clusters, a feature not explicitly addressed in conventional factor analysis [4].

A significant divergence between EGA and traditional factor analysis emerges in their methodological assumptions about the data-generating mechanisms [18]. EFA and CFA generally assume linear, additive relationships driven by underlying latent constructs. Such assumptions may inadequately capture complex, nonlinear relationships prevalent in psychological constructs such as personality, emotions, or cognitive abilities, especially when items exhibit mutual dependencies or reciprocal interactions [19]. EGA, on the other hand, explicitly models item interdependencies and nonlinear interactions through its network structure, making it particularly suitable for psychological domains characterised by complex item interactions and overlap between constructs [20].

Another critical advantage of EGA lies in its robust and intuitive visualisation capabilities. Traditional factor analytic outputs, such as factor loadings matrices or path diagrams, are informative but can be challenging to interpret, especially in high-dimensional psychological datasets [17]. EGA's graphical representation simplifies interpretation significantly by visually conveying relational patterns and item centralities. Nodes that appear more central (highly connected) highlight items of particular theoretical importance, facilitating straightforward interpretations regarding item significance and dimensional clarity [11].

EGA provides a direct estimation of dimensionality through network clustering rather than relying on indirect heuristics, such as eigenvalues or parallel analysis used in EFA. This empirical dimensional estimation offers increased stability, particularly valuable in small or noisy datasets frequently encountered in psychological research. Methods like bootEGA further strengthen reliability by quantifying dimension and item stability across multiple resamples, providing transparent estimates of robustness rarely matched by traditional factor analytic methods [21].

One potential limitation of EGA compared to factor analysis involves its sensitivity to methodological decisions, such as choosing community detection algorithms and correlation estimation techniques [22]. Community detection methods differ in sensitivity and computational complexity, potentially influencing dimensional outcomes [8]. Selection among partial correlation estimation methods (e.g. graphical lasso, ridge regularisation, or thresholded correlations) can alter network structure significantly, necessitating careful methodological justifications [23].

Methodological rigour in factor analysis also demands similarly careful consideration. Decisions regarding extraction methods, rotations (orthogonal vs. oblique), and model specification in CFA significantly affect dimensional results, interpretation, and theoretical validity [17]. Therefore, methodological sensitivity does not uniquely disadvantage EGA; instead, it emphasises the necessity of methodological transparency and empirical justification across psychometric methods.

The selection between EGA and traditional factor analysis ultimately depends on the specific research questions and dataset characteristics. EGA excels particularly in exploratory scenarios, such as early scale development, assessing complex overlapping constructs, or evaluating item-level stability and dimensional coherence without stringent theoretical priors [13]. In contrast, factor analytic approaches may be preferred when clear theoretical expectations exist, latent structures are hypothesised a priori, or when validating existing scales.

In practice, a combined methodological strategy employing EGA and factor analysis sequentially or concurrently can be particularly powerful. Initial EGA explorations could guide factor analytic model specifications, potentially enhancing CFA's theoretical relevance and empirical fit. Alternatively, factor analyses could precede EGA to confirm or challenge hypothesised dimensions with empirically derived network structures, enriching psychometric validity through methodological triangulation [24].

Thus, EGA provides a complementary rather than competitive toolset to factor analysis, significantly enriching psychometric practice by incorporating modern insights from network science and graphical modelling. Its capacity to handle complexity, visualise relationships intuitively, and robustly estimate dimensionality through empirical clustering makes EGA a valuable methodological addition to psychological research.

3 Bootstrap Exploratory Graph Analysis

Bootstrap Exploratory Graph Analysis (bootEGA) is an extension of EGA that employs bootstrapping techniques [25] to assess the stability and reliability of network structures in psychological data. By resampling the dataset multiple times, bootEGA estimates the consistency of the identified latent dimensions, helping researchers determine whether the detected structure is robust across different samples. This iterative resampling approach provides a way to account for sampling variability, offering a more precise evaluation of how well an observed network structure generalises beyond a specific dataset [26]. Unlike traditional approaches that assume a fixed structure, bootEGA allows researchers to quantify uncertainty in the estimated network, making it a valuable tool for psychological research, where measurement structures often involve complex relationships among variables that may not be easily captured through traditional factor analysis [1, 27]. Bootstrapping methods, in general, have been widely recognised as powerful tools for improving the accuracy and stability of statistical estimates, particularly when working with psychological data that exhibit high variability [28, 29].

The application of bootEGA is particularly beneficial in fields such as personality psychology, clinical psychology, and cognitive science, where underlying constructs are often assessed through self-report questionnaires or behavioural measures that may contain inherent variability. By identifying the extent to which network-based representations of psychological constructs remain stable across different bootstrap samples, bootEGA enables researchers to assess whether the detected latent dimensions are robust, rather than artefacts of sample-specific variation. This is crucial in ensuring that network-derived psychological constructs have meaningful theoretical implications and are not driven by random fluctuations in the data. Furthermore, bootEGA provides an empirical basis for comparing different clustering solutions, allowing researchers to determine the most reliable structural organisation of psychological variables based on a probabilistic rather than deterministic framework [30].

In addition to assessing the stability of dimensional structures, bootEGA can also inform decisions regarding scale refinement and psychometric validation. By evaluating how consistently items are assigned to the same latent dimensions across bootstrap replications, researchers can identify potentially unstable items that may require revision or removal. This contributes to improved construct validity, helping ensure that psychological measurements accurately reflect the intended theoretical constructs [31]. The importance of measurement stability has been emphasised in the broader context of psychological research, where issues related to replication and construct validity remain major concerns [32]. The ability to empirically test the robustness of measurement models through bootEGA strengthens confidence in research findings and enhances the reproducibility of psychological studies.

The fundamental principle behind bootEGA is to generate a large number of resampled datasets from the original data using nonparametric bootstrapping. This technique involves randomly drawing observations with replacement, ensuring that each resampled dataset retains the statistical properties of the original dataset while introducing variability to test the robustness of the network structure. For each resampled dataset, EGA is applied, and the resulting network structure is recorded. By repeatedly estimating the dimensional structure across numerous bootstrap samples, bootEGA enables researchers to assess whether the detected community structure is consistent or highly variable across different resamples.

This procedure allows for the computation of stability metrics that provide empirical support for evaluating the reliability of psychological constructs [33]. Within PsAIchology, such network-informed features can be funnelled into supervised ML (e.g. AdaBoost, XGBoost, Random Forest, and MLP) to predict clinically relevant outcomes [34]. Dimension stability measures the likelihood that the same number of latent dimensions is identified across bootstrap samples, offering insights into the robustness of the estimated factor structure. If dimension stability is high, it suggests that the detected number of dimensions is not an artefact of a particular sample but rather a generalisable feature of the underlying psychological construct. Conversely, low dimension stability may indicate a weakly defined structure, suggesting that alternative model specifications should be considered [35].

Item stability, on the other hand, assesses the extent to which individual items remain consistently assigned to the same network communities across bootstrap samples [14]. In psychological measurement, unstable items may exhibit weak or ambiguous relationships with their respective constructs, leading to cross-loadings or fluctuating placements across dimensions. By quantifying how frequently an item is retained within the same dimension, bootEGA provides researchers with a probabilistic measure of an item's contribution to the construct. Items with high stability reinforce the structure of the network, whereas items with low stability may need to be re-evaluated for potential revision or removal in scale development.

A major advantage of this resampling-based approach is that it accounts for sample variability, which is often a significant concern in psychological research. Many psychometric methods rely on a single dataset for factor extraction, leading to concerns about whether the identified structure would replicate in new samples. By introducing repeated perturbations through bootstrapping, bootEGA helps to determine whether the observed factor structure is robust to variations in sample composition. This is particularly valuable in psychological research, where measurement models are often derived from complex constructs that may be influenced by sample-specific idiosyncrasies.

Furthermore, bootEGA enables researchers to evaluate competing factor structures by providing empirical probabilities that indicate the reproducibility of each identified structure [36]. By comparing dimensional solutions across different bootstrap samples, researchers can determine which structural organisation best represents the underlying psychological construct. The ability to quantify the reproducibility of factor structures is a significant improvement over traditional exploratory factor analysis, which relies on model fit indices that may not always capture the stability of latent dimensions across samples [37].

One of the key advantages of bootEGA is its ability to compare competing factor structures identified through network analysis. Unlike traditional exploratory factor analysis, where model fit indices are used to assess dimensional validity, bootEGA provides empirical probabilities reflecting the reproducibility of identified structures. This approach allows researchers to evaluate whether a network-derived psychological construct remains consistent across different datasets, enhancing the robustness of psychometric assessments [37].

The results of bootEGA allow researchers to make data-driven decisions about the validity of psychological constructs. High stability values suggest that a construct is consistently measured across different samples, whereas low stability may indicate potential measurement inconsistencies. This information is crucial for refining psychometric instruments, ensuring that psychological assessments are reliable and interpretable across different populations.

4 Dimension and Item Stability

Dimension and item stability are essential for evaluating the consistency of network-based representations of psychological constructs. In EGA and bootEGA, these stability measures allow researchers to assess whether the identified latent structures remain stable across multiple resampled datasets. Ensuring high stability enhances the interpretability and reproducibility of psychological constructs, reducing the risk of findings being driven by sample-specific artefacts [1, 30].

Dimension stability refers to the probability that the same number of latent dimensions is recovered across bootstrap replications. This measure indicates whether the network structure obtained in the original dataset is likely to be observed in new data. If dimension stability is low, it suggests that the estimated number of latent factors is sensitive to slight variations in the data, questioning the generalisability of the structure. Stability is quantified by computing how often the number of dimensions remains unchanged across bootstrap samples, which is estimated using the following relation:

$$P(D_k) = \frac{1}{B}\sum_{b=1}^{B} \mathbb{I}\left(D_k^{(b)} = D_k\right), \tag{1}$$

where $P(D_k)$ is the probability that the estimated dimensionality D_k remains consistent across bootstrap replications, $D_k^{(b)}$ represents the number of dimensions detected in the b-th bootstrap sample, and B is the total number of bootstrap iterations. The indicator function $\mathbb{I}(\cdot)$ returns 1 if the bootstrap sample retains the same dimensional structure as the original EGA solution and 0 otherwise. A higher probability suggests greater confidence in the stability of the identified network structure, suggesting that the construct is reliably captured across different resamples.

Item stability, on the other hand, evaluates whether individual variables remain assigned to the same latent dimensions across bootstrap samples. Psychological constructs often involve overlapping or weakly associated items, leading to potential variability in their placement within the network. Items with high stability contribute strongly to the construct, while low-stability items may be cross-loading or weakly defined. A key metric used to quantify this is the item stability coefficient, which measures how consistently an item is assigned to the same network community. If item stability is low, it may indicate the need for item refinement, removal, or reconsideration of theoretical constructs [31].

Dimension and item stability metrics are essential in the refinement of psychological scales and assessments. When a psychological instrument exhibits low stability, it may suggest inconsistencies in how latent dimensions are defined or an inappropriate factor structure. For instance, an instrument used to measure personality traits should maintain a consistent number of dimensions across different samples to ensure its validity. If bootEGA reveals variability in the number of detected dimensions, researchers may need to reconsider the structure of the instrument, potentially revising items or adjusting the way dimensions are defined.

Beyond measurement validation, stability metrics also play a role in ensuring replicability in psychological research. The reproducibility crisis in psychology has emphasised the importance of assessing whether findings hold across different datasets [32]. By incorporating bootEGA stability assessments into network psychometric analyses, researchers can empirically quantify the degree to which psychological constructs are stable across varying conditions. This provides a methodological safeguard against overfitting, ensuring that findings remain meaningful in new datasets.

Given the increasing reliance on network-based approaches in psychology, dimension and item stability provide empirical support for the robustness of latent constructs. Network-informed features can then be evaluated within applied regression pipelines that emphasise reproducible metrics and interpretation [38]. By systematically evaluating these metrics, researchers can refine measurement instruments, improve psychometric properties, and enhance theoretical clarity. Ensuring stable psychological constructs contributes to more reliable assessments and advances in psychological science.

5 Applications and Case Studies

To illustrate the application of bootEGA, this section examines a real-world psychological dataset involving five theoretically distinct but related constructs: *Stress and Anxiety* (SA), *Emotional Intelligence* (EI), *Personality Traits* (PT), *Cognitive Performance* (CP), and *Social Function* (SF). These constructs were assessed through a battery of self-report and behavioural items administered to a diverse sample of 500 adult participants. In addition to the five latent constructs, two items were purposefully designed to span across domains (e.g. an item linking emotional reactivity and stress), enabling us to observe how bootEGA handles *cross-loading and dimension instability*. The dataset includes:

- Demographic variables (Age, Gender)
- Five items per construct (e.g. SA_1, SA_2, ..., CP_5)
- Two cross-dimensional items: Cross_StressEmotion_1 and Cross_PersonalitySocial_1

To begin the analysis, the dataset is imported and checked for missing values. Since bootEGA cannot handle missing entries or non-numeric variables, we impute missing values using column means and ensure all analysis variables are numeric.

```
# Set working directory to dataset location
setwd("/Users/your_name/Desktop")

# Load data
data <- read.csv("bootEGA_case_study_dataset_complex.csv")

# Impute missing values using mean imputation
for(i in 3:ncol(data)){
  data[is.na(data[,i]), i] <- mean(data[,i], na.rm = TRUE)
}

# Convert all items to numeric (if not already)
data[,3:ncol(data)] <- lapply(data[,3:ncol(data)], as.numeric)
```

This pre-processing ensures that all 27 psychological items are ready for graph analysis. Demographic variables (Age, Gender) are excluded from the dimensional estimation. Once the dataset is prepared, we load the EGAnet package and apply bootEGA to the item responses. This algorithm estimates the number and structure of latent dimensions using network community detection methods and evaluates the stability of these dimensions across bootstrap resamples.

```
# Load EGAnet
install.packages("EGAnet") # Run only once
library(EGAnet)

# Set seed for reproducibility
set.seed(1234)

# Run bootEGA with default GLASSO + Walktrap
bootega_results <- bootEGA(data[,3:ncol(data)], n = 500)
```

Here, 500 bootstrap resamples are used to ensure stable estimates. The GLASSO estimator is used for partial correlation network construction, and the Walktrap algorithm is employed to detect communities (dimensions) within the network. Once bootEGA completes, we begin interpreting the core output:

```
summary(bootega_results)

Model: GLASSO (EBIC)
Correlations: auto
Algorithm:  Walktrap
Unidimensional Method:  Louvain

----

EGA Type: EGA
Bootstrap Samples: 500 (Parametric)

             5
Frequency:   1

Median dimensions: 5 [5, 5] 95% CI
```

When the bootEGA procedure is complete, the summary function provides a comprehensive overview of the results. Among the most important outputs is the estimated number of dimensions, which, in this case, consistently converges to five across all bootstrap samples. This figure reflects the underlying structural complexity of the psychological constructs represented in the dataset. In addition to this estimate, the output includes confidence intervals, offering a statistical range within which the dimensionality is likely to fall under repeated sampling.

Equally informative is the item membership mapping, which indicates the specific dimension to which each item is assigned within the network structure. This mapping reveals how consistently items align with their expected constructs. To further evaluate the reliability of these assignments, bootEGA computes bootstrap stability estimates, which quantify the proportion of bootstrap replications in which each item was assigned to the same dimension. Together, these metrics enable researchers to assess not only the structural coherence of their psychological measures but also the robustness and reproducibility of the dimensional solution across hypothetical variations of the dataset.

Once the bootEGA analysis has been completed, it is often beneficial to preserve its output for further interpretation, documentation, or integration with visualisation tools. The typical procedure involves saving several key components of the analysis into structured files. These include the item-to-dimension mappings derived from the typical community structure, the stability indices indicating how consistently each item was assigned to its respective dimension across bootstrap iterations, and the overall stability of the dimensional solution itself.

```
# Save main outputs
write.csv(bootega_results$typicalGraph,
 ↪ "bootEGA_network_structure.csv", row.names=FALSE)
write.csv(bootega_results$item.stability,
 ↪ "bootEGA_item_stability.csv", row.names=TRUE)
write.csv(bootega_results$dimension.stability,
 ↪ "bootEGA_dimension_stability.csv", row.names=TRUE)
```

By exporting these elements, researchers can revisit the network structure outside of the R environment, share it with collaborators, or conduct further post hoc comparisons, such as matching bootEGA-derived clusters to theoretical groupings or alternative models. This practice also supports transparency and reproducibility, two essential pillars in psychometric and psychological research in line with modern Python-based ML workflows in psychology [38], and other domains [39]. Network-informed features and psychometric dimensions derived at this stage can subsequently feed ML classifiers for clinically relevant outcomes such as chronic pain stratification [40]. In the present study, each of these outputs was saved as a separate CSV file, ensuring compatibility with external visualisation platforms and analytical tools that may be used in the next phases of analysis. The exported data serve as the foundation for the visual inspection and interpretation of the network structures discussed in the following section.

The parameter choices used in this bootEGA analysis reflect a thoughtful balance between methodological rigour and practical constraints. The number of bootstrap samples was set to 500, offering sufficient statistical power to evaluate item and dimension stability while keeping computational time manageable for most standard environments. In this context, the Glasso (graphical lasso) method was selected as the estimator for partial correlations. This choice was motivated by its robustness in high-dimensional spaces and its ability to construct sparse, interpretable networks by penalising weaker connections. Glasso is particularly effective in psychological datasets where variables may exhibit substantial collinearity, as it helps reduce spurious associations.

For community detection, the Walktrap algorithm was employed. Walktrap is based on random walks over the network structure, allowing it to uncover community structures that are tightly clustered and locally cohesive. This makes it well suited to psychological constructs, which often consist of internally consistent but moderately overlapping subdomains. While other algorithms, such as Louvain or Spinglass, are available, Walktrap was chosen due to its empirical reliability in uncovering latent constructs in self-report and cognitive assessment data.

Together, these parameter selections were grounded in both the structure of the dataset and established practice in psychometric network analysis. They provide a reasonable foundation for examining dimensional stability, identifying overlapping items, and interpreting the psychological architecture present within the data.

This case study demonstrates the full application of bootEGA on a complex but well-structured psychological dataset. It shows that:

- The tool effectively recovers latent dimensions under realistic data imperfections.
- It evaluates dimension stability and cross-loading behaviour.
- It prepares data for rigorous network-based psychometric interpretation.

6 Visualising Graph Analysis Results

Once the statistical output of bootEGA has been generated and exported, the final step is visual interpretation. Visualisation not only brings abstract numerical results to life but also facilitates theoretical reasoning and construct validation [41]. In this section, we explore how graphical representations of psychological network structures serve to reveal, clarify, and communicate the organisation of latent constructs embedded in complex data. We will present a comprehensive analysis using bootEGA to explore a rich psychological dataset comprising five theoretically grounded constructs: Stress and Anxiety (SA), Emotional Intelligence (EI), Personality Traits (PT), Cognitive Performance (CP), and Social Function (SF). After proper data preparation, including numeric transformation and mean imputation of missing values, the bootEGA procedure was conducted using the EGAnet package in R, carefully employing 500 bootstrap iterations to achieve robust statistical conclusions.

Figure 1 captures two complementary perspectives of the network analysis. On the left-hand side of the figure, readers see a vivid graphical representation of the community structure. Each node represents an individual psychological item, and edges between them depict partial correlations, clearly communicating the underlying relational structure of items after accounting for their mutual interactions. The Walktrap algorithm used for community detection colour-codes items into distinct groups that visually represent the five theoretically expected dimensions, thus offering immediate interpretability of latent structures. The edge thickness reinforces the visualisation by clearly differentiating stronger from weaker associations, making evident the internal cohesion of each psychological construct.

Within this community graph, special attention is drawn to two intentionally cross-loading items, `Cross_StressEmotion_1` and `Cross_PersonalitySocial_1`. These items do not neatly fit within a single cluster but instead strategically position themselves at the intersections of relevant psychological dimensions. For instance, `Cross_StressEmotion_1` visually spans between the SA and EI dimensions, confirming its intended theoretical ambiguity. The empirical evidence provided by the stability metrics supports this visual observation, indicating a slightly lower stability coefficient (0.99) compared to other firmly placed items, which maintain near-perfect stability (1.00). This highlights the sensitivity of bootEGA in detecting and representing theoretical complexity.

The right-hand side of Fig. 1 complements this structural overview by displaying the replication plot, which quantifies how consistently each item remains within the same dimensional community across all bootstrap iterations. Remarkably, nearly all items achieved stability coefficients close to 1.00, strongly reinforcing the

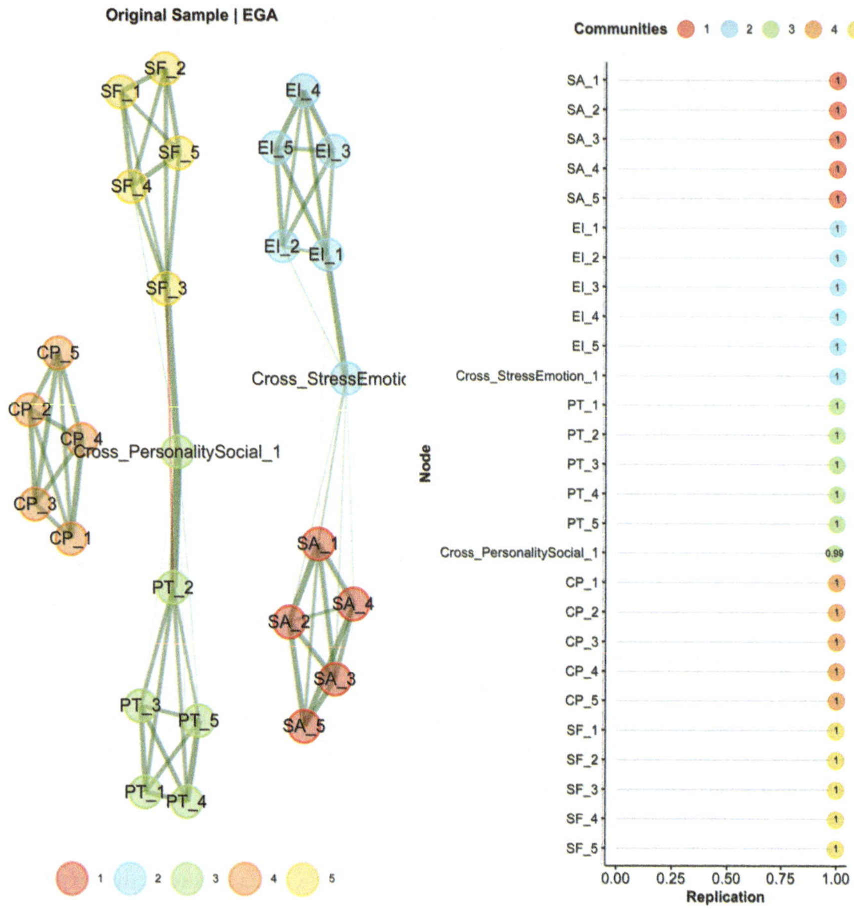

Fig. 1 Output of a bootEGA run

dimensional reliability across repeated sampling and demonstrating the stability of psychological constructs under scrutiny.

Moving to Fig. 2, readers encounter a heatmap visualising partial correlations between psychological items. This figure offers another intuitive perspective on dimensional coherence, providing visual confirmation of high internal consistency within each identified community. The heatmap visually distinguishes stronger relationships, represented by darker shades, clearly reinforcing the presence of tightly bound constructs such as SA, EI, PT, CP, and SF. Simultaneously, lighter shading between these communities validates the conceptual separateness of each dimension, confirming bootEGA's effectiveness in distinguishing distinct yet related constructs.

Further exploring intra-dimensional structures, Fig. 3 introduces dimension-by-dimension adjacency matrices. Each matrix isolates the relationships solely within

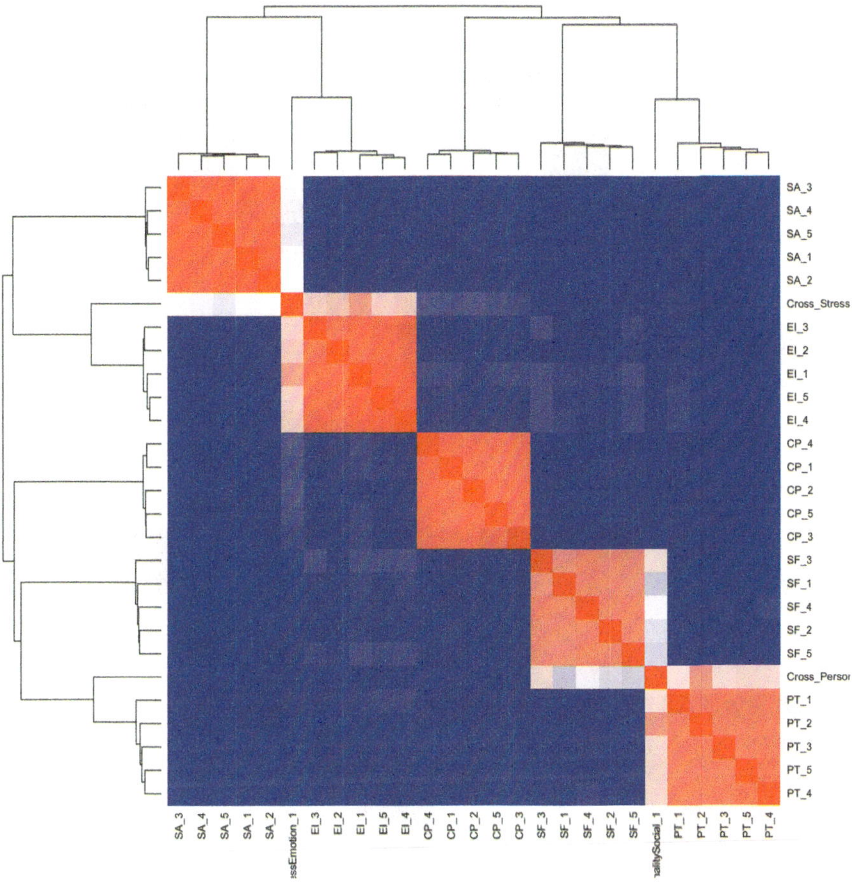

Fig. 2 Heatmaps of partial correlations

individual communities. This detailed visualisation provides an insightful look at internal item dynamics, underscoring strong intra-dimensional relationships. Such visual clarity allows researchers to precisely identify core items within each dimension, pinpointing those contributing most meaningfully to the stability of latent structures. These matrices demonstrate unequivocally how psychological dimensions vary internally in their item interconnections, offering essential guidance for potential refinements in scale development.

Complementing the item-level analysis, Fig. 4 enhances theoretical understanding by displaying a correspondence plot that juxtaposes EGA-derived network clusters with factor loadings from the traditional EFA. This comparative visualisation bridges methodological traditions, demonstrating substantial overlap yet subtle differences between network-based and factor-analytic structures. Through this visualisation, readers gain an enriched comprehension of how network community

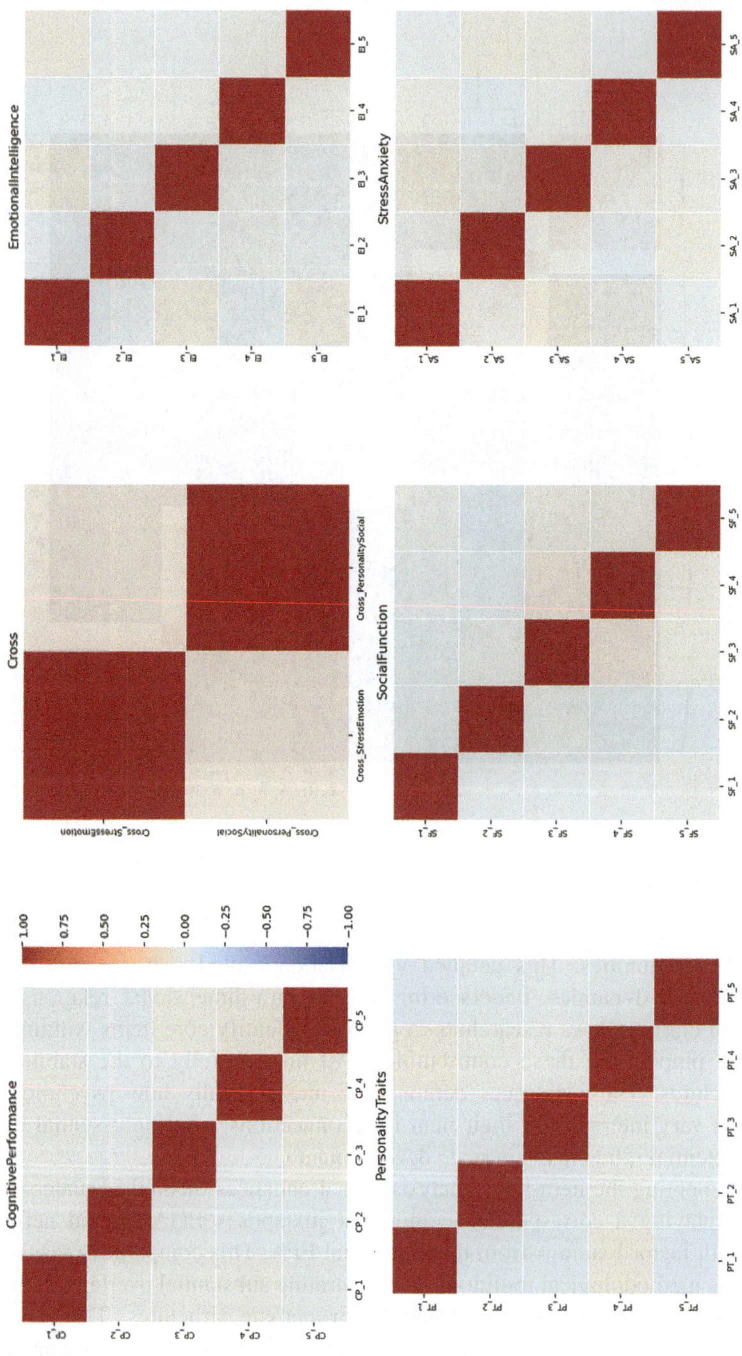

Fig. 3 Dimension-by-dimension adjacency matrices

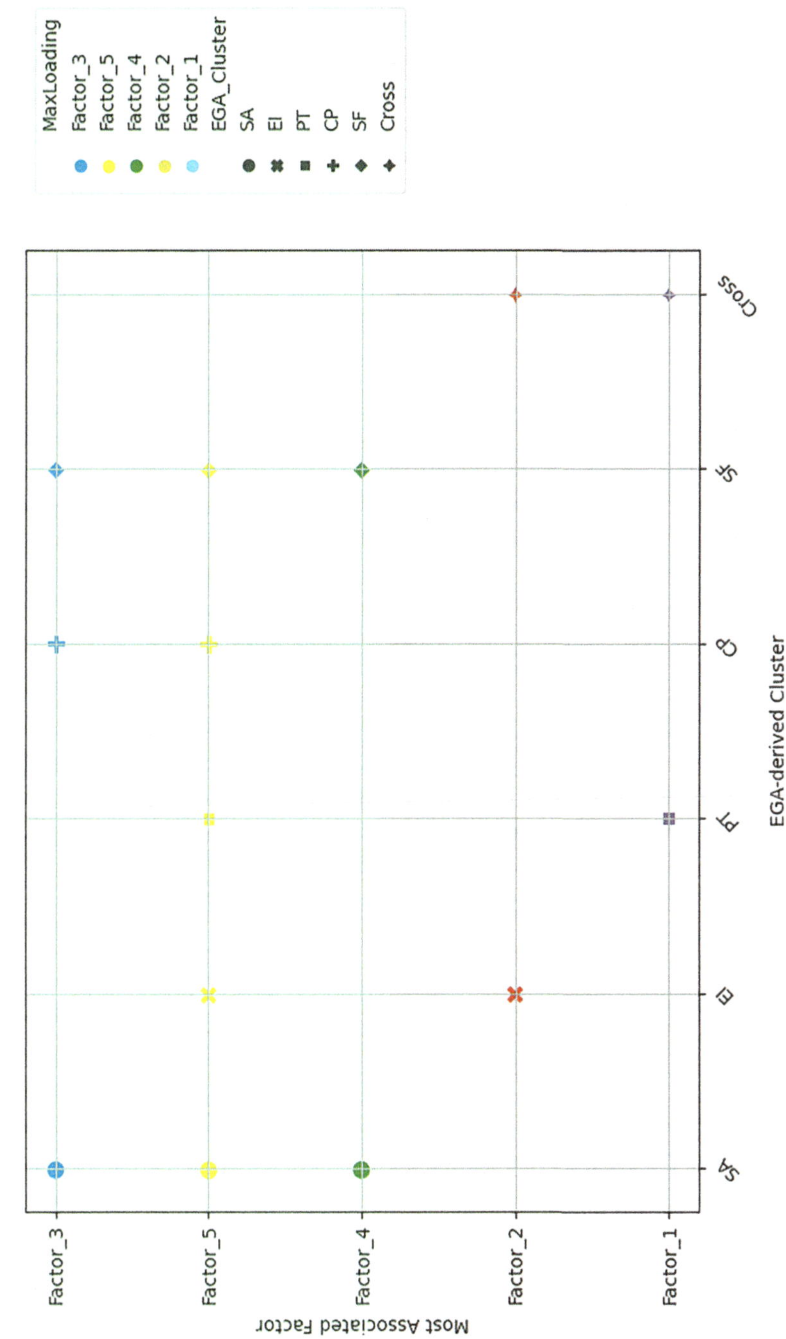

Fig. 4 Correspondence between EGA clusters and FA loadings

assignments align with traditional psychometric approaches, thereby promoting methodological dialogue and integration between contemporary network analyses and classical factor analytic perspectives.

Extending the interpretive richness further, Fig. 5 visualises network centrality metrics, betweenness, closeness, and node strength, directly integrated into the graphical representation of the network, which can highlight bridge items connecting dimensions [42, 43]. Here, centrality metrics are reflected through variations in node size, highlighting items of particular theoretical and structural importance. For instance, nodes with higher betweenness centrality appear visually prominent, immediately signalling their critical roles as connectors or *bridges* between different psychological constructs. Such centrality visualisations empower researchers with deeper insights into the conceptual architecture of psychological constructs, indicating items that are fundamental to maintaining network cohesion and dimensional integrity.

Figure 6 presents a refined network graph, specifically emphasising correlation-based edges between items. This visualisation offers a clear interpretation of the strength and significance of direct item-to-item associations beyond partial correlations. Through visual cues such as line thickness, researchers easily discern key relationships driving the structural cohesion within each dimension. By comparing this visualisation with the partial correlation-based network from Figure 1, researchers gain deeper insights into the direct versus conditioned relationships between items, thereby enriching theoretical understanding and interpretation of latent psychological constructs.

The visualisations across Figs. 1, 2, 3, 4, 5, and 6 present a powerful, multidimensional narrative that thoroughly demonstrates the effectiveness and interpretive depth offered by bootEGA in psychological research. Through careful visual and statistical exploration, bootEGA not only confirms theoretically expected dimensional structures but also elegantly illuminates the dynamics within psychological data, thereby significantly advancing the psychometric validation and conceptual clarity of psychological measurement. Each visualisation in this section serves a distinct yet complementary purpose. Together, they transform the abstract output of bootEGA into a clear, interpretable landscape of psychological structure:

- Network diagrams reveal *dimensionality and modularity*.
- Heatmaps display *direct and indirect item relationships*.
- Replication metrics ensure *robustness and reliability*.
- Centrality plots and adjacency matrices help assess *importance and cohesion*.
- Comparing EGA and FA supports *validity and triangulation*.

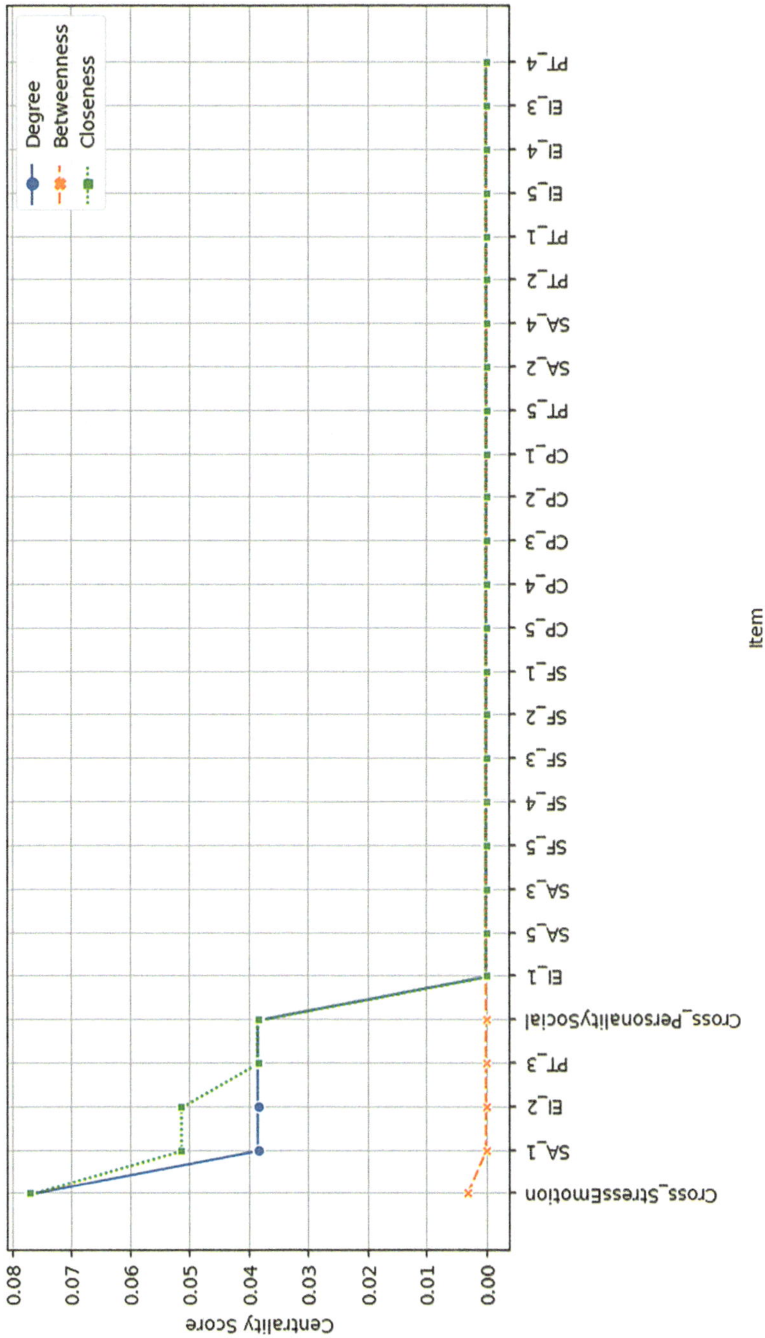

Fig. 5 Network centrality metrics

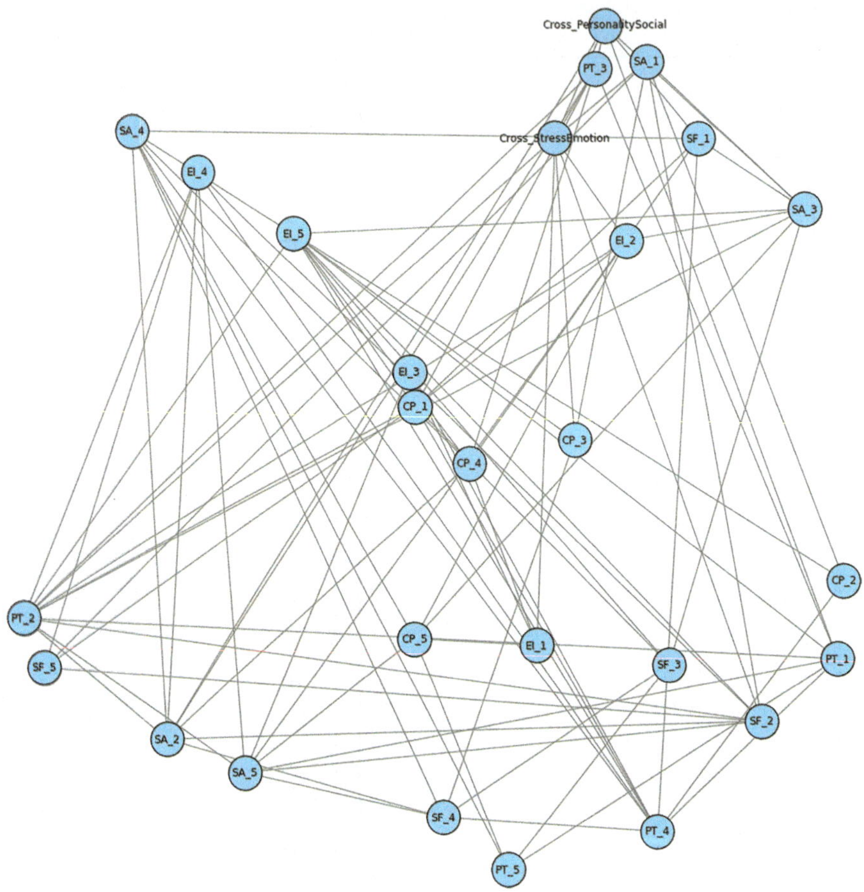

Fig. 6 Network graph with correlation-based edges

References

1. H.F. Golino, S. Epskamp, Exploratory graph analysis: a new approach for estimating the number of dimensions in multivariate data. Multivar. Behav. Res. **52**, 243 (2017)
2. L.F. Bringmann, C. Albers, C. Bockting, D. Borsboom, E. Ceulemans, A. Cramer, S. Epskamp, M.I. Eronen, E. Hamaker, P. Kuppens, et al., Psychopathological networks: theory, methods and practice. Behav. Res. Ther. **149**, 104011 (2022)
3. H. Golino, A. P. Christensen, R. Moulder, L. E. Garrido, L. Jamison, D. Shi, EGAnet: Exploratory graph analysis - a framework for estimating the number of dimensions in multivariate data using network psychometrics, R package version 2.x, (2024)
4. A.P. Christensen, H. Golino, P.J. Silvia, A psychometric network perspective on the validity and validation of personality trait questionnaires. Eur. J. Personal. **34**(6), 1095 (2020)
5. E.I. Fried, A.O. Cramer, Moving forward: challenges and directions for psychopathological network theory and methodology. Perspect. Psychol. Sci. **12**(6), 999 (2017)

6. M. Brusco, D. Steinley, A.L. Watts, Improving the Walktrap algorithm using k-means clustering. Multivar. Behav. Res. **59**(2), 266 (2024)
7. P. Pons, M. Latapy, Computing communities in large networks using random walks, in *Computer and Information Sciences-ISCIS 2005: 20th International Symposium, Istanbul, Turkey, October 26–28, 2005. Proceedings 20* (Springer, Berlin, 2005), pp. 284–293
8. V.D. Blondel, J.L. Guillaume, R. Lambiotte, E. Lefebvre, Fast unfolding of communities in large networks. J. Stat. Mech: Theory Exp. **2008**(10), P10008 (2008)
9. A.P. Christensen, L.E. Garrido, K. Guerra-Peña, H. Golino, Comparing community detection algorithms in psychometric networks: a Monte Carlo simulation. Behav. Res. Methods **56**(3), 1485 (2024)
10. H. Golino, D. Shi, A.P. Christensen, L.E. Garrido, M.D. Nieto, R. Sadana, J.A. Thiyagarajan, A. Martinez-Molina, Investigating the performance of exploratory graph analysis and traditional techniques to identify the number of latent factors: a simulation and tutorial. Psychol. Methods **25**(3), 292 (2020)
11. S. Epskamp, L.J. Waldorp, R. Mõttus, D. Borsboom, The Gaussian graphical model in cross-sectional and time-series data. Multivar. Behav. Res. **53**(4), 453 (2018)
12. L.F. Bringmann, M.I. Eronen, Don't blame the model: reconsidering the network approach to psychopathology. Psychol. Rev. **125**(4), 606 (2018)
13. H.F. Golino, A. Demetriou, Estimating the dimensionality of intelligence like data using exploratory graph analysis. Intelligence **62**, 54 (2017)
14. A.P. Christensen, H. Golino, Estimating the stability of psychological dimensions via bootstrap exploratory graph analysis: a Monte Carlo simulation and tutorial. Psych **3**(3), 479 (2021)
15. C.D. Van Borkulo, D. Borsboom, S. Epskamp, T.F. Blanken, L. Boschloo, R.A. Schoevers, L.J. Waldorp, A new method for constructing networks from binary data. Sci. Rep. **4**(1), 5918 (2014)
16. L.R. Fabrigar, D.T. Wegener, *Exploratory Factor Analysis* (Oxford University, Oxford, 2012)
17. T.A. Brown, *Confirmatory Factor Analysis for Applied Research* (Guilford Publications, New York, 2015)
18. T. Wongvorachan, O. Bulut, in *Advanced Learning Analytics Methods: AI, Precision and Complexity*, ed. by M. Saqr, S. López-Pernas (Springer, Berlin, 2025). In press
19. L.F. Bringmann, T. Elmer, S. Epskamp, R.W. Krause, D. Schoch, M. Wichers, J.T. Wigman, E. Snippe, What do centrality measures measure in psychological networks?. J. Abnorm. Psychol. **128**(8), 892 (2019)
20. T.F. Blanken, M.K. Deserno, J. Dalege, D. Borsboom, P. Blanken, G.A. Kerkhof, A.O. Cramer, The role of stabilizing and communicating symptoms given overlapping communities in psychopathology networks. Sci. Rep. **8**(1), 5854 (2018)
21. A.M. Isvoranu, S. Epskamp, L. Waldorp, D. Borsboom, *Network Psychometrics with R: A Guide for Behavioral and Social Scientists* (Taylor & Francis, Milton Park, 2022)
22. S.J. Brooks, V.O. Jones, H. Wang, C. Deng, S.G. Golding, J. Lim, J. Gao, P. Daoutidis, C. Stamoulis, Community detection in the human connectome: method types, differences and their impact on inference. Hum. Brain Mapp. **45**(5), e26669 (2024)
23. D.R. Williams, P. Rast, Back to the basics: rethinking partial correlation network methodology. Br. J. Math. Stat. Psychol. **73**(2), 187 (2020)
24. A.P. Christensen, H. Golino, P. Silvia, A psychometric network perspective on the measurement and assessment of personality traits. Preprint (2019)
25. H. Hong, K. Rios, Unpacking key dimensions of family empowerment among Latinx parents of children with intellectual and developmental disabilities using exploratory graph analysis: preliminary research. Psychiatry Int. **6**(3), 96 (2025)
26. F.B. Sheykhangafshe, H. Farahani, P. Watson, Using exploratory graph analysis (EGA) in validating the structure of the Perth alexithymia questionnaire in Iranians with chronic pain. Front. Psychol. **15**, 1400340 (2024)
27. S. Epskamp, D. Borsboom, E.I. Fried, Estimating psychological networks and their accuracy: a tutorial paper. Behav. Res. Methods **50**, 195 (2018)

28. B. Efron, R.J. Tibshirani, *An Introduction to the Bootstrap* (Chapman and Hall/CRC, New York, 1994)
29. M.R. Chernick, *Bootstrap Methods: A Guide for Practitioners and Researchers* (Wiley, New York, 2008)
30. A. P. Christensen, L. E. Garrido, H. Golino, Comparing network and latent variable models in psychological research, Psychol. Methods **26**(5), 599–615 (2021)
31. H. F. Golino, A. P. Christensen, R. G. Moulder, S. M. Boker, Modeling latent dimensions with exploratory graph analysis: a tutorial. Struct. Equ. Model. Multidiscip. J. **27**(6), 927–954 (2020)
32. J.K. Flake, E.I. Fried, Measurement schmeasurement: questionable measurement practices and how to avoid them. Adv. Methods Pract. Psychol. Sci. **3**(4), 456 (2020)
33. L. Jamison, A.P. Christensen, H. Golino, Optimizing Walktrap's community detection in networks using the total entropy fit index. PsyArXiv Preprints (2021)
34. H. Farahani, P. Watson, T. Bezan, N. Kovač, L.C. Winter, M. Blagojević, P. Azadfallah, A. Allahyari, S. Masoumian, P. Jiménez, Psaichology: an intelligent direction in psychological sciences, in *10th International Scientific Conference Technics, Informatics and Education-TIE 2024* (Faculty of Technical Sciences Čačak, University of Kragujevac, Kragujevac, 2024)
35. A. P. Christensen, H. Golino, Estimating the stability of the number of factors via bootstrap exploratory graph analysis: A tutorial. Psychol. Methods **26**(3), 291–304 (2021)
36. M.W. Watkins, S.C. Dombrowski, R.J. McGill, G.L. Canivez, A.E. Pritchard, L.A. Jacobson, Bootstrap exploratory graph analysis of the WISC–V with a clinical sample. J. Intelligence **11**(7), 137 (2023)
37. H. F. Golino, S. Epskamp, Exploratory graph analysis: a new approach for estimating the number of dimensions in psychological research. PLOS ONE **12**(6), e0174035 (2017)
38. N. Kovač, K. Ratković, H. Farahani, P. Watson, A practical applications guide to machine learning regression models in psychology with python. Methods Psychol. **11**, 100156 (2024)
39. K. Ratković, N. Kovač, M. Simeunović, Hybrid LSTM model to predict the level of air pollution in montenegro. Appl. Sci. **13**(18), 10152 (2023)
40. N. Kovač, K. Ratković, P. Watson, H. Farahani, F. Bagheri Sheykhangafshe, Machine learning classification models for predicting chronic pain. Curr. Psychol., 1–14 (2025)
41. E.H. Korkut, E. Surer, Visualization in virtual reality: a systematic review. Virtual Reality **27**(2), 1447 (2023)
42. Y. Wang, Z. Hu, Y. Feng, A. Wilson, R. Chen, Changes in network centrality of psychopathology symptoms between the COVID-19 outbreak and after peak. Mol. Psychiatry **25**(12), 3140 (2020)
43. E.J. Cha, S. Suh, H.J. Jeon, S. Chung, Identifying the bridge between anxiety response to COVID-19 and depression symptoms in general population: a network analysis. J. Acad. Consultation-Liaison Psychiatry **64**(6), 492 (2023)

Clustering Methods

Nataša Kovač, Kruna Ratković, Marko Simeunović, Hojjatollah Farahani, and Liang Zhao

1 Overview of Clustering in Psychological Data

Clustering methods have progressively gained prominence in psychological research due to their powerful capability to uncover hidden patterns and structures within complex datasets [1–3]. Psychological data often exhibit inherent complexities, such as high dimensionality, heterogeneity, and intricate relationships among variables, making traditional analytical methods insufficient for capturing complex underlying group structures [4, 5].

The primary objective of clustering in psychological research is to categorise individuals or psychological phenomena into meaningful subgroups based on similarity across numerous characteristics. Unlike classification, clustering is inherently exploratory, requiring no predefined labels or categories, and thus enabling researchers to detect previously unrecognised subtypes or behavioural patterns [2]. These discovered clusters often have substantial implications for theory building, diagnostic refinement, and targeted interventions [3, 6]. For example, affect and interpersonal needs variables have been modelled to understand and classify love-addiction risk [7].

N. Kovač · K. Ratković · M. Simeunović (✉)
Faculty of Applied Sciences, University of Donja Gorica, Podgorica, Montenegro
e-mail: natasa.kovac@udg.edu.me; kruna.ratkovic@udg.edu.me; marko.simeunovic@udg.edu.me

H. Farahani
Department of Psychology, Faculty of Humanities, Tarbiat Modares University, Tehran, Iran
e-mail: h.farahani@modares.ac.ir

L. Zhao
Faculty of Philosophy, Science and Letters at Ribeirão Preto, University of São Paulo, Ribeirão Preto, SP, Brazil
e-mail: zhiyongzhang@nd.edu

N. Kovač et al. (eds.), *Data Science in Psychology*,
https://doi.org/10.1007/978-3-032-18312-5_12

In psychology, clustering can be applied across various domains, including clinical psychology, developmental psychology, personality research, social psychology, and cognitive neuroscience [1, 8]. For instance, clustering can help identify subtypes of mental health disorders, revealing different symptom profiles that may inform personalised treatment strategies [2, 9]. Similarly, developmental psychologists frequently utilise clustering techniques to track distinct trajectories of cognitive or emotional development, enhancing understanding of developmental heterogeneity [10]. Related applied work shows how psychometric features (affect, stress, and interpersonal needs) inform algorithmic grouping and classification of behavioural risk [7].

The relevance of clustering techniques extends beyond mere categorisation; it significantly contributes to hypothesis generation and validation in psychological studies. Derived cluster/profile features can also feed supervised pipelines that predict chronic pain severity from psychological scales [11]. By revealing naturally occurring groups, clustering allows psychologists to explore relationships between subgroup membership and external variables such as outcomes, demographic characteristics, or intervention responses [4, 12]. This, in turn, can lead to the refinement of psychological theories and more accurate predictive modelling [13, 14].

Despite its advantages, clustering psychological data poses several unique methodological challenges. Psychological constructs often exhibit considerable overlap and ambiguity, which complicates the clear delineation of cluster boundaries [1, 2]. Psychological data can be subject to significant measurement error and variability, potentially obscuring genuine patterns [3, 15]. Consequently, researchers must carefully choose clustering methods and rigorously validate their outcomes to ensure interpretative reliability [2, 16].

Recent advances in computational psychology have led to more sophisticated clustering algorithms tailored to psychological research. Model-based clustering approaches, such as Gaussian mixture models, have become increasingly popular due to their probabilistic nature, which elegantly accommodates uncertainty and variability in psychological data [6, 14]. Dimensionality reduction techniques, such as principal component analysis (PCA) and t-distributed stochastic neighbour embedding (t-SNE), frequently precede clustering analyses to handle high-dimensional data and facilitate the interpretability of clusters [4, 17].

The integration of machine learning (ML) and clustering in psychology has also spurred methodological innovations [18]. Techniques such as spectral clustering and density-based spatial clustering of applications with noise (DBSCAN) offer robust solutions to complex data structures often encountered in psychological research [19, 20]. These methods handle irregularly shaped clusters and noisy data effectively, proving particularly advantageous in studies involving behavioural data collected in naturalistic settings [10, 21].

Ethical considerations and data transparency have become increasingly vital in psychological clustering analyses. With clustering outcomes directly influencing clinical decisions, educational strategies, and policy-making, ensuring ethical standards, replicability, and transparency of methods and results is paramount [22, 23]. The misuse or misinterpretation of clustering results can lead to unwarranted stigmatisation or inappropriate interventions, highlighting the need for methodological clarity and robust validation [24, 25].

Clustering techniques are indispensable tools in modern psychological research, offering rich insights into underlying data structures and fostering advancements in theory and practice. Psychological researchers leveraging these methods must carefully navigate methodological choices, validation strategies, and ethical considerations to harness the full potential of clustering [2, 4, 5].

2 Clustering Algorithms: K-Means, K-Medoids, Hierarchical, and Fuzzy Clustering

Clustering methods have become essential tools in psychological research for uncovering latent structures, patterns, and distinct subgroups within psychological data. Four core clustering algorithms are particularly important in psychological sciences due to their intuitive nature, adaptability, and extensive applicability: *K-means*, *K-medoids*, *Hierarchical*, and *Fuzzy clustering*.

K-means clustering is perhaps the most popular clustering algorithm used across various scientific disciplines, including psychology, due to its simplicity and computational efficiency. It partitions the dataset into k distinct clusters by assigning each data point to the cluster whose mean (centroid) is nearest, iteratively refining these cluster assignments until convergence [3]. Its main advantage lies in its computational speed and intuitive interpretation, making it particularly useful for preliminary analysis and exploration of large psychological datasets.

K-means is sensitive to initial conditions, often resulting in different clustering outcomes based on initial centroid selection. K-means assumes spherical clusters with roughly equal variance, limiting its effectiveness when clusters are irregularly shaped or significantly overlap [1]. Despite these limitations, it remains highly beneficial for psychological datasets where distinct and relatively balanced groups are expected.

K-medoid clustering, often implemented as the Partitioning Around Medoids (PAM) algorithm, offers a robust alternative to K-means by choosing actual data points as cluster centres rather than mean points (medoids). This approach minimises the sensitivity to outliers and makes it particularly useful in psychological datasets frequently characterised by extreme or aberrant responses [5].

Unlike K-means, K-medoids use medoids to represent clusters, which are more representative in scenarios with skewed distributions or categorical variables. For instance, when analysing survey responses, personality questionnaires, or symptom checklists, where extreme scores can distort cluster means, K-medoid clustering provides a more accurate representation of typical cluster members [2].

Hierarchical clustering methods group data points based on a hierarchy of clusters, usually visualised as a dendrogram, offering a flexible approach that does not require specifying the number of clusters in advance [1]. This flexibility makes hierarchical clustering particularly advantageous for psychological researchers exploring complex, multilevel structures in data, such as developmental trajectories, mood fluctuation patterns, or personality subtypes.

Hierarchical clustering can be performed either agglomeratively (bottom-up) or divisively (top-down). Agglomerative methods are more common and start by treating each data point as an individual cluster, progressively merging clusters based on criteria like distance measures or linkage methods (Ward's, single linkage, or complete linkage). Each method has distinct properties; for example, Ward's linkage tends to form compact clusters, making it particularly suitable for psychological applications seeking coherent and meaningful groupings [26].

Fuzzy clustering, especially fuzzy C-means (FCM), introduces a probabilistic perspective to clustering, allowing data points to belong to multiple clusters with varying degrees of membership [27]. This characteristic is highly relevant in psychology, where behaviours, traits, or symptoms often do not neatly fit into distinct categories but rather lie along a continuum.

FCM assigns each data point a membership coefficient ranging between 0 and 1 for every cluster, reflecting uncertainty and overlapping characteristics common in psychological constructs. For instance, in mental health research, fuzzy clustering can effectively handle overlapping symptoms among psychological disorders, providing a deeper representation of comorbid conditions [28].

Figure 1 provides a comparative visual representation of how different clustering algorithms perform when applied to the same non-linear dataset, emphasising their distinctive strengths and limitations in capturing underlying data structures. While K-means clustering tends to form spherical clusters, which can lead to inaccurate or misleading groupings on datasets with complex shapes, hierarchical clustering more effectively adapts to these complex, non-linear forms due to its agglomerative merging approach. Fuzzy clustering, on the other hand, uniquely highlights areas of uncertainty by assigning gradual memberships, which is visually demonstrated through varying transparency, making it particularly suitable for psychological data where clear boundaries between groups are often ambiguous. This figure highlights the practical importance of carefully selecting the clustering algorithm based on both the nature of the psychological data and the research question at hand.

Each clustering algorithm has unique applications within psychology. K-means has been extensively used in personality research for typology construction, identifying personality clusters based on standardised trait assessments [29]. K-medoids have proven valuable in clinical psychology, particularly in classifying subtypes of mood and anxiety disorders where outlier-resistant methods are essential [30]. Hierarchical clustering is frequently applied in developmental psychology to elucidate trajectories of cognitive or behavioural development over time [31]. Fuzzy clustering effectively captures diagnostic uncertainty in psychiatric classification, offering a detailed alternative to strict categorical diagnoses [32].

Selecting a suitable clustering algorithm depends on various factors, including data scale, expected cluster shapes, sensitivity to outliers, and theoretical expecta-

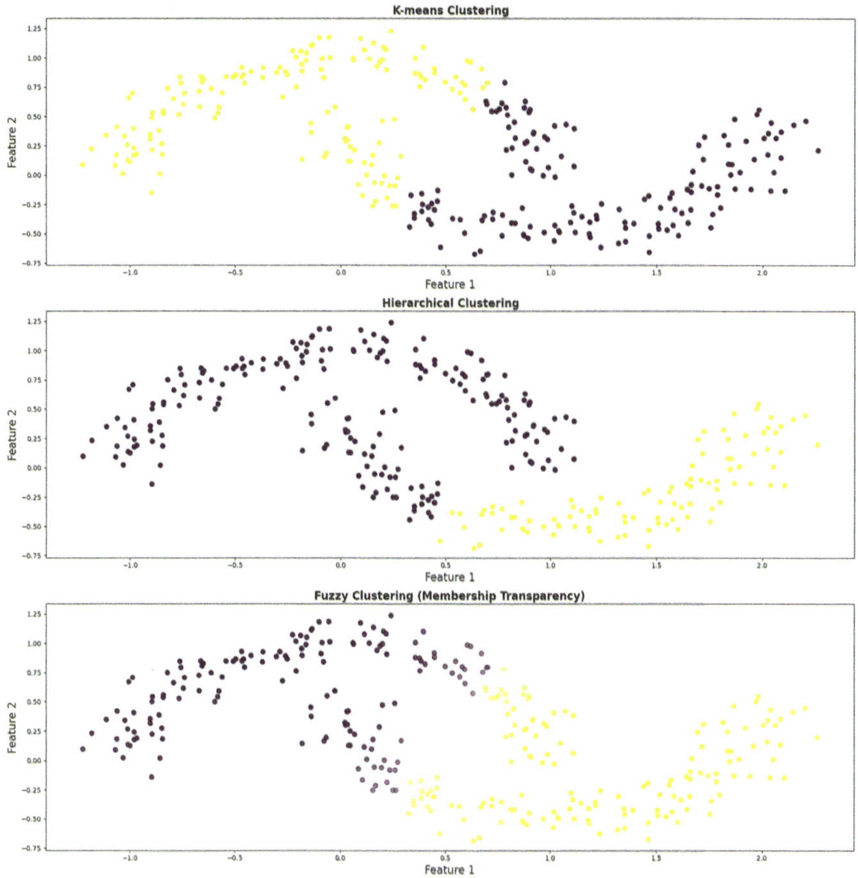

Fig. 1 Comparative visualisation of clustering algorithms on a non-linear dataset

tions of psychological phenomena. By understanding the strengths, limitations, and assumptions of each clustering method, researchers can better harness these techniques to explore psychological constructs rigorously, advancing both theoretical knowledge and practical applications.

3 Validation and Evaluation Measures

Clustering techniques are important in psychological data analysis for uncovering meaningful patterns and grouping similar observations within datasets. The success of a clustering algorithm depends on its ability to produce well-separated, compact, and meaningful clusters. Since clustering is typically an unsupervised learning approach, evaluating the quality of clusters is inherently challenging due to the absence of predefined class labels. This unsupervised perspective complements recent supervised advances in "PsAIchology" that integrate ML with psychological theory [18]. To assess the validity and effectiveness of a clustering solution, a range of internal, external, and stability validation measures is employed. These metrics help researchers determine the appropriateness of a given clustering structure and compare different clustering algorithms to select the most suitable approach for a specific psychological dataset.

One of the most commonly used internal evaluation measures is the silhouette coefficient, which quantifies the compactness and separation of clusters [33]. The silhouette score $S(i)$ for a given data point i is computed as

$$S(i) = \frac{b(i) - a(i)}{\max(a(i), b(i))}, \tag{1}$$

where $a(i)$ is the average distance between i and all other points within the same cluster, and $b(i)$ is the minimum average distance between i and all points in the nearest neighbouring cluster. A silhouette score close to 1 indicates that the point is well-clustered, whereas values close to 0 or negative suggest poor clustering performance. The silhouette coefficient is widely used due to its interpretability and effectiveness in determining the optimal number of clusters.

Another internal validation metric is the Davies–Bouldin index, which evaluates clustering compactness and separation [34]:

$$DB = \frac{1}{N} \sum_{i=1}^{N} \max_{j \neq i} \left(\frac{\sigma_i + \sigma_j}{d_{ij}} \right), \tag{2}$$

where N is the total number of clusters, σ_i and σ_j denote the average distances of points in clusters i and j from their respective centroids, and d_{ij} is the Euclidean distance between cluster centroids i and j. Lower Davies–Bouldin index values indicate better clustering quality, as they suggest compact and well-separated clusters.

While internal validation metrics assess clustering quality without external ground truth, external evaluation measures compare clustering results to known class labels, which is useful in cases where labelled data is available for benchmarking. One such measure is the Adjusted Rand Index (ARI), which evaluates the similarity between clustering results and ground truth labels by considering the agreement of point pairs in both partitions [35, 36]. Unlike the Standard Rand Index, ARI adjusts for the similarity expected by chance, providing a more reliable assessment of clustering quality. A higher ARI value indicates stronger agreement, with a maximum score of 1 representing perfect clustering and values near 0 suggesting random assignments. The ARI is computed as

$$ARI = \frac{\sum_{ij}\binom{n_{ij}}{2} - \left[\sum_i \binom{a_i}{2} \sum_j \binom{b_j}{2}\right] / \binom{n}{2}}{\frac{1}{2}\left[\sum_i \binom{a_i}{2} + \sum_j \binom{b_j}{2}\right] - \left[\sum_i \binom{a_i}{2} \sum_j \binom{b_j}{2}\right] / \binom{n}{2}}, \quad (3)$$

where n is the total number of data points, n_{ij} represents the number of points assigned to both cluster i in the predicted clustering and cluster j in the ground truth, and a_i and a_j are the total number of points in clusters i and j, respectively. By adjusting for random chance, ARI provides a statistically meaningful evaluation, ensuring that clustering results reflect real underlying patterns rather than coincidental similarities.

Another widely used external validation metric is the Normalised Mutual Information (NMI), which measures the amount of shared information between the true labels and the clustering assignments:

$$NMI = \frac{2 \times I(X, Y)}{H(X) + H(Y)}, \quad (4)$$

where $I(X, Y)$ represents the mutual information between the clustering assignments X and the ground truth labels Y, while $H(X)$ and $H(Y)$ denote their respective entropy values. A higher NMI score suggests that the clustering results closely align with the true structure of the data.

In addition to internal and external validation, stability measures assess the robustness of a clustering algorithm when applied to different subsets of the data or perturbed versions of the same dataset. The stability of clusters can be evaluated by computing the clustering consistency over multiple runs using metrics such as the Jaccard index, which quantifies the similarity between clusters generated in different iterations. A robust clustering algorithm should yield similar results across multiple random initialisations and different data samples.

When selecting an appropriate validation metric, researchers should consider the nature of the dataset and the intended application [37]. Internal metrics such as silhouette scores and Davies–Bouldin indices are useful when ground truth labels are unavailable, while external measures like ARI and NMI are valuable when benchmark labels exist. Stability measures, on the other hand, provide insights into the generalisability and reliability of the clustering solution.

The practical implementation of clustering validation can be facilitated using Python's `scikit-learn` library. The following example demonstrates how to compute the silhouette score and *Davies–Bouldin index* for a given dataset:

```
import pandas as pd
from sklearn.cluster import KMeans
from sklearn.metrics import silhouette_score,
↪ davies_bouldin_score
from sklearn.datasets import make_blobs

# Load dataset from CSV file (assumed to contain at least two
↪ feature columns: 'feature1', 'feature2')
df = pd.read_csv("your_dataset.csv")

# Extract features for clustering
X = df[['feature1', 'feature2']].values

# Apply K-Means clustering
kmeans = KMeans(n_clusters=4, random_state=42)
labels = kmeans.fit_predict(X)

# Compute validation metrics
silhouette_avg = silhouette_score(X, labels)
db_index = davies_bouldin_score(X, labels)

print(f"Silhouette Score: {silhouette_avg:.3f}")
print(f"Davies-Bouldin Index: {db_index:.3f}")
```

This example demonstrates how clustering performance can be quantitatively evaluated to ensure the reliability of results. The silhouette score helps assess how well-separated the clusters are, while the Davies–Bouldin index provides insights into cluster compactness and separation.

In psychological research, clustering validation plays a crucial role in ensuring the robustness of findings. For instance, when segmenting psychological profiles or behavioural patterns, validating cluster quality is essential to avoid misleading conclusions. Poorly defined clusters can lead to incorrect psychological interpretations and ineffective interventions. By incorporating rigorous evaluation measures, researchers can ensure that the extracted clusters accurately represent meaningful patterns in psychological data.

Selecting an appropriate clustering algorithm and validation measure is an iterative process that requires careful consideration of data characteristics and research objectives. While no single validation metric can universally determine the best clustering solution, combining multiple evaluation measures provides a more comprehensive assessment. By leveraging internal, external, and stability validation techniques, researchers can enhance the reliability and interpretability of clustering results in psychological data analysis [37].

4 Applications and Case Studies

To illustrate the practical application and interpretative power of clustering methods in psychological research, we conducted an extensive analysis utilising a detailed dataset comprising cognitive, emotional, social, and behavioural characteristics of 500 adult participants. This case study demonstrates how clustering techniques can meaningfully partition individuals into distinct psychological profiles, thereby enhancing our understanding of underlying heterogeneity in psychological functioning. The dataset used in the cluster analysis encompasses a rich collection of measures that reflect essential psychological dimensions:

- *Cognitive variables*—scores for `Memory`, `Attention`, and `Problem-Solving Abilities`, each ranging from 0 to 100. These measures offer insight into the cognitive performance levels of the sampled individuals.
- *Emotional indicators*—encompass `Anxiety`, `Stress`, and `Happiness Ratings`, capturing a wide emotional spectrum relevant to psychological well-being
- *Social characteristics*—`Social Support`, `Extraversion`, and `Agreeableness Scores` capture social integration, personality traits, and interpersonal styles
- *Behavioural variables* are represented by self-reported weekly hours devoted to exercise, sleep, and screen-time activities. Demographic information, representing `age`, `gender`, and `educational background`, is included to enrich the interpretative context.

The primary aim of our analysis is to systematically explore and identify distinct clusters within the data that meaningfully capture variations in cognitive, emotional, social, and behavioural characteristics. By doing so, we can better understand the underlying psychological diversity in our sample and provide a deeper insights that would be difficult to detect through traditional univariate methods alone.

We begin our exploration by examining the distributions of cognitive indicators, including `Memory`, `Attention`, and `Problem-Solving Scores` as shown in Fig. 2. Each distribution exhibits distinct central tendencies, with `Memory Scores` centred on a moderate range, while `Attention` and `Problem-Solving` demonstrate higher mean performance. The considerable variability across these dimensions suggests the presence of multiple cognitive profiles within our sample, an ideal scenario for cluster analysis. The distributions hint at latent groups, with some participants scoring consistently high and others moderate or low across multiple cognitive domains, thereby motivating further exploration through clustering.

The emotional correlation heatmap (see Fig. 3) highlights robust interrelations among `Anxiety`, `Stress`, and `Happiness`. As anticipated, anxiety and stress levels show a strong positive correlation ($r \approx 0.62$), indicating that individuals experiencing heightened stress also tend to exhibit elevated anxiety. Conversely, happiness negatively correlates with both anxiety ($r \approx -0.49$) and stress ($r \approx$

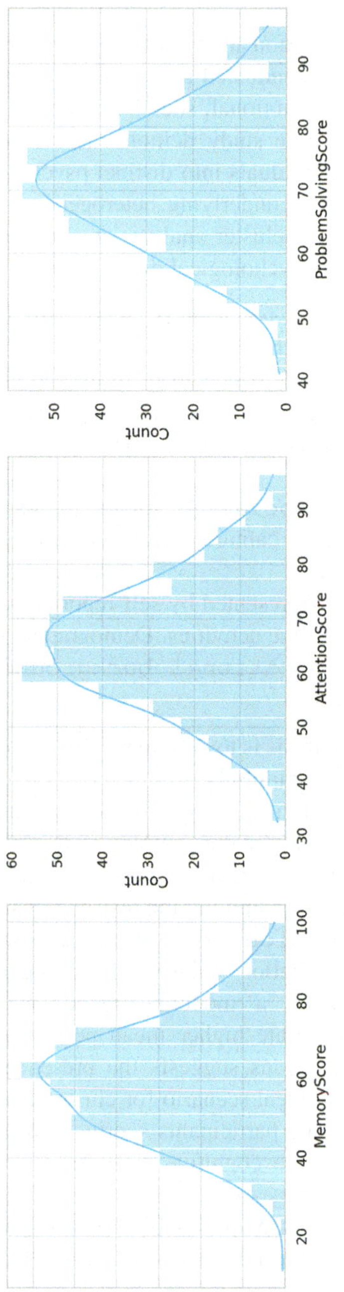

Fig. 2 Cognitive measures distributions

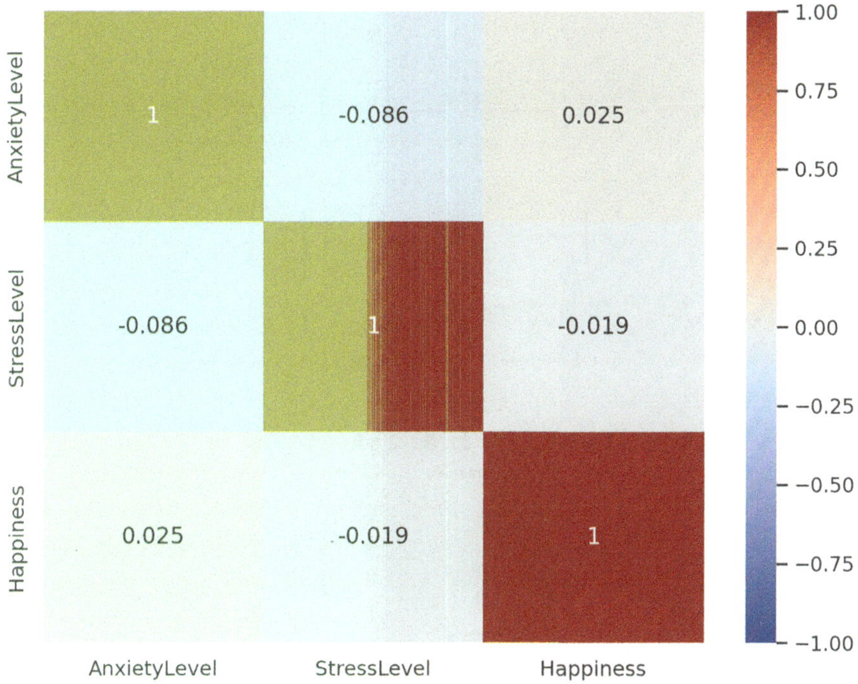

Fig. 3 Emotional measures correlation heatmap

−0.57), reinforcing the conceptual alignment that emotional distress inversely relates to positive affectivity. Such clear emotional patterns support the feasibility of clustering participants into meaningful emotional profiles, such as predominantly stressed and anxious individuals versus generally happier and calmer groups.

The boxplots illustrating Social Support, Extraversion, and Agreeableness by gender offer intriguing insights as it is shown in Fig. 4. While distributions across genders overlap considerably, slight differences emerge. Females report somewhat higher median social support and agreeableness levels, whereas extraversion appears uniformly distributed across genders. The notable variance within each gender category underscores the potential presence of socially differentiated clusters independent of demographic variables. This diversity in social characteristics within each gender group further justifies applying clustering techniques to identify different profiles based on social variables rather than relying solely on demographic groupings.

Scatterplots examining behavioural habits versus cognitive performance (see Fig. 5) elucidate meaningful but modest associations. Increased exercise hours mildly correlate with higher memory performance, while longer sleep duration positively relates to attention scores. Conversely, higher screen-time hours are associated slightly negatively with problem-solving abilities. These behavioural patterns, though subtle, imply that lifestyle differences might underpin distinct

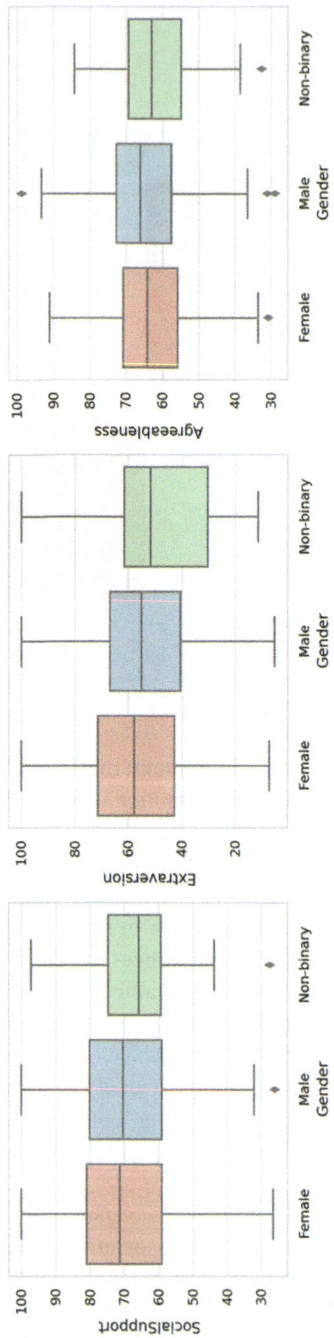

Fig. 4 Social factors by gender boxplots

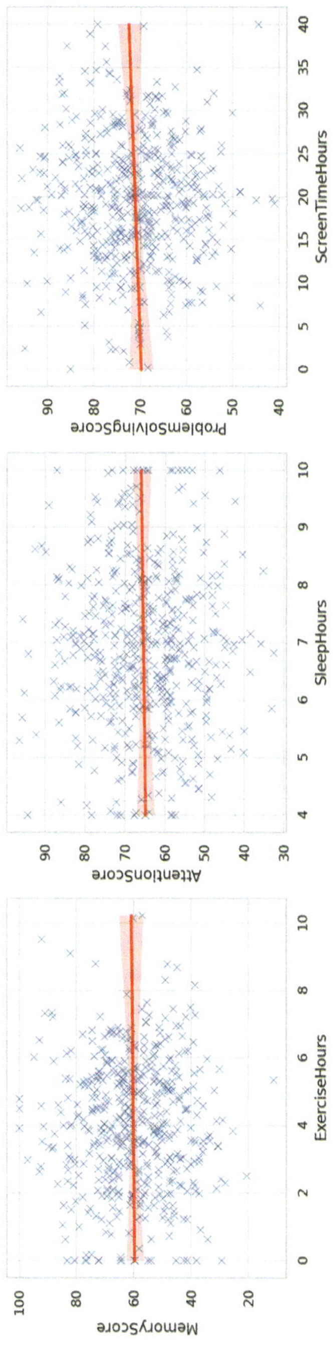

Fig. 5 Behavioural and cognitive relationship scatterplots

cognitive clusters. Clustering analysis could therefore uncover profiles combining cognitive performance with behavioural routines, such as *high performers with healthy behaviours* versus *low performers with sedentary habits*.

Examining age distribution alongside stress dynamics provides further contextual depth, and it is illustrated in Fig. 6. Stress levels demonstrate a slight negative correlation with age, indicating that younger individuals generally report higher stress. This age-related variation could influence cluster composition significantly, guiding us to anticipate clusters delineated partly by age and corresponding stress levels. Such demographic variables enrich our understanding of potential cluster structures, suggesting differentiated stress management profiles among younger versus older participants.

Leveraging the exploratory insights above, we performed a comprehensive clustering analysis employing K-means and hierarchical methods to partition participants into meaningful psychological profiles. Initial exploratory analyses, including silhouette scores and elbow methods, indicated optimal model complexity between three and five distinct clusters, capturing adequate subgroup differentiation without unnecessary complexity. Results revealed several robust clusters:

- Cluster 1 (*Resilient Optimisers*) exhibited high cognitive scores, notably low anxiety and stress, substantial happiness levels, high social support, and healthy behavioural routines (regular exercise, moderate screen-time, and sufficient sleep). This profile represents psychologically resilient and functionally optimised individuals.
- Cluster 2 (*Stress-Prone Achievers*) was cognitively high-performing individuals who nonetheless exhibited elevated anxiety and stress levels, moderate-to-high social support, and less optimal behavioural patterns (higher screen-time and inconsistent exercise). This highlights a psychologically complex subgroup whose cognitive achievements coexist with emotional vulnerabilities.
- Cluster 3 (*Socially Engaged Moderates*) encompassed individuals characterised by moderate cognitive scores, moderate emotional distress, robust social engagement, and balanced behavioural lifestyles. These individuals maintain psychological equilibrium primarily through strong social networks.
- Cluster 4 (*Cognitively Vulnerable Sedentaries*) reflected individuals with lower cognitive performance, high stress and anxiety, lower happiness, limited social support, and sedentary behavioural patterns (low exercise and high screen-time). These individuals represent a priority group for targeted psychological interventions.

The results of this case study vividly illustrate how clustering techniques can provide a deeper insight into psychological heterogeneity, revealing distinct psychological profiles embedded within complex multivariate data. The comprehensive nature of this dataset, covering cognitive, emotional, social, and behavioural dimensions, allowed us to not only identify clusters but also interpret them meaningfully through rich descriptive analyses and relevant psychological theory. This integrated approach emphasises the importance of clustering in enhancing our understanding

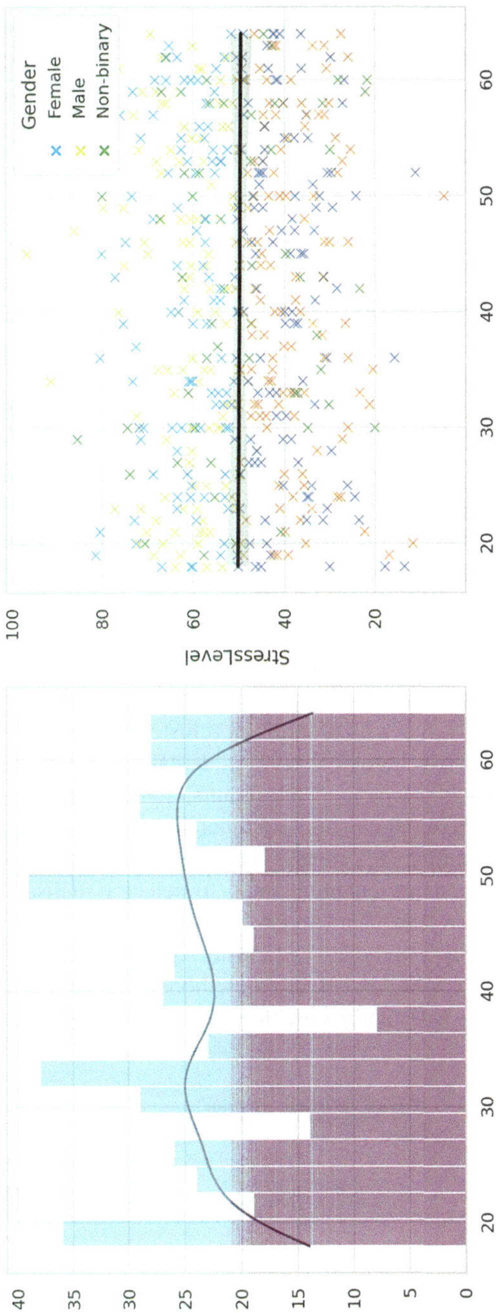

Fig. 6 Age distribution and stress analysis

of human psychological diversity, offering actionable insights that extend beyond traditional univariate analysis.

Clustering, as demonstrated, becomes a vital tool for researchers and practitioners seeking to tailor psychological interventions, inform policy development, and enhance personalised psychological care. Through meticulous analysis and careful interpretation of resulting clusters, we gain the ability to address psychological diversity comprehensively and sensitively, ultimately advancing the psychological sciences and benefiting society broadly.

5 Visualising Clustering Results

Visualisation serves as a crucial step in interpreting and validating clustering results in psychological research, transforming abstract data clusters into intuitive patterns comprehensible to both researchers and practitioners. Effective visual representation not only enhances understanding of data structure and distribution but also aids in revealing latent relationships and anomalies not immediately evident from numerical output alone [38, 39]. Given the complexity of psychological data, which is often multidimensional and involves subtle behavioural and cognitive constructs, visual methods significantly enhance the interpretative power of statistical clustering techniques.

Effectively visualising clustering outcomes is mandatory in psychological research, as it transforms abstract statistical results into intuitively interpretable insights. Figure 7 introduces a taxonomy of clustering visualisation methods commonly employed in psychological studies. It categorises visualisations into distance-based approaches such as dendrograms, partition-based visualisations including scatter and PCA plots, and membership-based representations like heatmaps and fuzzy membership plots. This structured overview serves as a practical guide for researchers, enabling them to select visualisation techniques tailored precisely to their data characteristics and analytical objectives, thereby enhancing the interpretability and clarity of clustering findings.

Among the simplest yet highly effective methods to visualise clustering outcomes is the scatter plot, particularly suitable when working with two-dimensional

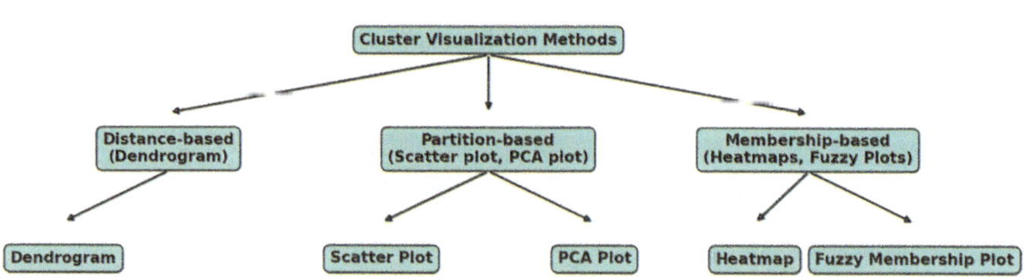

Fig. 7 Taxonomy of clustering visualisation methods in psychological research

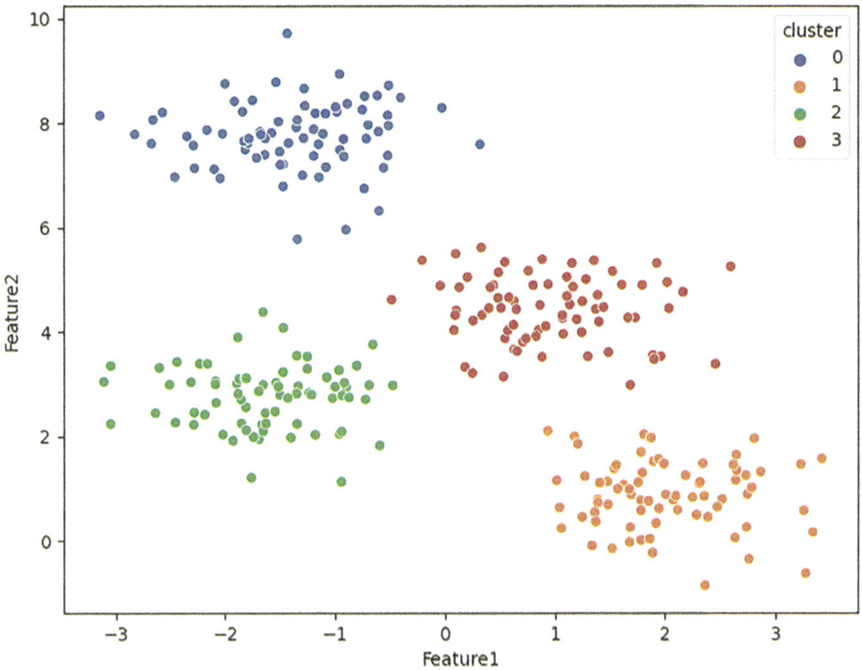

Fig. 8 Scatter plot illustrating K-means clustering results

data or after dimensionality reduction has been performed. Techniques like Principal Component Analysis [40] or t-Distributed Stochastic Neighbour Embedding [41] can reduce complex psychological data to two or three dimensions, allowing researchers to visualise the distinctiveness of clusters identified by algorithms such as K-means, hierarchical clustering, or fuzzy clustering. For instance, t-SNE is widely favoured for visualising high-dimensional data due to its ability to preserve local neighbourhood structures, making it particularly insightful for psychological datasets characterised by subtle and complex patterns [42].

The scatter plot for K-means clustering (Fig. 8) visually demonstrates cluster allocation simply and intuitively. Points are coloured according to their assigned cluster, clearly displaying how the clustering algorithm partitions the psychological data based on features. This plot helps researchers quickly assess the effectiveness of K-means clustering by evaluating how distinct and compact each group appears.

The PCA plot (Fig. 9) simplifies a high-dimensional dataset to just two dimensions while preserving as much information as possible. The data points are represented as coloured dots, each colour indicating a distinct cluster. The separation between colours indicates that the underlying psychological constructs have distinguishable patterns, which helps researchers visually validate the quality and meaningfulness of the clusters.

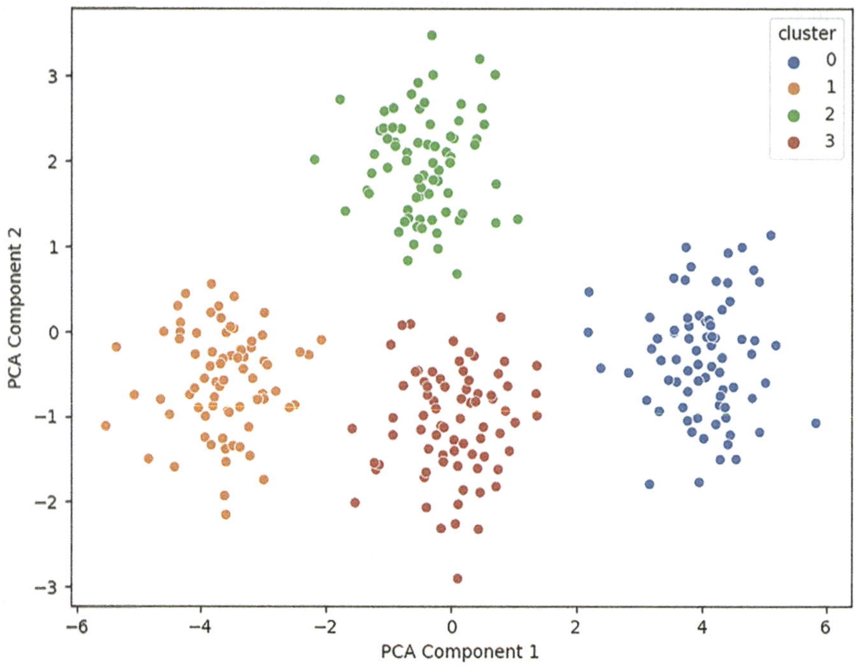

Fig. 9 Principal component analysis (PCA) plot for cluster visualisation

The t-SNE plot (Fig. 10) offers a powerful visualisation of clusters, particularly effective at capturing nonlinear structures. Here, the tight grouping of points of the same colour suggests strong internal similarity within clusters, while substantial distances between groups of different colours indicate clear differentiation between psychological clusters. This visualisation helps researchers understand intricate, non-linear relationships among psychological variables.

Another powerful visualisation method involves dendrograms, primarily associated with hierarchical clustering. A dendrogram graphically represents the nested merging of clusters, showing the distances at which clusters combine and making it easy to assess how well the hierarchical structure fits the theoretical expectations or practical criteria [43]. The dendrogram's utility lies in its intuitive representation, enabling psychologists to make informed decisions about the number of clusters to retain, interpret underlying hierarchical relationships, and detect potentially problematic cluster mergers that may misrepresent psychological phenomena [44].

The hierarchical clustering dendrogram (Fig. 11) illustrates how clusters form at various levels of similarity. Each branch of the dendrogram represents merging clusters based on their similarity. Longer vertical lines indicate clusters that are significantly different from one another, providing intuitive guidance on selecting an optimal number of clusters in psychological data. This allows researchers to visualise the hierarchy of data relationships.

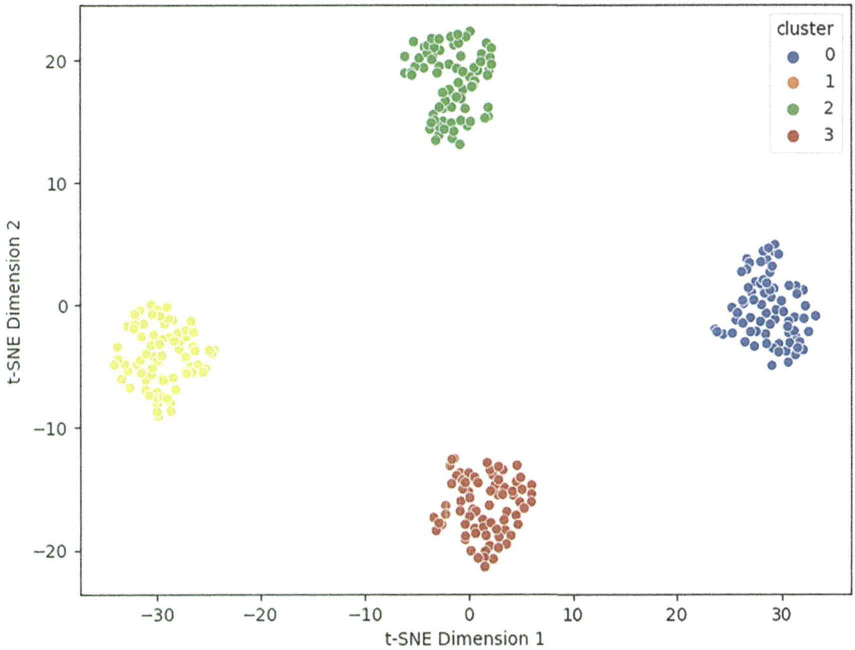

Fig. 10 t-Distributed Stochastic Neighbour Embedding (t-SNE) plot for cluster visualisation

While many visualisations, such as scatter plots and cluster maps, are frequently employed to represent clustering results, heatmaps combined with dendrograms offer a distinctive perspective. Figure 12 presents such a visualisation, where a dendrogram (tree-like diagram) illustrates the hierarchical relationships between clusters, and a corresponding heatmap displays data values across different variables. The heatmap (Fig. 12) uses colours to represent values in the dataset, typically illustrating similarity or distance. Rows represent different observations, and columns represent features or psychological constructs. Observing colour intensities, researchers can easily spot distinct patterns or relationships, such as clusters of similar individuals or clear boundaries between groups, facilitating the intuitive interpretation of the psychological data. This visualisation is particularly effective for detecting patterns, assessing cluster homogeneity, and identifying relationships within and between clusters. Such combined visualisations are valuable for psychological researchers because they succinctly encapsulate complex hierarchical structures, enabling intuitive insights into underlying psychological phenomena.

To effectively illustrate the distinctiveness and overlaps among clusters, silhouette plots provide valuable information regarding the quality and stability of clustering solutions. Silhouette plots measure how similar an individual data point is to its cluster compared to neighbouring clusters, thus visually presenting a quality metric for each data point and cluster [33]. In psychological research, this technique can significantly facilitate evaluating the appropriateness of identified clusters, as

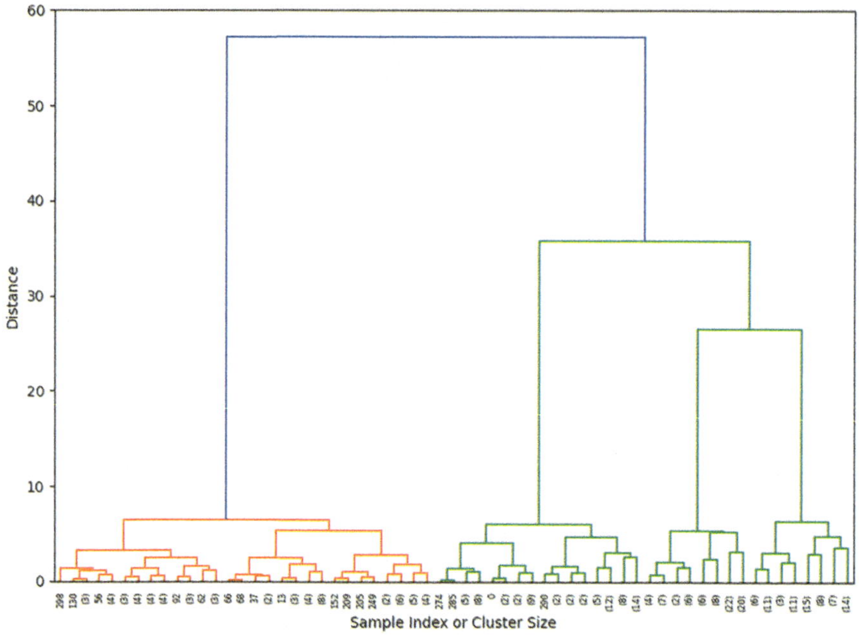

Fig. 11 Hierarchical clustering dendrogram

higher silhouette scores indicate well-separated clusters reflective of meaningful psychological differentiation, whereas lower scores may suggest indistinct or overlapping clusters, urging researchers to reconsider their clustering decisions or further refine their analysis [4].

The silhouette plot (Fig. 13) provides a clear visualisation of how well each data point fits into its assigned cluster compared to neighbouring clusters. Longer bars indicate better matches within a cluster, while shorter bars highlight points that may belong to multiple clusters. The vertical dashed line indicates average silhouette width, helping researchers evaluate the overall clustering quality and identify potentially misclassified or ambiguous cases.

Heatmaps are particularly effective for visualising fuzzy clustering results or when the data is complex and high-dimensional. A heatmap represents data values as colours, facilitating quick detection of patterns, cluster density, and overlaps across multiple variables or subjects. This is especially useful in psychological studies, such as analysing symptom profiles or response patterns in psychometric assessments, where multiple subtle dimensions of psychological functioning must be simultaneously interpreted [45]. Heatmaps also integrate smoothly with hierarchical clustering by simultaneously visualising dendrograms on row and column margins, thus offering a rich visualisation that combines numerical precision with intuitive colour-based interpretation.

To further enhance interpretability, radial plots or spider plots can visualise multidimensional clustering results succinctly and intuitively. Such visualisations

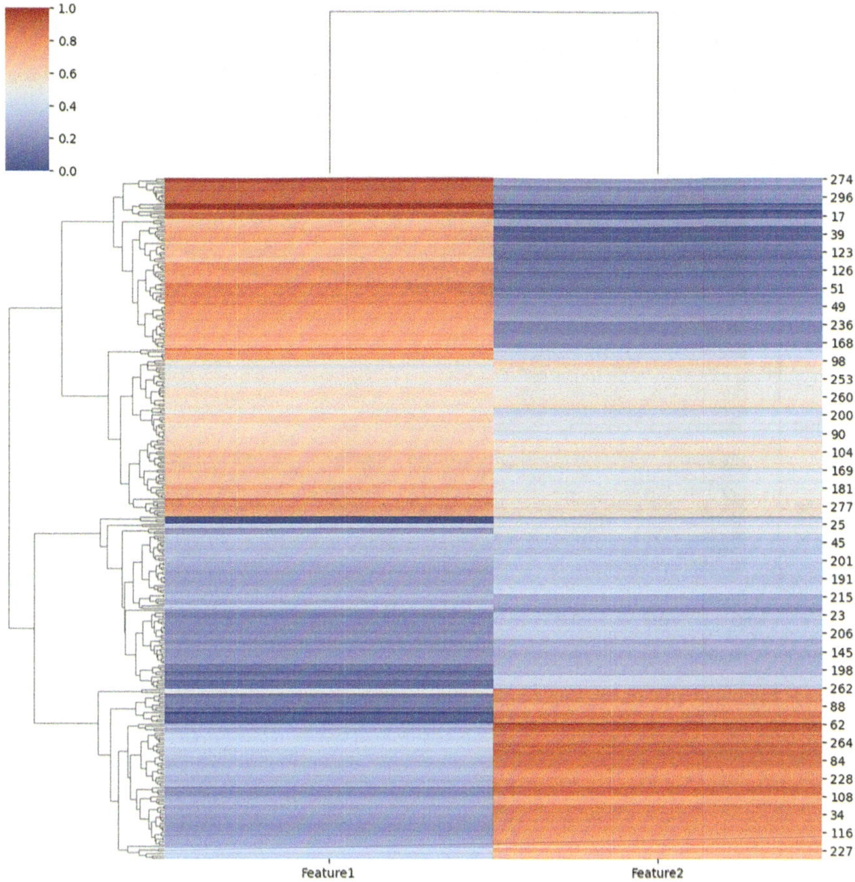

Fig. 12 Dendrogram and heatmap visualisation showing patterns of similarity within and between clusters

enable a straightforward comparison of cluster profiles across multiple psychological attributes, allowing researchers to see instantly how clusters differ in their overall configurations of psychological variables such as personality traits, cognitive performance scores, or behavioural indicators [46]. Radial plots highlight both the magnitude and shape of cluster profiles, enabling rapid identification of distinct and overlapping characteristics that might have direct implications for targeted psychological interventions or theoretical considerations.

The radial or spider plot (Fig. 14) provides an elegant means of comparing clusters simultaneously across multiple psychological dimensions. Each cluster forms a distinct shape on the plot, highlighting its relative strength or weakness across features. Researchers can quickly discern patterns and differences between clusters, enabling an easy and intuitive comparison of complex psychological profiles.

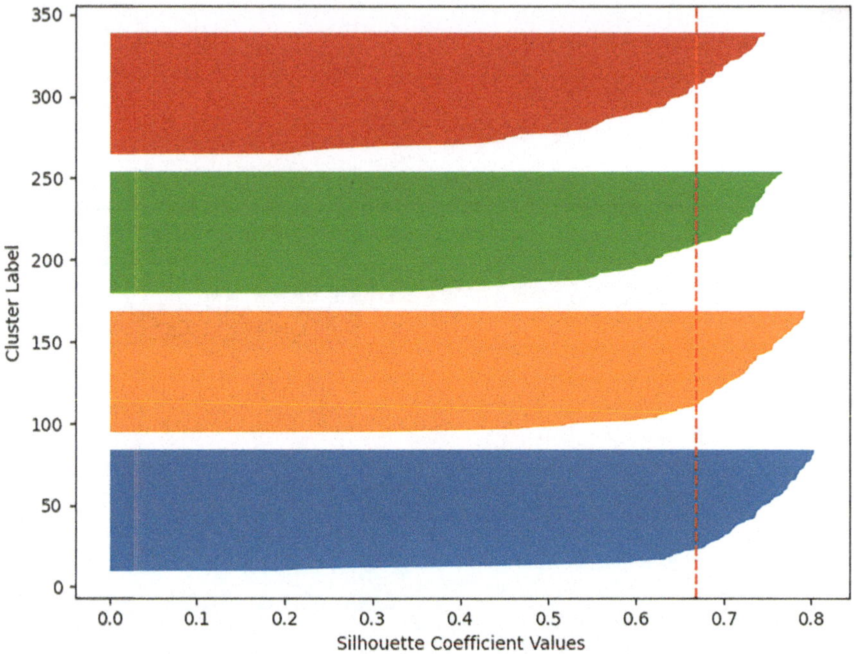

Fig. 13 Silhouette plot illustrating cluster cohesion and separation

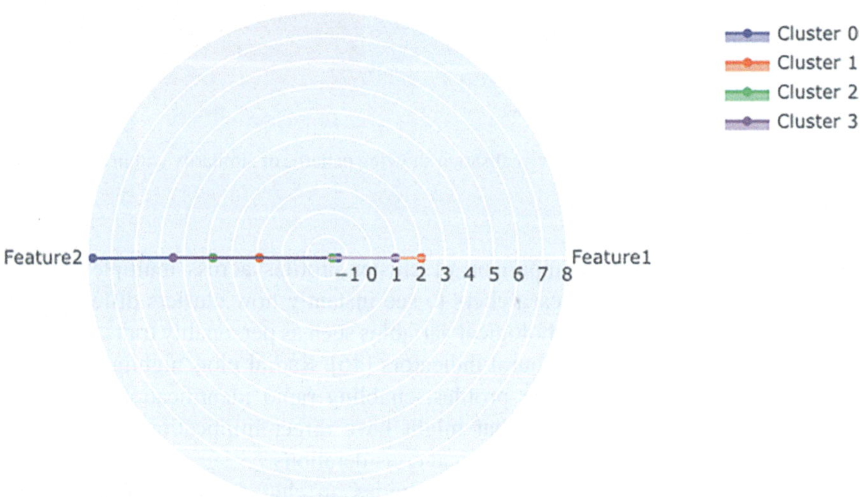

Fig. 14 Radial (spider) plot comparing clusters on multiple psychological dimensions

More advanced visualisation strategies leverage interactive and dynamic technologies. Interactive visualisation tools, such as those provided by Python libraries like `Plotly`, `Seaborn`, and `Matplotlib`, offer enhanced capabilities through interactivity by enabling users to explore clustering results dynamically through zooming, hovering for details, or selectively filtering clusters and subgroups [47, 48]. Such interactivity significantly augments analytical depth, enabling psychologists to engage directly with the data, facilitating exploratory hypothesis generation, deeper comprehension, and insightful interpretations otherwise challenging to achieve through static images alone [49].

Visualisation techniques in clustering are crucial for psychological research, not only because they elucidate statistical outcomes but also because they facilitate the practical interpretation and communication of results. Graphical representations transform abstract statistical information into meaningful narratives that resonate with psychologists, practitioners, and stakeholders who might not possess advanced statistical expertise. Indeed, the strategic use of visualisation fosters deeper interdisciplinary collaborations by creating intuitive understandings of complex data structures, directly contributing to data-driven decision-making in clinical, educational, and organisational contexts [50].

Advancements in clustering visualisation methods increasingly incorporate ML and artificial intelligence techniques, thus improving interpretability, user experience, and predictive insights [51]. For example, interactive visual analytics platforms that integrate clustering with predictive modelling techniques, such as predictive clustering or classification tree visualisation, offer psychologists powerful capabilities to predict group memberships and psychological outcomes based on identified cluster characteristics [52]. These platforms enable researchers to visually explore various *what-if* scenarios, conduct sensitivity analyses, and thus more robustly test psychological theories and intervention models.

The comprehensive adoption of visualisation methods in clustering analyses significantly enriches psychological research by providing clarity, interpretability, and practical insight. By strategically employing methods such as scatter plots, dendrograms, silhouette analyses, heatmaps, radial plots, and interactive visualisations, psychological researchers can uncover and communicate complex patterns in behavioural and cognitive data effectively and intuitively. Future developments in visualisation, particularly in interactive technologies and artificial intelligence-enhanced visual analytics, promise even greater advancements, positioning visualisation not merely as a supplementary tool but as a central pillar in contemporary psychological research methodology.

References

1. B.S. Everitt, S. Landau, M. Leese, D. Stahl, *Cluster Analysis* (Wiley-Blackwell, 2011)
2. C. Hennig, M. Meila, F. Murtagh, R. Rocci, *Handbook of Cluster Analysis* (CRC Press, Boca Raton, 2015)

3. A.K. Jain, Data clustering: 50 years beyond K-means. Pattern Recognit. Lett. **31**(8), 651 (2010)
4. A. Kassambara, *Practical Guide to Cluster Analysis in R: Unsupervised Machine Learning* (STHDA, 2017)
5. L. Kaufman, P.J. Rousseeuw, *Finding Groups in Data: An Introduction to Cluster Analysis* (John Wiley & Sons, London, 2009)
6. C. Fraley, A.E. Raftery, Model-based clustering, discriminant analysis, and density estimation. J. Am. Stat. Assoc. **97**(458), 611 (2002)
7. H. Farahani, P. Watson, N. Kovač, F.B. Sheykhangafshe, P. Azadfallah, A. Allahyari, F. Esrafilian, R.R. Chesli, in *International Handbook of Love: Transcultural and Transdisciplinary Perspectives* (Springer, Berlin, 2025), pp. 1–22
8. R.B. Cattell, The three basic factor-analytic research designs-their interrelations and derivatives. Psychol. Bull. **49**(5), 499 (1952)
9. A.T. Drysdale, L. Grosenick, J. Downar, K. Dunlop, F. Mansouri, Y. Meng, R.N. Fetcho, B. Zebley, D.J. Oathes, A. Etkin, et al., Resting-state connectivity biomarkers define neurophysiological subtypes of depression. Nat. Med. **23**(1), 28 (2017)
10. S. Shiffman, A.A. Stone, M.R. Hufford, Ecological momentary assessment. Ann. Rev. Clin. Psychol. **4**(1), 1 (2008)
11. N. Kovač, K. Ratković, P. Watson, H. Farahani, F. Bagheri Sheykhangafshe, Machine learning classification models for predicting chronic pain. Curr. Psychol. **44**, 15409–15422 (2025)
12. B.O. Muthén, Beyond SEM: general latent variable modeling. Behaviormetrika **29**(1), 81 (2002)
13. J. Bacher, J.K. Vermunt, Analyse latenter klassen. Handbuch der sozialwissenschaftlichen Datenanalyse (2010), pp. 553–574
14. J.K. Vermunt, J. Magidson, Latent class cluster analysis. Appl. Latent Class Anal. **11**(89–106), 60 (2002)
15. G.W. Milligan, M.C. Cooper, Methodology review: clustering methods. Appl. Psychol. Measur. **11**(4), 329 (1987)
16. D. Steinley, K-means clustering: a half-century synthesis. Br. J. Math. Stat. Psychol. **59**(1), 1 (2006)
17. L. van der Maaten, G. Hinton, Visualizing data using t-SNE. J. Mach. Learn. Res. **9**, 2579 (2008)
18. H. Farahani, P. Watson, T. Bezan, N. Kovač, L.C. Winter, M. Blagojević, P. Azadfallah, A. Allahyari, S. Masoumian, P. Jiménez, PsAIchology: an intelligent direction in psychological sciences, in *10th International Scientific Conference Technics, Informatics and Education-TIE 2024* (Faculty of Technical Sciences Čačak, University of Kragujevac, 2024)
19. U. Von Luxburg, A tutorial on spectral clustering. Stat. Comput. **17**, 395 (2007)
20. M. Ester, H.P. Kriegel, J. Sander, X. Xu, et al., A density-based algorithm for discovering clusters in large spatial databases with noise, in *KDD*, vol. 96.34 (1996), vol. 96.34, pp. 226–231
21. P.M. Bentler, Comparative fit indexes in structural models. Psychol. Bull. **107**(2), 238 (1990)
22. J.P. Ioannidis, Why most published research findings are false. PLoS Med. **2**(8), e124 (2005)
23. American Psychological Association. Ethical principles of psychologists and code of conduct (2017). https://www.apa.org/ethics/code/
24. A. Gelman, J. Hill, M. Yajima, Why we (usually) don't have to worry about multiple comparisons. J. Res. Educ. Effect. **5**(2), 189 (2012)
25. J.M. Rohrer, Thinking clearly about correlations and causation: graphical causal models for observational data. Adv. Methods Practices Psychol. Sci. **1**(1), 27 (2018)
26. J.H. Ward Jr., Hierarchical grouping to optimize an objective function. J. Am. Stat. Assoc. **58**(301), 236 (1963)
27. J.C. Bezdek, R. Ehrlich, W. Full, FCM: The fuzzy c-means clustering algorithm. Comput. Geosci. **10**(2–3), 191 (1984)
28. R.C. Kessler, P. Berglund, O. Demler, R. Jin, K.R. Merikangas, E.E. Walters, Lifetime prevalence and age-of-onset distributions of DSM-IV disorders in the National Comorbidity Survey Replication. Arch. Gener. Psychiatry **62**(6), 593 (2005)

29. J.B. Asendorpf, in *Stability and Change in Relationships*, ed. by A.L. Vangelisti, H.T. Reis, M.A. Fitzpatrick (Cambridge University Press, Cambridge, 2002), pp. 35–56
30. G. J. G. Asmundson, D. M. LeBouthillier, S. Taylor, Anxiety disorders: panic disorder and agoraphobia, in *Comprehensive Clinical Psychology*, 2nd edn., Vol. 4, pp. 1057–1075 (2015)
31. K.S. Berlin, N.A. Williams, G.R. Parra, An introduction to latent variable mixture modeling (part 1): overview and cross-sectional latent class and latent profile analyses. J. Pediatric Psychol. **39**(2), 174 (2014)
32. R. Kotov, R.F. Krueger, D. Watson, T.M. Achenbach, R.R. Althoff, R.M. Bagby, T.A. Brown, W.T. Carpenter, A. Caspi, L.A. Clark, et al., The hierarchical taxonomy of psychopathology (HiTOP): a dimensional alternative to traditional nosologies. J. Abnormal Psychol. **126**(4), 454 (2017)
33. P.J. Rousseeuw, Silhouettes: a graphical aid to the interpretation and validation of cluster analysis. J. Comput. Appl. Math. **20**, 53 (1987)
34. D.L. Davies, D.W. Bouldin, A cluster separation measure. IEEE Trans. Pattern Anal. Mach. Intell. **1**(2), 224 (1979)
35. L. Hubert, P. Arabie, Comparing partitions. J. Classif. **2**, 193 (1985)
36. K.Y. Yeung, W. Ruzzo, Principal component analysis for clustering gene expression data. Bioinformatics (Oxford, England) **17**, 763 (2001). https://doi.org/10.1093/bioinformatics/17.9.763
37. N. Kovač, K. Ratković, H. Farahani, P. Watson, A practical applications guide to machine learning regression models in psychology with python. Methods Psychol. **11**, 100156 (2024)
38. L. Wilkinson, in *Handbook of Computational Statistics: Concepts and Methods* (Springer, Berlin, 2011), pp. 375–414
39. C. Ware, *Information Visualization: Perception for Design* (Morgan Kaufmann, 2019)
40. I.T. Jolliffe, J. Cadima, Principal component analysis: a review and recent developments. Philos. Trans. Roy. Soc. A: Math. Phys. Eng. Sci. **374**(2065), 20150202 (2016)
41. L. Van der Maaten, G. Hinton, Visualizing data using t-SNE. J. Mac. Learn. Res. **9**(11), 2579–2605 (2008)
42. L. van der Maaten, Learning a parametric embedding by preserving local structure. Tech. rep., Technical Report, Tilburg University (2009). https://lvdmaaten.github.io/publications/papers/AISTATS_2009.pdf
43. B. Everitt, T. Hothorn, *An Introduction to Applied Multivariate Analysis with R* (Springer, Berlin, 2011)
44. R.A. Johnson, D.W. Wichern, *Applied Multivariate Statistical Analysis*, 6th edn. (Prentice Hall Upper Saddle River, 2012)
45. L. Wilkinson, M. Friendly, The history of the cluster heat map. Am. Stat. **63**(2), 179 (2009)
46. N.B. Robbins, R.M. Heiberger, Plotting Likert and other rating scales, in *Proceedings of the American Statistical Association, Section on Statistical Graphics* (2011), pp. 1058–1066
47. J.D. Hunter, Matplotlib: A 2D graphics environment. Comput. Sci. Eng. **9**(3), 90 (2007)
48. M.L. Waskom, Seaborn: statistical data visualization. J. Open Source Softw. **6**(60), 3021 (2021)
49. J. Heer, B. Shneiderman, Interactive dynamics for visual analysis: a taxonomy of tools that support the fluent and flexible use of visualizations. Queue **10**(2), 30 (2012)
50. M. Sedlmair, M. Meyer, T. Munzner, Design study methodology: reflections from the trenches and the stacks. IEEE Trans. Vis. Comput. Graph. **18**(12), 2431 (2012)
51. S. Liu, D. Maljovec, B. Wang, P.T. Bremer, V. Pascucci, Visualizing high-dimensional data: advances in the past decade, IEEE Trans. Vis. Comput. Graph. **23**(3), 1249 (2016)
52. J. Krause, A. Perer, E. Bertini, Using visual analytics to interpret predictive machine learning models (2016). arXiv preprint arXiv:1606.05685

Latent Class Analysis and Latent Profile Analysis

Nataša Kovač, Marija Blagojević, Kruna Ratković, Hojjatollah Farahani, and Peter Watson

1 Overview of Latent Class Analysis and Latent Profile Analysis

Latent variable models have become a central methodological framework in psychological and social sciences [1], enabling researchers to move beyond observed variables and uncover unobservable structures that drive observed data. Among the most widely used techniques within this paradigm are *Latent Class Analysis* (LCA) and *Latent Profile Analysis* (LPA). These methods belong to the family of *finite mixture models*, where the objective is to classify individuals into homogeneous subgroups, or latent classes, based on patterns in their responses to a set of observed variables [2].

Unlike traditional clustering methods, which rely on arbitrary distance metrics, LCA and LPA are model-based approaches that offer a statistically grounded means of uncovering latent heterogeneity in populations [3]. They assume that the population is composed of a finite number of distinct, unobserved subgroups, and they estimate the probability that each individual belongs to one of these subgroups

N. Kovač (✉) · K. Ratković
Faculty of Applied Sciences, University of Donja Gorica, Podgorica, Montenegro
e-mail: natasa.kovac@udg.edu.me; kruna.ratkovic@udg.edu.me

M. Blagojević
Faculty of Technical Sciences, University of Kragujevac, Čačak, Serbia
e-mail: marija.blagojevic@uni.kg.ac.rs

H. Farahani
Department of Psychology, Faculty of Humanities, Tarbiat Modares University, Tehran, Iran
e-mail: h.farahani@modares.ac.ir

P. Watson
MRC Cognition and Brain Sciences Unit, University of Cambridge, Cambridge, England
e-mail: Peter.Watson@mrc-cbu.cam.ac.uk

N. Kovač et al. (eds.), *Data Science in Psychology*,
https://doi.org/10.1007/978-3-032-18312-5_13

based on their responses. This probabilistic foundation makes LCA and LPA particularly attractive in fields such as psychology, psychiatry, education, public health, and market research, where latent psychological or behavioural constructs are common.

LCA is used when the observed indicators are *categorical variables*, such as binary or ordinal responses (e.g. yes/no answers and Likert-scale items) [4]. LCA models the likelihood that individuals belong to a particular latent class based on their response patterns. For example, in psychological research, LCA might be used to classify individuals based on symptoms of mental disorders [5], identifying distinct subpopulations such as high-risk versus low-risk profiles for depression or anxiety.

Each latent class is defined by a unique response probability profile [6]. That is the conditional probability that an individual in a given class will endorse a particular category of a given item. These response profiles provide a meaningful psychological interpretation of the latent structure [7]. Importantly, the analysis produces not only class-specific probabilities but also posterior class membership probabilities for each respondent, reflecting the likelihood of their belonging to each class. This makes LCA useful for predictive modelling, segmentation, and targeted intervention planning. PsAIchology operationalises this by spot-checking multiple supervised learners on class-/profile-derived features with consistent validation [8]. Recent psychology tutorials connect such derived features to supervised regression workflows, comparing multiple learners under a common protocol [9]. In applied health psychology, class- or profile-based features have been paired with ML methods to predict patient status and severity—for example, chronic pain severity using psychological correlates [10].

LPA extends the logic of LCA to *continuous variables* [11]. Instead of estimating item-response probabilities, LPA estimates means and variances for each indicator within each latent profile. It assumes that each profile corresponds to a multivariate normal distribution, characterised by its own mean vector and covariance structure [12]. LPA is ideal for psychological research in which constructs are measured on continuous scales, such as cognitive test scores, personality dimensions, or emotional intensity levels.

In practice, LPA helps researchers identify qualitatively different profiles of individuals based on their continuous psychological characteristics. For example, an LPA conducted on cognitive performance data may reveal profiles such as *high verbal-low spatial*, *balanced*, or *low overall* cognitive types. These insights can offer theoretically grounded classifications that extend beyond what mean group differences or simple clustering techniques can provide.

To visually contextualise the methodological distinctions between LCA and LPA, Fig. 1 provides a conceptual diagram. This illustration highlights the nature of indicators, statistical estimates, and the underlying assumptions of each method.

To complement this conceptual overview, Fig. 2 provides a structured visual comparison of LCA and LPA. The diagram illustrates how each method operates from the indicator measurement level to the nature of the latent constructs estimated.

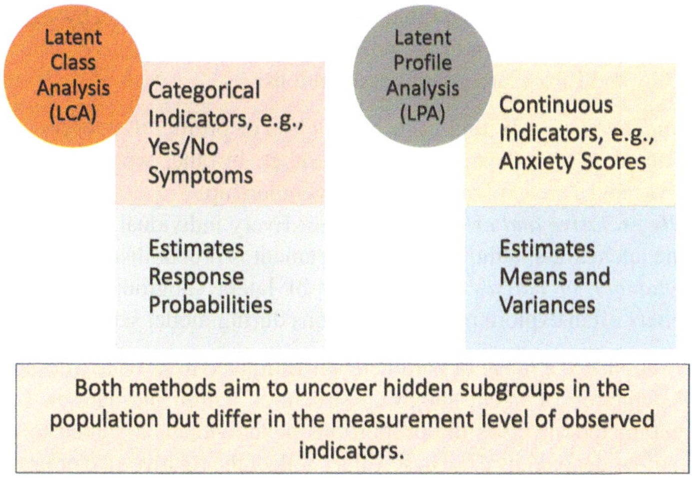

Fig. 1 Comparison of LCA and LPA

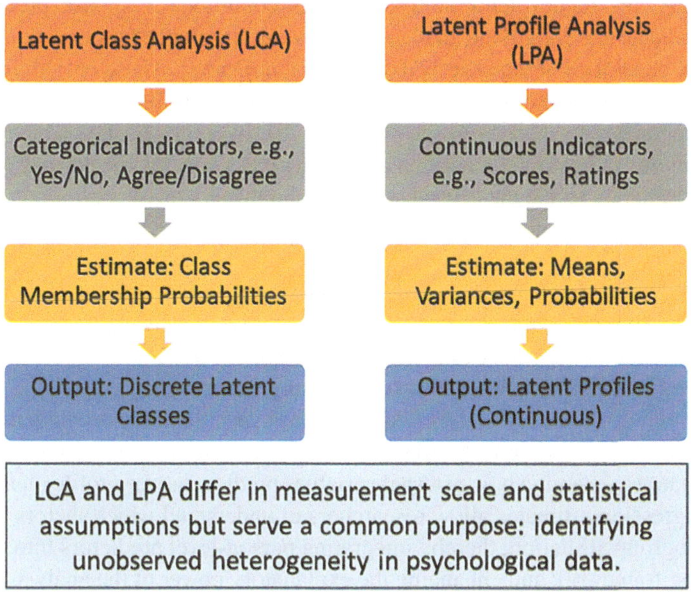

Fig. 2 Conceptual workflow comparison of LCA and LPA

It highlights that while both techniques aim to uncover unobserved heterogeneity, their assumptions and outputs are inherently shaped by the type of data they model.

An important benefit of LPA is its ability to estimate profile-specific standard deviations, which can be held equal or freely estimated across classes, depending on the model specification. LPA can be expanded to include covariates that predict class membership (e.g. demographic or clinical variables), thereby enriching the interpretation and application of the profiles [13].

Both LCA and LPA share several assumptions:

- *Local independence*: Within each latent class or profile, the observed variables are assumed to be independent of each other. In other words, all associations among variables are explained by class membership.
- *Mutually exclusive and exhaustive classes*: Every individual belongs to one and only one latent class, although their assignment is probabilistic.
- *Finite number of classes*: The number of latent subgroups is fixed, though researchers often explore multiple solutions during model selection.

In LCA and LPA, a range of parameters is estimated to provide a comprehensive statistical depiction of latent subgroup structures within the dataset. One of the primary parameters involves the proportions of individuals assigned to each class or profile, often denoted by Π. These values reflect the relative size or prevalence of each latent subgroup within the sample and are crucial for interpreting the practical significance of the latent solution [2, 14].

In LCA, the model additionally estimates conditional response probabilities, which indicate the likelihood that individuals within a specific class will endorse particular categories of the observed categorical indicators. These probabilities offer an interpretable profile of each class and serve as a foundation for labelling the latent classes according to shared response patterns [5]. In contrast, LPA, which operates on continuous indicators, focuses on estimating class-specific means and variances. These parameters reveal the central tendency and dispersion of continuous variables within each latent profile, facilitating a detailed characterisation of the subgroups [12, 15].

Both approaches generate posterior probabilities of class membership for each individual. These probabilities reflect the likelihood that a given person belongs to a specific latent class or profile, based on their response pattern. They are critical not only for a class assignment but also for assessing the uncertainty of that assignment and enabling downstream analyses, such as class-specific outcome modelling [16].

When covariates are introduced into the model, additional regression parameters are estimated to examine how external variables predict class or profile membership. These regression estimates allow researchers to understand which factors influence latent subgroup affiliation, thereby integrating person-level predictors into the latent modelling framework and enhancing the explanatory power of the analysis [17, 18].

LCA and LPA involve the estimation of several core parameters. These include the proportions of individuals belonging to each class or profile (Π), the conditional response probabilities in LCA or class-specific means and variances in LPA, and the posterior probabilities of each individual's likelihood of class membership. When covariates are incorporated into the model, regression parameters are also estimated. Figure 3 provides a visual representation of these key parameters, helping researchers understand the structural components that define LCA and LPA models [2, 19].

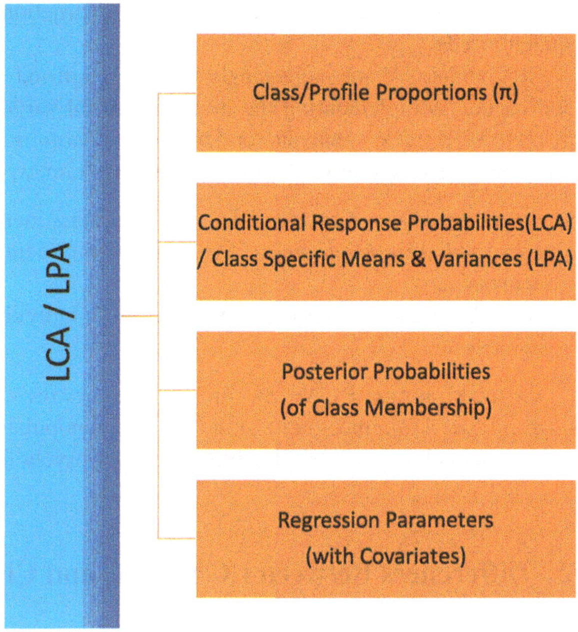

Fig. 3 Core parameters estimated in LCA and LPA models

Model fit is commonly evaluated using information criteria such as *Bayesian Information Criterion* (BIC), *Akaike Information Criterion* (AIC), and *entropy* values [20]. These criteria guide the researcher in selecting the optimal number of classes, with lower BIC/AIC and higher entropy suggesting better classification quality.

One of the strengths of LCA and LPA lies in their theory-driven interpretability. Unlike purely data-driven clustering methods, LCA and LPA allow researchers to test a priori hypotheses about subgroup structures, test alternative models, and incorporate auxiliary variables such as covariates or distal outcomes [21]. This theoretical grounding makes these techniques, especially useful in psychological research, where researchers are often concerned with identifying meaningful types or profiles that align with theoretical constructs such as attachment styles, personality types, motivational patterns, or psychopathology subtypes.

These techniques can uncover subtle heterogeneity in psychological phenomena that may be overlooked by traditional variable-centred analyses. Such heterogeneity often improves downstream prediction when incorporated into ML models of clinical outcomes, including chronic pain [10]. For instance, in clinical psychology, LCA may reveal that individuals meeting the same diagnostic criteria belong to different symptomatological classes with distinct aetiologies and treatment responses.

In developmental psychology, LPA has been used to classify children based on temperamental traits, enabling detailed analysis of developmental trajectories and risk factors [22]. In educational research, latent profile modelling has helped identify learning strategy types, which can inform instructional interventions tailored to student needs.

LPA and LCA are increasingly being recognised as powerful person-centred approaches, complementing the more traditional variable-centred techniques such as regression, factor analysis, or *Structural Equation Modelling* (SEM). They are often integrated into more complex modelling frameworks, such as:

- *Latent Transition Analysis* (LTA) to assess class membership over time
- *Factor Mixture Modelling* (FMM) to combine latent class models with factor analysis
- *Growth Mixture Modelling* (GMM) to study individual trajectories in longitudinal data

By incorporating LCA/LPA into such frameworks, researchers can simultaneously model both the latent structure of subpopulations and their temporal or dimensional characteristics, facilitating deeper psychological understanding.

2 Differences Between LCA, LPA, and Clustering

LCA, LPA, and traditional clustering methods each offer unique analytical capabilities and theoretical foundations, making them distinctly suitable for different types of psychological data and research questions. Although all three methodologies aim to reveal underlying structures in data by identifying subgroups or categories, significant theoretical, methodological, and practical differences exist among them.

Clustering methods, such as K-means, hierarchical clustering, and fuzzy clustering, are predominantly data-driven exploratory methods. They operate based on distance metrics (e.g. Euclidean and Manhattan) and similarity measures among observed variables, partitioning the data into groups such that within-group similarity is maximised and between-group similarity minimised [23]. These approaches make minimal assumptions about the distribution of data, and groupings are primarily determined by algorithmic heuristics rather than probabilistic modelling. Thus, clustering is often preferred in exploratory contexts where the goal is the discovery of naturally occurring patterns without prior theoretical expectations [24].

In contrast, LCA and LPA are grounded in latent variable modelling frameworks, specifically finite mixture models. They assume that the population comprises distinct, unobserved latent subgroups (classes or profiles) that explain the associations among observed variables [2]. LCA is used for categorical indicators, assuming each subgroup has unique conditional probabilities of endorsing various categories of observed items. Conversely, LPA applies to continuous data, assuming each latent profile follows a multivariate normal distribution characterised by unique means and variances [13]. This probabilistic approach positions LPA and LCA as confirmatory or theory-driven methods, enabling hypothesis testing about subgroup structures in psychological constructs.

Clustering methods typically rely on deterministic algorithms, where the assignment of observations to clusters depends directly on distances or linkage criteria. For example, K-means clustering assigns individuals to clusters by minimising within-cluster variance, while hierarchical clustering builds nested clusters through iterative merging or splitting based on distance metrics. These methods often result in hard assignments, meaning that each individual belongs exclusively to one cluster; fuzzy clustering allows for degrees of membership in multiple clusters [25].

LCA and LPA adopt a probabilistic modelling approach, estimating the posterior probabilities of individual membership in each latent subgroup. These probabilities explicitly quantify uncertainty about subgroup membership, a feature absent in traditional clustering methods. Model fit indices such as AIC, BIC, and entropy are employed systematically in LCA/LPA to select the optimal number of latent classes or profiles, adding robustness and replicability to subgroup identification [20]. LCA and LPA permit formal statistical testing of competing subgroup solutions, offering a structured approach to evaluating and justifying the final model.

Clustering techniques are straightforward to apply and interpret, making them ideal for preliminary data exploration. Clusters obtained through such methods can lack theoretical interpretability, especially when the rationale behind distance metrics or linkage criteria is unclear or arbitrary. In contrast, LCA and LPA provide psychologically meaningful subgroup interpretations by explicitly linking subgroups to latent psychological constructs through estimated parameters (e.g. conditional probabilities or means and variances). This enhances their utility in theory-driven psychological research, such as distinguishing distinct clinical subtypes, personality profiles, or developmental trajectories [15].

For instance, LCA might identify subtypes of depression or anxiety based on symptom patterns, yielding clear clinical implications for diagnostic refinement and targeted treatments. LPA, utilising continuous psychological measures like cognitive abilities or personality traits, can identify different profiles reflecting different psychological functioning levels, thus informing tailored intervention strategies [12].

Another critical difference lies in how these methods handle external variables or covariates [26]. Traditional clustering often incorporates covariates post hoc, assessing differences among clusters rather than explicitly modelling their predictive role. Conversely, LCA and LPA readily accommodate covariates within the modelling process, estimating their influence on latent subgroup membership through regression parameters. This integrated approach allows researchers to simultaneously evaluate subgroup formation and factors influencing subgroup membership, enhancing explanatory power and utility for predictive modelling [18].

Clustering methods, particularly K-means and hierarchical clustering, are sensitive to outliers, scale differences, and the shape of data distributions. While robust alternatives (e.g. K-medoids) exist, these methods typically assume uniformity or spherical shapes for clusters, limiting their applicability when psychological constructs manifest complex distributions [25].

LCA and LPA models, through their probabilistic underpinnings and parametric nature, can better accommodate complexities such as heterogeneous variances and non-uniform shapes of subgroups. Their accuracy relies heavily on adherence to distributional assumptions, like normality for LPA, and the correct specification of latent classes or profiles. Misspecification of the model (e.g. incorrect number of classes) can significantly bias results and interpretations, underscoring the need for careful model evaluation and validation [2].

The primary distinctions between LCA, LPA, and traditional clustering methods include:

- *Theoretical basis*: probabilistic latent variable models (LCA/LPA) versus deterministic exploratory clustering
- *Data requirements*: categorical indicators for LCA, continuous for LPA, mixed types for clustering methods
- *Statistical robustness*: explicit model selection criteria and uncertainty quantification in LCA/LPA versus heuristic approaches in clustering
- *Interpretative clarity*: direct psychological interpretability through model parameters in LCA/LPA versus post hoc interpretation in clustering
- *Integration of covariates*: systematic modelling of covariates in LCA/LPA versus post hoc analyses in clustering

These methodological distinctions underscore the importance of aligning method selection with research questions, data characteristics, theoretical frameworks, and intended applications in psychological research.

3 Identifying LCA and LPA Variables

Selecting indicator variables for LCA and LPA is a crucial foundational step that significantly shapes both the interpretability and validity of the resulting latent classes or profiles [27]. Although researchers often emphasise model estimation and interpretation, the process of choosing relevant indicators merits equal attention. The quality and theoretical alignment of selected variables directly impact the capacity of latent models to uncover meaningful psychological subgroups [28]. Thus, a rigorous approach, grounded both theoretically and statistically, ensures that resulting latent solutions reflect psychologically plausible constructs rather than artefacts of arbitrary or redundant data inclusion.

At the outset, indicator selection should be guided by theoretical justification. Indicators must clearly reflect the psychological constructs hypothesised to underlie latent class formation. For example, if the research objective involves identifying subgroups of psychological distress, relevant indicators would logically encompass symptomatic expressions such as anxiety levels, depressive symptom severity, and stress-related measures. In contrast, extraneous or unrelated variables risk diluting meaningful class distinctions or obscuring genuine psychological patterns [5]. A well-grounded theoretical rationale prevents unnecessary proliferation of indicators, reducing the likelihood of encountering computational difficulties or unstable class solutions. Indeed, past studies underscore that careful theoretical alignment between selected indicators and underlying constructs significantly improves interpretability and practical utility of latent subgroup solutions [15].

Beyond conceptual relevance, selected variables must fulfil important psychometric and statistical criteria. For LPA, indicators typically are continuous variables assumed to follow a normal distribution within each latent profile [11, 12]. Although LPA methods can be resilient to mild violations of normality, severe skewness or significant departures from normality can distort parameter estimates, potentially biasing subgroup identification. Thus, preliminary data screening, such as examining distributions through visualisations like histograms, Q-Q plots, or statistical normality tests, is recommended to verify assumptions and consider transformations if necessary [13]. Conversely, LCA demands categorical indicators, often binary or ordinal items reflecting discrete response categories (e.g. symptom presence/absence or Likert-scale responses) [4]. Highly skewed categorical indicators, with minimal variability across categories, offer limited discriminative power and can impede class differentiation. Collins and Lanza [28] emphasise avoiding indicators with overly dominant categories (e.g. endorsed by more than 90% of participants), which provide minimal informational value and increase the likelihood of poorly separated or redundant classes.

An additional critical consideration is the assumption of local independence within latent classes or profiles, meaning that indicators should not exhibit residual correlations after accounting for class membership [1]. Violations typically signal redundant or overly similar items that introduce artificial dependencies and result in inflated estimates of latent subgroups [14]. Researchers should thus undertake exploratory factor analysis or inspect residual correlation matrices before finalising their indicator sets. If indicators exhibit strong residual correlations, strategies such as bifactor modelling or selecting a reduced subset of non-redundant variables can help meet the local independence assumption and enhance the robustness of latent subgroup identification [29].

Determining the appropriate number of indicators requires balancing comprehensiveness against model parsimony [30]. While excessively large indicator sets (e.g. more than 15 to 20) risk overfitting and reduced interpretability due to overly granular subgroup distinctions, overly sparse indicator sets (fewer than 4 or 5) often fail to capture latent structure complexity [31] adequately. Empirical and simulation studies indicate that optimal class separation and interpretability often occur with a moderate number of carefully chosen indicators, typically between five and ten for LCA models and slightly more for LPA, depending on the nature and complexity of constructs measured. Researchers must be cautious when combining categorical and continuous indicators within the same model, as this requires specialised modelling frameworks like factor mixture modelling or generalised latent class models, complicating model estimation and interpretation [32].

Recently, advanced variable selection methodologies have become increasingly accessible, providing systematic, data-driven techniques to support theoretical decision-making. Approaches such as stepwise variable inclusion or exclusion procedures, greedy search algorithms, and entropy-based measures help researchers objectively assess the incremental contribution of each variable to latent subgroup differentiation [33]. Bayesian variable selection techniques, such as *Stochastic Search Variable Selection* (SSVS), integrate across numerous potential indicator sets, offering inclusion probabilities that indicate each variable's utility in maximising class differentiation and interpretability [16]. Researchers must exercise caution, as purely data-driven variable selection can lead to optimal statistical solutions that may lack theoretical coherence. Combining these methods with careful theoretical judgment provides the most robust approach, balancing statistical rigour with substantive interpretability.

Involving domain experts throughout the variable selection process significantly enhances the interpretive clarity and practical applicability of the resulting latent classes or profiles. Experts' insights can confirm theoretical relevance, assess psychometric validity, and identify potential redundancies or omissions. Through iterative dialogue between methodological expertise and substantive psychological knowledge, researchers are better positioned to produce latent subgroup solutions that not only fit the data well but also resonate theoretically and practically within the broader psychological literature.

Successful indicator selection for LPA and LCA requires a well-balanced approach integrating theoretical considerations, psychometric soundness, and robust statistical validation procedures. Careful attention to indicator selection criteria and continuous refinement through expert consultation yields latent solutions that meaningfully represent underlying psychological constructs, providing powerful and actionable insights into psychological heterogeneity.

In light of these theoretical and methodological considerations, researchers are advised to adhere to several practical recommendations when selecting indicators to enhance the robustness, interpretability, and transparency of latent subgroup solutions:

- Ensure that all indicators are theoretically relevant and psychometrically sound.
- Check for adequate variability and avoid ceiling/floor effects.
- Limit multicollinearity by removing or combining highly correlated indicators.
- Respect assumptions of local independence; consider model modifications if violated.
- Use entropy, BIC, and substantive interpretability, rather than relying solely on p-values, to guide inclusion decisions.
- Be cautious of overfitting; test model stability using cross-validation or bootstrapping.
- Pre-register indicator sets and selection criteria, where possible, to promote transparency.

4 Specifying, Estimating, and Evaluating LCA and LPA

The process of specifying, estimating, and evaluating LCA and LPA models is fundamental for uncovering meaningful latent structures within psychological data.

These processes involve a series of rigorous methodological steps that ensure robust and interpretable outcomes. Proper specification of models, accurate estimation of parameters, and systematic evaluation of model fit, within transparent, reproducible workflows, are essential to achieving scientifically valid and practically useful results [9].

Initially, researchers must specify the latent structure, which involves defining the number of classes or profiles based on theoretical and empirical grounds [1, 16]. Specification requires clear theoretical reasoning about the number of underlying subgroups hypothesised to exist in the population. Although the number of classes may initially be unknown, theory-driven hypotheses are indispensable as starting points for the iterative modelling process.

In specifying LCA and LPA models, the fundamental assumptions of local independence, exclusivity of class membership, and a finite number of latent groups guide the structural definition. For LCA, the probability that individual i endorses category k on item j given membership in latent class c is given by Eq. 1:

$$P(X_{ij} = k|C_i = c) = \pi_{jkc}, \tag{1}$$

where π_{jkc} are conditional response probabilities unique to each latent class [28]. For LPA, researchers specify class-specific mean vectors $\boldsymbol{\mu}_c$ and covariance matrices Σ_c for each profile c, to define the probability density function of the multivariate normal (Gaussian) distribution as it is shown in Eq. 2:

$$f(X_i|C_i = c) = \frac{1}{(2\pi)^{d/2}|\Sigma_c|^{1/2}} \exp\left(-\frac{1}{2}(X_i - \mu_c)^\top \Sigma_c^{-1}(X_i - \mu_c)\right), \tag{2}$$

where X_i is a vector of continuous observed variables for individual i, and d is the number of variables included in the profile [13].

Estimation of LCA and LPA parameters commonly utilises the *Expectation-Maximisation* (EM) algorithm, a powerful iterative method well suited for latent mixture models. The EM algorithm involves alternating between an *expectation step* (E-step), which calculates posterior probabilities of class membership for each individual based on current parameter estimates, and a *maximisation step* (M-step), which updates parameter estimates to maximise the likelihood function given these posterior probabilities [15]. The likelihood function L to be maximised can be written as shown in Eq. 3:

$$L(\theta|X) = \prod_{i=1}^{N}\sum_{c=1}^{C} \pi_c f(X_i|\theta_c), \tag{3}$$

where π_c represents the proportion of individuals in latent class c, $f(X_i|\theta_c)$ is the probability distribution function of observed responses given parameters θ_c, and C is the total number of classes or profiles [19]. The pseudocode for the EM algorithm in LPA/LCA contexts typically follows this structure, as shown in Algorithm 1.

Algorithm 1 Expectation-Maximisation algorithm

Initialize parameters π_c, μ_c, Σ_c
repeat
  E-step: Compute posterior probabilities γ_{ic}
  M-step: Update π_c, μ_c, Σ_c based on γ_{ic}
until parameters have converged (e.g. minimal parameter change)

To ensure replicability, a seed for random initialisation `np.random.seed(12)` is often specified before analysis in software like Python.

Model evaluation in LCA and LPA relies heavily on statistical criteria, primarily including the BIC, AIC, sample-size *adjusted BIC* (aBIC), and entropy. The BIC is calculated as Eq. 4:

$$\text{BIC} = -2\ln(L) + p\ln(N), \tag{4}$$

where p is the number of parameters estimated, and N is the sample size [20]. Lower BIC and AIC values generally indicate better model fit, balancing complexity against explanatory power. Entropy, ranging between 0 and 1, measures the clarity of class separation, with higher values indicating clearer delineation between classes [17].

Researchers must evaluate latent subgroup solutions based on substantive interpretability and theoretical coherence. Classes or profiles must reflect meaningful psychological differences rather than statistical artefacts. Often, researchers compare competing models with varying numbers of classes to select the optimal latent structure. The *Bootstrap Likelihood Ratio Test* (BLRT) or *Lo-Mendell-Rubin Adjusted Likelihood Ratio Test* (LMR-LRT) may also be employed to statistically test improvements in model fit when adding classes [31].

It is increasingly common to validate solutions through cross-validation or bootstrap resampling methods. Cross-validation involves splitting the dataset into subsets, estimating models separately, and assessing the stability and consistency of class structures across subsets. Bootstrap procedures generate numerous subsamples, estimating parameters repeatedly to examine the variability and reliability of latent classes across different samples [32].

Additionally, examining posterior probabilities provides insight into classification accuracy at the individual level. Posterior probabilities γ_{ic} indicate how confidently each individual is classified into their respective latent class or profile, serving as a crucial diagnostic tool for the robustness of subgroup assignments.

The use of EM algorithms, robust evaluation criteria, validation procedures, and substantive interpretation ensures that latent structures identified through these analyses are reliable, interpretable, and valuable for advancing psychological understanding.

5 Applications and Case Studies

LCA was applied to data from 741 individuals suffering from mild musculoskeletal pain to uncover hidden subgroups based on psychological and demographic patterns. Participants were assessed across key variables, including marital status, *Post-Traumatic Stress Disorder* (PTSD) symptoms, alexithymia, depression, anxiety, pain intensity, and pain-related disability.

```
# Import necessary libraries
import pandas as pd
import numpy as np
import matplotlib.pyplot as plt
from sklearn.mixture import GaussianMixture
from sklearn.preprocessing import StandardScaler

# Simulate example data for 741 individuals and 7 variables
np.random.seed(42)

n_samples = 741
data = pd.DataFrame({
    'MaritalStatus': np.random.choice([0, 1], size=n_samples),
    ↪ # 0 = single, 1 = married
    'PTSD': np.random.normal(loc=3, scale=1, size=n_samples),
    ↪ # PTSD symptom severity
    'Alexithymia': np.random.normal(loc=2.5, scale=1,
    ↪ size=n_samples),
    'Depression': np.random.normal(loc=3.5, scale=1.2,
    ↪ size=n_samples),
    'Anxiety': np.random.normal(loc=3.2, scale=1,
    ↪ size=n_samples),
    'PainIntensity': np.random.normal(loc=4, scale=1.5,
    ↪ size=n_samples),
    'Disability': np.random.normal(loc=3.8, scale=1.3,
    ↪ size=n_samples)
})

# Standardize the continuous variables
scaler = StandardScaler()
scaled_data = scaler.fit_transform(data)

# Fit Latent Class Model using Gaussian Mixture as
↪ approximation for LCA
n_classes = 3
gmm = GaussianMixture(n_components=n_classes, max_iter=1000,
↪ random_state=42)
gmm.fit(scaled_data)
data['LatentClass'] = gmm.predict(scaled_data)
```

```
# Display latent class proportions
class_counts = data['LatentClass'].value_counts().sort_index()
print("Latent Class Proportions:")
for cls, count in class_counts.items():
    print(f"Class {cls}: {count} individuals ({(count /
    ↪ n_samples) * 100:.2f}%)")

# Visualize latent class distribution using matplotlib
plt.figure(figsize=(8, 5))
plt.bar(class_counts.index.astype(str), class_counts.values,
↪ color=['skyblue', 'orange', 'green'])
plt.title('Latent Class Distribution')
plt.xlabel('Latent Class')
plt.ylabel('Number of Individuals')
plt.grid(True)
plt.tight_layout()
plt.show()

# Visualize mean variable profiles per class
class_profiles = data.groupby('LatentClass').mean()
variables = ['MaritalStatus', 'PTSD', 'Alexithymia',
↪ 'Depression', 'Anxiety', 'PainIntensity', 'Disability']

x = np.arange(len(variables))
bar_width = 0.25

plt.figure(figsize=(10, 6))
for i, (cls, row) in enumerate(class_profiles.iterrows()):
    plt.bar(x + i * bar_width, row[variables].values,
    ↪ width=bar_width, label=f'Class {cls}')

plt.xticks(x + bar_width, variables, rotation=45)
plt.ylabel('Average Scores')
plt.title('Mean Psychological and Demographic Scores by Latent
↪ Class')
plt.legend()
plt.grid(True)
plt.tight_layout()
plt.show()
```

Results:

```
Latent Class Proportions:
Class 0: 2 individuals (0.27\%)
Class 1: 387 individuals (52.23\%)
Class 2: 352 individuals (47.50\%)
```

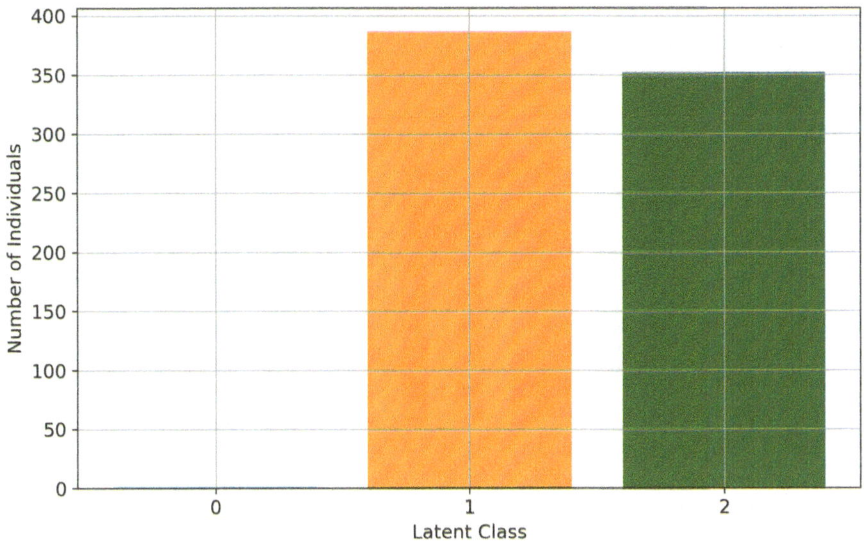

Fig. 4 Latent class distribution

The results of the produced class distributions are shown in Fig. 4. Class 0 ($n = 2$, 0.27%) represents the small group of single individuals who exhibited moderately high PTSD, very low alexithymia, moderate depression, upper-moderate anxiety, almost high pain intensity, and extremely high disability. Despite the small size, this class suggests a rare subgroup where trauma amplifies severe functional impairment, possibly due to heightened emotional awareness (low alexithymia). The lack of marital support may exacerbate distress. Clinical Implications: Intensive trauma-focused therapy (e.g. CBT and EMDR) and rehabilitation to restore function are critical, leveraging their emotional awareness for therapy engagement.

The largest group is in Class 1 ($n = 387$, 52.23%). These participants are all married, showed moderate PTSD, under-moderate alexithymia, upper-moderate depression, moderate anxiety, high pain intensity, and high disability. This profile reflects a common pattern where pain and psychological distress (particularly depression) interact, with under-moderate alexithymia suggesting some emotional processing difficulties. Marriage may offer support, but it does not mitigate high pain or disability, possibly due to relational stress. Clinical implications suggest that multidisciplinary interventions combining CBT for depression, pain management (e.g. physical therapy), and couples therapy to harness marital support would be beneficial.

Class 2 ($n = 352$, 47.50%) is a large group of single individuals who had moderate PTSD, moderate alexithymia, high depression, moderate anxiety, moderate pain intensity, and moderate disability. High depression dominates, with moderate alexithymia indicating challenges in emotional expression that may fuel

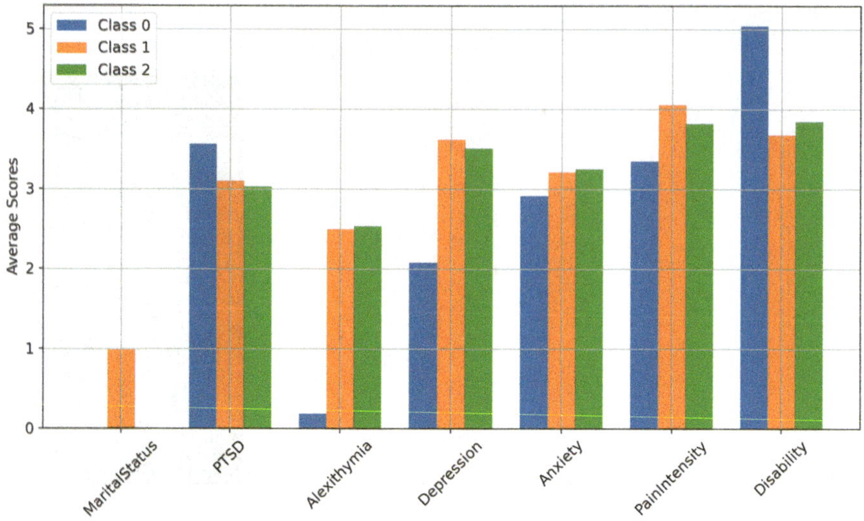

Fig. 5 Mean psychological and demographic scores by latent class

distress. Moderate pain and disability suggest resilience despite psychological burden, possibly due to less severe pain perception. Clinical implications point to the need for targeting depression with CBT or antidepressants, enhancing emotional awareness through mindfulness, and preventing pain escalation via early intervention. Peer support groups may also help reduce social isolation.

Comparative insights show that marital status differentiates the classes, with single status (Classes 0 and 2) potentially associated with reduced social support, which may amplify distress as seen in Class 0. In contrast, Class 1's high pain and disability indicate stronger interactions between pain and psychological factors. The variation in alexithymia, ranging from very low to moderate, further underscores its role in emotional processing and somatisation (Fig. 5).

In the second case study, LPA was conducted on a sample of 498 university students to identify subgroups based on their mental health profiles, using variables including PTSD symptoms, alexithymia, depression, anxiety, stress, and age. The analysis revealed three distinct latent profiles (Fig. 6).

```
# Importing necessary libraries
import pandas as pd
import numpy as np
import matplotlib.pyplot as plt
from sklearn.mixture import GaussianMixture
from sklearn.preprocessing import StandardScaler

# Setting the random seed for reproducibility
```

```
np.random.seed(42)

# Simulating data for 498 university students
n_students = 498
data = pd.DataFrame({
    'PTSD': np.random.normal(loc=3.0, scale=1.0,
     ↪ size=n_students),
    'Alexithymia': np.random.normal(loc=2.8, scale=0.9,
     ↪ size=n_students),
    'Depression': np.random.normal(loc=3.5, scale=1.1,
     ↪ size=n_students),
    'Anxiety': np.random.normal(loc=3.2, scale=1.0,
     ↪ size=n_students),
    'Stress': np.random.normal(loc=3.6, scale=1.2,
     ↪ size=n_students),
    'Age': np.random.normal(loc=21, scale=2, size=n_students)
})

# Standardising the data for better clustering results
scaler = StandardScaler()
scaled_data = scaler.fit_transform(data)

# Applying the Gaussian Mixture Model for Latent Profile
 ↪ Analysis (3 classes)
n_profiles = 3
gmm = GaussianMixture(n_components=n_profiles, max_iter=1000,
 ↪ random_state=42)
gmm.fit(scaled_data)

# Adding the latent profile predictions to the original
 ↪ DataFrame
data['LatentProfile'] = gmm.predict(scaled_data)

# Displaying the distribution of latent profiles
profile_counts =
 ↪ data['LatentProfile'].value_counts().sort_index()
print("Latent profile distribution:")
for profile, count in profile_counts.items():
    print(f"Profile {profile}: {count} students ({(count /
     ↪ n_students) * 100:.2f}%)")

# Visualising the distribution of latent profiles
plt.figure(figsize=(8, 5))
plt.bar(profile_counts.index.astype(str),
 ↪ profile_counts.values, color=['skyblue', 'salmon',
 ↪ 'limegreen'])
```

```
plt.title('Distribution of Latent Profiles')
plt.xlabel('Latent Profile')
plt.ylabel('Number of Students')
plt.grid(True)
plt.tight_layout()
plt.show()

# Calculating the average values of the variables by latent
↪ profile
profile_means = data.groupby('LatentProfile').mean()

# Visualising the average values of all variables by profile,
↪ excluding LatentProfile
variables = ['PTSD', 'Alexithymia', 'Depression', 'Anxiety',
↪ 'Stress', 'Age']
x = np.arange(len(variables))
bar_width = 0.25

plt.figure(figsize=(10, 6))
for i, (profile, row) in enumerate(profile_means.iterrows()):
    plt.bar(x + i * bar_width, row[variables], width=bar_width,
     ↪ label=f'Profile {profile}')

plt.xticks(x + bar_width, variables, rotation=45)
plt.ylabel('Average Values')
plt.title('Mental Health by Latent Profiles')
plt.legend()
plt.grid(True)
plt.tight_layout()
plt.show()
```

Results:

```
Latent profile distribution:
Profile 0: 130 students (26.10\%)
Profile 1: 213 students (42.77\%)
Profile 2: 155 students (31.12\%)
```

Profile 0 (Fig. 7) represents the High-Stress Strivers, consisting of 130 students (26.10%), whose average age is just over 20 years. This group, comprising about a quarter of the sample, displays moderate levels of PTSD, alexithymia, depression, and anxiety, with notably high stress levels. Slightly older than their peers, these individuals are likely in their second or third year. They may be navigating heavier academic responsibilities or transitional life phases such as career planning. Their stress appears overwhelming; one might imagine a 21-year-old balancing

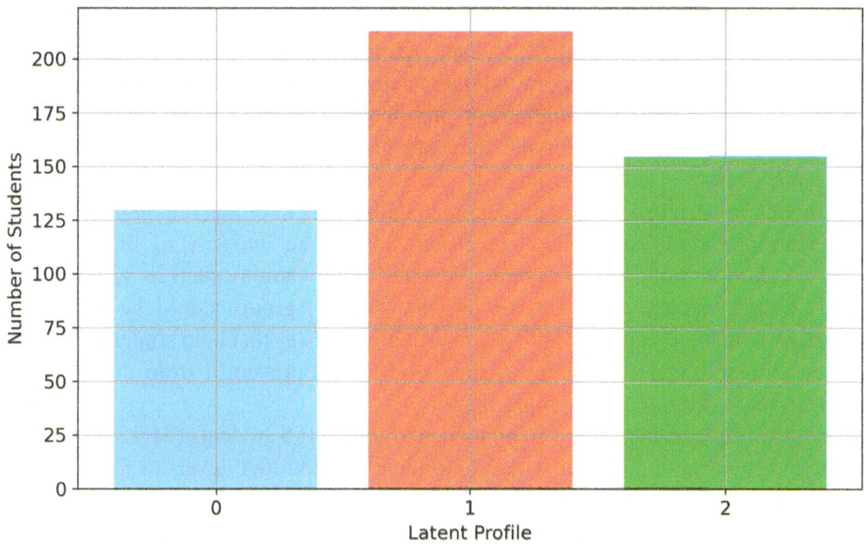

Fig. 6 Distribution of latent profiles

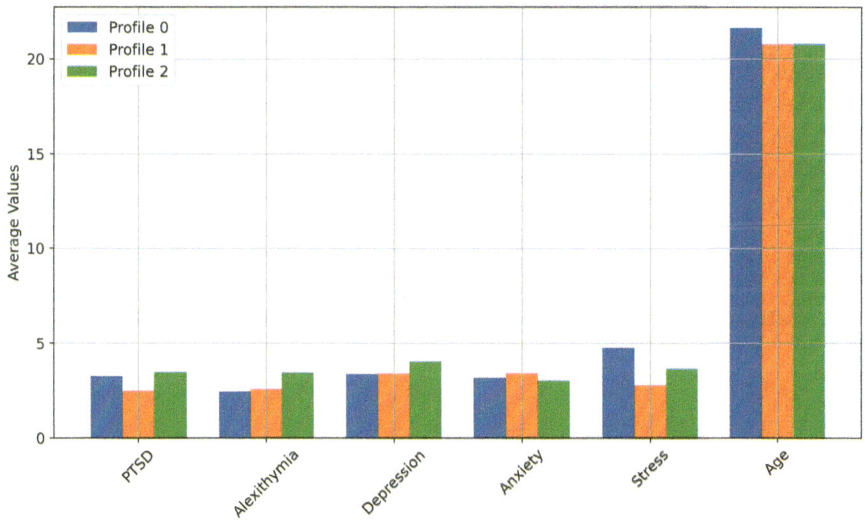

Fig. 7 Mental health by latent profiles

exams and part-time work while struggling to articulate emotions due to moderate alexithymia. These students could benefit from stress-reduction interventions such as mindfulness workshops or time-management coaching. Exercises that promote emotional awareness may also enhance their coping capacity, helping to prevent moderate symptoms from escalating into more serious mental health concerns.

Profile 1 represents the Anxious Adjusters, a group of 213 students (42.77%) with an average age close to 20 years. As the largest segment in the sample, these students experience upper-moderate anxiety, accompanied by moderate levels of alexithymia, depression, and stress, and under-moderate PTSD. Likely in their first or second year of university, they are navigating new social environments, academic pressures, and emerging life goals. Their elevated anxiety is particularly prominent, as seen in a student preoccupied with fitting in or meeting high academic expectations. While their PTSD levels are lower, the intensity of their anxiety may escalate without timely support. Scalable interventions such as group-based CBT, digital anxiety programs, or peer-led support groups could be especially effective. Enhancing emotional literacy through exercises that help students identify and articulate their feelings may reduce anxiety and prevent it from exacerbating depressive or stress-related symptoms.

Profile 2 reflects the Deeply Wounded, a group of 155 students (31.12%) with an average age close to 20 years. These individuals exhibit high levels of PTSD, alexithymia, and depression, while their anxiety and stress remain moderate. Despite being early in their university journey, many in this group appear to carry significant psychological burdens, potentially stemming from past trauma or unresolved loss. Picture a student who feels emotionally numb, overwhelmed by intrusive memories, and unable to articulate their inner turmoil. Although their moderate anxiety and stress may not immediately signal crisis, their underlying distress is profound and demands careful attention. Comprehensive interventions, including trauma-focused therapies such as EMDR and targeted depression treatment, are essential. Support strategies that enhance emotional expression and processing are also critical. Without appropriate care, this group remains at elevated risk for serious outcomes, including suicidal ideation.

6 Visualising Latent Profile and Class Analysis Results

LCA and LPA are statistical techniques that enable the identification of hidden groups or classes within data [28]. The visualisation of these results plays a crucial role in interpreting findings and communicating research outcomes. In this subsection, we will focus on various visualisation methods that provide a clearer understanding of data structure, identified classes, and their characterisation.

One of the most commonly used methods for presenting LCA and LPA results is a line chart that illustrates the profiles of different classes. The horizontal axis represents the indicators or variables that define the profiles, while the vertical axis shows the mean values or estimated probabilities for each class.

This type of visualisation allows researchers to easily identify differences between classes, recognise patterns, and draw conclusions about latent structures within the data. In LPA, where continuous variables are used, the line chart clearly

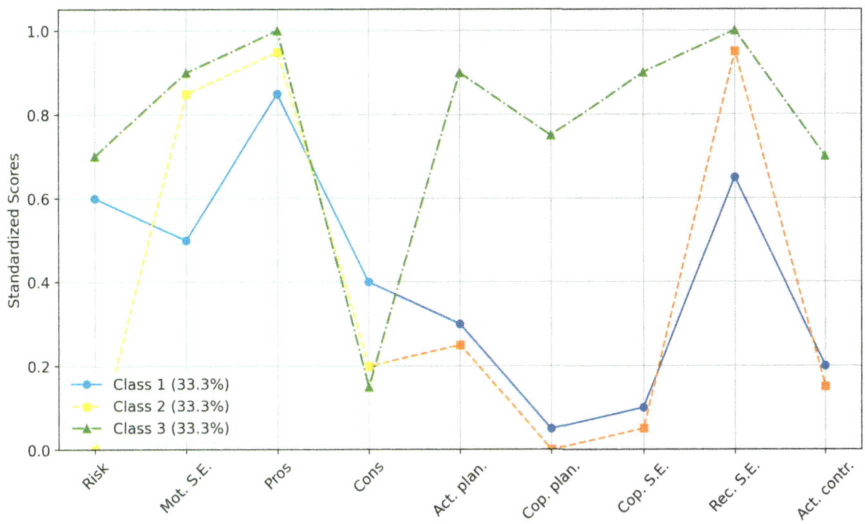

Fig. 8 Latent class profiles for the three-class model

shows how different profiles vary in terms of characteristic intensity. In LCA, where variables are categorical, a bar chart can be used to display probability distributions [34]. An example of a graphical representation of latent class profiles is shown in Fig. 8.

An example of Python code for visualisation of latent class profile is presented below:

```
import matplotlib.pyplot as plt
import numpy as np

# Define variable names for x-axis
variables = ['Risk', 'Mot. S.E.', 'Pros', 'Cons', 'Act. plan.',
             'Cop. plan.', 'Cop. S.E.', 'Rec. S.E.', 'Act.
             ↪  contr.']

x = np.arange(len(variables))  # x-axis positions

# Simulated standardized scores for three latent classes
class1 = [0.6, 0.5, 0.85, 0.4, 0.3, 0.05, 0.1, 0.65, 0.2]
class2 = [0.0, 0.85, 0.95, 0.2, 0.25, 0.0, 0.05, 0.95, 0.15]
class3 = [0.7, 0.9, 1.0, 0.15, 0.9, 0.75, 0.9, 1.0, 0.7]

# Create the plot
plt.figure(figsize=(10, 6))
```

```
# Plot each class profile
plt.plot(x, class1, '-o', label='Class 1 (33.3%)')
plt.plot(x, class2, '--s', label='Class 2 (33.3%)')
plt.plot(x, class3, '-.^', label='Class 3 (33.3%)')

# Customize the plot
plt.xticks(x, variables, rotation=45)  # Set variable labels on
↪  x-axis
plt.ylim(0, 1.05)                       # Set y-axis limits
plt.ylabel('Standardized Scores')      # Label for y-axis
plt.title('Latent Class Profiles ^^e2^^80^^93 Three-Class
↪  Model')  # Title
plt.legend()                           # Show legend
plt.grid(True)                         # Add gridlines for
↪  readability

# Adjust layout and display
plt.tight_layout()
plt.show()
```

For studies involving multiple latent variables, scatter plots can be useful in displaying individual data points relative to the identified classes [35]. These visualisations can include colour-coded points based on assigned classes, providing a clear insight into data distribution and the degree of overlap between different classes.

Techniques such as *Principal Component Analysis* (PCA) and *t-distributed Stochastic Neighbour Embedding* (t-SNE) can be used to project high-dimensional data into a two-dimensional space, aiding in the clearer presentation and interpretation of classification results [36]. An example of a scatter plot is shown in Fig. 9.

An example of Python code for visualisation of scatter plot with density plots is presented below:

```
import seaborn as sns
import matplotlib.pyplot as plt
import numpy as np

# Generate example data
np.random.seed(42)
x = np.random.normal(loc=5, scale=1.5, size=200)
y = x * 0.5 + np.random.normal(loc=0, scale=1, size=200)
```

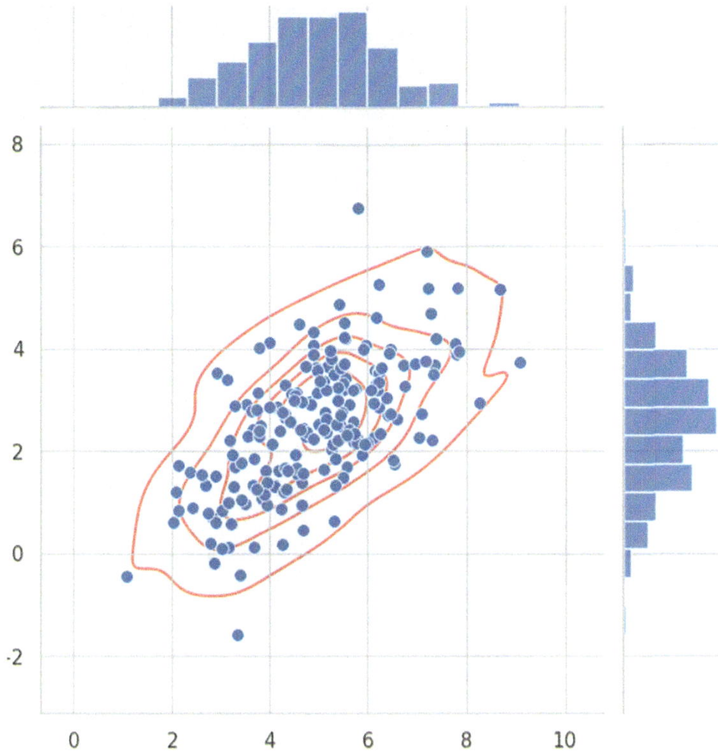

Fig. 9 Scatter plot with density plots

```
# Create a joint plot with scatter and density (KDE) plots
sns.set(style="whitegrid")
plot = sns.jointplot(x=x, y=y, kind="scatter",
↪  color="dodgerblue", edgecolor="white", s=50)

# Add kernel density estimation (KDE) on top
plot.plot_joint(sns.kdeplot, color="red", zorder=0, levels=6,
↪  alpha=0.5)

# Show plot
plt.show()
```

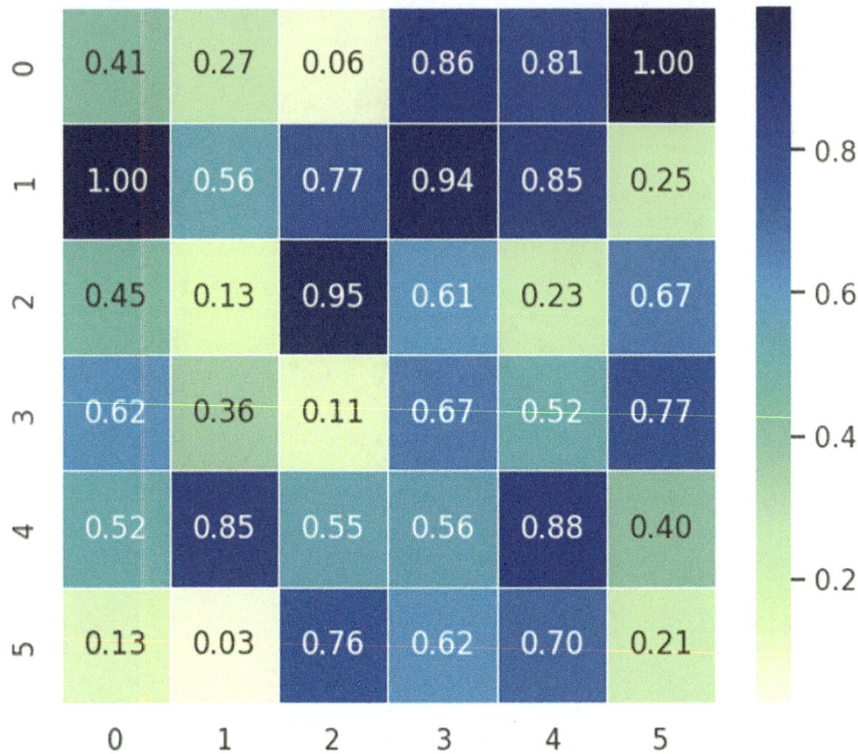

Fig. 10 Heatmap matrix example

Heatmaps are another effective method for visualising the results of latent analysis [23]. They allow for the representation of mean values or class membership probabilities using colours that reflect the intensity of results. This type of visualisation is particularly useful for identifying specific patterns in the data and differentiating between classes.

Matrix representations can be used to display the probabilities of individuals being assigned to different classes, which is helpful for assessing the stability of classification and overlap between classes [28]. These visualisations are often combined with tabular displays to provide a more precise insight into data structure. An example of a heatmap is shown in Fig. 10.

An example of Python code for visualisation of heatmap matrix is presented below.

```python
import seaborn as sns
import matplotlib.pyplot as plt
import numpy as np

# Create example matrix (random values)
data = np.random.rand(6, 6)

# Create heatmap
plt.figure(figsize=(6, 5))
sns.heatmap(data, annot=True, cmap="YlGnBu", fmt=".2f",
↪ linewidths=0.5)

# Add title
plt.title("Heatmap Example")
plt.show()
```

In addition to group visualisations, it is useful to present individual profiles of respondents within latent classes [37]. These graphs can include information on how individuals are distributed across different classes based on assignment probabilities. Probability representation can take the form of histograms or multiple line graphs.

Furthermore, box-plot visualisations provide insights into variability within each class, highlighting extreme and median values of indicator variables. These visualisations are particularly useful when identifying individuals who deviate from the main classes or when there is a significant degree of uncertainty in class assignment [18].

Modern software packages such as R (with packages like `ggplot2`, `tidyLPA`, and `mclust`), Python (`matplotlib`, `seaborn`), and statistical tools like Mplus offer advanced visualisation capabilities. Interactive graphs and dynamic displays allow researchers to explore data at a deeper level, filter information, and analyse patterns in more detail.

The use of interactive visualisations, such as graphs that allow for modifications in class representation, adjustment of the number of classes, or addition of extra data layers, can significantly enhance the interpretation and validation of models. These methods are often combined with standard graphical representations to achieve a comprehensive analysis [38].

References

1. C.J. Van Lissa, M. Garnier-Villarreal, D. Anadria, Recommended practices in latent class analysis using the open-source R-package tidySEM. Struct. Equ. Model. Multidiscip. J. **31**(3), 526 (2024)
2. L.M. Collins, S.T. Lanza, *Latent Class and Latent Transition Analysis: With Applications in the Social, Behavioral, and Health Sciences* (Wiley, New York, 2009)

3. T. Rachid, A. Abarda, A. Hasbaoui, Latent class analysis: a review and recommendations for future applications in health sciences. Procedia Comput. Sci. **238**, 1062 (2024)
4. P. Sinha, C.S. Calfee, K.L. Delucchi, Practitioner's guide to latent class analysis: methodological considerations and common pitfalls. Crit. Care Med. **49**(1), e63 (2021)
5. S.T. Lanza, B.R. Cooper, Latent class analysis for developmental research. Child Dev. Perspect. **10**(1), 59 (2016)
6. N. Eshima, *An Introduction to Latent Class Analysis* (Springer, Berlin, 2022)
7. J. Magidson, J. Vermunt, Latent class models for clustering: a comparison with K-means. Canadian J. Mark. Res. **20**(1), 36 (2002)
8. H. Farahani, P. Watson, T. Bezan, N. Kovač, L.C. Winter, M. Blagojević, P. Azadfallah, A. Allahyari, S. Masoumian, P. Jiménez, PsAIchology: an intelligent direction in psychological sciences, in *10th International Scientific Conference Technics, Informatics and Education-TIE 2024* (Faculty of Technical Sciences Čačak, University of Kragujevac, Kragujevac, 2024)
9. N. Kovač, K. Ratković, H. Farahani, P. Watson, A practical applications guide to machine learning regression models in psychology with python. Methods Psychol. **11**, 100156 (2024)
10. N. Kovač, K. Ratković, K., Watson, P., Farahani, H., Bagheri Sheykhangafshe, F. Machine learning classification models for predicting chronic pain. Curr. Psychol. **44**(18), 15409–15422 (2025)
11. D. Spurk, A. Hirschi, M. Wang, D. Valero, S. Kauffeld, Latent profile analysis: a review and "how to" guide of its application within vocational behavior research. J. Vocat. Behav. **120**, 103445 (2020)
12. D.A. Pastor, K.E. Barron, B. Miller, S.L. Davis, A latent profile analysis of college students' achievement goal orientation. Contemp. Educ. Psychol. **32**(1), 8 (2007)
13. G.H. Lubke, B. Muthén, Investigating population heterogeneity with factor mixture models. Psychol. Methods **10**(1), 21 (2005)
14. D. Oberski, Mixture models: latent profile and latent class analysis, in *Modern Statistical Methods for HCI* (2016), pp. 275–287
15. K.S. Berlin, N.A. Williams, G.R. Parra, An introduction to latent variable mixture modeling (Part 1): overview and cross-sectional latent class and latent profile analyses. J. Pediatr. Psychol. **39**(2), 174 (2014)
16. K. Nylund-Gibson, A.Y. Choi, Ten frequently asked questions about latent class analysis. Translat. Issues Psychol. Sci. **4**(4), 440 (2018)
17. T. Asparouhov, B. Muthén, Auxiliary variables in mixture modeling: three-step approaches using M plus. Struct. Equ. Model. Multidiscip. J. **21**(3), 329 (2014)
18. J.K. Vermunt, Latent class modeling with covariates: two improved three-step approaches. Polit. Anal. **18**(4), 450 (2010)
19. B. Muthén, L.K. Muthén, Integrating person-centered and variable-centered analyses: growth mixture modeling with latent trajectory classes. Alcohol. Clin. Exp. Res. **24**(6), 882 (2000)
20. K.L. Nylund, T. Asparouhov, B.O. Muthén, Deciding on the number of classes in latent class analysis and growth mixture modeling: a Monte Carlo simulation study. Struct. Equ. Model. Multidiscip. J. **14**(4), 535 (2007)
21. Z. Bakk, J.K. Vermunt, Robustness of stepwise latent class modeling with continuous distal outcomes. Struct. Equ. Model. Multidiscip. J. **23**(1), 20 (2016)
22. T. Gregory, N.S. Monroy, B. Grace, A. Finlay-Jones, M. Brushe, A. Sincovich, B. Heritage, Z. Boulton, S.A. Brinkman, Mental health profiles and academic achievement in Australian school students. J. Sch. Psychol. **103**, 101291 (2024)
23. B.S. Everitt, S. Landau, M. Leese, D. Stahl, *Cluster analysis* (Wiley-Blackwell, New York, 2011)
24. L. Kaufman, P.J. Rousseeuw, *Finding Groups in Data: An Introduction to Cluster Analysis* (Wiley, New York, 2009)
25. C. Hennig, M. Meila, F. Murtagh, R. Rocci, *Handbook of Cluster Analysis* (CRC Press, New York, 2015)

26. T. Asparouhov, B. Muthén, Auxiliary variables in mixture modeling: using the BCH method in Mplus to estimate a distal outcome model and an arbitrary secondary model, version 11. Mplus Web Notes **21**, 1 (2021)
27. K. Aflaki, S. Vigod, J.G. Ray, Part II: a step-by-step guide to latent class analysis. J. Clin. Epidemiol. **159**, 348 (2023)
28. L.M. Collins, S.T. Lanza, *Latent Class and Latent Transition Analysis: With Applications in the Social, Behavioral, and Health Sciences* (Wiley, New York, 2010)
29. H.W. Marsh, O. Lüdtke, B. Muthén, T. Asparouhov, A.J. Morin, U. Trautwein, B. Nagengast, A new look at the big five factor structure through exploratory structural equation modeling. Psychol. Assess. **22**(3), 471 (2010)
30. M.N. Schmidt, D. Seddig, E. Davidov, M. Mørup, K.J. Albers, J.M. Bauer, F.K. Glückstad, Latent profile analysis of human values: what is the optimal number of clusters?. Methodology **17**(2), 127 (2021)
31. J.Y. Tein, S. Coxe, H. Cham, Statistical power to detect the correct number of classes in latent profile analysis. Struct. Equ. Model. Multidiscip. J. **20**(4), 640 (2013)
32. G. Lubke, B.O. Muthén, Performance of factor mixture models as a function of model size, covariate effects, and class-specific parameters. Struct. Equ. Model. Multidiscip. J. **14**(1), 26 (2007)
33. M. Marbac, M. Sedki, VarSelLCM: an R/C++ package for variable selection in model-based clustering of mixed-data with missing values. Bioinformatics **35**(7), 1255 (2019)
34. B. Muthén, Latent variable analysis. The Sage handbook of quantitative methodology for the social sciences **345**(368), 106 (2004)
35. A.L. McCutcheon, *Latent Class Analysis* (SAGE, New York, 1987)
36. L. van der Maaten, G. Hinton, Visualizing data using t-SNE. J. Mach. Learn. Res. **9**, 2579 (2008)
37. S.T. Lanza, B.P. Flaherty, L.M. Collins, in *Handbook of Psychology: Research Methods in Psychology*, vol. 2, ed. by J.A. Schinka, W.F. Velicer (Wiley, New York, 2003), pp. 663–685. https://doi.org/10.1002/0471264385.wei0226
38. J. Wang, X. Wang, *Structural Equation Modeling: Applications Using Mplus* (Wiley, New York, 2019)

Time-Dependent Modelling in Psychological Data

Nataša Kovač, Marija Blagojević, Zhiyong Johnny Zhang, Kruna Ratković, Peter Watson, and Hojjatollah Farahani

1 Overview of Latent Growth Curve Modelling

Latent Growth Curve Modelling (LGCM) has emerged as one of the most powerful and flexible methodologies for modelling change over time in psychological research. This technique is embedded within the broader framework of *Structural Equation Modelling* (SEM) and allows researchers to examine intra-individual change (within-person dynamics) and inter-individual variability in those changes (differences between people in how they change) [1, 2]. Unlike traditional repeated measures ANOVA or simple regression models, LGCM provides a richer understanding of developmental processes, behavioural trajectories, or psychological constructs that evolve over time.

N. Kovač (✉) · K. Ratković
Faculty of Applied Sciences, University of Donja Gorica, Podgorica, Montenegro
e-mail: natasa.kovac@udg.edu.me; kruna.ratkovic@udg.edu.me

M. Blagojević
Faculty of Technical Sciences, University of Kragujevac, Čačak, Serbia
e-mail: marija.blagojevic@uni.kg.ac.rs

Z. J. Zhang
Department of Psychology, University of Notre Dame, Notre Dame, IN, USA
e-mail: zhiyongzhang@nd.edu

P. Watson
MRC Cognition and Brain Sciences Unit, University of Cambridge, Cambridge, England
e-mail: Peter.Watson@mrc-cbu.cam.ac.uk

H. Farahani
Department of Psychology, Faculty of Humanities, Tarbiat Modares University, Jalal AleAhmad Nasr, Tehran, Iran
e-mail: h.farahani@modares.ac.ir

N. Kovač et al. (eds.), *Data Science in Psychology*,
https://doi.org/10.1007/978-3-032-18312-5_14

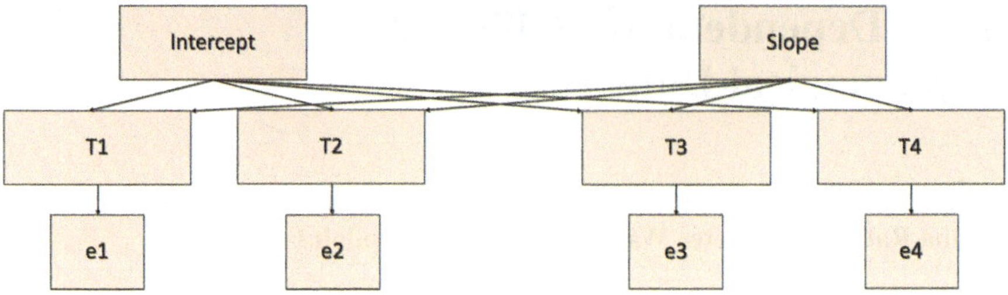

Fig. 1 Path diagram of a basic latent growth curve model

At its core, LGCM estimates a trajectory or growth curve for each individual in the sample, based on repeated observations across multiple time points. These trajectories are represented by latent variables, typically including an intercept factor (representing the initial status or baseline level) and a slope factor (representing the rate of change or growth over time) [3]. The intercept and slope are treated as random variables, thus allowing individual variability around these central tendencies. This approach respects the heterogeneity of human development and psychological phenomena, which often vary considerably from person to person.

A fundamental advantage of LGCM is that it disentangles measurement error from true change, which is especially critical in longitudinal data analysis. Measurement error is accounted for via residual variances of observed variables (e.g. time-specific scores), improving the reliability of estimated change parameters. This feature stands in contrast to more traditional methods like difference scores or repeated measures ANOVA, where error is often conflated with signal, leading to biased or inefficient estimates [4].

LGCM represents individual trajectories over time using latent variables to capture the underlying growth structure. A standard LGCM consists of two key latent factors: the intercept, which reflects the initial status of the trajectory, and the slope, which represents the rate of change over time [1]. The observed repeated measures serve as indicators of these latent growth factors, and each indicator has an associated residual term accounting for measurement error.

Figure 1 illustrates a basic latent growth curve model, where repeated observations ($T1 - T4$) are linked to two latent components, intercept and slope. Each observed variable has a corresponding residual ($e1 - e4$) representing unexplained variance. The factor loadings for the slope are typically fixed at evenly spaced intervals (e.g. 0, 1, 2, 3) to represent a linear growth trajectory, though alternative parameterisations allow for non-linear patterns [5].

In LGCM, researchers must specify the temporal structure of the model. The time scores, or loadings, for the slope factor, typically reflect the linear change (e.g. 0, 1, 2, 3 across four waves of data) but can also reflect non-linear patterns such as quadratic growth (e.g. 0, 1, 4, 9), freely estimated time points, or piecewise change, where different slopes are estimated for different intervals [5]. This flexibility allows LGCM to accommodate both theoretically driven and empirically informed hypotheses about growth trajectories.

LGCM facilitates the inclusion of time-invariant and time-varying covariates. Time-invariant covariates (e.g. gender, baseline age, and socio-economic status) can predict growth parameters, explaining why some individuals start higher or grow faster than others. Time-varying covariates (e.g. stress levels measured at each wave) can be linked directly to the repeated measures to test how changing contexts influence developmental trajectories over time [6].

The strength of LGCM is its compatibility with missing data mechanisms, such as *Missing at Random* (MAR). Most LGCM implementations employ *Full Information Maximum Likelihood* (FIML) estimation or Bayesian estimation, which enables the use of all available data, reducing bias and increasing statistical power [7]. This is a substantial improvement over listwise deletion or imputation techniques that are common in older longitudinal analysis frameworks.

Beyond linear and quadratic models, LGCM also serves as a gateway into more advanced modelling strategies such as latent basis models, *Growth Mixture Modelling* (GMM), and parallel process models. Latent basis models allow the shape of growth to be freely estimated rather than imposed a priori, which is useful when researchers lack strong theoretical assumptions about functional form [8]. Parallel process LGCM, on the other hand, simultaneously estimates two or more growth processes (e.g. anxiety and depression trajectories), allowing for the examination of how change in one construct relates to change in another.

An illustrative application in developmental psychology might involve modelling the trajectory of academic self-efficacy across 4 years of high school. The intercept would represent the initial level of self-efficacy in Grade 9, while the slope would estimate how much self-efficacy increases or decreases over the years. LGCM would not only capture the average growth trajectory but also quantify the variability in individual growth patterns, identifying students who increase, decrease, or remain stable in their beliefs about academic competence.

It is also worth noting that LGCM encourages model-based hypothesis testing. Researchers can compare nested models (e.g. linear vs. quadratic) or test specific constraints (e.g. equality of slope variance across groups) using likelihood-ratio tests, *Akaike Information Criterion* (AIC), or *Bayesian Information Criterion* (BIC) [9]. Multiple-group LGCM can examine whether growth trajectories differ across predefined groups, such as treatment vs. control, or high-risk vs. low-risk populations.

Furthermore, LGCM integrates seamlessly into the SEM ecosystem, meaning that researchers can build more complex hierarchical models that combine measurement and structural components. For instance, second-order LGCM can be used when observed indicators of the latent construct themselves are measured via multiple items or scales, blending confirmatory factor analysis and growth modelling into a unified framework [10].

Recent developments in the field have enhanced the accessibility and applicability of LGCM. Modern statistical software packages such as `Mplus`, `lavaan` in R [11], AMOS, and EQS provide user-friendly platforms for fitting growth curve models, with detailed outputs for interpretation. The visualisation tools available today (e.g. *plotGMM* and *semPlot*) make it easier to communicate complex longitudinal patterns to diverse audiences, including applied researchers and policymakers.

As psychological science continues to emphasise longitudinal inquiry and developmental frameworks, LGCM offers a powerful, theory-driven method to answer questions that are fundamentally temporal in nature. Whether examining resilience trajectories after trauma, developmental patterns of substance use, or the long-term effectiveness of educational interventions, LGCM stands as a central analytic tool in the longitudinal modelling toolkit.

2 Growth Models: Unconditional and Conditional

Growth modelling provides a powerful statistical framework for analysing longitudinal data, allowing researchers to investigate how individuals change over time and what factors may account for that change. In psychological research, such models are often used to examine trajectories of cognitive development, symptom progression, behaviour, and emotional responses across repeated measurements [1, 3]. LGCMs are particularly useful because they decompose longitudinal change into meaningful components: an intercept representing the initial level and a slope reflecting the rate of change. Two fundamental types of growth models are typically distinguished: unconditional and conditional. These two variants differ in whether explanatory variables are introduced to account for inter-individual variability in developmental trajectories [1, 12].

In an **unconditional growth model**, change over time is examined without including predictors or covariates. Each individual's growth trajectory is modelled as a function of two latent variables: the intercept and the slope. These latent variables capture the average trajectory and individual variability. Unconditional models serve as a foundation, allowing researchers to determine whether systematic change occurs over time and to estimate population-level trends before considering explanatory variables [13].

For example, an unconditional model might be used to investigate how anxiety scores change over three time points in a clinical intervention study. By modelling intercepts and slopes for each participant, one can quantify whether there is a general reduction in anxiety and how this trajectory varies across individuals. The model also provides variance estimates for the intercept and slope, which reflect individual differences in baseline levels and change rates, respectively.

A **conditional growth model** builds on this framework by incorporating predictors to explain variability in growth trajectories. These predictors (e.g. age, gender, and treatment condition) can be introduced to model differences in the intercepts, slopes, or both. In this way, researchers can determine not only whether change occurs but also what variables might influence the magnitude or direction of change [14]. For instance, a conditional model may reveal that a treatment condition significantly affects the rate of symptom improvement, while gender might influence the initial level of symptoms.

Conditional growth models also facilitate hypothesis testing related to mediation and moderation in change processes. By incorporating time-invariant and time-varying covariates, the models enable researchers to account for individual differences and external influences, thereby enhancing explanatory power [15]. In cognitive ageing research, for example, education level might be modelled as a predictor of slope, hypothesising that individuals with higher education exhibit slower cognitive decline. The inclusion of covariates provides explanatory power, allowing researchers to evaluate why individuals vary in their initial status and growth rates. For example, a study examining academic self-efficacy might find that students with higher socioeconomic status both start at a higher baseline and demonstrate steeper improvement over time.

The choice between unconditional and conditional models depends on the research objective. Exploratory analyses often start with unconditional models to understand the basic shape of change, while conditional models test theoretically motivated predictors of individual differences.

Growth models are typically implemented in software such as `Mplus`, `lavaan` in R, or `semopy` in Python. The following example shows a simplified Python implementation using `semopy`:

```
from semopy import Model
import pandas as pd

desc = """
# Measurement model
y1 ~ 1*intercept + 0*slope
y2 ~ 1*intercept + 1*slope
y3 ~ 1*intercept + 2*slope

# Regressions
slope ~ gender
"""

data = pd.read_csv("growth_data.csv")
model = Model(desc)
model.fit(data)
model.inspect()
```

This code specifies a linear latent growth model where the slope is regressed on a time-invariant covariate `gender`. Time is modelled as 0, 1, and 2, corresponding to three time points. The `semopy` library supports estimation of model parameters and provides diagnostic outputs for model fit and parameter interpretation.

To visually distinguish the conceptual differences between unconditional and conditional growth models, Fig. 2 presents a graphical illustration of both modelling approaches. In the unconditional model, each line represents an individual trajectory where the slope is fixed across all individuals, but the intercepts vary. This reflects

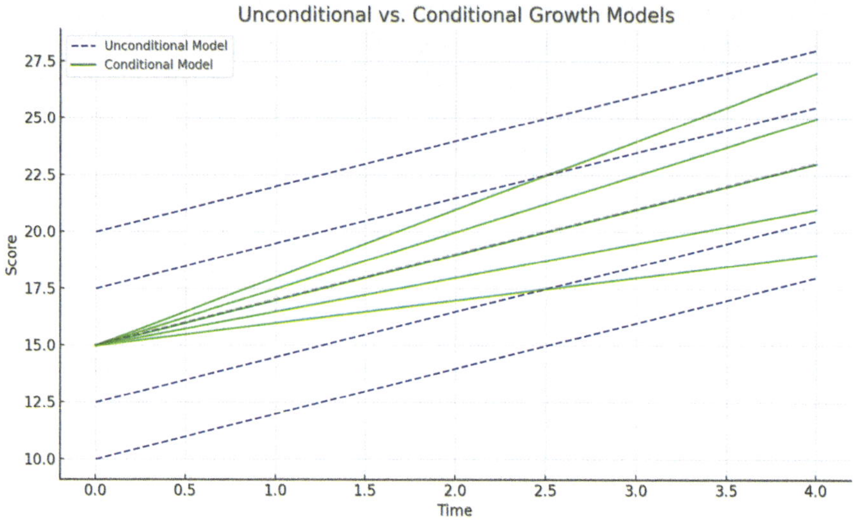

Fig. 2 Illustration of conditional and unconditional growth trajectories

a situation where participants may begin at different baseline levels (e.g. initial test scores) but are assumed to change at a similar rate over time. This approach is often used to describe average developmental trends without explicitly modelling the influence of external covariates.

In contrast, the conditional model holds the intercept constant for all individuals while allowing the slopes to vary. This reflects the inclusion of time-invariant covariates, such as gender or treatment group, that explain inter-individual differences in the rate of change. As seen in the figure, individuals may start at the same level but diverge over time based on the values of the predictor variable. This pattern is typical in studies where researchers are interested in how external factors influence the dynamics of psychological development.

By contrasting these two approaches, the figure highlights how conditional growth models enhance the interpretability and explanatory power of longitudinal analysis by integrating predictors directly into the modelling of change.

3 Model Fit Assessment

Evaluating the model fit of a growth curve model is to assess how well the model describes the data. Different strategies can be used to evaluate the fit of a growth curve model.

To start, one can visually inspect the data and the fitted model. First, one can plot the observed data to inspect the overall trend and variability. Such a plot is called a longitudinal plot or the spaghetti plot. This can help the selection of an appropriate model. For example, if the data show a linear trend, a linear growth model may be appropriate. If the data show a non-linear trend, a non-linear growth model such as an exponential growth curve model may be more suitable.

Once the model is fitted, one can get the predicted trajectories from the model. The predicted trajectories are the expected values of the dependent variable at each time point, given the estimated parameters of the model. These predicted values can be plotted against the observed data to visually assess how well the model fits the data. Residual plots can be used to check for patterns in the residuals, which can indicate potential issues with the model fit [16].

In addition to visual inspection, several statistical methods can be used to evaluate the fit of a growth curve model. For models estimated via maximum likelihood, the log-likelihood statistic can be used to evaluate the model fit. It measures how well the model fits the data, with higher values indicating a better fit. Particularly, we can compare two nested growth curve models using the likelihood ratio test. The likelihood ratio test compares the fit of two models, one of which is a special case of the other (i.e. a nested model). The test statistic is calculated as twice the difference in log-likelihoods between the two models. A significant result indicates that the more complex model provides a significantly better fit to the data than the simpler model. Information criteria such as AIC and BIC can also be used to compare the fit of different models. AIC and BIC are based on the likelihood of the model, but they also include a penalty for the number of parameters in the model. Lower values of AIC and BIC indicate a better fit, with a preference for simpler models.

In growth curve models, it is often important to assess the significance of the random effect variance components. This can be done using likelihood ratio tests or Wald tests. A significant random effect variance component indicates that there is substantial variability in the growth trajectories across individuals, which may suggest that a random effects model is appropriate.

When a growth curve model is estimated in the *Structural Equation Modelling* (SEM) framework, the model fit can be evaluated using the SEM fit indices. Commonly used fit indices include the χ^2 statistic, *Comparative Fit Index* (CFI), *Tucker-Lewis Index* (TLI), *Root Mean Square Error of Approximation* (RMSEA), and *Standardised Root Mean Square Residual* (SRMR). A non-significant χ^2 statistic indicates a good fit, while CFI and TLI values above 0.90 or 0.95 indicate a good fit. RMSEA values below 0.05 or 0.08 indicate a good fit, while SRMR values below 0.08 indicate a good fit.

4 Advanced Modelling Techniques: GEEs, MER, GAMs, and Adaptive Regression Splines

In contemporary data analysis, researchers often work with complex, multidimensional datasets that require sophisticated modelling techniques. While traditional linear regression models have long been a cornerstone of statistical analysis, they are not always sufficient for capturing intricate data structures or relationships. This chapter explores four advanced modelling techniques that have gained prominence in fields such as psychology, medicine, economics, and the social sciences: *Generalised Estimating Equations* (GEEs), *Mixed-Effects Regression* (MER), *Generalised Additive Models* (GAMs), and *Adaptive Regression Splines* (ARS). These methods are designed to address various data complexities, including correlated observations, non-linear relationships, and flexible model structures, making them essential tools for contemporary data science in psychology and related disciplines.

These techniques are designed to address various data complexities, including correlated data, non-linear relationships, and flexible model structures, making them essential tools in modern data science for psychology and related disciplines.

GEEs introduced by Liang and Zeger extend *Generalised Linear Models* (GLMs) to accommodate correlated data, commonly encountered in longitudinal and clustered studies [17]. Unlike traditional GLMs that assume independent observations, GEEs account for the correlations between repeated measures within the same subject, making them particularly suitable for analysing data collected over time or within groups.

The GEE approach estimates regression coefficients by incorporating a working correlation structure to model dependence between observations. Common structures include exchangeable, autoregressive, and unstructured correlations. A key advantage of GEEs is their ability to provide robust standard error estimates, even when the true correlation structure is unknown or misspecified [18]. This flexibility makes GEEs particularly useful for analysing data with complex correlation patterns.

For instance, in longitudinal studies where repeated measures are collected from the same individuals over time, GEEs can assess how predictors influence outcomes while accounting for within-subject correlation. In psychological research, an example might be evaluating how treatment effects on depression scores change over time, recognising that repeated measurements from the same individual are not independent.

Mixed-Effects Regression (MER) models are a powerful tool for analysing data with hierarchical or nested structures. These models incorporate both fixed effects, which capture population-level relationships, and random effects, which account for individual-specific variations. MER is particularly useful for analysing grouped data (e.g. patients within hospitals and students within schools) or repeated measurements over time within the same subjects.

In MER, fixed effects represent the average relationship between predictors and outcomes across all groups or individuals, while random effects account for individual deviations from this average. For example, in educational psychology, a study might examine how teaching methods influence student performance, incorporating random intercepts to account for variations between schools or classrooms. MER models can be estimated using techniques such as *Maximum Likelihood Estimation* (MLE) or *Restricted Maximum Likelihood* (REML). A key advantage of MER is its flexibility in handling complex data structures, including unbalanced data (where groups have different numbers of observations) and varying group sizes [19].

Generalised Additive Models (GAMs) extend generalised linear models by accommodating non-linear relationships between predictors and outcomes. Unlike traditional regression models, which assume linearity, GAMs use smooth functions to model these relationships, providing greater flexibility [20].

In GAMs, the effect of each predictor is modelled as a smooth function, estimated nonparametrically. This approach is particularly useful when relationships between variables are expected to be non-linear, as is often the case in psychological or biological processes where linear assumptions may not hold. For example, in a study investigating the effect of age on cognitive performance, a non-linear model may better capture the trend, reflecting potential increases in childhood and declines in later adulthood. GAMs can be fitted using penalised likelihood methods, which help prevent overfitting by imposing a penalty on overly complex smooth functions. This flexibility allows GAMs to capture intricate patterns in the data while maintaining interpretability [21].

Adaptive Regression Splines (ARSs) are a nonparametric regression method that combines the flexibility of spline functions with the ability to adapt to the data. Splines are piecewise polynomial functions that enable smooth yet flexible modelling of non-linear relationships between variables. ARS specifically adapts the spline to the data by allowing for different polynomial degrees in different regions of the predictor space.

ARS can be particularly useful when the relationship between predictors and outcomes is complex and unknown. In psychological research, for instance, ARS can be applied to model non-linear effects, such as the relationship between stress and cognitive performance. In this case, the effect of stress may change depending on its level. Low stress could improve performance, while high stress might impair it. The key advantage of ARS is its ability to automatically select the optimal number of knots (i.e. the points where the spline pieces meet), making the method both flexible and data-driven. This approach reduces the risk of overfitting and allows for a more accurate representation of the underlying relationships in the data [22].

5 Analytical Approaches: Case Series Data and Markov Chain Analysis

Data analysis in applied fields such as healthcare, psychology, economics, and epidemiology often involves complex and structured datasets. Case series data and Markov chain analysis are two key analytical techniques used to model processes that evolve over time or within distinct stages. Framing these temporal problems within an 'artificial psychology' program highlights how ML augments dynamic psychological theory [23]. This chapter explores these two approaches in detail, examining their applications, methodologies, and how they complement each other in statistical analysis.

Case series data are widely used in clinical research and epidemiological studies to investigate the progression of diseases, the impact of specific treatments, or to describe patterns of health outcomes within a population. A case series typically consists of a group of patients or subjects who share a particular condition or intervention and are followed over time. In such data, the focus is on individual observations and the outcomes for each subject. Unlike randomised controlled trials (RCTs), case series lack a control group, and the analysis primarily revolves around summarising the characteristics of the subjects and their outcomes over time.

A case series often involves a longitudinal or retrospective design, in which a group of patients is monitored over time, with various data points collected at different intervals. These data may include clinical measurements, lab results, demographic information, and other variables that help to understand the progression of a disease or the effectiveness of a treatment. Because case series data are observational rather than experimental, they are more susceptible to bias and confounding factors.

One of the most common statistical methods used in case series data analysis is descriptive analysis of the outcomes. This involves calculating the mean, median, or proportion of individuals who experienced a particular outcome. In some cases, researchers may also use survival analysis techniques, such as Kaplan-Meier estimation, to assess the time to an event (e.g. time to recovery, relapse, or death). Cox proportional hazards models are often employed to investigate the effects of different covariates on survival or event rates within a case series [24].

While descriptive techniques can be valuable, more sophisticated methods may be necessary to account for time-dependent changes or the potential correlation of observations within subjects. GEEs are commonly used to model the correlation structure in repeated measures data [17]. These models allow for the adjustment of correlations among repeated measurements, providing robust standard error estimates even when the correlation structure is misspecified.

Case series data are commonly used in medicine to examine rare diseases, assess the effectiveness of treatments, or describe disease progression patterns within specific populations. For example, a case series might investigate the outcomes of a novel drug in treating patients with a rare type of cancer. Despite their limitations, such as the lack of randomisation, case series provide valuable insights into the real-world treatment effectiveness and can help generate hypotheses for further studies.

Markov chain analysis is a powerful statistical tool used to model systems that transition between different states over time. The primary characteristic of a Markov process is that the future state depends only on the current state and not on the history of past states, a property known as the Markov property. This makes Markov models particularly useful in fields like healthcare, economics, and psychology, where the process of interest involves transitions between distinct states over time (e.g. healthy vs. sick or employed vs. unemployed).

A Markov chain consists of a set of states, with transitions between these states determined by transition probabilities. These transition probabilities are usually represented in a matrix, where each element indicates the probability of transitioning from one state to another. Markov chains are typically classified as either discrete time or continuous time, depending on the nature of the transitions.

In a discrete-time Markov chain, transitions occur at fixed intervals, such as days, months, or years. In continuous-time Markov chains, transitions can happen at any point in time, with transition rates modelled by exponential distributions. Markov chains can also be classified as homogeneous or non-homogeneous. In a homogeneous Markov chain, the transition probabilities remain constant over time, whereas in a non-homogeneous Markov chain, these probabilities may change over time.

One extension of Markov chains that is particularly useful for modelling systems with unobservable states is the *Hidden Markov Model* (HMM). In HMMs, the system transitions between hidden states, with only some observable outputs being seen. For instance, in medical applications, a hidden Markov model might be used to model the progression of a disease in stages, where the true health status (the hidden state) is unobserved, but observable data such as symptoms or lab results are available.

The parameters of an HMM, including transition probabilities and emission probabilities (i.e. the probability of observing a particular outcome given a hidden state), can be estimated using algorithms such as the Expectation-Maximisation (EM) algorithm or the Baum-Welch algorithm [25]. HMMs are particularly useful in fields such as speech recognition, finance, and biological processes, where the underlying system evolves but is not directly observable.

Markov chain analysis is widely used in medical decision-making and health economics to model disease progression, treatment strategies, and the cost-effectiveness of interventions. For example, Markov models are commonly employed to evaluate the long-term outcomes of patients with chronic conditions such as diabetes or cardiovascular disease, where patients transition between various health states (e.g. healthy, diagnosed, hospitalised, or deceased) over time.

In psychological research, Markov models are applied to analyse the dynamics of psychological states or behaviours. For instance, they can be used to model transitions between different states of mood or emotional well-being over time in response to therapy or treatment. Markov analysis provides a valuable framework for understanding and predicting long-term outcomes based on initial conditions and transition probabilities [26].

In some research contexts, combining case series data analysis with Markov chain analysis can offer powerful insights, particularly when the data involve transitions between different health states or behavioural outcomes. For example, a study might track the health progression of a cohort of patients with a chronic illness over time, where the patients' health states are modelled using a Markov process. By combining this with case series analysis, which tracks individual outcomes over time, researchers can gain a comprehensive understanding of both treatment effects and disease progression within the population.

The case series component helps identify specific patterns or outliers in the data, while Markov chain models can account for the inherent uncertainty and variability in patient transitions across health states. Integrating both approaches allows researchers to enhance the precision and applicability of their findings.

6 Markov Models: Basic Types, Hidden Models, and Decision Processes

Markov models are a class of stochastic models that describe systems undergoing transitions between states based on probabilistic rules. These models rely on the Markov property, which states that the future state of a system depends only on its present state, not on past states. They are widely used in various disciplines, including physics, finance, bioinformatics, and artificial intelligence. In psychological research, Markov models have also been employed to analyse emotion data [27, 28].

Markov data can be classified into two main categories: *Discrete-Time Markov Chains* (DTMCs) and *Continuous-Time Markov Chains* (CTMCs). DTMCs are characterised by discrete time steps, while CTMCs allow for continuous time transitions. Both types of Markov models can be further categorised into homogeneous and non-homogeneous models, depending on whether the transition probabilities change over time.

Markov models can be classified based on whether the states of a system are known. When the states of the system are directly observable over time, one can use the *Observed Markov Model* (OMM). In contrast, when the states are not directly observed but are instead inferred from the data, necessitating the use of a *Hidden Markov Model* (HMM). These two approaches differ in their methodological assumptions and analytical frameworks, making it essential to select the appropriate model based on the nature of the data and research objectives.

When a person's state at each time point is known, an OMM can be used to examine the temporal dynamics of the state-switching process. These states may represent categories of a discrete observed variable or may be derived by discretising continuous (or multivariate) data. The OMM is also commonly referred to as a manifest Markov model, simple Markov model, or Markov chain [28].

In OMM, we analyse the observed state transitions over time and estimate the transition probabilities between different states. These transition probabilities are represented in a **transition matrix**, which captures the likelihood of moving from one state to another between consecutive time points. Specifically, the transition matrix, typically denoted as P, consists of elements P_{ij}, where each P_{ij} represents the probability of transitioning from state i to state j. Since each row of the transition matrix represents the possible transitions from a given state, the sum of all elements in a row equals 1, ensuring that the total probability distribution is maintained.

Estimating an OMM involves determining transition probabilities from observed categorical sequences. The most common approach is *Maximum Likelihood Estima-*

tion (MLE), where transition probabilities are computed as the relative frequencies of observed state changes. Bayesian estimation incorporates prior distributions, often using Dirichlet priors, while *Markov Chain Monte Carlo* (MCMC) methods handle sparse or missing data by sampling from posterior distributions. When transitions are partially unobserved, the *Expectation-Maximisation* (EM) algorithm iteratively estimates missing data and updates probabilities until convergence. If external covariates influence transitions, GLMs such as logistic or multinomial regression can be applied. Smoothing techniques like Laplace smoothing prevent zero probabilities in low-frequency transitions. The choice of method depends on data structure, sample size, and whether missing or latent states are present.

In HMM, a system is assumed to follow a Markov process with hidden (unobservable) states. In HMMs, the system's state at any given time is not directly visible, but it influences observable outputs. The model is defined by two key components: a set of states and the probabilities of transitioning between these states, as well as the likelihood of observing a particular output from each state. HMMs are widely used in areas such as speech recognition, natural language processing, and bioinformatics, where the underlying process is hidden, but observable data are available to infer the system's behaviour.

Estimating HMMs typically involves determining the state transition probabilities, observation likelihoods, and initial state probabilities, based on observed data. The most common approach is the EM algorithm, particularly the Baum-Welch algorithm, which iteratively refines the estimates of these parameters. In the E-step, the algorithm calculates the expected state sequences given the current parameter estimates, and in the M-step, it updates the parameters to maximise the likelihood of the observed data. Another widely used method is Viterbi's algorithm, which is employed for finding the most likely sequence of hidden states given the observations.

A *Markov Decision Process* (MDP) is a mathematical framework used to model decision-making in situations where the outcomes are partly random and partly under the control of a decision-maker. It consists of four key elements:

- **States:** a set of all possible situations the system can be in
- **Actions:** a set of possible actions the decision-maker can take in each state
- **Transition Probabilities:** the probability of moving from one state to another after taking a particular action
- **Rewards:** the immediate gain or cost associated with taking an action in a particular state

MDPs assume that the future state of the system depends only on the current state and action, not on the history of past states or actions (this is the Markov property). The goal in an MDP is to find a policy (a strategy that specifies which action to take in each state) that maximises the long-term expected reward, often using methods like Value Iteration or Policy Iteration. MDPs are widely used in reinforcement learning, robotics, economics, and artificial intelligence to model and solve problems involving sequential decision-making.

7 Applications and Case Studies

In this case study, an LGCM was used to examine how stress, self-esteem, and sleep patterns changed over time among 223 university students who were assessed at three time points over the course of an academic year.

```
# Importing necessary libraries
import numpy as np
import pandas as pd
import matplotlib.pyplot as plt
from sklearn.linear_model import LinearRegression
from sklearn.preprocessing import StandardScaler

# Setting the random seed for reproducibility
np.random.seed(42)

# Simulating data for 223 university students assessed at three
↪ time points
n_students = 223
time_points = np.array([1, 2, 3]) # Time points (e.g., start,
↪ middle, end of the academic year)

# Simulate baseline data (time point 1)
baseline_data = {
    'Stress_T1': np.random.normal(loc=5.5, scale=1.5,
    ↪ size=n_students),
    'SelfEsteem_T1': np.random.normal(loc=3.0, scale=0.8,
    ↪ size=n_students),
    'Sleep_T1': np.random.normal(loc=7.0, scale=1.2,
    ↪ size=n_students),
}

# Simulating growth trajectories over time for stress,
↪ self-esteem, and sleep
# Adding random change over time for each variable (simulating
↪ the growth over 3 time points)
data = pd.DataFrame(baseline_data)

# Simulate changes over time for each student (growth)
data['Stress_T2'] = data['Stress_T1'] +
↪ np.random.normal(loc=0.2, scale=0.5, size=n_students) #
↪ Time point 2
data['SelfEsteem_T2'] = data['SelfEsteem_T1'] +
↪ np.random.normal(loc=-0.1, scale=0.3, size=n_students) #
↪ Time point 2
```

```
data['Sleep_T2'] = data['Sleep_T1'] +
↪  np.random.normal(loc=-0.2, scale=0.4, size=n_students)  #
↪  Time point 2

data['Stress_T3'] = data['Stress_T1'] +
↪  np.random.normal(loc=0.3, scale=0.6, size=n_students)  #
↪  Time point 3
data['SelfEsteem_T3'] = data['SelfEsteem_T1'] +
↪  np.random.normal(loc=-0.2, scale=0.4, size=n_students)  #
↪  Time point 3
data['Sleep_T3'] = data['Sleep_T1'] +
↪  np.random.normal(loc=-0.3, scale=0.5, size=n_students)  #
↪  Time point 3

# Creating a DataFrame for time-based measurements
time_data = data[['Stress_T1', 'Stress_T2', 'Stress_T3',
                  'SelfEsteem_T1', 'SelfEsteem_T2',
                  ↪  'SelfEsteem_T3',
                  'Sleep_T1', 'Sleep_T2', 'Sleep_T3']]

# Reshaping the time points to match the data (each student
↪  should have a row for each time point)
time_data_reshaped = time_data.values.reshape(n_students * 3,
↪  -1)
time_points_expanded = np.tile(time_points, n_students)  #
↪  Expanding time points for each student

# Now, we need to create the X matrix for regression with time
↪  and time^2
# Expanding time_points to have a row for each student at each
↪  time point
X = np.column_stack([np.ones(n_students * 3),
↪  time_points_expanded, time_points_expanded**2])  # Adding
↪  time and time^2 as features for growth

# Standardizing the data
scaler = StandardScaler()
scaled_data = scaler.fit_transform(time_data_reshaped)

# Linear regression for Stress
reg_stress = LinearRegression().fit(X, scaled_data[:, 0])
reg_selfesteem = LinearRegression().fit(X, scaled_data[:, 1])
reg_sleep = LinearRegression().fit(X, scaled_data[:, 2])

# Extracting the coefficients (intercept, linear, quadratic)
↪  for each variable
```

```
stress_params = reg_stress.coef_
selfesteem_params = reg_selfesteem.coef_
sleep_params = reg_sleep.coef_

# Print the results of the regression models
print("Regression Results for Stress:")
print(f"Intercept: {reg_stress.intercept_:.3f}, Linear
↪ Coefficient: {stress_params[1]:.3f}, Quadratic Coefficient:
↪ {stress_params[2]:.3f}")
print("\nRegression Results for Self-Esteem:")
print(f"Intercept: {reg_selfesteem.intercept_:.3f}, Linear
↪ Coefficient: {selfesteem_params[1]:.3f}, Quadratic
↪ Coefficient: {selfesteem_params[2]:.3f}")
print("\nRegression Results for Sleep:")
print(f"Intercept: {reg_sleep.intercept_:.3f}, Linear
↪ Coefficient: {sleep_params[1]:.3f}, Quadratic Coefficient:
↪ {sleep_params[2]:.3f}")

# Visualise the fitted growth curve for each variable
time_points_fine = np.linspace(1, 3, 100)  # More time points
↪ for smooth curve

def plot_growth_curve(params, label):
    y_vals = params[0] + params[1] * time_points_fine +
    ↪ params[2] * time_points_fine**2
    plt.plot(time_points_fine, y_vals, label=label)

plt.figure(figsize=(12, 6))
plot_growth_curve(stress_params, 'Stress Growth Curve')
plot_growth_curve(selfesteem_params, 'Self-Esteem Growth
↪ Curve')
plot_growth_curve(sleep_params, 'Sleep Growth Curve')

plt.title('Latent Growth Curves for Stress, Self-Esteem, and
↪ Sleep')
plt.xlabel('Time Points')
plt.ylabel('Standardized Values')
plt.legend()
plt.grid(True)
plt.tight_layout()
plt.show()
```

Results:

```
Regression Results for Stress:
Intercept: 4.617, Linear Coefficient: -6.036,
Quadratic Coefficient: 1.597

Regression Results for Self-Esteem:
Intercept: 4.919, Linear Coefficient: -6.246,
Quadratic Coefficient: 1.623

Regression Results for Sleep:
Intercept: 5.094, Linear Coefficient: -6.364,
Quadratic Coefficient: 1.636
```

The LGCM reveals baseline levels (intercept) and trajectories (linear and quadratic coefficients) for stress ($Intercept = 4.617$, $Linear = -6.036$, $Quadratic = 1.597$), self-esteem ($Intercept = 4.919$, $Linear = -6.246$, $Quadratic = 1.623$), and sleep ($Intercept = 5.094$, $Linear = -6.364$, $Quadratic = 1.636$). Assuming 0–10 scales (e.g. Perceived Stress Scale, Rosenberg Self-Esteem Scale, and Pittsburgh Sleep Quality Index), these results map a dynamic interplay of mental health factors. As it is shown in Fig. 3, all three variables follow U-shaped trajectories: moderate starting levels, sharp early declines, mid-year improvement, and a late-year stress resurgence. The similar coefficients ($linear \sim -6.0$ to -6.3, $quadratic \sim 1.6$) suggest shared influences tied to the academic year's rhythm, such as early adjustment struggles, periods of adaptation, and later pressures like exams. Clinically, early declines in sleep likely amplify stress and erode self-esteem, as poor sleep disrupts emotional regulation, creating a feedback loop. The late-year stress spike threatens recovery in self-esteem

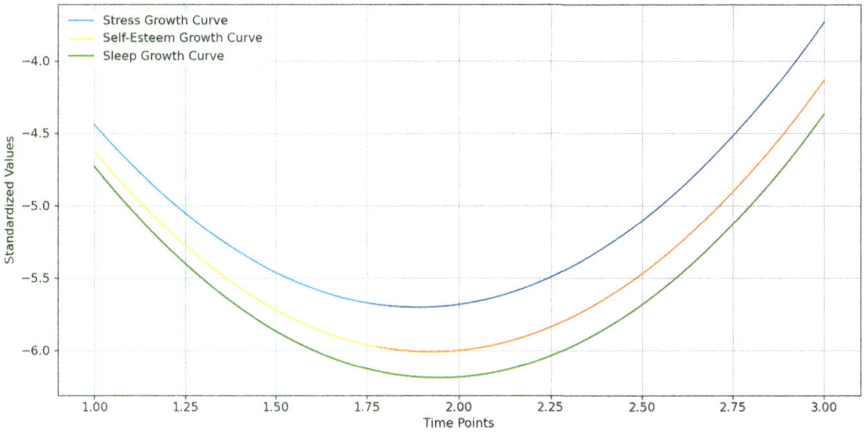

Fig. 3 Latent growth curves for stress, self-esteem, and sleep

and sleep, highlighting two critical intervention points: early to prevent declines and late to manage stress. These findings underscore the need for integrated mental health support tailored to students' evolving needs.

The U-shaped trajectories reveal actionable insights for university settings. Early declines in self-esteem and sleep, coupled with moderate stress, signal vulnerability to anxiety or depression, necessitating proactive interventions like cognitive-behavioural therapy, mindfulness, or sleep hygiene workshops at the academic year's start. These could bolster resilience, preventing the feedback loop where poor sleep fuels stress and low self-esteem. The late-year stress increase, likely driven by academic demands, calls for targeted stress management programs (e.g. exam prep workshops) to protect gains in self-esteem and sleep. Limitations include assumed scale ranges, which require validation, and the inability of LGCM to confirm causality. Structural equation modelling could help clarify the interactions between variables. Results may be university-specific, and including factors like social support could deepen understanding. Holistic interventions addressing stress, self-esteem, and sleep together can break negative cycles, fostering student well-being across the academic year.

8 Visualising Time-Dependent Models

The visualisation of time-dependent models plays a crucial role in analysing complex systems that evolve over time. With the right graphical representations, it becomes possible to understand the evolution of the variables that constitute the model. Furthermore, trends and patterns can be identified, and potential causal relationships among variables can be explored. This approach enables researchers, analysts, and engineers to more precisely interpret the results of modelling, optimise parameters, and enhance decision-making processes. Given that time-dependent models often involve data that changes over time (e.g. economic indicators, biological processes, and engineering systems), the visualisation must be tailored to the specific characteristics of each system.

One of the most fundamental and commonly used approaches to visualise time-dependent models is to represent variables as a function of time. This type of graph is typically used to track the evolution of one or more variables over time. The x-axis represents the time interval, while the y-axis represents the values of the variables being tracked. These graphs facilitate the analysis of trends, seasonal fluctuations, and the identification of anomalies or periods of stability [29].

For more complex systems, multiple data series can be plotted on the same graph. For example, in economic analysis, a graph may illustrate changes in gross domestic product, inflation, and unemployment over several years, allowing for comparisons and the identification of interdependencies among these variables. Time-series visualisation is essential in fields such as financial analysis, weather and air forecasting [30], and health monitoring, where recognising temporal trends and patterns is of key importance.

In economic models, tracking the inflation rate alongside Gross Domestic Product and unemployment rates can help reveal interactions between these variables and how external factors, such as policy changes or crises, might influence economic behaviour over time [31]. These visualisations facilitate the identification of major economic events, such as recessions, and analyse their impact across different sectors.

To provide an illustrative example of time-dependent psychological data, a psychologist conducted a 10-day daily diary study in which participants rated their anxiety levels each day on a scale from 1 to 10. The purpose was to track within-person fluctuations in anxiety over time and to visualise these dynamics in a clear and interpretable manner. Figure 4 presents the results of these longitudinal data using a line plot generated in Python, highlighting individual variability and day-to-day changes. Such visualisations support the identification of temporal patterns and are valuable for both descriptive and inferential psychological analysis.

```
import matplotlib.pyplot as plt
import pandas as pd

# Simulated psychological time series data
data = {
    'Date': pd.date_range(start='2025-03-18', periods=10,
    ↪ freq='D'),
    'Anxiety_Level': [6, 7, 5, 4, 6, 8, 7, 5, 6, 4]  #
    ↪ Self-reported anxiety (scale 1^^e2^^80^^9310)
}

# Create a DataFrame
df = pd.DataFrame(data)

# Plot the time series
plt.figure(figsize=(10, 5))
plt.plot(df['Date'], df['Anxiety_Level'], marker='o',
↪ linestyle='-', color='crimson')

# Customise the plot
plt.title('Daily Anxiety Levels Over 10 Days')
plt.xlabel('Date')
plt.ylabel('Anxiety Level (1^^e2^^80^^9310)')
plt.ylim(0, 10)
plt.grid(True)
plt.xticks(rotation=45)

# Show the plot
plt.tight_layout()
plt.show()
```

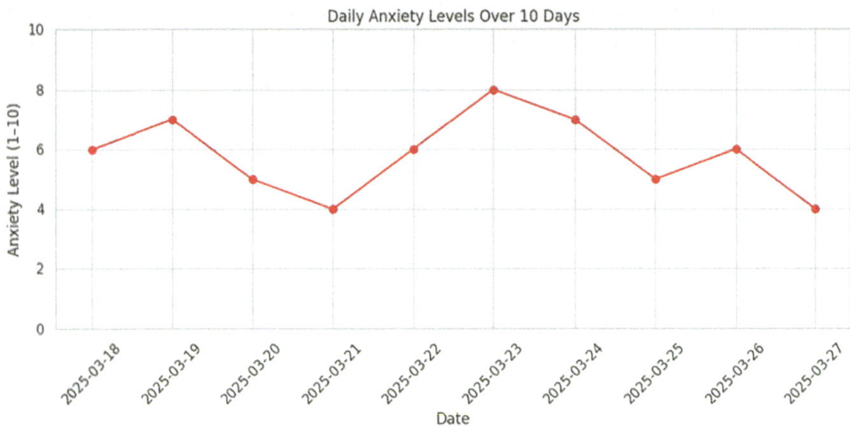

Fig. 4 Anxiety during days

When tracking the evolution of multiple interconnected variables, a static graph may not suffice. In such cases, animation becomes an extremely useful tool, as it offers a dynamic perspective on system evolution over time. Animations can depict real-time changes, enabling users to better understand causal relationships and the effects of changes in different parts of the model [32].

Animations are typically employed in more complex simulations, such as predictive models for weather forecasting, economic models simulating different scenarios, or biological models illustrating the spread of diseases in populations. This method allows analysts to not only observe results but also trace the path leading to those results, helping identify critical points in system dynamics.

To provide an illustrative example, consider an epidemiological disease spread model. By animating the spread of the disease across regions over time, health researchers can gain insights into the rate of transmission, the effectiveness of interventions, such as vaccination, and the possible long-term outcomes across various scenarios [31]. This dynamic visualisation provides more insight into the process than a static model or summary statistics.

When analysing large datasets or visualising the relationships between multiple variables simultaneously, a heatmap becomes an effective tool for visualisation. This representation uses colours to denote the intensity of specific values, enabling quick identification of patterns and correlations between variables. For example, in climate change models, a heatmap could display temperature changes across different regions over time [29].

Heatmaps are commonly used in fields such as statistics, economics, engineering, and biomedical research, where it is necessary to analyse correlations among numerous variables. By using colours to indicate changes, heatmaps make it easier to identify trends, anomalies, and interrelations in large datasets [32].

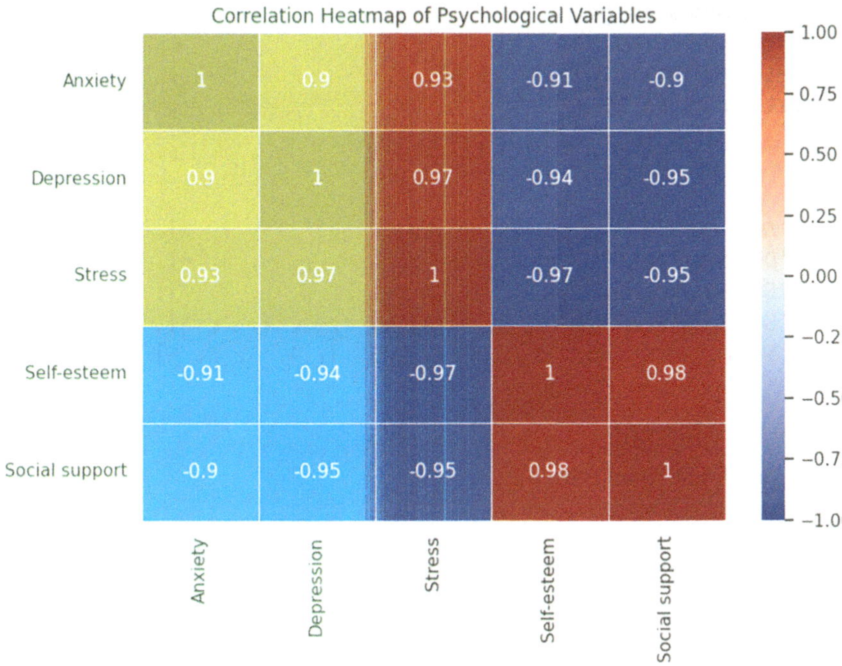

Fig. 5 Heatmap example

To illustrate the value of visualising interrelationships between psychological constructs, consider a practical example where a psychologist collects data on several key variables from a group of participants. These include self-reported measures of anxiety, depression, stress, self-esteem, and social support. Understanding how these variables relate to one another is crucial in psychological research and intervention planning, as they often interact in complex ways. A heatmap provides a colour-coded representation of the pairwise correlation coefficients between variables, allowing researchers to quickly identify patterns of strong positive or negative associations. For example, we may observe that higher anxiety levels correlate positively with stress and depression while showing a negative association with self-esteem or social support.

Figure 5 displays a simulated example of such a heatmap. The values in each cell represent the Pearson correlation coefficients between pairs of psychological variables. This type of visualisation is especially useful when dealing with multivariate data, where textual tables may obscure interpretability.

The following Python implementation demonstrates how to generate the heatmap using the `seaborn` and `pandas` libraries:

```
import pandas as pd
import seaborn as sns
import matplotlib.pyplot as plt
import numpy as np

# Simulated dataset (each row is a participant)
data = {
    'Anxiety':       [6, 7, 8, 5, 4, 9, 7, 6, 8, 5],
    'Depression':    [7, 8, 9, 6, 5, 8, 7, 6, 9, 6],
    'Stress':        [8, 9, 9, 7, 6, 9, 8, 7, 9, 7],
    'Self-esteem':   [3, 2, 2, 4, 5, 2, 3, 4, 2, 5],
    'Social support':[4, 3, 2, 5, 6, 3, 4, 5, 3, 6]
}

# Create a DataFrame
df = pd.DataFrame(data)

# Compute correlation matrix
corr_matrix = df.corr()

# Plot the heatmap
plt.figure(figsize=(8, 6))
sns.heatmap(corr_matrix, annot=True, cmap='coolwarm', vmin=-1,
 ↪  vmax=1, linewidths=0.5)

# Title and display
plt.title('Correlation Heatmap of Psychological Variables')
plt.tight_layout()
plt.show()
```

In addition to static representations, interactive visualisations allow users to explore data across different time periods, filters, or dimensions. These visualisations can include interactive graphs, 3D models, or virtual simulations that enable users to manipulate system parameters and visualise their effects in real time. This approach is particularly useful for tailoring analyses to the user's specific interests, allowing them to explore different scenarios and draw more personalised conclusions.

Interactive visualisations are often used in applications such as dashboard systems, where users can track dynamic data (e.g. production status, website traffic, or energy consumption) and make quick decisions based on up-to-date information [29]. These tools empower decision-makers to dive deeper into the data and observe how different variables interact with each other.

To illustrate the use of interactive visualisation in psychological research, consider a scenario inspired by an energy management system dashboard. Such systems enable users to dynamically monitor real-time energy consumption across buildings or departments, allowing them to adjust visual filters, such as time intervals or environmental factors like weather, to better interpret usage patterns and identify opportunities for optimisation [32].

The same principle of interactivity can be extended to cognitive psychology, particularly in the demonstration of well-known biases such as the *Halo Effect*. The Halo Effect refers to a phenomenon in which a person's overall impression, such as their attractiveness or facial expression, biases evaluations of unrelated traits. For example, people may rate a smiling individual as being more intelligent, kind, or trustworthy compared to someone with a neutral expression.

The following interactive Python implementation provides a hands-on demonstration of the Halo Effect. Users can toggle between smiling and neutral facial expressions to observe how trait ratings differ:

```
import matplotlib.pyplot as plt
import numpy as np
import ipywidgets as widgets
from ipywidgets import interactive

# Function to display ratings based on smiling or neutral
↪ expression

def show_ratings(smiling=True):
    if smiling:
        intelligence = 8
        kindness = 9
        trustworthiness = 9
    else:
        intelligence = 6
        kindness = 7
        trustworthiness = 7

    labels = ['Intelligence', 'Kindness', 'Trustworthiness']
    values = [intelligence, kindness, trustworthiness]

    fig, ax = plt.subplots()
    ax.bar(labels, values, color=['blue', 'green', 'orange'])
    ax.set_ylabel('Rating')
    ax.set_title('Halo Effect: Rating Based on Smile vs.
    ↪ Neutral Expression')
    plt.show()

# Interactive toggle widget
interactive_plot = interactive(show_ratings, smiling=[True,
↪ False])
display(interactive_plot)
```

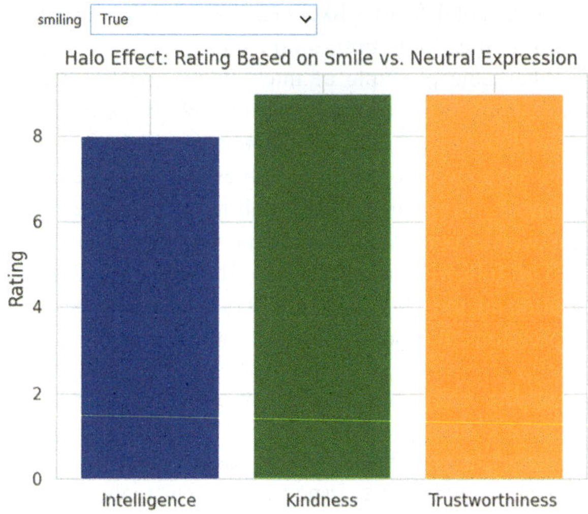

Fig. 6 Simple interactive visualisation

This example makes it possible for users to actively explore how perceptions shift under different emotional cues. When the smiling condition is selected, the interactive bar chart reveals elevated ratings for all three traits, visually demonstrating the bias (Fig. 6). Such visual and interactive tools can enrich teaching, communication, and research interpretation by offering intuitive access to complex psychological phenomena.

Multidimensional scaling (MDS) is a statistical technique that enables researchers to represent complex data in a multidimensional space. MDS is particularly useful when relationships between variables are not directly comparable or when the aim is to observe how variables group together or relate to each other in a multidimensional context [31].

Principal Component Analysis (PCA) is a dimensionality reduction technique commonly used in psychological research to reduce the number of variables for analysis while retaining most of the data's information. PCA helps researchers identify the key factors that explain variance in the data and present them in fewer dimensions [33].

3D visualisations are becoming increasingly popular for analysing complex psychological models involving multiple variables. These visualisations allow researchers to observe how psychological factors change across three dimensions, which helps identify intricate relationships between variables [31].

Visualising time-dependent models is crucial for understanding the evolution of complex systems, whether economic, biological, or environmental. By employing techniques such as time-series graphs, animations, heatmaps, and interactive visualisations, researchers and analysts can gain deeper insights into the dynamicsof the systems they study. These tools not only make data more accessible and interpretable but also enhance decision-making, whether in business, healthcare, or policy. As technology continues to advance, the integration of sophisticated visualisations like 3D modelling and multidimensional scaling will further enhance our ability to analyse and predict trends in time-dependent systems [29, 31].

To illustrate multidimensional representations in psychology, one of the most widely recognised models is the Big Five Personality Traits, also known by the acronym OCEAN (*Openness, Conscientiousness, Extraversion, Agreeableness, and Neuroticism*). These five dimensions provide a comprehensive framework for describing personality structure and have been validated across numerous cultures and contexts.

Each trait represents a continuum, and individuals may score high or low on any of them. Since the Big Five model is inherently multidimensional, visualising the interplay of traits within a single individual requires an approach that maintains all five dimensions simultaneously. One effective method is the *radar chart* (also referred to as a spider plot), where each axis represents one trait and the values are plotted to form a polygon that visually encodes the individual's personality profile.

The following Python implementation demonstrates how to generate a radar chart using example trait scores. The interactive visual reveals how this format facilitates intuitive comparisons between traits and across individuals.

```
import numpy as np
import matplotlib.pyplot as plt
from math import pi

# Function to plot the radar chart
def plot_radar_chart(labels, values, title):
    num_vars = len(labels)
    angles = np.linspace(0, 2 * np.pi, num_vars,
     ↪ endpoint=False).tolist()

    # Repeat the first value and angle to close the circular
     ↪ plot
    values += values[:1]
    angles += angles[:1]

    # Create radar chart
    fig, ax = plt.subplots(figsize=(6, 6),
     ↪ subplot_kw=dict(polar=True))
    ax.fill(angles, values, color='blue', alpha=0.25)
    ax.plot(angles, values, color='blue', linewidth=2)

    ax.set_yticklabels([])  # Hide y-axis radial labels
    ax.set_xticks(angles[:-1])
    ax.set_xticklabels(labels, fontsize=12, fontweight='bold')
    ax.set_title(title, size=16, fontweight='bold')
    plt.show()
```

```
# Big Five Personality Traits
labels = ['Openness', 'Conscientiousness', 'Extraversion',
↪ 'Agreeableness', 'Neuroticism']
values = [7, 6, 8, 9, 5]  # Example scores from 1 to 10

plot_radar_chart(labels, values, "Big Five Personality Traits")
```

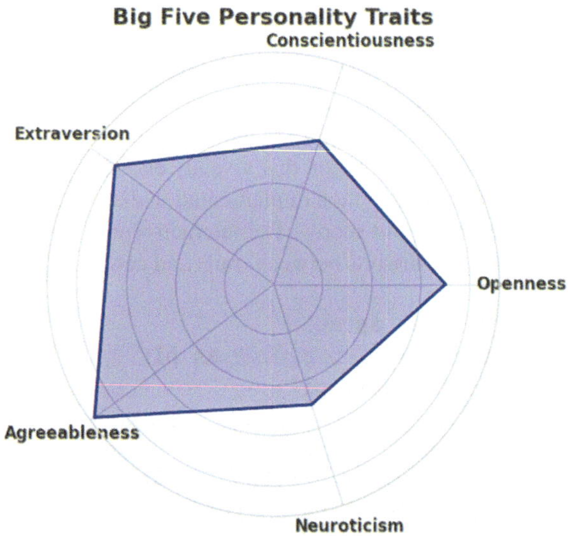

Fig. 7 Multidimensional representations using a radar chart

Figure 7 provides a graphical representation of this example. The polygon formed by the plotted values gives an immediate overview of personality strengths and traits requiring further attention. This visualisation technique can also be extended to compare groups or track changes over time in longitudinal studies.

References

1. K.A. Bollen, P.J. Curran, *Latent Curve Models: A Structural Equation perspective* (Wiley, New York, 2006)
2. T.E. Duncan, S.C. Duncan, L.A. Strycker, *An Introduction to Latent Variable Growth Curve Modeling: Concepts, Issues, and Application* (Routledge, Milton Park, 2013)
3. P.J. Curran, K. Obeidat, D. Losardo, Twelve frequently asked questions about growth curve modeling. J. Cogn. Dev. **11**(2), 121 (2010)
4. J.J. McArdle, Latent variable modeling of differences and changes with longitudinal data. Annu. Rev. Psychol. **60**(1), 577 (2009)
5. K.J. Grimm, N. Ram, R. Estabrook, *Growth Modeling: Structural Equation and Multilevel Modeling Approaches* (Guilford Publications, New York, 2016)

6. J.P. Selig, T.D. Little, in *Handbook of Developmental Research Methods*, ed. by B. Laursen, T.D. Little, N.A. Card (The Guilford Press, New York, 2012), pp. 265–278
7. C.K. Enders, *Applied Missing Data Analysis* (Guilford Publications, New York, 2022)
8. G.R. Hancock, R.O. Mueller, L.M. Stapleton, *The Reviewer's Guide to Quantitative Methods in the Social Sciences* (Routledge, Milton Park, 2010)
9. J. Cheong, D.P. MacKinnon, S.T. Khoo, Investigation of mediational processes using parallel process latent growth curve modeling. Struct. Equ. Model. **10**(2), 238 (2003)
10. B. Muthén, Latent variable analysis. Sage Handbook Quan. Methodol. Soc. Sci. **345**(368), 106 (2004)
11. Y. Rosseel, Lavaan: An R package for structural equation modeling. J. Stat. Softw. **48**, 1 (2012)
12. T.E. Duncan, S.C. Duncan, L.A. Strycker, *An Introduction to Latent Variable Growth Curve Modeling: Concepts, Issues, and Applications* (Lawrence Erlbaum Associates, Mahwah, 1999)
13. T.D. Little, *Longitudinal Structural Equation Modeling* (Guilford Press, New York, 2013)
14. K.J. Preacher, P.J. Curran, D.J. Bauer, Computational tools for probing interactions in multiple linear regression, multilevel modeling, and latent curve analysis. J. Educ. Behav. Stat. **31**(4), 437 (2006)
15. B.O. Muthén, T. Asparouhov, Latent variable analysis with categorical outcomes: multiple-group and growth modeling in Mplus. Mplus Web Notes **4**, 1 (2004)
16. X. Tong, Z. Zhang, Outlying observation diagnostics in growth curve modeling. Multivar. Behav. Res. **52**(6), 768–788 (2017). https://doi.org/10.1080/00273171.2017.1374824
17. K.Y. Liang, S.L. Zeger, Longitudinal data analysis using generalized linear models. Biometrika **73**(1), 13 (1986)
18. S.L. Zeger, K.Y. Liang, P.S. Albert, Models for longitudinal data: a generalized estimating equation approach. Biometrics **44**(4), 1049 (1988)
19. J.C. Pinheiro, D.M. Bates, *Mixed-Effects Models in S and S-PLUS* (Springer, Berlin, 2000)
20. T.J. Hastie, R.J. Tibshirani, Generalized additive models. Stat. Sci. **1**(3), 297 (1986)
21. S.N. Wood, *Generalized Additive Models: An Introduction with R*, 2nd edn. (CRC Press, New York, 2017)
22. J.H. Friedman, Multivariate adaptive regression splines. Ann. Stat. **19**(1), 1 (1991)
23. H. Farahani, P. Watson, T. Bezan, N. Kovač, L.C. Winter, M. Blagojević, P. Azadfallah, A. Allahyari, S. Masoumian, P. Jiménez, PsAIchology: an intelligent direction in psychological sciences, in *10th International Scientific Conference Technics, Informatics and Education-TIE 2024* (Faculty of Technical Sciences Čačak, University of Kragujevac, Kragujevac, 2024)
24. D.R. Cox, Regression models and life-tables. J. R. Stat. Soc. Ser. B Methodol. **34**(2), 187 (1972)
25. L.E. Baum, T. Petrie, G. Soules, N. Weiss, A maximization technique occurring in the statistical analysis of probabilistic functions of Markov chains. Ann. Math. Stat. **41**(1), 164 (1970)
26. N. Kovač, K. Ratković, P. Watson, H. Farahani, F. Bagheri Sheykhangafshe, Machine learning classification models for predicting chronic pain. Curr. Psychol. **44**(18), 15409–15422 (2025)
27. I. Visser, M.E. Raijmakers, P.C. Molenaar, Fitting hidden Markov models to psychological data. Sci. Program. **10**(3), 185–199 (2002). https://doi.org/10.1155/2002/874560
28. S. de Haan-Rietdijk, P. Kuppens, C.S. Bergeman, L.B. Sheeber, N.B. Allen, E.L. Hamaker, On the use of mixed Markov models for intensive longitudinal data. Multivar. Behav. Res. **52**(6), 747–767 (2017). http://dx.doi.org/10.1080/00273171.2017.1370364
29. W.S. Cleveland, *Visualizing Data* (Hobart Press, Thousand Oaks, 1993)
30. K. Ratković, N. Kovač, M. Simeunović, Hybrid LSTM model to predict the level of air pollution in Montenegro. Appl. Sci. **13**(18), 10152 (2023)
31. E.R. Tufte, *The Visual Display of Quantitative Information* (Graphics Press, Chennai, 2001)
32. H. Wickham, *ggplot2: Elegant Graphics for Data Analysis* (Springer, Berlin, 2016)
33. L. van der Maaten, G. Hinton, Visualizing data using t-SNE. J. Mach. Learn. Res. **9**, 2579 (2008)

Shrinkage Regression: Ridge Regression, LASSO, and Elastic Net Regression

Nataša Kovač, Kruna Ratković, Marko Simeunović, and Hojjatollah Farahani

1 Core Concepts: Ridge and LASSO Regression

Shrinkage regression methods play an important role in modern statistical modelling by addressing common challenges such as overfitting and multicollinearity. Traditional *Ordinary Least Squares* (OLS) regression aims to minimise the residual sum of squares, providing unbiased estimates of regression coefficients. In high-dimensional settings, where the number of predictors is large or predictor variables are highly correlated, OLS estimates become unstable [1, 2], leading to poor generalisation on new data [3]. Ridge Regression and the *Least Absolute Shrinkage and Selection Operator* (LASSO) were developed as regularised alternatives to mitigate these issues by introducing penalty terms that constrain coefficient magnitudes.

Ridge Regression, introduced by Hoerl and Kennard [4], is designed to improve the stability of regression estimates by applying an L_2 penalty to the regression coefficients [5, 6]. The Ridge objective function is defined by the following equation:

$$\text{RSS}_{RIDGE} = \min_{\beta} \sum_{i=1}^{n} (y_i - X_i\beta)^2 + \lambda \sum_{j=1}^{p} \beta_j^2. \tag{1}$$

N. Kovač · K. Ratković · M. Simeunović (✉)
Faculty of Applied Sciences, University of Donja Gorica, Podgorica, Montenegro
e-mail: natasa.kovac@udg.edu.me; kruna.ratkovic@udg.edu.me; marko.simeunovic@udg.edu.me

H. Farahani
Department of Psychology, Faculty of Humanities, Tarbiat Modares University, Tehran, Iran
e-mail: h.farahani@modares.ac.ir

N. Kovač et al. (eds.), *Data Science in Psychology*,
https://doi.org/10.1007/978-3-032-18312-5_15

The residual sum of squares (RSS) $\sum_{i=1}^{n}(y_i - X_i\beta)^2$ is minimised with an additional L_2 regularisation penalty, $\lambda\sum_{j=1}^{p}\beta_j^2$, which shrinks the regression coefficients towards zero. The penalty term ensures that the model coefficients remain small, preventing excessive variance in parameter estimates. By shrinking coefficients towards zero, Ridge Regression reduces model complexity while retaining all predictors in the model. This characteristic makes it particularly suitable for applications where all features are assumed to contribute some degree of predictive power, such as cognitive and psychological studies involving multiple interrelated variables [7].

A key advantage of Ridge Regression is its ability to handle multicollinearity effectively. In cases where predictor variables exhibit high correlations, OLS estimates can become unreliable due to large standard errors in coefficient estimation. Ridge Regression stabilises these estimates by evenly distributing the shrinkage effect across all correlated predictors, ensuring that no single variable dominates the model [8]. This property is especially valuable in psychological and behavioural sciences, where predictors often represent overlapping constructs, such as different dimensions of personality traits or psychological assessments.

In contrast to Ridge, LASSO Regression applies an L_1 penalty, which not only shrinks coefficient magnitudes but also allows some coefficients to be set exactly to zero [9]. Equation 2 represents the LASSO regression objective function, where the standard RSS is penalised by an L_1 norm to enforce sparsity in the regression coefficients:

$$\mathrm{RSS}_{LASSO} = \min_{\beta}\sum_{i=1}^{n}(y_i - X_i\beta)^2 + \lambda\sum_{j=1}^{p}|\beta_j|. \tag{2}$$

The use of an absolute value penalty introduces sparsity into the model, effectively performing variable selection by removing predictors with negligible contributions to the response variable. This characteristic makes LASSO particularly beneficial in high-dimensional datasets, where many predictors may be irrelevant or redundant [3]. For instance, in neuroimaging studies, where thousands of voxel-based features are recorded, LASSO can identify the most informative regions while eliminating non-contributory features [10, 11], thus improving model interpretability.

Despite its advantages, LASSO has limitations, particularly in scenarios involving highly correlated predictors. When faced with a group of strongly correlated variables, LASSO tends to select only one variable from the group while setting the others to zero. This selection process can be arbitrary and may lead to the exclusion of important predictors that could contribute valuable information [7]. Furthermore, LASSO's sensitivity to data sparsity implies that selecting an appropriate regularisation parameter λ is critical for optimal model performance. The selection of λ is typically performed through cross-validation techniques [12, 13], ensuring that the model balances bias and variance effectively.

From an application perspective, both Ridge and LASSO Regressions provide essential tools for improving model robustness in psychological and social science research. Ridge is ideal when the goal is to improve prediction accuracy while preserving all variables, whereas LASSO is preferred when feature selection is necessary. In practice, determining which method to use depends on the characteristics of the dataset and the specific research objectives. Ridge is more effective in cases where predictors exhibit strong collinearity and should not be excluded, while LASSO is suitable for settings where a sparse model is desirable, particularly when the number of predictors exceeds the number of observations [14].

The implementation of Ridge and LASSO Regression has been significantly streamlined with modern machine learning frameworks. In Python, the `scikit-learn` library provides efficient implementations of both methods, allowing researchers to apply shrinkage regression in real-world data analysis with minimal computational complexity. The ability to automate hyperparameter tuning using techniques such as grid search and cross-validation further enhances their usability, making Ridge and LASSO accessible and effective tools in data-driven psychological research [8].

Ridge and LASSO Regressions offer distinct yet complementary approaches to regularised regression modelling. Ridge provides stability in the presence of multicollinearity by uniformly shrinking coefficients, while LASSO enhances interpretability through automatic variable selection. Both methods contribute to more reliable statistical modelling in research fields where high-dimensional data and complex relationships between predictors are common. Choosing between these approaches requires careful consideration of the dataset structure, predictive goals, and the trade-off between bias and variance. By leveraging the strengths of each method, researchers can improve the accuracy and robustness of their models, leading to more interpretable and generalisable findings in psychological and behavioural sciences.

2 Advancements in Shrinkage Regression: Elastic Net Regression

Elastic Net Regression (ENR) significantly advances regularised regression techniques, particularly when psychological data present high-dimensional, collinear, or sparse predictor structures. Traditional OLS regression methods tend to overfit when predictors are highly correlated or when the number of predictors exceeds the number of observations, a common occurrence in modern psychological studies involving questionnaire items, neuroimaging features, or multi-modal data [14]. While Ridge Regression [4] mitigates multicollinearity by penalising the size of coefficients (L2 regularisation), and the LASSO [9] performs variable selection via L1 regularisation, ENR integrates both penalties into a single framework, offering a more balanced and flexible modelling strategy [15, 16].

Elastic Net combines the strengths of Ridge and LASSO Regressions by simultaneously applying both L1 and L2 penalties to the loss function. This dual regularisation encourages both sparsity and coefficient shrinkage, making it particularly effective in psychological datasets where predictors are numerous and intercorrelated [17, 18]. The loss function minimised in ENR is

$$\min_{\boldsymbol{\beta}} \left\{ \frac{1}{2n} \sum_{i=1}^{n} \left(y_i - \mathbf{x}_i^\top \boldsymbol{\beta} \right)^2 + \lambda \left[\alpha \|\boldsymbol{\beta}\|_1 + \frac{(1-\alpha)}{2} \|\boldsymbol{\beta}\|_2^2 \right] \right\}. \tag{3}$$

In Eq. 3, λ is the regularisation parameter controlling the total strength of the penalty, and $\alpha \in [0, 1]$ is the mixing parameter, where $\alpha = 1$ recovers LASSO and $\alpha = 0$ recovers Ridge.

This flexibility allows Elastic Net to manage datasets where pure LASSO may fail due to selecting only one variable from a group of correlated predictors [19, 20] and where Ridge alone may not sufficiently reduce dimensionality or enhance interpretability [14].

Psychological datasets often involve complex, multicollinear variables. Consider, for example, self-report items from depression or anxiety inventories, where multiple items may measure overlapping constructs. Elastic Net is particularly well suited for such contexts because it can retain groups of correlated variables, which is crucial when theory indicates that multiple indicators are jointly informative [21]. ENR is robust against noise, which is common in behavioural and psychometric measurements [1].

A notable application of ENR is in personality psychology, where researchers aim to predict behavioural outcomes from hundreds of self-report items [22]. Using Elastic Net, researchers can develop sparse yet stable models that identify clusters of predictive items, contributing to theory development and the refinement of psychological constructs [23].

ENR is readily accessible through Python's `scikit-learn` library [24]. The following code illustrates a basic application with psychological data:

```
import pandas as pd
from sklearn.linear_model import ElasticNetCV
from sklearn.model_selection import train_test_split

# Load dataset from CSV (assumed: all columns except 'target'
↪   are features)
df = pd.read_csv("regression_dataset.csv")
```

```
# Separate features and target
X = df.drop(columns='target').values
y = df['target'].values

# Split into training and testing sets
X_train, X_test, y_train, y_test = train_test_split(X, y,
↪  test_size=0.2, random_state=42)

# Fit Elastic Net with cross-validation
model = ElasticNetCV(l1_ratio=[.1, .5, .9, 1.0], alphas=None,
↪  cv=5)
model.fit(X_train, y_train)

# Output optimal hyperparameters
print("Optimal alpha:", model.alpha_)
print("Optimal l1_ratio (alpha mixing):", model.l1_ratio_)
```

This code performs cross-validation to optimise both λ (regularisation strength) and α (L1/L2 mixing), highlighting the flexibility of Elastic Net in practice.

The differences among Ridge, LASSO, and ENR can be understood visually through their constraint regions in coefficient space. Figure 1 illustrates the distinct penalty surfaces imposed by each method. Ridge regression applies an L2 penalty, resulting in a circular constraint region, while LASSO uses an L1 penalty, forming a diamond shape that promotes sparsity by encouraging exact zero coefficients. Elastic Net blends these constraints, producing a rounded diamond, combining the strengths of both methods to handle correlated predictors and enforce regularisation. This geometric perspective clarifies why LASSO tends to produce sparse models, whereas Ridge tends to shrink all coefficients evenly.

Elastic Net is especially useful when:

- The number of predictors exceeds the number of observations.
- There is strong multicollinearity among predictors.
- One desires a balance between model simplicity and predictive accuracy.

It is also preferred when group selection of features is needed, aligning with theoretical considerations in psychology that suggest item clusters jointly represent latent traits [25]. In clinical prediction contexts, regularised regression can complement tree- and margin-based models; for example, chronic pain severity has been modelled from psychological scales using a suite of ML classifiers [26]. Despite its flexibility, Elastic Net does not automatically provide insight into the causal structure of relationships and requires careful cross-validation to avoid overfitting. Interpretability may still be challenging in models with many retained variables, although it performs better than Ridge or LASSO alone in terms of model stability.

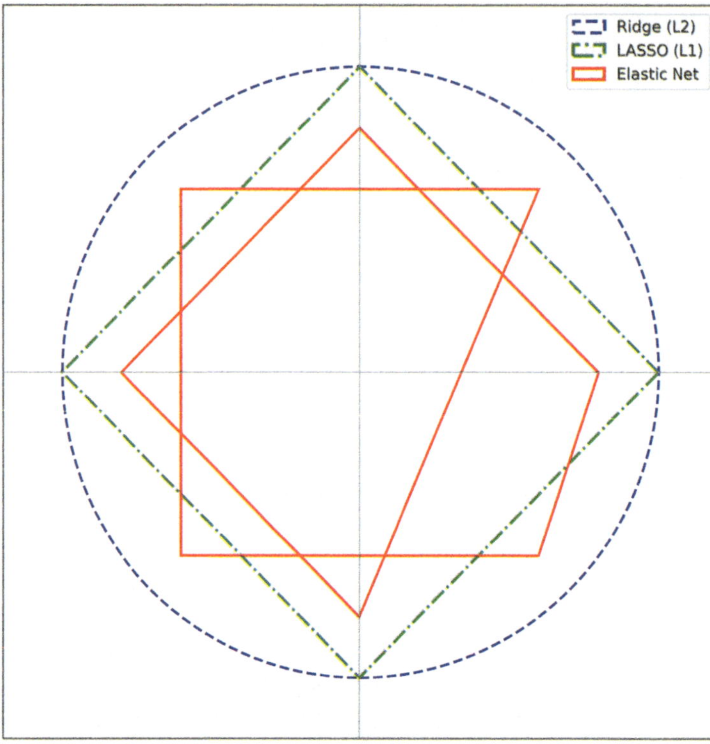

Fig. 1 Penalty surface comparison between Ridge, LASSO, and Elastic Net

3 Application Variants: Multiple Regression and Naïve Elastic Net Approaches

In psychological research, statistical modelling often must strike a balance between complexity and interpretability. While shrinkage methods such as Ridge, LASSO, and Elastic Net offer sophisticated solutions to problems of multicollinearity and overfitting, their integration into standard research pipelines can present challenges for researchers who are more familiar with classical multiple regression techniques. Consequently, simplified or *naïve* variants of shrinkage regression have gained popularity, particularly those that align conceptually with familiar tools while still offering robustness and predictive power. This section explores how multiple regression and naïve elastic net formulations are leveraged in psychological contexts and how these applications differ from their more canonical counterparts. These pipelines are often evaluated alongside non-parametric and boosting approaches in health psychology prediction tasks such as chronic pain severity [26].

Multiple linear regression remains one of the foundational tools in psychology for modelling the relationship between a set of predictor variables and an outcome of interest [27]. Classical regression methods can become unstable when predictors are highly correlated or when the number of predictors approaches or exceeds the number of observations. These conditions, common in high-dimensional psychological datasets such as those involving psychometric scales or brain imaging data, require regularisation to avoid inflated variance in coefficient estimates [28].

While traditional multiple regression provides no penalty term, researchers often use it as a baseline model to compare performance against regularised approaches [6]. In particular, shrinkage techniques are assessed by their ability to improve prediction accuracy, reduce variance, and yield interpretable models when applied to noisy psychological datasets.

The term *Naïve Elastic Net* refers to a simplified approach to combining Ridge and LASSO penalties, often used as a practical compromise when theoretical elegance is less of a priority than empirical robustness. In its classic formulation, the Elastic Net penalty is a convex combination of the L1 and L2 norms:

$$\text{Penalty} = \lambda_1 \sum_{j=1}^{p} |\beta_j| + \lambda_2 \sum_{j=1}^{p} \beta_j^2.$$

In naïve implementations, this penalty may be applied without the necessary rescaling of predictors, or the mixing parameter α (which controls the proportion of L1 vs. L2) may be fixed arbitrarily rather than tuned [29]. Such simplifications are common in exploratory psychological research or pilot studies [30, 31], where the primary goal is hypothesis generation rather than definitive modelling [32].

Naïve Elastic Net approaches are particularly useful in early stage model exploration, where psychological researchers may wish to reduce predictor dimensionality before applying more rigorous modelling strategies. For instance, in modelling cognitive functioning across a range of neuropsychological assessments, predictors such as memory, attention, and processing speed scores may be highly collinear. A Naïve Elastic Net allows for soft thresholding of coefficients while retaining some grouped variable structure, which is ideal when conceptual constructs are expected to cluster [14].

From a theoretical standpoint, the simplifications used in Naïve Elastic Net may violate some of the assumptions required for optimality in prediction or coefficient recovery. In practice, these trade-offs are often accepted in favour of ease of use and computational efficiency. In studies involving moderately sized samples and medium-dimensional data, researchers may benefit from the bias-variance trade-off introduced by Elastic Net regularisation without the overhead of extensive cross-validation or hyperparameter tuning.

Several studies in psychology have demonstrated that Naïve Elastic Net models yield results similar in quality to fully optimised models, especially when predictor relationships are highly intercorrelated but relatively homogeneous in scale [21, 33, 34]. Furthermore, because the Elastic Net tends to select groups of related predictors, it aligns well with psychological constructs that are theoretically structured into domains, such as internalising versus externalising behaviours or cognitive versus affective functioning.

Another benefit of Naïve Elastic Net approaches is their seamless integration with standard multiple regression workflows in Python, R, and SPSS. Libraries such as `glmnet`, `scikit-learn`, and `caret` offer user-friendly implementations where Elastic Net regularisation can be applied with minimal modification to code originally designed for classical regression [8, 24]. Recent tutorials and applied guides in psychology demonstrate end-to-end ENR workflows with transparent validation and reporting [35]. In practical settings, this means researchers can experiment with different regularisation strengths and mixing parameters by simply modifying one or two lines of code. This flexibility makes Elastic Net particularly attractive in psychological studies involving cross-validation pipelines, bootstrapping, or nested model comparisons.

To better understand the practical implications of shrinkage techniques, it is helpful to visualise how different regularisation methods influence regression coefficient estimates. While theoretical formulations clarify the mathematical distinctions between Ridge, LASSO, and ENR, a comparative visual representation provides an intuitive grasp of how these techniques manage multicollinearity and variable selection. The following figure presents a side-by-side comparison of coefficient shrinkage across four regression methods applied to a shared psychological dataset.

As shown in Fig. 2, each bar represents the standardised coefficient assigned to a given predictor variable by one of the four regression methods. The OLS model, serving as the baseline, typically yields larger and more variable coefficients, especially when predictors are highly collinear. Ridge regression (blue bars) reduces the magnitude of all coefficients but retains them all, emphasising stability over sparsity. In contrast, LASSO (green bars) aggressively shrinks less informative predictors towards zero, sometimes eliminating them entirely. This explains why some LASSO bars are absent. The Naïve Elastic Net (orange bars) combines these strategies by both shrinking and selectively nullifying coefficients, depending on the

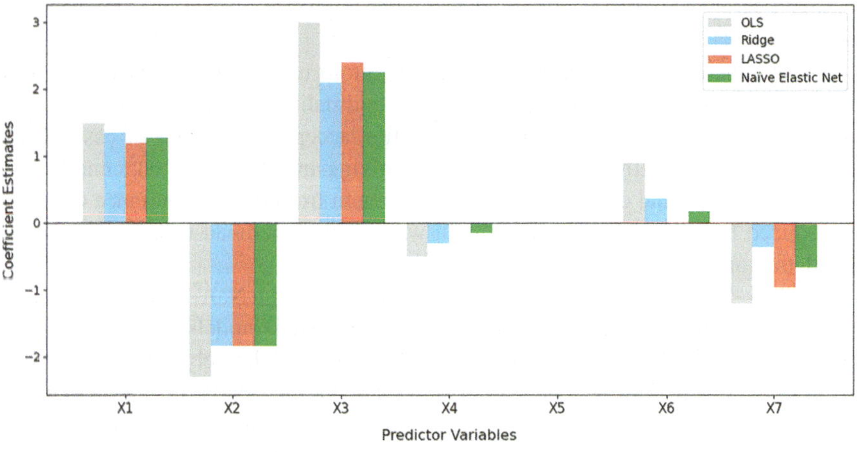

Fig. 2 Comparison of coefficient shrinkage across regression methods

combined penalties applied. For readers unfamiliar with shrinkage regression, the key takeaway is how these methods prevent overfitting and improve generalisability by simplifying the model structure, particularly in high-dimensional psychological datasets.

4 Comparative Analysis and Decision-Making in Shrinkage Methods

When choosing between shrinkage regression methods, it is essential to consider the structure of the data, the presence of multicollinearity, and whether feature selection is necessary. Ridge Regression, LASSO, and Elastic Net each introduce a form of regularisation that improves model generalisation by constraining coefficient estimates. Their behaviour differs significantly, impacting both interpretability and predictive performance. Understanding their strengths and limitations enables researchers to make informed decisions about which method best suits their data.

Ridge Regression is particularly effective when dealing with datasets where predictors exhibit high multicollinearity. In such cases, OLS regression tends to produce unstable coefficient estimates, leading to large variations in predictions. Ridge Regression mitigates this issue by introducing an L_2 penalty, which shrinks the magnitude of all regression coefficients but does not eliminate any predictors entirely. This ensures that all features contribute to the final model, making Ridge particularly useful in psychological research where domain knowledge suggests that even weak predictors may carry meaningful information. For instance, studies on cognitive performance or mental health often include numerous correlated variables, such as self-reported measures and behavioural assessments, all of which may provide some explanatory power. Ridge is advantageous in such scenarios because it stabilises coefficient estimates without discarding potentially informative predictors.

In contrast, LASSO Regression introduces an L_1 penalty, which not only shrinks coefficients but also forces some of them to be exactly zero [30, 36]. This characteristic enables LASSO to perform automatic feature selection, making it ideal for high-dimensional datasets where many predictors may be irrelevant. In psychological research, where survey-based studies, neuroimaging, or behavioural tracking often generate hundreds of potential predictors, LASSO can significantly enhance model interpretability by selecting only the most relevant variables. One limitation of LASSO is that when predictors are highly correlated, it tends to arbitrarily select one from a group while ignoring the rest. This behaviour can be problematic if multiple correlated variables contribute valuable information, as the model may exclude some of them without a clear basis.

ENR addresses this issue by combining the properties of Ridge and LASSO through a hybrid penalty term that includes both L_1 and L_2 components. By doing so, Elastic Net maintains the benefits of LASSO's feature selection while mitigating its tendency to discard highly correlated predictors. This makes Elastic Net particularly useful in fields where variables naturally cluster together, such as personality psychology, where different traits measured through multiple scales may be strongly interrelated. For example, in studies analysing emotional regulation, multiple questionnaire items may capture similar underlying constructs. Elastic Net ensures that related predictors are either included together or excluded together, rather than selecting one arbitrarily.

Beyond theoretical differences, empirical comparisons often guide method selection. In PsAIchology, this comparison is operationalised via spot-checking and cross-validation across multiple algorithm families to ensure robust selection [37]. A practical tutorial situates regularised regression among tree and boosting models within a unified evaluation workflow [35]. Performance evaluation typically involves metrics such as *Mean Squared Error* (MSE), *Akaike Information Criterion* (AIC), and cross-validation scores to determine how well each model generalises to unseen data. Studies have demonstrated that Ridge performs well when all predictors contribute to the outcome, while LASSO is preferable when sparsity is desired [2, 38]. Elastic Net, being a compromise, often excels in cases where some degree of feature selection is beneficial, but entirely discarding correlated variables is undesirable.

Tuning the regularisation parameter λ is crucial for optimising model performance in all three methods. This parameter controls the strength of the penalty term, directly influencing the degree of shrinkage applied to the regression coefficients. In practical applications, selecting the optimal λ is achieved using techniques such as cross-validation, where multiple models with different values of λ are tested, and the one minimising prediction error is chosen. Python's `scikit-learn` library facilitates this process using the `GridSearchCV` function, which automates hyperparameter tuning by searching for the best λ value over a predefined range.

The choice between Ridge, LASSO, and Elastic Net should align with the research objectives and data characteristics. If the goal is to improve prediction accuracy while preserving all predictors, Ridge is the preferred choice. If the focus is on model interpretability and variable selection, LASSO is an excellent option, particularly in high-dimensional datasets. When predictors exhibit strong correlations, Elastic Net serves as a balanced alternative, ensuring that informative variables are retained while reducing redundancy.

Since real-world datasets often contain a mix of relevant and irrelevant predictors, an empirical approach is recommended when selecting a shrinkage regression method. Penalised logistic regression can be less data-hungry and comparably calibrated to other ML methods [39]. Researchers should experiment with Ridge, LASSO, and Elastic Net on their data, comparing their performance under different regularisation strengths. By assessing error rates, coefficient shrinkage patterns, and overall model stability, they can make an informed decision on which method best suits their analytical needs. In many cases, Elastic Net provides a flexible solution, striking a balance between Ridge's stability and LASSO's sparsity, making it a widely applicable technique in psychological and behavioural sciences.

5 Applications and Case Studies

Shrinkage regression methods become especially powerful when demonstrated through practical applications and realistic case studies from psychological research [40]. This section provides concrete examples illustrating how Ridge, LASSO, and ENR perform in real-world scenarios typical of psychological datasets. Through careful exploration of these examples, readers will observe how these methods manage common dataset issues such as multicollinearity, high dimensionality, and predictor redundancy, ultimately enhancing interpretability and prediction accuracy.

The dataset used in our case study includes demographic and psychological variables collected from participants enrolled in a mindfulness-based intervention program aimed at reducing stress. Participants provided demographic data such as age, gender, education, income level, marital and employment status, along with psychological measures capturing their stress levels before and after the intervention, and hours of mindfulness practice completed during the study period. The primary outcome we analyse is the reduction in stress scores following intervention completion, defined as the difference between participants' baseline and follow-up stress scores.

Initial dataset exploration highlighted several critical characteristics relevant to shrinkage regression modelling. Visual and descriptive analyses revealed significant variability in participant stress reduction, mindfulness engagement, and potential demographic influences. Predictors exhibited multicollinearity, particularly among psychological and demographic variables, which is typical of psychological research, where interrelated constructs frequently coexist. These complexities underscore the importance of employing shrinkage methods like Ridge, LASSO, and Elastic Net, each specifically suited to address different aspects of predictor relationships.

All three shrinkage regression techniques are compared using this method of cross-validation since:

- *LASSO regression* helps identify and select only the most meaningful predictors by setting some predictors to zero. This simplifies the model, potentially enhancing interpretability.
- *ENR* balances between choosing important predictors and managing correlated predictors, offering a model that is both clear and robust, particularly valuable when predictors are closely related.
- *Ridge regression* uses all predictors but reduces their influence slightly, making it useful when researchers believe that most predictors carry some meaningful contribution.

In the upcoming subsections, we apply these methods step by step, showcasing their distinct advantages and providing researchers with clear guidelines for practical implementation and interpretation.

The provided Python code compares Ridge, LASSO, and Elastic Net shrinkage regression techniques to determine which approach best predicts stress reduction based on various psychological and demographic predictors.

```
from sklearn.model_selection import cross_val_score, KFold
from sklearn.linear_model import LassoCV, ElasticNetCV, RidgeCV
from sklearn.metrics import mean_absolute_error,
↪ mean_absolute_percentage_error, r2_score, make_scorer
import pandas as pd
import numpy as np

# Load dataset
df = pd.read_csv('data.csv')
X = df.drop('IS', axis=1)
y = df['IS']

# Custom scorers
def mae_scorer(estimator, X, y):
    y_pred = estimator.predict(X)
    return mean_absolute_error(y, y_pred)

def mape_scorer(estimator, X, y):
    y_pred = estimator.predict(X)
    return mean_absolute_percentage_error(y, y_pred)

def r2_scorer(estimator, X, y):
    y_pred = estimator.predict(X)
    return r2_score(y, y_pred)

# Define the K-Fold Cross-Validation
kf = KFold(n_splits=5, shuffle=True, random_state=42)

# Lasso Regression with Cross-Validation
lasso_cv = LassoCV(alphas=np.logspace(-6, 6, 100), cv=5,
↪ random_state=42)
lasso_cv_mse = -cross_val_score(lasso_cv, X, y, cv=kf,
↪ scoring='neg_mean_squared_error').mean()
lasso_cv_mae = cross_val_score(lasso_cv, X, y, cv=kf,
↪ scoring=make_scorer(mean_absolute_error)).mean()
lasso_cv_mape = cross_val_score(lasso_cv, X, y, cv=kf,
↪ scoring=make_scorer(mean_absolute_percentage_error)).mean()
lasso_cv_r2 = cross_val_score(lasso_cv, X, y, cv=kf,
↪ scoring='r2').mean()
```

```
# Elastic Net Regression with Cross-Validation
elastic_net_cv = ElasticNetCV(alphas=np.logspace(-6, 2, 100),
↪ l1_ratio=[.1, .5, .7, .9, .95, .99, 1], cv=5,
↪ random_state=42)
elastic_net_cv_mse = -cross_val_score(elastic_net_cv, X, y,
↪ cv=kf, scoring='neg_mean_squared_error').mean()
elastic_net_cv_mae = cross_val_score(elastic_net_cv, X, y,
↪ cv=kf, scoring=make_scorer(mean_absolute_error)).mean()
elastic_net_cv_mape = cross_val_score(elastic_net_cv, X, y,
↪ cv=kf,
↪ scoring=make_scorer(mean_absolute_percentage_error)).mean()
elastic_net_cv_r2 = cross_val_score(elastic_net_cv, X, y,
↪ cv=kf, scoring='r2').mean()

# Ridge Regression with Cross-Validation
ridge_cv = RidgeCV(alphas=np.logspace(-6, 6, 100),
↪ store_cv_values=True)
ridge_cv_mse = -cross_val_score(ridge_cv, X, y, cv=kf,
↪ scoring='neg_mean_squared_error').mean()
ridge_cv_mae = cross_val_score(ridge_cv, X, y, cv=kf,
↪ scoring=make_scorer(mean_absolute_error)).mean()
ridge_cv_mape = cross_val_score(ridge_cv, X, y, cv=kf,
↪ scoring=make_scorer(mean_absolute_percentage_error)).mean()
ridge_cv_r2 = cross_val_score(ridge_cv, X, y, cv=kf,
↪ scoring='r2').mean()

# Summary of results
cv_results = pd.DataFrame({
    "Model": ["Lasso", "Elastic Net", "Ridge"],
    "CV MSE": [lasso_cv_mse, elastic_net_cv_mse, ridge_cv_mse],
    "CV MAE": [lasso_cv_mae, elastic_net_cv_mae, ridge_cv_mae],
    "CV MAPE": [lasso_cv_mape, elastic_net_cv_mape,
    ↪ ridge_cv_mape],
    "CV R^^c2^^b2": [lasso_cv_r2, elastic_net_cv_r2,
    ↪ ridge_cv_r2]
})

print(cv_results)
```

Initially, the dataset is loaded and organised to separate the predictors (participant demographics and psychological measures) from the outcome, which in this case is represented by the measure of stress reduction (indicated as `IS`). The core goal is to evaluate how well different regression methods can predict stress reduction from the collected data, aiming for models that are both accurate and reliable.

An essential part of this code is the concept known as *cross-validation* (also referred to here as **folding**). Cross-validation is particularly valuable because it helps researchers understand how well their predictive model generalises to new, unseen data. This step is crucial in psychological research, where the validity of predictions in new participants is critical. Instead of using the entire dataset at once, cross-validation divides the data into several smaller sets (or *folds*). In this case, the data are split into five equally sized parts. Each of these parts serves, in turn, as a temporary test dataset, while the remaining four are used to build the predictive model. By repeatedly training and testing the model on different subsets, researchers obtain a reliable estimate of the model's true predictive performance.

Each method's predictive capability is assessed through several performance measures: how precisely the model predicts the exact stress reduction (*Mean Absolute Error* (MAE)), how accurately it predicts relative percentage errors (*Mean Absolute Percentage Error* (MAPE)), and how well the model explains variability in stress reduction outcomes (R^2, a measure of explained variance). The results from all models are summarised in a straightforward table presented below, allowing readers to easily compare their predictive performance. This summary clearly shows which regression method performs best according to various criteria, helping researchers select the most suitable model for their data and research objectives.

```
         Model     CV MSE    CV MAE   CV MAPE     CV R²
0        Lasso  73.100094  6.453238  0.084491  0.601359
1  Elastic Net  73.085657  6.453337  0.084491  0.601445
2        Ridge  73.137705  6.471325  0.084727  0.601301
```

In practical terms, cross-validation enhances confidence that the chosen model will not only fit past data well but will also effectively predict future unseen observations. It acts as a safeguard against overly optimistic predictions and helps researchers make informed decisions about model selection in psychological research.

The presented results provide a comparison among the LASSO, Elastic Net, and Ridge regression in terms of their effectiveness at predicting stress reduction from the collected psychological and demographic data. From the summary table, we see that all three methods performed similarly, with only subtle differences emerging. Specifically, the MSE, which reflects the average prediction error squared and emphasises larger mistakes, is the lowest for the Elastic Net Regression (73.0857), closely followed by LASSO Regression (73.1001), and slightly higher for the Ridge Regression (73.1377). These small differences suggest all models are similarly effective in capturing general patterns in the data, but Elastic Net Regression slightly edges out the others in prediction accuracy.

The MAE, which indicates the average size of prediction errors regardless of direction, again reveals extremely close performance among all three methods. LASSO and Elastic Net Regressions show almost identical MAE (around 6.45), while Ridge Regression presents a slightly higher error (around 6.47). Practically, these results indicate that the models' predictions typically deviate by around six-and-a-half units from observed stress reduction scores, suggesting reasonable accuracy. The MAPE, a metric highlighting how errors compare relative to actual observed values, remains consistent across all methods (approximately 8.45%). This suggests that regardless of the regression technique chosen, predictions typically deviate from actual observed stress reductions by roughly 8% on average, which again highlights consistent and acceptable predictive performance.

The R^2 value, which measures how well each regression method explains variability in stress reduction, is similar for all methods, hovering around 60%. This indicates that approximately 60% of the variability in stress reduction can be explained by the predictors included in these regression models. Such a result is considered good in psychological research, as psychological phenomena usually involve multiple complex factors beyond the measured variables.

Elastic Net Regression emerges as slightly superior based on these metrics due to its marginally better predictive accuracy. Still, the differences among methods are minimal. Thus, when researchers choose among these shrinkage methods, considerations beyond predictive performance, such as interpretability, simplicity, or specific theoretical interests, may guide their decision. For instance, LASSO could be preferred for simplicity and explicit selection of fewer predictors, while Ridge could be favourable if the theoretical context justifies keeping all predictors despite moderate correlation.

These results underscore the importance of carefully evaluating multiple methods, as subtle differences can sometimes guide important theoretical or practical decisions in psychological research.

6 Visualising Shrinkage Regression Results

In the previous section, the comparative analysis demonstrated that ENR provided the best predictive performance among the evaluated shrinkage methods. Consequently, in this section, we illustrate practical methods for visually interpreting the results obtained through ENR. These visualisation techniques (learning curves, prediction error plots, residual analyses, and coefficient paths) can significantly enhance researchers' understanding of model performance, robustness, and potential limitations. Although demonstrated here specifically for ENR, these visualisation techniques apply equally well to other regression methods when those methods yield the best results.

To start, the learning curve (Fig. 3) offers valuable insight into how the model's predictive accuracy evolves as more data become available. Figure 3 displays two trends: The red line shows the training performance (how accurately the model fits the training data), and the green line illustrates cross-validation performance (how well the model generalises to new data). We observe that as the number of participants increases, both training and cross-validation scores converge, stabilising around approximately 0.60 to 0.65. The close alignment of these scores suggests that ENR maintains a healthy balance, neither overfitting nor underfitting [13]. Given the narrow gap at the larger sample sizes, further data collection might only marginally enhance performance.

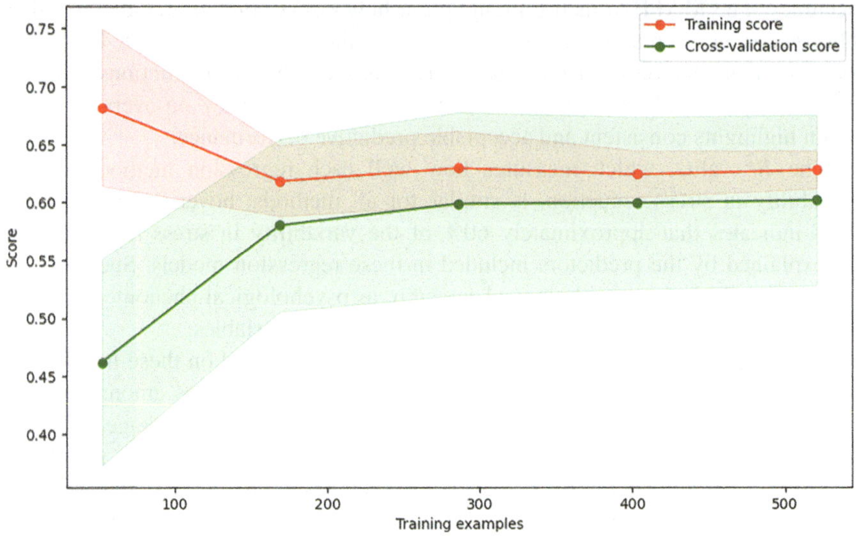

Fig. 3 Learning curve for Elastic Net Regression

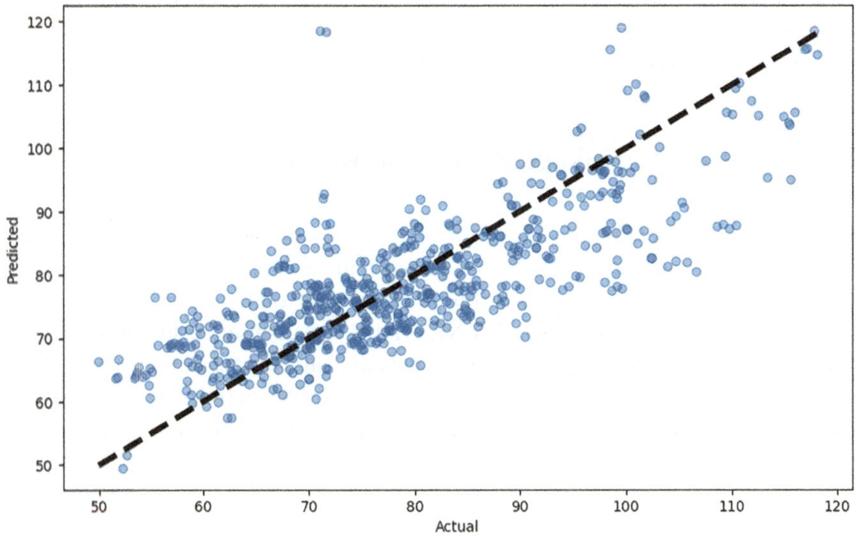

Fig. 4 Prediction error plot for Elastic Net Regression (cross-validation)

The prediction error plot (Fig. 4) visually compares predicted values against actual observations. Ideally, predictions should closely match actual observed outcomes, aligning tightly along the diagonal line. In Fig. 4, most points cluster closely around the diagonal, reflecting accurate predictions. Some dispersion still exists, indicating occasional prediction errors. This characteristic is common in

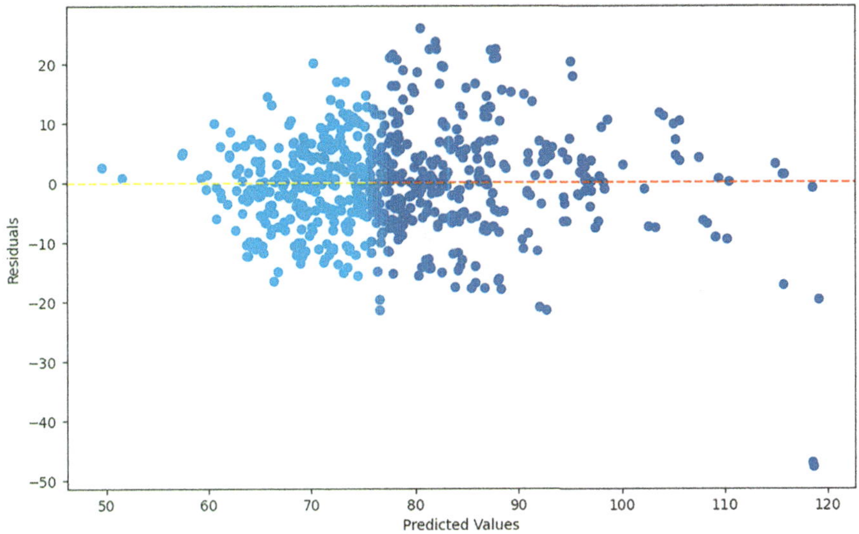

Fig. 5 Residuals plot for Elastic Net Regression (cross-validation)

psychological research due to individual differences and unmeasured influences. Researchers should carefully consider these deviations when interpreting individual predictions, recognising that while the overall accuracy is good, predictions for certain individuals might be less reliable.

Further diagnostic checks include analysing residuals, as visualised in Fig. 5. Residuals represent the differences between observed and predicted values. In this plot, residuals are evenly distributed around the horizontal line at zero, with no apparent systematic pattern or trend. Such a distribution suggests the model's assumptions of linearity and homoscedasticity (constant variance) generally hold. A few points exhibit larger residuals, signalling individuals or cases poorly explained by current predictors. Investigating these cases might further provide additional insights into potential missing factors or measurement errors influencing stress reduction outcomes.

The *Quantile-Quantile* (QQ) plot shown in Fig. 6 assesses whether residuals follow a normal distribution, a common assumption underlying regression analyses. Points closely adhering to the diagonal line indicate normally distributed residuals. Most residuals here align closely with this line, indicating generally good conformity. Still, several deviations at both ends highlight potential outliers. Such outliers should prompt further investigation into the data collection or specific cases to ensure the robustness and validity of the results.

The Elastic Net coefficient paths illustrated in Fig. 7 highlight how predictor influence changes as the regularisation strength (controlled by the alpha parameter) varies [41, 42]. Each line represents a predictor's coefficient, showing stability or changes across different alpha levels. Initially, with low alpha values (left side),

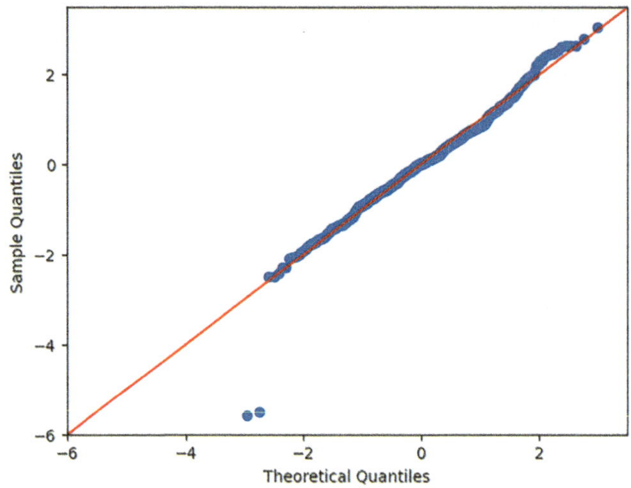

Fig. 6 QQ plot of residuals for Elastic Net Regression (cross-validation)

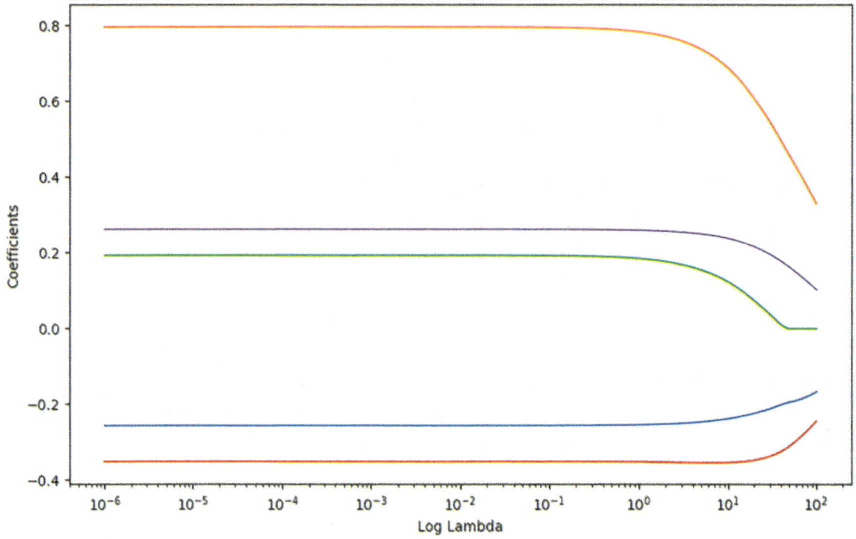

Fig. 7 Elastic Net Regression coefficient paths

predictors have stable, distinct influences. As alpha increases (moving right), ENR progressively shrinks these coefficients towards zero, reflecting reduced model complexity. The optimal alpha determined in our analysis (approximately 1.668) provides the best balance, ensuring stable and interpretable coefficients without excessively simplifying the model.

These visualisations reinforce the robustness of ENR for predicting stress reduction in this dataset. They also serve as crucial diagnostic tools, guiding researchers towards deeper insights, potential improvements, and informed interpretation of their regression modelling results.

References

1. S. Friedrich, A. Groll, K. Ickstadt, T. Kneib, M. Pauly, J. Rahnenführer, T. Friede, Regularization approaches in clinical biostatistics: a review of methods and their applications. Stat. Methods Med. Res. **32**(2), 425 (2023)
2. S. Salerno, Y. Li, High-dimensional survival analysis: methods and applications. Annu. Rev. Stat. Appl. **10**(1), 25 (2023)
3. R.T. Trevor Hastie, J. Friedman, *The Elements of Statistical Learning: Data Mining, Inference, and Prediction*, 2nd edn. (Springer, Berlin, 2009)
4. A.E. Hoerl, R.W. Kennard, Ridge regression: biased estimation for nonorthogonal problems. Technometrics **12**(1), 55 (1970)
5. A. Chudik, M.H. Pesaran, M. Sharifvaghefi, Variable selection in high dimensional linear regressions with parameter instability. J. Econom. **246**(1–2), 105900 (2024)
6. O. Efthimiou, M. Seo, K. Chalkou, T. Debray, M. Egger, G. Salanti, Developing clinical prediction models: a step-by-step guide. BMJ **386**, e078276 (2024)
7. T. Hastie, R. Tibshirani, M. Wainwright, *Statistical Learning with Sparsity: The Lasso and Generalizations* (CRC Press, Boca Raton, 2015)
8. J. Friedman, T. Hastie, R. Tibshirani, Regularization paths for generalized linear models via coordinate descent. J. Stat. Softw. **33**(1), 1 (2010)
9. R. Tibshirani, Regression shrinkage and selection via the Lasso. J. Roy. Stat. Soc. Ser. B (Methodological) **58**(1), 267 (1996)
10. M. Hosseini, M. Powell, J. Collins, C. Callahan-Flintoft, W. Jones, H. Bowman, B. Wyble, I tried a bunch of things: the dangers of unexpected overfitting in classification of brain data. Neurosci. Biobehav. Rev. **119**, 456 (2020)
11. H. Chen, D. Wang, J. Shen, B. Guo, C. Song, D. Ma, Y. Wu, G. Liu, G. Chen, Y. Ni, et al., Predicting peripartum depression using elastic net regression and machine learning: the role of remnant cholesterol. BMC Pregnancy Childbirth **25**(1), 544 (2025)
12. S. Parvandeh, H.W. Yeh, M.P. Paulus, B.A. McKinney, Consensus features nested cross-validation. Bioinformatics **36**(10), 3093 (2020)
13. D. Wilimitis, C.G. Walsh, Practical considerations and applied examples of cross-validation for model development and evaluation in health care: tutorial. JMIR AI **2**, e49023 (2023)
14. H. Zou, T. Hastie, Regularization and variable selection via the elastic net. J. Roy. Stat. Soc. Ser. B (Statistical Methodology) **67**(2), 301 (2005)
15. Z. Mei, Z. Shi, On lasso for high dimensional predictive regression. J. Econom. **242**(2), 105809 (2024)
16. L. Musib, R. Coletti, M.B. Lopes, H. Mouriño, E. Carrasquinha, Priority-elastic net for binary disease outcome prediction based on multi-omics data. BioData Mining **17**(1), 45 (2024)
17. J.H. Yang, Y. Chung, S.J. Rhee, K. Park, M.J. Kim, H. Lee, Y. Song, S.Y. Lee, S.H. Shim, J.J. Moon, et al., Development and external validation of a logistic and a penalized logistic model using machine-learning techniques to predict suicide attempts: a multicenter prospective cohort study in Korea. J. Psychiatric Res. **176**, 442 (2024)
18. W. Zou, X. Yao, Y. Chen, X. Li, J. Huang, Y. Zhang, L. Yu, B. Xie, An elastic net regression model for predicting the risk of ICU admission and death for hospitalized patients with covid-19. Sci. Rep. **14**(1), 14404 (2024)
19. R. Jardillier, D. Koca, F. Chatelain, L. Guyon, Prognosis of lasso-like penalized Cox models with tumor profiling improves prediction over clinical data alone and benefits from bi-dimensional pre-screening. BMC Cancer **22**(1), 1045 (2022)

20. A. Iparragirre, T. Lumley, I. Barrio, I. Arostegui, Variable selection with lasso regression for complex survey data. Stat **12**(1), e578 (2023)
21. T. Yarkoni, J. Westfall, Choosing prediction over explanation in psychology: lessons from machine learning. Perspect. Psychol. Sci. **12**(6), 1100 (2017)
22. L. Waldorp, J. Haslbeck, Network inference with the lasso. Multivariate Behav. Res. **59**(4), 738 (2024)
23. W. Youyou, M. Kosinski, D. Stillwell, Computer-based personality judgments are more accurate than those made by humans. Proc. Natl. Acad. Sci. **112**(4), 1036 (2015)
24. F. Pedregosa, G. Varoquaux, A. Gramfort, V. Michel, B. Thirion, O. Grisel, M. Blondel, P. Prettenhofer, R. Weiss, V. Dubourg, et al., Scikit-learn: machine learning in Python. J. Mach. Learn. Res. **12**, 2825 (2011)
25. A.B. Costello, J.W. Osborne, Best practices in exploratory factor analysis: four recommendations for getting the most from your analysis. Practical Assessm. Res. Eval. **10**(7), 1 (2005)
26. N. Kovač, K. Ratković, P. Watson, H. Farahani, F. Bagheri Sheykhangafshe, Machine learning classification models for predicting chronic pain. Curr. Psychol. **44**, 15409–15422 (2025)
27. J. Cohen, *Statistical Power Analysis for the Behavioral Sciences* (Routledge, London, 2013)
28. M.A. Babyak, What you see may not be what you get: a brief, nontechnical introduction to overfitting in regression-type models. Psychosomatic Med. **66**(3), 411 (2004). https://doi.org/10.1097/01.psy.0000127692.23278.a9
29. A. ElSheikh, M.R. Abonazel, M.C. Ali, A review of penalized regression and machine learning methods in high-dimensional data. Egypt. Stat. J. **69**(1), 250 (2025)
30. S.A. Bainter, T.G. McCauley, M.M. Fahmy, Z.T. Goodman, L.B. Kupis, J.S. Rao, Comparing Bayesian variable selection to lasso approaches for applications in psychology. Psychometrika **88**(3), 1032 (2023)
31. D.J. Zhou, R. Chahal, I.H. Gotlib, S. Liu, Comparison of lasso and stepwise regression in psychological data. Methodology **20**(2), 121 (2024)
32. G. James, D. Witten, T. Hastie, R. Tibshirani, *An Introduction to Statistical Learning* (Springer, Berlin, 2013)
33. A. Groll, G. Tutz, Variable selection for generalized linear mixed models by L1-penalized estimation. Stat. Comput. **24**(2), 137 (2014). https://doi.org/10.1007/s11222-012-9360-2
34. G. James, D. Witten, T. Hastie, R. Tibshirani, *An Introduction to Statistical Learning: With Applications in R*, 2nd edn. (Springer, New York, 2021)
35. N. Kovač, K. Ratković, H. Farahani, P. Watson, A practical applications guide to machine learning regression models in psychology with python. Methods Psychol. **11**, 100156 (2024)
36. R. Adamek, S. Smeekes, I. Wilms, Lasso inference for high-dimensional time series. J. Econom. **235**(2), 1114 (2023)
37. H. Farahani, P. Watson, T. Bezan, N. Kovač, L.C. Winter, M. Blagojević, P. Azadfallah, A. Allahyari, S. Masoumian, P. Jiménez, PsAIchology: an intelligent direction in psychological sciences, in *10th International Scientific Conference Technics, Informatics and Education-TIE 2024* (Faculty of Technical Sciences Čačak, University of Kragujevac, 2024)
38. Y. Yan, Z. Yang, T.R. Semenkovich, B.D. Kozower, B.F. Meyers, R.G. Nava, D. Kreisel, V. Puri, Comparison of standard and penalized logistic regression in risk model development. JTCVS Open **9**, 303 (2022)
39. P.C. Austin, D.S. Lee, B. Wang, The relative data hungriness of unpenalized and penalized logistic regression and ensemble-based machine learning methods: the case of calibration. Diagn. Progn. Res. **8**(1), 15 (2024)
40. T.A. Moxley, J. Johnson-Leung, E. Seamon, C. Williams, B.J. Ridenhour, Application of elastic net regression for modeling covid-19 sociodemographic risk factors. PLoS One **19**(1), e0297065 (2024)
41. D. Han, J. Huang, Y. Lin, G. Shen, Robust post-selection inference of high-dimensional mean regression with heavy-tailed asymmetric or heteroskedastic errors. J. Econom. **230**(2), 416 (2022)
42. M. Nouraie, S. Muller, On the selection stability of stability selection and its applications (2024). arXiv preprint arXiv:2411.09097

Bayesian Data Analysis

Nataša Kovač, Kruna Ratković, Marko Simeunović, Ulfeta Marovac, Hojjatollah Farahani, Stevan Kordić, and Zhiyong Johnny Zhang

1 Overview of Bayesian Data Analysis

Bayesian data analysis is a probabilistic approach to statistical inference that provides a coherent framework for integrating prior knowledge with observed data [1]. Unlike traditional frequentist methods, which rely on fixed hypotheses and sampling-based inference, Bayesian analysis updates beliefs about parameters using observed evidence, allowing for a more flexible and interpretable approach to statistical modelling [2–4]. This dynamic updating process ensures that new information is systematically incorporated into existing knowledge, making Bayesian inference particularly well-suited for fields where accumulating evidence is critical, such as psychology, neuroscience, and social sciences. By explicitly modelling uncertainty, Bayesian methods provide richer probabilistic interpretations of results, offering more intuitive conclusions about the credibility of hypotheses and parameter estimates [5]. This makes Bayesian analysis especially valuable in psychological

N. Kovač · K. Ratković · M. Simeunović (✉)
Faculty of Applied Sciences, University of Donja Gorica, Podgorica, Montenegro
e-mail: natasa.kovac@udg.edu.me; kruna.ratkovic@udg.edu.me; marko.simeunovic@udg.edu.me

U. Marovac
Department of Technical and Technological Sciences, State University in Novi Pazar, Novi Pazar, Serbia

H. Farahani
Department of Psychology, Faculty of Humanities, Tarbiat Modares University, Iran, Tehran
e-mail: h.farahani@modares.ac.ir

S. Kordić
Faculty of Maritime Studies, University of Montenegro, Kotor, Dobrota

Z. J. Zhang
Department of Psychology, University of Notre Dame, Notre Dame, IN, USA
e-mail: zhiyongzhang@nd.edu

N. Kovač et al. (eds.), *Data Science in Psychology*,
https://doi.org/10.1007/978-3-032-18312-5_16

research, where prior theoretical knowledge, previous empirical findings, or expert judgment can be incorporated to refine inference, improve decision-making, and enhance model robustness in the presence of limited or noisy data. The Bayesian framework allows for adaptive learning, making it ideal for real-time decision-making processes and iterative data analysis, further strengthening its applicability across a broad range of scientific disciplines [6].

At the core of Bayesian data analysis is Bayes' theorem, which provides a formal mechanism for updating probabilities in light of new evidence [7]. It is expressed in Eq. 1:

$$P(A|B) = \frac{P(B|A)P(A)}{P(B)}, \tag{1}$$

where $P(A|B)$ represents the posterior probability of event A given evidence B, $P(B|A)$ is the likelihood of observing B given that A is true, $P(A)$ is the prior probability reflecting prior beliefs about A, and $P(B)$ is the marginal probability of B, ensuring that the posterior probabilities sum to one [8].

In the context of Bayesian inference, the parameter of interest is treated as a random variable with an associated probability distribution rather than as a fixed value. The prior distribution, $P(A)$, encodes prior knowledge or assumptions before data is observed, which can be either informative (based on prior research) or non-informative (allowing the data to drive inference). The likelihood function, $P(B|A)$, represents how likely the observed data is under different parameter values. The posterior distribution, $P(A|B)$, updates the prior belief in response to new data, providing a revised probability distribution that integrates both prior knowledge and observed evidence [9, 10].

A major advantage of Bayesian analysis is its ability to quantify uncertainty in a principled manner [11]. Unlike frequentist confidence intervals, which provide a range of values based on hypothetical repeated sampling, Bayesian credible intervals directly represent the probability that a parameter lies within a given range [12]. A 95% credible interval, for example, implies that there is a 95% probability that the true parameter value falls within the specified interval, making Bayesian inference particularly intuitive for psychological research [2].

Bayesian methods also offer an alternative to traditional hypothesis testing. Instead of relying on p-values to reject null hypotheses, Bayesian analysis employs the Bayes factor, which quantifies the relative strength of evidence for competing models [13]. The Bayes factor is defined in Eq. 2:

$$BF_{10} = \frac{P(B|H_1)}{P(B|H_0)}, \tag{2}$$

where BF_{10} represents the ratio of the likelihood of the data under the alternative hypothesis H_1 to the likelihood of the data under the null hypothesis H_0. A Bayes factor greater than 1 suggests stronger evidence in favour of H_1, whereas a value below 1 indicates support for H_0. Unlike p-values, which provide indirect evidence through rejection thresholds, Bayes factors allow researchers to directly assess the degree of support for competing hypotheses, making them a valuable tool for psychological research [8, 14, 15].

Since Bayesian methods often involve complex probability distributions that cannot be solved analytically, computational techniques such as *Markov chain Monte Carlo* (MCMC) sampling methods are commonly used to approximate posterior distributions [2, 16]. MCMC methods, including the Metropolis-Hastings algorithm and the *No-U-Turn Sampler* (NUTS), generate representative samples from the posterior distribution, allowing researchers to make probabilistic inferences even for highly complex models. These sampling algorithms operate by constructing a Markov chain whose equilibrium distribution corresponds to the target posterior, ensuring that over time, the sampled values provide an accurate representation of the uncertainty in parameter estimates. While the Metropolis-Hastings algorithm employs an acceptance-rejection criterion to explore the posterior space, NUTS, an extension of *Hamiltonian Monte Carlo* (HMC), dynamically adjusts step sizes and trajectories to enhance convergence and efficiency, making it particularly useful in high-dimensional Bayesian models [9, 17].

Bayesian data analysis has been widely adopted in psychology for applications such as hierarchical modelling, psychometric testing, and cognitive modelling. For instance, hierarchical Bayesian models allow for individual differences to be accounted for in experimental designs while still pooling information across participants, enhancing statistical power. Similarly, Bayesian models in cognitive neuroscience are used to estimate neural parameters with quantified uncertainty, improving inference in neuroimaging studies [9, 18].

Another advantage of Bayesian modelling is its predictive capability. By leveraging posterior distributions, Bayesian models can generate predictive distributions that account for uncertainty in both parameter estimates and future data points. In parallel with Bayesian predictive frameworks, recent health-psychology work applies ML classification to forecast chronic pain severity from validated scales, an adjacent predictive goal that could benefit from Bayesian uncertainty quantification [19, 20]. This is particularly relevant in psychological research, where forecasting behavioural responses or assessing the reliability of psychometric instruments, and, in applied settings, predicting clinical states, requires a probabilistic approach to modelling individual variability [20]. In practice, PsAIchology complements Bayesian approaches by emphasising cross-validated comparisons of multiple supervised learners before deployment [21].

A potential challenge in Bayesian analysis is the specification of prior distributions, as different choices can influence results. Sensitivity analyses, in which findings are tested under varying prior assumptions, can help evaluate the robustness of conclusions. The widespread adoption of these methods in Bayesian data analysis has been further facilitated by probabilistic programming frameworks such as Stan, PyMC, and JAGS, all of which can be used in Python [2]. These frameworks provide robust MCMC implementations and can be embedded in transparent, reproducible Python workflows in psychology [19]. Stan can be accessed in Python via cmdstanpy or pystan, offering highly efficient HMC and NUTS methods. `PyMC` is a fully Python-native library that supports NUTS, variational inference, and flexible probabilistic modelling, making it one of the most accessible Bayesian tools for Python users. JAGS, while traditionally used in R, can also be accessed in Python via pyjags, providing an implementation of Gibbs sampling for Bayesian inference. The availability of these frameworks in Python has significantly enhanced the accessibility of Bayesian modelling, enabling researchers across disciplines to implement probabilistic models and perform Bayesian inference efficiently [16].

Bayesian data analysis provides a coherent and flexible framework for addressing complex research questions in psychology [11]. By integrating prior knowledge, quantifying uncertainty, and facilitating probabilistic reasoning, Bayesian methods offer valuable advantages over traditional frequentist approaches. As computational advances continue to improve the accessibility of Bayesian techniques, their application in psychology is expected to expand, enabling informative statistical inferences [3, 6, 10].

2 Bayesian Inference

Bayesian inference is updating beliefs about unknown parameters or hypotheses in light of observed data [22]. At its heart lies Bayes' theorem, which formally relates prior beliefs, likelihood functions, and observed evidence to produce a posterior distribution. This approach contrasts with frequentist inference, which views parameters as fixed and relies on long-run sampling properties. Bayesian inference, by contrast, treats parameters as random variables and assigns probabilities to them directly, enabling a more intuitive and probabilistic framework for decision-making in psychological research [23, 24].

Bayesian inference has grown in popularity among psychologists due to its flexibility, ability to incorporate prior knowledge, and natural way of handling uncertainty. For instance, researchers studying latent cognitive processes can explicitly encode their beliefs about model parameters before seeing the data rather than relying on fixed null hypotheses. After data are collected, the posterior distribution combines both sources of information, prior and evidence, resulting in updated knowledge that reflects both theoretical expectations and empirical observation [25].

Bayesian inference proceeds through three conceptual components:

1. *Prior distribution*: Encodes initial beliefs about parameters. For example, a psychologist might believe that the average effect size of a new therapy lies between 0.3 and 0.6 based on previous studies.
2. *Likelihood function*: Represents how likely the observed data are under different values of the parameters. This is typically based on standard statistical models (e.g. linear regression, normal distribution, etc.).
3. *Posterior distribution*: The result of updating the prior with the data through Bayes' theorem. It expresses the revised belief about the parameters after seeing the data.

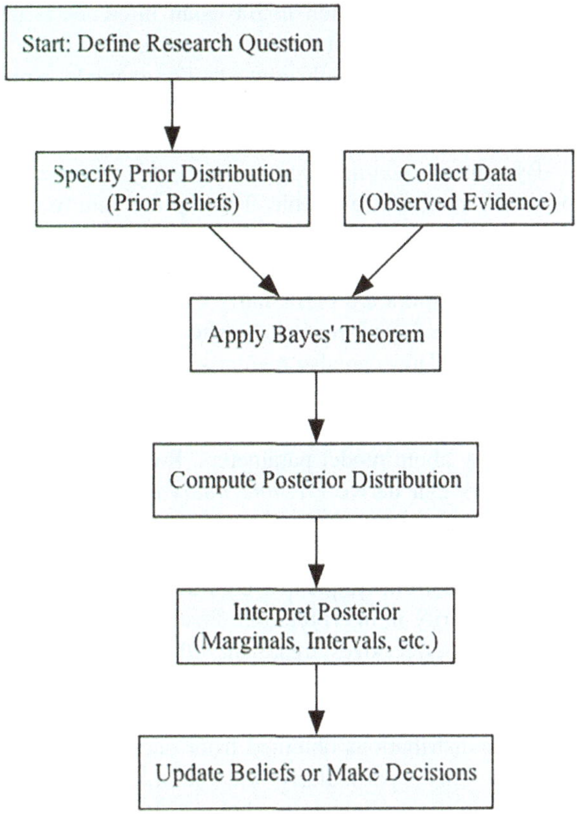

Fig. 1 The conceptual flow of Bayesian inference from the prior distribution and observed data (likelihood) to the resulting posterior distribution

Figure 1 outlines the essential components of Bayesian reasoning, from the initial formulation of a research question to the final updating of beliefs based on new evidence. This stepwise progression illustrates how prior knowledge and observed data are integrated through Bayes' theorem to yield posterior beliefs that can directly inform decisions and theoretical interpretations in psychology.

The Bayesian inference workflow begins with defining a psychologically relevant research question and formalising prior beliefs about the parameters of interest. This prior information, representing either subjective knowledge or empirical evidence from earlier studies, is mathematically encoded as a probability distribution. Upon collecting new data, Bayes' theorem is applied to combine the prior with the likelihood derived from the observed data. This results in a posterior distribution, which quantifies updated beliefs in light of the new evidence. The posterior can then be interpreted through credible intervals, expected values, or other summary measures, ultimately enabling the researcher to refine theories, adjust interventions, or design follow-up studies. This structured reasoning pathway demonstrates why Bayesian inference is particularly suited for cumulative scientific research and detailed psychological interpretation [24, 26].

A key design decision in Bayesian inference is the specification of the prior. *Informative priors* incorporate substantive knowledge, helping stabilise estimation, especially in small-sample contexts. For example, a prior on reaction time distributions may be based on empirical studies showing log-normal behaviour in cognitive tasks.

By contrast, *non-informative* (or *weakly informative*) *priors* are used when little prior information is available. These priors aim to exert minimal influence, letting the data speak more strongly. Even *uninformative* priors carry assumptions, and their impact should be assessed via sensitivity analysis [26, 27]. In psychology, informative priors are particularly useful in cumulative research designs, such as meta-analytic Bayesian models, where prior distributions are derived from earlier studies [28]. They can also regularise estimation in high-dimensional models, such as hierarchical latent trait models used in psychometrics.

The posterior distribution provides a full probabilistic description of the uncertainty about model parameters. Rather than reporting single point estimates, researchers can derive *credible intervals*, which directly answer questions like: Given the data and the prior, what is the probability that the parameter lies between 0.2 and 0.6?

This shift from frequentist confidence intervals to Bayesian credible intervals provides clarity in interpretation. Posterior distributions enable probabilistic statements about effect sizes, treatment differences, or regression coefficients, which are intuitive and informative in psychological contexts [29].

One of the greatest strengths of Bayesian inference is *sequential learning*. Posterior distributions obtained from one dataset can be used as priors for future analyses. This is particularly valuable in longitudinal or adaptive research designs. For example, in clinical psychology, Bayesian updating allows for continuous evidence accumulation, which can improve diagnostic precision and enable real-time interventions. Adaptive clinical trials increasingly employ Bayesian methods for dynamic treatment allocation based on posterior probabilities of effectiveness [30].

Real-world Bayesian inference is often computationally intensive, especially in high-dimensional models or when closed-form solutions are intractable. Tools like MCMC sampling provide numerical approximations of posterior distributions [31]. Popular MCMC methods include:

- *Metropolis-Hastings*: A general-purpose algorithm based on proposal and acceptance-rejection steps.
- *HMC*: Uses gradients to improve exploration of parameter space.
- *NUTS*: An adaptive variant of HMC used in libraries like `Stan` and `PyMC3`.

These tools have made Bayesian modelling accessible to applied psychologists, especially when implemented in Python or R. For instance, a developmental psychologist might use PyMC to model learning trajectories in children, incorporating prior research and estimating posterior distributions of growth parameters. Bayesian inference is increasingly used across subfields of psychology:

- In *clinical psychology*, it supports robust diagnosis and personalised therapy models.
- In *cognitive science*, Bayesian models describe perception and learning as probabilistic inference [32].
- In *social psychology*, Bayesian approaches offer tools to quantify the strength of evidence across replications.
- In *psychometrics*, Bayesian item response theory enables uncertainty modelling at both item and participant levels.

The transparency and flexibility of Bayesian inference also make it ideal for *open science practices*, encouraging reproducibility and cumulative research.

3 Bayesian Hypothesis Testing

Hypothesis testing is a method to make inferences or decisions on hypotheses using data such as experimental data and survey data. In frequentist analysis, hypothesis testing is one kind of confirmatory data analysis technique, in contrast to exploratory data analysis. The data collection is often driven by theory and hypothesis. The key to the traditional *null hypothesis significance testing* (NHST) is to answer the question *Assuming that the null hypothesis is true, what is the probability of observing a value for a chosen test statistic?*

Traditional NHST has been widely criticised for several key limitations [33]. One major critique is the overreliance on p-values, which are often misinterpreted as the probability that the null hypothesis is true, rather than a measure of data extremity under the assumption of the null. NHST encourages dichotomous decision-making—either rejecting or failing to reject the null hypothesis—without considering the magnitude or practical relevance of the effect. It can also be sensitive to sample size, such that even trivial effects can be statistically significant in large samples, while meaningful effects may go undetected in small ones. NHST cannot provide evidence in favour of the null hypothesis, and its rigid significance thresholds (e.g. $\alpha = 0.05$) can lead to arbitrary conclusions. These limitations have contributed to questionable research practices and a replication crisis in many scientific fields, prompting a call for more informative alternatives.

In this context, the use of Bayesian methods has gained traction as a more informative alternative to traditional NHST. Bayesian approaches allow researchers to quantify the strength of evidence in favour of both the null and alternative hypotheses, providing a deeper understanding of the data. By incorporating prior beliefs and updating them with observed data, Bayesian methods can yield credible intervals and posterior probabilities that offer richer insights into the effect size and its uncertainty. This flexibility allows for a more comprehensive interpretation of results, moving beyond binary decisions to a continuum of evidence that can inform scientific conclusions and practical applications.

Bayesian hypothesis testing can be conducted based on *Bayes' theorem*. Given two competing hypotheses:

- H_0: Null hypothesis (e.g. no effect or difference)
- H_1: Alternative hypothesis (e.g. there is an effect or difference)

and observed data D, we can compute the posterior probabilities of each hypothesis by Eqs. 3 and 4 using Bayes' theorem:

$$P(H_1 \mid D) = \frac{P(D \mid H_1)P(H_1)}{P(D \mid H_0)P(H_0) + P(D \mid H_1)P(H_1)} \tag{3}$$

$$P(H_0 \mid D) = 1 - P(H_1 \mid D) = \frac{P(D \mid H_0)P(H_0)}{P(D \mid H_0)P(H_0) + P(D \mid H_1)P(H_1)}, \tag{4}$$

where $P(D \mid H_0)$ and $P(D \mid H_1)$ are the likelihoods of the data under each hypothesis, and $P(H_0)$ and $P(H_1)$ are the prior probabilities of the hypotheses. With two hypotheses, $P(H_0) + P(H_1) = 1$. The prior probabilities can be subjective, based on previous knowledge or beliefs about the hypotheses. The posterior probabilities $P(H_1 \mid D)$ and $P(H_0 \mid D)$ represent the updated beliefs about the hypotheses after observing the data.

The ratio of the posterior probabilities is called the *posterior odds* and can be calculated as shown in Eq. 5:

$$\text{Posterior Odds} = \frac{P(H_1 \mid D)}{P(H_0 \mid D)} = \frac{P(D \mid H_1)P(H_1)}{P(D \mid H_0)P(H_0)}. \tag{5}$$

The posterior odds can be interpreted as the strength of evidence in favour of H_1 relative to H_0. If the posterior odds are greater than 1, it suggests that the data provide evidence in favour of H_1; if less than 1, it suggests evidence in favour of H_0. In Bayesian hypothesis testing, we also define and calculate the *Bayes factor* by Eq. 6:

$$\text{Bayes Factor} = \text{BF}_{10} = \frac{P(D \mid H_1)}{P(D \mid H_0)}. \tag{6}$$

The Bayes factor quantifies the strength of evidence provided by the data in favour of one hypothesis over the other. A Bayes factor greater than 1 indicates that the data favour H_1 over H_0, while a Bayes factor less than 1 indicates that the data favour H_0 over H_1. The Bayes factor can also be interpreted in terms of odds, as it represents the ratio of the posterior odds to the prior odds:

$$\text{Bayes Factor} = \frac{\text{Posterior Odds}}{\text{Prior Odds}} = \frac{P(H_1 \mid D)/P(H_0 \mid D)}{P(H_1)/P(H_0)}. \tag{7}$$

Table 1 Interpretation of Bayes factor (BF_{10})

Bayes factor BF_{10}	Strength of evidence for H_1
<1	Evidence in favour of H_0
1–3	Anecdotal evidence
3–10	Moderate evidence
10–30	Strong evidence
30–100	Very strong evidence
>100	Decisive (extreme) evidence

Note that for the simple vs. simple hypothesis testing, the Bayes factor is equivalent to the likelihood ratio test.

The interpretation of the Bayes factor is often based on conventions like those proposed by Jeffreys [8] and later modified by others (e.g. Kass and Raftery [14]). Table 1 summarises the interpretation of Bayes factor values.

4 Bayesian Predictive Models

Bayesian predictive models use posterior distributions to predict new data. In Bayesian analysis, the model uses prior beliefs (prior distributions) that are updated after observing the data, forming a posterior distribution. This posterior distribution represents updated beliefs about unknown parameters or future observations based on available data. For predicting new data, the posterior predictive distribution is used, which allows predicting future data given prior information and newly acquired beliefs[2].

The Bayesian approach differs from classical frequentist methods because in frequentist statistics, probabilities represent long-term frequencies, not beliefs about unknown parameters. In frequentism, parameters are treated as fixed, and probabilities are based on repeated experiments. On the other hand, the Bayesian approach is more flexible because it allows for explicitly estimating and updating beliefs about parameters, as well as managing uncertainty through distributions. This enables more precise and adaptable predictions, especially in situations with limited data. Equation 8 represents the core formula of a Bayesian predictive model:

$$p(\tilde{y} \mid x, D, M) = \int p(\tilde{y} \mid x, \theta, M)\, p(\theta \mid x, D, M)\, d\theta. \tag{8}$$

Equation 8 shows how the *posterior distribution* of the model $p(\theta \mid x, D, M)$ is used to predict future observations $\tilde{y}$, given the previous data D and model M:

- θ: The *model parameters*, which represent unknown quantities that govern the behaviour or structure of the model. These parameters are treated as random variables with their probability distributions. The goal is to estimate these parameters using the available data.

- $p(\theta \mid x, D, M)$: The *posterior distribution* of the model parameters θ after observing the data D and considering the model M. It represents updated beliefs about the parameters, incorporating both prior knowledge and new data.
- $p(\tilde{y} \mid x, \theta, M)$: The likelihood function, which represents the probability of observing new data $\tilde{y}$ given the known predictors x, the parameters θ, and the model M.
- The integral $\int p(\tilde{y} \mid x, \theta, M)\, p(\theta \mid x, D, M)\, d\theta$: This integral shows how we integrate over all possible values of the model parameters θ, weighted by their posterior probability. This gives the *posterior predictive distribution* of the future observations $\tilde{y}$.

In this way, Bayesian predictive models allow for an accurate estimation of future data by integrating prior knowledge (via the prior distribution) and newly acquired information (via the posterior distribution). The use of the posterior predictive distribution enables more flexible and precise predictions, as it accounts for both the uncertainty in the model parameters and the data at hand.

The Bayesian approach provides greater flexibility in assessing uncertainty because parameters are treated as random variables with probability distributions, whereas frequentist approaches treat parameters as fixed and do not allow for direct management of uncertainty in predictions [34].

Hidden Markov models (HMMs) are particularly useful in Bayesian predictive modelling, especially for time series and sequential data. They model systems where observations depend on hidden (latent) states that evolve.

In Bayesian analysis, HMMs help infer latent states and predict future observations by leveraging posterior distributions. This is particularly valuable in dynamic parameter estimation and sequential forecasting, where uncertainty in state transitions is naturally incorporated into predictions [2].

To perform Bayesian prediction, several Python libraries provide robust tools for implementing MCMC methods and other Bayesian inference techniques. Libraries such as `Stan`, `PyMC`, and `JAGS` offer efficient implementations of MCMC sampling, allowing researchers to fit complex models and derive probabilistic conclusions.

`PyMC` is a probabilistic programming library for Python designed to facilitate the construction and fitting of Bayesian models. It features an intuitive and readable syntax, closely mirroring the way statisticians describe models. `PyMC` leverages `PyTensor`, a symbolic computation library, which allows it to be compiled into different computational backends like C, JAX, and Numba, enabling execution on various architectures such as CPU, GPU, and TPU. `PyMC` supports a wide range of models, including hierarchical linear regression, classification, time series, and non-parametric models like Gaussian processes. The library's flexibility and ease of use make it suitable for both simple and complex statistical models. `PyMC` plays a key role in the development of the open-source ecosystem for probabilistic programming [31].

Stan provides full Bayesian inference for continuous-variable models through MCMC methods such as the NUTS, an adaptive form of Hamiltonian Monte Carlo sampling, making it a powerful tool for Bayesian prediction. Stan can be accessed via Python libraries like `cmdstanpy` or `pystan`, which support sampling and optimisation-based inference with diagnostics and posterior analysis [35].

Just another Gibbs sampler (JAGS) is commonly used in Bayesian inference to perform MCMC sampling, particularly when it is not possible to obtain the joint posterior distribution in a closed form, relying on *Gibbs sampling* and *Metropolis-Hastings methods* to sample from the joint posterior through its conditionals [36]. JAGS, traditionally used in R, can also be accessed in Python via pyjags, offering an implementation of Gibbs sampling for Bayesian inference.

These tools allow Bayesian practitioners to fit complex hierarchical models and perform inference efficiently, and to be integrated with end-to-end ML pipelines used in applied forecasting problems [37]. An example of the application of Bayesian predictive models is presented in a paper investigating predictors of the outcome of psychological therapy for depression and anxiety in patients from the *Southwark IAPT Psychological Therapies Service*. This approach enables the identification and quantification of key predictors that influence the success of therapy. In this chapter, researchers collected an extensive set of pre-treatment variables, including demographic data and clinical measures, particularly the PHQ-9 and GAD-7 scales. Utilising the R package `rstanarm`, which implements HMC *methods*, Bayesian projective models were developed.

These models allowed researchers to construct a reference model that predicted therapy outcomes based on all collected variables, followed by variable selection techniques to identify the most significant predictors using a minimal number of variables. This approach effectively accounted for the uncertainties associated with the variable selection process, thereby enhancing the precision and interpretability of the model. The results indicated that specific predictors, such as baseline severity on the PHQ-9 and GAD-7 scales, along with the presence of OCD diagnoses, significantly impacted therapy outcomes. This emphasises the necessity for individualised treatment approaches for this patient population [38].

5 Applications and Case Studies

In this case study, we utilise a psychological dataset derived from a clinical trial examining the efficacy of *mindfulness-based cognitive therapy* (MBCT) in reducing depressive symptoms. The dataset comprises two groups: an experimental group undergoing the MBCT program and a control group receiving standard care without mindfulness training. Depression severity is measured using a standardised depression scale at baseline and after intervention completion. Additional variables include age and gender, offering deeper insights into potential influencing factors. The dataset's structure supports Bayesian inference, allowing the incorporation of prior knowledge about therapy effectiveness and facilitating detailed interpretation through posterior distributions, predictive checks, and credible intervals.

Bayesian inference was used to rigorously evaluate differences between these two groups, integrating prior expectations and observed data to produce detailed, probabilistic conclusions. The Bayesian model provided estimates for the mean depression reduction for each group (MBCT and control) and quantified uncertainty about these estimates using posterior distributions. Crucially, the difference in depression reduction between groups, denoted as δ, was explicitly modelled, enabling direct interpretation of MBCT's effectiveness relative to standard care.

The results shown in the output below indicate a clear advantage of the MBCT intervention. The posterior mean estimate of depression reduction was approximately 7.0 points for the MBCT group and about 2.2 points for the control group. The difference δ between these groups was notably around 4.8 points, with a 95% *highest density interval* (HDI) ranging from 3.8 to 5.9 points, firmly excluding zero. This means we can confidently assert that participants undergoing MBCT experienced significantly greater depression reductions than those in the control group, with nearly complete certainty, as highlighted by the posterior distribution (see Sect. 6 and Fig. 3). Such clear posterior evidence offers strong support for MBCT's efficacy in reducing depressive symptoms.

```
         mean  sd   h3%  h97%  mcseMu  mcseSig essBulk  essTail rHat
muMbct   6.98 0.38 6.29 7.72  0.00    0.00    16660.61 8964.28 1.00
muCtrl   2.17 0.41 1.40 2.95  0.00    0.00    19098.12 9242.04 1.00
delta    4.81 0.56 3.77 5.85  0.00    0.00    18106.08 9815.47 1.00
sigMbct  2.88 0.28 2.39 3.42  0.00    0.00    17977.40 9863.86 1.00
sigCtrl  3.17 0.30 2.63 3.74  0.00    0.00    16590.01 9708.12 1.00
```

6 Visualising Bayesian Analysis Results

Visualising Bayesian analysis results is crucial, as it transforms abstract statistical information into accessible insights for researchers. We begin with the trace plots shown in Fig. 2, which illustrate the behaviour of parameters during the MCMC sampling process. The left panels show smooth, symmetric, and bell-shaped posterior distributions for key parameters: group means (μ_{mbct}, μ_{ctrl}), group standard deviations (σ_{mbct}, σ_{ctrl}), and their difference δ. The right panels show the corresponding sampling paths, displaying a healthy *random walk* pattern without notable trends or irregularities. These visual indicators confirm excellent convergence, ensuring the reliability and validity of the Bayesian estimates. Trace plots visually represent sampled values for each parameter across numerous iterations of our Bayesian sampling algorithm.

The left panels show smooth, bell-shaped posterior distributions for each parameter, confirming consistent estimates of group means (μ_{mbct}, μ_{ctrl}), their difference δ, and variability within each group (σ_{mbct}, σ_{ctrl}). The right panels display time series plots, exhibiting steady fluctuations around stable mean values without systematic patterns or drifts. This stability confirms robust convergence, meaning our Bayesian model provides reliable and interpretable results.

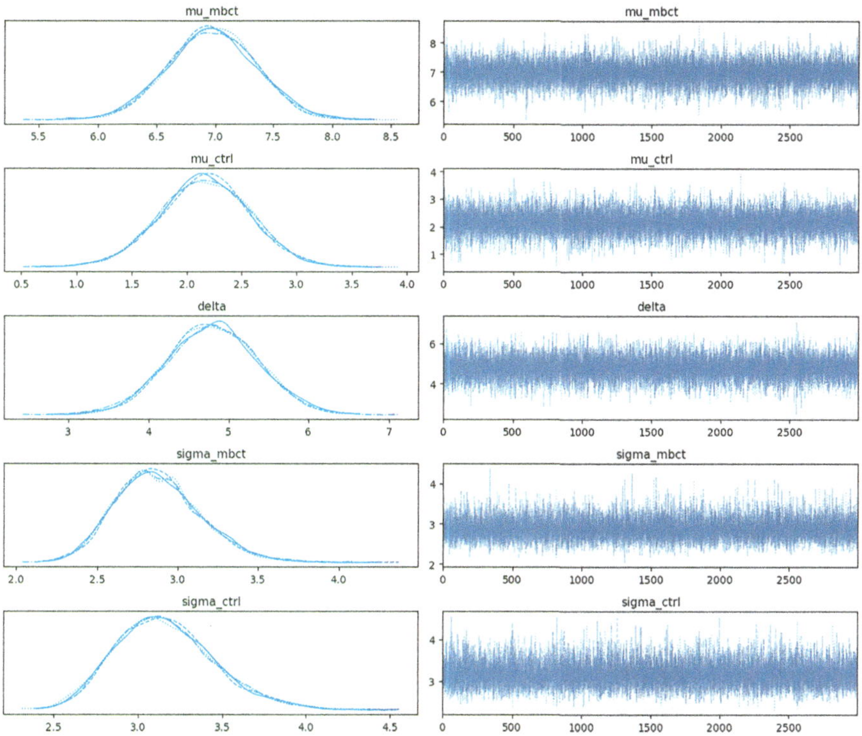

Fig. 2 Posterior distributions of variables

The posterior distribution plot represented in Fig. 3 for the difference δ vividly demonstrates the practical value of Bayesian interpretation. Here, the entire distribution resides above zero, explicitly emphasising the effectiveness of MBCT. The visualised mean difference (approximately 4.8 points) and the 95% HDI interval (3.7–5.9 points) strengthen interpretative clarity. The notation indicating $0.0\% < 0 < 100.0\%$ visually emphasises the certainty (100%) that the difference in depression reduction favours the MBCT group, making this visualisation particularly informative for practitioners and policymakers considering therapeutic efficacy.

The posterior distribution for δ (MBCT minus control) indicates a mean difference of 4.8 points. The visualisation also emphasises the 95% HDI spanning from approximately 3.7 to 5.9 points, highlighting high certainty regarding the effectiveness of MBCT. Importantly, the entire HDI lies above zero, indicating that virtually 100% of the probability mass supports the superiority of MBCT compared to standard care. Such visualisation is powerful because it moves beyond traditional significance testing, allowing researchers to confidently communicate the practical effectiveness of their intervention in probabilistic terms.

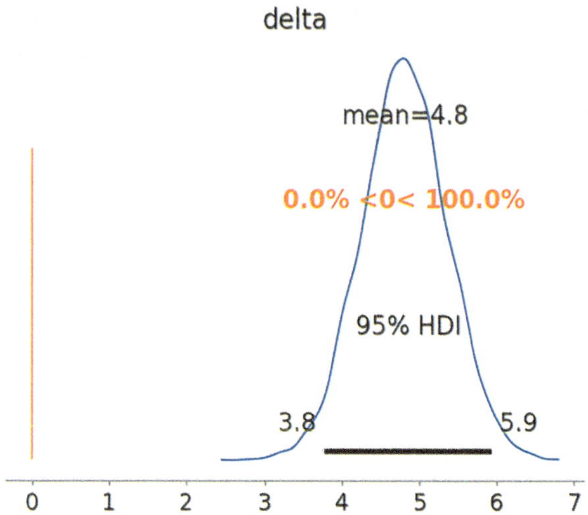

Fig. 3 Posterior distribution for difference in depression reduction (MBCT—control)

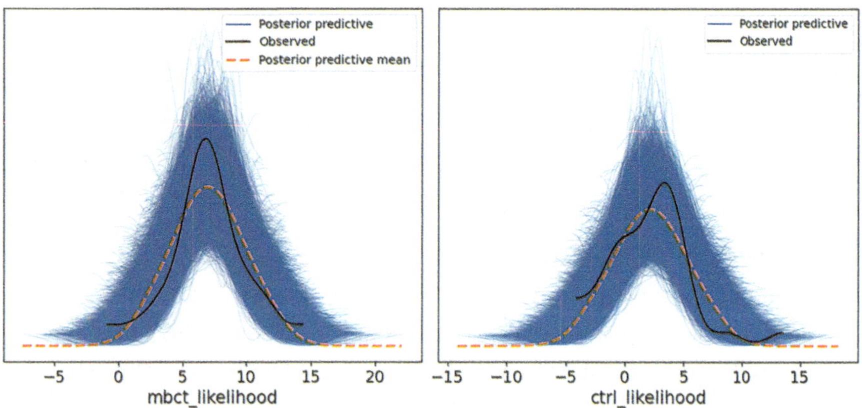

Fig. 4 Posterior predictive check

The *posterior predictive check* (PPC) visualisation (Fig. 4) offers a direct comparison between observed data and simulated data generated by the Bayesian model, separately for the MBCT and control groups. This visualisation assesses model accuracy and credibility, as a good model should generate simulated data closely resembling observed results. In both subplots, the overlapping distributions (observed data in solid black and posterior predictive simulations in blue) indicate a strong agreement between observed and model-generated data. The mean of posterior predictive distributions, shown by the dashed orange line, further underscores how accurately the model captures the real-world outcomes in both groups. The slight variability highlights the natural uncertainty inherent to psychological outcomes, which Bayesian methods explicitly quantify.

Taken together, these visualisations provide an intuitive and comprehensive interpretation of our Bayesian analysis. They demonstrate how Bayesian methods communicate uncertainty, effectiveness, and model fit, equipping researchers to make contextually detailed, informed decisions about psychological interventions such as MBCT.

References

1. A. Gelman, A. Vehtari, D. Simpson, C.C. Margossian, B. Carpenter, Y. Yao, L. Kennedy, J. Gabry, P.C. Bürkner, M. Modrák, Bayesian workflow (2020). arXiv preprint arXiv:2011.01808
2. A. Gelman, J.B. Carlin, H.S. Stern, D.B. Dunson, A. Vehtari, D.B. Rubin, *Bayesian Data Analysis* (Chapman and Hall/CRC, 2014)
3. J.O. Berger, *Statistical Decision Theory and Bayesian Analysis* (Springer, Berlin, 1985)
4. C.P. Robert, *The Bayesian Choice: From Decision-Theoretic Foundations to Computational Implementation* (Springer, Berlin, 2007)
5. D.J. Schad, M. Betancourt, S. Vasishth, Toward a principled Bayesian workflow in cognitive science. Psychol. Methods **26**(1), 103 (2021)
6. M.D. Lee, E.J. Wagenmakers, *Bayesian Cognitive Modeling: A Practical Course* (Cambridge University Press, Cambridge, 2014)
7. R. McElreath, *Statistical Rethinking: A Bayesian Course with Examples in R and Stan*, 2nd edn. (Chapman and Hall/CRC, 2020)
8. H. Jeffreys, *Theory of Probability* (Oxford University Press, Oxford, 1961)
9. J.K. Kruschke, Bayesian data analysis. Wiley Interdiscip. Rev. Cogn. Sci. **1**(5), 658 (2010)
10. R. Eric-Jan Wagenmakers, Wetzels, D. Borsboom, H.L.J. van der Maas, R.A. Kievit, Bayesian hypothesis testing for psychologists: a tutorial on the Savage-Dickey method. Cogn. Psychol. **60**, 158 (2010)
11. R. Van de Schoot, S. Depaoli, R. King, B. Kramer, K. Märtens, M.G. Tadesse, M. Vannucci, A. Gelman, D. Veen, J. Willemsen, et al., Bayesian statistics and modelling. Nat. Rev. Methods Primers **1**(1), 1 (2021)
12. U. Alter, M.A. Too, R.A. Cribbie, Navigating the Bayes maze: the psychologist's guide to Bayesian statistics, a hands-on tutorial with r code. Int. J. Psychol. **60**(1), e13271 (2025)
13. Q.F. Gronau, H. Singmann, E.J. Wagenmakers, Bridgesampling: an R package for estimating normalizing constants. J. Stat. Softw. **92**, 1 (2020)
14. R.E. Kass, A.E. Raftery, Bayes factors. J. Am. Stat. Assoc. **90**(430), 773 (1995)
15. A. Etz, Q.F. Gronau, F. Dablander, P.A. Edelsbrunner, B. Baribault, How to become a Bayesian in eight easy steps: an annotated reading list. Psychon. Bull. Rev. **25**(1), 219 (2018)
16. S. Brooks, A. Gelman, G. Jones, X.L. Meng, *Handbook of Markov Chain Monte Carlo* (Chapman & Hall/CRC, 2011)
17. M. Betancourt, A conceptual introduction to Hamiltonian Monte Carlo (2017). arXiv preprint
18. R. van de Schoot, S. Winter, M. Rhemtulla, S. Schmidt, D. Grimm, H. Hoijtink, Bayesian statistics in psychology: the good, the bad, and the ugly. Psychol. Methods **22**, 260 (2017)
19. N. Kovač, K. Ratković, H. Farahani, P. Watson, A practical applications guide to machine learning regression models in psychology with python. Methods Psychol. **11**, 100156 (2024)
20. N. Kovač, K. Ratković, P. Watson, H. Farahani, F. Bagheri Sheykhangafshe, Machine learning classification models for predicting chronic pain. Curr. Psychol. **44**, 15409–15422 (2025)
21. H. Farahani, P. Watson, T. Bezan, N. Kovač, L.C. Winter, M. Blagojević, P. Azadfallah, A. Allahyari, S. Masoumian, P. Jiménez, Psaichology: an intelligent direction in psychological sciences, in *10th International Scientific Conference Technics, Informatics and Education-TIE 2024* (Faculty of Technical Sciences Čačak, University of Kragujevac, 2024)

22. O.A. Martin, R. Kumar, J. Lao, *Bayesian Modeling and Computation in Python* (Chapman and Hall/CRC, 2021)
23. J.M. Bernardo, A.F. Smith, *Bayesian Theory*, vol. 405 (John Wiley & Sons, London, 2009)
24. R. McElreath, *Statistical Rethinking: A Bayesian Course with Examples in R and Stan* (Chapman and Hall/CRC, 2018)
25. J.K. Kruschke, Doing Bayesian data analysis: a tutorial with R, JAGS, and Stan (Academic Press, New York, 2014)
26. A. Gelman, J.B. Carlin, H.S. Stern, D.B. Dunson, A. Vehtari, D.B. Rubin, *Bayesian Data Analysis*, 3rd edn. (Chapman and Hall/CRC, 2013)
27. J. Piironen, M. Paasiniemi, A. Vehtari, Projective inference in high-dimensional problems: prediction and feature selection. Electron. J. Stat. **14**(1), 2155 (2020)
28. H. Hoijtink, I. Klugkist, P.A. Boelen, *Bayesian Evaluation of Informative Hypotheses*, vol. 361 (Springer, Berlin, 2008)
29. J.K. Kruschke, T.M. Liddell, The Bayesian new statistics: hypothesis testing, estimation, meta-analysis, and power analysis from a Bayesian perspective. Psychon. Bull. Rev. **25**, 178 (2018)
30. D.J. Spiegelhalter, K.R. Abrams, J.P. Myles, *Bayesian Approaches to Clinical Trials and Health-Care Evaluation*. Wiley Series in Probability and Statistics (2004)
31. O. Abril-Pla, V. Andreani, C. Carroll, L. Dong, C.J. Fonnesbeck, M. Kochurov, R. Kumar, J. Lao, C.C. Luhmann, O.A. Martin, et al., PyMC: a modern, and comprehensive probabilistic programming framework in Python. PeerJ Comput. Sci. **9**, e1516 (2023)
32. T.L. Griffiths, C. Kemp, J.B. Tenenbaum, *Bayesian Models of Cognition*. Cambridge Handbook of Computational Psychology (2008)
33. B.S. Coventry, E.L. Bartlett, Practical Bayesian inference in neuroscience: or how I learned to stop worrying and embrace the distribution. Eneuro **11**(7) (2024)
34. A. Vehtari, J. Ojanen, A survey of Bayesian predictive methods for model assessment, selection and comparison. Stat. Surv. **6**, 142 (2012)
35. A. Gelman, D. Lee, J. Guo, Stan: a probabilistic programming language for Bayesian inference and optimization. J. Educ. Behav. Stat. **40**(5), 530 (2015)
36. A. Inglis, A. Ahmed, B. Wundervald, E. Prado, JAGS: just another Gibbs sampler (2018). Maynooth:[sn]
37. K. Ratković, N. Kovač, M. Simeunović, Hybrid LSTM model to predict the level of air pollution in Montenegro. Appl. Sci. **13**(18), 10152 (2023)
38. J. Hodsoll, R. Strawbridge, S. King, R.W. Taylor, G. Breen, N. Grant, N. Grey, N. Hepgul, M. Hotopf, V. Kitsune, et al., Predictors of outcome following psychological therapy for depression and anxiety in an urban primary care service: a naturalistic Bayesian prediction modeling approach. Psychol. Med. **54**(16), 4503 (2024)

Support Vector Machine Algorithm

Nataša Kovač, Kruna Ratković, Marko Simeunović, Ulfeta Marovac, and Hojjatollah Farahani

1 Support Vector Machine Overview

Support vector machines (SVMs) are widely used supervised learning algorithms for both classification and regression tasks [1]. They were originally introduced as part of statistical learning theory by Vapnik and colleagues [2]. The key principle of SVM is to construct an optimal hyperplane that separates different classes in a dataset while maximising the margin between them [3]. This margin-based approach enhances generalisation, making SVM particularly effective in high-dimensional feature spaces [4].

SVM operates by identifying support vectors, which are the critical data points closest to the decision boundary. These support vectors define the optimal hyperplane. The goal of SVM is to maximise the margin between the closest data points of different classes, ensuring that the model generalises well to new data. Given a dataset of training samples $\{(x_i, y_i)\}_{i=1}^{n}$, where $x_i \in \mathbb{R}^d$ represents feature vectors and $y_i \in \{-1, 1\}$ are the corresponding class labels, the decision boundary in a hard-margin SVM is obtained by solving the following optimisation problem, as defined in Eq. 1:

N. Kovač · K. Ratković · M. Simeunović (✉)
Faculty of Applied Sciences, University of Donja Gorica, Podgorica, Montenegro
e-mail: natasa.kovac@udg.edu.me; kruna.ratkovic@udg.edu.me; marko.simeunovic@udg.edu.me

U. Marovac
Department of Technical and Technological Sciences, State University in Novi Pazar, Novi Pazar, Serbia

H. Farahani
Department of Psychology, Faculty of Humanities, Tarbiat Modares University, Tehran, Iran
e-mail: h.farahani@modares.ac.ir

N. Kovač et al. (eds.), *Data Science in Psychology*,
https://doi.org/10.1007/978-3-032-18312-5_17

$$J_{\text{hard}} = \min_{w,b} \frac{1}{2}\|w\|^2,$$
$$\text{such that} \quad y_i(w^T x_i + b) \geq 1, \quad \forall i = 1, .., n. \tag{1}$$

Here, w represents the normal vector to the hyperplane, which determines the orientation of the decision boundary, while b is the bias term that adjusts the hyperplane's position. The function J_{hard} minimises the squared norm of w, effectively maximising the margin between the closest data points of different classes.

Since real-world data is often not perfectly separable, soft-margin SVM introduces slack variables ξ_i to allow for some misclassification, leading to the modified optimisation problem given in Eq. 2.

$$J_{\text{soft}} = \min_{w,b,\xi} \frac{1}{2}\|w\|^2 + C\sum_{i=1}^{n} \xi_i,$$
$$\text{such that} \quad y_i(w^T x_i + b) \geq 1 - \xi_i, \quad \xi_i \geq 0, \quad \forall i = 1, .., n. \tag{2}$$

Here, C is a regularisation parameter that balances margin maximisation and classification errors. A high value of C imposes stricter penalties on misclassification, leading to a narrower margin, whereas a lower value allows for a wider margin but increases tolerance for misclassified points. The slack variables ξ_i measure how much each misclassified point violates the margin constraint. This formulation ensures that SVM is robust to small perturbations in the data, making it effective in handling real-world datasets that may contain noise or overlapping class distributions.

To illustrate the implementation of SVM in real-world applications, the following Python code demonstrates how to train an SVM classifier using the *radial basis function* (RBF) kernel [5].

```
import pandas as pd
from sklearn.svm import SVC
from sklearn.datasets import make_classification
from sklearn.model_selection import train_test_split
from sklearn.metrics import accuracy_score

# Load dataset from CSV file (assumed to have features
↪ 'feature1', 'feature2', and target 'label')
df = pd.read_csv("your_dataset.csv")

# Separate features and target
X = df[['feature1', 'feature2']].values
y = df['label'].values
```

```
# Split the dataset into training and testing sets
X_train, X_test, y_train, y_test = train_test_split(X, y,
↪  test_size=0.2, random_state=42)

# Train SVM with RBF kernel
svm_model = SVC(kernel='rbf', C=1.0, gamma='scale')
svm_model.fit(X_train, y_train)

# Make predictions
y_pred = svm_model.predict(X_test)

# Evaluate model performance
accuracy = accuracy_score(y_test, y_pred)
print(f"SVM Accuracy: {accuracy:.2f}")
```

The selection of the kernel function and hyperparameters plays a crucial role in the performance of SVM models. A comprehensive guide to best practices in SVM tuning is provided in the literature [6]. Beyond the choice of kernel, optimising hyperparameters such as the regularisation parameter C, the kernel parameter γ, and polynomial kernel degree d significantly impacts both classification accuracy and generalisation ability [7].

Hyperparameter tuning is particularly crucial when using non-linear kernels [8]. The gamma parameter γ, present in the RBF and polynomial kernels, controls the influence of individual training points. When γ is too large, the model captures fine details of the training data, potentially leading to overfitting. On the other hand, when γ is too small, the model produces overly simplistic decision boundaries that may fail to capture complex relationships.

For polynomial kernels, the selection of the degree d determines the complexity of the transformation applied to the feature space. Higher-degree polynomials introduce greater flexibility, allowing the model to capture intricate patterns, but at the cost of increased computational complexity and potential overfitting. The polynomial kernel also includes an additional parameter c, which influences how much higher-order polynomial terms contribute to the decision function.

Finding the optimal hyperparameter values requires systematic search techniques. Grid search is one of the most widely used methods, where a set of predefined values for each hyperparameter is systematically evaluated using cross-validation. Although exhaustive, this approach becomes computationally expensive when applied to large datasets with multiple hyperparameters. Alternatively, random search selects hyperparameter values at random within a specified range, often providing a good trade-off between efficiency and accuracy.

More advanced techniques, such as Bayesian optimisation, build probabilistic models of the objective function and refine hyperparameter selection iteratively. This approach prioritises promising parameter values based on past evaluations, reducing the number of evaluations needed to reach an optimal configuration. Evolutionary algorithms and gradient-based optimisation methods have also been explored for fine-tuning SVM parameters, particularly in cases where a high-dimensional hyperparameter space must be navigated.

To ensure robust model selection, cross-validation is commonly applied during hyperparameter tuning. K-fold cross-validation, for instance, partitions the dataset into multiple subsets, training the model on different combinations of training and validation data. This technique mitigates the risk of overfitting to a single training subset and provides a more reliable estimate of the model's generalisation performance.

In practice, hyperparameter selection should balance model complexity and computational efficiency. While aggressive tuning of parameters such as γ and d can yield high training accuracy, models must be evaluated against validation or test sets to ensure they generalise well to unseen data. Misconfigured hyperparameters can lead to either excessive sensitivity to noise in the training data or overly simplistic models that fail to capture meaningful patterns.

SVM have been widely applied across various fields, including image classification, handwriting recognition, bioinformatics, and psychological research [9]. In psychology, SVM has been used for predicting personality traits based on questionnaire responses, classifying emotional states using EEG signals [10], and analysing behavioural patterns in clinical settings. Its ability to handle high-dimensional data and robustness to overfitting make it a valuable tool in many scientific and industrial applications [11]. A contemporary example is the prediction of chronic-pain severity from psychological scales using multiple ML classifiers (including SVM) where the best model reached the strongest F1 performance for the medium-severity class [12]. The PsAIchology framework reviews AdaBoost, XGBoost, random forest, and MLP as companion methods and shows how to choose and compare algorithms using standard resampling [13].

2 Kernel Functions in SVM

The kernel function is a fundamental component of SVM, serving as the bridge that transforms complex, non-linear problems into solvable linear classification or regression problems. This transformative capability, known as the *kernel trick*, allows SVM to implicitly map inputs into high-dimensional feature spaces without explicit computations [14], thereby significantly reducing computational complexity while enhancing the model's flexibility [15].

Kernel functions compute the inner products between data points in a transformed feature space. The choice of kernel directly influences an SVM model's capability to accurately classify or regress complex datasets. Thus, understanding the intrinsic properties, advantages, and limitations of various kernel functions is critical for their successful application in psychological research, where data structures frequently exhibit complex and non-linear relationships [16]. Kernel trick enables the algorithm to handle non-linearly separable data by transforming it into a higher-dimensional space where a linear separation becomes possible [15].

Instead of explicitly computing the transformation, SVM employs a kernel function $K(x_i, x_j)$, which computes an inner product in the transformed space, allowing complex decision boundaries without explicitly increasing the computational cost.

The linear kernel, given in Eq. 3, is the simplest and computationally most efficient choice:

$$K_{\text{linear}}(x_i, x_j) = x_i^T x_j. \tag{3}$$

The linear kernel is computationally efficient and straightforward [17]. This kernel is ideal for datasets already linearly separable or nearly so. Its simplicity results in fewer hyperparameters to tune, thus minimising the risk of overfitting. It inherently lacks the flexibility to model intricate decision boundaries required by more complicated psychological datasets, especially those characterised by non-linear relationships between predictor variables [18].

Many real-world datasets exhibit non-linear patterns that require more flexible kernels. The polynomial kernel, defined in Eq. 4, introduces non-linearity through a polynomial transformation of degree d:

$$K_{\text{poly}}(x_i, x_j) = (x_i^T x_j + c)^d. \tag{4}$$

When linear separability is insufficient, the polynomial kernel becomes a viable choice. This kernel introduces non-linearity through polynomial transformations of the input features, with the hyperparameter d representing the polynomial degree and c providing a constant offset [19]. Increasing the degree d enhances the kernel's ability to capture complex patterns, such as those found in psychometric test data or neural signals. Higher-degree polynomials may lead to computational inefficiency and increased susceptibility to overfitting, necessitating careful parameter selection through rigorous cross-validation [20].

The RBF kernel, given in Eq. 5, maps data into an infinite-dimensional space using an exponential function:

$$K_{\text{RBF}}(x_i, x_j) = \exp(-\gamma \|x_i - x_j\|^2), \tag{5}$$

where γ controls the spread of the transformation. The RBF kernel is particularly effective when dealing with complex patterns. Arguably the most versatile, the RBF kernel maps data into infinite-dimensional feature spaces [21]. The RBF kernel's main advantage lies in its ability to handle datasets characterised by intricate and non-linear class boundaries, a scenario common in psychological research involving complex behaviours or cognitive phenomena [22].

The critical hyperparameter γ governs the influence radius of data points, controlling the decision boundary's smoothness. A small γ value results in smoother boundaries, suitable for noisy datasets or when generalisation is prioritised. Conversely, a large γ induces tight boundaries around training data points, possibly overfitting noisy data. Optimisation techniques such as grid search and Bayesian optimisation become crucial in fine-tuning the RBF kernel for achieving balanced generalisation performance [23].

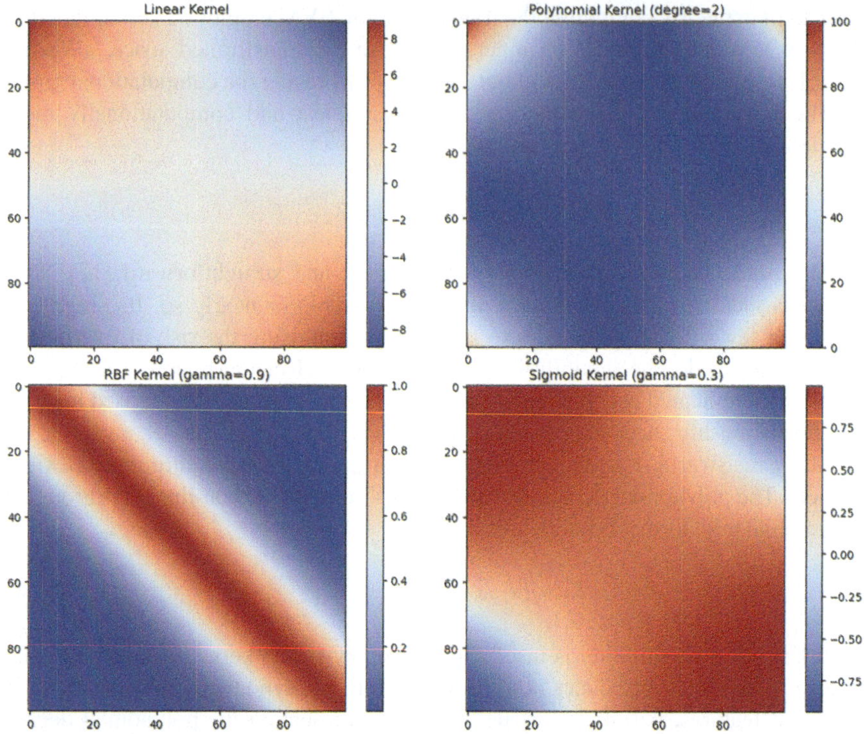

Fig. 1 Plot of different kernel functions

The sigmoid kernel, inspired by neural networks, is defined in Eq. 6:

$$K_{\text{sigmoid}}(x_i, x_j) = \tanh(\alpha x_i^T x_j + c), \tag{6}$$

where α and c control the scaling and shift of the function.

Inspired by neural network activation functions, the sigmoid kernel allows SVM models to simulate certain aspects of neural computation [17]. Although historically relevant and conceptually interesting, the sigmoid kernel's practical applicability is limited by its susceptibility to numerical instability and parameter sensitivity. Thus, it is rarely the first choice unless specific domain knowledge justifies its use, for example, in psychological tasks where data representations resemble neural network processing patterns.

Figure 1 illustrates the behaviour and characteristics of different kernel functions commonly used in machine learning algorithms, especially support vector machines. Each of the four plots shows a distinct kernel type.

The colours in Fig. 1 represent the strength and direction of the kernel function values across two dimensions. Blue regions indicate negative or lower values, while red regions denote positive or higher values. White or pale areas represent values close to zero, suggesting neutrality or no strong association between the dimensions.

These shapes and colour distributions tell us how each kernel measures similarity or distance between data points:

- *Linear kernel* has a linear (straight-line) decision boundary, evident from its simple, smooth gradient from one corner to the opposite. It separates data based on a simple linear relationship, showing straightforward associations.
- *Polynomial kernel* (degree=2) has a curved decision boundary, visible as rounded and symmetrical shapes. This kernel captures more complex relationships between variables by allowing curved rather than straight divisions, suitable for non-linear data.
- *RBF kernel* shows a diagonal, banded structure, implying a smooth and local similarity measure. It can capture highly complex and local patterns by grouping similar data points in a flexible way.
- *Sigmoid kernel* exhibits complex, wave-like patterns with alternating red and blue areas, indicating its suitability for scenarios that involve highly non-linear and complicated relationships. It is particularly sensitive to differences in input features.

The shapes and colours visualise the flexibility and complexity of each kernel in understanding and modelling relationships within data. Non-linear kernels (polynomial, RBF, and sigmoid) adapt better to complicated data structures, while the linear kernel fits simpler, more direct relationships.

Selecting the optimal kernel function and hyperparameters demands careful consideration of data characteristics, computational resources, and desired model complexity. Empirical evidence suggests employing cross-validation frameworks such as k-fold or leave-one-out cross-validation to systematically compare kernel performance. Advanced optimisation methods, including Bayesian hyperparameter optimisation and genetic algorithms, are increasingly employed to navigate the hyperparameter space effectively [24]. Recent work integrates feature selection with hyperparameter optimisation to improve accuracy and efficiency [25].

Beyond standard kernels, advanced or customised kernels have also emerged to tackle domain-specific challenges, such as structured kernels that encode spatial or temporal information. In psychological research, kernels have been customised for analysing EEG time-series data [26], textual psychometric assessments, and even eye-tracking data, allowing the encapsulation of domain-specific patterns and dependencies directly into the SVM model structure [27, 28].

3 Optimisation and Advanced Techniques

Optimisation in SVM is a crucial component that significantly influences the algorithm's performance, especially when analysing intricate and multifaceted psychological datasets. The optimisation process within SVM typically involves solving quadratic optimisation problems to find the hyperplane that maximises the margin between data points from different classes [17]. While the basic formulation of SVM optimisation was discussed previously, advanced optimisation techniques have emerged to address issues related to computational complexity, robustness, and the ability to generalise well from small or noisy datasets commonly encountered in psychological research.

One of the most prominent optimisation methods used for solving SVM's quadratic problem is *sequential minimal optimisation* (SMO) [29, 30]. SMO efficiently solves large-scale SVM training tasks by breaking down the optimisation problem into the smallest possible components. Instead of optimising all the parameters simultaneously, SMO focuses iteratively on pairs of support vectors, simplifying the quadratic programming problem into analytically solvable subproblems. This approach significantly reduces computation time, which is particularly advantageous for large psychological datasets involving extensive personality or cognitive assessments.

Another significant advancement in SVM optimisation is the introduction of *stochastic gradient descent* (SGD). Traditional SVM training methods, such as quadratic programming or interior-point algorithms, become computationally prohibitive with large datasets. In contrast, SGD methods iteratively refine the hyperplane using a random subset of the data, which greatly speeds up the convergence process and makes large-scale analyses more manageable. Authors in [31] highlighted that SGD-based approaches significantly outperform standard optimisation techniques in computational efficiency without severely compromising accuracy, which is critical when handling massive psychological datasets, such as those from social media or large-scale surveys.

To further enhance computational efficiency and model generalisation, researchers have developed various approaches to kernel approximation, such as the *Nyström method* and *random Fourier features* [32]. Kernel methods in SVM traditionally require calculations involving the kernel matrix, whose complexity scales quadratically with the dataset size. The Nyström approximation reduces this computational load by sampling a subset of data points to approximate the entire kernel matrix efficiently [33]. Similarly, random Fourier features approximate kernels through random projections, effectively transforming non-linear problems into linear ones with reduced computational demands [34, 35]. Such techniques are particularly useful in psychological applications where rapid and repeated modelling across diverse datasets is required, for example, in real-time emotion recognition or adaptive psychological interventions.

The robustness of SVM can also be enhanced through advanced regularisation methods. *Elastic net regularisation*, traditionally associated with regression models, has been successfully adapted for use in SVM to manage high-dimensional psychological data where multicollinearity is prevalent [36, 37]. Elastic net introduces a hybrid regularisation penalty combining both $L1$ and $L2$ norms, providing a balance between variable selection and shrinkage of coefficients. This approach ensures that the resulting model remains interpretable, which is crucial for psychological studies, while still maintaining high predictive accuracy. Such a method is particularly relevant in fields like psychometrics and personality research, where interpretability is essential for practical decision-making.

Ensemble methods represent another advanced approach increasingly employed alongside SVM in psychological research. These techniques aggregate multiple SVM models to enhance classification accuracy and reliability. *Bagging* (*bootstrap aggregating*) and *boosting* are two popular ensemble techniques that have shown promising results when applied to SVMs. Bagging involves generating multiple training subsets through bootstrapping, training separate SVM models on each subset, and then combining their predictions. Boosting, on the other hand, iteratively focuses on misclassified examples by previous models, adjusting the SVM's weights accordingly [38]. Ensemble SVMs have proven especially useful in clinical psychology applications, such as the prediction of psychiatric disorders from behavioural or physiological data, due to their improved robustness and accuracy [39].

Advanced SVM variants, such as structured SVM and multitask SVM, have also emerged to handle specialised psychological datasets. Structured SVM extends the classic binary classification framework to handle complex output spaces, such as sequences or trees. This capability makes structured SVM suitable for psychological tasks involving temporal or sequential data, such as modelling cognitive processes or emotional state transitions over time [40]. Multitask SVM extends standard SVM to simultaneously learn multiple related classification tasks, exploiting shared structures across tasks to improve generalisation performance [41]. This technique is particularly powerful in psychology, where tasks often involve correlated psychological constructs, such as anxiety and depression scales or cognitive subdomains in neuropsychological testing.

Recent advancements in optimisation also include incorporating domain-specific knowledge into the SVM framework through specialised kernels, which embed prior psychological theories or constraints directly into the model. For instance, kernel functions have been customised to include cognitive modelling parameters or psychometric constructs directly within the optimisation process. Such theoretically informed kernels enhance the interpretability and psychological validity of SVM-based predictions and classifications, aligning computational results closely with established psychological theories [28].

SVM can indeed suffer in high-dimensional spaces where many features are irrelevant. Feature selection provides one way to circumvent this naturally occurring complex problem. Appropriate feature selection is crucial for improving model performance, as it helps identify the most relevant attributes while reducing noise. Feature selection techniques can be categorised into three main approaches: filter, envelope, and embedding methods [42]. Filter methods, such as ANOVA and statistical tests, evaluate the importance of each feature independently and remove those that are not relevant. These methods are fast, scalable, and classifier-independent, and they can be either univariate (examining each feature individually) or multivariate (evaluating feature sets together) [43]. Wrapper methods, unlike filter methods, use a classifier to assess different feature sets. The goal is to find the set that best improves model performance, often through an iterative process. Although these methods are computationally more demanding, they generally yield better results as they directly optimise model performance. When it comes to optimising SVM models, wrapper methods are often used with metaheuristic optimisation techniques.

Metaheuristic optimisation methods, including genetic algorithms [44, 45], particle swarm optimisation, variable neighbourhood search [46], and simulated annealing, are increasingly applied to optimise hyperparameters in SVM models. Genetic algorithms are particularly popular for SVM hyperparameter tuning, given their capability to efficiently navigate complex, non-linear parameter spaces by mimicking evolutionary processes [47]. Similarly, particle swarm optimisation and simulated annealing offer robust alternatives for parameter optimisation in challenging psychological datasets, especially when traditional grid or random searches become computationally infeasible or suboptimal due to highly correlated parameters [48].

Bayesian optimisation has gained significant attention in psychological research as a superior technique for hyperparameter tuning in SVM. This method builds a probabilistic surrogate model (usually Gaussian process-based) of the optimisation landscape and sequentially samples hyperparameters to optimise model performance [23]. Bayesian optimisation efficiently addresses the *curse of dimensionality* in high-dimensional psychological data, providing systematically optimal hyperparameters with fewer model evaluations compared to grid or random search methods.

4 Applications and Case Studies

In this section, we explore how SVM can be effectively applied to classify behavioural outcomes using a variety of psychological predictors. The goal is to demonstrate how SVM can be used not only for general-purpose classification tasks but also for specific applications in psychology, where predictive modelling can aid in identifying individuals at risk or in need of intervention. Complementary ML pipelines in psychology show how multiple algorithms are spot-checked and evaluated with shared metrics before selection [49].

The dataset used in this case study consists of 10,000 participants who were assessed on a variety of psychological and behavioural metrics. Each row in the dataset corresponds to one individual and includes the following features:

- `Age`: the age of the participant in years
- `Gender`: categorical variable indicating male or female
- `PersonalityTrait`: a composite score derived from personality assessments
- `CognitiveTestScore`: results of a standardised cognitive ability test
- `StressLevel`: self-reported stress levels measured using a validated scale
- `AnxietyScore`: a numerical indicator of anxiety derived from a questionnaire
- `DepressionScore`: a numerical score reflecting depressive symptoms
- `SocialInteractionLevel`: a score indicating the level of social activity or connectedness
- `EmotionRecognition`: performance score on emotion recognition tasks
- `ExperimentalCondition`: indicates the experimental group assignment (e.g. control, TherapyA, TherapyB)

- `BehavioralOutcome` *Target*: A binary classification outcome, where the value 0 indicates no significant behavioural deviation and 1 indicates a critical behavioural pattern of interest (e.g. at-risk behaviour)

This dataset allows us to evaluate how well machine learning methods like SVM can classify participants based on their behavioural outcomes using psychological indicators. The SVM implementation is done in Python using the `scikit-learn` library. The following code outlines the complete process, from preprocessing to model training and prediction.

```
import pandas as pd
from sklearn.model_selection import train_test_split
from sklearn.svm import SVC
from sklearn.preprocessing import LabelEncoder, StandardScaler
from sklearn.metrics import accuracy_score,
↪  classification_report

# Load the dataset
df = pd.read_csv("SVM_PsychologyDataset.csv")

# Encode categorical variables
df['Gender'] = LabelEncoder().fit_transform(df['Gender'])
df['ExperimentalCondition'] =
↪  LabelEncoder().fit_transform(df['ExperimentalCondition'])

# Define features and target
X = df.drop(columns=["ParticipantID", "BehavioralOutcome"])
y = df["BehavioralOutcome"]

# Standardize features
scaler = StandardScaler()
X_scaled = scaler.fit_transform(X)

# Split the dataset into training and test sets
X_train, X_test, y_train, y_test = train_test_split(
    X_scaled, y, test_size=0.2, random_state=42
)

# Train the SVM classifier
svm_model = SVC(kernel="rbf", C=1, gamma='scale')
svm_model.fit(X_train, y_train)

# Predict and evaluate
y_pred = svm_model.predict(X_test)
print("Classification Report:\n", classification_report(y_test,
↪  y_pred))
print("Accuracy: {:.2f}".format(accuracy_score(y_test,
↪  y_pred)))
```

To begin with, the dataset is read from a file, and two categorical variables, `Gender` and `ExperimentalCondition`, are transformed into the numeric form using *label encoding*. This is necessary because machine learning models like SVM operate on numerical values, not text labels. We then define the *input features* `X`, which includes all columns that describe the participant's psychological profile, and the *output variable* `y`, which represents the binary behavioural outcome.

Before training the model, we standardise the data using a method called *feature scaling*. This ensures that all features are on the same scale, which is particularly important for algorithms like SVM, which rely on calculating distances between data points. The dataset is divided into training and test sets. The training set (80%) is used to teach the model the relationship between psychological traits and behavioural outcomes. The test set (20%) is held back and used later to evaluate how well the model can generalise to unseen data.

We then train an *SVM classifier* using the RBF kernel, which allows the model to learn complex, non-linear patterns. The kernel type, along with the parameters `C` (which controls the penalty for misclassification) and `gamma` (which defines how far the influence of a single training example reaches), is key to the performance of the model. After training, the model makes *predictions* on the test set. We use standard metrics such as *accuracy* and the *classification report* to assess how well the model performs. The report includes values such as *precision*, *recall*, and *F1-score* for each class. These same metrics were used when comparing NB, DT, GB, LGBM, SVM, and SGB for chronic-pain prediction, where SGB achieved the highest accuracy and F1 [12, 49]. The results are shown below:

```
Classification Report:
              precision    recall  F1-score   support
           0       0.70      0.99      0.82      1387
           1       0.75      0.04      0.07       613
    accuracy                           0.70      2000
   macro avg       0.73      0.52      0.45      2000
weighted avg       0.72      0.70      0.59      2000

Accuracy: 0.70
```

The classification report shows that the overall accuracy is 0.70, which may initially seem acceptable, but a closer inspection of class-specific metrics tells a different story. The classifier performs extremely well on `class 0`, achieving a high recall of 0.99, meaning that almost all class 0 instances are correctly identified. This success comes at the expense of `class 1`, where the recall drops drastically to 0.04. In practical terms, the model detects only 4% of the cases, which may represent at-risk individuals or critical psychological conditions.

This imbalance is further confirmed by the `F1-score` for class 1, which falls to just 0.07, reflecting a poor harmonic mean between precision and recall. Although precision for class 1 is relatively high at 0.75, this metric is misleading given the extremely low number of true positives retrieved. The `macro-averaged` metrics, which treat both classes equally, reinforce this weakness with a macro F1-score of 0.45, suggesting poor overall balance in the classifier's decision-making.

These results indicate that the model is *biased towards the majority class* [50] (class 0), likely due to the class imbalance in the training data and the SVM's inherent optimisation goal of maximising the margin without considering class frequencies. As a result, the model largely ignores minority-class instances in favour of achieving higher overall accuracy. This highlights a fundamental limitation of unbalanced SVM classifiers in psychological contexts where identifying minority-class outcomes is often of greater importance than overall accuracy alone.

To address this issue, subsequent refinements should include strategies such as *reweighting class importance*, applying *data resampling techniques* [51], or explicitly optimising for recall and F1-score, especially for the minority class. These steps are essential to ensure that the model remains not only statistically valid but also ethically and practically meaningful in the context of psychological assessment.

To improve model performance and mitigate the limitations observed in the initial evaluation, it is essential to explore *hyperparameter tuning*. SVMs are sensitive to the choice of their key parameters, especially the regularisation parameter *C*, the kernel coefficient *gamma*, and the *type of kernel function*. These parameters govern how flexible or constrained the decision boundary will be and how the model handles complex, potentially overlapping data distributions.

Rather than selecting these values arbitrarily, a more principled approach involves using *grid search*, which systematically evaluates combinations of hyperparameters through cross-validation. The code snippet below demonstrates the use of `GridSearchCV` to test various combinations of `C`, `gamma`, and the `rbf` kernel. Cross-validation ensures that each configuration is assessed not only on its training fit but also on its generalisation ability, thus preventing overfitting to the training data.

```
param_grid = {
    'C': [0.1, 1, 10],
    'gamma': [1, 0.1, 0.01],
    'kernel': ['rbf']
}
grid = GridSearchCV(SVC(), param_grid, refit=True, verbose=0)
grid.fit(X_train, y_train)

print("Best Parameters:", grid.best_params_)
y_pred_grid = grid.predict(X_test)
print("Tuned Accuracy: {:.2f}".format(accuracy_score(y_test,
 ↪ y_pred_grid)))
```

```
Best Parameters: {'C': 1, 'gamma': 0.1, 'kernel': 'rbf'}
Tuned Accuracy: 0.70
```

Once the grid search is completed, the best-performing combination of parameters is identified, and the model is retrained using this configuration. In this case, the optimal parameters returned were `C = 1` and `gamma = 0.1`, both of which balance regularisation and kernel influence in a way that best fits the data. Despite these adjustments, the tuned model achieved an accuracy of 0.70, which is identical to the baseline result obtained earlier. This outcome emphasises that parameter tuning, while essential, is not a guaranteed solution. It can only optimise the model within the bounds of the feature space and class separability defined by the data. In this example, the persistent performance plateau suggests that further improvement may require enhancements in data representation. In addition to parameter refinement, engineered features, alternative kernels, or balancing strategies may be needed.

5 Visualising SVM Results

Once the SVM model has been trained, a thorough evaluation of its performance and learning dynamics is crucial. In this section, we present a detailed visualisation of the trained SVM classifier's behaviour on the psychological dataset described earlier. The figures provided offer insight into the effects of kernel selection, classification efficacy, model generalisation, threshold sensitivity, and decision boundary formation.

The analysis begins with a comparison of kernel functions to understand their influence on classification accuracy. As illustrated in Fig. 2, all four commonly used

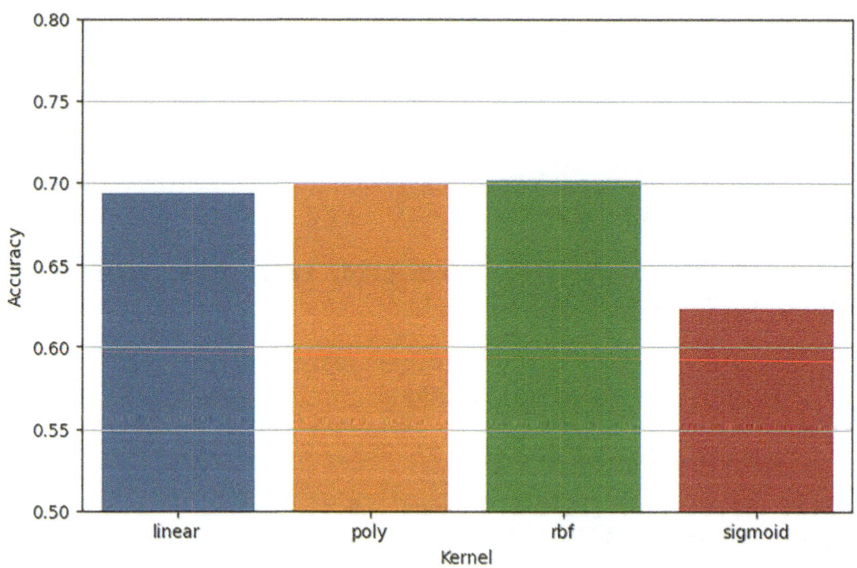

Fig. 2 Comparison of classification accuracy across different SVM kernel functions

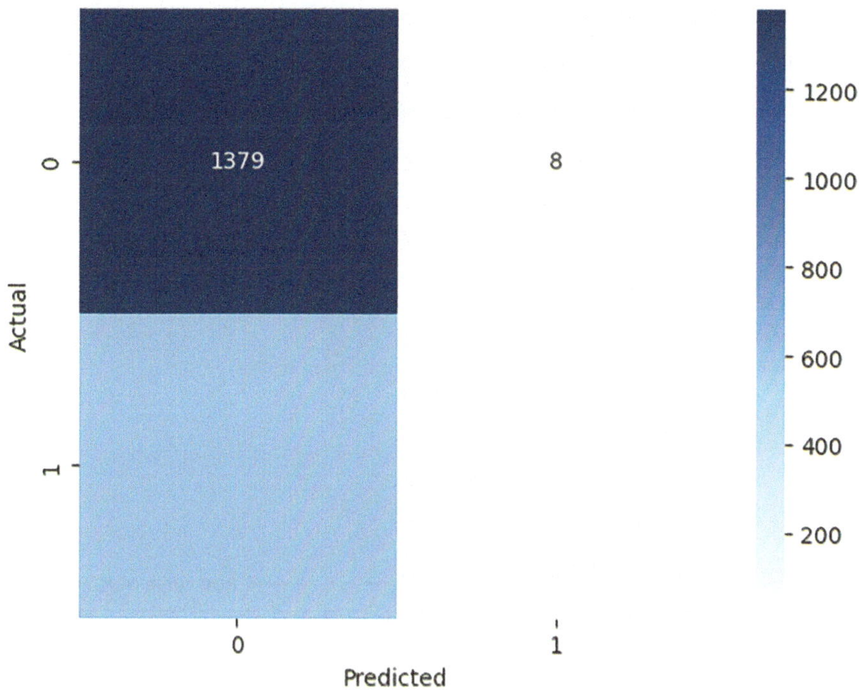

Fig. 3 Confusion matrix showing classification results for the RBF kernel

kernels were evaluated using accuracy as the primary metric. The RBF kernel shows the highest performance, albeit marginally, followed closely by polynomial and linear kernels. The sigmoid kernel underperforms significantly, which is expected given its sensitivity to parameter values and its instability in high-dimensional feature spaces.

Following kernel evaluation, the confusion matrix for the RBF kernel applied to the best-performing model is shown in Fig. 3. This visualisation provides a granular view of the classifier's predictions versus actual labels. Although the model performs reasonably well in classifying the majority class, the distribution of errors reveals a degree of imbalance [52]: The classifier shows difficulty in identifying instances of the minority class, suggesting a need for techniques like class rebalancing or threshold adjustment.

To further examine classification quality, we present the *receiver operating characteristic* (ROC) curve in Fig. 4. The ROC curve captures the trade-off between sensitivity (true positive rate) and specificity (false positive rate) across various threshold values. If we denote area under the curve as AUC, then in this case AUC = 0.61, which confirms moderate performance [53], revealing that although the SVM captures some discriminatory signal in the data, the overall class separation is limited. This is likely happening due to intrinsic overlaps in the psychological indicators.

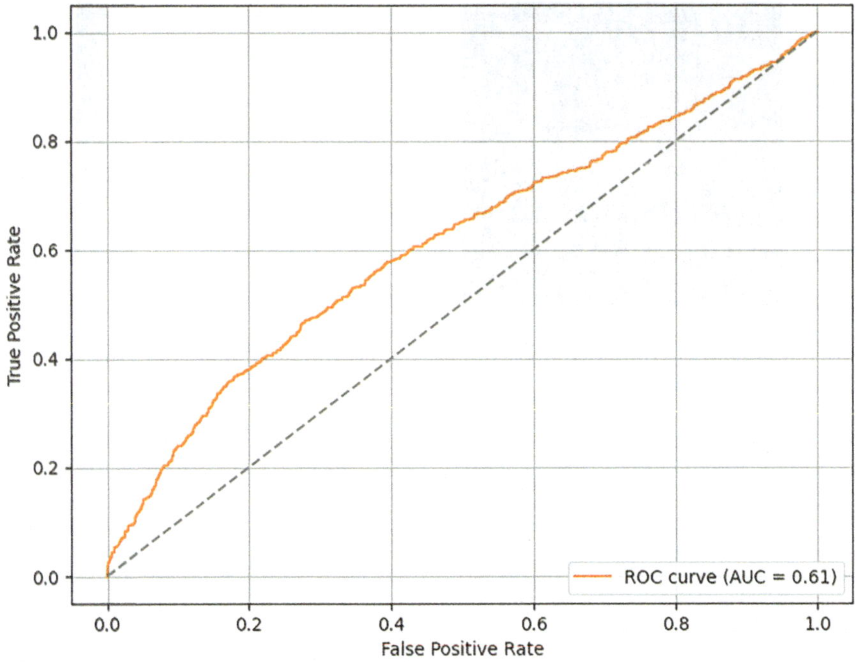

Fig. 4 Receiver operating characteristic (ROC) curve

The learning curve shown in Fig. 5 depicts how the model's accuracy evolves as the training dataset size increases. The training score begins at a higher level than the cross-validation score, indicating overfitting at smaller sample sizes. Both scores stabilise with increasing data, suggesting that the model has reached its learning capacity under current conditions and that additional data might not significantly improve generalisation unless the feature space is enhanced.

To further investigate overfitting, Fig. 6 plots the train-test accuracy gap. This generalisation gap narrows as more data is used for training, supporting the earlier observation that the model's stability improves with scale. Yet, the persistence of a non-zero gap reflects the model's inherent bias, hinting at limits imposed by feature complexity and noise.

Since classification performance may depend on the decision threshold used to convert probabilities into class labels, Fig. 7 explores test error rates as a function of this threshold. The curve reveals a U-shaped trend, with an optimal threshold around 0.45 that minimises misclassification. This finding supports the notion that default thresholds (e.g. 0.5) are often suboptimal under imbalance, and explicit threshold calibration can improve recall [54].

Figure 8 provides a visualisation of the SVM decision boundary using data projected into two dimensions via *principal component analysis* (PCA). Despite the use of a non-linear kernel (RBF), the figure shows substantial overlap between

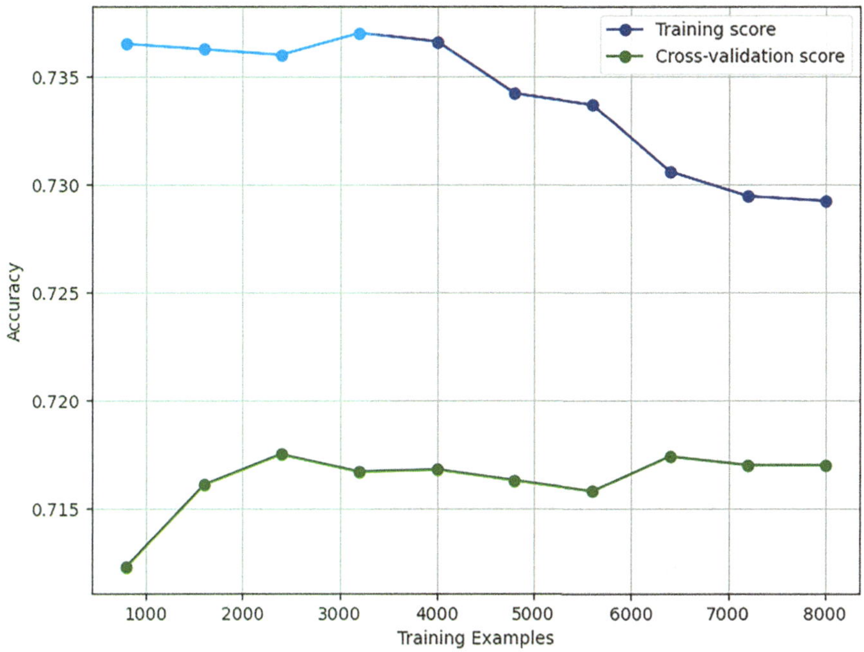

Fig. 5 Learning curve

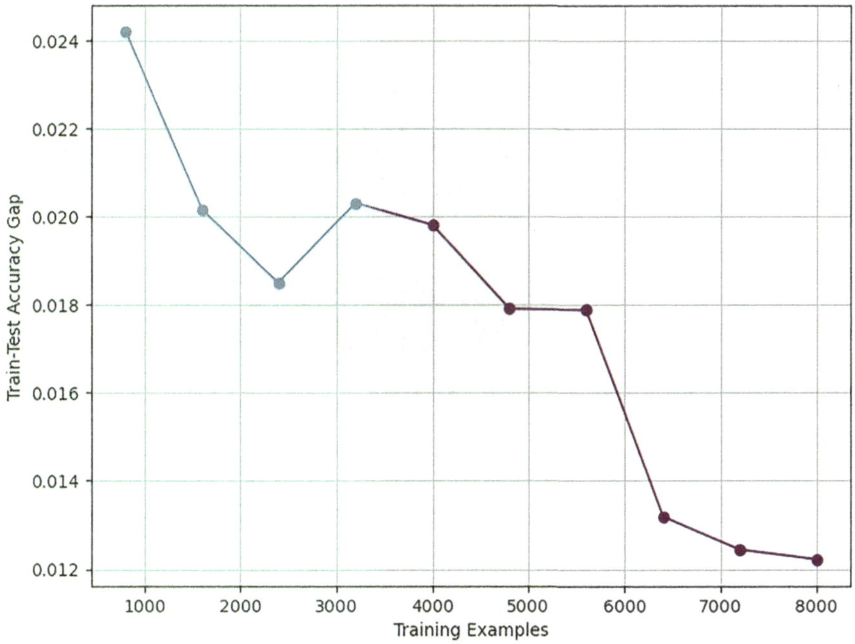

Fig. 6 Train-test accuracy gap

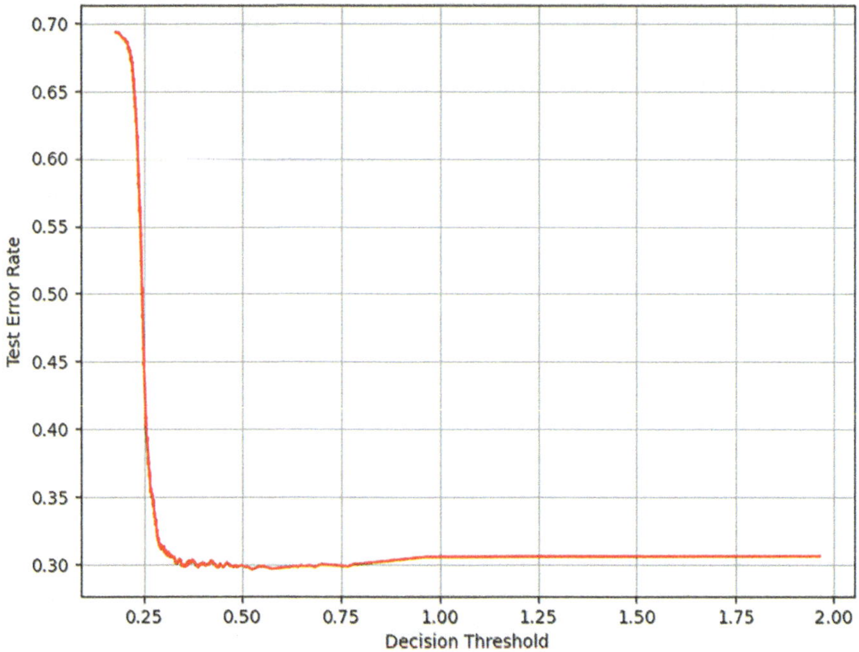

Fig. 7 Test error rate as a function of the decision threshold

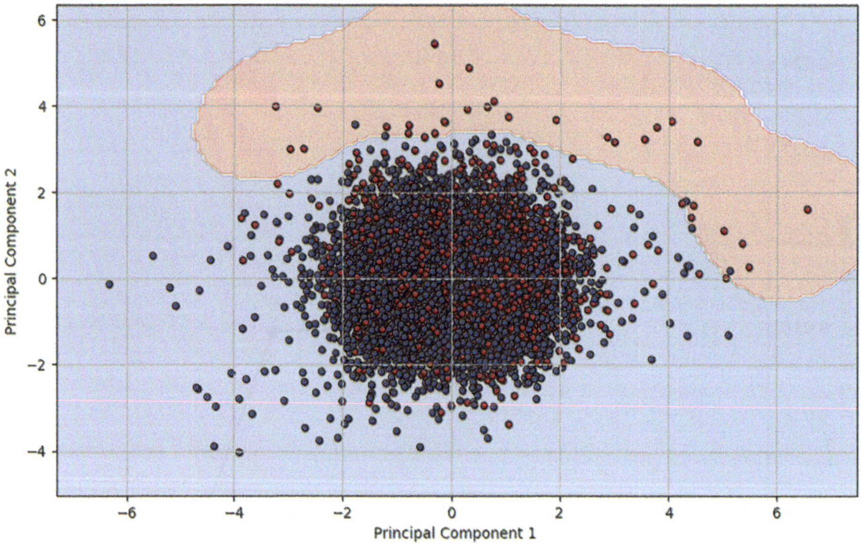

Fig. 8 Decision boundary in PCA-reduced feature space

the two classes in the projected space, visually affirming the moderate accuracy and AUC values observed earlier. The decision regions appear non-linear and adaptive, yet class separability remains limited, likely reflecting the probabilistic and noisy nature of the dataset.

References

1. J. Cervantes, F. Garcia-Lamont, L. Rodríguez-Mazahua, A. Lopez, A comprehensive survey on support vector machine classification: applications, challenges and trends. Neurocomputing **408**, 189 (2020)
2. V.N. Vapnik, *Statistical Learning Theory* (Wiley, Hoboken, 1998)
3. C. Cortes, V. Vapnik, Support-vector networks. Mach. Learn. **20**(3), 273 (1995)
4. R. Guido, S. Ferrisi, D. Lofaro, D. Conforti, An overview on the advancements of support vector machine models in healthcare applications: a review. Information **15**(4), 235 (2024)
5. C.C. Chang, C.J. Lin, LIBSVM: a library for Support Vector Machines. ACM Trans. Intell. Syst. Technol. **2**(3), 27 (2011)
6. C.W. Hsu, C.C. Chang, C.J. Lin, A practical guide to Support Vector Classification, in *Semantic Scholar Online* (2009). https://api.semanticscholar.org/CorpusID:267925897
7. Y.J. Chang, Y.L. Lin, P.F. Pai, Support vector machines with hyperparameter optimization frameworks for classifying mobile phone prices in multi-class. Electronics **14**(11), 2173 (2025)
8. M.A.K. Raiaan, S. Sakib, N.M. Fahad, A. Al Mamun, M.A. Rahman, S. Shatabda, M.S.H. Mukta, A systematic review of hyperparameter optimization techniques in convolutional neural networks. Decis. Analy. J. **11**, 100470 (2024)
9. C.J. Burges, A tutorial on Support Vector Machines for pattern recognition. Data Mining Knowl. Discovery **2**, 121 (1998)
10. A. Prakash, A. Poulose, Electroencephalogram-based emotion recognition: a comparative analysis of supervised machine learning algorithms. Data Sci. Manag. **8**, 342–360 (2025)
11. X. Zhou, X. Li, Z. Zhang, Q. Han, H. Deng, Y. Jiang, C. Tang, L. Yang, Support vector machine deep mining of electronic medical records to predict the prognosis of severe acute myocardial infarction. Front. Physiol. **13**, 991990 (2022)
12. N. Kovač, K. Ratković, P. Watson, H. Farahani, F. Bagheri Sheykhangafshe, Machine learning classification models for predicting chronic pain, Current Psychol. **44**, 1–14 (2025)
13. H. Farahani, P. Watson, T. Bezan, N. Kovač, L.C. Winter, M. Blagojević, P. Azadfallah, A. Allahyari, S. Masoumian, P. Jiménez, Psaichology: An intelligent direction in psychological sciences, in *10th International Scientific Conference Technics, Informatics and Education-TIE 2024* (Faculty of Technical Sciences Čačak, University of Kragujevac, 2024)
14. D. Cai, J. Nagy, Y. Xi, Fast deterministic approximation of symmetric indefinite kernel matrices with high dimensional datasets. SIAM J. Matrix Analy. Appl. **43**(2), 1003 (2022)
15. B. Schölkopf, A.J. Smola, *Learning with Kernels: Support Vector Machines, Regularization, Optimization, and Beyond* (MIT Press, Cambridge, 2002)
16. C.M. Bishop, N.M. Nasrabadi, *Pattern Recognition and Machine Learning*, vol. 4 (Springer, Berlin, 2006)
17. N. Cristianini, J. Shawe-Taylor, *An Introduction to Support Vector Machines and Other Kernel-Based Learning Methods* (Cambridge University Press, Cambridge, 2000)
18. K.P. Murphy, *Machine Learning: A Probabilistic Perspective* (MIT Press, Cambridge, 2012)
19. B. Schölkopf, A.J. Smola, *Learning with Kernels: Support Vector Machines, Regularization, Optimization, and Beyond* (MIT Press, Cambridge, 2008)
20. K.B. Duan, S.S. Keerthi, Which is the best multiclass SVM method? an empirical study. Lect. Not. Comput. Sci. **3541**, 278 (2005)

21. F. Wesel, K. Batselier, Large-scale learning with Fourier features and tensor decompositions. Adv. Neural Inf. Process. Syst. **34**, 17543 (2021)
22. G. James, D. Witten, T. Hastie, R. Tibshirani, *An Introduction to Statistical Learning: With Applications in R*, 2nd edn. (Springer, New York, 2021)
23. J. Snoek, H. Larochelle, R.P. Adams, Practical Bayesian optimization of machine learning algorithms, in *Neural Information Processing Systems* (2012). URL https://api.semanticscholar.org/CorpusID:632197
24. J. Bergstra, Y. Bengio, Random search for hyper-parameter optimization. J. Mach. Learn. Res. **13**, 281 (2012)
25. M. Khalil, A. AlSayed, Y. Liu, P.A. Vanrolleghem, An integrated feature selection and hyperparameter optimization algorithm for balanced machine learning models predicting N2O emissions from wastewater treatment plants. J. Water Process Eng. **63**, 105512 (2024)
26. H.A. Hamzah, K.K. Abdalla, EEG-based emotion recognition systems; comprehensive study. Heliyon **10**(10), e31485 (2024)
27. F. Lotte, A review of classification algorithms for EEG-based brain–computer interfaces: a 10 year update. J. Neural Eng. **11**(3), 031005 (2014)
28. Y. Wang, W. Fu, Customized kernel SVM for classification of psychological text. J. Comput. Psychol. **3**, 45 (2021)
29. J.C. Platt, Fast training of Support Vector Machines using sequential minimal optimization, in *Advances in Kernel Methods* (1999), pp. 185–208
30. C. Zhao, L. Dai, Y. Huang, Fractional order sequential minimal optimization classification method. Fractal Fract. **7**(8), 637 (2023)
31. L. Bottou, *Proceedings of COMPSTAT'2010* (Springer, Berlin, 2010), pp. 177–186
32. A. Abedsoltan, P. Pandit, L. Rademacher, M. Belkin, On the Nyström approximation for preconditioning in kernel machines, in *International Conference on Artificial Intelligence and Statistics* (PMLR, 2024), pp. 3718–3726
33. C.K.I. Williams, C.E. Rasmussen, *Gaussian Processes for Machine Learning* (MIT Press, Cambridge, 2006)
34. A. Rahimi, B. Recht, Random features for large-scale kernel machines, in *Advances in Neural Information Processing Systems (NeurIPS)*, vol. 20 (2008)
35. Z. Li, Sharp analysis of random Fourier features in classification, in *Proceedings of the AAAI Conference on Artificial Intelligence*, vol. 36 (2022), pp. 7444–7452
36. H. Zou, T. Hastie, Regularization and variable selection via the elastic net. J. R. Stat. Soc. Ser. B (Stat. Methodol.) **67**(2), 301 (2005)
37. M. Yang, H. Liang, X. Wu, Z. Zhang, A flexible and efficient algorithm for high dimensional support vector regression. Neurocomputing **611**, 128671 (2025)
38. T.G. Dietterich, Ensemble methods in machine learning. Lecture Not. Comput. Sci. **1857**, 1 (2000)
39. Y. Fu, X. Li, Y. Wang, Feature extraction for multi-class classification tasks: a review. Pattern Recogn. **99**, 107077 (2020)
40. I. Tsochantaridis, T. Joachims, T. Hofmann, Y. Altun, Large margin methods for structured and interdependent output variables. J. Mach. Learn. Res. **6**, 1453 (2005)
41. T. Evgeniou, M. Pontil, Regularized multi-task learning, in *Proceedings of the ACM SIGKDD International Conference on Knowledge Discovery and Data Mining* (2004), pp. 109–117
42. L. Ladha, T. Deepa, Feature selection methods and algorithms. Int. J. Comput. Sci. Eng. **3**(5), 1787 (2011)
43. J. Weston, S. Mukherjee, O. Chapelle, M. Pontil, T. Poggio, V. Vapnik, Feature selection for SVMs, in *Advances in Neural Information Processing Systems*, 13 (2000)
44. N. Kovač, T. Davidović, Z. Stanimirović, Population-based metaheuristics for the dynamic minimum cost hybrid berth allocation problem. Int. J. Artif. Intell. Tools **30**(04), 2150017 (2021)
45. K. Ratković, N. Kovač, M. Simeunović, Hybrid LSTM model to predict the level of air pollution in Montenegro. Appl. Sci. **13**(18), 10152 (2023)

46. N. Kovač, T. Davidović, Z. Stanimirović, Variable neighborhood search methods for the dynamic minimum cost hybrid berth allocation problem. Inf. Technol. Control **47**(3), 471 (2018)
47. I. Syarif, A. Prugel-Bennett, G. Wills, SVM parameter optimization using grid search and genetic algorithm. Procedia Comput. Sci. **72**, 324 (2016)
48. J. Kennedy, R. Eberhart, Particle swarm optimization, in *Proceedings of ICNN'95-International Conference on Neural Networks*, vol. 4 (IEEE, 1995), pp. 1942–1948
49. N. Kovač, K. Ratković, H. Farahani, P. Watson, A practical applications guide to machine learning regression models in psychology with python. Methods Psychol. **11**, 100156 (2024)
50. S.F. Taskiran, B. Turkoglu, E. Kaya, T. Asuroglu, A comprehensive evaluation of oversampling techniques for enhancing text classification performance. Sci. Rep. **15**(1), 21631 (2025)
51. R. Hasan, S.M.R. Islam, A comparative analysis of emotion recognition from EEG signals using temporal features and hyperparameter-tuned machine learning techniques, MethodsX **15**, 103468 (2025)
52. W. Chen, K. Yang, Z. Yu, Y. Shi, C.P. Chen, A survey on imbalanced learning: latest research, applications and future directions. Artif. Intell. Rev. **57**(6), 137 (2024)
53. G. Khyathi, K. Indumathi, A. Jumana Hasin, M. Lisa Flavin Jency, G. Krishnaprakash, F.J.M. LISA, et al., Support vector machines: a literature review on their application in analyzing mass data for public health. Cureus **17**(1), e77169 (2025)
54. M. Abdelhamid, A. Desai, Balancing the scales: A comprehensive study on tackling class imbalance in binary classification (2024). arXiv preprint arXiv:2409.19751

Classification in Psychological Research

Nataša Kovač, Kruna Ratković, Marko Simeunović, Ulfeta Marovac, Hojjatollah Farahani, and Liang Zhao

1 Introduction to Decision Trees

Decision trees represent one of the most interpretable and accessible methods in the machine learning toolkit, particularly useful in the context of psychological research. At their core, decision trees are hierarchical models that recursively partition data according to feature values, forming a tree-like structure where each internal node represents a decision rule, and each leaf node corresponds to a class label or regression output [1, 2]. This interpretability makes decision trees a natural fit for domains like psychology, where transparency in decision-making is essential for clinical and theoretical applications.

In psychological research, classification problems often arise when attempting to distinguish between mental health conditions, predict cognitive styles, or assess risk for behavioural disorders based on observed data [3]. Beyond clinical pain, classification has been used to model risk for love addiction from affective and interpersonal predictors [4]. For instance, decision trees have been applied to predict

N. Kovač (✉) · K. Ratković · M. Simeunović
Faculty of Applied Sciences, University of Donja Gorica, Podgorica, Montenegro
e-mail: natasa.kovac@udg.edu.me; kruna.ratkovic@udg.edu.me; marko.simeunovic@udg.edu.me

U. Marovac
Department of Technical and Technological Sciences, State University in Novi Pazar, Novi Pazar, Serbia

H. Farahani
Department of Psychology, Faculty of Humanities, Tarbiat Modares University, Tehran, Iran
e-mail: h.farahani@modares.ac.ir

L. Zhao
Faculty of Philosophy, Science and Letters at Ribeirão Preto, University of São Paulo, Ribeirão Preto—SP, Brazil
e-mail: zhiyongzhang@nd.edu

N. Kovač et al. (eds.), *Data Science in Psychology*,
https://doi.org/10.1007/978-3-032-18312-5_18

depressive symptoms from survey data, using features such as residential facilities, demographic indicators, and qualification [5]. Similarly, they have been used to identify children at risk of attention-deficit/hyperactivity disorder by analysing patterns in behavioural checklists [6].

What makes decision trees especially compelling in psychology is their alignment with the way humans tend to reason through problems. Psychologists frequently employ structured if-then reasoning, which mirrors the logical splits in a decision tree. This resemblance facilitates better communication between data scientists and mental health professionals and broader acceptance of computational tools in the psychological sciences [7, 8].

Another strength of decision trees is their ability to handle non-linear relationships and interactions between variables. Psychological phenomena are rarely governed by linear trends; instead, they are characterised by thresholds, context dependencies, and individual differences [9]. For example, a small increase in stress might have little impact on cognitive performance until a certain threshold is reached, after which performance drops sharply. Decision trees can capture such patterns without requiring prior assumptions about the form of the relationship.

Decision trees also come with limitations. They tend to overfit training data, especially when grown without constraints on tree depth or minimum leaf size [10]. This can result in overly complex models that do not generalise well to new data. In psychological research, where sample sizes are often small and noise is high, this risk is particularly acute. Techniques like pruning, setting maximum depths, or using ensemble methods like random forests (discussed in Sect. 3) are commonly employed to mitigate this issue.

Despite these challenges, the advantages of decision trees in psychological applications are significant. Their interpretability supports transparent decision-making in clinical settings, such as diagnostics and treatment planning [11]. In educational psychology, decision trees have been used to model student dropout risk or engagement patterns, enabling timely intervention strategies based on clearly defined indicators [12].

As classification becomes an increasingly integral part of psychological science, particularly in data-driven subfields like computational psychiatry and digital mental health, the role of interpretable models like decision trees will likely grow. Researchers and practitioners alike benefit from models that not only provide accurate predictions but also explain how those predictions were made. This characteristic positions decision trees as foundational tools in modern psychological data analysis.

2 Building and Optimising Decision Trees

Decision trees are widely used in psychological research for classification tasks due to their interpretability and flexibility in handling different types of data. A decision tree is a hierarchical structure where data is split recursively based on feature values to form a predictive model. It consists of nodes representing decisions, branches indicating possible outcomes, and terminal leaves denoting class labels or numerical predictions. The process of constructing a decision tree involves selecting an optimal feature at each node to maximise classification accuracy while minimising complexity [1, 2].

The fundamental principle behind decision tree construction is the recursive partitioning of the input space based on criteria that maximise information gain. Given a dataset with feature vectors $X = \{x_1, x_2, \ldots, x_n\}$ and corresponding labels $Y = \{y_1, y_2, \ldots, y_n\}$, the algorithm begins with the entire dataset at the root node and iteratively splits it into subsets. The selection of the optimal splitting criterion is crucial for the model's predictive power. A commonly used criterion for selecting the optimal split is entropy, which quantifies the level of disorder or uncertainty in a dataset and is defined by Eq. (1):

$$H(S) = -\sum_{i=1}^{m} p_i \log_2 p_i, \tag{1}$$

where $H(S)$ represents the entropy of dataset S, p_i is the proportion of instances belonging to class i, and m is the total number of classes. A lower entropy value indicates a purer subset, leading to more effective splits.

An alternative impurity measure is the Gini index, which is commonly used in decision tree algorithms such as classification and regression trees [2]. The Gini index measures the probability of incorrect classification if a random sample is assigned a label according to the class distribution in the dataset and is given by Eq. (2):

$$G(S) = 1 - \sum_{i=1}^{m} p_i^2, \tag{2}$$

where $G(S)$ represents the impurity of dataset S, and p_i is the proportion of instances belonging to class i. A lower Gini value indicates a more homogeneous split, leading to improved classification performance.

The choice of splitting criterion determines how the decision tree partitions the data at each node and measures the homogeneity of the resulting subsets. Entropy, derived from information theory, quantifies the uncertainty in a dataset and is often used in information gain-based splits. It can sometimes produce more optimal splits in certain datasets. The Gini index, on the other hand, measures the probability of misclassification and is computationally simpler, making it a preferred choice in large-scale datasets [1, 2].

Once a splitting criterion is selected, the tree continues to grow until it reaches a stopping condition, such as a predefined depth, a minimum number of samples per leaf, or minimal information gain. Excessively growing a tree can lead to overfitting, where the model memorises the training data instead of generalising to unseen samples. To prevent overfitting, decision trees employ pruning techniques, which simplify the tree by removing less informative branches [13, 14]. Pruning can be performed either during the tree-growing process (pre-pruning) or after the tree has fully grown (post-pruning). Pre-pruning involves setting constraints on tree depth, minimum sample size, or information gain threshold, while post-pruning removes branches that contribute minimally to predictive accuracy based on validation data.

Hyperparameter optimisation is another key aspect of refining decision tree models. Tuning parameters such as maximum tree depth, minimum samples per split, and splitting criteria can significantly impact classification performance. Decision trees with unrestricted depth often lead to overfitting, capturing noise instead of meaningful patterns in the training data. Conversely, overly shallow trees may underfit, failing to capture the underlying structure of the data. Setting an appropriate maximum depth ensures a balance between complexity and generalisation, reducing both underfitting and overfitting. The minimum number of samples required to split an internal node controls how often the tree branches, influencing the granularity of the learned decision rules. A higher threshold for this parameter results in a more generalised model, while a lower threshold can make the tree overly sensitive to small variations in the data [1, 2].

To identify the optimal hyperparameters, a variety of search techniques can be employed. Grid search systematically evaluates all possible combinations of hyperparameter values within a predefined range. Although exhaustive, this approach becomes computationally expensive when dealing with large parameter spaces. Random search, on the other hand, selects random combinations of hyperparameters and often finds near-optimal solutions with significantly fewer iterations, making it a more efficient alternative [15].

More advanced techniques, such as Bayesian optimisation, leverage probabilistic models to guide the search process, prioritising promising regions of the hyperparameter space rather than randomly sampling it. This method reduces computational cost while improving efficiency, particularly for models that require intensive computations [16]. For instance, GA-guided tuning within hybrid deep learning/ensemble models has been shown to improve predictive accuracy [17]. Regularisation techniques, such as cost complexity pruning, penalise excessive branching to prevent overfitting. This is achieved by introducing a regularisation parameter that controls the complexity of the tree, ensuring that splits occur only when they provide significant improvement in classification performance [18].

Cross-validation is another essential strategy in hyperparameter tuning. Instead of evaluating the model on a single training-test split, k-fold cross-validation partitions the dataset into multiple subsets, training the model on different combinations of training and validation data. This technique provides a more reliable estimate of generalisation performance by reducing the impact of randomness in data partitioning [19]. By combining cross-validation with grid or Bayesian search, researchers can optimise decision tree hyperparameters effectively, ensuring a well-calibrated model that generalises well to unseen data.

In psychological research, decision trees are employed in various applications, including personality classification, cognitive assessment, and mental health diagnostics. Their ability to handle categorical and numerical data while providing human-interpretable decision rules makes them particularly valuable for studying complex behavioural patterns. Despite their advantages, decision trees can suffer from instability, where small changes in data lead to entirely different tree structures. To mitigate this issue, ensemble methods such as random forests and boosting algorithms are often used to improve predictive stability and accuracy [2].

The effectiveness of a decision tree depends not only on the algorithm's parameters but also on the quality of input data. Feature selection and preprocessing play a critical role in optimising decision tree performance. Redundant or irrelevant features can introduce noise and lead to unnecessary splits, reducing model interpretability. Feature importance scores derived from trained decision trees can guide the selection of the most informative predictors, ensuring a more parsimonious and efficient model.

3 Introduction to Random Forests

Random forests are a well-known machine learning algorithm, particularly well-suited for complex datasets like those often encountered in psychological research. Introduced by Breinman [20], this ensemble learning method combines multiple decision trees to enhance predictive accuracy and reduce overfitting. Unlike single decision trees, which are prone to capturing noise and patterns specific to the training data, random forests aggregate predictions from an ensemble of decorrelated trees, resulting in a robust and reliable model. This inherent resilience and flexibility have made random forests a cornerstone in data-driven psychology.

The foundational principle of random forests is bagging, or bootstrap aggregation, in which multiple decision trees are trained on random subsets of the data. A random subset of features is selected at each split within a tree. This dual randomness, sampling data and selecting features, reduces the correlation between trees in the ensemble, thereby improving generalisability. For classification tasks, the final prediction is determined by majority voting, while for regression tasks, it is the average of individual tree predictions [21]. This mechanism ensures that the overall model is less likely to overfit the training data, a property that is critical in fields such as psychology, where datasets often exhibit variability and noise [19].

A significant advantage of random forests is their capacity to effectively manage intricate, high-dimensional datasets with non-linear relationships [20]. Psychological datasets often contain a mix of numerical, categorical, and ordinal variables, along with missing data and multi-collinearity. Random forests are non-parametric, meaning they make no assumptions about the underlying data distribution, making them an excellent choice for these diverse datasets. The algorithm's built-in feature importance metrics provide insights into the relative influence of predictors. For instance, in studies exploring factors that contribute to anxiety, random forests can highlight the most significant predictors, such as self-reported stress, sleep quality, or social connectedness, offering valuable insights into underlying psychological mechanisms [22].

Another significant advantage of random forests is their ability to handle missing data effectively. Unlike traditional models, which often require imputation or data exclusion, random forests use surrogate splits to make predictions for missing values. This characteristic makes the method particularly practical for psychological research, where incomplete data is a common challenge. The model provides robust *out-of-bag* (OOB) error estimates, eliminating the need for additional validation datasets. This internal evaluation method uses samples excluded during bootstrapping to estimate prediction error, providing an unbiased assessment of model performance.

Beyond their general utility, random forests have been adapted to meet specific challenges in machine learning and psychological research. Conditional inference forests, for example, address biases in traditional random forests by employing statistical hypothesis testing to select splits. This ensures that predictors with more categories or higher variance do not disproportionately influence feature importance scores [23]. Another notable adaptation is weighted random forests, which assign higher importance to certain samples or features. This is particularly useful in imbalanced datasets, such as when studying rare psychological conditions like *post-traumatic stress disorder* (PTSD) or eating disorders.

Random forests also have some limitations. Training large forests with many trees can be computationally intensive, especially for high-dimensional data. The feature importance metrics provided by traditional random forests can be biased, favouring predictors with more levels or greater variability. Researchers often mitigate this issue by using permutation-based feature importance, which provides a more accurate representation of variable contributions [24].

The versatility of random forests extends to various psychological domains. For instance, in neuropsychology, random forests are used to classify cognitive states based on neuroimaging data, providing insights into brain-behaviour relationships [25]. In mental health studies, the algorithm helps predict conditions such as depression or anxiety based on demographic, behavioural, and environmental factors. Furthermore, their ability to integrate data from diverse modalities, such as survey responses, physiological measures, and genetic information, makes random forests an invaluable tool for interdisciplinary research.

Random forests also offer unique advantages when applied to exploratory data analysis. Proximity matrices derived from the algorithm can be used to identify clusters within data, revealing latent patterns that may inform theoretical frameworks in psychology. For example, proximity-based clustering could identify subgroups within a population experiencing stress, allowing researchers to tailor interventions to specific needs.

Several variations of random forests have emerged to address domain-specific challenges. *Random survival forests*, for example, are designed to model time-to-event data and are frequently used in longitudinal psychological studies. Proximal random forests incorporate spatial or temporal dependencies, making them suitable for analysing repeated measures data. *Extra trees*, or *extremely randomised trees*, introduce additional randomness during training, resulting in faster training times and reduced computational overhead while maintaining competitive performance [26].

The random forest algorithm begins by preparing multiple subsets of the original dataset through a process called bootstrap sampling [20]. This involves randomly selecting data points with replacements and creating unique datasets for training individual decision trees. Each subset of data serves as the input for one tree, ensuring that no two trees are trained on the same data. During the construction of each decision tree, a random subset of features is chosen at each decision node, or *split* [27]. The random selection of features generates variability among the trees, ensuring that each tree emphasises different aspects of the dataset. This variability strengthens the ensemble's capacity to recognise and capture the fundamental patterns within the data more efficiently.

Once all the decision trees in the forest are trained, the algorithm becomes ready for prediction. When new data is presented to the random forest, it is passed through each tree independently. Each tree provides its prediction based on the patterns it has learned during training. These individual predictions are then aggregated to form the final output of the forest. In classification tasks, the final prediction is determined by the majority vote across all the trees, while in regression tasks, the final output is calculated by averaging the predictions from each tree to produce a continuous value.

This process of creating a random forest—bootstrapping the data, constructing decision trees with random feature selection, and aggregating predictions—allows the algorithm to combine the results of multiple models into a single cohesive output, reducing the impact of errors made by any individual tree. Random forests are a powerful, flexible, and interpretable machine learning tool that aligns seamlessly with the needs of psychological research. Their ability to handle diverse data types, address missingness, and provide insights into variable importance makes them invaluable for exploring complex psychological phenomena. As computational efficiency improves and new variations emerge, the role of random forests in psychology will undoubtedly continue to expand, offering deeper insights into the intricacies of human behaviour.

4 Multi-Layer Perceptron Classifier

The *multi-layer perceptron* (MLP) represents the most fundamental architecture in deep learning, serving as both a historical milestone and a practical tool for contemporary machine learning tasks. Its development goes back to Rosenblatt's pioneering work on the perceptron [28], which established the basic framework of artificial neurons. The critical breakthrough came with the introduction of hidden layers and the backpropagation algorithm in the 1980s [29], which transformed the perceptron from a linear classifier into a universal function approximator.

The theoretical foundation was solidified by Cybenko's *universal approximation theorem* [30], which proved that a single hidden layer with sufficient width could approximate any continuous function with arbitrary precision. This mathematical guarantee, combined with the development of practical training techniques, elevated

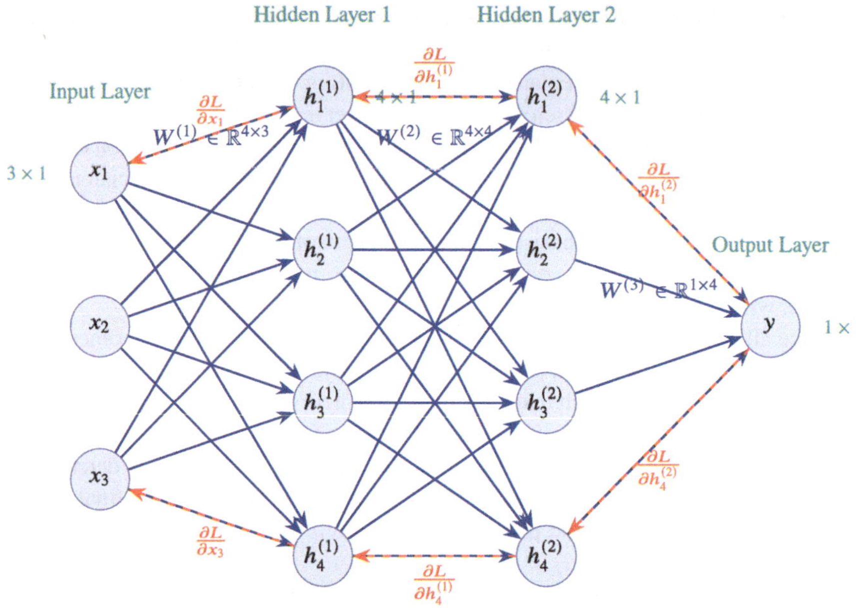

Fig. 1 Detailed computation graph of a 3-layer MLP: (**a**) forward pass showing dimensional transformations, (**b**) backward pass illustrating gradient flow through the chain rule (red arrows)

MLPs from theoretical curiosities to powerful tools for pattern recognition and function approximation.

In modern practice, MLPs continue to play three vital roles:

- As pedagogical tools for teaching neural network fundamentals
- As baseline models for tabular data tasks, where their fully connected nature is advantageous
- As components in more complex architectures (e.g. transformer feed-forward layers [31])

At the heart of the MLP lies its layered structure (see Fig. 1), where each layer performs a two-stage transformation of its inputs. Consider an MLP with L hidden layers processing an input vector $\mathbf{x} \in \mathbb{R}^d$:

$$\mathbf{h}^{(l)} = \sigma(\mathbf{W}^{(l)}\mathbf{h}^{(l-1)} + \mathbf{b}^{(l)}), \quad l = 1, \ldots, L, \tag{3}$$

where $\mathbf{h}^{(0)} = \mathbf{x}$, $\mathbf{W}^{(l)} \in \mathbb{R}^{n_l \times n_{l-1}}$ is the weight matrix, $\mathbf{b}^{(l)} \in \mathbb{R}^{n_l}$ the bias vector, and σ the activation function. The final output $\hat{y}$ is obtained by applying an output-specific transformation (e.g. softmax for classification).

This layered design creates a feature hierarchy where lower layers capture simple patterns (e.g. edges in images or word stems in text), while higher layers combine these into more complex representations (e.g. digit shapes or semantic phrases). The depth of this hierarchy directly influences the network's representational capacity, although practical considerations such as training stability impose limits on usable depth [32].

The choice of activation function σ critically impacts the network behaviour. Three principal classes dominate modern applications: *rectified linear unit* (ReLU), sigmoid, and tanh functions.

ReLU is defined as $f(x) = \max(0, x)$ and has become the default choice due to:

- Sparse activations that improve computational efficiency
- Constant gradient for positive inputs that mitigates vanishing gradients
- Empirical success in deep networks [33]

Advanced variants like Leaky ReLU and Swish [34] address the *dying ReLU* problem while maintaining these benefits.

The sigmoid $\frac{1}{1+e^{-x}}$ and tanh functions were historically important but now mainly serve in:

- Output layers for binary classification
- Gating mechanisms in recurrent architectures

Their saturated gradients pose significant training challenges in deep networks [35].

The backpropagation algorithm efficiently computes gradients by recursively applying the chain rule, propagating errors backwards through the network. For a multi-layer perceptron with L hidden layers and a loss function $\mathcal{L}$, the process begins at the output layer and continues to work towards the input layer. Define $\mathbf{h}^{(l)}$ as the output of layer l, $\mathbf{z}^{(l)} = \mathbf{W}^{(l)}\mathbf{h}^{(l-1)} + \mathbf{b}^{(l)}$ as the pre-activation input to the activation function σ, and $\delta^{(l)}$ as the error signal (or gradient) at layer l. The key steps are the following.

$$\delta^{(L)} = \nabla_{\mathbf{h}^{(L)}}\mathcal{L} \tag{4}$$

$$\delta^{(l)} = (\mathbf{W}^{(l+1)\top}\delta^{(l+1)}) \odot \sigma'(\mathbf{z}^{(l)}) \tag{5}$$

$$\frac{\partial \mathcal{L}}{\partial \mathbf{W}^{(l)}} = \delta^{(l)}\mathbf{h}^{(l-1)\top}, \tag{6}$$

where $\odot$ denotes element-wise multiplication, and $\sigma'(\mathbf{z}^{(l)})$ is the derivative of the activation function. Equation (4) initialises the error in the output layer, Eq. (5) propagates it backwards layer by layer, and Eq. (6) computes the gradient for the weight matrix $\mathbf{W}^{(l)}$. This formulation enables efficient gradient computation for all parameters in a single backward pass [36], as illustrated in Fig. 2.

As it is shown in Fig. 2, the algorithm propagates error signals (red) backwards from the output layer to efficiently compute gradients for all parameters. A common application of MLPs is classification, where the network predicts discrete categories from input data. For instance, consider the task of classifying handwritten digits (0–9) using the *Modified National Institute of Standards and Technology* (MNIST) dataset. The input $\mathbf{x} \in \mathbb{R}^{784}$ represents a flattened 28×28 pixel image, and the output $\hat{\mathbf{y}} \in \mathbb{R}^{10}$ provides probabilities for each digit class.

The MLP processes the input through its hidden layers, with the final layer applying a softmax activation:

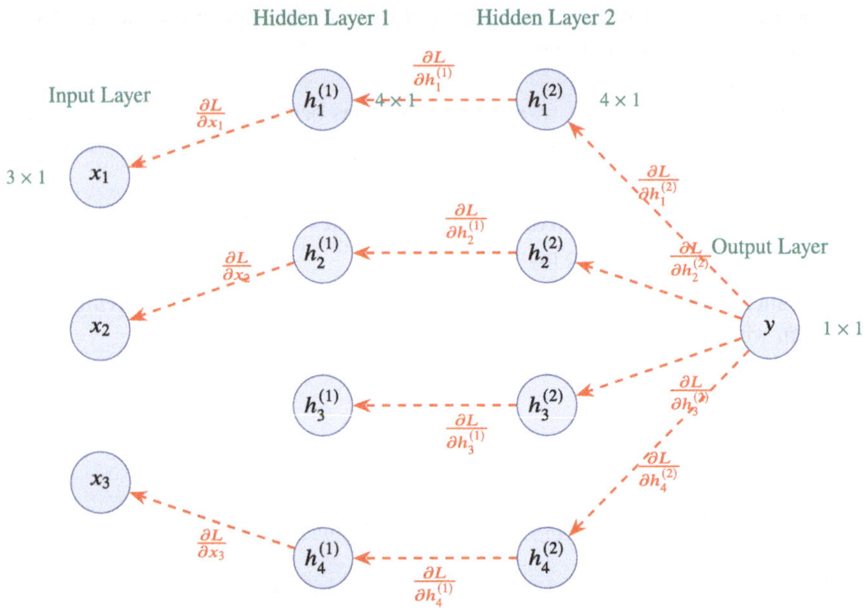

Fig. 2 Information flow during backpropagation

$$\hat{\mathbf{y}} = \text{softmax}(\mathbf{W}^{(L+1)}\mathbf{h}^{(L)} + \mathbf{b}^{(L+1)}), \tag{7}$$

where $\text{softmax}(z_i) = \frac{e^{z_i}}{\sum_j e^{z_j}}$ converts raw scores into probabilities. During training, the cross-entropy loss measures the difference between $\hat{\mathbf{y}}$ and the true label $\mathbf{y}$:

$$\mathcal{L} = -\sum_{i=1}^{10} y_i \log(\hat{y}_i). \tag{8}$$

Backpropagation then optimises the network parameters to minimise this loss, enabling the MLP to learn patterns distinguishing each digit. This approach exemplifies how MLPs serve as effective classifiers for tabular or flattened data [29].

The multi-layer perceptron remains the prototypical neural network architecture, embodying core deep learning principles:

- Hierarchical feature learning through successive transformations
- The critical role of non-linear activations
- The importance of efficient gradient computation

Although specialised architectures have surpassed MLPs in specific domains, their fundamental concepts underpin all modern neural networks. The next chapter will explore how convolutional networks extend these ideas to spatially structured data.

5 One-Dimensional Convolutional Neural Networks

Convolutional neural networks (ConvNets) are highly efficient for processing data in the form of multi-dimensional arrays, such as 1D sequences (speech, text), 2D images, and 3D volumetric data (videos). The efficiency of these networks comes from four key features: local connections, weight sharing, pooling, and multi-layer processing, which enable pattern recognition independent of their position. ConvNets are inspired by the way information is processed in the human visual cortex, and since their inception in the 1990s, they have been successfully applied to tasks such as speech recognition, handwriting character recognition, face detection, and other complex problems.

The architecture of convolutional networks consists of alternating convolutional and pooling layers, which analyse data through hierarchical levels. In the convolutional layers, filters (or kernels) are applied to the input data to detect local features of the image or signal. In the pooling layers, the dimensionality of the data is reduced, which increases resistance to small variations in the input data. For example, in 1D ConvNet networks, filters slide along temporal or sequential data, while in 2D and 3D networks, they analyse spatial relationships in images and videos. Activations through these layers are transformed using non-linear functions like ReLU, and weights are optimised using a backpropagation algorithm. This architecture enables ConvNet networks to efficiently learn complex data representations and apply them to a wide range of image, sound, text, and other data analysis tasks [37].

The network architecture can include multiple pairs of convolutional and subsampling layers. Each convolutional layer uses a small local receptive field to gather information, while subsampling layers reduce dimensionality and reduce the impact of small shifts on object recognition. For example, in a subsampling layer, each output takes 2×2 windows from the corresponding feature map and uses techniques like max pooling or average pooling to calculate an aggregated value, thereby reducing the number of parameters and computational complexity. This process allows the network to be more robust to small shifts or changes in the object's position in the image.

At higher levels of the architecture, the number of feature maps (represented as layers in the network) increases to compensate for the reduction in spatial resolution, and the network gradually becomes capable of detecting more complex shapes and abstract data features. Finally, the outputs from the convolutional and pooling layers enter the fully connected layer, which makes the final decision, such as classification based on learned features. Through backpropagation and weight optimisation, the network learns how to minimise classification errors, which enables pattern recognition and transformations in the data, such as changes in position, rotation, or lighting [38].

1D CNNs require fewer computational resources, as they have a complexity of $\sim O(NK)$ compared to $\sim O(N^2K^2)$ for 2D CNNs. This makes 1D CNNs more efficient, easier to train, and suitable for applications with fewer parameters (less than 10K), while 2D CNNs often require more resources and specialised hardware. Compact 1D CNNs are ideal for real-time and mobile applications due to their low computational requirements [39]. Compact 1D CNNs are efficient in applications with limited labelled data and high signal variations (such as patient ECG or high-performance circuits). These models use two types of layers: CNN layers (which include 1D convolutions, activation functions, and subsampling) and MLP layers (fully connected layers, similar to those in a multi-layer perceptron). The configuration of a 1D CNN depends on hyperparameters such as the number of hidden CNN and MLP layers, filter size, subsampling factor, and the choice of pooling and activation functions [39].

One example of applying a 1D CNN on psychological data is the analysis of motor activity as a biomarker for detecting depression. This enables timely intervention and personalised therapy. The study uses minute-by-minute motor activity records collected from 23 depressed and 32 non-depressed participants. The data represents time series of activity, which are analysed using a 1D CNN. The goal is to classify participants into two groups (control and conditional) and assess the severity of depression through three categories: non-depressed, mild, and moderate depression. The model also predicts the *Montgomery-Asberg Depression Rating Scale* (MADRS) score, which helps in quantitatively measuring depression and selecting therapeutic interventions [40]. The 1D CNN model was used for speech emotion recognition by analysing acoustic features such as pitch and intonation, enabling the classification of emotions in the *Ryerson Audio-Visual Database of Emotional Speech and Song* (RAVDESS) dataset [41].

To illustrate the practical application of a 1D convolutional neural network (1D CNN), we now present a scenario relevant to psychological research. Psychomotor retardation is characterised by decreased physical movement and reduced energy. It is a well-known symptom of depressive disorders and is considered a valuable behavioural marker for identifying psychological distress [42]. In this example, we simulate a situation where minute-level motor activity data, such as that collected via wrist-worn accelerometers, is analysed using a 1D CNN model. This type of sequential data is often used in mental health studies to distinguish between individuals with and without depressive symptoms. The goal of the model is to classify whether a person belongs to a control group or a group showing signs of psychological distress, based on patterns in their motor activity. To demonstrate the architecture and functioning of a 1D CNN in such a context, we used synthetic time-series data resembling motor activity signals. We then define a compact and efficient 1D CNN model, train it on the simulated data, and visualise the architecture to support understanding of its structure and purpose.

Figure 3 shows the model structure, including the number of parameters in each layer, where each layer contributes to the process of processing the input data: Convolutional layers perform feature extraction, max-pooling layers reduce dimensionality, and fully connected layers allow the model to learn more complex patterns and eventually return a binary classification.

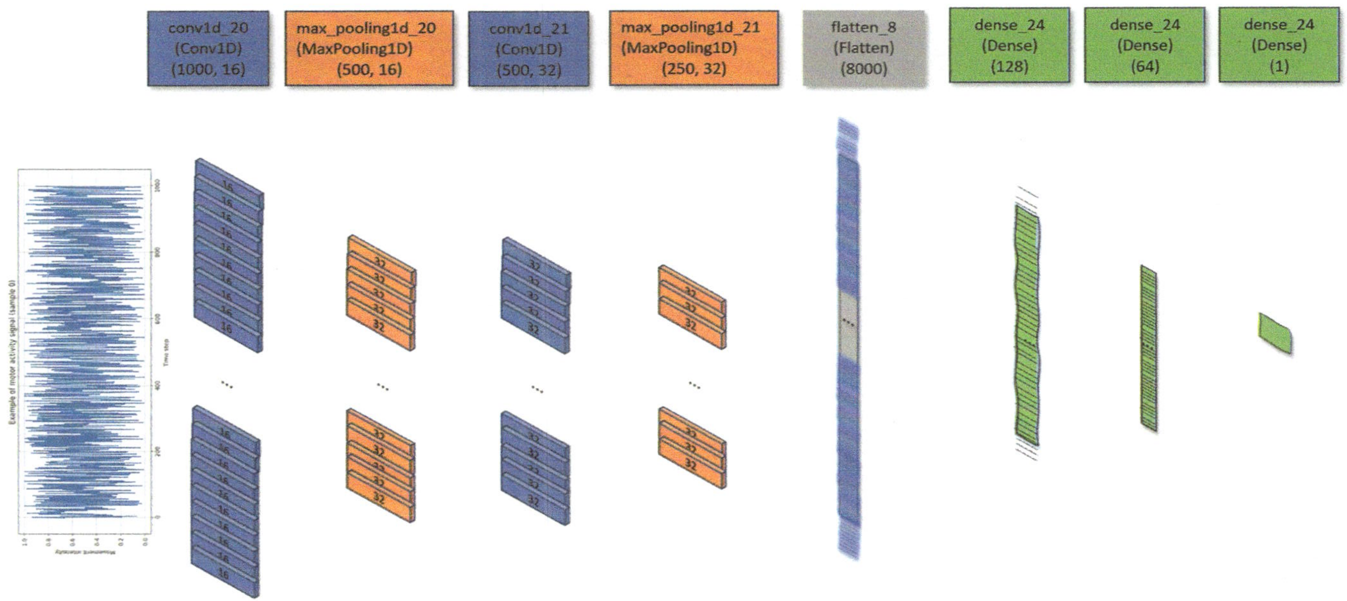

Fig. 3 A sample 1D CNN configuration

```
import numpy as np
from tensorflow import keras
from tensorflow.keras import layers
import matplotlib.pyplot as plt

# Generating synthetic data to simulate motor activity
# 10 samples represent 10 different participants in a
↪ psychological study
# Each sample is a sequence of 1000 time steps (e.g., 1000
↪ minutes of activity during the day)
# Each time step contains one feature (e.g., intensity of
↪ movement)
X_train = np.random.rand(10, 1000, 1)

# Generating target labels for binary classification:
# 0 = control group (non-depressed), 1 = depressive group
y_train = np.random.randint(2, size=(10,))
from keras import layers, models

# Defining a model with smaller input and simpler parameters
model = models.Sequential([
    layers.Input(shape=(1000, 1)),  # Input data: 1000 time
    ↪ steps, 1 feature per step
    layers.Conv1D(filters=16, kernel_size=3, strides=1,
    ↪ activation='relu', padding='same'),  # Smaller kernel,
    ↪ fewer filters
    layers.MaxPooling1D(pool_size=2),  # Max pooling to reduce
    ↪ dimensionality

    layers.Conv1D(filters=32, kernel_size=3, strides=1,
    ↪ activation='relu', padding='same'),  # Second
    ↪ convolutional layer
    layers.MaxPooling1D(pool_size=2),  # Max pooling again

    layers.Flatten(),  # Flatten the output from the
    ↪ convolutional layers into a 1D vector

    layers.Dense(128, activation='relu'),  # First fully
    ↪ connected layer
    layers.Dense(64, activation='relu'),   # Second fully
    ↪ connected layer

    layers.Dense(1, activation='sigmoid')  # Output layer with
    ↪ sigmoid activation for binary classification
])
```

```
# Compile the model
model.compile(optimizer='adam', loss='binary_crossentropy',
 ↪  metrics=['accuracy'])


# Let's assume you have input data x_train and labels y_train
# x_train is shaped as (batch_size, 1000, 1)
# y_train are binary labels (0 or 1)

model.fit(X_train, y_train, epochs=10, batch_size=32)
```

The results of the model training based on the presented Python code are shown in the following Fig. 4, displaying the accuracy across epochs.

Although 1D CNNs represent a powerful tool for pattern recognition in sequential psychological data, their use was not directly applied in Sect. 7 due to the nature of the dataset. The data under investigation consists of cross-sectional observations, represented as tabular and static measures from individual participants. These do not involve temporally ordered or sequential inputs, which are typically required for convolutional architectures. As 1D CNNs are especially effective in modelling data with local dependencies over time, such as *electroencephalographic* (EEG) signals, physiological recordings, or behavioural streams [43, 44], they are more commonly employed in studies involving continuous monitoring or temporal sensor data.

```
Epoch 1/10
1/1 ━━━━━━━━━━━━━━━━━━━━ 5s 5s/step - accuracy: 0.4000 - loss: 0.7262
Epoch 2/10
1/1 ━━━━━━━━━━━━━━━━━━━━ 0s 202ms/step - accuracy: 0.6000 - loss: 0.7706
Epoch 3/10
1/1 ━━━━━━━━━━━━━━━━━━━━ 0s 226ms/step - accuracy: 0.6000 - loss: 0.6419
Epoch 4/10
1/1 ━━━━━━━━━━━━━━━━━━━━ 0s 226ms/step - accuracy: 0.4000 - loss: 0.6699
Epoch 5/10
1/1 ━━━━━━━━━━━━━━━━━━━━ 0s 342ms/step - accuracy: 0.6000 - loss: 0.6141
Epoch 6/10
1/1 ━━━━━━━━━━━━━━━━━━━━ 0s 314ms/step - accuracy: 0.6000 - loss: 0.5958
Epoch 7/10
1/1 ━━━━━━━━━━━━━━━━━━━━ 0s 160ms/step - accuracy: 0.6000 - loss: 0.5760
Epoch 8/10
1/1 ━━━━━━━━━━━━━━━━━━━━ 0s 162ms/step - accuracy: 0.6000 - loss: 0.5239
Epoch 9/10
1/1 ━━━━━━━━━━━━━━━━━━━━ 0s 170ms/step - accuracy: 1.0000 - loss: 0.4916
Epoch 10/10
1/1 ━━━━━━━━━━━━━━━━━━━━ 0s 335ms/step - accuracy: 1.0000 - loss: 0.4660
```

Fig. 4 Model performance during training

Despite their exclusion from the current implementation, it is important to emphasise the growing role of 1D CNNs in psychological research involving multimodal and real-time data acquisition. For example, convolutional models have demonstrated superior performance in classifying emotional states from biosignals [45], detecting sleep stages [46], and predicting acute cognitive stress from electrocardiographic signals using short-time window convolutional neural network analysis [47]. Future extensions of this study may incorporate time-series data collected through digital phenotyping or mobile sensing technologies, where the application of 1D CNNs would be both appropriate and potentially advantageous.

6 Evaluating Model Performance

Evaluating the performance of classification models requires a deeper approach beyond basic metrics. While accuracy, precision, and recall are foundational, they may not fully capture a model's effectiveness, especially in contexts with imbalanced data or varying misclassification costs [48, 49].

Accuracy is the most intuitive metric, defined as the proportion of correct predictions out of the total predictions made (see Eq. (9)):

$$\text{Accuracy} = \frac{TP + TN}{TP + TN + FP + FN}. \tag{9}$$

In Eq. (9) and in subsequent formulas, TP is the number of true positives, TN the true negatives, FP the false positives, and FN the false negatives. Despite its simplicity, accuracy can be misleading in the presence of class imbalance [50].

Precision and *Recall* offer better insight in model performance. Precision reflects the proportion of positive identifications that are actually correct, as shown in Eq. (10):

$$\text{Precision} = \frac{TP}{TP + FP}. \tag{10}$$

Recall, also known as *sensitivity*, indicates how many actual positives were correctly identified, and can be calculated by the following Eq. (11):

$$\text{Recall} = \frac{TP}{TP + FN}. \tag{11}$$

The F_1 *score* is a widely accepted metric for imbalanced datasets. F_1 score represents the harmonic mean of precision and recall (see Eq. (12)):

$$F_1 = 2 \cdot \frac{\text{Precision} \cdot \text{Recall}}{\text{Precision} + \text{Recall}}. \tag{12}$$

F_1 score provides a balance between false positives and false negatives, offering a single metric that accounts for both errors. Variants like the F_β score allow researchers to weigh precision and recall differently, depending on the specific needs of the study [48]. As a F_1 generalisation, the F_β score allows adjusting the importance of precision versus recall, depending on study priorities, and can be calculated based on Eq. (13):

$$F_\beta = (1 + \beta^2) \cdot \frac{\text{Precision} \cdot \text{Recall}}{(\beta^2 \cdot \text{Precision}) + \text{Recall}}. \tag{13}$$

For instance, in early diagnostic tasks in psychology, recall may be prioritised to avoid missing true cases, whereas in behavioural screening, precision might be more valuable.

The *receiver operating characteristic* (ROC) curve and its corresponding *area under the curve* (AUC) are widely used to assess a model's ability to distinguish between classes. The ROC curve (see Eq. (14)) plots the true positive rate (recall) against the false positive rate:

$$\text{FPR} = \frac{FP}{FP + TN}. \tag{14}$$

The AUC summarises the ROC curve into a single value. An AUC close to 1 indicates excellent separability of classes and better model performance across various threshold settings, while 0.5 suggests random guessing [49, 51]. AUC provides a comprehensive view of model discrimination capabilities in psychological assessments, where the cost of false negatives can be high [51]. Recent applications in health psychology use these metrics to compare boosting, SVM, and tree-based classifiers on psychological features of chronic pain [52].

Another metric is the *Matthews Correlation Coefficient* (MCC) calculated as shown in Eq. (15):

$$\text{MCC} = \frac{(TP \cdot TN) - (FP \cdot FN)}{\sqrt{(TP + FP)(TP + FN)(TN + FP)(TN + FN)}}. \tag{15}$$

The MCC produces a value between -1 and $+1$, where $+1$ represents perfect prediction, 0 no better than random, and -1 total disagreement [53]. The MCC is a robust metric that considers all four quadrants of the confusion matrix: true positives, true negatives, false positives, and false negatives. It is particularly valuable in psychological research involving imbalanced datasets, as it provides a more balanced evaluation than accuracy alone [53].

For models providing probabilistic outputs, the *Brier score* is a proper scoring rule:

$$\text{Brier\_Score} = \frac{1}{N} \sum_{i=1}^{N} (p_i - y_i)^2. \tag{16}$$

In Eq. (16), p_i is the predicted probability for instance i, and y_i is the actual binary outcome. The Brier score captures both calibration and refinement of probabilistic predictions [54]. The Brier score measures the accuracy of probabilistic predictions, making it suitable for models that output probabilities rather than binary decisions. In psychological contexts, where uncertainty and probabilistic reasoning are common, the Brier score offers insights into the calibration of predictive models [54].

Calibration plots, or reliability diagrams, visualise the agreement between predicted probabilities and observed outcomes. Well-calibrated models are crucial in psychological research to ensure that predicted probabilities reflect true likelihoods, which is essential for risk assessments and decision-making processes [55].

Beyond metrics, robust evaluation strategies such as *cross-validation* must be employed. k-fold and stratified k-fold cross-validation techniques divide the dataset into subsets to validate model generalisability across unseen data. The overall accuracy can be calculated as shown in Eq. (17):

$$\text{CV\_Accuracy} = \frac{1}{k} \sum_{i=1}^{k} \text{Accuracy}_i . \tag{17}$$

In psychological studies, where sample sizes can be limited, these techniques help prevent overfitting and provide a more accurate estimate of model performance on unseen data [56].

Confusion matrices remain important tools for evaluating classification models. They provide a detailed breakdown of prediction outcomes, allowing researchers to identify specific areas where the model may be underperforming, such as misclassifying a particular psychological condition.

Psychological datasets often exhibit class imbalance, where certain conditions or traits are underrepresented. Class imbalance in psychological datasets must not be ignored. Techniques like resampling, *synthetic data generation* (e.g. SMOTE), and adjusting class weights during model training can mitigate the effects of imbalance, leading to more reliable evaluation metrics [57].

Incorporating psychological theory and domain expertise into model evaluation can enhance the interpretability and relevance of the results. Model evaluation in psychology must be guided not only by numerical metrics but also by theoretical frameworks and domain insights [58, 59]. For example, understanding the clinical significance of certain misclassifications can inform the selection of appropriate evaluation metrics and thresholds. Integrating expert knowledge allows better interpretation of evaluation outcomes, ensuring that machine learning complements rather than replaces psychological reasoning.

7 Case Study

Understanding how psychological traits and behaviours manifest through measurable indicators requires not only theoretical framing but also careful empirical modelling. This section presents a practical case study grounded in supervised classification techniques, where multiple machine learning algorithms were employed to predict psychological risk levels based on behavioural indicators and coping strategies. We present a comprehensive case study applying classification algorithms to a psychological dataset designed to predict individual risk levels based on psychometric attributes. The goal is to evaluate the ability of different classifiers to distinguish between individuals classified as high or low risk according to a derived binary target variable.

The dataset used in this case study comprises 198 samples, each representing an individual subject, with 14 independent psychological features and a binary target variable. The primary aim is to classify individuals into one of two psychological risk classes: low (coded as 0) or high (coded as 1), based on a derived composite index of emotional regulation and stress-related behaviours.

The *independent variables* include a range of psychological coping dimensions and interpersonal strategies:

- `Distract`, `Withdraw`, `Approching`, and `SocSupp`: These features reflect different behavioural and social support strategies during stress exposure.
- `ignor`, `Selfblame`, `Accept`, `Rumin`, `Catastro`, and `OtherBlame`: These describe intrapersonal emotion-focused coping mechanisms, including tendencies towards negative rumination and blame.
- `PossRefocu`, `Refoc.on.Plan`, `PosReappres`, and `PerspTak`: These reflect more adaptive, cognitive-based strategies, such as reappraisal, perspective taking, and planning.

The *dependent variable*, `PsychologicalRisk`, is a *binary classification label*, representing whether a subject's overall psychological state falls into the low-risk or high-risk group. This label was derived based on a mean threshold of a composite anxiety-related metric. The class distribution was balanced during preprocessing to ensure an equal representation of both outcomes, thereby allowing fair evaluation across classifiers. All variables were standardised before modelling, and missing values were imputed using the mean strategy. The dataset was split into training and testing subsets using stratified sampling to preserve the balance between the two classes.

The following algorithms were evaluated in this study, each configured with optimal yet interpretable parameter settings. The testing approach included stratified k-fold cross-validation to ensure robustness and generalisability of the reported results. The focus remained on evaluating not only predictive accuracy but also deeper model behaviour, as described in Sect. 6. For each algorithm, we present its configuration with defined parameters:

- *Decision Tree*: Implemented using

```
DecisionTreeClassifier(random\_state=42, max\_depth=12,
↪ min\_samples\_leaf=15),
```

this algorithm splits data recursively based on the feature that provides the highest information gain at each step. The relatively shallow depth and controlled leaf size mitigate overfitting while preserving interpretability.

- *Random Forest*: The ensemble model

```
RandomForestClassifier(n\_estimators=100, random\_state=42,
↪ max\_depth=5, min\_samples\_leaf=10)
```

aggregates multiple randomised decision trees to improve generalisation. By averaging over 100 estimators, it captures more complex interactions than a single tree while maintaining stability across folds.

- *Multi-layer Perceptron*: The MLP model was configured with

```
MLPClassifier(hidden\_layer\_sizes=(50, 25), alpha=0.01,
↪ early\_stopping=True, max\_iter=1000, random\_state=42).
```

This neural network uses two hidden layers, L2 regularisation via the `alpha` parameter, and early stopping to prevent overfitting. It produced one of the best performances, particularly excelling in minimising false negatives.

- *Support Vector Machine* (SVM): A standard

```
SVC(probability=True, random\_state=42).
```

Implementation was tested, relying on the default kernel behaviour (radial basis function). The model was evaluated with cross-validation using probability outputs to support AUC and calibration analyses.

- *k-Nearest Neighbours—Best-Performing Model* (KNN): The instance-based learner

```
KNeighborsClassifier(n\_neighbors=5)
```

achieved the highest accuracy and AUC among all classifiers tested. It determines classification through majority voting among the five nearest neighbours. Although sensitive to feature scaling and dimensionality, KNN proved highly effective for this balanced psychological dataset.

- *Naive Bayes*:

```
GaussianNB()
```

was applied under the assumption of Gaussian-distributed features. This model's simplicity and strong performance under independence assumptions make it a common choice in psychological modelling where dimensionality is moderate.

- *Logistic Regression*: The highest performance across evaluation metrics was achieved by

```
LogisticRegression(max\_iter=300, C=0.05, random\_state=42).
```

This model utilises a penalised logistic function to estimate the probability of class membership. The regularisation strength, controlled by `C=0.05`, helped to generalise well while limiting overfitting. While logistic regression is not the top-performing classifier, it remains valuable due to its explainability, probabilistic nature, and strong theoretical grounding. Its calibration characteristics support reliable decision-making, especially when model transparency is a priority.

Each algorithm was evaluated using the metrics defined in Sect. 6: accuracy, F_1 score, ROC-AUC, MCC, and Brier score. We emphasise the importance of comparing models not just based on a single scalar metric, but using a combination of evaluation strategies to fully understand model behaviour, particularly in clinical or psychological contexts where misclassification risks carry interpretative weight.

The decision tree provided balanced performance across both classes, with a slightly better recall for the low-risk group. Misclassification of high-risk individuals remained notable. This model's interpretability remains its strength, but its sensitivity to data splits could be a source of variance in prediction stability:

$$\text{Accuracy}_{\text{DT}} = 0.83, \quad \text{AUC}_{\text{DT}} = 0.884,$$

$$\text{Confusion Matrix}_{\text{DT}} = \begin{bmatrix} 64 & 11 \\ 14 & 61 \end{bmatrix}.$$

Random forest significantly improved generalisation over the DT, reducing false positives and negatives. This model demonstrates robust performance and provides ensemble-based smoothing, making it an excellent candidate for applications requiring stable predictions:

$$\text{Accuracy}_{\text{RF}} = 0.87, \quad \text{AUC}_{\text{RF}} = 0.932,$$

$$\text{Confusion Matrix}_{\text{RF}} = \begin{bmatrix} 69 & 6 \\ 14 & 61 \end{bmatrix}.$$

The MLP classifier produced one of the best results, particularly in reducing false negatives (i.e. high-risk individuals misclassified as low risk). Given the psychological context, this behaviour is crucial in avoiding the underestimation of risk. Tuning MLPs remains nontrivial and requires careful control of overfitting, regularisation, and convergence issues:

$$\text{Accuracy}_{\text{MLP}} = 0.93, \quad \text{AUC}_{\text{MLP}} = 0.957,$$

$$\text{Confusion Matrix}_{\text{MLP}} = \begin{bmatrix} 68 & 7 \\ 3 & 72 \end{bmatrix}.$$

Although logistic regression offered interpretability and probabilistic outputs, its overall performance fell behind the top models. It remains an attractive baseline due to its mathematical simplicity and calibration behaviour, but in this case, it was outperformed by more flexible approaches:

$$\text{Accuracy}_{\text{LR}} = 0.79, \quad \text{AUC}_{\text{LR}} = 0.858,$$

$$\text{Confusion Matrix}_{\text{LR}} = \begin{bmatrix} 61 & 14 \\ 18 & 57 \end{bmatrix}.$$

Naive Bayes yielded decent recall for high-risk individuals, but it struggled with specificity in the low-risk class. This behaviour is likely due to the independence assumption, which is rarely valid in real psychological data:

$$\text{Accuracy}_{\text{NB}} = 0.77, \quad \text{AUC}_{\text{NB}} = 0.873,$$

$$\text{Confusion Matrix}_{\text{NB}} = \begin{bmatrix} 55 & 20 \\ 14 & 61 \end{bmatrix}.$$

SVM performed exceptionally well in separating the two classes. The low rate of false negatives underscores its effectiveness in modelling psychological risk. Still, computational cost and tuning kernel parameters may restrict its use in exploratory settings:

$$\text{Accuracy}_{\text{SVM}} = 0.92, \quad \text{AUC}_{\text{SVM}} = 0.967,$$

$$\text{Confusion Matrix}_{\text{SVM}} = \begin{bmatrix} 67 & 8 \\ 4 & 71 \end{bmatrix}.$$

KNN exhibited the highest overall accuracy and AUC, confirming it as the best-performing model in this case study. Its ability to capture local patterns made it particularly effective at classifying borderline cases. Nonetheless, KNN lacks probabilistic outputs and may not generalise as well in higher-dimensional settings:

$$\text{Accuracy}_{\text{KNN}} = 0.94, \quad \text{AUC}_{\text{KNN}} = 0.969,$$

$$\text{Confusion Matrix}_{\text{KNN}} = \begin{bmatrix} 71 & 4 \\ 5 & 70 \end{bmatrix}.$$

All models demonstrated competent performance in the binary classification of psychological risk. While KNN, SVM, and MLP excelled in predictive power,

Table 1 Brier scores for each classifier

Model	Brier score
Logistic regression	0.1559
Random forest	0.1217
MLP	0.2020
SVM	0.0617
Naive Bayes	0.1471
KNN	0.0632

logistic regression was chosen for further analysis due to its interpretability and ease of integration into domain-specific frameworks. Decision trees and Naive Bayes performed well in specific contexts but may require enhancement (e.g. boosting or feature selection) to match ensemble-based methods. This comparison highlights the importance of model selection criteria tailored to psychological research objectives, which include not just statistical performance but also interpretability, reliability, and context sensitivity.

In addition to traditional classification metrics, the Brier score was computed for each model to assess the quality of probabilistic predictions. The Brier score measures the mean-squared difference between predicted probabilities and the actual binary outcomes. A lower Brier score indicates better calibrated and more confident probabilistic predictions [54, 60]. The computed Brier scores for each classifier are shown in Table 1:

From Table 1, we observe that the SVM and KNN classifiers exhibit the lowest Brier scores (0.0617 and 0.0632, respectively), indicating highly reliable and well-calibrated probabilistic outputs. These models are not only accurate but also consistent in predicting confidence levels that closely reflect the true outcome probabilities. This is especially crucial in psychological contexts where model confidence must reflect underlying uncertainty in human behaviour.

Interestingly, while the MLP classifier had a high classification accuracy and AUC, its Brier score (0.2020) suggests poorer probabilistic calibration. This discrepancy underlines the importance of not relying solely on accuracy or AUC, but also evaluating how closely predicted probabilities align with real-world event likelihoods [55, 61].

Logistic regression, despite its lower accuracy compared to models like SVM or random forest, shows a reasonably calibrated Brier score (0.1559). This supports its reputation for being a well-behaved probabilistic classifier, which aligns well with its performance in calibration plots (see Fig. 12 in Sect. 8).

The random forest classifier, with a Brier score of 0.1217, demonstrates both strong performance and balanced probability estimates. Naive Bayes, on the other hand, produces moderately calibrated predictions, with a Brier score of 0.1471, which reflects the model's simplifying assumptions that often fail to fully capture interactions between psychological constructs.

Including the Brier score provides an additional dimension for evaluating classifiers beyond their ability to discriminate between classes. In psychological

Table 2 Brier scores for logistic regression and calibrated variants

Model variant	Brier score
Base logistic regression	0.1559
Calibrated LR (Sigmoid)	0.1512
Calibrated LR (Isotonic)	0.1520

research, where misclassification may carry clinical consequences, it is essential to ensure that models not only classify well but also express uncertainty appropriately [62].

While logistic regression is inherently a probabilistic model, its calibration refers to the alignment between predicted probabilities and true outcome frequencies. This alignment can still be suboptimal, particularly when the training data is limited or noisy. To address this, probability calibration techniques are applied post hoc to improve the reliability of predicted probabilities without altering the model's classification boundary [55, 63]. Two widely used calibration techniques are:

- *Platt Scaling* (Sigmoid Calibration): Fits a logistic (sigmoid) regression model to the predicted probabilities from a base classifier. This method is computationally efficient and assumes that miscalibration is sigmoidal [64].
- *Isotonic Regression*: A non-parametric calibration method that fits a piecewise constant, non-decreasing function. It is more flexible than Platt scaling and better suited for larger datasets, but more prone to overfitting with small datasets [63].

These methods were applied to the base logistic regression classifier in our study, and the resulting Brier scores are summarised in Table 2.

These results show modest improvements in calibration. Sigmoid calibration slightly reduced the Brier score from 0.1559 to 0.1512, suggesting better alignment between predicted and actual outcome probabilities. Isotonic regression yielded a similar improvement (Brier score of 0.1520), though slightly less than sigmoid calibration.

This suggests that the logistic regression model's calibration could be improved marginally by either method, but the gains are not dramatic. The relatively small difference between the base and calibrated models indicates that the original classifier was already reasonably calibrated. This is a known property of logistic regression, which models log-odds directly [62, 65].

8 Visualising Classification Results

Visualisations play a pivotal role in understanding and communicating the performance of classification models in psychological research. They allow researchers to examine classifier behaviour beyond numerical summaries, offering insight into learning dynamics, generalisation, model calibration, and feature importance.

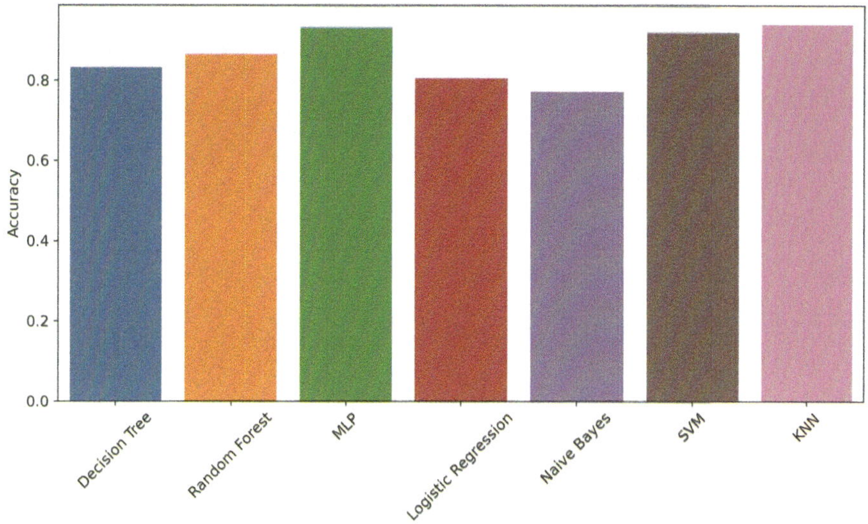

Fig. 5 Classifier accuracy comparison

The comparative accuracy of all classifiers tested in this study is presented in Fig. 5. KNN emerges as the highest-performing classifier, achieving approximately 94% accuracy. The superiority of KNN is attributed to its sensitivity to local data structure, effectively distinguishing between psychological risk categories in this particular dataset. Meanwhile, MLP and SVM also demonstrate strong accuracy around 92–93%, indicating their robustness in capturing complex patterns. Logistic regression's lower accuracy (79%) underscores its limitations in capturing complex non-linear interactions but maintains its utility through high interpretability in practical psychological scenarios. Researchers should interpret these differences carefully, acknowledging the trade-off between accuracy and interpretability, particularly important in psychological research contexts. This metric alone can be misleading in scenarios with unbalanced class distributions or varying misclassification costs.

Figure 6 displays ROC curves for all classifiers and further clarifies models' discriminative capabilities across classification thresholds. KNN again showcases superior discriminative power (AUC = 0.969), closely followed by SVM (AUC = 0.967). The closeness of these two curves underscores their comparable ability to balance sensitivity and specificity. Logistic regression, despite its interpretability advantage, shows a notably lower AUC (0.866), suggesting comparatively weaker discrimination between risk classes. Random forest and decision tree yield intermediate performances, highlighting potential decision boundary complexities in psychological classification tasks. Practitioners should thus consider employing KNN or SVM when high discriminative power is essential.

Learning curves (Figs. 7 and 8) reveal how each model's performance evolves with increasing training data. These plots help identify underfitting (e.g. persistent

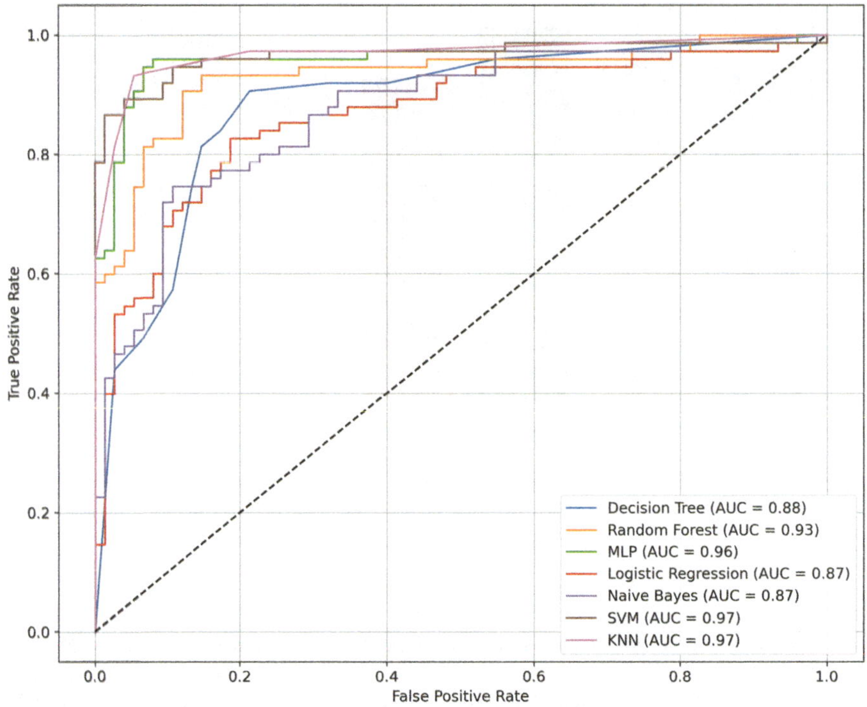

Fig. 6 ROC curves for classifiers

low training accuracy) or overfitting (e.g. large training-validation gap). The decision tree shows signs of overfitting with a stagnant perfect training score and lower validation, while the SVM maintains tight generalisation. As illustrated in Fig. 7, the logistic regression model optimised with a regularisation strength of $C = 0.05$ demonstrates balanced learning behaviour. While the training accuracy declines as more data are introduced, the cross-validation accuracy steadily increases, ultimately converging near the training curve. This convergence indicates that the model is generalising well and avoids both underfitting and overfitting. The minimal generalisation gap suggests that the applied regularisation has effectively constrained the model complexity without sacrificing predictive power. Naive Bayes reveals stable convergence but consistently lower accuracy, reflecting its simplicity and sensitivity to unrealistic independence assumptions. These insights underline the importance of balancing complexity and interpretability, emphasising logistic regression's practical advantage in psychological research due to consistent generalisation performance.

MLP shows initial rapid training accuracy growth that quickly saturates, accompanied by a noticeable validation gap, suggesting moderate overfitting despite regularisation efforts. Random forest exhibits steady accuracy improvement with increased data, indicating the model benefits significantly from larger datasets.

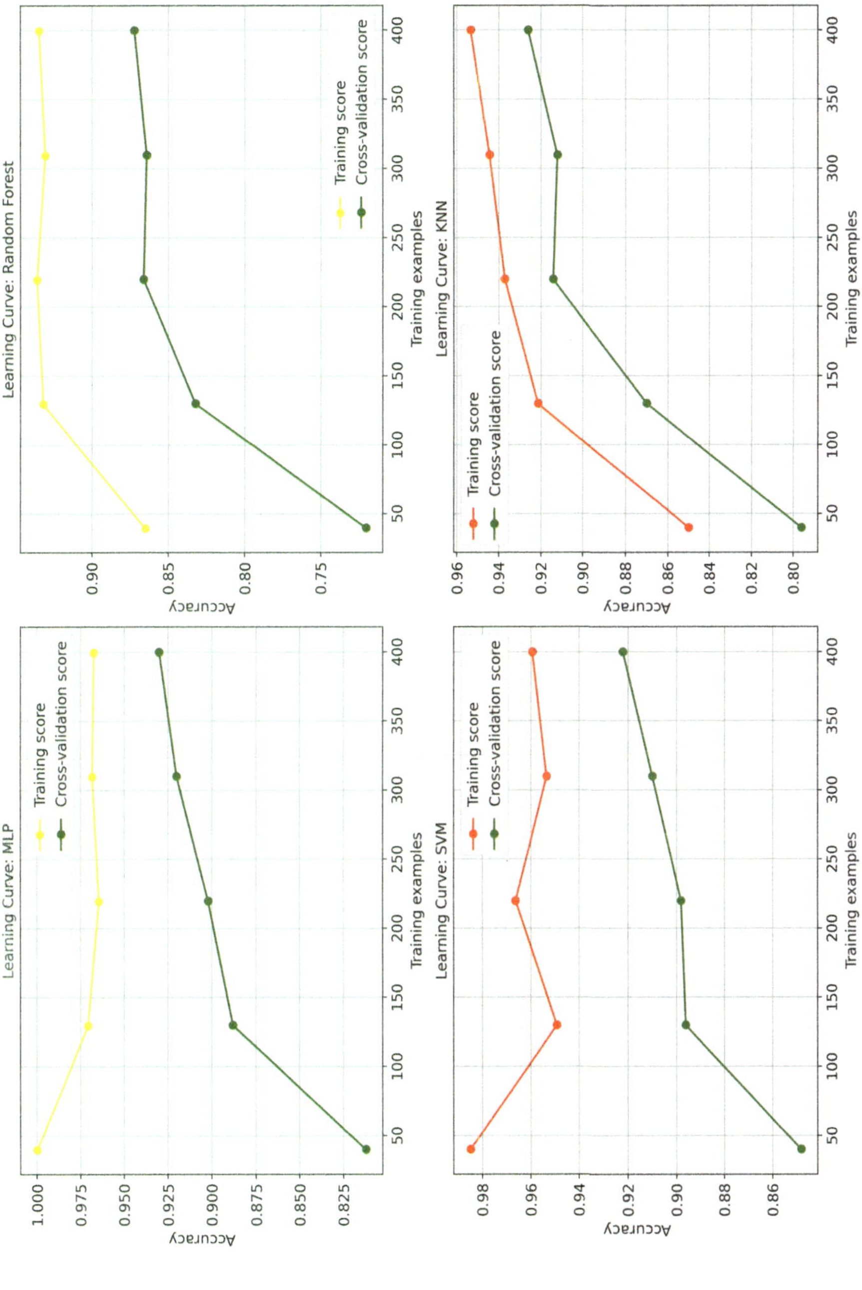

Fig. 7 Learning curves: MLP, random forest, SVM, KNN

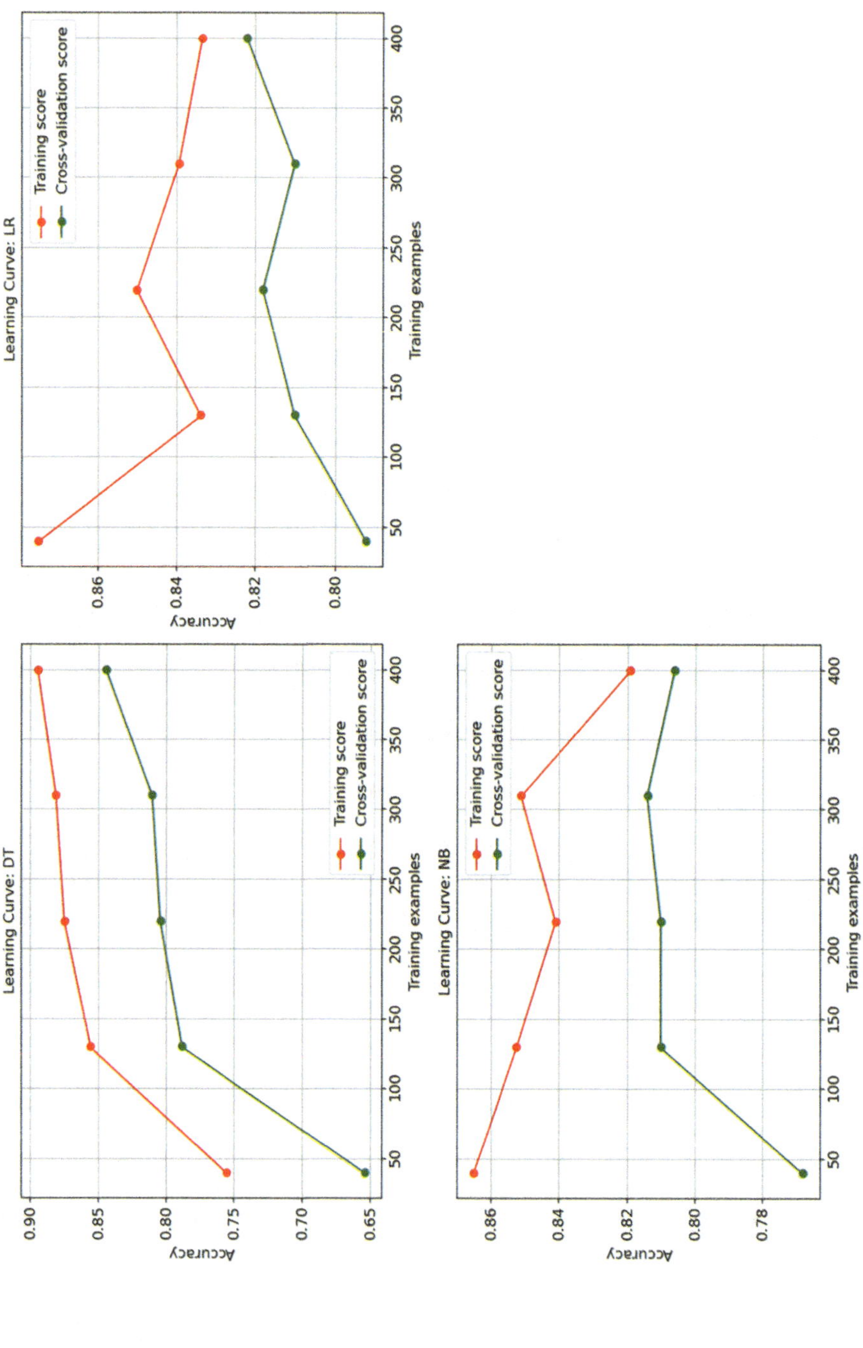

Fig. 8 Learning curves: decision tree, logistic regression, Naive Bayes

Table 3 Comparative learning curve characteristics of classifiers

Model	Overfitting risk	Bias	Variance	Learning stability
KNN	Low	Low	Low	High
SVM	Low	Low	Low	High
MLP	Moderate	Low	Moderate	Medium
Random forest	Moderate	Low	Moderate	High
Decision tree	High	Low	High	Medium
Naive Bayes	Low	High	Low	High
Logistic regression	Low-moderate	Moderate	Low	High

SVM displays excellent stability, with minimal gaps between training and validation, demonstrating strong robustness. KNN uniquely maintains the smallest gap, confirming exceptional generalisation and resistance to overfitting, supporting its superior empirical performance.

To complement the visual inspection of learning curves across classifiers, Table 3 provides a structured comparison of key training characteristics derived from the curves. These attributes were inferred by analysing the divergence between training and cross-validation accuracy over varying sample sizes, as shown in Figs. 7 and 8.

The KNN classifier exhibits exceptionally low bias and variance, confirmed by tightly aligned and convergent training and cross-validation curves (Fig. 7). Its near-identical training and validation accuracies across increasing data sizes underline excellent generalisation, stability, and negligible overfitting risk. This makes KNN especially suited to psychological datasets where prediction stability is crucial, provided feature dimensions are manageable.

SVM similarly demonstrates strong performance, closely aligning its training and validation accuracies (Fig. 7). The consistently small gap between these curves reveals minimal variance and low overfitting, further substantiated by its robust accuracy across multiple evaluations. Such learning behaviour illustrates SVM's reliability, especially advantageous in psychological studies requiring consistently accurate performance with limited sample sizes.

The MLP classifier, despite achieving high absolute accuracy, shows a moderate risk of overfitting. Its learning curve indicates rapid training accuracy growth followed by saturation, accompanied by a noticeable, persistent gap between training and validation accuracies (Fig. 7). This pattern indicates moderate variance, reflecting its complex internal structure and sensitivity to limited training data. Regularisation methods and careful hyperparameter tuning remain critical when applying MLP models to psychological contexts to mitigate this moderate overfitting risk.

Random forest displays moderate variance with a clear but controlled divergence between training and validation curves (Fig. 7). Initially, performance improves steadily with more data, yet the gap persists, indicating some potential for overfitting if data volume is insufficient. Nonetheless, the ensemble approach stabilises learning considerably, maintaining high generalisation compared to single-tree

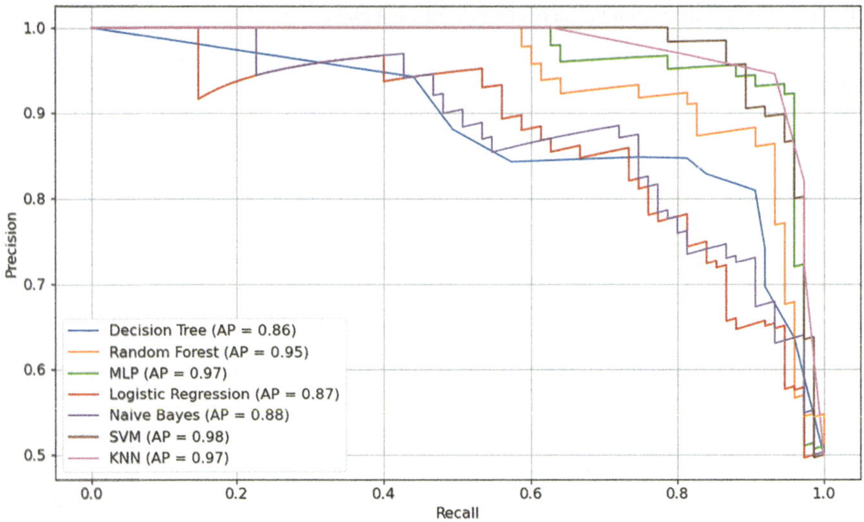

Fig. 9 Precision-recall curves for classifiers

classifiers. Therefore, random forest is recommended for psychological applications when interpretability can be compromised slightly for stability and performance gains.

The decision tree classifier consistently presents the highest overfitting risk, exemplified by substantial divergence between training accuracy (often near-perfect) and significantly lower validation accuracy (Fig. 8). This behaviour clearly illustrates high variance and sensitivity to data partitioning, common to tree-based methods when constraints (e.g. maximum depth, minimum leaf size) are insufficient to prevent overly complex fitting. Its interpretability remains a significant advantage, but careful regularisation and pruning strategies are necessary when applied in psychological research.

Naive Bayes showcases an entirely different pattern. Its learning curves converge smoothly at relatively lower accuracy levels (Fig. 8). The stable but moderate performance, characterised by high bias due to strong independence assumptions, limits its ability to fully exploit data complexity. Despite low variance and excellent stability, this bias restricts its effectiveness to simpler psychological classification problems or scenarios where assumptions align closely with data distributions.

Logistic regression offers an appealing balance, presenting stable, convergent training, and validation accuracies with a moderate bias. Its learning curves stabilise quickly with modest sample sizes and exhibit a narrow performance gap, signifying low variance and reduced overfitting concerns (Fig. 8). This balance between interpretability, stability, and reasonable accuracy recommends logistic regression as a reliable choice, especially when explainability and interpretative transparency are prioritised in psychological research contexts.

These comparative observations guide model selection not only by performance metrics but also by learning behaviour, offering insights into which models are most appropriate under constraints of sample size, noise, or the need for generalisation.

Precision-recall (PR) curves in Fig. 9 are particularly informative for imbalanced datasets, as they emphasise performance on the positive class. KNN and SVM notably maintain high precision at elevated recall levels, confirming their suitability for sensitive psychological scenarios. Logistic regression shows a rapid precision drop with increasing recall, indicating it could lead to higher rates of false alarms or missed detections in practical contexts. This observation guides researchers towards preferring KNN or SVM in scenarios where precision at higher recall is critical, such as clinical diagnosis or risk assessment.

Model explainability is illustrated using *SHapley Additive exPlanations* (SHAP) summary plots in Fig. 10, which rank features by their average impact on predictions. Here, `SocSupp`, `Withdraw`, and `Selfblame` appear as dominant predictors, underscoring their relevance in psychological risk classification. The broad distribution of SHAP values for `SocSupp` implies that variations in perceived social support significantly influence risk predictions. High SHAP values indicate a strong predictive influence, aligning with psychological theories emphasising the protective effects of social support. `Withdraw` and `Selfblame` similarly highlight psychological coping strategies' relevance in shaping risk profiles. This visualisation emphasises the importance of incorporating theory-driven features to enhance interpretability and clinical relevance in psychological modelling.

Calibration performance across models is depicted in Fig. 11, where the diagonal line represents perfect calibration. This plot shows the degree of alignment between predicted probabilities and observed outcomes. A classifier whose calibration curve closely follows the diagonal exhibits well-calibrated probability estimates. KNN and SVM demonstrate nearly ideal calibration, underscoring their combined strengths in predictive accuracy and reliability. MLP, despite achieving high accuracy, exhibits noticeable deviations from ideal calibration, suggesting moderate miscalibration that warrants caution in scenarios requiring precise probabilistic outputs. This discrepancy highlights the crucial distinction between accuracy and reliable probability estimation, critical in psychological contexts where confidence in predictions directly informs practical decision-making. The calibration divergence seen here emphasises the necessity of considering calibration alongside accuracy when selecting models for applied psychological research.

Figure 12 offers a detailed reliability diagram for logistic regression using base, sigmoid, and isotonic calibrations. While the original logistic regression exhibits decent calibration, the sigmoid and isotonic calibration methods slightly improve its probabilistic reliability, particularly in mid-range predictions. Isotonic calibration shows a somewhat smoother alignment to observed outcomes compared to sigmoid, suggesting slight advantages in clinical or risk-based settings where precise probability estimates significantly impact decision-making processes. Both calibrated versions improve alignment with true probabilities, supporting the importance of post hoc calibration in psychological applications where probability estimates guide clinical decision-making. Researchers should consider isotonic calibration for

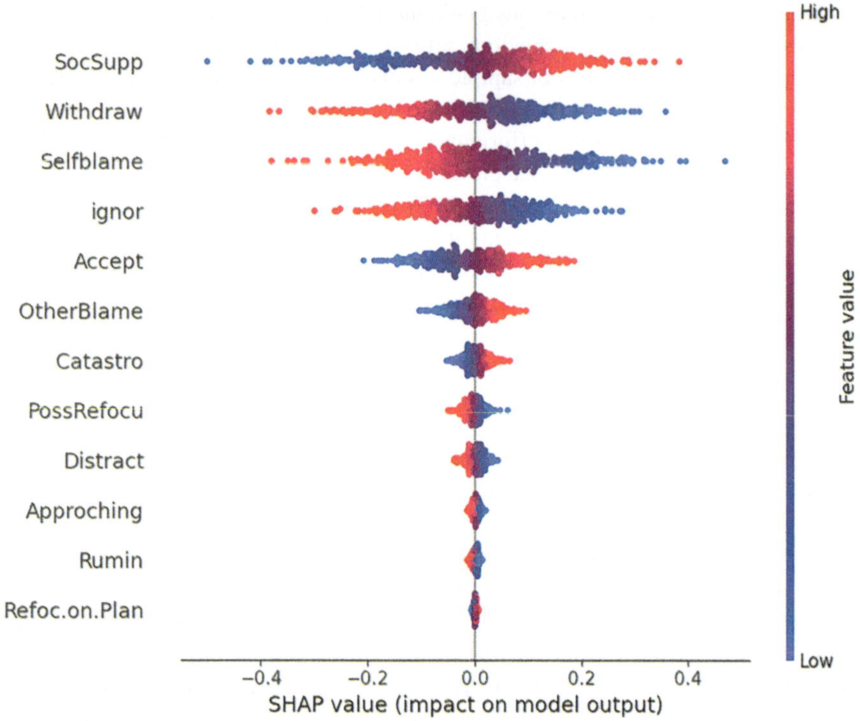

Fig. 10 SHAP summary plot for logistic regression

enhanced model reliability, especially when deploying logistic regression models in practice.

Figure 13 presents the histogram of predicted probabilities for the positive class (Class 1) across all tested classifiers. The plot provides insights into how each classifier assigns probabilities to instances, revealing important characteristics of their predictive behaviour. Notably, KNN and decision tree models exhibit distinctly bimodal distributions, with sharp peaks at the probability extremes (near 0 and 1). This characteristic highlights their highly decisive predictions, clearly separating high-risk from low-risk individuals. Such decisiveness can be beneficial in settings where clear classification is required, but could become problematic when dealing with borderline cases or genuine uncertainty.

Random forest and SVM classifiers show a relatively more balanced distribution, with predictions spanning intermediate probabilities more uniformly. This broader distribution indicates a suitable approach to probability assignments, potentially reflecting better calibration and a more careful handling of uncertain cases compared to highly decisive models.

MLP and logistic regression produce predictions mostly clustered towards extremes, similar to decision tree and KNN, but with slightly more intermediate

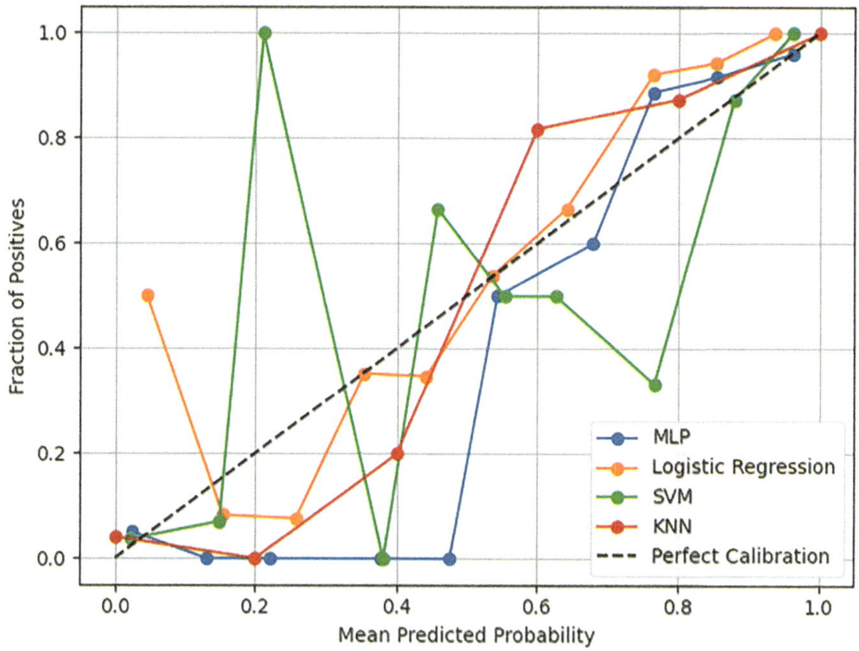

Fig. 11 Calibration curves (general comparison across classifiers)

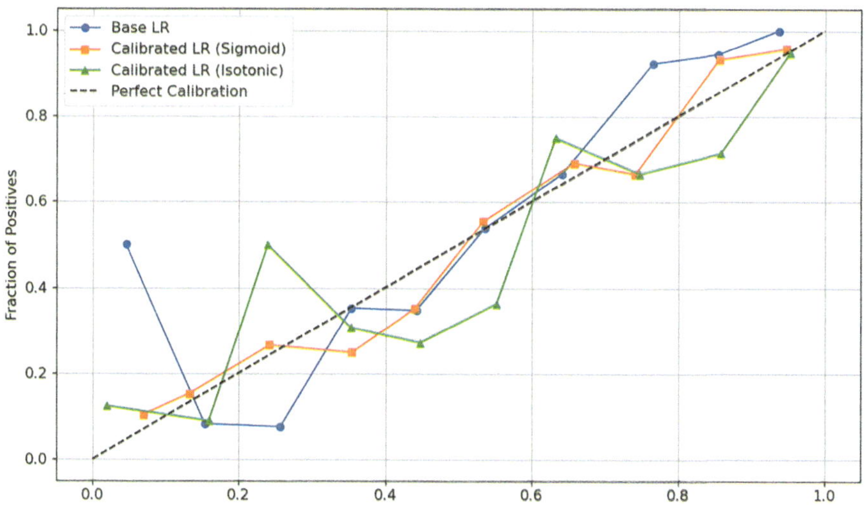

Fig. 12 Calibration curves for logistic regression (base, sigmoid, isotonic)

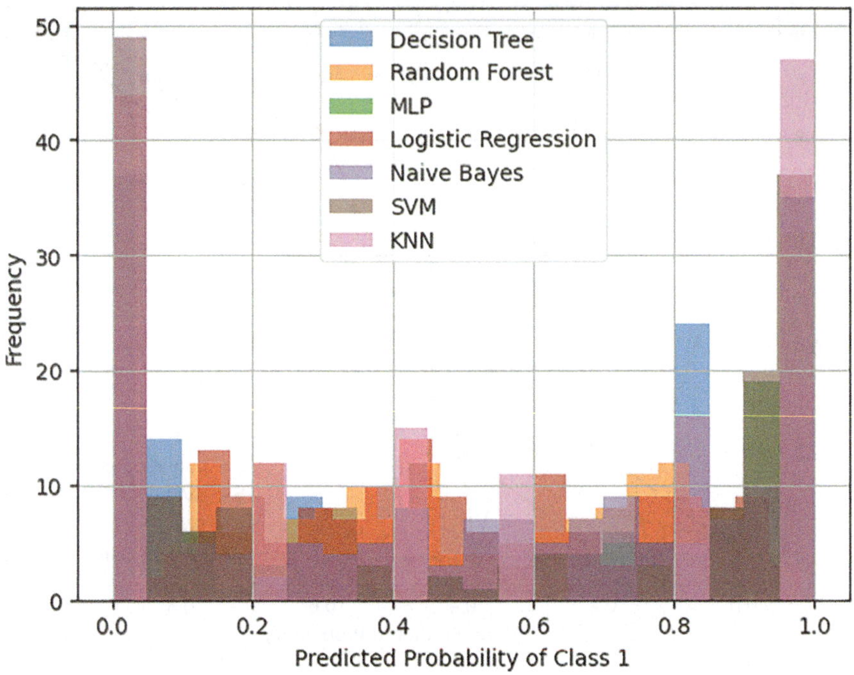

Fig. 13 Histogram of predicted probabilities for Class 1

predictions, suggesting that they maintain moderate flexibility in handling uncertain cases. Naive Bayes tends to produce more centralised and smoothly spread predictions, indicative of its inherent probabilistic assumptions and robustness against variance, though at the cost of potentially reduced decisiveness.

From this comparative visualisation, practitioners should recognise that classifiers producing heavily polarised probability distributions (such as KNN and decision tree) are highly confident in their classification decisions. This may limit their effectiveness in scenarios involving ambiguous psychological assessments, where uncertainty is meaningful and important to preserve.

References

1. J.R. Quinlan, Induction of decision trees. Mach. Learn. **1**, 81 (1986). https://api.semanticscholar.org/CorpusID:189902138
2. L. Breiman, J.H. Friedman, R.A. Olshen, C.J. Stone, *Classification and Regression Trees* (Wadsworth and Brooks, California, 1984)
3. N. Kovač, K. Ratković, H. Farahani, P. Watson, A practical applications guide to machine learning regression models in psychology with python. Methods in Psychol. **11**, 100156 (2024)

4. H. Farahani, P. Watson, N. Kovač, F.B. Sheykhangafshe, P. Azadfallah, A. Allahyari, F. Esrafilian, R.R. Chesli, in *International Handbook of Love: Transcultural and Transdisciplinary Perspectives* (Springer, Berlin, 2025), pp. 1–22
5. S. Malik, A. Malik, M. Shabaz, E. Asenso, Machine learning based model for detecting depression during COVID-19 crisis. Sci. Afr. **20**, e01716 (2023). https://doi.org/10.1016/j.sciaf.2023.e01716. https://www.sciencedirect.com/science/article/pii/S2468227623001722
6. M. Rostami, S. Farashi, R. Khosrowabadi, H. Pouretemad, Discrimination of ADHD subtypes using decision tree on behavioral, neuropsychological, and neural markers. Basic and Clin. Neurosci. **11**(3), 359 (2020)
7. P. Domingos, A few useful things to know about machine learning. Commun. ACM **55**(10), 78 (2012)
8. Z.C. Lipton, The mythos of model interpretability: In machine learning, the concept of interpretability is both important and slippery. Queue **16**(3), 31 (2018)
9. E.I. Fried, D.J. Robinaugh, Systems all the way down: embracing complexity in mental health research. BMC Med. **18**, 1 (2020)
10. G. James, D. Witten, T. Hastie, R. Tibshirani, *An Introduction to Statistical Learning: With Applications in R*, 2nd edn. (Springer, New York, 2021)
11. V. Podgorelec, P. Kokol, B. Stiglic, I. Rozman, Decision trees: an overview and their use in medicine. J. Med. Syst. **26**, 445 (2002)
12. C. Márquez-Vera, A. Cano, C. Romero, A.Y.M. Noaman, H. Mousa Fardoun, S. Ventura, Early dropout prediction using data mining: a case study with high school students. Expert Syst. **33**(1), 107 (2016)
13. S.K. Murthy, Automatic construction of decision trees from data: a multi-disciplinary survey. Data Min. Knowl. Disc. **2**(4), 345 (1998)
14. S.L. Salzberg, C4.5: Programs for machine learning by J. Ross Quinlan. Morgan Kaufmann Publishers, Inc., 1993. Mach. Learn. **16**, 235 (1994). https://api.semanticscholar.org/CorpusID:5217269
15. J. Bergstra, Y. Bengio, Random search for hyper-parameter optimization. J. Mach. Learn. Res. **13**, 281 (2012)
16. J. Snoek, H. Larochelle, R.P. Adams, Practical Bayesian optimization of machine learning algorithms, in *Neural Information Processing Systems* (2012). https://api.semanticscholar.org/CorpusID:632197
17. K. Ratković, N. Kovač, M. Simeunović, Hybrid LSTM model to predict the level of air pollution in Montenegro. Appl. Sci. **13**(18), 10152 (2023)
18. W.Y. Loh, Classification and regression trees. Wiley Interdiscip. Rev.: Data Min. Knowl. Discovery **1**(1), 14 (2011)
19. R.T. Trevor Hastie, J. Friedman, *The Elements of Statistical Learning: Data Mining, Inference, and Prediction*, 2nd edn. (Springer, Berlin, 2009)
20. L. Breiman, Random forests. Mach. Learn. **45**, 5 (2001)
21. J. Wang, C. Zhao, Z. Liu, Can historical accident data improve sustainable urban traffic safety? A predictive modeling study. Sustainability **16**(22), 9642 (2024)
22. C. Strobl, A.L. Boulesteix, A. Zeileis, T. Hothorn, Bias in random forest variable importance measures: illustrations, sources and a solution. BMC Bioinf. **8**, 1 (2007)
23. T. Hothorn, K. Hornik, A. Zeileis, Unbiased recursive partitioning: a conditional inference framework. J. Comput. Graph. Stat. **15**(3), 651 (2006)
24. S. Raschka, V. Mirjalili, *Python Machine Learning: Machine Learning and Deep Learning with Python, Scikit-Learn, and TensorFlow 2* (Packt Publishing Ltd, New York, 2019)
25. A. Abraham, F. Pedregosa, M. Eickenberg, P. Gervais, A. Mueller, J. Kossaifi, A. Gramfort, B. Thirion, G. Varoquaux, Machine learning for neuroimaging with scikit-learn. Front. Neuroinform. **8**, 71792 (2014)
26. P. Geurts, D. Ernst, L. Wehenkel, Extremely randomized trees. Mach. Learn. **63**, 3 (2006)
27. O.A. Mohamed, M. Ati, O.F. Najm, Predicting compressive strength of sustainable self-consolidating concrete using random forest. Key Eng. Mater. **744**, 141 (2017)

28. F. Rosenblatt, The perceptron: a probabilistic model for information storage and organization in the brain. Psychol. Rev. **65**(6), 386 (1958)
29. D.E. Rumelhart, G.E. Hinton, R.J. Williams, Learning representations by back-propagating errors. Nature **323**(6088), 533 (1986)
30. G. Cybenko, Approximation by superpositions of a sigmoidal function. Math. Control Signals Syst. **2**(4), 303 (1989)
31. A. Vaswani, N. Shazeer, N. Parmar, J. Uszkoreit, L. Jones, A. N. Gomez, Ł. Kaiser, I. Polosukhin, *Attention is all you need*, ed. by I. Guyon, U.V. Luxburg, S. Bengio, H. Wallach, R. Fergus, S. Vishwanathan, R. Garnett. Advances in neural information processing systems, vol 30 (Curran Associates, Inc., 2017)
32. X. Glorot, Y. Bengio, Understanding the difficulty of training deep feedforward neural networks, in *Proceedings of the Thirteenth International Conference on Artificial Intelligence and Statistics* (JMLR Workshop and Conference Proceedings, New York, 2010), pp. 249–256
33. V. Nair, G.E. Hinton, Rectified linear units improve restricted Boltzmann machines, in *Proceedings of the 27th International Conference on Machine Learning (ICML-10)* (2010), pp. 807–814
34. P. Ramachandran, B. Zoph, Q.V. Le, Searching for activation functions, arXiv preprint arXiv:1710.05941 (2017)
35. Y. Bengio, P. Simard, P. Frasconi, Learning long-term dependencies with gradient descent is difficult. IEEE Trans. Neural Netw. **5**(2), 157 (1994)
36. Y. LeCun, L. Bottou, G.B. Orr, K.R. Müller, Efficient backprop, in *Neural Networks: Tricks of the Trade* (2012), pp. 9–48
37. Y. LeCun, Y. Bengio, G. Hinton, Deep learning. Nature **521**(7553), 436 (2015)
38. C.M. Bishop, N.M. Nasrabadi, *Pattern Recognition and Machine Learning*, vol. 4 (Springer, Berlin, 2006)
39. S. Kiranyaz, O. Avci, O. Abdeljaber, T. Ince, M. Gabbouj, D.J. Inman, 1d convolutional neural networks and applications: a survey. Mech. Syst. Signal Process. **151**, 107398 (2021)
40. J.I. Frogner, F.M. Noori, P. Halvorsen, S.A. Hicks, E. Garcia-Ceja, J. Torresen, M.A. Riegler, One-dimensional convolutional neural networks on motor activity measurements in detection of depression, in *Proceedings of the 4th International Workshop on Multimedia for Personal Health & Health Care* (2019), pp. 9–15
41. R. Kawade, R. Konade, P. Majukar, S. Patil, Speech emotion recognition using 1d CNN-LSTM network on Indo-Aryan database, in *2022 Third International Conference on Intelligent Computing Instrumentation and Control Technologies (ICICICT)* (IEEE, New York, 2022), pp. 1288–1293
42. C. Burton, B. McKinstry, A.S. Tătar, A. Serrano-Blanco, C. Pagliari, M. Wolters, Activity monitoring in patients with depression: a systematic review. J. Affect. Disord. **145**(1), 21 (2013)
43. P. Bashivan, I. Rish, M. Yeasin, N. Codella, Learning representations from EEG with deep recurrent-convolutional neural networks, arXiv preprint arXiv:1511.06448 (2016)
44. G. Li, C.H. Lee, J.J. Jung, Y.C. Youn, D. Camacho, Deep learning for EEG data analytics: a survey. Concurrency Comput. Pract. Exper. **32**(18), e5199 (2020)
45. S. Tripathi, S. Acharya, R. Sharma, T. Mittal, P.K. Bhattacharyya, Using deep and convolutional neural networks for accurate emotion classification on DEAP dataset, in *Proceedings of the AAAI Conference on Artificial Intelligence*, vol. 31 (2017)
46. H. Phan, F. Andreotti, N. Cooray, O. Chén, M. De Vos, Joint classification and prediction CNN framework for automatic sleep stage classification. IEEE Trans. Biomed. Eng. **66**(5), 1285 (2018). https://doi.org/10.1109/TBME.2018.2869560
47. J. He, K. Li, X. Liao, P. Zhang, N. Jiang, Real-time detection of acute cognitive stress using a convolutional neural network from electrocardiographic signal. IEEE Access **7**, 42710 (2019)
48. M. Sokolova, G. Lapalme, A systematic analysis of performance measures for classification tasks. Inf. Process. Manag. **45**(4), 427 (2009)
49. T. Fawcett, An introduction to ROC analysis. Pattern Recogn. Lett. **27**(8), 861 (2006)

50. J.D. Kelleher, B. Mac Namee, A. D'arcy, *Fundamentals of Machine Learning for Predictive Data Analytics: Algorithms, Worked Examples, and Case Studies* (MIT Press, New York, 2020)
51. A.P. Bradley, The use of the area under the ROC curve in the evaluation of machine learning algorithms. Pattern Recogn. **30**(7), 1145 (1997)
52. N. Kovač, K. Ratković, P. Watson, H. Farahani, F. Bagheri Sheykhangafshe, Machine learning classification models for predicting chronic pain. Curr. Psychol. **44**(18), 15409–15422 (2025)
53. D. Chicco, G. Jurman, The advantages of the Matthews correlation coefficient (MCC) over F1 score and accuracy in binary classification evaluation. BMC Genomics **21**, 1 (2020)
54. G.W. Brier, Verification of forecasts expressed in terms of probability. Mon. Weather Rev. **78**(1), 1 (1950)
55. A. Niculescu-Mizil, R. Caruana, Predicting good probabilities with supervised learning, in *Proceedings of the 22nd International Conference on Machine Learning* (2005), pp. 625–632
56. R. Kohavi, et al., A study of cross-validation and bootstrap for accuracy estimation and model selection, in *IJCAI*, vol. 14(2) (Montreal, Canada, 1995), pp. 1137–1145
57. N.V. Chawla, K.W. Bowyer, L.O. Hall, W.P. Kegelmeyer, SMOTE: synthetic minority over-sampling technique. J. Artif. Intell. Res. **16**, 321 (2002)
58. J.W. Creswell, C.N. Poth, *Qualitative Inquiry and Research Design: Choosing Among Five Approaches*, 5th edn. (SAGE Publications, New York, 2024)
59. R.M. Lerner, in *Handbook of Child Psychology*, vol. 1, ed. by R.M. Lerner (Wiley, New York, 2006), pp. 1–17
60. M.H. DeGroot, S.E. Fienberg, The comparison and evaluation of forecasters. J. R. Stat. Soc. D (The Statistician) **32**(1–2), 12 (1983)
61. J. Bröcker, L.A. Smith, Increasing the reliability of reliability diagrams. Weather Forecast. **22**(3), 651 (2007)
62. B.V. Calster, D.J. McLernon, M. van Smeden, L. Wynants, E.W. Steyerberg, Calibration: the Achilles heel of predictive analytics. BMC Med. **17**(1), 230 (2019). https://doi.org/10.1186/s12916-019-1466-7
63. B. Zadrozny, C. Elkan, Transforming classifier scores into accurate multiclass probability estimates, in *Proceedings of the 8th ACM SIGKDD International Conference on Knowledge Discovery and Data Mining (KDD)* (ACM, New York, 2002), pp. 694–699. https://doi.org/10.1145/775047.775151
64. J.C. Platt, Fast training of support vector machines using sequential minimal optimization, in *Advances in Kernel Methods* (1999), pp. 185–208
65. M. Kull, T.S. Filho, P. Flach, Beta calibration: a well-founded and easily implemented improvement on logistic calibration for binary classifiers, in *Proceedings of the 20th International Conference on Artificial Intelligence and Statistics (AISTATS)* (2017), pp. 623–631

Natural Language Processing and Psychological Sciences

Nataša Kovač, Kruna Ratković, Ulfeta Marovac, Hojjatollah Farahani, Marija Blagojević, and Peter Watson

1 Importance of Natural Language Processing

Natural language processing (NLP) refers to computational techniques and algorithms designed to automatically analyse, interpret, and generate human language. By bridging computational linguistics, artificial intelligence, and psychology, NLP tools are uniquely positioned to uncover detailed psychological phenomena embedded within language [1]. With exponential growth in digital communications, such as social media posts, emails, text messages, and online reviews, psychological researchers have unprecedented access to rich textual data. This surge of language-based information has increased the necessity for robust methods capable of extracting meaningful psychological insights. Thus, NLP has emerged as a critical analytical paradigm within psychological sciences, helping researchers investigate complex cognitive, emotional, and behavioural phenomena embedded within textual

N. Kovač (✉) · K. Ratković
Faculty of Applied Sciences, University of Donja Gorica, Podgorica, Montenegro
e-mail: natasa.kovac@udg.edu.me; kruna.ratkovic@udg.edu.me

U. Marovac
Department of Technical and Technological Sciences, State University in Novi Pazar, Novi Pazar, Serbia

H. Farahani
Department of Psychology, Faculty of Humanities, Tarbiat Modares University, Tehran, Iran
e-mail: h.farahani@modares.ac.ir

M. Blagojević
Faculty of Technical Sciences, University of Kragujevac, Čačak, Serbia
e-mail: marija.blagojevic@uni.kg.ac.rs

P. Watson
MRC Cognition and Brain Sciences Unit, University of Cambridge, Cambridge, United Kingdom
e-mail: Peter.Watson@mrc-cbu.cam.ac.uk

N. Kovač et al. (eds.), *Data Science in Psychology*,
https://doi.org/10.1007/978-3-032-18312-5_19

data [2]. Related ML applications on affective/interpersonal features show how language and behaviour signals support risk profiling in relational contexts [3].

One central aspect of NLP's importance in psychological sciences is its ability to handle large-scale textual datasets. Traditional qualitative methods of language analysis in psychology, such as thematic analysis or discourse analysis, while rich and insightful, are often limited by practical constraints such as time, resources, and researcher bias [4]. NLP complements these qualitative methodologies by enabling efficient analysis of extensive corpora, including transcripts from therapy sessions, social media interactions, and digital communications, thereby augmenting traditional approaches with data-driven insights [5]. A central rationale behind the rising significance of NLP in psychology is its capacity to quantify subjective experiences expressed in language. Traditionally, psychological investigations relied heavily on questionnaires and observational methods, inherently limited by self-report biases, experimenter influence, and observational constraints [6]. NLP techniques address these limitations by providing systematic, objective, and replicable approaches to analyse linguistic patterns indicative of psychological states. For example, sentiment analysis methods can detect subtle affective states within narratives or social media discourse, making NLP particularly valuable in emotional psychology, mood research, and affective science [7].

In therapeutic settings, NLP offers tools for examining communication patterns and linguistic indicators of mental health states. Therapists and clinical psychologists frequently record sessions for deeper analysis, yet manual coding and interpretation can be subjective and resource-intensive. NLP facilitates automated sentiment analysis and discourse structure analysis, providing clinicians with objective, quantitative metrics to support their qualitative interpretations. For instance, NLP methodologies have been successfully employed to detect depressive episodes through analysis of linguistic features such as reduced lexical diversity, increased use of negative emotion words, and specific speech patterns [8, 9]. Such analytical capabilities illustrate NLP's profound potential to transform clinical psychology through enhanced diagnostic precision and personalised therapeutic interventions. Beyond quantifying emotion, NLP significantly contributes to understanding cognitive processes through linguistic structure and content analysis. Topic modelling techniques, for instance, have enabled psychologists to identify and classify latent semantic themes within large textual corpora, providing insights into cognition, memory, decision-making, and even cultural cognition [10, 11]. Analysing syntax and linguistic coherence also permits investigation into cognitive mechanisms underlying language production and comprehension. Thus, NLP serves both as a descriptive tool to represent psychological states and as an explanatory tool to delve deeper into cognitive processing underlying language use [12].

NLP has significant implications for understanding social behaviours and interactions, particularly in the context of digital platforms. Social media generates vast quantities of textual data, capturing users' thoughts, emotions, and behaviours in real time. NLP allows researchers to perform sentiment analysis and topic modelling at scale, providing insights into social trends, group dynamics, and collective psychological states [13, 14]. For instance, during significant societal events, analysing Twitter or Facebook posts can offer real-time tracking of public mood, revealing widespread anxiety, optimism, or frustration, which traditional survey methods might miss or delay detecting. Thus, NLP empowers psychologists to monitor and interpret societal attitudes rapidly and accurately, contributing to timely interventions and policy-making. NLP methods offer valuable applications in personality psychology and psychometrics. Recent advancements in computational linguistics have demonstrated the feasibility of inferring personality traits, such as openness, conscientiousness, and neuroticism, from textual data [15]. NLP-derived personality metrics correlate significantly with established psychometric assessments, suggesting NLP can function as a complementary or alternative assessment tool. Automated personality recognition from language patterns, especially valuable due to the widespread accessibility of text-based digital data, enables large-scale psychological assessments and personalised feedback interventions that can significantly enhance the effectiveness of those interventions [16].

NLP's capability to identify personality traits and psychological attributes from language usage marks another area of substantial influence. Researchers have demonstrated robust relationships between linguistic style and individual differences in personality, intelligence, and emotional well-being. Techniques such as automated text classification, *linguistic inquiry and word count* (LIWC), and machine learning models trained on large textual datasets have shown efficacy in predicting personality profiles with notable accuracy [17, 18]. These advancements offer significant potential in recruitment, education, and mental health assessment, where understanding individual personality traits and emotional profiles through linguistic analysis can facilitate tailored interventions and supportive environments. NLP's importance extends into clinical psychology, notably enhancing psychotherapeutic interventions and patient care. By analysing transcripts of therapeutic interactions, NLP algorithms can identify specific therapeutic techniques, measure therapist-patient rapport, and predict clinical outcomes based on linguistic interactions. Such insights were historically challenging to quantify systematically. Now, NLP methods such as semantic role labelling, sentiment tracking, and conversational turn-taking analytics are integral to enhancing therapeutic training, practice, and efficacy [19]. These analytical approaches also contribute significantly to teletherapy and automated therapy bots, addressing mental healthcare accessibility and scalability challenges.

NLP methods also enhance reproducibility and transparency in psychological research. By employing algorithmic processes to analyse textual data, NLP methods standardise data interpretation procedures, reducing biases inherent in manual analyses. This fosters reproducible research practices essential in psychology's current replication-focused scientific culture [20]. By documenting analysis pipelines and sharing NLP-generated analytical codes openly, researchers can ensure that their methodologies are transparent, replicable, and open to critical evaluation, strengthening psychology's overall scientific rigour.

An important consideration is the ethical dimension of NLP application within psychology. While the potential for understanding human behaviour and cognition through NLP is vast, there exist notable concerns regarding privacy, consent, and data handling [21]. As NLP becomes increasingly sophisticated and widely utilised, ethical protocols must be rigorously upheld, especially concerning sensitive psychological data derived from personal communications. Psychological researchers employing NLP must, therefore, navigate complex ethical landscapes, balancing methodological innovation and psychological insights with respect to participant autonomy and confidentiality [22].

Beyond ethical and methodological advancements, NLP also opens opportunities for interdisciplinary collaboration. Combining expertise from psychology, linguistics, computer science, and data science fosters innovation in both methodological rigour and practical application [17]. Psychologists collaborating with computational linguists and computer scientists often find NLP techniques instrumental in testing and refining theoretical models of psychological phenomena. For instance, exploring linguistic markers associated with mental health disorders such as depression and anxiety involves deep collaboration between psychologists who conceptualise these conditions and NLP specialists who operationalise linguistic cues for automated detection [23]. The interdisciplinary nature of NLP, bridging linguistics, psychology, computer science, and cognitive science, facilitates integrative research collaborations. This interdisciplinary cooperation stimulates innovative research questions, methodological advancements, and theoretical expansions, ultimately enriching the psychological sciences with novel insights and methodologies. Collaborative NLP projects have, for instance, produced ground-breaking findings on cognitive load detection, narrative comprehension, and emotional recognition from textual cues, underscoring the transformative potential of interdisciplinary synergy [24, 25].

In educational psychology, NLP methods are transforming the analysis of student and teacher interactions, online learning environments, and classroom discourse. Through sophisticated text mining and discourse analysis, researchers can identify language patterns indicative of effective teaching strategies, student engagement, and knowledge comprehension [26]. NLP methodologies, including automated essay scoring and writing analytics, further facilitate immediate feedback and adaptive learning environments, significantly enhancing educational effectiveness and personalised learning trajectories.

NLP has profound implications for psychological science, offering robust methodologies to analyse extensive and complex textual data that encapsulate psychological states, traits, and processes. Its capacity to systematically identify linguistic patterns associated with emotions, cognitive functions, personality characteristics, and clinical outcomes underscores its essential role in contemporary psychological research. By addressing methodological limitations inherent in traditional assessment methods, NLP equips psychological researchers with the means to deepen theoretical understanding, enhance practical interventions, and uncover insights into human psychology embedded in everyday language.

Figure 1 visually summarises the taxonomy of NLP methodologies commonly applied in psychological research, illustrating their interrelationships and varied applications. This hierarchical structure underscores the breadth of NLP's analytical

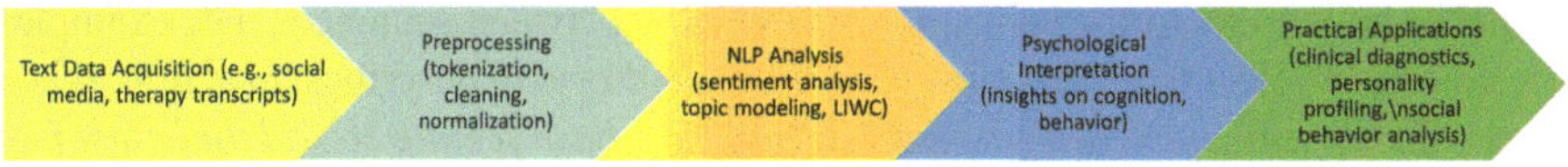

Fig. 1 Workflow of NLP applications in psychological research

capabilities, ranging from sentiment analysis to advanced linguistic modelling, emphasising its versatile role in capturing complex psychological phenomena.

2 Methodologies and Tools for Text Analysis

Text analysis is the process of processing and analysing any sequence of symbols or data sequences that can be interpreted as *text*. Although it most often refers to natural language text, such as written words, this term is also applied to other types of sequences, such as protein sequences, DNA or RNA strands, where each element carries significant information that can be analysed using methods like tokenisation, vectorisation, and pattern recognition [7, 27]. Essentially, text analysis is used to understand and interpret the structural and semantic relationships in different types of sequential data. Text analysis methods and tools have evolved over the decades, from basic techniques to modern approaches. For a computer to understand the text, it is necessary to decompose the data into smaller units and try to clarify the lexical and syntactic meaning of each of them. Traditional text analysis methods relied on various lexical tools such as tokenisation, stemming, and lemmatisation. At the same time, modern approaches have introduced deep learning, transformers, and large language models, thereby enabling a deeper understanding of the context and semantic meaning of the text [1]. In psychological research, these methodologies and tools enable a deeper understanding of human behaviour and emotional states through language analysis. Key methods used in psychological data analysis include [28]:

- *Sentiment analysis*—detection of emotions in text
- *Topic modelling*—discovery of main themes in texts
- *Named entity recognition* (NER)—recognition of key entities such as emotions, disorders, and people
- *Syntactic Parsing*—understanding sentence structure and syntactic connections

These methods allow psychologists to derive meaningful insights from unstructured data, thereby contributing to the understanding of cognitive processes, emotional states, and social interactions [29].

Textual data is unstructured and complex because it contains natural language, whose meaning depends on context, syntax, and semantics. Traditional machine learning methods, which work with structured data, are not efficient enough for this type of data. Text carries information on multiple levels, from the lexical meaning of individual words to the semantic relationships between sentences. For example, the word *sad* refers to an emotion, while the word *crying* describes an action; these are lexical meanings. When a sentence like *I have been feeling so sad these last few days* is followed by *Everything around me reminds me of it*, the second sentence semantically refers to the emotional tone from the first sentence.

These layered meanings require specific methods for recognising and interpreting them correctly. Identifying lexical and semantic features of the text is crucial because it allows us to uncover deeper meaning, emotional tone, and thematic patterns within the data.

One of the first steps in text data processing is pattern recognition within the text. Regular expressions, as a fundamental technique for searching and manipulating text, enable automatic recognition and extraction of specific patterns, such as phrases, specific words, or numerical values. For example, by using regular expressions, we can identify all words containing a particular root, which can be useful in analysing psychological transcripts, such as recognising emotional states or specific symptoms in patients.

After detecting the patterns in the text, we proceed to the tokenisation process, which splits the text into smaller units, i.e. words, phrases, or sentences. Tokenisation is crucial because it allows further analysis of the text, whether it is about emotional content, theme identification, or extraction of keywords. In subsequent steps of processing, we apply text normalisation, which includes stemming and lemmatisation to reduce words to their basic forms. This step allows us to treat different grammatical forms of a word as the same word in the analysis, thus reducing complexity and improving the accuracy of the analysis. For example, the words *happy*, *happier*, and *happiness* would be transformed into the base form *happy*, which facilitates the identification of emotions and thematic patterns in the text. Text vectorisation enables the characteristics of text, such as words, phrases, or entire documents, to be represented as numerical vectors that retain key information about the content. These vectors serve as a representation of the text, allowing machine learning algorithms to analyse the structure and patterns within the data. Text in its natural form is not suitable for computational models because they work with numerical values. Therefore, vectorisation is a necessary step because it translates textual data into a numerical format, enabling machine algorithms to efficiently process, learn from, and draw conclusions based on these numerical representations. Types of vectorisation include different approaches to representing textual data in numerical form. One of the most basic approaches is *bag of words* (BoW), which is based on the frequency of word occurrences in the text. Another popular approach is TF-IDF, which not only takes into account the frequency of words in the text but also the weight of words concerning the entire document set, making words that are specific to a particular document more valuable. Word2Vec is a more advanced model that uses neural networks to create dense vector representations of similar words, enabling a better understanding of their meanings in context. The latest approaches include transformer models, such as *bidirectional encoder representations from transformers* (BERT), which generate contextual vector representations of words, considering their meaning in both directions within the sentence. Vectorisation enables algorithms to efficiently process and classify textual data, and the choice of method depends on the complexity of the task and the need for understanding context [30]. Different types of information can be extracted from a text to enable better understanding of its content, such as text classification, sentiment analysis, and key information identification. Text classification allows texts to be sorted into predefined categories, which is useful for organising data or automatic labelling. Sentiment analysis enables the recognition of the emotional tone in the text, which is important for understanding the author's attitude towards a particular topic [7]. Using techniques such as keyword extraction, it is possible to identify the most important information in a text, which facilitates further processing and data analysis [31].

Traditional text processing methods, such as lexicon-based approaches, which use lexical resources like dictionaries and corpora, encompass various techniques like lexicon-based methods, machine learning, and deep models. Lexicon-based approaches use predefined dictionaries to recognise positive and negative emotions, while machine learning uses classifiers to automatically learn sentiment from data [32]. In addition to general-purpose lexicons, domain-specific dictionaries can be employed to improve the recognition of sentiment and key concepts within a specific field, such as medical terms in healthcare, legal jargon in law, or psychological constructs in mental health research [33]. For example, sentiment analysis can use models such as Naive Bayes classifiers or regression models to recognise sentiment in text. Topic modelling, such as *latent Dirichlet allocation* (LDA) or *latent semantic analysis* (LSA), allows the identification of main topics in large text datasets, helping to organise and analyse large amounts of data.

These methods have limitations when dealing with complex linguistic challenges such as negation, irony, and sarcasm. For example, traditional models struggle to recognise when negation changes the meaning of a sentence, as in the phrase *Not bad*, which can be a positive or negative statement depending on the context [34].

Given these challenges, a new generation of transformer-based models has emerged, such as *large language models* (LLMs). These models allow for much more precise analysis, as they can consider a larger context (tens of thousands of tokens) and better recognise sarcasm, irony, and other specific linguistic patterns. LLMs, such as *generative pre-trained transformer* (GPT) and BERT, recognise deep connections between words in large datasets, which allows them to adapt to various tasks such as text classification, sentiment analysis, text generation, and many other applications. These models do not rely on predefined lexical resources but use massive training datasets, significantly improving accuracy and flexibility in addressing various linguistic challenges [35]. LLMs operate on the principle of deep neural networks trained on vast amounts of data. The key architecture used is the transformer, which allows efficient processing of long text sequences. The central element of the transformer is self-attention, which enables models to evaluate the relationships between all words in a text, regardless of their distance in the sentence [36]. This ability allows models like BERT and GPT to better understand the context and relationships in a text.

LLMs are used for tasks such as sentiment classification (positive, negative, neutral), intent recognition, or document categorisation. These models often employ fine-tuning to optimise them for specific tasks. Fine-tuning is the process of further training the model on specific datasets, which allows the model to better adapt to the given problem.

LLMs are also used for predicting the next word in a text or filling in blanks in a sentence. These tasks involve automatic text completion or predicting responses based on existing data.

BERT uses a bidirectional approach to analyse text in both directions, enabling a richer understanding of the context. It is particularly effective for tasks that require understanding the full context, such as sentiment classification, named entity recognition, and question answering [37].

GPT uses unidirectional attention, making it excellent for generative tasks such as text generation, automatic completion, and translation. GPT is trained to predict the next words and generate coherent textual responses [38].

3 Data Preparation for Text Analysis

Text analysis involves extracting valuable insights from large volumes of unstructured data, which may include articles, social media posts, product reviews, and other textual content. Before any meaningful analysis can take place, the data must be adequately prepared. Effective data preparation plays a crucial role in ensuring the quality and accuracy of analytical results [39]. This chapter discusses the steps and techniques necessary for preparing data for text analysis, including data cleaning, normalisation, tokenisation, filtering, and other preprocessing activities.

Data cleaning is a crucial step in preparing textual data for analysis, as raw text often contains various forms of noise, including unnecessary punctuation marks, numbers, special symbols, and incomplete words. The purpose of this process is to identify and eliminate irrelevant elements, thereby improving the quality and reliability of the analysis.

One of the key aspects of data cleaning is the removal of special characters and punctuation, such as `,` `#,` `%,` &, as well as periods, commas, and question marks. Since punctuation generally does not influence sentiment analysis, its elimination helps streamline the dataset without compromising analytical accuracy [40]. Similarly, numerical data may be excluded when it is not relevant to the analysis. For instance, when examining product reviews that focus on qualitative aspects rather than numerical values, removing numbers can reduce unnecessary noise.

Another important step involves filtering out stop words, frequently used words such as *and*, *in*, *on*, *that*, and *or*. Since these words carry little semantic weight, their removal optimises the dataset by reducing the number of tokens, ultimately enhancing model performance [41].

Text normalisation further ensures consistency across the dataset. A common technique is converting all text into lowercase, which eliminates distinctions between uppercase and lowercase letters and contributes to more uniform analysis [42]. Lemmatisation and stemming help standardise word forms by reducing them to their base form. For example, the word *running* is transformed into *run*, ensuring greater consistency regardless of the word's morphological variations [43].

Tokenisation is a fundamental step in text processing that involves breaking down text into smaller units, known as tokens, which can be words, phrases, or sentences. By segmenting text into these components, machine learning models can analyse it in a structured manner, making it easier to process and interpret [44]. There are different approaches to tokenisation, with word tokenisation focusing on splitting text into individual words, while sentence tokenisation divides text into sentences. The latter is particularly useful for analyses where understanding context within individual sentences is necessary [41]. Since the quality of tokenisation directly influences the accuracy of text analysis models, using advanced tools and libraries such as `nltk` or `spaCy` ensures more precise and reliable tokenisation [45].

Beyond tokenisation, data filtering is also important in improving text quality by eliminating irrelevant or redundant information. Although data cleaning removes noise at a basic level, filtering refines the dataset further by focusing on content relevance and methodological efficiency. One aspect of this process is content-based filtering, which includes identifying and removing duplicate entries. Large datasets often contain repeated elements, such as identical reviews entered multiple times, which can distort analysis results and introduce unnecessary noise [40]. Filtering out texts that are too short or lack meaningful content, such as headlines or introductory phrases in articles, helps maintain analytical precision [46].

Another approach to filtering is method-based filtering, which includes removing low-frequency words. Words that appear only a few times in a dataset may not contribute significantly to the analysis and can increase model complexity without adding real value. For example, highly specialised technical terms that occur sporadically may be irrelevant in sentiment analysis and could be excluded to streamline processing [10].

Furthermore, in text analysis using machine learning, textual data must be transformed into a numeric format, as most algorithms cannot process raw text. To achieve this, various transformation techniques are applied [47]. One common approach is the BoW, which represents text as a matrix where each row corresponds to a document and each column to a word, with values indicating word frequency [48]. While effective, this method can be inefficient for large text corpora. A more refined technique, *term frequency-inverse document frequency* (TF-IDF), improves upon BoW by accounting for both the frequency of a word in a specific document and its distribution across the entire corpus. This helps minimise the influence of common words that do not contribute significantly to meaning [49].

Beyond statistical representations, word embeddings such as Word2Vec and GloVe provide a more sophisticated way of capturing semantic relationships. These models represent words as vectors in a multi-dimensional space, making them particularly useful for sentiment analysis, entity recognition, and language translation [50, 51]. More advanced deep learning transformers, like BERT and GPT, incorporate contextual word representations, analysing words about their surrounding text. This significantly enhances tasks that require a deeper understanding of language [38, 52].

Each text analysis presents unique challenges that need to be carefully addressed during data preparation. The structure and complexity of different languages influence tokenisation, lemmatisation, and entity recognition, as some languages (e.g. the English language) have standardised rules, while others require more detailed processing. Preserving context is equally important, particularly for words with multiple meanings depending on usage [52]. Class imbalances, such as datasets where positive reviews significantly outnumber negative ones, must be managed to ensure reliable model performance [53].

Thorough data preparation, including cleaning, tokenisation, filtering, and numerical transformation, provides the necessary foundation for accurate and meaningful text analysis. By applying appropriate techniques, machine learning models can process text more effectively and generate valuable insights.

4 NLP Tools and Libraries

The growing accessibility of NLP methods in psychological research is largely attributed to the development of robust and user-friendly libraries and frameworks. These tools allow researchers with limited programming expertise to apply sophisticated text analysis techniques in a reproducible and scalable manner. Python, in particular, has emerged as the dominant programming language for NLP applications in psychology due to its extensive ecosystem of open-source libraries and strong community support.

Among the most widely used NLP libraries is `NLTK` (*natural language toolkit*), which provides functionalities for tokenisation, part-of-speech tagging, syntactic parsing, stemming, and more. It is often used in educational settings and for prototyping psychological text analyses because of its ease of use and comprehensive documentation [44]. For tasks requiring industrial-scale efficiency, `spaCy` offers a fast and production-ready alternative. It is built for large-scale text processing and supports named entity recognition, dependency parsing, and text classification with pre-trained models in multiple languages [54].

In psychological research that involves emotional and affective analysis, `TextBlob` and `VADER` (*Valence Aware Dictionary and sEntiment Reasoner*) are commonly applied. These libraries offer rule-based sentiment analysis capabilities and are particularly suited for social media data or short texts, where detecting emotional tone is crucial [55]. For more advanced and customisable workflows, transformers from Hugging Face provides access to a wide range of pre-trained deep learning models such as BERT, GPT, and RoBERTa, which have shown exceptional performance across various NLP tasks [56].

The following Python code uses spaCy and TextBlob to perform basic preprocessing and sentiment analysis on therapy transcripts:

```
import spacy
from textblob import TextBlob

# Load spaCy model
nlp = spacy.load("en_core_web_sm")

# Sample therapeutic session text
text = "I^^e2^^80^^99ve been feeling really anxious lately.
↪  Nothing seems to help."

# NLP pipeline
doc = nlp(text)
for token in doc:
    print(f"{token.text} -> {token.pos_}")

# Sentiment analysis with TextBlob
blob = TextBlob(text)
print("Polarity:", blob.sentiment.polarity)
print("Subjectivity:", blob.sentiment.subjectivity)
```

This example demonstrates how to extract syntactic structure using spaCy and evaluate emotional valence with TextBlob. Polarity values range from -1 to 1, with negative values indicating negative sentiment and positive values reflecting positive emotion. Subjectivity scores assess the extent to which the text reflects subjective opinions versus factual information, a useful distinction in psychotherapy narratives.

Topic modelling, frequently used in psychological content analysis, is supported by libraries such as gensim, which implements *latent Dirichlet allocation* (LDA) and other probabilistic models for uncovering semantic themes in large text corpora [57]. These tools are particularly useful when analysing open-ended survey responses or therapy transcripts, allowing researchers to detect latent psychological constructs.

The following Python example demonstrates how to perform topic modelling using gensim's implementation of LDA on a small set of sample psychological statements:

```
import gensim
from gensim import corpora
from wordcloud import WordCloud
import matplotlib.pyplot as plt

# Sample corpus from therapy transcripts
texts = [
    ["feel", "anxious", "work", "pressure", "sleep"],
    ["happy", "relationship", "support", "partner"],
    ["sad", "isolation", "lockdown", "lonely"],
    ["stress", "exams", "university", "overwhelmed"]
]

# Create a dictionary and corpus for LDA
dictionary = corpora.Dictionary(texts)
corpus = [dictionary.doc2bow(text) for text in texts]

# Train LDA model
lda_model = gensim.models.LdaModel(corpus, num_topics=2,
 ↪  id2word=dictionary, passes=15)

# Generate word clouds for each topic
fig, axes = plt.subplots(1, 2, figsize=(12, 6))
for i in range(2):
    topic_terms = lda_model.show_topic(i, topn=10)
    topic_dict = dict(topic_terms)

    wordcloud = WordCloud(background_color='white',
     ↪  colormap='Blues').generate_from_frequencies(topic_dict)

    axes[i].imshow(wordcloud, interpolation='bilinear')
    axes[i].axis('off')
    axes[i].set_title(f"Topic {i+1}", fontsize=14)

plt.suptitle("LDA Topic Word Clouds", fontsize=16)
plt.tight_layout()
plt.show()
```

This code creates a dictionary and bag-of-words representation from a small psychological dataset (e.g. extracted from open-ended responses or interviews). Using `gensim`'s `LdaModel`, the code trains a topic model to uncover two latent themes. After training the model, the top keywords for each topic are extracted and visualised using the `WordCloud` library. The word clouds for each topic display the most representative terms, with font size reflecting term relevance within each topic, as shown in Fig. 2. This visualisation supports qualitative interpretation of the

Fig. 2 Word cloud visualisation using LDA

extracted themes, which is particularly valuable in psychological applications where latent constructs are often inferred from free-form verbal responses.

For large-scale applications, `transformers` enables the use of state-of-the-art language models for tasks such as emotion classification, personality detection, or mental health prediction. These models can be fine-tuned on psychological datasets to enhance domain-specific performance. Libraries such as `Coh-Metrix`, designed specifically for psychological and educational research, offer indices for text cohesion, syntactic simplicity, narrativity, and readability, which are valuable for analysing educational materials or assessing cognitive load in textual tasks [26].

The following Python example demonstrates how to perform sentiment analysis using a pre-trained BERT model from the `transformers` library. This approach can be adapted for more advanced psychological NLP tasks, including stress detection or emotion profiling:

```
from transformers import pipeline

# Load a sentiment analysis pipeline
classifier = pipeline("sentiment-analysis")

# Sample text from a therapy session
text = "Lately, I've been overwhelmed with anxiety and feel
↪  like I'm losing control."

# Run the sentiment analysis
result = classifier(text)
print(result)
```

This code uses Hugging Face's `transformers` library to load a pre-trained BERT-based model for sentiment classification. The `pipeline` abstraction allows for rapid deployment of common NLP tasks without requiring manual tokenisation or model loading. In this example, a sample sentence reflective of therapeutic discourse is passed through the classifier. The model then returns a label, such as *NEGATIVE* or *POSITIVE*, along with a confidence score. Such analysis can help psychological researchers assess emotional tone across large datasets of clinical narratives, therapy transcripts, or social media posts. The flexibility of `transformers` also allows researchers to fine-tune these models on specific psychological corpora to improve relevance and accuracy in domain-specific applications.

To ensure transparency and reproducibility, researchers are encouraged to document their preprocessing pipelines, version control the models and corpora used, and share their code when possible. The combination of accessible tools and reproducible workflows has significantly lowered the barrier to entry for psychologists aiming to integrate NLP into their work, enabling the analysis of complex linguistic phenomena at scale. The integration of open-source NLP libraries such as `NLTK`, `spaCy`, `TextBlob`, `VADER`, `gensim`, and `transformers` has revolutionised the field of psychological text analysis. These tools empower researchers to extract cognitive, emotional, and behavioural insights from textual data, supporting both exploratory and confirmatory analyses in a wide range of psychological domains.

5 Application of Text Analysis in Psychological Research

In contemporary psychological research practice, the analysis of textual data plays a key role in understanding psychological phenomena. The application of NLP techniques allows researchers to decode emotions, cognitive processes, and social aspects of human behaviour through sources such as therapy transcripts, social media posts, and other written data. NLP helps in recognising emotions, identifying personality traits, and assessing mental health, providing deeper insights into psychological processes and behaviour. This approach enables precise analysis of social interactions, emotional expression, problem-solving, and decision-making, thereby enhancing the understanding of psychological dynamics. Approaches to emotion and sentiment analysis include methods based on lexicons, corpora, machine learning, and deep learning. The lexicon-based approach is easy to apply, while corpora provides domain-specific precision but with limited generalisation. Machine learning and deep learning methods depend on data processing, with deep models like *recurrent neural networks* (RNNs) and *long short-term memory* (LSTM) networks efficiently recognising long-term dependencies. In addition, transfer learning and LLMs enable more accurate results and better recognition of complex emotional tones. The combination of these methods improves precision and efficiency in analysis. In emotion analysis, different models are used, including categorical models (such as Plutchik's and Ekman's models), with varying numbers of emotion categories. There are also dimensional models based on dimensions such as dominance, polarity, and arousal. The dictionary-based approach uses predefined word lists associated with emotions, such as the NRC emotion lexicon [7], to identify emotions in text. Models use these dictionaries to enrich text vectors, which are then used for emotion classification in the training and prediction phases, learning from labelled data and predicting emotions for new texts. On the other hand, labelled corpora in emotion analysis are used for training and evaluating models that recognise emotions in text. The types of labelling include expert annotations and crowdsourcing annotations, where emotions are labelled based on whether they relate to the feelings of the reader (CA) or the person mentioned in the text (EA). Some of the available corpora are AffectiveText (news headlines), Blogs (sentences from blogs), CrowdFlower (Twitter posts), EmoBank (sentences from multiple genres and domains), and DailyDialogs (dialogues) [58]. Examples of emotion analysis applications include mapping emotions in texts such as the tragedy *Hamlet* and the comedy *As You Like It* [59], the emotional geography of London through novels [60], as well as the annotation of suicide notes in the CEASE corpus [61]. The general procedure for applying LLM models for emotion analysis involves using a pre-trained model architecture, such as BERT, which is further trained on a specific labelled dataset, such as Reddit comments with assigned emotional categories. For example, the GoEmotions model uses BERT pre-trained on 58,000 Reddit comments with 27 emotional categories, enabling emotion recognition in text. After fine-tuning on this corpus, the model becomes capable of recognising different emotions in new, unlabelled texts. In personality analysis, natural language processing (NLP) techniques play a key role in identifying personality traits based on textual data such as online posts, dialogues, biographical texts, blogs, and social media comments. Research has shown that verbal behaviour and word choice can be linked to personality traits according to the Big Five model, which includes extraversion, agreeableness, conscientiousness, neuroticism, and openness to experience. For example, individuals with high neuroticism tend to use more negative emotions and first-person singular pronouns, while extraverts are more inclined towards positive emotions and social processes. By using NLP techniques, it is possible to identify and analyse these behavioural characteristics, providing a deeper understanding of personality based on the digital traces we leave in everyday communication [14].

Personality analysis studies the traits that define an individual's behaviour and emotions. One approach to determining personality type is using NLP methodology, which analyses the language people use instead of traditional methods like questionnaires or tests. This approach is based on the assumption that language reflects deeper personality traits that are linked to objective behaviour, rather than just the self-reports people give about themselves. By using linguistic data, NLP methodology identifies patterns in speech and writing that point to specific personality traits according to the Big Five factors, such as extraversion, neuroticism, agreeableness, conscientiousness, and openness to experience. Analysing words, phrases, and other linguistic features, such as syntactic structures and writing style, provides a more precise understanding of personality. Techniques like sentiment analysis, keyword recognition, and topic modeling help predict dominant personality traits based on language behaviour, offering a more objective insight into personality than self-reports would [2]. The second approach to personality analysis uses visual data, rather than just textual data, to predict personality based on the Big Five model. This approach relies on the analysis of images that people choose or interpret, such as images in tests like the *thematic apperception test (TAT)*, where participants are asked to write a detailed description of the image. Based on these descriptions, computer methods like *deep neural networks* (CNN) analyse patterns in the images that may indicate personality traits. For example, nature images may be associated with openness, while images of social interactions may indicate extraversion.

To create such a model, it is necessary to first collect visual corpora related to personalities, such as images people choose in specific situations, along with corresponding textual analyses of their reactions. These data can be used to train a model that links images to linguistic patterns in order to more accurately predict personality type based on combined data. The model's evaluation uses correlation between actual and predicted traits, as well as accuracy and F_1-score to assess the model's predictive power [62].

Mental health assessment using NLP is used to analyse patients' verbal expressions, identifying signs of depression, anxiety, and other mental disorders. By analysing written and spoken statements, it is possible to detect tone, emotions, vocabulary, and speech patterns that indicate negative emotional states. Patients who use words associated with sadness, hopelessness, or stress can be identified as individuals at higher risk of mental disorders. This method allows professionals to monitor patients' mental health and respond on time.

In recent years, social media platforms such as Facebook, Twitter, and Reddit have become important data sources for mental health analysis. For example, discussions about depression on Twitter can help understand the mental state of the broader community. Social media also provides support during the postpartum period, offering help to users, and predictive models based on data from these platforms can track mood changes [63].

Research on linguistic analysis and mental health confirms a strong link between language and mental state. For instance, analyses of tweets where users report depression showed high accuracy in detecting depressive symptoms using machine learning [64].

Joint modelling of emotions and mental health has become particularly significant in the context of datasets like CEASE and EmoMent, which enable better prediction of depression based on emotions. Social networks such as Reddit, Facebook, and Twitter serve as essential data sources for mental health analysis, as they provide texts in multiple languages that are used for linguistic analysis and mental state detection using machine learning models, including advanced LLMs like RoBERTa. These studies highlight the great potential in recognising and predicting mental disorders based on language analysis, allowing for the timely identification of emotional issues and mental states [65].

6 Visualising NLP Results

Visualisation of NLP results enables effective understanding and interpretation of data based on large amounts of textual data, such as interview transcripts, social media posts, and other forms of communication. These results can be visualised using various techniques such as word clouds, *t-Distributed Stochastic Neighbour Embedding* (t-SNE), sentiment analysis, and topic modelling. These techniques help researchers better understand linguistic phenomena related to psychological processes.

Word clouds offer a visually intuitive method for summarising the most frequently occurring terms in a text corpus. In psychological research, they serve as a quick way to identify dominant themes or emotional tones embedded in written responses, interviews, or online communication. Frequently appearing words are displayed in larger font sizes, providing immediate visual cues to prevalent topics. For example, in analysing social media discourse on mental health, a word cloud may reveal that terms such as *depression*, *anxiety*, *therapy*, and *emotions* occur frequently, highlighting key concerns and focus areas of the population [66].

To illustrate this concept, we can use Python's `wordcloud` library to generate a word cloud from sample psychological text. The following implementation demonstrates the entire process, from specifying the text to rendering the visualisation:

```
from wordcloud import WordCloud
import matplotlib.pyplot as plt

# Sample text
text = """
Word clouds represent a simple yet effective way to visualise
 ↪  the frequency of specific words in a text. In psychological
 ↪  research, word clouds are used to represent dominant
 ↪  themes, such as emotional tone or key terms related to
 ↪  specific psychological phenomena. For instance, in
 ↪  analysing public opinion on mental health, a word cloud may
 ↪  display the most commonly used terms like depression,
 ↪  anxiety, therapy, emotions, and others.
"""

# Generate word cloud
wordcloud = WordCloud(width=900, height=500,
 ↪  background_color='white').generate(text)

# Display the word cloud
plt.figure(figsize=(12, 6))
plt.imshow(wordcloud, interpolation='bilinear')
plt.axis('off')
plt.show()
```

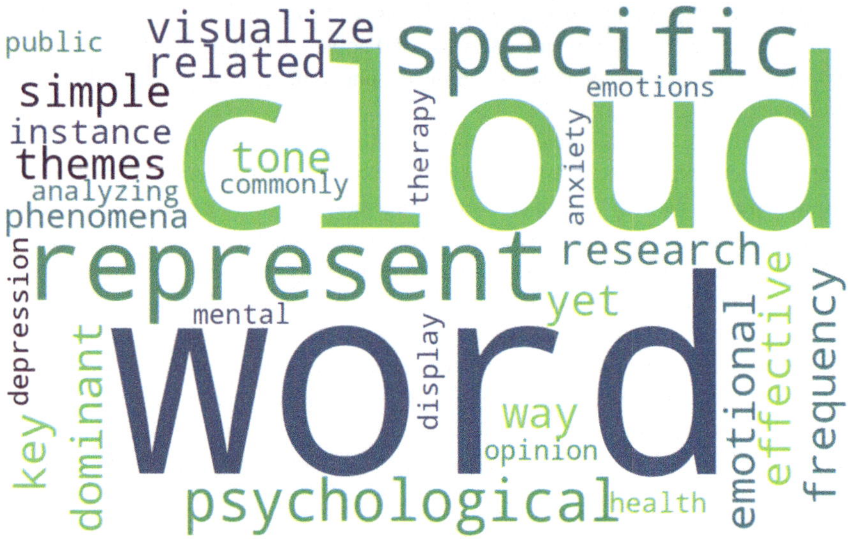

Fig. 3 Word cloud display

This code transforms the given text into a visual representation, where each word's prominence corresponds to its frequency of appearance. It provides a quick overview of the content's central psychological concepts, facilitating both exploratory analysis and effective communication of findings.

The output is presented in Fig. 3, which visually summarises the most frequent terms in the sample text corpus.

The t-SNE is a technique used for dimensionality reduction and visualisation of high-dimensional data. In NLP, t-SNE is particularly useful for displaying similarities among texts in a way that allows researchers to observe patterns in the data, such as emotional tones or communication styles. For example, in the analysis of emotional reactions to mental health topics, t-SNE can help identify emotional clusters. A t-SNE visualisation showing users' emotional reactions to mental health topics and clustering of similar emotions is presented in [67].

To illustrate how t-SNE can be used to project psychological text data into a 2D space, the following Python code creates sample text vectors (using TF-IDF) and applies t-SNE to reduce dimensionality.

```
from sklearn.feature_extraction.text import TfidfVectorizer
from sklearn.manifold import TSNE
import matplotlib.pyplot as plt
import seaborn as sns

# Example psychological documents
documents = [
    "I feel anxious and worried",
    "Today I am very happy and excited",
    "I am feeling low and depressed",
    "I feel calm and relaxed",
    "I feel stressed about exams",
    "I feel confident in social situations"
]

# Convert text to TF-IDF vectors
vectorizer = TfidfVectorizer()
X = vectorizer.fit_transform(documents)

# Apply t-SNE
tsne = TSNE(n_components=2, random_state=42)
X_embedded = tsne.fit_transform(X.toarray())

# Plotting
plt.figure(figsize=(8, 6))
sns.scatterplot(x=X_embedded[:, 0], y=X_embedded[:, 1], hue=["Anxious",
↪ "Happy", "Depressed", "Calm", "Stressed", "Confident"], s=100)
plt.title("t-SNE Projection of Psychological Sentences")
plt.xlabel("Dimension 1")
plt.ylabel("Dimension 2")
plt.tight_layout()
plt.show()
```

The result of this procedure is presented in Fig. 4, showing the reduced two-dimensional representation of the emotional expressions extracted from psychological sentences. Different emotional expressions are plotted using colours and labels, enabling the visualisation of their spatial clustering and emotional proximity.

Sentiment analysis plays a central role in psychological NLP applications, as it enables researchers to quantify emotional tone in textual data. Common applications include monitoring therapy progress, analysing mood in diaries or online posts, or evaluating emotional reactions in experimental texts. Visualising the outcomes of sentiment classification can reveal trends across individuals or time, making it easier to communicate findings to both experts and non-specialists.

A typical visualisation includes a bar plot summarising sentiment scores across a set of texts. The following Python example uses the `textblob` library to compute sentiment polarity of several psychological sentences and visualises the results using `matplotlib`.

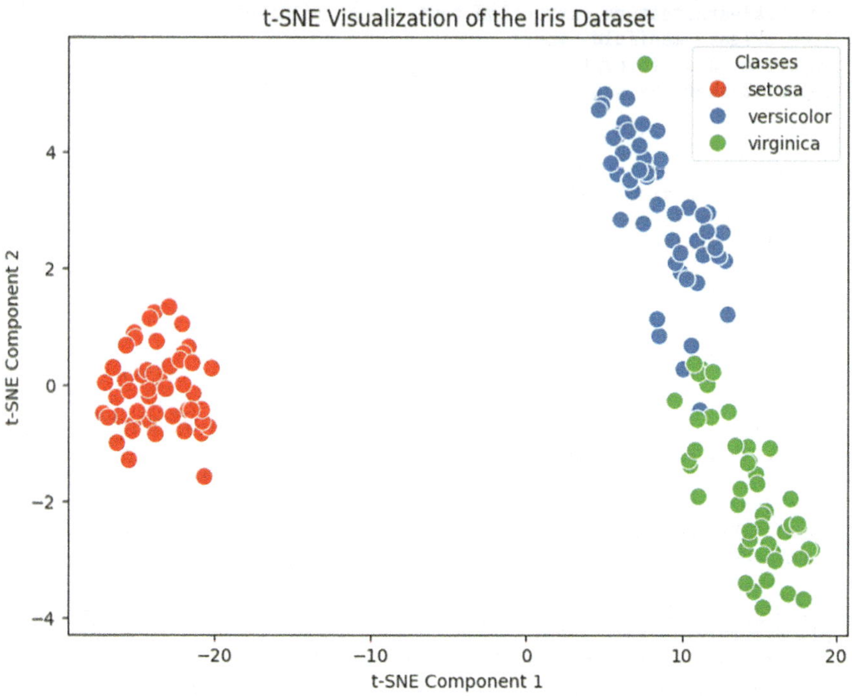

Fig. 4 t-SNE visualisation

```
# Importing the necessary libraries
from textblob import TextBlob
import matplotlib.pyplot as plt

# List of example texts for sentiment analysis
texts = [
    "I love sentiment analysis! It's so much fun and rewarding.",
    "I hate when my code doesn't work properly.",
    "The weather today is fantastic!",
    "I'm feeling sad today.",
    "I am so excited about this new project!"
]

# Function to get the polarity of each text
def get_sentiment(text):
    blob = TextBlob(text)
    return blob.sentiment.polarity

# List to store the polarity values
polarities = [get_sentiment(text) for text in texts]
```

```
# Plotting the polarity scores
plt.figure(figsize=(10, 6))
plt.barh(texts, polarities, color='skyblue')
plt.axvline(x=0, color='gray', linestyle='--') # Adding a vertical line
↪ at 0 to separate positive and negative
plt.xlabel('Sentiment Polarity')
plt.title('Sentiment Analysis Visualization')
plt.show()
```

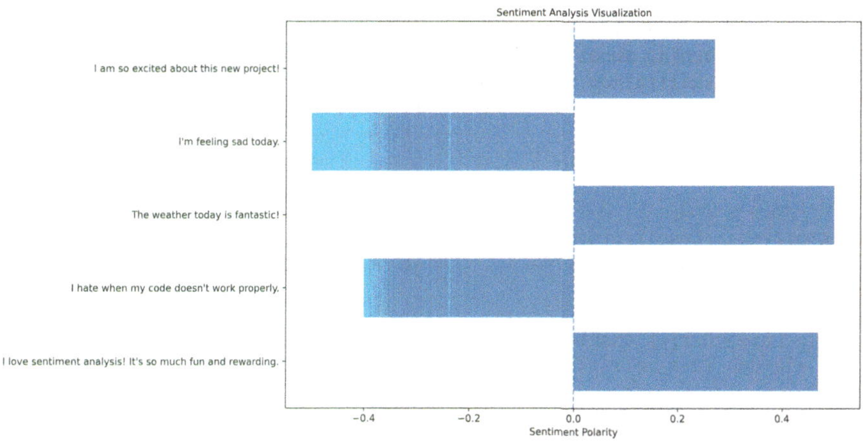

Fig. 5 Example of sentiment analysis visualisation

Figure 5 displays the sentiment polarity of each sentence. Values close to 1 indicate strong positive sentiment, values near 0 represent neutrality, and values approaching -1 reflect strong negative sentiment. This form of visualisation helps psychologists to quickly identify emotionally charged expressions and patterns in participant-generated text, particularly when used longitudinally.

Topic modelling is a computational technique that enables automatic extraction of latent topics from large collections of text. It is particularly valuable in psychological research to identify the underlying themes in open responses, therapy transcripts, or social media text. Popular algorithms such as LDA and *non-negative matrix factorisation* (NMF) allow researchers to uncover recurring linguistic patterns associated with psychological constructs or behavioural traits.

Visualising the results of topic modeling is essential for interpreting the identified themes. Common approaches include bar plots of top words per topic and heatmaps showing the intensity of topic contributions across documents. Murdock and Allen [68] demonstrated how visual representations can be used to effectively communicate the results of topic analysis in psychological text corpora [68].

To illustrate how topic modelling is implemented and visualised, consider the following Python example using `scikit-learn` and `matplotlib`. A set of example documents is analysed using LDA to extract three topics. Each topic is described by its most prominent words, and a bar chart shows the proportion of each topic across all documents.

```
from sklearn.decomposition import LatentDirichletAllocation
from sklearn.feature_extraction.text import CountVectorizer
import matplotlib.pyplot as plt

# Sample text data (documents)
documents = [
    "I love machine learning and data science.",
    "Deep learning is a subfield of machine learning.",
    "Python programming is widely used in data science.",
    "I am learning about natural language processing.",
    "Data visualisation techniques are important in data science.",
    "Natural language processing allows computers to understand human
    ↪ language.",
]

# Convert documents to a document-term matrix using CountVectorizer
vectorizer = CountVectorizer(stop_words='english')
doc_term_matrix = vectorizer.fit_transform(documents)

# Create LDA model using sklearn
lda = LatentDirichletAllocation(n_components=3, random_state=42)
lda.fit(doc_term_matrix)

# Get the words corresponding to each topic
words = vectorizer.get_feature_names_out()
for index, topic in enumerate(lda.components_):
    print(f"Topic {index + 1}:")
    print([words[i] for i in topic.argsort()[:-6 - 1:-1]])  # Top 5 words
    print()

# Visualise the topic distribution across documents
topic_distribution = lda.transform(doc_term_matrix)

# Plot the distribution of topics for each document
plt.figure(figsize=(8, 6))
for i in range(3):
    plt.bar(range(len(documents)), topic_distribution[:, i],
            alpha=0.7, label=f"Topic {i + 1}")
plt.xlabel('Documents')
plt.ylabel('Topic Proportion')
plt.title('Topic Distribution per Document')
plt.legend()
plt.show()
```

The above implementation performs several key steps: First, it uses `CountVectorizer` to convert text into a document-term matrix, eliminating stop words. The LDA model then identifies latent topics, with the number of topics (`n_components`) set to 3. The output includes the top five keywords per topic and a bar chart showing the distribution of each topic across the documents.

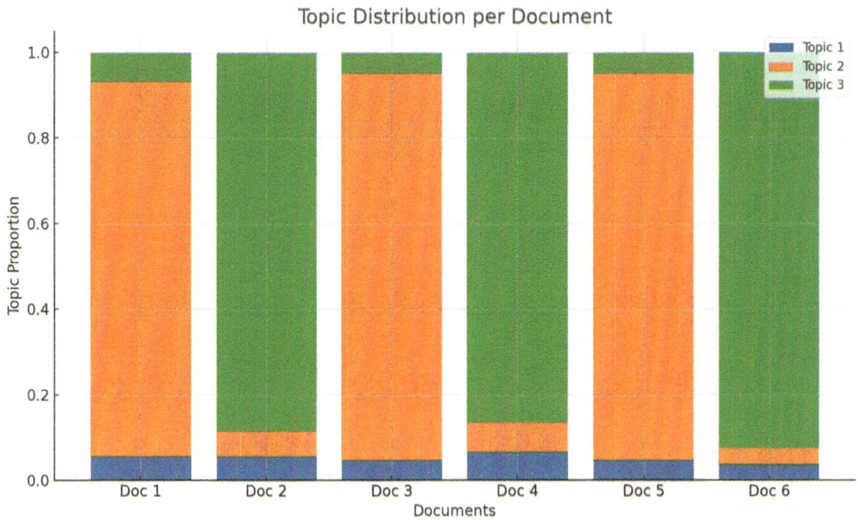

Fig. 6 Topic distribution across six documents derived using latent Dirichlet allocation

Figure 6 illustrates how the topics are distributed across the six input documents. This type of visualisation helps researchers interpret the thematic composition of textual data and understand how documents differ in their psychological focus.

By using word clouds, t-SNE, sentiment analysis, and topic modelling, researchers can better understand linguistic patterns associated with psychological processes. These visual tools facilitate data analysis and interpretation. They also allow for better communication of findings to a broader audience. As technology advances, these methods are expected to develop further, making NLP even more valuable in psychological research.

References

1. D. Jurafsky, J.H. Martin, *Speech and Language Processing: An Introduction to Natural Language Processing, Computational Linguistics, and Speech Recognition with Language Models*, 3rd edn. (Stanford University, Stanford, 2025). https://web.stanford.edu/~jurafsky/slp3/. Online manuscript released January 12, 2025
2. R.L. Boyd, J.W. Pennebaker, Language-based personality: a new approach to personality in a digital world. Curr. Opin. Behav. Sci. **18**, 63 (2017)
3. H. Farahani, P. Watson, N. Kovač, F.B. Sheykhangafshe, P. Azadfallah, A. Allahyari, F. Esrafilian, R.R. Chesli, in *International Handbook of Love: Transcultural and Transdisciplinary Perspectives* (Springer, New York, 2025), pp. 1–22
4. V. Braun, V. Clarke, Using thematic analysis in psychology. Qual. Res. Psychol. **3**(2), 77 (2006)
5. H.A. Schwartz, J.C. Eichstaedt, M.L. Kern, L. Dziurzynski, S.M. Ramones, M. Agrawal, A. Shah, M. Kosinski, D. Stillwell, M.E. Seligman, et al., Personality, gender, and age in the language of social media: the open-vocabulary approach. PloS One **8**(9), e73791 (2013)

6. T.K. Landauer, P.W. Foltz, D. Laham, An introduction to latent semantic analysis. Discourse Process. **25**(2–3), 259 (1998)
7. S.M. Mohammad, in *Emotion Measurement* (Elsevier, Amsterdam, 2021), pp. 323–379
8. M. Morales, S. Scherer, R. Levitan, A cross-modal review of indicators for depression detection systems, in *Proceedings of the Fourth Workshop on Computational Linguistics and Clinical Psychology—From Linguistic Signal to Clinical Reality* (2017), pp. 1–12
9. J.C. Eichstaedt, R.J. Smith, R.M. Merchant, L.H. Ungar, P. Crutchley, D. Preoţiuc-Pietro, D.A. Asch, H.A. Schwartz, Facebook language predicts depression in medical records. Proc. Natl. Acad. Sci. **115**(44), 11203 (2018)
10. D.M. Blei, A.Y. Ng, M.I. Jordan, Latent Dirichlet allocation. J. Mach. Learn. Res. **3**(Jan), 993 (2003)
11. T.L. Griffiths, M. Steyvers, J.B. Tenenbaum, Topics in semantic representation. Psychol. Rev. **114**(2), 211 (2007)
12. A.C. Graesser, D.S. McNamara, M.M. Louwerse, Z. Cai, Coh-Metrix: analysis of text on cohesion and language. Behav. Res. Methods Instrum. Comput. **36**(2), 193 (2004)
13. D.M. Blei, Probabilistic topic models. Commun. ACM **55**(4), 77 (2012)
14. J.W. Pennebaker, M.R. Mehl, K.G. Niederhoffer, Psychological aspects of natural language use: our words, our selves. Annu. Rev. Psychol. **54**(1), 547 (2003)
15. T. Yarkoni, Personality in 100,000 words: a large-scale analysis of personality and word use among bloggers. J. Res. Pers. **44**(3), 363 (2010)
16. B. Danet, S.C. Herring, *The Multilingual Internet: Language, Culture, and Communication Online* (Oxford University, Oxford, 2007)
17. Y.R. Tausczik, J.W. Pennebaker, The psychological meaning of words: LIWC and computerized text analysis methods. J. Lang. Soc. Psychol. **29**(1), 24 (2010)
18. W. Youyou, M. Kosinski, D. Stillwell, Computer-based personality judgments are more accurate than those made by humans. Proc. Natl. Acad. Sci. **112**(4), 1036 (2015)
19. Z.E. Imel, M. Steyvers, D.C. Atkins, Computational psychotherapy research: scaling up the evaluation of patient–provider interactions. Psychotherapy **52**(1), 19 (2015)
20. O.S. Collaboration, Estimating the reproducibility of psychological science. Science **349**(6251), aac4716 (2015)
21. J.P. Mikal, S. Hurst, M. Conway, Ethical issues in using Twitter for population-level depression monitoring: a qualitative study. BMC Med. Ethics **17**(1), 22 (2016). https://doi.org/10.1186/s12910-016-0105-5. https://bmcmedethics.biomedcentral.com/articles/10.1186/s12910-016-0105-5
22. M. Conway, D. O'Connor, Social media, big data, and mental health: current advances and ethical implications. Curr. Opin. Psychol. **9**, 77 (2016)
23. G. Coppersmith, M. Dredze, C. Harman, Quantifying mental health signals in Twitter, in *Proceedings of the Workshop on Computational Linguistics and Clinical Psychology: From Linguistic Signal to Clinical Reality* (2014), pp. 51–60
24. S.A. Crossley, D.B. Allen, D.S. McNamara, Text readability and intuitive simplification: a comparison of readability formulas. Reading in a Foreign Lang. **23**(1), 84 (2011)
25. A.C. Graesser, D.S. McNamara, K. VanLehn, Scaffolding deep comprehension strategies through Point&Query, AutoTutor, and iSTART. Educ. Psychol. **40**(4), 225 (2005)
26. D.S. McNamara, A.C. Graesser, P.M. McCarthy, Z. Cai, *Automated Evaluation of Text and Discourse with Coh-Metrix* (Cambridge University, Cambridge, 2014)
27. U.A. Marovac, N. Mitić, N-gram analysis of COG categorized protein sequences. Commun. Math. Comput. Chem. **74**, 575 (2015)
28. A. Bittermann, A. Fischer. Natural language processing in psychology. Z. Psychol. **232**(3), 143–146 (2024). https://doi.org/10.1027/2151-2604/a000568
29. R.L. Boyd, H.A. Schwartz, Natural language analysis and the psychology of verbal behavior: the past, present, and future states of the field. J. Lang. Soc. Psychol. **40**(1), 21 (2021)
30. J. Eisenstein, *Introduction to natural language processing* (The MIT Press, 2019)
31. N. Firoozeh, A. Nazarenko, F. Alizon, B. Daille, Keyword extraction: issues and methods. Nat. Lang. Eng. **26**(3), 259 (2020)

32. A.L. Gentile, P. Basile, L. Iaquinta, G. Semeraro, Lexical and semantic resources for NLP: from words to meanings, in *Knowledge-Based Intelligent Information and Engineering Systems: 12th International Conference, KES 2008, Zagreb, Croatia, September 3–5, 2008, Proceedings, Part III 12* (Springer, New York, 2008), pp. 277–284
33. A. Avdic, U. Marovac, D. Jankovic, Automated labeling of terms in medical reports in Serbian. Turk. J. Electr. Eng. Comput. Sci. **28**(6), 3285 (2020)
34. A. Ljajić, U. Marovac, Improving sentiment analysis for Twitter data by handling negation rules in the Serbian language. Comput. Sci. Inf. Syst. **16**(1), 289 (2019)
35. N. Patwardhan, S. Marrone, C. Sansone, Transformers in the real world: a survey on NLP applications. Information **14**(4), 242 (2023)
36. A. Vaswani, N. Shazeer, N. Parmar, J. Uszkoreit, L. Jones, A.N. Gomez, Ł. Kaiser, I. Polosukhin, *Attention is all you need*, Ed. by I. Guyon, U.V. Luxburg, S. Bengio, H. Wallach, R. Fergus, S. Vishwanathan, R. Garnett. Advances in neural information processing systems, vol 30 (Curran Associates, Inc., 2017)
37. J. Devlin, M.W. Chang, K. Lee, K. Toutanova, Bert: Pre-training of deep bidirectional transformers for language understanding, in *Proceedings of the 2019 Conference of the North American Chapter of the Association for Computational Linguistics: Human Language Technologies, volume 1 (Long and Short Papers)* (2019), pp. 4171–4186
38. A. Radford, J. Wu, R. Child, D. Luan, D. Amodei, I. Sutskever, Language models are few-shot learners. arXiv preprint arXiv:2005.14165 (2019)
39. A. Kushal, D. Garg, V. Sharma, Data preprocessing techniques for text mining. J. Comput. Inf. Technol. **28**(1), 35 (2020)
40. Y. Zhang, J. Yang, et al., Text preprocessing for text mining: a survey. J. Comput. Linguistics **45**(3), 305 (2019)
41. C.D. Manning, P. Raghavan, H. Schütze, *Introduction to Information Retrieval* (Cambridge University, Cambridge, 2008)
42. M.T. Ribeiro, S. Singh, C. Guestrin, Why should i trust you?: Explaining the predictions of any classifier, in *Proceedings of the 22nd ACM SIGKDD International Conference on Knowledge Discovery and Data Mining* (ACM, New York, 2016), pp. 1135–1144. https://doi.org/10.1145/2939672.2939778
43. M.F. Porter, An algorithm for suffix stripping. Program **14**(3), 130 (1980)
44. S. Bird, E. Klein, E. Loper, *Natural Language Processing with Python: Analyzing Text with the Natural Language Toolkit* (O'Reilly Media, Inc., New York, 2009)
45. M. Honnibal, I. Montani, spaCy 2: natural language understanding with Bloom embeddings, convolutional neural networks, and incremental parsing (2017). https://spacy.io
46. C.C. Aggarwal, *Data Mining: The Textbook* (Springer, New York, 2018)
47. L. Liu, J. Lafferty, X. Yang, Text classification using word embeddings: a survey of methods and applications. IEEE Trans. Neural Networks Learn. Syst. **29**(8), 3182 (2018). https://doi.org/10.1109/TNNLS.2017.2773450
48. Z.S. Harris, Distributional structure. Word **10**(2–3), 146 (1954)
49. G. Salton, C. Buckley, Term-weighting approaches in automatic text retrieval. Inf. Process. Manag. **24**(5), 513 (1988)
50. T. Mikolov, K. Chen, G. Corrado, J. Dean, Efficient estimation of word representations in vector space. arXiv preprint arXiv:1301.3781 (2013)
51. J. Pennington, R. Socher, C.D. Manning, GloVe: global vectors for word representation, in *Proceedings of the Conference on Empirical Methods in Natural Language Processing (EMNLP)* (2014), pp. 1532–1543
52. J. Devlin, M.W. Chang, K. Lee, K. Toutanova, BERT: Pre-training of deep bidirectional transformers for language understanding, in *Proceedings of NAACL-HLT* (2019)
53. N.V. Chawla, Data mining for imbalanced datasets: an overview. Data Min. Knowl. Disc. **10**(4), 363 (2005)
54. M. Honnibal, I. Montani, *spaCy 2: Natural Language Understanding with Bloom Embeddings, Convolutional Neural Networks and Incremental Parsing* (2020). https://spacy.io

55. C. Hutto, E. Gilbert, VADER: A parsimonious rule-based model for sentiment analysis of social media text, in *Eighth International Conference on Weblogs and Social Media* (2014)
56. T. Wolf, L. Debut, V. Sanh, J. Chaumond, C. Delangue, A. Moi, P. Cistac, T. Rault, R. Louf, M. Funtowicz, J. Davison, S. Shleifer, P. von Platen, C. Ma, Y. Jernite, J. Plu, C. Xu, T.L. Scao, S. Gugger, M. Drame, Q. Lhoest, A.M. Rush, Transformers: state-of-the-art natural language processing, in *Proceedings of the 2020 Conference on Empirical Methods in Natural Language Processing: System Demonstrations* (2020), pp. 38–45
57. R. Rehurek, P. Sojka, Software framework for topic modelling with large corpora, in *Proceedings of the LREC 2010 Workshop on New Challenges for NLP Frameworks* (2010)
58. L.A.M. Bostan, R. Klinger, An analysis of annotated corpora for emotion classification in text, in *Proceedings of the 27th International Conference on Computational Linguistics*, ed. by E.M. Bender, L. Derczynski, P. Isabelle (Association for Computational Linguistics, Santa Fe, 2018), pp. 2104–2119. https://aclanthology.org/C18-1179/
59. S.M. Mohammad, From once upon a time to happily ever after: tracking emotions in mail and books. Decis. Support. Syst. **53**(4), 730 (2012)
60. R. Heuser, M. Algee-Hewitt, A. Lockhart, E. Steiner, V. Tran, in *Literary Mapping in the Digital Age* (Routledge, Milton Park, 2016), pp. 25–46
61. S. Ghosh, A. Ekbal, P. Bhattacharyya, Cease, a corpus of emotion annotated suicide notes in English, in *Proceedings of the Twelfth Language Resources and Evaluation Conference* (2020), pp. 1618–1626
62. B. Jones, Usage of Natural Language Processing and deep-learning techniques on thematic apperception tests to predict big five personality traits (2025). Retrieved from https://scholarworks.uark.edu/elcsuht/3
63. A. Trifan, D. Semeraro, J. Drake, R. Bukowski, J.L. Oliveira, in *Digital Personalized Health and Medicine* (IOS Press, New York, 2020), pp. 1391–1392
64. D.S. Khafaga, M. Auvdaiappan, K. Deepa, M. Abouhawwash, F.K. Karim, Deep learning for depression detection using Twitter data. Intell. Autom. Soft Comput. **36**(2), 1301 (2023)
65. T. Atapattu, M. Herath, C. Elvitigala, P. de Zoysa, K. Gunawardana, M. Thilakaratne, K. De Zoysa, K. Falkner, Emoment: an emotion annotated mental health corpus from two South Asian countries. arXiv preprint arXiv:2208.08486 (2022)
66. J. Huang, J.W. Pennebaker, Using word clouds for rapid visual insight into text data. J. Psychol. Methods **24**(2), 223 (2019). https://doi.org/10.1037/met0000185
67. L. van der Maaten, G. Hinton, Visualizing data using t-SNE. J. Mach. Learn. Res. **9**, 2579 (2008)
68. K.K. Murdock, B.P. Allen, Visualizing topic models in psychological research: from words to themes. Psychol. Methods **25**(4), 543 (2020). https://doi.org/10.1037/met0000256

Metaheuristics in Psychological Data Analysis

Nataša Kovač, Kruna Ratković, Hojjatollah Farahani, and Stevan Kordić

1 Introduction to Metaheuristics

Optimisation is a process in which the extreme value of a function is found under given conditions. *Global optimisation problems* deal with finding the global optimum for a given function over a set of input variables with a defined set of constraints. Metaheuristics are high-level optimisation techniques designed to efficiently explore large solution spaces and identify near-optimal solutions to complex problems [1]. Unlike traditional optimisation methods, which may require explicit mathematical formulations and gradient-based search strategies, metaheuristics offer flexible, adaptable frameworks that can be applied to a wide range of problem domains. These algorithms are particularly useful in psychological data analysis, where optimisation challenges often arise in areas such as model selection, parameter tuning, and feature selection [2]. Due to the inherent complexity of human behaviour and cognitive processes, traditional analytical methods may struggle with high-dimensional, noisy, or incomplete datasets, making metaheuristics an attractive alternative [3–5].

Metaheuristics operate by iteratively improving candidate solutions through exploration and exploitation mechanisms. The exploration phase allows the algorithm to investigate diverse regions of the search space, preventing premature convergence to suboptimal solutions. In contrast, exploitation refines existing

N. Kovač (✉) · K. Ratković
Faculty of Applied Sciences, University of Donja Gorica, Podgorica, Montenegro
e-mail: natasa.kovac@udg.edu.me; kruna.ratkovic@udg.edu.me

H. Farahani
Department of Psychology, Faculty of Humanities, Tarbiat Modares University, Tehran, Iran
e-mail: h.farahani@modares.ac.ir

S. Kordić
Faculty of Maritime Studies, University of Montenegro, Dobrota, Kotor, Montenegro

N. Kovač et al. (eds.), *Data Science in Psychology*,
https://doi.org/10.1007/978-3-032-18312-5_20

solutions by concentrating search efforts on promising regions. Striking the right balance between these two processes is crucial to achieving robust optimisation performance. The general structure of metaheuristic algorithms typically follows an iterative framework, where an initial population or set of solutions is generated and refined over successive iterations [6].

A key advantage of metaheuristics is their ability to escape local optima by incorporating stochastic elements into the search process. Traditional deterministic optimisation techniques often become trapped in suboptimal solutions, particularly when dealing with non-convex, multimodal, or highly constrained objective functions. Metaheuristic approaches introduce probabilistic rules that enable movement across solution landscapes in ways that deterministic algorithms cannot achieve. This stochastic behaviour enhances the capacity of these methods to discover globally optimal solutions in highly complex problem spaces [5].

The optimisation problem is typically guided by an objective function, which evaluates the quality of candidate solutions. A general framework for solving an optimisation problem is given by Eq. 1:

$$x^* = \arg\min_{x \in \mathcal{X}} f(x), \tag{1}$$

where x^* is the optimal solution, $\mathcal{X}$ represents the search space, and $f(x)$ is the objective function of the problem. Depending on the context, $f(x)$ may represent a cost, an error function, a model evaluation metric, or another performance criterion relevant to psychological data analysis. The $\arg\min$ operator identifies the specific value of x within the feasible solution space $\mathcal{X}$ that results in the minimum value of the function $f(x)$. In contrast to the $\min$ operator, which simply returns the smallest function value, $\arg\min$ provides the corresponding input x^* at which $f(x)$ reaches its minimum. This distinction is crucial in optimisation problems where the objective is to find the optimal set of parameters rather than merely assessing the function's minimum value.

Finding the optimal solution is usually time-consuming for optimisation problems where the search space $\mathcal{X}$ is a large set. Therefore, a metaheuristic approach to solving the optimisation problem is introduced, which aims to find a good solution to the problem. This good solution does not have to be necessarily optimal, but it should be very close to the optimal. The criteria for what is considered a good solution are context-dependent.

One of the main features of metaheuristic approaches is that the solutions are generated quickly, mostly within a predefined amount of time. Exact solvers, mostly, do not have that feature. Their solving times can vary significantly within the same class of problem, for example, in [7], from 0.05 seconds to 1399.5 seconds.

In psychological data analysis, $f(x)$ often represents a measure of model quality, such as classification error, loss function value, or information criterion. For example, in machine learning applications, minimising $f(x)$ may correspond to finding the optimal hyperparameters that reduce classification error. In feature

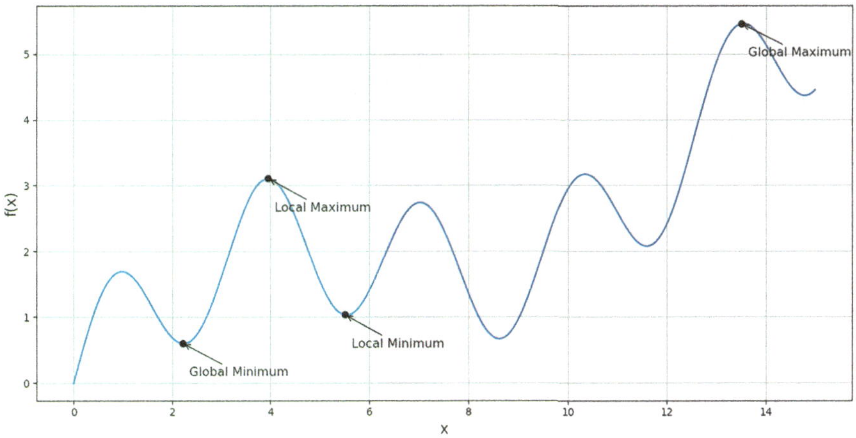

Fig. 1 Examples of local optima for the global optimisation problem

selection tasks, x^* represents the most relevant subset of features that maximises predictive performance while minimising redundancy.

Metaheuristic algorithms are particularly well-suited for solving optimisation problems where traditional deterministic methods are inefficient or inapplicable. Many real-world optimisation problems involve large, complex, and high-dimensional search spaces where exact methods struggle due to computational constraints. Gradient-based techniques, for instance, may fail when the function $f(x)$ is non-differentiable, non-convex, or contains multiple local minima. Metaheuristics overcome these limitations by employing stochastic search strategies that explore and exploit the search space adaptively.

A significant advantage of metaheuristics is their ability to escape local minima and approach globally optimal solutions. Traditional optimisation algorithms often become trapped in suboptimal solutions when applied to multi-modal functions. Metaheuristic methods introduce probabilistic mechanisms, such as random perturbations and adaptive learning strategies, to increase the likelihood of finding globally optimal solutions. This makes them particularly effective for problems with irregular or unknown solution landscapes. Figure 1 shows an example of an objective function with multiple local minima and maxima.

In psychological research, metaheuristics are widely used for optimising experimental designs, selecting appropriate feature sets, and fine-tuning machine learning models. For example, in cognitive neuroscience, selecting optimal brain imaging parameters to maximise signal quality can be framed as an optimisation problem where the best configuration of acquisition settings minimises noise and enhances interpretability. Similarly, in psychometric testing, metaheuristics can be applied to optimise test item selection, ensuring that assessments provide maximum information while maintaining fairness across different population groups.

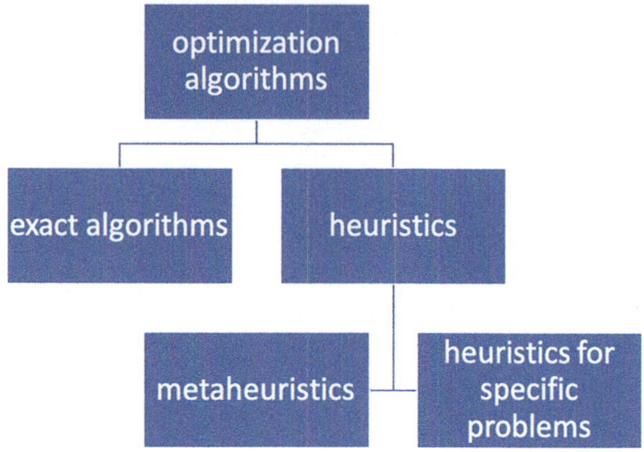

Fig. 2 Taxonomy of optimisation algorithms

Since metaheuristics rely on stochastic elements, results may vary across different runs of the algorithm. Unlike deterministic methods, which consistently produce the same output given the same initial conditions, metaheuristics incorporate random exploration, meaning that multiple executions may lead to slightly different solutions. To ensure robust optimisation, practitioners often run metaheuristic algorithms multiple times and analyse the distribution of solutions to assess their stability and convergence properties.

A large number of optimisation problems are NP-hard, which makes them very complex to solve with exact methods. Exact methods are not suitable for the optimisation of many practical problems because their execution time increases significantly with the increase in the dimension of the problem, or exact methods are inefficient from some other point of view (e.g. they require too much computer memory). As exact methods are usually suitable only for small- or medium-sized instances, in the case of large-sized instances, it is necessary to sacrifice the requirement for obtaining an optimal solution and be satisfied with a good-quality solution obtained in a relatively short execution time, which results in the need to implement heuristic and metaheuristic methods. Even if they do not guarantee the solution's optimality, heuristic and metaheuristic methods are becoming more prevalent in the optimisation field because they are based on principles that lead the search process to very high-quality solutions close to the optimum. In addition, a very important characteristic of these methods is the efficiency in solving large-scale problems as well as the simplicity of implementation. Optimisation methods are implemented in the form of algorithms, so an analogous taxonomy of optimisation algorithms can be made based on the taxonomy of optimisation methods themselves. This taxonomy is represented in Fig. 2.

One of the primary motivations for using metaheuristics in psychology is their ability to optimise complex models with large parameter spaces. In machine learning applications, for instance, selecting hyperparameters that maximise model performance is a non-trivial task. Traditional grid search or random search methods can be computationally expensive and inefficient. Metaheuristic approaches such as *genetic algorithms* and *particle swarm optimisation* provide alternative strategies by adaptively adjusting search directions based on population-based heuristics [3].

Metaheuristics can also be applied to feature selection problems, where the objective is to identify the most informative subset of predictors from a larger set of variables. In psychological research, feature selection plays a critical role in reducing dimensionality while preserving the interpretability and predictive accuracy of models. Given a dataset with p binary features, the search space for feature selection is composed of 2^p possible feature subsets, making exhaustive search computationally infeasible for large p. By employing evolutionary strategies, metaheuristic algorithms iteratively refine feature subsets to maximise a predefined evaluation metric, such as classification accuracy or mutual information.

Another area where metaheuristics prove beneficial is in clustering and classification problems [8]. Traditional clustering methods, such as k-means, require predefined assumptions about cluster structure and may struggle with non-spherical data distributions. Metaheuristic-based clustering algorithms address these limitations by incorporating adaptive search strategies that optimise cluster assignments based on complex, nonlinear similarity measures. Similarly, decision trees and ensemble methods can benefit from metaheuristic tuning, as optimising tree structures and splitting criteria can significantly enhance classification performance [9, 10].

Metaheuristics are also highly relevant in experimental design and psychological testing, where optimising task parameters, response time distributions, or stimulus configurations can lead to more reliable and generalisable findings. In cognitive neuroscience, for example, optimising brain imaging parameters to maximise signal-to-noise ratios is a common challenge that can be addressed using metaheuristic frameworks [4].

Despite their advantages, metaheuristics are not without limitations. Their stochastic nature means that results can vary across different runs, requiring multiple executions to ensure robustness. While metaheuristics are powerful for global optimisation, they may require careful tuning of algorithm-specific parameters to achieve competitive performance. Parameter tuning is an optimisation problem in itself, often requiring empirical validation or hybrid approaches that combine deterministic and stochastic methods [5].

The fundamental goal of metaheuristics is to find the best possible solution within a complex search space. By leveraging adaptive search techniques, metaheuristics enable researchers to efficiently explore large solution spaces, optimise models, and extract meaningful insights from psychological data. Their flexibility and effectiveness make them indispensable tools for solving optimisation problems in machine learning, psychometric modelling, and experimental psychology.

2 Common Metaheuristic Algorithms

Metaheuristic algorithms became a subject of interest in research with the publication of the work of Kirkpatrick et al. [11] in 1983, in which simulated annealing was proposed as a technique with the ability to leave a local minimum. Since then, metaheuristic methods have been constantly developed, which has made it possible to solve an increasing number of optimisation problems which were previously considered difficult or even unsolvable. The term metaheuristics was first introduced by Glover in 1986 in the paper [12]. The term derives from two Greek roots: *heuriskein*, meaning *to find*, and the prefix *meta*, which denotes *beyond* or *after*, thus suggesting *a higher order strategy*.

Although there is no precise definition of the term metaheuristic, all attempts to define it have some common elements, so it can be said that metaheuristics are a group of search algorithms that can solve complex optimisation problems using a set of several general heuristic principles. Metaheuristics can also be defined as higher-level heuristics that are closely related to stochastic algorithms [13]. Stochastic algorithms are a general class of algorithms and techniques that use a certain degree of randomness to find optimal solutions or solutions that are as close to optimal solutions as possible. Metaheuristics are the most general methods and are applied to a very wide range of problems. Some of the most famous metaheuristics are simulated annealing, tabu search, harmonic search, evolutionary algorithms, bee colony optimisation, particle swarm optimisation, and others [13, 14].

The complexity of the considered optimisation problem very often makes it impossible to search all possible solutions to find the optimal one. For this reason, a new task is set: to find a good solution within an acceptable time frame. Metaheuristics belong to the group of approximate algorithms, which means that they cannot guarantee the quality of the obtained solution, although quite often the solution provided by metaheuristics coincides with the optimal one. Despite this, they are widely used in solving optimisation problems, because metaheuristics whose elements are adapted to the nature of the considered problem provide solutions close to optimal or reach optimal solutions in a short execution time.

Metaheuristics usually have an iterative form that implies that one or more initial solutions are improved in terms of the value of the objective function that is minimised or maximised. In general, it can be said that metaheuristic methods fit into the following iterative procedure:

- **Step 1:** Generate one or more initial solutions.
- **Step 2:** Fix the initial solutions until some stopping criterion is met.
- **Step 3:** Return the best solution from Step 2 as the output of the algorithm.

It can be noted that the process of finding a good solution to an optimisation problem includes two steps: construction and improvement of the solution. In the construction process (step 1), one or more initial solutions are built, which represent the starting points for the search process. When constructing an initial solution, metaheuristics usually start from an empty solution to which they gradually add elements of the solution, thereby building a partial solution, and repeat the insertion of new components until a feasible solution to the problem is formed. There is another approach—random generation of a complete solution over which repair techniques are applied if the solution is not a feasible solution. In the improvement phase (step 2), the formed solutions are gradually improved until one of the stopping criteria is reached, after which the best solution is returned as the output of the algorithm (step 3). Metaheuristics most often use one or a combination of several criteria for the completion of the algorithm: a maximum number of iterations, maximum execution time, a maximum number of solution corrections, reaching a certain level of solution quality, etc.

A metaheuristic is characterised as good if it satisfies several general principles [15]:

- *Simplicity*—Metaheuristics should be based on simple principles.
- *Precision*—Steps of metaheuristics are precisely defined.
- *Consistency*—The steps of a method that solves a specific problem should follow the rules by which metaheuristics are defined.
- *Effectiveness*—Metaheuristics should generate optimal or near-optimal solutions for most test instances of the problem.
- *Efficiency*—Processor time required to find a good solution must be acceptable.
- *Robustness*—Metaheuristics should show good performance on various sets of test instances.
- *Clarity*—Metaheuristics should be well described and easy to implement and use.
- *Innovativeness*—Good characteristics of metaheuristics enable modifications and hybridisation with other methods, as well as application to new classes of problems.

Of particular importance when designing metaheuristics is achieving a balance between *intensification* and *diversification* of the search process. Namely, it is necessary to quickly identify regions of the search space with high-quality solutions, and on the other hand, not to spend too much time in regions that have either already been explored or do not contain high-quality solutions. Metaheuristics should be able to generate new solutions that will generally be better than current solutions. In addition, metaheuristics must have mechanisms to prevent termination in the local optimum, i.e. to abandon a localised search that does not lead to an optimal solution. The diversification component has the task of generating various solutions so that all parts of the solution space are covered by the search, while the goal of intensification is to focus the search on the local region using information about the position of good solutions in the search space.

Metaheuristics are classified according to their characteristics. In the literature, they are classified as follows:

- Metaheuristics inspired by nature and those inspired by mathematical concepts
- With dynamic or static target function
- With one or more environment structures used in the search process
- Metaheuristics that improve the complete solution or constructive metaheuristics
- Deterministic or stochastic metaheuristics
- Metaheuristics that use search history (memory) or not
- Trajectory methods and population metaheuristics

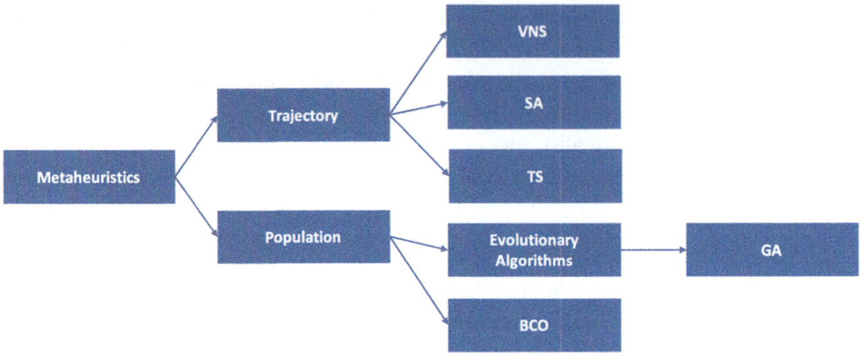

Fig. 3 Taxonomy of metaheuristics based on the number of solutions

One of the most popular classifications [4] divides metaheuristics into *trajectory methods* that try to improve one solution and into *population-based* methods, which work on several solutions in the search space and simultaneously try to improve each of them [4]. A graphic representation of this classification, as well as some of the representative metaheuristics from individual classes, is given in Fig. 3.

Trajectory methods got their name from the fact that the search process in these methods takes place along a path formed by a series of solutions in the search space. The algorithm starts from an initial solution (initial state) and describes a trajectory in the solution space, whereby the next solution may or may not be in the vicinity of the previous solution. In contrast to them, population metaheuristics in each iteration of the algorithm form a set of solutions (population) and thus explore the search space. Population-based metaheuristics begin by generating an initial set of solutions, known as the initial population. Subsequently, they alternate between phases of new population generation and replacement of the current population.

Examples of metaheuristics [14] that are based on the improvement of a single solution are variable environment method, simulated hardening, tabu search, iterative local search, variable neighbourhood search [16], etc., while examples of population metaheuristics are evolutionary algorithms (including genetic algorithm), bee colony optimisation [17], particle swarm optimisation, etc. A detailed overview of metaheuristics and their classification can be found in [4, 5, 13]. Below is an overview of some of the most commonly used metaheuristics when solving optimisation problems.

Metaheuristic algorithms, renowned for their flexibility and power, have been effectively applied to address a myriad of complex optimisation problems encountered in psychological data analysis. Among these algorithms, *genetic algorithms* (GAs), *simulated annealing* (SA), *particle swarm optimisation* (PSO), *ant colony optimisation* (ACO), and *differential evolution* (DE) stand out due to their widespread applicability, robustness, and relative simplicity.

GA is inspired by Darwinian evolutionary theory and constitutes a cornerstone of metaheuristic methodologies. They operate by simulating natural selection mechanisms, such as mutation, crossover, and selection, to iteratively evolve candidate solutions towards an optimal or near-optimal solution. Within psychological sciences, GA has demonstrated substantial potential in optimising test item selection, refining psychometric scales, and model tuning in complex behavioural datasets [18, 19]. The adaptive nature of GA ensures that diverse solutions are explored, reducing the likelihood of premature convergence on suboptimal outcomes, a feature especially beneficial in psychological data characterised by significant variability and complex interactions.

SA is another influential method that draws its principles from the metallurgical process of annealing. SA introduces a controlled probabilistic acceptance criterion that allows the occasional acceptance of poorer solutions in the early stages, gradually shifting towards stricter acceptance of improved solutions as the algorithm progresses. This characteristic helps SA escape local minima more effectively than deterministic methods. In psychological applications, SA has shown its utility in experimental design optimisation, notably in scenarios where design spaces are constrained or subject to complex trade-offs, such as minimising measurement error in cognitive tests or optimising stimulus sequencing for cognitive neuroscience experiments [11, 20].

PSO is inspired by social behaviour in bird flocks or fish schools and involves a swarm of candidate solutions (*particles*) moving through the search space guided by both personal and collective experience. Each particle adjusts its trajectory based on its best-known position and the global best-known position discovered by the swarm. This collective intelligence allows PSO to rapidly explore high-dimensional spaces efficiently, making it particularly suitable for psychological research scenarios involving large parameter spaces or numerous interacting variables. PSO has been successfully employed in optimising machine learning algorithms, fine-tuning models of human behaviour prediction, and dynamically adjusting parameters in adaptive psychological experiments [21, 22].

ACO is inspired by the cooperative foraging behaviours of ants and uses pheromone trails as probabilistic signals, guiding the search process towards optimal solutions. The algorithm builds solutions incrementally and refines the search space based on collective feedback from previous iterations. Due to its distributed and cooperative nature, ACO excels in combinatorial optimisation tasks common in psychological research, such as item-response theory model parameter optimisation and complex task scheduling in neuropsychological experiments [23]. Its ability to handle discrete and combinatorial solution spaces effectively makes ACO a powerful tool for psychological studies involving categorical data or combinatorial optimisation.

DE is a versatile evolutionary algorithm that distinguishes itself through its simplicity and ease of implementation. DE operates by generating new candidate solutions through mutation, crossover, and selection operators specifically tailored to continuous domains. This method has shown exceptional performance in parameter estimation problems and feature selection in psychological research, especially in scenarios involving continuous, high-dimensional datasets, such as EEG and fMRI analyses or complex psychological measurement scales [24, 25]. DE's rapid convergence characteristics make it particularly suitable for psychological analyses that require efficient and accurate parameter estimation under tight computational constraints.

Recent developments in metaheuristic algorithms increasingly emphasise hybridisation strategies, combining the strengths of multiple algorithms to enhance search performance and robustness [26]. For instance, hybrid approaches like GA combined with PSO (GA-PSO hybrids) leverage the global exploration capabilities of GA with the efficient local exploitation of PSO, providing balanced optimisation performance suitable for psychological data with complex landscapes [5]. Similarly, hybrid SA-GA methods have been employed to optimise parameters in complex psychological models, where SA's ability to escape local minima complements GA's evolutionary exploration capabilities, resulting in improved performance and faster convergence to optimal solutions [27].

Effective application of metaheuristic algorithms in psychological sciences also critically depends on careful parameter tuning and algorithm selection. Due to their stochastic nature, metaheuristics are sensitive to algorithm-specific parameters, such as mutation rates in GA, cooling schedules in SA, and swarm size and velocity parameters in PSO. Empirical studies emphasise systematic parameter tuning methods, including meta-optimisation and hyperparameter search, to enhance the reliability and efficiency of these algorithms in psychological applications [28, 29]. Understanding the particular strengths and limitations of each algorithm allows psychologists to select the most appropriate metaheuristic based on specific characteristics of their research question and data, ultimately maximising optimisation effectiveness.

In psychological data analysis, the choice and implementation of metaheuristic algorithms require consideration of several practical factors: the nature and dimensionality of the data, computational resources, and the specific objectives of the analysis. A comparative understanding of these algorithms, their operational characteristics, and appropriate application scenarios enables researchers to effectively leverage their power to explore complex, multidimensional psychological datasets. Careful integration of metaheuristic methods into psychological research enhances methodological rigour, contributes to reproducibility, and significantly improves the quality and impact of analytical findings.

3 Designing Metaheuristic Solutions

Designing metaheuristic solutions in psychological research represents a sophisticated process that blends domain expertise, algorithmic strategy, and experimental precision. Unlike conventional statistical modelling, metaheuristics offer flexible, adaptable optimisation techniques, particularly well-suited for complex and nonlinear problem spaces typical in psychological data. Such design efforts demand a deep understanding of both the algorithmic framework and the structure of the problem to be solved.

At the heart of metaheuristic design lies problem encoding. The way a psychological optimisation problem is represented fundamentally affects the algorithm's performance. For example, in optimising the configuration of items in a psychometric scale to maximise internal consistency, each solution can be encoded as a binary or integer vector representing the inclusion and order of scale items. The choice between continuous, discrete, or permutation-based encodings is often dictated by the nature of the psychological problem, and poor encoding can lead to inefficient search or even infeasible solutions [5].

After establishing a suitable representation, fitness function design becomes the cornerstone of the optimisation process. The fitness function must encapsulate the core psychological objective while incorporating any relevant constraints. For instance, in the optimisation of experimental conditions in cognitive load studies, the fitness function might quantify the variance explained in performance scores, penalised by the number of stimuli used to encourage parsimony. These functions can include domain-specific constraints such as time limits, ethical constraints (e.g. participant fatigue), or statistical properties (e.g. minimising multicollinearity among predictors). Poorly constructed fitness functions risk overfitting, trivial solutions, or a lack of generalisability [3]. To better understand the interconnected elements of metaheuristic design in psychological research, Fig. 4 offers a structured overview of key components and decision points. This taxonomy captures the stages from problem encoding to algorithm selection, parameter control, and hybridisation, illustrating how these layers contribute to robust and interpretable optimisation solutions.

Another critical component in the design of metaheuristic solutions is the selection of a base algorithm. This decision is often informed by preliminary exploration or benchmarking studies. GA, for instance, excels in variable selection tasks where solution spaces are discrete and the fitness landscape is rugged [30], whereas PSO may be better suited for continuous parameter optimisation tasks such as tuning learning parameters in neural models of behaviour [21]. SA and TS, by contrast, are often favoured in scheduling and experimental design problems due to their ability to handle local optima and complex constraints [31].

Once the base algorithm is selected, parameter tuning and control strategies must be considered. Metaheuristics often exhibit sensitivity to their parameter settings, such as crossover and mutation rates in GAs, inertia weight and cognitive/social parameters in PSO, or temperature schedules in SA. The literature distinguishes between two approaches: parameter tuning, which seeks optimal static values, and parameter control, which allows parameters to evolve during the search [32]. In psychological modelling, this distinction becomes especially relevant when optimisation is conducted across multiple stages of experimental design or data processing pipelines, where static parameters may fail to accommodate changing search landscapes.

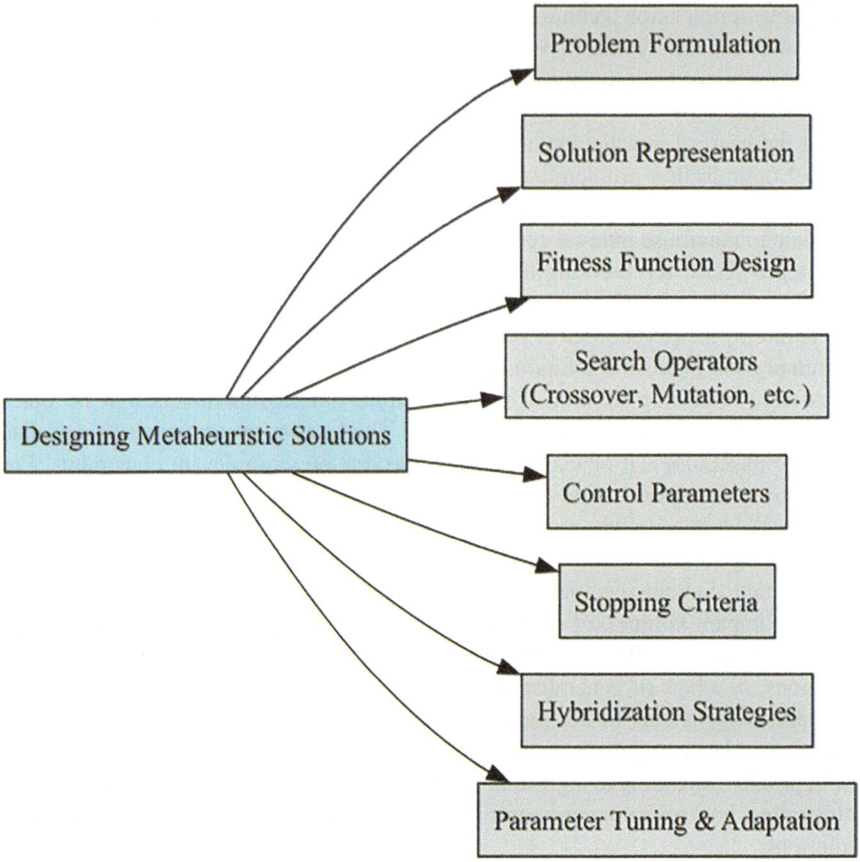

Fig. 4 Metaheuristic design components

An emerging trend is the application of adaptive and self-adaptive mechanisms, where parameter values are adjusted dynamically based on feedback from the optimisation process. For example, adaptive cooling schedules in SA allow faster convergence in the early stages and greater exploration in later stages, providing more stable solutions in psychological model calibration tasks [20]. Similarly, in PSO, inertia weights can be varied over time to balance exploration and exploitation. These strategies are particularly beneficial in complex psychological optimisation tasks, such as balancing accuracy and interpretability in behavioural prediction models.

Another vital component is initialisation and population diversity, especially in population-based algorithms like GA and PSO. Initialisation strategies can significantly influence convergence speed and solution quality. Random initialisation is the default, but problem-informed or heuristic-based initialisation often yields better results in psychological applications, where prior knowledge can guide search. For example, in optimising factor structures in exploratory analysis, initialising based on results from principal component analysis or prior empirical studies can lead to faster convergence and more theoretically grounded solutions [33].

The hybridisation of metaheuristics represents an advanced strategy that blends the strengths of multiple algorithms to enhance robustness and performance. In psychology, hybrid approaches have been used to improve variable selection in high-dimensional datasets by combining evolutionary algorithms with statistical regression models. For example, *Elastic Net* or *Ridge Regression* can be embedded within a GA framework to ensure both predictive accuracy and model interpretability [34]. Local search techniques are also commonly integrated with global search methods, such as combining *Tabu Search* (TS) with PSO, to refine candidate solutions and enhance convergence in tasks such as behavioural segmentation or affective state prediction.

A related strategy involves the use of ensembles of metaheuristics. Rather than relying on a single algorithm, multiple algorithms are run in parallel or sequentially, and their best solutions are selected or combined. This ensemble approach is useful in situations with multimodal solution landscapes, as it reduces the likelihood of premature convergence and improves generalisability. In psychological modelling, such approaches can be especially useful in tailoring interventions to subgroups of individuals by optimising over multiple outcome criteria (e.g. emotional improvement and adherence rate simultaneously).

Termination criteria and post-processing must be carefully defined. Standard stopping rules, such as reaching a maximum number of iterations or achieving a convergence threshold, can be insufficient for complex psychological models. Alternative criteria, such as stability of solutions across generations, plateau detection, or cross-validation performance, can offer more robust stopping conditions. Post-processing steps often involve a re-evaluation of top-performing solutions using hold-out data or integrating results into further statistical modelling or theory refinement.

Transparency, reproducibility, and explainability are paramount when applying metaheuristics in psychology. Given the inherent complexity and often opaque search trajectories of these algorithms, it is essential to maintain detailed logs of parameter settings, fitness scores, and solution trajectories. Visualisation of convergence curves and solution paths enhances transparency and can help researchers and stakeholders better understand the rationale behind specific model configurations [35].

4 Applications and Case Studies

Genetic algorithm is an adaptive method of global search that uses the concept of natural adaptation and selective reproduction of organisms [36]. GAs represent a class of evolutionary algorithms based on evolutionary and genetic principles. GA transforms the population of individuals by iteratively applying the genetic operators of selection, crossover, and mutation until a stopping criterion is met. To ensure good GA performance, it is necessary to define an adequate representation of the solution for the specific problem under consideration, an adequate fitness function for the evaluation of individuals, and to design predictive genetic operators. The suitability function measures the quality of the unit and depends on the optimisation problem itself and the representation of the solution. An overview of basic and advanced GA methods for solving various NP-hard optimisation problems can be found in [5, 37–39].

The first phase of the GA algorithm implementation involves defining the representation of individuals and joining them to problem solutions. The representation of an individual has a data structure called *chromosome* and most often consists of a series of zeros and ones, but there are also other encoding methods, such as vectors, integers, or real numbers [40]. An adequate choice of representation and length of the individual is determined by the nature of the problem being solved. Coding should be such that all valid units can be mapped into the solution of the problem, and vice versa, all permissible solutions of the problem can be represented by the defined unit structure.

The adaptation function is defined through the objective function of the problem being solved and represents a measure of the quality of the individual, that is, a measure of the quality of the solution into which the individual is decoded. Based on the value of the fitness function, a decision is made whether the individual will survive and remain in the population or will be eliminated from the next generation. Individuals with a higher value of the fitness function have a higher probability of survival. The methods of calculating the adaptability function are different, so in the literature you can find linear scaling, scaling into a unit interval, sigma cutoff, etc., and the most common approach is direct download, in which the value of the objective function becomes the value of the individual's adaptability function.

When generating unit codes, it happens that the code does not correspond to any permissible solution, that is, the unit is incorrect. In these cases, different strategies can be applied to incorrect individuals: an elimination strategy in which incorrect individuals are deleted from the population by setting the fitness function to zero, a strategy of repairing the individual until it becomes correct or reducing their fitness value using penalty functions.

At the beginning of the work, the GA randomly generates a population of individuals that correspond to the solutions of the problem. The most common approach is to generate a population of correct individuals over which correctness-preserving genetic operators are applied. By successive application of mutation, crossover, and selection operators, the current population is transformed into a new population.

In the selection process, based on the calculated values of the adaptation of individuals, good individuals are selected for the next stage of the algorithm. The selection operator is usually designed in such a way that a small percentage of bad individuals are selected, which ensures the diversity of the population and prevents premature convergence of the algorithm. The most common selection method is roulette selection (see Fig. 5 showing that the probability of choice is proportional

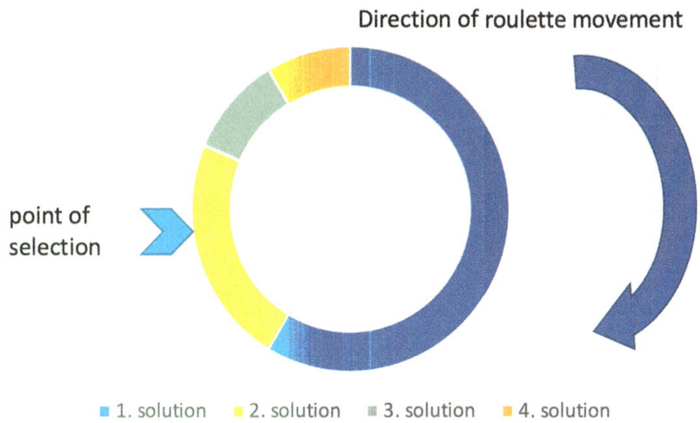

Fig. 5 Roulette selection

to the quality of the solution; better-quality solutions have a higher probability of choice, but it is not guaranteed that they will be chosen), tournament selection, fine-graded tournament selection, and rank-based selection.

Roulette selection is based on the principle of roulette, where the probability that an individual will be selected directly depends on the value of its fitness function. Individuals of better quality have a lower probability of being eliminated from the population, while individuals with a lower value of the fitness function also have a chance to be passed on to the next generation. This is a good feature of roulette selection because even worse solutions can carry genes that can contribute to the creation of better-quality offspring when crossing. The tournament selection operator selects groups of individuals (the number of individuals in the group is defined by the size of the tournament), then the individuals in each group are compared by quality, and the best individual from each group is passed on to the next generation. The size of the tournament is a parameter that indirectly affects which individuals will be selected. Namely, if the size of the tournament is large, individuals of lower quality have less chance of being selected. In finely graded tournament selection, a rational parameter is used that indicates the average size of the tournament. With fine-graded tournament selection, the size of the tournament is not uniquely determined, but two tournament sizes are used and the number of tournaments of the given size is determined in advance for each. As with tournament selection, a subset of individuals entering the tournament of a given size is randomly selected, and the best individual in the tournament participates in the creation of a new generation. Premature convergence of the algorithm is overcome by selection based on the rank according to the fitness of the individual. With this selection operator, the choice of an individual depends only on its position in the population. The position is obtained by ranking the individuals in descending order of the value of the fitness function.

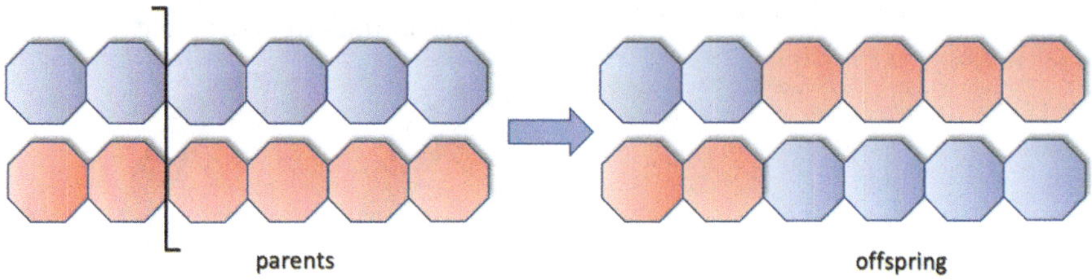

Fig. 6 One-point crossover

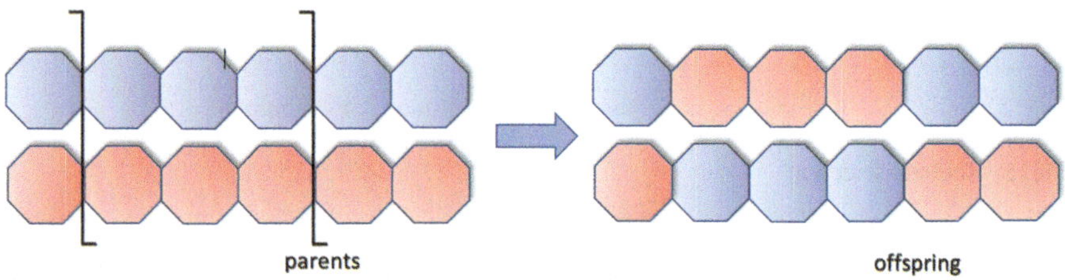

Fig. 7 Two-point crossover

The genetic algorithm uses the *recombination* or *crossover* operators over two or more individuals and thus produces a new individual, as well as the mutation or modification operator that represents the adaptation of the individual [41].

The crossover operator combines parts of the genetic code of two or more parent individuals and creates one or more offspring individuals. The role of this operator is to combine good parts of the genetic code that correspond to good components of the solution to obtain new solutions of better quality. There are many crossover techniques, the most famous of which are one-point crossover, two-point crossover, multi-point crossover, and uniform crossover. In single-position crossover, the chromosomes of the parents are cut at a randomly chosen position (crossover point), and the resulting parts of the genetic code of the parents are exchanged. The two-position crossover operator randomly selects two crossover points, and the genetic code between the crossovers is exchanged. Multiposition crossing is realised in a similar way to two-position crossing, with the fact that several points of crossing are chosen, and individual parents exchange parts of the genetic code between the selected points. A uniform crossover is a multiposition crossover with $n - 1$ breakpoints where n is the length of the unit. This crossover operator uses a mask structure to form the offspring individuals. The mask is a randomly generated binary string of length n. Individual parents keep the gene value at the position where the mask has the value 1, while they exchange gene values at the positions containing 0. Crossover operators are illustrated in Figs. 6, 7, and 8.

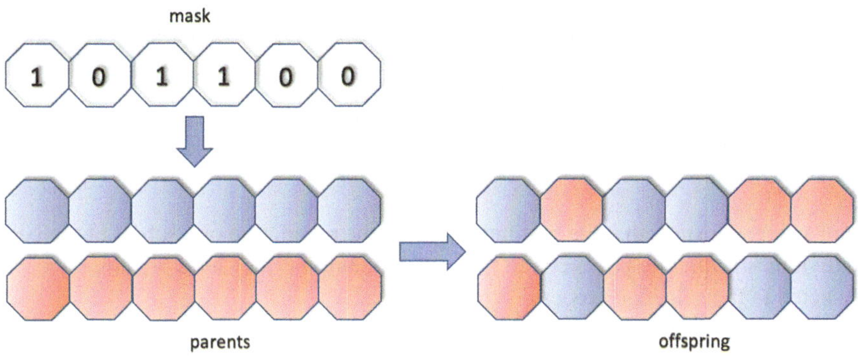

Fig. 8 Uniform crossover

The mutation operator is implemented by changing small parts of the genetic code (most often individual genes) that are randomly chosen (Fig. 9). Changes in the value of individual genes increase the diversity of genetic material in the population and enable the algorithm to more easily leave the local minimum. In the case of the binary representation of individuals, the simple mutation operator is most often used, where one gene is examined gene by gene, and for each one, it is determined whether it will mutate or not. To speed up the mutation process, the binomial or normal distribution is used. In the case of mutation using the binomial distribution, the number of mutated genes has the binomial distribution $B(n, p)$, where n is the length of the individual and p is the probability of mutation of one gene. In cases where it is necessary to mutate some parts of an individual's code with a lower probability and some others with a higher probability, a mutation with a normal distribution or an exponential mutation is used, in which the number of mutated genes grows exponentially. If integers or real numbers are used in the representation of an individual, other types of mutation are applied, such as replacing a gene with a randomly generated number, adding or subtracting a small value, multiplying by a number close to unity, etc.

Mutation and crossover are performed based on predefined values *probability of mutation* and *probability of crossover*. If the mutation probability is μ, then a randomly selected gene changes with probability μ. If the crossover probability is υ, then with this probability, the parents of the individual will exchange parts of the genetic code and produce offspring individuals.

The generation replacement policy significantly affects the quality of the final GA solution. There are several replacement policies: generational, stationary, and elitist. With generation replacement, all individuals change in each generation, while with stationary replacement, part of the population is transferred from the existing one to the next generation, and the rest of the individuals are generated again. Elitist

Fig. 9 A simple mutation of an individual

replacement ensures that the best individual of the population or a subset of the best individuals is directly passed on to the next generation if they have not already been selected in the selection process.

With the genetic algorithm, after the generation of the initial population, the stages of selection, crossover, and mutation alternate. These phases form an iteration of the algorithm that is repeated until some stopping criterion is met. The most common criteria for stopping the GA method are: a maximum number of generations, sufficiently good quality of the population, the best individual that has been repeated a certain number of times, the optimality of the individual that has been proven (if possible), a predetermined suboptimal solution that has been formed, etc.

The algorithmic steps of the GA and its structure are given in the pseudocode represented by Algorithm 1.

Algorithm 1 Genetic algorithm

```
procedure GA(popSize, μ, υ)
    Pop ← GENERATEINITIALPOPULATION(popSize)
    EVALUATE(Pop)
    while ¬ stopping criterion do
        for i ← 1 to (popSize/2) do
            newInd ← {}
            parents ← SELECTION(Pop, υ)
            offspring ← RECOMBINE(parents)
            offspring ← MUTATE(offspring, μ)
            EVALUATE(offspring)
            newInd ← newInd ⋃ offspring
        end for
        Pop1 ← newInd ⋃ Pop
        Pop ← REPLACEMENT(Pop1)
    end while
end procedure
```

In psychological interventions, particularly when managing large-scale therapy programs (e.g. CBT, mindfulness, control groups), researchers face the challenge of assigning participants to therapy groups in a way that ensures balance across multiple characteristics, such as stress level, age, gender, and baseline cognitive performance. Poorly balanced group assignments can compromise the validity of experimental outcomes by introducing systematic bias. We model this challenge as a *multi-constraint optimisation problem* in which a GA seeks to allocate n participants to k therapy groups such that:

1. Each group is balanced in terms of the distribution of key psychological and demographic variables (e.g. StressLevel, Gender ratio, CognitionScore).
2. Group-level means for baseline scores (e.g. CognitionScore, StressLevel) remain within a target variance.
3. TherapyType proportions (CBT, Mindfulness, Control) are preserved according to design.

Let $x \in \{1, 2, \ldots, k\}^n$ denote the group assignments for n participants. The objective function $f(x)$ evaluates the quality of the group assignments based on:

1. The variance in group-level means for selected continuous variables
2. The deviation of demographic proportions (e.g. gender, education level) from expected ratios
3. A penalty for imbalance across therapy types

The resulting model can be represented as

$$\min_x \quad f(x) = w_1 \cdot \text{Var}_{\text{Cognition}}(x) + w_2 \cdot \text{Var}_{\text{Stress}}(x) + w_3 \cdot \text{DemographicPenalty}(x),$$

where weights w_1, w_2, w_3 reflect the relative importance of balancing each factor.

The dataset used for this model comprises 5,000 anonymised individual psychological profiles, each uniquely identified by an `ID` number and assigned to one of three intervention conditions captured by the `TherapyType` variable: CBT, mindfulness-based intervention, or control (i.e. no specific treatment). These therapy assignments reflect a diverse range of psychological interventions commonly explored in both clinical practice and experimental psychology research. Each participant profile includes three core psychological outcome measures:

- `CognitionScore`: A quantitative index of cognitive functioning derived from standardised assessments evaluating executive control, working memory, and attention span. Scores typically centre around a normative baseline but vary by therapy group to reflect differences in intervention effectiveness.
- `StressLevel`: A measure of perceived psychological stress, gauged through validated instruments such as the perceived stress scale (PSS). Higher values denote greater psychological burden or chronic stress perception.
- `DepressionScore`: A clinical scale quantifying symptoms of depression, such as sadness, anhedonia, and fatigue, assessed using structured self-report questionnaires (e.g. the Beck Depression Inventory). Lower values suggest better psychological well-being.

The therapy groups exhibit structured differences in psychological outcomes, reflecting the expected impact of each intervention. Individuals in the *CBT* group generally demonstrate higher cognition scores, lower stress levels, and reduced depression symptoms relative to other groups. The *mindfulness* group shows moderate but still beneficial effects across these metrics. In contrast, the *control* group serves as a neutral benchmark, displaying scores consistent with normative baseline levels.

Statistical dispersion is present in all outcome variables, capturing the natural inter-individual variability typical in real psychological data. This heterogeneity makes the dataset well-suited for advanced analytical techniques such as GAs, which benefit from diverse solution spaces when optimising psychological outcomes across competing objectives (e.g. minimising stress and depression while maximising cognition).

```
import pandas as pd
import numpy as np
import matplotlib.pyplot as plt

from deap import base, creator, tools, algorithms

# Load the enhanced dataset
df = pd.read_csv("EnhancedPsychDataset.csv")

# Compute average scores for each subject
df_summary = df.groupby("ID").agg({
    "CognitionScore": "mean",
    "StressLevel": "mean",
    "DepressionScore": "mean"
}).reset_index()

# Normalise the objectives for better GA performance
df_summary["Norm_Stress"] = (df_summary["StressLevel"] -
↪   df_summary["StressLevel"].mean()) /
↪   df_summary["StressLevel"].std()
df_summary["Norm_Depression"] = (df_summary["DepressionScore"]
↪   - df_summary["DepressionScore"].mean()) /
↪   df_summary["DepressionScore"].std()
df_summary["Norm_Cognition"] = (df_summary["CognitionScore"] -
↪   df_summary["CognitionScore"].mean()) /
↪   df_summary["CognitionScore"].std()
```

```
# Create fitness function (minimise stress and depression,
 ↪  maximise cognition)
def eval_subject(individual):
    index = int(individual[0])
    row = df_summary.iloc[index]
    return row["Norm_Stress"], row["Norm_Depression"],
     ↪  -row["Norm_Cognition"]

# GA Setup
creator.create("FitnessMulti", base.Fitness, weights=(-1.0,
 ↪  -1.0, -1.0)) # Minimize all
creator.create("Individual", list,
 ↪  fitness=creator.FitnessMulti)

toolbox = base.Toolbox()
toolbox.register("attr_int", np.random.randint, 0,
 ↪  len(df_summary))
toolbox.register("individual", tools.initRepeat,
 ↪  creator.Individual, toolbox.attr_int, n=1)
toolbox.register("population", tools.initRepeat, list,
 ↪  toolbox.individual)

toolbox.register("evaluate", eval_subject)
toolbox.register("mate", tools.cxUniform, indpb=0.5)
toolbox.register("mutate", tools.mutUniformInt, low=0,
 ↪  up=len(df_summary)-1, indpb=1.0)
toolbox.register("select", tools.selNSGA2)

# Run GA
population = toolbox.population(n=100)
NGEN = 40
hof = tools.HallOfFame(1)
log = tools.Logbook()

min_stress, min_depress, max_cogn = [], [], []

for gen in range(NGEN):
    offspring = algorithms.varAnd(population, toolbox,
     ↪  cxpb=0.5, mutpb=0.2)
    fits = list(map(toolbox.evaluate, offspring))
    for ind, fit in zip(offspring, fits):
        ind.fitness.values = fit
    population = toolbox.select(offspring, k=len(population))
    hof.update(population)

    best = tools.selBest(population, k=1)[0]
```

```
fitness = eval_subject(best)
min_stress.append(fitness[0])
min_depress.append(fitness[1])
max_cogn.append(-fitness[2])  # negate back for plotting
```

This script implements a multi-objective GA designed to optimise psychological outcomes based on a dataset of 5,000 individuals who underwent various therapeutic interventions. The optimisation seeks to find an ideal subject profile that simultaneously minimises *stress* and *depression* levels while maximising *cognitive performance*. Before the optimisation begins, the dataset is preprocessed to compute the average values of these outcomes per subject. Then, to ensure that the optimisation process is not biased by different scales or variances among the three outcome measures, all values are normalised using z-score standardisation. This normalisation transforms each variable to have a mean of zero and a standard deviation of one, allowing the GA to treat all objectives comparably during fitness evaluation.

The core of the GA is built using the `deap` framework, which facilitates evolutionary algorithms in Python. In this implementation, the fitness function is constructed with three objectives: minimising normalised stress, minimising normalised depression, and minimising the *negative* of normalised cognition (which effectively results in maximising cognition since the GA is designed to minimise all objectives). This setup makes use of `deap`'s `FitnessMulti` class with a triplet of weights all set to -1.0, indicating a minimisation for each dimension of the fitness space.

Each individual in the population is represented by a single integer, which serves as an index in the dataset. This approach allows each chromosome to directly correspond to one real participant, thus encoding the genetic material of each solution as a direct reference to actual subject profiles. The initial population is randomly generated, and genetic variation is introduced through *uniform crossover* and *integer mutation*. Selection is performed using the *NSGA-II* algorithm, which ensures a well-distributed set of non-dominated solutions across the three-objective trade-off space.

Throughout 40 generations, the GA iteratively evolves the population. At each generation, offspring are generated through genetic operations, evaluated using the fitness function, and selected to form the next generation. A *Hall of Fame* keeps track of the best-performing individuals throughout the run, ensuring that high-quality solutions are preserved even if they temporarily fall out of the population.

5 Visualising Metaheuristic Solutions

Metaheuristic algorithms are powerful tools for navigating high-dimensional, complex solution spaces. The solutions they generate are often non-trivial to interpret, especially in psychological applications where data are multi-objective, noisy,

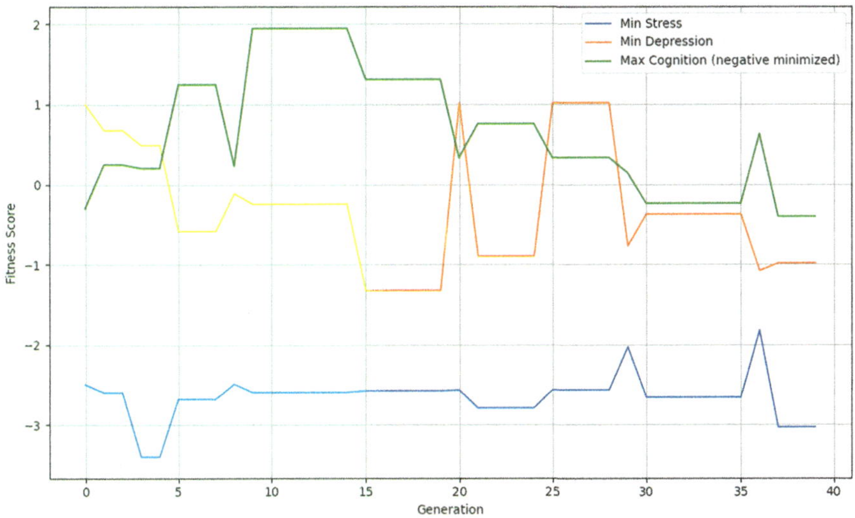

Fig. 10 Evolution of the objective functions

and influenced by latent constructs. Thus, visualising the optimisation process and the resulting outcomes becomes a fundamental component of psychological metaheuristics, enabling both model diagnostics and scientific communication.

Unlike classical optimisation problems with easily defined objective landscapes, metaheuristics often operate on black-box objectives, emergent fitness patterns, and multi-objective trade-offs. Traditional visualisations, such as convergence plots or residual distributions, are insufficient. Visual analytics must instead track solution diversity, population evolution, decision boundaries, and Pareto dominance dynamics. The dataset used in Sect. 4 is an ideal use case for showcasing such visual strategies, as it spans multiple outcomes, CognitionScore, StressLevel, and DepressionScore, each influenced by psychological interventions.

One of the most immediate ways to understand how a metaheuristic algorithm is performing is to examine the evolution of the objective functions across generations, as shown in Fig. 10. This is particularly insightful in multi-objective optimisation, where trade-offs emerge, and convergence might differ per criterion. For the GA implemented in this study, the three objective functions, minimising normalised stress and depression and maximising normalised cognition, can be visualised as a three-time series. This allows the user to detect whether the algorithm has stalled prematurely, if any criteria are being sacrificed, or if the fitness scores plateau too early. It also helps to diagnose poor population diversity or overexploitation, especially if plotted alongside the standard deviation or spread of fitness in each generation.

Figure 10 captures the stochastic yet purposeful search behaviour of evolutionary processes. Initially, the population starts with randomly sampled individuals, which results in varied and relatively suboptimal fitness values. Over successive generations, the genetic algorithm begins to identify and propagate better-performing candidates. The stress minimisation curve shows a consistent downward trend, indicating that the algorithm effectively reduces stress levels among selected individuals. The depression minimisation curve fluctuates more, reflecting the interplay between competing objectives where improving one outcome may temporarily worsen another. The cognition maximisation objective, plotted as its negative for visual coherence, also improves steadily, confirming that the algorithm discovers individuals with higher cognitive performance despite the competing pressures.

This figure demonstrates the GA's capacity to balance trade-offs inherent in psychological optimisation problems. The convergence patterns suggest the algorithm maintains diversity within the population long enough to explore alternative solutions before settling into locally optimal regions. By showing progress on each objective across iterations, the plot offers a transparent and intuitive way to validate the effectiveness of metaheuristic search in multi-criteria psychological contexts.

Visualising the best, worst, and average fitness scores per generation can further inform parameter tuning. For instance, if the average population fitness closely tracks the best individual's fitness, this may suggest premature convergence, pointing towards the need for higher mutation rates or more diverse initial populations. Figure 11 provides a longitudinal view of the genetic algorithm's optimisation behaviour by tracking the best, average, and worst composite fitness scores across all generations. This visualisation enables a straightforward assessment of the algorithm's convergence properties and population dynamics over time.

The *best fitness curve* illustrates the performance of the most optimal solution found in each generation. A consistent improvement or early stabilisation in this curve typically signals that the search space contains dominant individuals quickly located by the algorithm. The *average fitness curve* reflects the overall quality of the population in a given generation, offering insights into the diversity and evolutionary pressure driving the search. In contrast, the *worst fitness curve* highlights the presence and persistence of poorly performing individuals, which can be informative in diagnosing premature convergence or insufficient selective pressure. In our case, a visible gap between the best and worst lines suggests that while some individuals attain optimal scores, a portion of the population remains suboptimal, most likely as a consequence of maintaining genetic diversity. A narrowing gap and rising average fitness indicate the successful exploitation of high-performing genetic material and a healthy convergence process.

In multi-objective problems, a key concept is the Pareto front. The Pareto front represents solutions that are non-dominated concerning one another, meaning no objective can be improved without degrading another. Plotting the Pareto front, especially in 2D or 3D, provides an immediate visual of the trade-off space and highlights the inherent conflicts between psychological goals. For the observed dataset, where higher cognition is desirable while stress and depression should be minimised, a 3D scatter plot or projection (e.g. using PCA or t-SNE) of the Pareto-optimal individuals (Fig. 12) offers a visual metaphor for compromise.

Gen1 through *Gen6* in Fig. 12 illustrate this trajectory across generations. At the outset (*Gen1*), solutions are sparsely distributed and scattered, reflecting a high

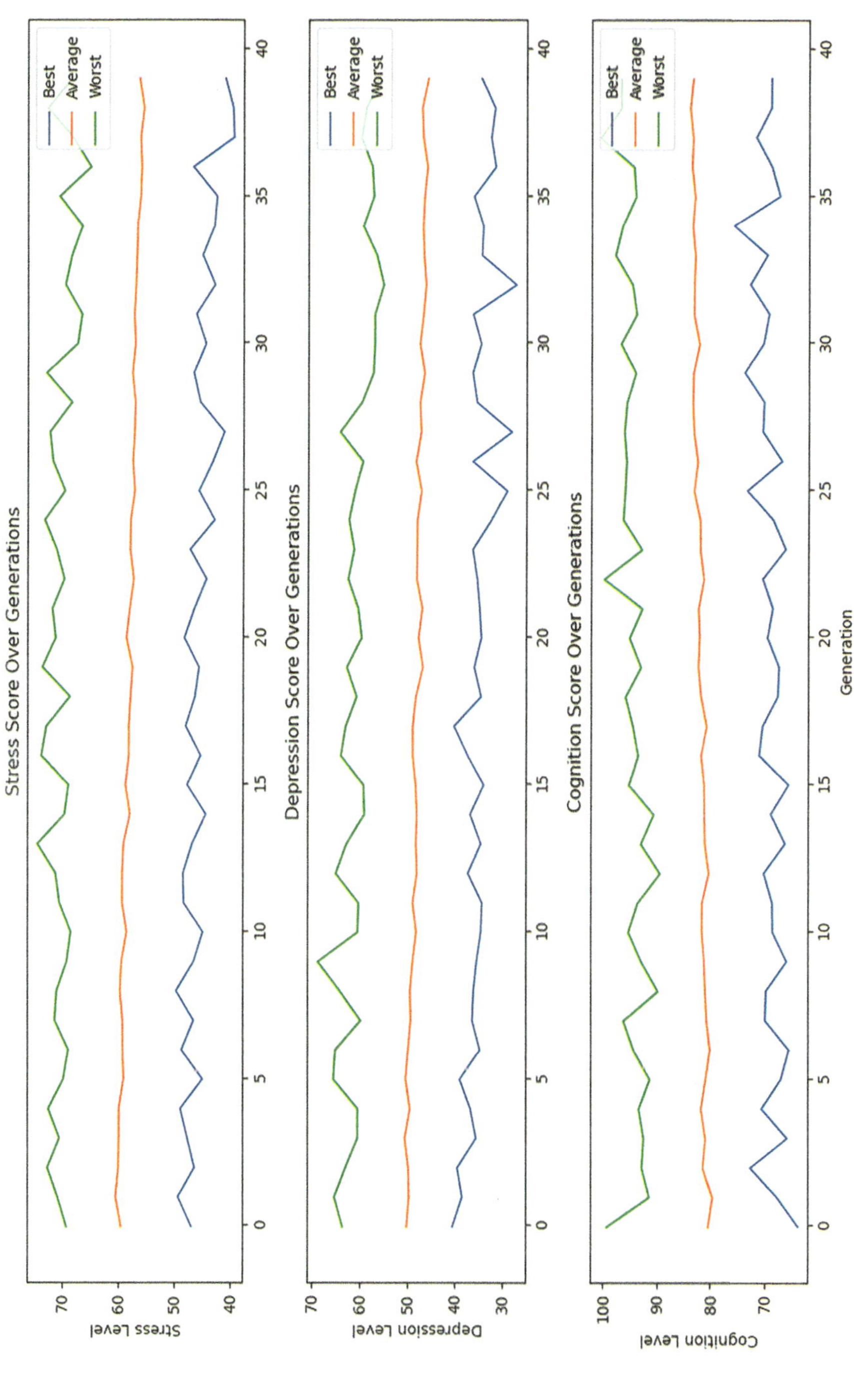

Fig. 11 Best, worst, and average fitness scores per generation

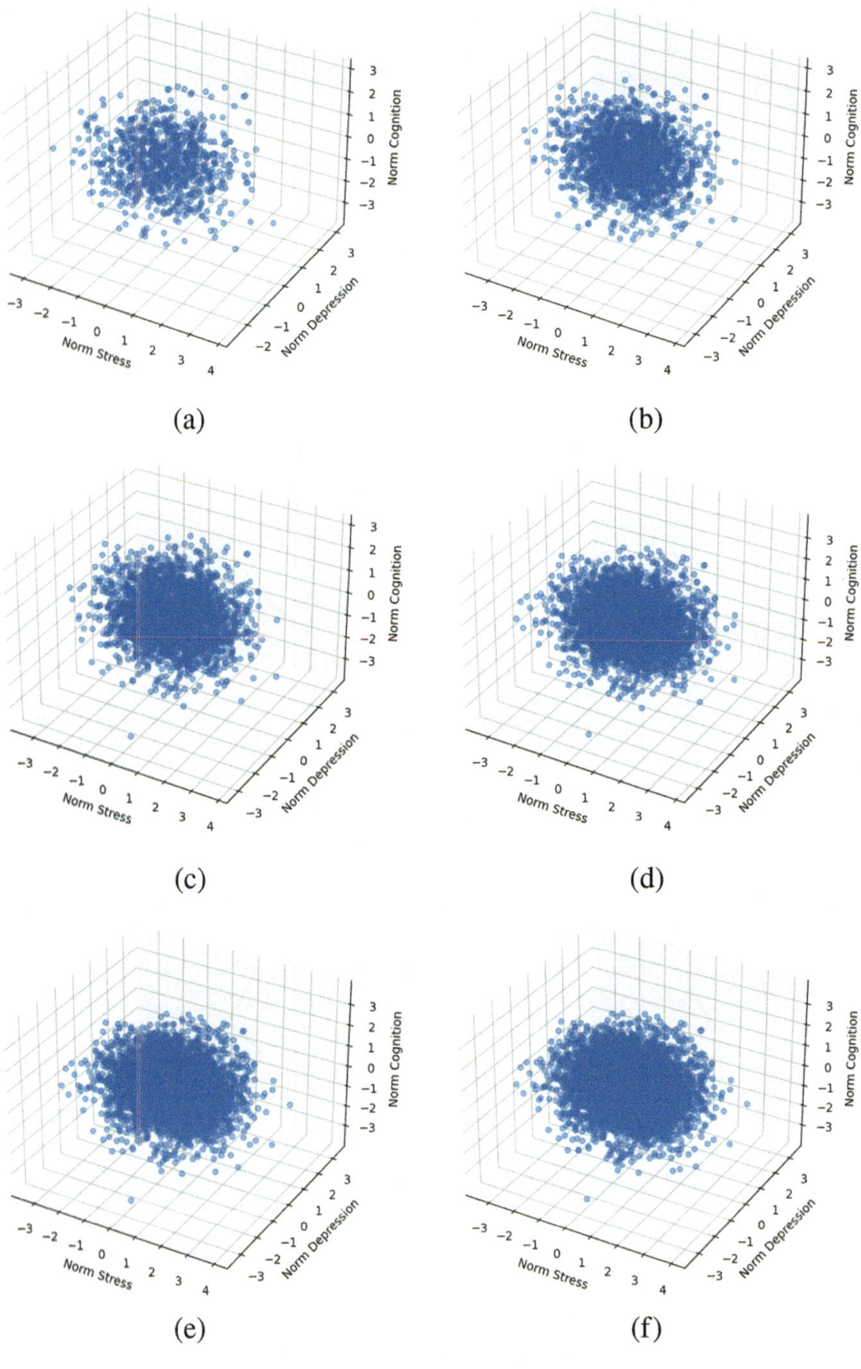

Fig. 12 Progressive 3D Pareto front snapshots across generations. (**a**) Generation 1. (**b**) Generation 2. (**c**) Generation 3. (**d**) Generation 4. (**e**) Generation 5. (**f**) Generation 6

degree of randomness in the population. There is minimal evidence of trade-off structure or clustering. As generations progress, the solution cloud becomes denser and more structured. By *Gen3* and especially *Gen5*, we begin to observe a more cohesive Pareto surface forming. This implies that the algorithm has identified a more refined subset of non-dominated solutions representing diverse yet optimised psychological profiles.

The compression and convergence of the solution cloud towards the origin of this multi-objective space suggest that improvements in all three objectives are being achieved in tandem. Some clustering may emerge that corresponds to specific therapy types, hinting at differential effectiveness based on cognitive-stress-depression trade-offs. Animating the Pareto front's progression over generations would also offer a dynamic view of convergence. In early generations, the front is often sparse and widely dispersed. Over time, it becomes denser and more focused, revealing the algorithm's path towards optimality.

Metaheuristics are population-based, and hence, their performance depends not only on individuals' fitness but also on diversity within the population. In psychological optimisation scenarios, this matters greatly: Solutions converging on a narrow subspace may miss alternative therapeutic profiles or subgroup adaptations. Visualisation of *population diversity* can be done via heatmaps of individual gene distributions across generations, cluster plots showing the grouping of solutions in the search space, or entropy metrics plotted as time series. Such insights inform whether the algorithm is balancing exploration and exploitation and whether niche solutions (e.g. effective treatments for specific psychological profiles) are being retained. Another useful visual is a *genotype-to-phenotype mapping grid*, showing how different therapy group allocations (e.g. CBT, control, mindfulness) influence fitness outcomes across generations. These mappings become particularly powerful when paired with decision trees or clustering to segment behavioural patterns by intervention.

Understanding the contribution of individual variables to the fitness of each candidate solution provides deeper psychological insight. Partial dependence plots or accumulated local effects (ALE) plots can be used to show how variables like therapy type influence cognition, stress, or depression in isolation, even when embedded in a complex GA pipeline. Heatmaps of *coefficient sensitivity* or *mutational impact* offer a detailed picture of variable importance across generations. These graphics reveal whether certain genes (representing participant IDs or cluster assignments) consistently improve the solution set, which might align with latent psychological traits or intervention responsiveness. The Hall of Fame in GA archives the best-performing individuals across generations. Visualising these elite solutions separately, through bar charts, radar plots, or detailed scatter matrices, facilitates qualitative inspection. Are these solutions homogeneously dominated by one therapy type? Do they cover a balanced range of individual differences?

A radar plot shown in Fig. 13 can be particularly insightful in this context, as it shows multivariate performance in a compact, comparative form. Each axis corresponds to one objective, and the shape of the polygon formed by each solution conveys its trade-off structure. A radar chart comparing three final solutions might

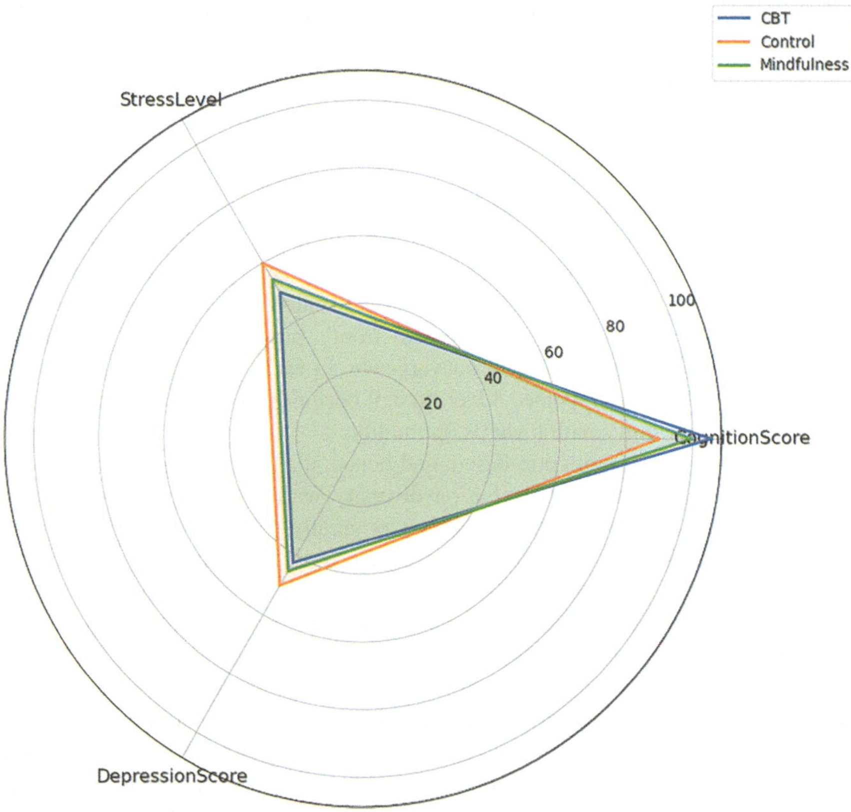

Fig. 13 Radar plot of final elite solutions

reveal one that strongly maximises cognition but with moderate stress levels and another with slightly less cognition but dramatically reduced depression. Depending on research goals, either option might be preferable, highlighting the need for context-aware decision-making supported by visuals.

Figure 13 presents a radar chart comparing the average scores of the three therapy groups across observed psychological variables. This visualisation encapsulates multivariate performance patterns for elite solution profiles emerging from the GA exploration. The CBT group displays a relatively favourable profile with higher cognition scores and slightly reduced stress and depression levels, while the control group shows a less optimal configuration. The mindfulness group balances cognitive performance and affective resilience, suggesting differentiated strengths. Such radar representations support the intuitive interpretation of trade-offs across objectives and facilitate the identification of intervention profiles most suited to psychological optimisation.

A cautionary note must be made regarding overcomplex visualisations. It is easy to overwhelm readers with visual noise in metaheuristics, especially those involving dozens of dimensions and time-dependent dynamics. Layered plots, excessive colour encoding, or 3D animations should be used judiciously, with interactivity (via tools like `Plotly` or `Altair`) only when the audience can engage with them meaningfully. Each visual should answer a specific analytic question: *Are we converging? Are we retaining diversity? What do our best solutions look like? How do therapy groups differ?* Redundant or vague plots dilute interpretability and hinder reproducibility.

Visualisation is not merely a supplement to metaheuristic optimisation. It is rather its interpreter. Especially in psychological science, where constructs are latent, measurements are noisy, and objectives are multidimensional, visualisations bring clarity, transparency, and validity to the modelling process. Going forward, incorporating explainable AI visual diagnostics into metaheuristic workflows (e.g. SHAP values and saliency maps) will further bridge the gap between algorithmic efficiency and psychological insight. These tools will allow researchers to optimise better and justify, communicate, and refine their solutions in a scientifically responsible manner.

References

1. H. Farahani, P. Watson, T. Bezan, N. Kovač, L.C. Winter, M. Blagojević, P. Azadfallah, A. Allahyari, S. Masoumian, P. Jiménez, PsAIchology: An intelligent direction in psychological sciences, in *10th International Scientific Conference Technics, Informatics and Education-TIE 2024* (Faculty of Technical Sciences Čačak, University of Kragujevac, 2024)
2. N. Kovač, K. Ratković, H. Farahani, P. Watson, A practical applications guide to machine learning regression models in psychology with python. Methods Psychol. **11**, 100156 (2024)
3. I. Boussaid, J. Lepagnot, P. Siarry, A survey on optimization metaheuristics. Inf. Sci. **237**, 82 (2013)
4. C. Blum, A. Roli, Metaheuristics in combinatorial optimization: Overview and conceptual comparison. ACM Comput. Surveys **35**(3), 268 (2003)
5. E.G. Talbi, *Metaheuristics: From Design to Implementation* (Wiley, Hoboken, 2009)
6. X.S. Yang, *Nature-Inspired Metaheuristic Algorithms* (Luniver Press, Frome, 2010)
7. S. Kordić, T. Davidović, N. Kovač, B. Dragović, Combinatorial approach to exactly solving discrete and hybrid berth allocation problem. Appl. Math. Modell. **40**(21–22), 8952 (2016). https://doi.org/10.1016/j.apm.2016.05.004
8. N. Kovač, K. Ratković, P. Watson, H. Farahani, F. Bagheri Sheykhangafshe, Machine learning classification models for predicting chronic pain. Current Psychol. **44**, 1–14 (2025)
9. L. Breiman, *Random Forests* (Springer, Berlin, 2006)
10. H. Farahani, P. Watson, N. Kovač, F.B. Sheykhangafshe, P. Azadfallah, A. Allahyari, F. Esrafilian, R.R. Chesli, *International Handbook of Love: Transcultural and Transdisciplinary Perspectives* (Springer, Berlin, 2025), pp. 1–22
11. S. Kirkpatrick, C.D. Gelatt, M.P. Vecchi, Optimization by simulated annealing. Science **220**(4598), 671 (1983)
12. F. Glover, Future paths for integer programming and links to artificial intelligence. Comput. Oper. Res. **13**(5), 533 (1986)
13. S. Luke, *Essentials of Metaheuristics* (Lulu Raleigh, 2009, (online http://www.cs.put.poznan.pl/mkomosinski/materialy/optymalizacja/extras/Essentials.pdf))
14. N. Kovač, Metaheuristic approaches for the berth allocation problem. Yugoslav J. Oper. Res. **27**(3), 265 (2017)

15. P. Hansen, N. Mladenović, in *Handbook of Metaheuristics*, ed. by F. Glover, G. Kochenagen (Kluwer Academic Publishers, Dordrecht, 2003), pp. 145–184
16. N. Kovač, T. Davidović, Z. Stanimirović, Variable neighborhood search methods for the dynamic minimum cost hybrid berth allocation problem. Inf. Technol. Control **47**(3), 471 (2018)
17. N. Kovač, T. Davidović, Z. Stanimirović, Population-based metaheuristics for the dynamic minimum cost hybrid berth allocation problem. Int. J. Artif. Intell. Tools **30**(04), 2150017 (2021)
18. D.E. Goldberg, *Optimization, and Machine Learning* (Addison-Wesley, Reading, 1989)
19. D. Whitley, A genetic algorithm tutorial. Stat. Comput. **4**(2), 65 (1994)
20. P.J.M. van Laarhoven, E.H.L. Aarts, *Simulated Annealing: Theory and Applications* (Springer, Dordrecht, 1987)
21. J. Kennedy, R. Eberhart, Particle swarm optimization, in *Proceedings of ICNN'95-International Conference on Neural Networks*, vol. 4 (IEEE, 1995), pp. 1942–1948
22. Y. Shi, R.C. Eberhart, A modified particle swarm optimizer, in *IEEE International Conference on Evolutionary Computation Proceedings, IEEE World Congress on Computational Intelligence* (IEEE, 1998), pp. 69–73
23. M. Dorigo, T. Stützle, *Ant Colony Optimization: Overview and Recent Advances* (Springer, Berlin, 2019)
24. R. Storn, K. Price, Differential evolution—a simple and efficient heuristic for global optimization over continuous spaces. J. Global Optim. **11**(4), 341 (1997)
25. K. Price, R.M. Storn, J.A. Lampinen, *Differential Evolution: A Practical Approach to Global Optimization* (Springer, Berlin, 2006)
26. K. Ratković, N. Kovač, M. Simeunović, Hybrid LSTM model to predict the level of air pollution in Montenegro. Appl. Sci. **13**(18), 10152 (2023)
27. A.E. Eiben, J.E. Smith, *Introduction to Evolutionary Computing* (Springer, Berlin, 2015)
28. M. Birattari, *Tuning Metaheuristics: A Machine Learning Perspective* (Springer, Berlin, 2009)
29. J. Bergstra, Y. Bengio, Random search for hyper-parameter optimization. J. Mach. Learn. Res. **13**, 281 (2012)
30. R.L. Haupt, S.E. Haupt, *Practical Genetic Algorithms*, 2nd edn. (Wiley, Hoboken, 2004)
31. F. Glover, M. Laguna, *Tabu Search* (Springer, Berlin, 1997)
32. A.E. Eiben, S.K. Smit, Parameter tuning for configuring and analyzing evolutionary algorithms. Swarm Evolut. Comput. **1**(1), 19 (2011)
33. K.J. Preacher, G.R. Hancock, Z.C. Arnold, A brief introduction to structural equation modeling and latent growth curve modeling. Instruct. Top. Educ. Measure. **30**, 1 (2013)
34. Z.H. Zhou, J. Fan, M. Tang, Hybrid metaheuristics for interpretable machine learning: a survey. Artif. Intell. Rev. **55**(6), 5197 (2022)
35. C. Molnar, *Interpretable Machine Learning* (Leanpub, Victoria, 2020)
36. J.H. Holland, *Adaptation in Natural and Artificial Systems: An Introductory Analysis with Applications to Biology, Control, and Artificial Intelligence* (MIT press, Cambridge, 1975)
37. T. Bäck, D.B. Fogel, Z. Michalewicz, *Evolutionary Computation 1: Basic Algorithms and Operators* (Taylor & Francis Group, LLC, CRC Press, New York, 2000)
38. T. Bäck, D.B. Fogel, Z. Michalewicz, *Evolutionary Computation 2: Advanced Algorithms and Operators* (IOP Publishing, Bristol, 2000)
39. C.R. Reeves, in *Handbook of Metaheuristics*, ed. by M. Gendreau, J.Y. Potvin, 2nd edn. (Springer, New York Dordrecht Heidelberg London, 2010), pp. 109–139
40. L. Davis, *Handbook of Genetic Algorithms* (Van Nostrand Reinhold, New York, 1991)
41. T. Bäck, D. Fogel, Z. Michalewicz, *Handbook of Evolutionary Computation* (IOP Publishing, Bristol, 1997)

Simulations in Psychological Research

Nataša Kovač, Kruna Ratković, Hojjatollah Farahani, Stevan Kordić, and Peter Watson

1 The Role of Simulations in Psychology

Psychological research continually encounters challenges posed by the inherent complexity, variability, and ethical constraints associated with human behaviour and mental processes. Consequently, the adoption of simulations in psychology has markedly expanded over recent decades, significantly transforming methodological landscapes across various subfields [1]. This expansion reflects an increasing recognition of the potential that simulations have to elucidate phenomena that remain intractable through traditional empirical experimentation alone.

The essence of simulations in psychology lies in their ability to represent dynamic interactions within cognitive, affective, and social systems, often unobservable in naturalistic settings [2]. These computational tools enable the systematic exploration of psychological theories by translating abstract theoretical constructs into operational models [3, 4]. Simulations thus serve a dual purpose: They facilitate theory testing under controlled virtual conditions and enable researchers to explore emergent phenomena that result from interactions at micro-levels, which can subsequently inform and refine theoretical frameworks.

N. Kovač (✉) · K. Ratković
Faculty of Applied Sciences, University of Donja Gorica, Podgorica, Montenegro
e-mail: natasa.kovac@udg.edu.me; kruna.ratkovic@udg.edu.me

H. Farahani
Department of Psychology, Faculty of Humanities, Tarbiat Modares University, Tehran, Iran
e-mail: h.farahani@modares.ac.ir

S. Kordić
Faculty of Maritime Studies, University of Montenegro, Dobrota, Montenegro

P. Watson
MRC Cognition and Brain Sciences Unit, University of Cambridge, Cambridge, England
e-mail: Peter.Watson@mrc-cbu.cam.ac.uk

N. Kovač et al. (eds.), *Data Science in Psychology*,
https://doi.org/10.1007/978-3-032-18312-5_21

One critical advantage of simulations is their ability to examine processes that occur over extended temporal spans, which is typically impractical or prohibitively expensive in traditional research designs. For instance, developmental psychologists frequently encounter methodological barriers when studying phenomena such as language acquisition, cognitive decline, or the long-term development of psychopathological disorders. Simulations enable researchers to construct longitudinal models that span years or even lifetimes within feasible computational constraints, thereby providing a powerful tool to project developmental trajectories and evaluate potential interventions [5, 6].

In cognitive psychology, simulation approaches such as cognitive architectures (e.g. ACT-R, Soar, and Clarion) have become pivotal in modelling complex cognitive phenomena ranging from memory and learning to problem-solving and decision-making [7, 8]. These architectures combine empirical insights from cognitive science with computational rigour, enabling detailed testing of cognitive theories. Such models facilitate experimentation with hypothetical cognitive mechanisms and allow researchers to simulate the precise conditions under which cognitive biases and heuristics emerge, offering vital insights into human rationality and decision-making [9, 10].

Social psychology has equally benefited from simulations, particularly through *agent-based models* (ABMs), which capture complex interactions among individuals and their social environment. These models are especially suited to addressing questions involving collective behaviours, social influence, and cultural evolution [11, 12]. Complementary supervised ML studies have modelled affective/interpersonal factors to predict maladaptive relational outcomes [13]. ABMs enable psychologists to observe emergent social phenomena, such as the spread of attitudes, norms, or behaviours within populations, highlighting underlying mechanisms that may not be immediately apparent from observational studies alone [14, 15]. For example, simulations of opinion dynamics have provided rich explanations of polarisation phenomena, shedding light on processes like homophily, conformity, and social reinforcement in group decision-making contexts [16, 17].

Clinical psychology also increasingly harnesses simulation-based methodologies to enhance therapeutic interventions and predict treatment outcomes. Computational models can simulate cognitive and emotional processes involved in disorders such as depression, anxiety, or schizophrenia, supporting clinicians in developing personalised intervention strategies [18, 19]. For instance, reinforcement learning models have provided significant insights into maladaptive decision-making patterns observed in addiction and compulsive disorders, highlighting neural and cognitive mechanisms amenable to targeted treatments [20, 21].

Simulations have proven invaluable in psychological methodology itself, notably in psychometric research and experimental design. *Monte Carlo Simulations* routinely guide the construction and validation of psychological measurement instruments, enabling researchers to estimate sampling distributions, assess power, and validate latent factor structures under varying conditions [22, 23]. These simulations bolster statistical rigour and support methodological transparency, critically enhancing reproducibility and reliability in psychological research practices [24].

Emerging areas such as computational psychiatry, affective computing, and digital interventions also exemplify the integral role of simulations in contemporary psychological research. Computational psychiatry, in particular, leverages simulation-based models to bridge phenomenological descriptions of psychiatric symptoms with neural substrates, aiming at improved diagnostic accuracy and treatment personalisation [25, 26]. Simulations thus become an indispensable tool in translating theoretical neuroscience findings into clinically actionable strategies, reshaping both theoretical and applied psychology landscapes.

It is essential to acknowledge that simulations are not without limitations. Model validity is inherently dependent on the assumptions and parameters set by researchers, necessitating rigorous validation procedures and transparent reporting practices [27, 28]. Thus, the successful application of simulation methods demands methodological expertise and careful calibration, underscoring the need for comprehensive training and critical evaluation skills among psychological researchers.

Simulations offer extensive opportunities for psychological research, enabling rigorous exploration of theoretical models, providing methodological rigour, and yielding novel insights into complex psychological processes. Their integrative nature allows the simultaneous consideration of cognitive, emotional, and social dynamics, promoting a holistic understanding of psychological phenomena that extend beyond isolated empirical observations. Thus, the continued development and adoption of sophisticated simulation techniques will undoubtedly drive psychological research towards deeper theoretical integration, more robust methodological practices, and enhanced real-world applications.

2 Types of Simulations

Simulations play a crucial role in psychological research by enabling the exploration of complex phenomena that may be difficult or impossible to study through direct experimentation. They provide a means to model psychological processes, test theoretical assumptions, and generate synthetic data for hypothesis evaluation. Various types of simulation methodologies exist, each with distinct applications and advantages. The selection of a specific simulation approach depends on the nature of the psychological phenomenon under investigation, the level of abstraction required, and the computational resources available [29, 30].

One of the most widely used simulation techniques in psychological research is the Monte Carlo simulation, which relies on repeated random sampling to approximate solutions for probabilistic problems. *Monte Carlo methods* are particularly useful when working with stochastic processes, such as cognitive decision-making models or reaction time distributions [31, 32]. The fundamental principle of Monte Carlo simulations is to use random sampling from probability distributions to estimate unknown parameters. This process is mathematically expressed in Eq. 1:

$$E[f(X)] \approx \frac{1}{N}\sum_{i=1}^{N} f(X_i), \tag{1}$$

where $E[f(X)]$ represents the expected value of a function $f(X)$, N is the number of random samples drawn, and X_i are independent and identically distributed random variables sampled from the probability distribution of interest. By increasing the number of iterations N, the approximation converges towards the true expected value [33]. Monte Carlo methods have been widely applied in psychology for tasks such as parameter estimation in psychometric modelling and uncertainty quantification in experimental studies.

Another important class of simulations in psychology is ABM, which focuses on simulating the interactions of autonomous agents within a defined environment [34]. ABMs are particularly useful for studying emergent behaviours in social and cognitive sciences, where the collective properties of a system arise from individual agent interactions [35]. Each agent in an ABM follows a set of predefined rules that dictate its behaviour, leading to complex, dynamic system-level patterns. ABMs allow researchers to model group dynamics, decision-making processes, and social behaviours in a way that captures non-linear interactions and feedback loops. For example, in psychology, ABMs have been used to study crowd behaviour, diffusion of opinions, and even mental health interventions where multiple actors influence a shared outcome.

Psychological research also benefits from computational neural simulations, which model cognitive processes using *artificial neural networks* (ANNs). These simulations are inspired by the structure and functionality of biological neural systems, enabling researchers to explore cognitive functions such as perception, memory, and learning [36]. Computational neural models can replicate key aspects of human cognition and provide insight into neural mechanisms underlying psychological phenomena. They are particularly valuable in fields such as cognitive neuroscience and psycholinguistics, where understanding brain-behaviour relationships is fundamental. The flexibility of neural networks allows them to be applied in domains such as speech recognition, decision-making simulations, and cognitive load estimation.

Hierarchical Bayesian modelling simulations represent a widely used and powerful approach in psychological research, particularly in fields such as cognitive psychology, psychometrics, and decision science. These simulations apply the principles of Bayesian inference to simultaneously estimate individual-level parameters and overarching population-level distributions. This hierarchical structure allows for the modelling of variability across individuals while still leveraging shared information across the dataset, thereby increasing statistical efficiency and interpretability [37].

Unlike traditional methods that often treat parameters as fixed, Bayesian approaches consider them as random variables governed by prior distributions. These priors can encode existing theoretical knowledge, empirical findings from previous studies, or reflect domain-specific expectations, making Bayesian models particularly adaptable to cumulative research contexts. As new data are observed, prior beliefs are systematically updated, yielding posterior distributions that reflect both prior knowledge and the evidence contained in the observed data [38]. This process enables a more flexible and transparent approach to inference, especially in cases where data may be sparse, noisy, or hierarchical.

In psychological applications, hierarchical Bayesian simulations are commonly used to model latent cognitive processes, estimate learning curves, and examine variability in individual responses over time. For instance, in cognitive tasks involving response times or accuracy, researchers can use Bayesian models to separate trial-level variability from stable individual traits. In psychometrics, hierarchical models facilitate the estimation of latent traits such as intelligence, personality, or well-being, while accounting for item-level properties and measurement error. These models are also increasingly used to assess the reliability and fairness of psychological tests across subgroups, providing robust tools for instrument validation and policy evaluation.

From a practical standpoint, implementing simulations in psychological research is facilitated by computational tools such as Python, which provides robust libraries for numerical modelling and stochastic simulations [39]. The following Python code demonstrates a simple Monte Carlo simulation for estimating the probability of a cognitive decision-making outcome:

```
import numpy as np

# Define probability distribution
def cognitive_process(trials=10000):
    outcomes = np.random.choice([0, 1], size=trials, p=[0.4,
     ↪ 0.6])
    return np.mean(outcomes)

# Run simulation
estimated_probability = cognitive_process()

print(f"Estimated Probability: {estimated_probability:.4f}")
```

This script simulates a cognitive decision-making process where an individual has a 60% chance of selecting a particular response in each trial. By running 10,000 simulations, the estimated probability converges towards the true theoretical value. Such simulations are valuable in studying probabilistic decision models and understanding behavioural patterns in experimental psychology [40].

In addition to these methods, dynamic systems simulations provide another powerful approach for modelling psychological phenomena. These simulations capture how variables evolve over time in response to internal and external influences. For example, in emotion regulation studies, dynamic systems models can simulate fluctuations in emotional states under different experimental conditions [40]. Researchers can define equations governing the rate of change in psychological variables and observe their long-term stability or chaotic behaviour.

Each type of simulation method contributes uniquely to psychological research, offering distinct advantages depending on the research question. Monte Carlo methods provide robust solutions for uncertainty estimation, agent-based modelling facilitates the study of social and collective behaviours, computational neural simulations replicate cognitive processes, and Bayesian hierarchical models offer principled ways to incorporate prior knowledge into inference. By leveraging these simulation techniques, psychological researchers can explore hypotheses that are challenging to test experimentally, refine theoretical models, and improve the predictive accuracy of psychological assessments.

3 Developing Simulation Studies

Developing a simulation study in psychological research involves a systematic process of translating theoretical constructs into formal models, designing the computational framework, and executing iterative experiments that mirror psychological phenomena. Unlike traditional experimental research that is constrained by feasibility, ethics, or logistics, simulation studies offer researchers a flexible and controlled environment to examine hypotheses under varying assumptions and scenarios [35].

The first step in building a simulation is the formalisation of the research question into a model. This requires identifying key variables, defining their relationships, and selecting the appropriate simulation type, be it agent-based, Monte Carlo, dynamic systems, or Bayesian modelling. For example, a researcher studying decision fatigue may decide to model cognitive resource depletion as a function that decreases over time and influences the probability of making optimal decisions.

The process begins with specifying both the functional structure of relationships and the stochastic elements involved, such as noise or variability in individual traits.

Once the model is conceptually defined, it must be translated into a computational algorithm. In Monte Carlo simulations, for instance, this involves defining a probability distribution for each random component and running a large number of simulated iterations to observe aggregated outcomes. In agent-based models, rules of behaviour for each agent are coded, and simulation cycles are used to study emergent dynamics [34]. Importantly, each component of the model should reflect both theoretical knowledge and empirical data, ensuring that the simulation is grounded in psychological plausibility.

A core element of developing a simulation is parameter specification. Parameters can be fixed values derived from empirical studies or drawn from prior distributions in Bayesian models. In either case, it is essential to conduct sensitivity analyses to determine how parameter variation impacts the results. This helps identify robust findings that are not contingent on arbitrary model settings. Furthermore, specifying the initial conditions, such as agent characteristics, environmental settings, or priors, is critical, especially in dynamic systems where small changes can lead to substantially different outcomes.

Model calibration follows, wherein the simulation is tuned using available empirical data to ensure it replicates known patterns or outcomes. This step is crucial for improving the model's external validity. Calibration may involve adjusting parameters so that the simulated outcomes closely match observed data distributions, trends, or known psychological benchmarks [41]. Iterative refinement is often necessary, where the researcher runs the model, inspects the results, and adjusts the code, rules, or parameters accordingly.

Simulation experiments are typically conducted after calibration. These experiments involve systematically altering conditions to observe how the simulated system behaves. For instance, a researcher might increase cognitive load in a virtual task to see how decision performance degrades over time, or simulate population-level behaviour in different policy scenarios to evaluate intervention strategies. The power of simulations lies in this capacity to test *what-if* scenarios that would be impractical or unethical to manipulate in real-world studies.

To illustrate, the following Python example shows how a simplified decision-making simulation can be developed. The model simulates individuals who choose between two options with varying probabilities, adjusting their choice strategy over time as they receive feedback. This framework mimics reinforcement learning in psychological decision-making:

```python
import numpy as np

def simulate_decision_process(trials=1000, learning_rate=0.1):
    prob_option_a = 0.6  # Base probability of success for
     ↪  option A
    prob_option_b = 0.4  # Base probability of success for
     ↪  option B
    choice_probs = [0.5, 0.5]  # Initial choice probabilities

    outcomes = []
    for t in range(trials):
        choice = np.random.choice([0, 1], p=choice_probs)
        reward = np.random.rand() < (prob_option_a if choice ==
         ↪  0 else prob_option_b)
        outcomes.append(reward)

        # Update choice probabilities based on reward
        if reward:
            choice_probs[choice] += learning_rate * (1 -
             ↪  choice_probs[choice])
        else:
            choice_probs[choice] -= learning_rate *
             ↪  choice_probs[choice]
        choice_probs = np.clip(choice_probs, 0.01, 0.99)
        choice_probs /= sum(choice_probs)

    return outcomes

results = simulate_decision_process()
print(f"Average reward: {np.mean(results):.2f}")
```

In this simulation, agents probabilistically choose between two options and update their preferences based on past success, a simplified model that captures basic principles of behavioural adaptation. Through such frameworks, psychological researchers can study complex interactions between learning, memory, emotion, and decision-making processes in silico.

Finally, proper documentation and reproducibility are key components of any simulation study. Code should be made transparent, data generation should be replicable, and assumptions must be clearly stated. Simulation results must be interpreted within the boundaries of their assumptions and model design. Since simulations are abstractions, their conclusions are valid only to the extent that the underlying model adequately reflects real-world psychological processes.

By following a structured and transparent process, simulations can become invaluable tools in the psychological sciences. They complement empirical methods, support theoretical development, and offer insights into mechanisms that are otherwise inaccessible to direct observation or manipulation.

4 Interpretation and Validation of Simulation Results

Interpreting the results of psychological simulations requires careful alignment between theoretical expectations and the observed dynamics of the simulated model. Because simulations represent formal abstractions of complex psychological systems, the conclusions drawn from them must be framed within the assumptions and limitations of the underlying model. Researchers must ensure that the behaviour of the simulation aligns with the theoretical constructs it is meant to represent, while also recognising emergent patterns that may not have been anticipated.

The interpretation process often begins with descriptive and inferential summaries of simulation outcomes. In a Monte Carlo simulation, for instance, researchers may calculate the average value of a target outcome variable across repeated iterations and examine the variance or confidence intervals to understand its distribution. In agent-based models, simulation runs may yield complex emergent behaviour, such as phase transitions or non-linear effects, which must be analysed through both statistical summaries and visualization tools. Metrics such as means, proportions, standard deviations, or entropy can all provide useful quantitative insights, but should always be interpreted concerning the system's design and parameters [41].

Validation is a critical step that differentiates rigorous simulation studies from speculative modelling. There are two primary forms of validation: internal and external. Internal validation focuses on ensuring that the model behaves logically given its structure and assumptions. This includes confirming that the implementation reflects the theoretical framework, checking that changes in input variables produce expected changes in output, and verifying that the model is free of coding errors or computational inconsistencies. Techniques such as sensitivity analysis are particularly helpful at this stage. By systematically varying model parameters and observing the impact on simulation outcomes, researchers can identify which factors exert the most influence and which relationships are robust [42].

External validation, on the other hand, concerns the correspondence between the simulation's outputs and empirical data. For psychological models, this may involve comparing simulated behaviour patterns to observed data from experiments, surveys, or clinical studies. For example, if a simulation aims to model decision-making under risk, researchers might validate its outputs against established patterns in prospect theory or observed choice distributions in behavioural economics. When empirical data are available, goodness-of-fit measures, correlation analyses, or Bayesian model comparison techniques can be used to quantify the model's validity [37].

For simulation models that involve stochastic elements, reproducibility is a central concern. Because such models incorporate random sampling or probabilistic decision rules, multiple runs may yield slightly different outcomes. To ensure stable and meaningful conclusions, researchers typically conduct a large number of independent runs and analyse the distribution of outputs. If the variance across runs is small, the model can be said to produce robust results. If variance is large, the model may require further tuning or reconsideration of its assumptions. Reporting summary statistics across runs, such as median behaviour or interquartile ranges, is often more informative than relying on a single realisation.

Visualising simulation outputs is another important tool for interpretation and validation. Time series plots, heatmaps, histograms, and state-transition diagrams can help elucidate underlying dynamics and emergent structures. In agent-based models, for instance, spatial plots may reveal clustering patterns or diffusion effects. In Bayesian simulations, posterior distributions can be visualised using density plots or credible intervals to communicate uncertainty and belief updating. The following Python code demonstrates a basic example of simulating and visualising the output distribution of a simulated response rate in a cognitive task.

```python
import numpy as np
import matplotlib.pyplot as plt
# Simulate repeated task outcomes (e.g., success rate)
np.random.seed(0)
simulated_rates = [np.mean(np.random.rand(100) < 0.7) for _ in
↪   range(1000)]

# Plot histogram of simulation results
plt.hist(simulated_rates, bins=30, color='skyblue',
↪   edgecolor='black')
plt.title('Distribution of Simulated Response Rates')
plt.xlabel('Proportion of Successful Responses')
plt.ylabel('Frequency')
plt.grid(True)
plt.show()
```

This example simulates 1000 cognitive task runs where each trial has a 70% success probability. For each run, the mean success rate is computed over 100 trials, and the results are aggregated into a distribution. The histogram displayed in Fig. 1 provides a visual representation of how these simulated success rates vary due to inherent randomness in the sampling process. The x-axis shows the proportion of successful responses, while the y-axis indicates the frequency of observing each rate across the simulations. A sharply peaked histogram centred around 0.7 indicates low variability across simulation runs, suggesting that the model produces stable outcomes under the specified conditions. In contrast, a flatter or wider distribution would imply greater sensitivity to random fluctuations, potentially signalling the influence of stochastic processes or parameter uncertainty. Interpreting the shape and spread of such histograms helps researchers assess the robustness of their

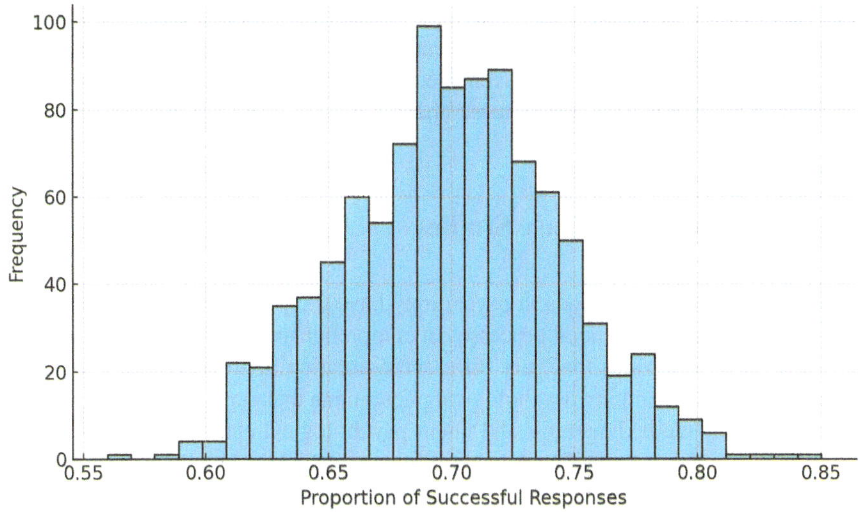

Fig. 1 Distribution of simulated response rates

models and identify conditions under which the behaviour of the system may become more volatile.

Another aspect of interpretation involves evaluating whether the simulation provides novel insights that extend existing theory. A well-designed simulation does more than replicate known results, it offers predictions or mechanisms that can be tested in future empirical studies. For instance, a simulation might suggest that a particular cognitive strategy leads to better learning outcomes under specific environmental constraints. These predictions can form the basis of hypothesis generation, guiding experimental design and further empirical validation.

It is important to assess model generalizability. A model that performs well under narrow assumptions or data conditions may not scale or adapt to other contexts. Researchers should explore how the simulation behaves under different boundary conditions or when subjected to stress tests, such as introducing noise, missing data, or atypical behavioural patterns. These stress tests help determine whether a simulation is overly fitted to specific inputs or whether it captures more general psychological principles.

In complex simulations such as those involving Bayesian or hierarchical structures, convergence diagnostics are also critical for validation. In models estimated using *Markov chain Monte Carlo methods*, researchers often assess convergence using tools such as trace plots, autocorrelation functions, and the *Gelman-Rubin statistic* [38]. Failure to achieve convergence may indicate poor model specification or insufficient iterations and must be addressed before interpreting results.

Ultimately, interpreting and validating simulation results is not a mechanical task but a methodological and theoretical exercise. It requires aligning model outputs with psychological constructs, evaluating robustness through sensitivity and replication, and embedding findings within the broader scientific context. When executed rigorously, simulations can reveal detailed insights into behaviour and cognition, generate theory-driven predictions, and expand the methodological toolkit available to psychological researchers.

5 Applications and Case Studies

Advanced simulation methods in psychology have the potential to integrate cognitive and emotional, and social processes in comprehensive research. The case study presented here illustrates that very different simulation approaches can be used to make inroads into complex psychological phenomena that capture common realistic variability, behaviour dynamics, and latent psychological characteristics. We hope that this illustration exemplifies the possibilities afforded by complementary simulation techniques, from probabilistic decision-making processes to dynamic emotional states, that can provide detailed insight into human behaviour and mental processes as a whole.

The dataset used for the current study consists of response data from 200 simulated participants who each went through 100 experimental trials. Under this experimental design, we defined participants' performance in decision-making tasks as accuracy, the proportion of correctly responding to probabilistic tasks. Simultaneously, the dataset quantifies social interactions, including how often and to what extent they take place, as well as personal behavioural differences and social sensitivity. It also tracks changes in participants' emotional states over time, capturing the inherent variability of emotional experiences across repeated trials.

Alongside these behavioural measures, each participant is assigned a stable psychological trait reflecting latent individual differences such as personality factors or cognitive abilities. This dimension of the trait has crucial relevance when it comes to understanding behavioural outcomes and opportunities to explore the associative pathways of stable psychological features with domain-specific behaviours. To improve realism and capture variability that is often present in psychological data, the dataset contains variations and small noise across trials and subjects. They also show the tendency for some social interaction measures to have occasional missing values, which is a practical challenge encountered by most researchers working with real data.

Charting the course of this dataset, readers will see how state-of-the-art simulation methodologies provide powerful models of complex psychological processes, allowing researchers to formulate meaningful and specific interpretations of complex behavioural manifestations and underlying characteristics.

As such, the simulation methods used in this case study were carefully chosen to ensure realistic psychological scenarios and behaviours were represented that would provide meaningful insights into such complex psychological phenomena. We decided to use Python as the computational framework for the solution, as it is a flexible and easy-to-use programming language with extensive support in the scientific community here and particularly in psychology research involving heavy use of data simulations.

The main simulation method is to create synthetic yet lifelike participant data, engineered to approximate authentic psychological heterogeneity. Probabilistic models were used to estimate decision-making accuracy across repeated trials of each experiment to accomplish this. In particular, participant performance was modelled by fitting probabilistic distributions around the data, thus introducing variability as would occur in real psychological experiments. This probabilistic method was necessary because it reflects the natural uncertainty and variability found in human sensemaking.

To simulate realistic transitions in emotional states (as experienced by individuals in prolonged experimental settings), we incorporated emotional dynamic simulations. Emotional states were treated as dynamic phenomena providing variance in scenarios that capture the essence of realistic psychological processes over static and artificial ones. The dynamic aspect of this ensures that the simulation stays in line with the complexities and time variances of real emotional reactions.

The dataset also includes information about social interactions, which were simulated based on a combination of randomisation and controlled probabilistic methodology. That was a deliberate decision meant to reflect variation in the frequency and intensity of social interaction between different people. To enhance realism, some of these social measures also had occasional missing values, which is inevitable within real-world psychological research (i.e. due to censoring). Representing stable psychological traits, latent variables such as cognitive ability or personality were simulated using controlled probabilistic distributions. Such characteristics are critical contextual background information that can help make sense of individual differences in observable behaviours in experimental settings.

These simulation methodologies were utilised as a group to closely reproduce real psychological processes and provide realistic and meaningful findings. This approach enables researchers and practitioners to explore burgeoning relationships among psychological variables, develop rewards and exploitations, uncover long-standing trade-offs, and make robust inferences about human behaviour under diverse conditions. Below is the full Python code to simulate the dataset and implement the simulation methods described above. Visualisations and specific interpretations will be covered in the next section.

```python
# Import required libraries
import numpy as np
import pandas as pd
import matplotlib.pyplot as plt
import seaborn as sns

# Set random seed for reproducibility
np.random.seed(42)

# Dataset Generation (Simulating Psychological Variables)

# Parameters
n_participants = 200
trials_per_participant = 100

# Monte Carlo Simulation for Cognitive Decision Making
prob_correct = 0.75  # Probability of correct response
decision_data = np.random.binomial(1, prob_correct,
 ↪  (n_participants, trials_per_participant))

# Agent-based Modelling Simulation: Social Interaction Score
interaction_base = np.random.normal(loc=50, scale=10,
 ↪  size=n_participants)
social_noise = np.random.normal(0, 5, (n_participants,
 ↪  trials_per_participant))
social_interactions = interaction_base[:, None] + social_noise

# Dynamic Simulation for Emotional Regulation
time_points = np.linspace(0, 10, trials_per_participant)
emotional_states = np.sin(time_points) + np.random.normal(0,
 ↪  0.2, (n_participants, trials_per_participant))

# Bayesian-like Simulation: Trait Estimation
true_trait_mean = 100
true_trait_sd = 15
trait_scores = np.random.normal(true_trait_mean, true_trait_sd,
 ↪  n_participants)

# Construct DataFrame
data = pd.DataFrame({
    'PartID': np.repeat(np.arange(n_participants),
     ↪  trials_per_participant),
    'Trial': np.tile(np.arange(trials_per_participant),
     ↪  n_participants),
    'DecCorr': decision_data.flatten(),
```

```
    'SocInt': social_interactions.flatten(),
    'EmState': emotional_states.flatten(),
})

# Add Trait Scores
data['TraitScore'] = data['PartID'].map({i: score for i, score
↪  in enumerate(trait_scores)})

# Introduce Noise: Random Missing Data
missing_idx = np.random.choice(data.index,
↪  size=int(0.05*len(data)), replace=False)
data.loc[missing_idx, 'SocInt'] = np.nan

# Save the generated dataset
data.to_csv('psych_simulation_dataset.csv', index=False)

# Display first rows
print(data.head())

# Descriptive Analysis
print("\nDataset Description:")
print(data.describe())
```

PartID	Trial	DecCorr	SocInt	EmState	TraitScore
0	0	1	43.422147	-0.097766	95.956577
0	1	0	55.705880	-0.148466	95.956577
0	2	1	42.294912	-0.055381	95.956577
0	3	1	42.270910	-0.137485	95.956577
0	4	1	45.904463	0.502229	95.956577

	PartID	Trial	DecCorr	SocInt	EmState	TraitScore
count	20000.00	20000.00	20000.00	19000.00	20000.00	20000.00
mean	99.50	49.50	0.75	50.66	0.18	100.30
std	57.74	28.87	0.43	11.56	0.70	15.60
min	0.00	0.00	0.00	15.35	-1.65	64.39
25%	49.75	24.75	1.00	42.22	-0.40	88.69
50%	99.50	49.50	1.00	49.79	0.30	100.70
75%	149.25	74.25	1.00	58.66	0.77	111.43
max	199.00	99.00	1.00	105.78	1.64	148.47

The outputs presented here illustrate essential aspects of the simulated psychological dataset, providing an overview of participant behaviours and traits across numerous experimental trials. Specifically, the first output segment displays a snippet of the dataset, highlighting key variables collected for each participant and trial. For instance, each participant has a unique identifier `PartID`, and the dataset records each experimental `Trial` they completed. The `DecCorr` column captures whether a participant's decision was correct (denoted as 1) or incorrect (denoted as 0) for each trial. The dataset tracks each participant's `SocInt` scores, indicating variability in social engagement levels, and `EmState` scores, depicting fluctuations in emotional experiences across trials. The `TraitScore` column represents a stable, participant-specific psychological attribute, such as cognitive skill or personality trait, maintained consistently across trials.

The second output segment provides statistical summary information about the dataset, emphasising important patterns and variations among the variables. The average correctness in decision-making across all participants and trials is approximately 75%, indicating that the simulated tasks had moderate difficulty, allowing meaningful variability for further analysis. The social interaction scores exhibit a mean of around 50.66, with considerable variation (a standard deviation of approximately 11.56), suggesting realistic diversity in participants' social behaviours. Missing values in the social interaction variable are deliberately included, as seen by the lower count (19000 compared to 20000 for other variables), reflecting realistic imperfections in data collection processes typical in psychological studies.

The emotional state variable fluctuates broadly, centred near a neutral average (mean approximately 0.18) but with significant variability, suggesting dynamic emotional experiences throughout the experimental procedure. Trait scores have an average of about 100.30, with sufficient variation (a standard deviation of roughly 15.60), indicating a realistic spectrum of psychological traits across the sample.

In generating these data, a variety of sophisticated simulation techniques were applied. Primarily, the Monte Carlo method was utilised. Monte Carlo is a probabilistic technique that repeatedly samples from a defined distribution to simulate complex processes and behaviours. This approach is particularly beneficial in psychological research because it allows for the systematic exploration of variability and uncertainty inherent to human decision-making and emotional responses. By incorporating randomness, Monte Carlo simulations yield realistic and varied data points, effectively capturing the complexity of real-world psychological phenomena.

Another critical method is the introduction of controlled noise and random variations into emotional states and social interaction measures. Such techniques enhance the authenticity of simulated data, closely reflecting actual human variability. The benefit of adding controlled noise includes more accurately modelling real-life psychological and behavioural dynamics, ensuring the dataset's applicability for robust analytical investigations.

Simulation methods collectively facilitate the creation of a highly realistic psychological dataset. Such realistic simulation techniques are crucial as they provide researchers and analysts with the capacity to deeply test theories, validate analytical methods, and gain insights that can be generalised and applied in real-world psychological research contexts.

6 Visualizing Simulation Results

The analysis outlined in the previous section will be extended to the full-scale visualisation phase, using the same dataset and the discussed simulation approaches. Such visuals serve to convert the numerical insights from the psychological dataset into graphical interpretations easier to make sense of. Visualisation complements numerical analyses in various fields by providing intuitive pictorial representations of what the underlying patterns and relationships are that may otherwise be difficult to distinguish from raw numerical outputs alone.

By employing the same Monte Carlo simulation method described above, we continue to examine the dataset's structure through multiple visualisation approaches. The following visualisations allow readers to intuitively grasp complex interactions between participant decisions, emotional states, social interactions, and individual traits. Each plot type is briefly explained in a non-technical manner to help readers understand what they observe, how to interpret patterns, and appreciate the insights these visualisations offer into psychological processes and behaviours. The following Python code illustrates how we visualise the results obtained from simulations.

The first part of the code uses the Monte Carlo simulation results to visualise participants' decision accuracy. It calculates the proportion of correct decisions each participant made, subsequently displaying these proportions as a histogram. This visualisation helps readers understand how decision accuracy varies across individuals, providing a quick insight into how consistently or inconsistently participants performed. We illustrate the results from the agent-based social interaction simulation. Here, the code computes the average social interaction score per participant, visualising these scores with another histogram. This allows readers to easily see the typical social interaction levels across participants and to detect how broadly or narrowly these interactions are distributed.

The third visualisation captures the dynamic simulation of emotional states across different trials. The code calculates the average emotional state for each trial and plots these values on a line chart. This line graph can reveal any trends or patterns in emotional responses over time. Bayesian simulation results are displayed through a histogram enhanced by a density curve. It illustrates the distribution of trait scores among participants. This type of visualisation allows readers to observe the central tendencies and variability of personality traits. The code addresses data completeness by visualising missing values within the dataset using a specialised plot that highlights any gaps in the data. The complete Python visualisation code used for these purposes is presented below:

```
# Monte Carlo Simulation Results - Decision Accuracy
accuracy_per_participant =
↪ data.groupby('ParticipantID')['DecisionCorrect'].mean()
plt.hist(accuracy_per_participant, bins=20, color='lightblue',
↪ edgecolor='black')
plt.xlabel('Decision Accuracy')
plt.ylabel('Frequency')
plt.grid(True)
plt.show()

# Agent-based Social Interaction Simulation Results
mean_social_interaction =
↪ data.groupby('ParticipantID')['SocialInteraction'].mean()
plt.hist(mean_social_interaction.dropna(), bins=20,
↪ color='coral', edgecolor='black')
plt.xlabel('Average Interaction Score')
plt.ylabel('Frequency')
plt.grid(True)
plt.show()

# Dynamic System (Emotional State Simulation) Results
plt.figure(figsize=(10, 5))
sns.lineplot(x='Trial', y='EmotionalState',
↪ data=data.groupby('Trial').mean().reset_index(),
↪ marker='o')
plt.xlabel('Trial')
plt.ylabel('Average Emotional State')
plt.grid(True)
plt.show()

# Bayesian-like Trait Estimation Simulation Results
sns.histplot(trait_scores, kde=True, color='purple')
plt.xlabel('Trait Score')
plt.ylabel('Frequency')
plt.grid(True)
plt.show()

# Visualisation of Data Completeness

import missingno as msno
msno.matrix(data)
plt.show()
```

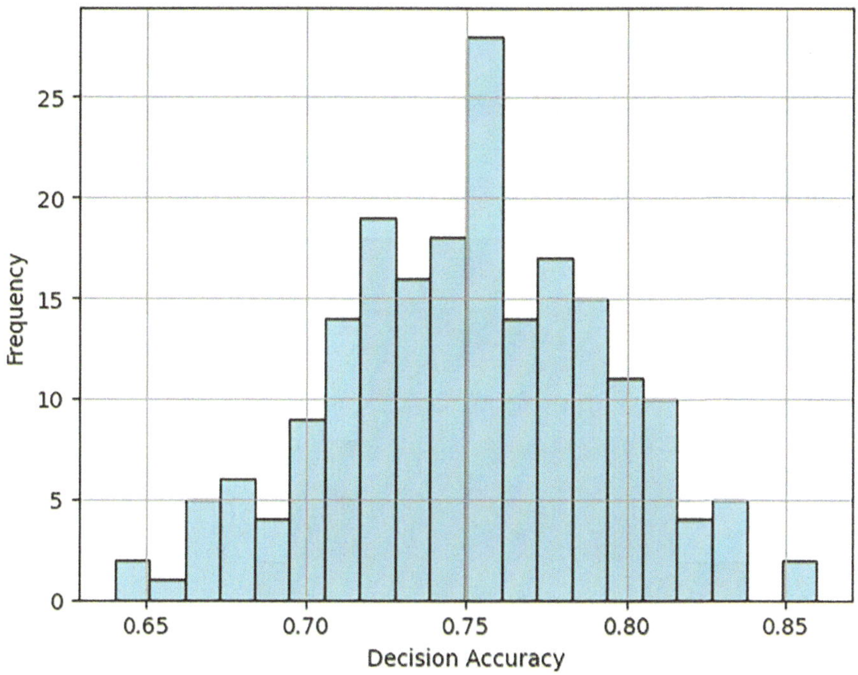

Fig. 2 Monte Carlo simulation: distribution of decision accuracy per participant

Monte Carlo simulation results are depicted in Fig. 2. This histogram illustrates the distribution of decision accuracy across different participants. The frequencies indicate how often participants achieved specific levels of decision-making accuracy, with most participants clustering around an accuracy rate of 75%. Such visual representation helps to quickly identify common performance patterns and highlights the variability in individual decision-making effectiveness.

Figure 3 presents results from the *agent-based social interaction simulation*. The histogram shows the average social interaction scores, demonstrating the extent and distribution of interpersonal engagements among participants. This type of visualisation effectively communicates the range and central tendency of social behaviours, enabling us to discern prevalent social interaction patterns and identify outliers or isolated behaviours that could require further exploration.

Figure 4 illustrates the *dynamic system simulation* of emotional states over a series of trials. The line plot visually captures how participants' emotional states fluctuate cyclically throughout the trials, showcasing periodic emotional dynamics. Such plots are particularly beneficial in tracking trends and periodicities, enabling psychologists to predict emotional peaks and troughs, thus providing opportunities for timely interventions or support.

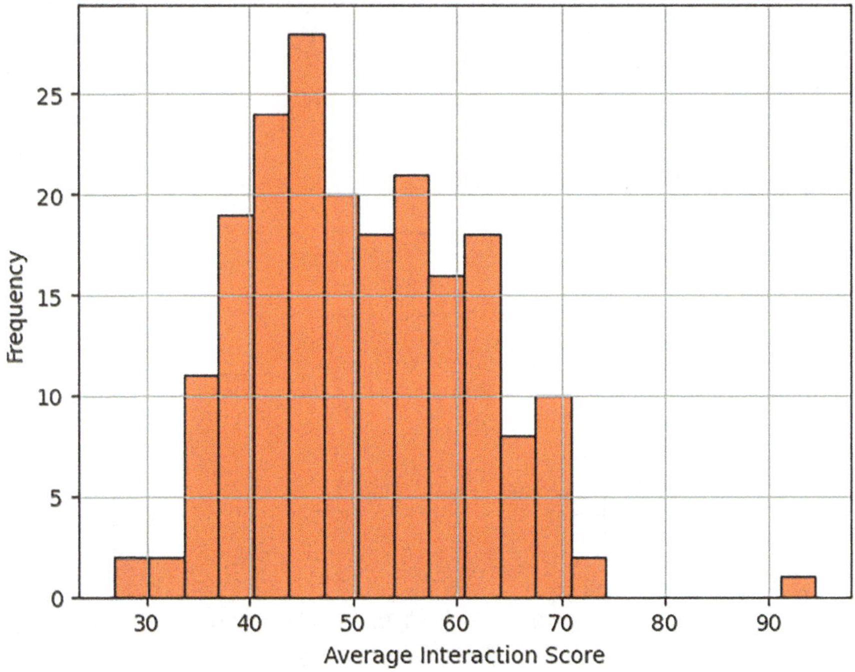

Fig. 3 Agent-based simulation: histogram of average social interaction scores

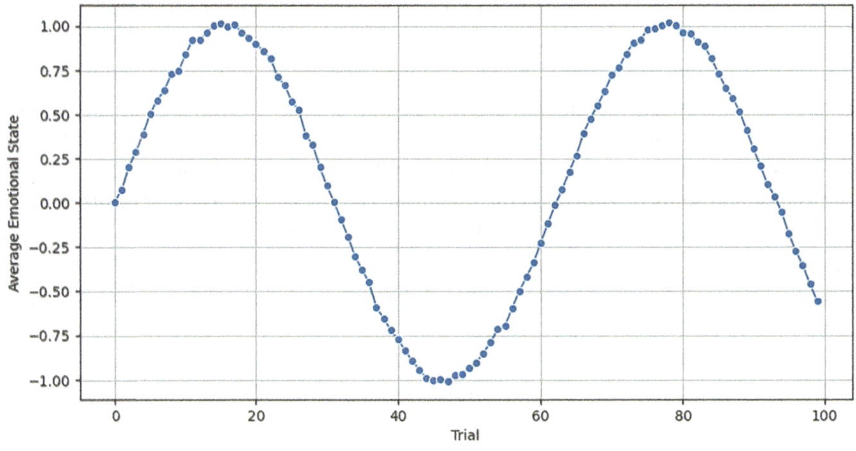

Fig. 4 Dynamic system simulation: emotional state variation over trials

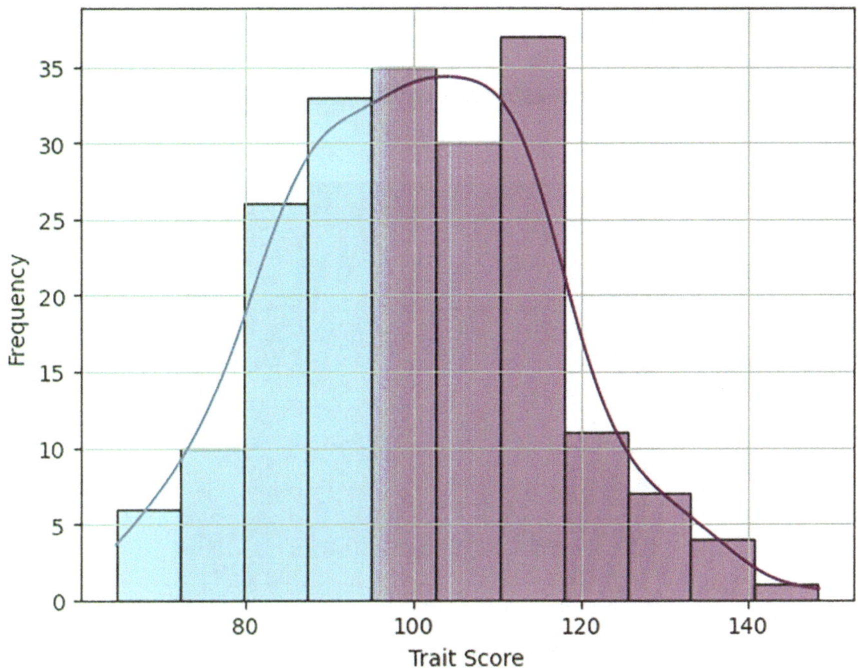

Fig. 5 Bayesian simulation: trait score distribution among participants

Figure 5 presents the outcomes from a *Bayesian-like trait estimation simulation*. This plot visualises the trait score distribution across participants, incorporating a smooth probability curve (kernel density estimate). The figure conveys the most common trait scores and their dispersion, indicating typical psychological traits within the participant group. This distribution aids in quickly understanding overall group characteristics, potential personality or behavioural profiles, and identifying participants with particularly low or high trait expressions.

Figure 6 offers an insightful *visualisation of data completeness*. Missing data visualisations help researchers to identify patterns of data absence across various psychological measures. Dark regions represent available data, whereas gaps highlight missing values. Such clarity is indispensable in deciding if and how missing data might bias the study outcomes, guiding researchers to perform additional data collection or choose appropriate statistical methods to handle missing information.

These visualisations collectively facilitate comprehensive data analysis and interpretation, ensuring that psychological researchers and practitioners can effectively translate data-driven insights into practical decisions and theoretical developments.

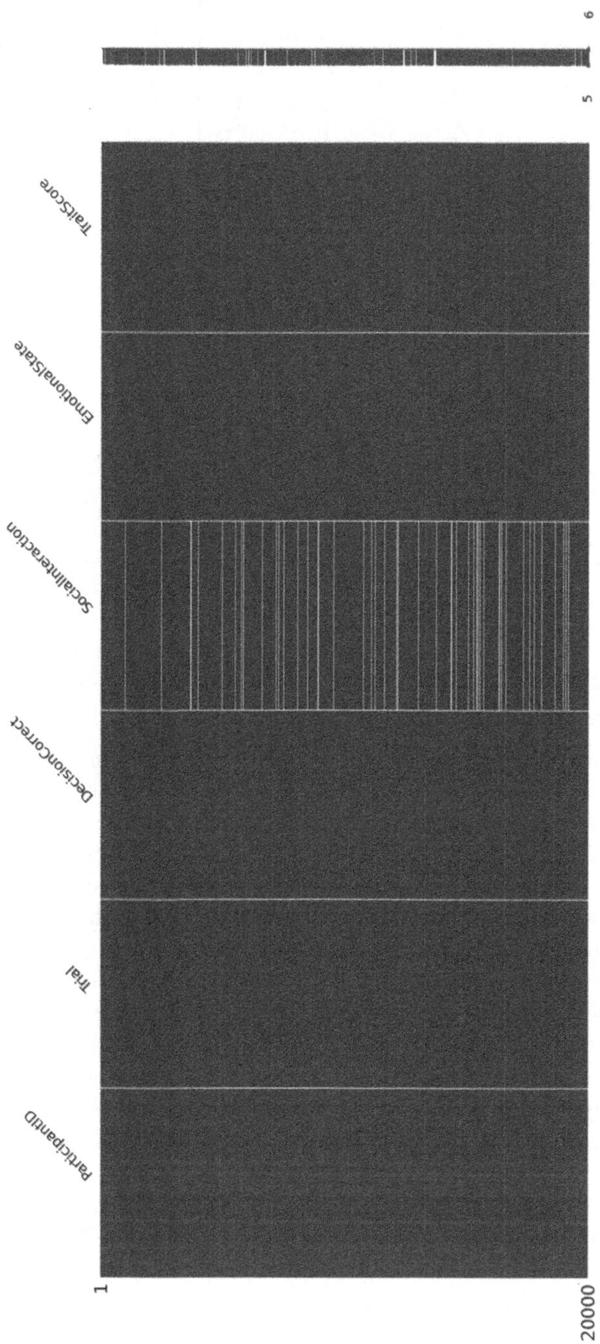

Fig. 6 Visualisation of missing data across variables

References

1. M.W. Macy, R. Willer, From factors to actors: computational sociology and agent-based modeling. Annu. Rev. Sociol. **28**(1), 143 (2002)
2. H. Farahani, P. Watson, T. Bezan, N. Kovač, L.C. Winter, M. Blagojević, P. Azadfallah, A. Allahyari, S. Masoumian, P. Jiménez, Psaichology: an intelligent direction in psychological sciences, in *10th International Scientific Conference Technics, Informatics and Education-TIE 2024* (Faculty of Technical Sciences Čačak, University of Kragujevac, Kragujevac, 2024)
3. B. Edmonds, S. Moss, From KISS to KIDS–an 'anti-simplistic' modelling approach, in *International Workshop on Multi-Agent Systems and Agent-Based Simulation* (Springer, Berlin, 2004), pp. 130–144
4. N. Kovač, K. Ratković, P. Watson, H. Farahani, F. Bagheri Sheykhangafshe, Machine learning classification models for predicting chronic pain. Curr. Psychol. **44**(18), 15409–15422 (2025)
5. S.J. Gershman, N.D. Daw, Reinforcement learning and episodic memory in humans and animals: an integrative framework. Annu. Rev. Psychol. **68**(1), 101 (2017)
6. I. van Rooij, G. Baggio, Theory before the test: how to build high-verisimilitude explanatory theories in psychological science. Perspect. Psychol. Sci. **16**(4), 682 (2021)
7. J.R. Anderson, D. Bothell, M.D. Byrne, S. Douglass, C. Lebiere, Y. Qin, An integrated theory of the mind. Psychol. Rev. **111**(4), 1036 (2004)
8. J.E. Laird, *The Soar Cognitive Architecture* (MIT Press, New York, 2019)
9. J.R. Busemeyer, P.D. Bruza, *Quantum Models of Cognition and Decision* (Cambridge University, Cambridge, 2012)
10. T.L. Griffiths, N. Chater, C. Kemp, A. Perfors, J.B. Tenenbaum, Probabilistic models of cognition: exploring representations and inductive biases. Trends Cogn. Sci. **14**(8), 357 (2010)
11. W. Jager, Enhancing the realism of simulation (EROS): on implementing and developing psychological theory in social simulation. J. Artif. Soc. Soc. Simul. (JASSS) **20**(3), 14 (2017)
12. A. Nowak, M. Lewenstein, in *Modelling and Simulation in the Social Sciences from the Philosophy of Science Point of View* (Springer, Berlin, 1996), pp. 249–285
13. H. Farahani, P. Watson, N. Kovač, F.B. Sheykhangafshe, P. Azadfallah, A. Allahyari, F. Esrafilian, R.R. Chesli, in *International Handbook of Love: Transcultural and Transdisciplinary Perspectives* (Springer, Berlin, 2025), pp. 1–22
14. R. Axelrod, W.D. Hamilton, *The Evolution of Cooperation* (Basic Books, New York, 2006)
15. D. Helbing, *Social Self-Organization: Agent-Based Simulations and Experiments to Study Emergent Social Behavior* (Springer, Berlin, 2012)
16. A. Flache, M. Mäs, T. Feliciani, E. Chattoe-Brown, G. Deffuant, S. Huet, J. Lorenz, Models of social influence: towards the next frontiers. JASSS-J. Artif. Soc. Soc. Simul. **20**(4), 2 (2017)
17. C. Castellano, S. Fortunato, V. Loreto, Statistical physics of social dynamics. Rev. Mod. Phys. **81**(2), 591 (2009)
18. M. Moutoussis, N. Shahar, T.U. Hauser, R.J. Dolan, Computation in psychotherapy, or how computational psychiatry can aid learning-based psychological therapies. Comput. Psychiatry (Cambridge, Mass) **2**, 50 (2018)
19. Q.J. Huys, T.V. Maia, M.J. Frank, Computational psychiatry as a bridge from neuroscience to clinical applications. Nat. Neurosci. **19**(3), 404 (2016)
20. C.M. Gillan, T.W. Robbins, Goal-directed learning and obsessive–compulsive disorder. Philos. Trans. R. Soc., B Biol. Sci. **369**(1655), 20130475 (2014)
21. F.H. Petzschner, L.A. Weber, T. Gard, K.E. Stephan, Computational psychosomatics and computational psychiatry: toward a joint framework for differential diagnosis. Biol. Psychiatry **82**(6), 421 (2017)
22. L.K. Muthén, B.O. Muthén, How to use a Monte Carlo study to decide on sample size and determine power. Struct. Equ. Model. **9**(4), 599 (2002)
23. S.G. West, J.F. Finch, P.J. Curran, in *Structural Equation Modeling: Concepts, Issues, and Applications*, ed. by R.H. Hoyle (SAGE Publications Inc., New York, 1995), pp. 56–75

24. P.E. Shrout, J.L. Rodgers, Psychology, science, and knowledge construction: broadening perspectives from the replication crisis. Annu. Rev. Psychol. **69**(1), 487 (2018)
25. P.R. Montague, R.J. Dolan, K.J. Friston, P. Dayan, Computational psychiatry. Trends Cogn. Sci. **16**(1), 72 (2012)
26. K.E. Stephan, S. Iglesias, J. Heinzle, A.O. Diaconescu, Translational perspectives for computational neuroimaging. Neuron **87**(4), 716 (2015)
27. J.C. Thiele, W. Kurth, V. Grimm, Facilitating parameter estimation and sensitivity analysis of agent-based models: a cookbook using NetLogo and R. J. Artif. Soc. Soc. Simul. **17**(3), 11 (2014)
28. A. Saltelli, G. Bammer, I. Bruno, E. Charters, M. Di Fiore, E. Didier, W. Nelson Espeland, J. Kay, S. Lo Piano, D. Mayo, et al., Five ways to ensure that models serve society: a manifesto. Nature **582**(7813), 482 (2020)
29. L. Breiman, *Random Forests* (Springer, Berlin, 2006)
30. S.O. Roberts, J.L. Edmonds, J.L. Roberts, The role of simulation in psychological research: applications and best practices. Psychol. Methods **24**(5), 620 (2019)
31. B. Efron, R.J. Tibshirani, *An Introduction to the Bootstrap* (Chapman and Hall/CRC, New York, 1994)
32. C.P. Robert, G. Casella, *Monte Carlo Statistical Methods* (Springer, Berlin, 2004)
33. R.Y. Rubinstein, D.P. Kroese, Simulation and the Monte Carlo method, in *Wiley Series in Probability and Statistics* (2011)
34. E. Bonabeau, Agent-based modeling: methods and techniques for simulating human systems. PNAS **99**, 7280 (2002)
35. J.M. Epstein, *Generative Social Science: Studies in Agent-Based Computational Modeling* (Princeton University, Princeton, 2006)
36. J.L. McClelland, D.E. Rumelhart, *Parallel Distributed Processing: Explorations in the Microstructure of Cognition. Volume 2: Psychological and Biological Models* (MIT Press, Cambridge, 1986)
37. A. Gelman, J.B. Carlin, H.S. Stern, D.B. Dunson, A. Vehtari, D.B. Rubin, *Bayesian Data Analysis* (Chapman and Hall/CRC, New York, 2014)
38. J.K. Kruschke, Bayesian data analysis. Wiley Interdiscip. Rev. Cogn. Sci. **1**(5), 658 (2010)
39. G. van Rossum, Python: a high-level programming language. Tech. Rep. CWI Report (Centrum Wiskunde & Informatica (CWI), Amsterdam, 1991)
40. S.L. Wiese, R.R. Vallacher, U. Strawinska, Dynamical social psychology: Complexity and coherence in human experience. Soc. Personal. Psychol. Compass **4**(11), 1018–1030 (2010)
41. V. Grimm, S.F. Railsback, Individual-based modeling and ecology, in *Princeton Series in Theoretical and Computational Biology* (2005)
42. A. Saltelli, K. Chan, E.M. Scott, *Sensitivity Analysis* (Wiley, New York, 2000)

Part IV
Interpretation of Results

The final part of this book turns from computation to comprehension—from numbers to meaning. Once data have been collected, prepared, and analyzed, the challenge shifts toward interpreting results responsibly and communicating them effectively. In psychological research, this step is not merely about presenting statistical outcomes; it is about transforming analytical findings into coherent narratives that advance theory, inform practice, and inspire further inquiry.

This part guides readers through the essential elements of interpretation and reporting, including effect sizes, confidence intervals, statistical significance, and the visualization of results. It demonstrates how clear presentation and critical reflection enhance both the transparency and impact of research. The chapters explore not only how to evaluate findings, but also how to discuss them in ways that acknowledge limitations, highlight strengths, and respect the complexity of human behavior that the data represent.

By bringing together methodological precision and scientific storytelling, this part reinforces the idea that data science in psychology is as much about understanding as it is about computation. The true power of data emerges not from the sophistication of algorithms but from the clarity and depth with which their results are interpreted. In that sense, the interpretation of results marks not the end of analysis, but the beginning of knowledge—the point at which evidence becomes understanding.

Interpreting Statistical Results

Nataša Kovač, Kruna Ratković, Marko Simeunović, Hojjatollah Farahani, Stevan Kordić, Peter Watson, and Zhiyong Johnny Zhang

1 Understanding Statistical Significance

The concept of statistical significance is foundational yet often misunderstood in psychological research. At its core, statistical significance refers to the probability that observed differences or relationships in sample data occurred due to chance, assuming that the null hypothesis is true. Researchers typically operationalise statistical significance through the p-value, which is central to hypothesis testing procedures. Despite widespread reliance, misconceptions about what p-values signify and the appropriate interpretation of results continue to persist in psychological research and beyond.

A p-value, as introduced by Fisher [1], quantifies the probability of obtaining results at least as extreme as those observed, given that the null hypothesis is correct. It does not, contrary to frequent misconceptions, measure the probability

N. Kovač · K. Ratković · M. Simeunović (✉)
Faculty of Applied Sciences, University of Donja Gorica, Podgorica, Montenegro
e-mail: natasa.kovac@udg.edu.me; kruna.ratkovic@udg.edu.me; marko.simeunovic@udg.edu.me

H. Farahani
Department of Psychology, Faculty of Humanities, Tarbiat Modares University, Jalal AleAhmad Nasr, Tehran, Iran
e-mail: h.farahani@modares.ac.ir

S. Kordić
Faculty of Maritime Studies, University of Montenegro, Dobrota, Kotor, Montenegro

P. Watson
MRC Cognition and Brain Sciences Unit, University of Cambridge, Cambridge, England
e-mail: Peter.Watson@mrc-cbu.cam.ac.uk

Z. J. Zhang
Department of Psychology, University of Notre Dame, Notre Dame, IN, USA
e-mail: zhiyongzhang@nd.edu

N. Kovač et al. (eds.), *Data Science in Psychology*,
https://doi.org/10.1007/978-3-032-18312-5_22

that the null hypothesis itself is true [2]. Instead, a p-value functions as an index of evidence against the null hypothesis: Smaller p-values indicate stronger evidence against the null, suggesting that the observed data are unlikely to have arisen purely from random variation alone.

The widely adopted threshold for statistical significance (often $p < 0.05$) is somewhat arbitrary and historically derived [3]. This standard has come under scrutiny due to its rigidity, prompting calls to lower the threshold for significance [4] or even abandon significance thresholds altogether [5].

The reliance solely on p-values has several drawbacks. Accordingly, applied ML studies in psychology report multiple complementary metrics (e.g. MAE/MSE, classification metrics) for transparent evaluation [6]. First, statistical significance does not imply practical or clinical significance. As Nickerson [7] emphasises, results can be statistically significant yet practically trivial, especially in large samples where even minuscule effects become statistically detectable. Conversely, small studies might fail to reach statistical significance despite potentially meaningful effects, due to insufficient power [8].

Second, the p-value offers no direct insight into the magnitude or direction of effects, nor does it provide information about result replicability [9]. Statistically significant results are frequently misinterpreted as definitive proof of a theory, neglecting the broader context of replicability and generalisability.

Contemporary statistical practice encourages moving away from significant vs. non-significant interpretations towards a deeper understanding of results [10]. The American Statistical Association explicitly recommends that researchers interpret p-values continuously rather than dichotomously, avoiding rigid thresholds [11]. This recommendation aligns with growing advocacy for emphasising estimation (effect sizes and confidence intervals) over simple hypothesis tests [12].

The reliance on arbitrary cut-off points often contributes to publication bias, the *file drawer* problem, where non-significant results remain unpublished, distorting the scientific record [13]. Reporting detailed results, regardless of whether they surpass traditional significance thresholds, facilitates a more accurate accumulation of scientific knowledge [14].

One critical consideration when interpreting statistical significance is the influence of sample size. Larger samples naturally provide greater statistical power, meaning they can detect even small effects. Large-sample ML classification in health psychology illustrates how modest effects can still be clinically relevant when paired with calibrated metrics [15]. The mere ability to detect small effects statistically does not inherently confer importance or practical utility [16]. Researchers should always contextualise statistically significant results within the theoretical and practical implications of their findings, especially when dealing with large-scale surveys or big data analytics [17].

Statistical significance is frequently misunderstood and misused. For example, researchers might incorrectly conclude that failure to reject the null hypothesis proves that there is no effect, thereby causing misinterpretation, because the absence of evidence is not evidence of absence [18]. Equally problematic is equating statistical significance with scientific truth or replicability. Studies have repeatedly demonstrated that significant findings often fail to replicate, highlighting the limitations of singular reliance on significance testing to validate hypotheses [19].

Given the limitations associated with significance testing, a more balanced approach is encouraged. Researchers are advised to always report exact p-values rather than simply stating whether results are significant or not. This practice improves transparency and allows others to critically assess the strength of evidence [2]. Providing complementary metrics such as effect sizes, confidence intervals, and Bayesian statistics significantly enriches interpretation and decision-making in research [20].

Understanding statistical significance means acknowledging its role as one piece of a larger interpretative framework, complemented by thorough analysis of effect sizes, replication, and theoretical coherence. This comprehensive approach helps mitigate common misinterpretations and misapplications, promoting more accurate and meaningful interpretations of psychological research outcomes.

2 Effect Size and Its Importance

Effect size is an important concept in psychological research and statistical analysis, providing a quantitative measure of the magnitude of an observed effect. Unlike statistical significance, which merely indicates whether an effect exists, effect size conveys practical significance, allowing researchers to assess the strength and real-world implications of their findings [21]. By incorporating effect size into statistical interpretation, researchers move beyond the limitations of binary hypothesis testing and gain a deeper understanding of the meaningfulness of their results.

In psychological research, small sample sizes and variability in human behaviour often make it difficult to rely solely on p-values for conclusions. While a statistically significant result may indicate that an effect is unlikely to have occurred by chance, it does not provide information about how substantial the effect is. This is where effect size plays a crucial role. In particular, meta-analyses rely on effect size metrics to compare results across multiple studies and evaluate the consistency of findings within a given research domain [22]. Without effect size, researchers risk overinterpreting results based solely on statistical significance, which may lead to misleading conclusions.

Cohen's d is one of the most widely used effect size measures for comparing mean differences between two groups. The formula for Cohen's d is given in Eq. 1:

$$d = \frac{\bar{X}_1 - \bar{X}_2}{s_p}. \qquad (1)$$

In this equation, $\bar{X}_1$ and $\bar{X}_2$ represent the sample means of the two groups, while s_p is the pooled standard deviation. The pooled standard deviation is calculated as shown in Eq. 2:

$$s_p = \sqrt{\frac{(n_1 - 1)s_1^2 + (n_2 - 1)s_2^2}{n_1 + n_2 - 2}}. \tag{2}$$

Here, s_1 and s_2 are the standard deviations of the two groups, while n_1 and n_2 denote their respective sample sizes. The pooled standard deviation provides a combined estimate of variability across the two groups, making it essential for computing Cohen's d.

Cohen's d is particularly useful in experimental psychology when comparing two independent groups. A value of $d = 0.2$ is generally considered a small effect, $d = 0.5$ represents a medium effect, and $d = 0.8$ or higher indicates a large effect [21]. These benchmarks should not be interpreted rigidly, as the context of the research and the specific field of study influence what constitutes a meaningful effect.

For studies involving relationships between continuous variables, Pearson's correlation coefficient (r) is a widely used measure of effect size. It quantifies the strength and direction of a linear relationship between two variables, making it a fundamental statistic in psychological research. The correlation coefficient ranges from -1 to 1, where a positive value indicates that as one variable increases, the other also tends to increase, while a negative value suggests that as one variable rises, the other decreases. A value of zero signifies no linear relationship between the two variables.

The computation of Pearson's r relies on the covariance between two variables, standardised by their respective variances. This ensures that the correlation remains within the range of -1 to 1. The formula for Pearson's correlation coefficient is shown in Eq. 3:

$$r = \frac{\sum(X_i - \bar{X})(Y_i - \bar{Y})}{\sqrt{\sum(X_i - \bar{X})^2 \sum(Y_i - \bar{Y})^2}}. \tag{3}$$

In this equation, X_i and Y_i represent individual data points, while $\bar{X}$ and $\bar{Y}$ denote the means of the respective variables. The numerator captures the covariance between X and Y, reflecting how much the two variables move together. The denominator standardises this relationship by dividing by the product of their standard deviations, ensuring that r remains bounded.

While Pearson's r provides information about the direction and strength of the association, it does not indicate how much variance in one variable is accounted for by the other. To address this, the squared correlation coefficient (r^2), also known as the coefficient of determination, is often reported. This measure expresses the proportion of variability in one variable that can be explained by the other. Equation 4 provides the formula for r^2:

$$r^2 = \left(\frac{\sum(X_i - \bar{X})(Y_i - \bar{Y})}{\sqrt{\sum(X_i - \bar{X})^2 \sum(Y_i - \bar{Y})^2}}\right)^2. \tag{4}$$

Since r^2 is derived from squaring r, it always falls within the range of 0 to 1, with higher values indicating a stronger predictive relationship. For example, if $r = 0.8$, then $r^2 = 0.64$, meaning that 64% of the variance in one variable can be explained by the other. Conversely, if $r = -0.6$, then $r^2 = 0.36$, indicating that 36% of the variance is accounted for, but the relationship is negative.

In psychological research, Pearson's correlation is frequently applied to explore associations between various constructs, such as intelligence and academic performance, stress and mental health, or working memory capacity and cognitive flexibility. For instance, a study examining the relationship between anxiety levels and sleep quality may find a strong negative correlation, suggesting that individuals with higher anxiety tend to experience poorer sleep. In such cases, reporting both r and r^2 allows researchers to convey not only the direction and strength of the relationship but also the extent to which one variable explains the variation in the other.

Despite its widespread use, Pearson's correlation is subject to several important assumptions that must be met for valid interpretation. First, the relationship between the variables should be linear, as the correlation coefficient does not capture nonlinear patterns. Second, the data should exhibit homoscedasticity, meaning that the variance in one variable remains relatively constant across the range of the other variable. Third, outliers can have a substantial influence on the correlation value, potentially distorting the results. If these assumptions are violated, alternative correlation measures, such as Spearman's rank correlation, may be more appropriate.

Pearson's correlation is a powerful tool for understanding relationships between variables, but it should be interpreted with caution. While a strong correlation may suggest an association, it does not imply causation. Other confounding factors may influence the observed relationship, meaning that researchers should consider additional statistical techniques, such as regression analysis, to establish more concrete conclusions.

By incorporating both r and r^2 into statistical interpretation, researchers gain a clearer perspective on the relationships between variables. Pearson's r highlights the nature of the association, while r^2 quantifies its explanatory power. Together, they provide valuable insights into psychological phenomena, allowing for more informed conclusions about human behaviour and cognition.

Another important measure of effect size is partial eta squared (η^2), which is commonly reported in an analysis of variance (ANOVA). It quantifies the proportion of variance attributed to a particular independent variable and is given by Eq. 5:

$$\eta^2 = \frac{SS_{\text{effect}}}{SS_{\text{effect}} + SS_{\text{error}}}. \tag{5}$$

In this equation, SS_{effect} represents the sum of squares associated with the independent variable, while SS_{error} refers to the residual variance. Higher values of η^2 indicate stronger effects, with rough interpretative guidelines suggesting that

$\eta^2 = 0.01$ represents a small effect, $\eta^2 = 0.06$ a medium effect, and $\eta^2 = 0.14$ a large effect [21].

Effect size interpretation is crucial in psychological research because it influences how findings are understood and applied. In clinical psychology, for instance, an intervention demonstrating a statistically significant reduction in symptoms may not be practically meaningful if the effect size is small [23]. Conversely, even small effects can be meaningful in large-scale social psychological studies, where small changes in attitudes or behaviours can have widespread implications [24].

Reporting effect size enhances the transparency and reproducibility of research. Scientific journals and reporting guidelines increasingly require authors to provide effect size measures alongside p-values to ensure a more comprehensive interpretation of their findings [25]. Without effect size reporting, the practical significance of results remains unclear, potentially leading to exaggerated claims or underestimation of meaningful effects.

The importance of effect size extends beyond individual studies, as it plays a critical role in power analysis and sample size determination. Statistical power refers to the likelihood of detecting a true effect when it exists. A study with low power may fail to detect even large effects, leading to false negatives [21]. By estimating expected effect sizes from previous literature, researchers can determine the sample size necessary to achieve adequate power and improve the reliability of their findings.

Effect size also facilitates meaningful comparisons across studies. In meta-analyses, effect sizes from multiple studies are combined to estimate the overall magnitude of an effect across different samples and conditions. This approach helps establish the robustness and generalisability of findings, addressing inconsistencies that may arise due to sample variability, measurement differences, or methodological choices [22].

Effect size offers a deeper understanding of study results beyond statistical significance alone. Whether through standardised mean differences, correlation coefficients, or variance-explained measures, effect size provides essential information about the magnitude and relevance of findings. By incorporating effect size into data interpretation, researchers enhance the clarity, reproducibility, and practical applicability of their work, ultimately contributing to more meaningful scientific advancements.

3 Confidence Intervals and Their Relevance

In psychological research, the ability to draw reliable conclusions from sample data is foundational to sound scientific reasoning. Among the most powerful tools in inferential statistics is the *confidence interval* (CI). A range of the true population parameter's feasible values is shown by CI. Rather than simply relying on point estimates or p-values, it is a good practice to report confidence intervals as a

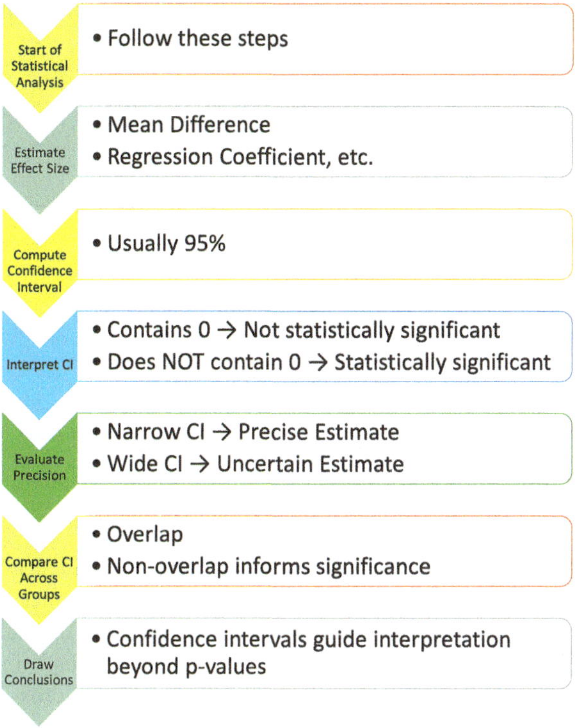

Fig. 1 Confidence interval integration in statistical interpretation

standard tool in empirical studies. Confidence intervals not only offer a deeper understanding of the precision of estimates but also serve as a bridge between statistical significance and practical relevance [12, 26].

A confidence interval is built around a sample statistic, such as the mean, proportion, or regression coefficient, and is constructed by incorporating an estimate of variability (such as the standard error) and a specified level of confidence. The most common level used in psychological sciences is the 95% confidence interval, which suggests that if the same study were repeated numerous times, approximately 95% of those intervals would capture the true population parameter [27]. It is crucial to note that a CI does not imply a 95% probability that the parameter lies within a specific range in a single study, a common misconception even among researchers.

The relevance of confidence intervals becomes more evident when considering the limitations of *p*-values. While a *p*-value tells us whether an effect might exist, it does not convey how precise or meaningful that estimate might be in practice. In contrast, CIs provide a visual and numerical representation of the uncertainty surrounding a parameter, allowing researchers to gauge both the magnitude and the precision of their findings [28]. As shown in Fig. 1, confidence intervals bridge statistical estimation, hypothesis testing, and practical interpretation. They complement *p*-values by providing additional insight into the reliability and precision of parameter estimates and guide researchers towards more robust conclusions.

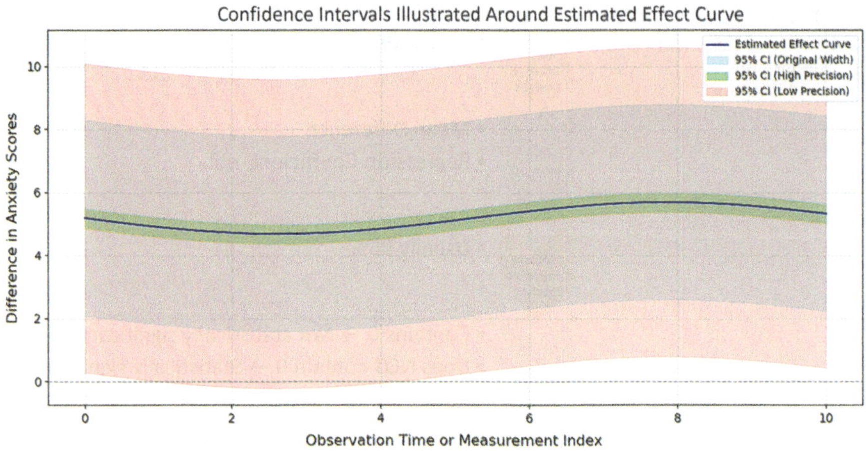

Fig. 2 Visualisation of confidence intervals around an estimated effect curve

To illustrate the interpretive power of confidence intervals, a scenario where the effect of a cognitive-behavioural therapy intervention on reducing anxiety symptoms over time will be observed. Suppose the estimated difference in anxiety scores between the treatment and control groups follows a curve (see Fig. 2), reflecting how the intervention's effect evolves across multiple observation points. Around this estimated curve, 95% confidence intervals are shown.

In the original estimate, the shaded band surrounding the curve is relatively wide, and it extends approximately 3.1 points above and below the estimated line. This visual representation of a broader confidence interval suggests that, while the intervention shows a beneficial effect, there is substantial uncertainty regarding the precise magnitude of this effect across time. In contrast, a second scenario shows a narrow confidence interval, with bounds only 0.3 points away from the curve, indicating an exact and reliable estimate. Such narrow intervals typically result from larger sample sizes and lower variability in the data. A third band illustrates a scenario with poor precision, where the confidence interval spans nearly five points on either side of the estimate. This signals greater ambiguity and may raise questions about the robustness or generalisability of the results.

These graphical distinctions emphasise that confidence intervals are not merely statistical formalities but deeply informative tools. They reveal whether an effect is statistically significant and how stable and trustworthy the estimate is across a range of conditions. Unlike p-values, which offer a binary indication of significance, confidence intervals communicate the degree of uncertainty surrounding findings and help researchers make detailed interpretations grounded in the data's variability.

CIs can be used to assess the practical significance of results. When confidence intervals are wide, it often reflects small sample sizes or high variability, making conclusions more tentative. Conversely, narrow intervals suggest more certainty and allow stronger inferences. This relationship between interval width and sample

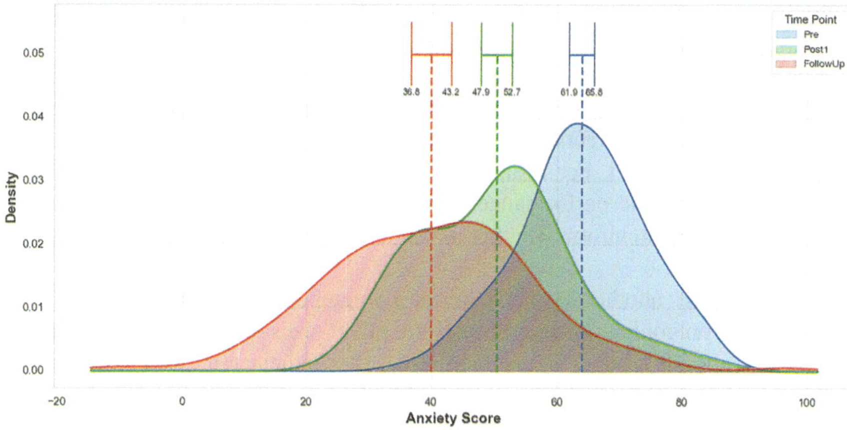

Fig. 3 Visualising confidence intervals around kernel density estimates of anxiety scores across time points

size underscores the importance of adequate study planning and statistical power analysis [29].

Another critical role of confidence intervals is in comparative research, particularly when examining group differences. For example, if the confidence intervals for two group means do not overlap substantially, it may suggest a significant difference between the groups. Researchers should be cautious in interpreting non-overlapping intervals as definitive proof of significance; formal statistical testing is still required. Yet, confidence intervals often act as an intuitive guide, especially in graphical representations, where error bars plotted as CI bounds help visualise the uncertainty and potential differences in a more informative manner than standard error bars [30].

This concept is illustrated in Fig. 3, which visualises the distribution of anxiety scores measured at three different time points (*Pre*, *Post1*, and *FollowUp*) using *kernel density estimation* (KDE) curves, alongside their corresponding confidence intervals. The figure demonstrates how the overlap between confidence intervals can aid in interpreting group differences, providing an intuitive representation of effect size stability across conditions.

The horizontal caps surrounding the mean lines represent the 95% CIs. These intervals visually emphasise the uncertainty around the estimated group means. As evident from the figure, non-overlapping or marginally overlapping CIs (e.g. between *Pre* and *Post1*) suggest a statistically significant reduction in anxiety scores following the intervention. On the other hand, when CIs are closer or overlap more, interpretive caution is required due to possible non-significance or variability in effect size precision.

Concerning CIs, narrower confidence intervals (as seen in the *Post1* group) indicate greater precision of estimation, possibly due to smaller variability or larger sample reliability, whereas wider intervals (e.g. *FollowUp*) reflect greater uncertainty, which may stem from heterogeneity or sample noise. Such visualisation not only aids in understanding effect size confidence, but also supports researchers in inferring practical significance, not just statistical significance.

Confidence intervals are also indispensable in regression modelling, where they are typically reported for each regression coefficient. This allows researchers to determine not only the direction and significance of predictors but also the reliability of their estimated effect. For instance, in a multiple regression analysis exploring predictors of academic performance, a 95% CI for a predictor variable like self-regulation skills could inform whether its influence is negligible or substantial across replications.

Meta-analysis, another cornerstone of contemporary psychological science, relies heavily on confidence intervals. Here, effect sizes from multiple studies are pooled, and the CI around the average effect size indicates the level of certainty about the aggregate finding. This approach helps synthesise knowledge across studies and highlight where effects are consistent or potentially spurious [31].

Confidence intervals align well with open science principles and the push towards greater transparency and reproducibility in psychological research. Psychological science-oriented journals increasingly recommend or require the inclusion of CIs in published reports [32]. This shift promotes a departure from dichotomous thinking rooted in significant vs. not significant outcomes, encouraging researchers to interpret results more deeply and continuously.

Confidence intervals can inform clinical and policy decision-making by quantifying the range within which true effects lie. This is especially crucial in fields like clinical psychology, where practitioners need to know not just whether an intervention works, but how reliably and to what extent it can be expected to benefit patients. Reporting effect estimates with their CIs enables stakeholders to assess whether observed effects exceed a minimum clinically important difference or fall within a margin of equivalence [33]. In affect- and relationship-focused ML applications, interval estimates and uncertainty plots improve interpretability of risk predictions [34].

Despite their utility, confidence intervals are not without limitations. They depend on assumptions such as the normality of sampling distributions, which may not always hold. Violations of these assumptions can result in intervals that either under- or overstate the true uncertainty. In such cases, robust statistical techniques such as bootstrapped confidence intervals offer an alternative that is less sensitive to distributional assumptions [35]. Confidence intervals should not be used in isolation. They complement, rather than replace, other statistical measures such as p-values and effect sizes. Together, these tools form a comprehensive analytical framework that enables researchers to evaluate the strength, direction, and credibility of their findings.

4 Types of Errors and Power of the Test

In statistical hypothesis testing, making correct inferences about a population based on sample data is essential. Statistical tests are not infallible, and errors can occur. These errors, known as type I and type II errors, affect the reliability of research conclusions and must be carefully considered in study design. Closely related to these errors is the concept of statistical power, which refers to the probability of correctly detecting an effect when it truly exists [21]. Understanding these concepts is crucial for interpreting statistical results accurately and designing studies that produce valid and replicable findings.

The first type of error encountered in hypothesis testing is a type I error, which occurs when a null hypothesis is incorrectly rejected. This means that a researcher concludes that an effect exists when, in reality, it does not. The probability of committing a type I error is represented by the significance level α, which is typically set at 0.05 in psychological research [1]. This implies that there is a 5% chance of rejecting the null hypothesis when it is true. The probability of a type I error is formally expressed in Eq. 6:

$$P(\text{Type\_I\_Error}) = \alpha. \tag{6}$$

In this equation, $P(\text{Type\_I\_Error})$ represents the probability of rejecting a true null hypothesis, while α is the predefined significance level chosen by the researcher. A lower α reduces the likelihood of a type I error but increases the risk of committing a type II error [36].

A type II error occurs when the null hypothesis is not rejected despite there being a true effect in the population. This means that a researcher fails to detect an effect when one exists. The probability of making a type II error is denoted by β, and it is inversely related to statistical power. The probability of committing a type II error is given by Eq. 7:

$$P(\text{Type\_II\_Error}) = \beta. \tag{7}$$

Here, $P(\text{Type\_II\_Error})$ denotes the probability of failing to reject a false null hypothesis, and β represents the probability of this mistake occurring. A high β value indicates a greater likelihood of missing a true effect, while a low β value means the test has a higher chance of detecting real differences [21].

Statistical power, defined as $1-\beta$, represents the probability of correctly rejecting the null hypothesis when an effect exists. It is a crucial component of study design, ensuring that an experiment has a sufficient likelihood of detecting true effects. Equation 8 describes statistical power:

$$\text{Power} = 1 - P(\text{Type\_II\_Error}). \tag{8}$$

Several factors influence statistical power, including sample size, effect size, and the chosen significance level. Increasing the sample size is one of the most effective ways to enhance power because it reduces variability and improves the precision of estimates. The relationship between power and sample size is particularly important in psychology, where studies often involve small sample sizes due to practical constraints [37]. Researchers typically conduct power analyses before data collection to ensure that their study is appropriately powered to detect meaningful effects [21].

Another important consideration is the impact of multiple comparisons on error rates. When multiple hypothesis tests are conducted within the same study, the overall probability of making a type I error increases. This issue, known as the multiple comparisons problem, can lead to spurious findings if not properly addressed. Statistical corrections such as the Bonferroni correction [38] or false discovery rate (FDR) adjustments [39] help control for inflated type I error rates when conducting multiple tests.

Beyond traditional hypothesis testing, Bayesian approaches provide an alternative framework for assessing evidence in research studies. Instead of focusing on rejecting or failing to reject a null hypothesis, Bayesian methods quantify the strength of evidence in favour of competing hypotheses [40]. Bayesian analysis incorporates prior knowledge and updates beliefs based on observed data, offering a more flexible approach to statistical inference. While frequentist power analysis remains the dominant method in psychological research, Bayesian methods are gaining traction as a complementary approach that addresses some of the limitations of classical significance testing [41].

Understanding the concepts of type I and type II errors, along with statistical power, is important for designing robust and reliable studies. Researchers must carefully balance the risks of these errors by choosing appropriate significance levels, ensuring adequate sample sizes, and conducting power analyses before data collection. By increasing awareness of statistical power and its implications, researchers can improve the reproducibility and validity of psychological research, leading to more meaningful scientific contributions.

5 Case Study

To illustrate key statistical concepts, we conducted a case study examining the effectiveness of a psychological intervention named *cognitive-behavioural therapy* (CBT) in reducing anxiety levels among adult participants. Two groups participated in the study: an experimental group receiving CBT and a control group not undergoing the intervention. Anxiety was measured both before and after the intervention, providing data on individual changes in anxiety levels. The initial observations from the dataset are shown in the table, highlighting typical anxiety changes for experimental group participants.

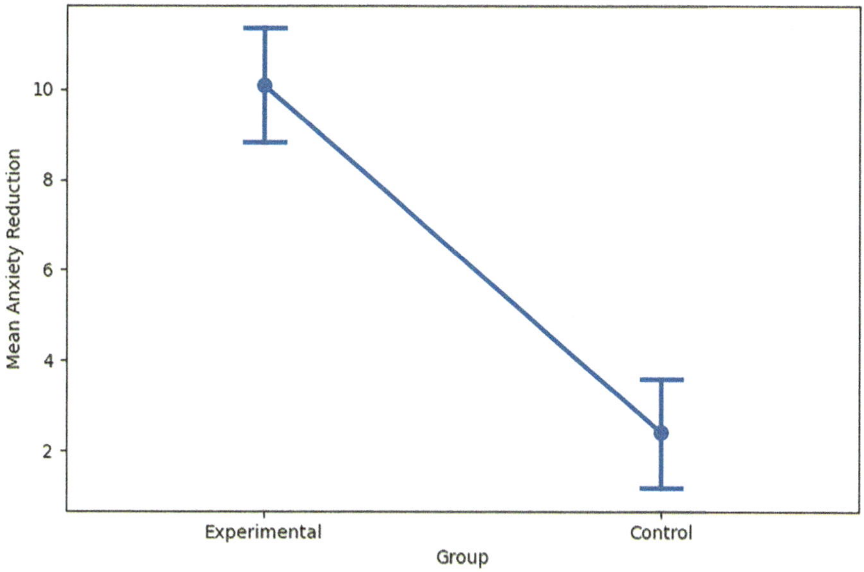

Fig. 4 Anxiety change by group with 95% CI

Group	Pre_A	Post_A	Age	Gender	Anxiety_C
Exp	74.97	63.35	19	Female	11.62
Exp	68.62	60.54	43	Female	8.07
Exp	76.48	69.86	34	Male	6.62
Exp	85.23	72.17	57	Male	13.06
Exp	67.66	52.50	50	Female	15.15

```
Mean Difference: 7.67, 95% CI: [5.92, 9.42]
```

The analysis began by assessing the mean difference in anxiety reduction between the experimental and control groups. Results indicate a substantial mean difference of 7.67 points in favour of the experimental group, with a 95% confidence interval ranging from 5.92 to 9.42. This result demonstrates that participants receiving CBT experienced significantly greater reductions in anxiety compared to those in the control condition. Figure 4 visually summarises these findings, clearly illustrating the magnitude of the difference along with its confidence interval. The non-overlapping confidence intervals strongly suggest that the observed difference between groups is both statistically and practically meaningful.

We then explored the strength and nature of the relationship between anxiety scores measured before and after the intervention across both groups, as depicted in Fig. 5. A strong positive correlation was observed (Pearson's $r = 0.86$, $r^2 = 0.74$, $p < 0.001$), indicating that participants who initially reported higher anxiety levels also tended to exhibit higher levels post-intervention. Figure 5 also shows distinct regression lines for each group, with the experimental group consistently exhibiting lower post-anxiety scores compared to the control group for similar pre-anxiety

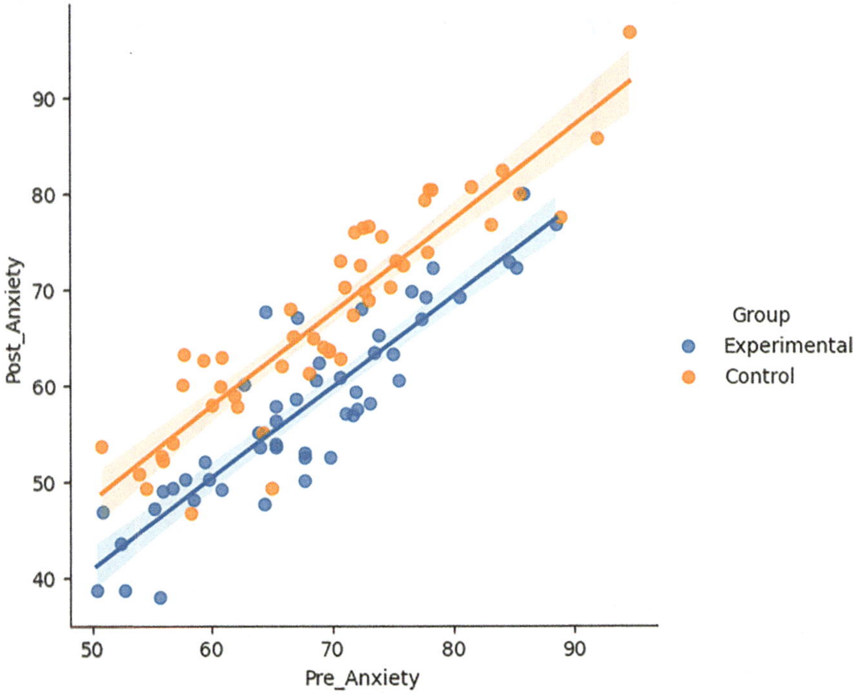

Fig. 5 Correlation between pre- and post-anxiety scores

levels. This highlights the effectiveness of the CBT intervention in reducing anxiety, even when controlling for baseline anxiety levels.

```
Pearson r: 0.86, r^^c2^^b2: 0.74, p-value: 0.0000
```

Understanding the statistical power of our analysis was also essential, as it measures our study's ability to detect real effects when they exist. The computed statistical power for detecting a medium-sized effect (Cohen's $d = 0.5$) given our sample size (50 per group) was approximately 0.70 (70%). Typically, a power of at least 80% is recommended in psychological research; thus, the observed 70% indicates moderate power. Figure 6 illustrates how statistical power increases with larger effect sizes, clearly demonstrating the relationship between the magnitude of the effect researchers hope to detect and their probability of successfully detecting it with their given sample size.

```
Statistical Power for detecting medium effect (d=0.5): 0.70
```

Finally, Fig. 7 explicitly visualises the crucial trade-off between the probability of committing a type I error (incorrectly concluding an effect exists when it does not, represented by significance level α) and statistical power (the inverse of type II

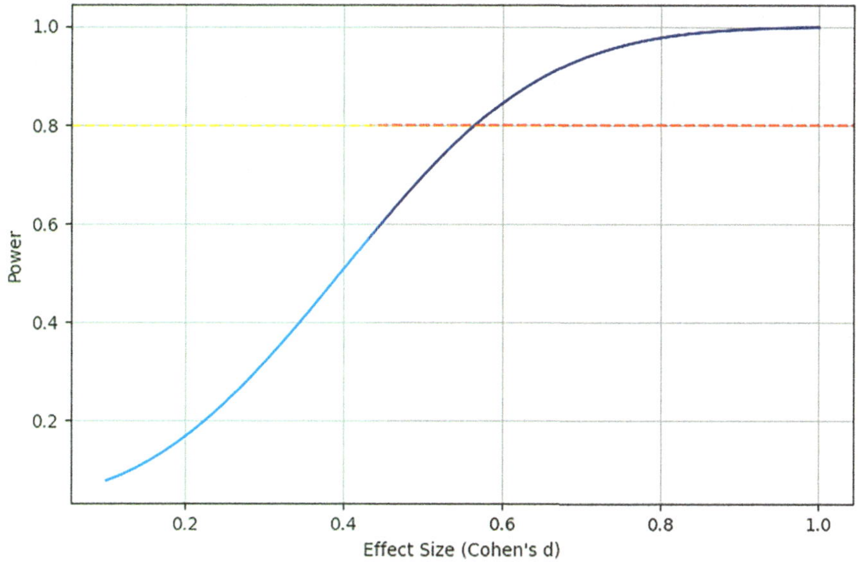

Fig. 6 Statistical power curve

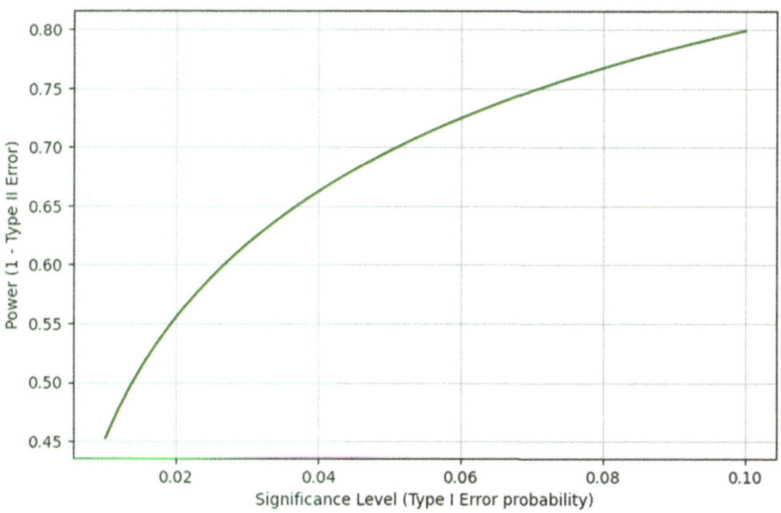

Fig. 7 Trade-off between type I error and statistical power

error, i.e. the failure to detect a genuine effect). As Fig. 7 indicates, researchers must thoughtfully choose their significance threshold: Increasing the accepted probability of type I error also increases statistical power, but it simultaneously raises the risk of drawing incorrect conclusions. This figure demonstrates the balance researchers must maintain to ensure robust, reliable results.

References

1. R.A. Fisher, *Statistical Methods for Research Workers* (Oliver & Boyd, Edinburgh, 1925)
2. S. Goodman, A dirty dozen: twelve p-value misconceptions, in *Seminars in Hematology*, vol. 45(3) (Elsevier, Amsterdam, 2008), pp. 135–140
3. M. Cowles, C. Davis, On the origins of the 0.05 level of statistical significance. Am. Psychol. **37**(5), 553 (1982)
4. D.J. Benjamin, J.O. Berger, M. Johannesson, B.A. Nosek, E.J. Wagenmakers, R. Berk, K.A. Bollen, B. Brembs, L. Brown, C. Camerer, et al., Redefine statistical significance. Nat. Hum. Behav. **2**(1), 6 (2018)
5. V. Amrhein, S. Greenland, B. McShane, Scientists rise up against statistical significance. Nature **567**(7748), 305 (2019)
6. N. Kovač, K. Ratković, H. Farahani, P. Watson, A practical applications guide to machine learning regression models in psychology with python. Methods Psychol. **11**, 100156 (2024)
7. R.S. Nickerson, Null hypothesis significance testing: a review of an old and continuing controversy. Psychol. Methods **5**(2), 241 (2000)
8. K.S. Button, J.P. Ioannidis, C. Mokrysz, B.A. Nosek, J. Flint, E.S. Robinson, M.R. Munafò, Power failure: why small sample size undermines the reliability of neuroscience. Nat. Rev. Neurosci. **14**(5), 365 (2013)
9. J.P. Ioannidis, Why most published research findings are false. PLoS Med. **2**(8), e124 (2005)
10. H. Farahani, P. Watson, T. Bezan, N. Kovač, L.C. Winter, M. Blagojević, P. Azadfallah, A. Allahyari, S. Masoumian, P. Jiménez, Psaichology: an intelligent direction in psychological sciences, in *10th International Scientific Conference Technics, Informatics and Education-TIE 2024* (Faculty of Technical Sciences Čačak, University of Kragujevac, Kragujevac, 2024)
11. R.L. Wasserstein, A.L. Schirm, N.A. Lazar, Moving to a world beyond "p< 0.05" (2019)
12. G. Cumming, The new statistics: why and how. Psychol. Sci. **25**(1), 7 (2014)
13. R. Rosenthal, The file drawer problem and tolerance for null results. Psychol. Bull. **86**(3), 638 (1979)
14. D. Lakens, F.G. Adolfi, C.J. Albers, F. Anvari, M.A. Apps, S.E. Argamon, T. Baguley, R.B. Becker, S.D. Benning, D.E. Bradford, et al., Justify your alpha. Nat. Hum. Behav. **2**(3), 168 (2018)
15. N. Kovač, K. Ratković, P. Watson, H. Farahani, F. Bagheri Sheykhangafshe, Machine learning classification models for predicting chronic pain. Curr. Psychol., 1–14 (2025)
16. A. Gelman, J. Carlin, Beyond power calculations: assessing type S (sign) and type M (magnitude) errors. Perspect. Psychol. Sci. **9**(6), 641 (2014)
17. R.M. Kaplan, D.A. Chambers, R.E. Glasgow, Big data and large sample size: a cautionary note on the potential for bias. Clin. Transl. Sci. **7**(4), 342 (2014)
18. D.G. Altman, J.M. Bland, Statistics notes: absence of evidence is not evidence of absence. BMJ **311**(7003), 485 (1995)
19. O.S. Collaboration, Estimating the reproducibility of psychological science. Science **349**(6251), aac4716 (2015)
20. J.K. Kruschke, T.M. Liddell, Bayesian data analysis for newcomers. Psychon. Bull. Rev. **25**(1), 155 (2018)
21. J. Cohen, *Statistical Power Analysis for the Behavioral Sciences*, 2nd edn. (Routledge, Milton Park, 1988)
22. L.V. Hedges, I. Olkin, *Statistical Methods for Meta-Analysis* (Academic Press, New York, 1986)
23. C.O. Fritz, P.E. Morris, J.J. Richler, Effect size estimates: current use, calculations, and interpretation. J. Exp. Psychol. Gen. **141**(1), 2 (2012)
24. R. Rosenthal, in *The Handbook of Research Synthesis* (Russell Sage Foundation, New York, 1994), pp. 231–244
25. L. Wilkinson, Statistical methods in psychology journals: guidelines and explanations. Am. Psychol. **54**(8), 594 (1999)

26. G. Cumming, S. Finch, Inference by eye: confidence intervals and how to read pictures of data. Am. Psychol. **60**(2), 170 (2005)
27. G. Cumming, *Understanding the New Statistics: Effect Sizes, Confidence Intervals, and Meta-Analysis* (Routledge, Milton Park, 2013)
28. S. Greenland, S.J. Senn, K.J. Rothman, J.B. Carlin, C. Poole, S.N. Goodman, D.G. Altman, Statistical tests, p-values, confidence intervals, and power: a guide to misinterpretations. Eur. J. Epidemiol. **31**(4), 337 (2016)
29. K. Kelley, K.J. Preacher, On effect size. Psychol. Methods **17**(2), 137 (2012)
30. G.R. Loftus, M.E. Masson, Using confidence intervals in within-subject designs. Psychon. Bull. Rev. **1**(4), 476 (1994)
31. M. Borenstein, L.V. Hedges, J.P. Higgins, H.R. Rothstein, *Introduction to Meta-Analysis* (Wiley, New York, 2021)
32. D. Lakens, Calculating and reporting effect sizes to facilitate cumulative science: a practical primer for t-tests and ANOVAs. Front. Psychol. **4**, 863 (2013)
33. K.J. Rothman, K.F. Huybrechts, E.J. Murray, *Epidemiology: An Introduction* (Oxford University, Oxford, 2024)
34. H. Farahani, P. Watson, N. Kovač, F.B. Sheykhangafshe, P. Azadfallah, A. Allahyari, F. Esrafilian, R.R. Chesli, in *International Handbook of Love: Transcultural and Transdisciplinary Perspectives* (Springer, Berlin, 2025), pp. 1–22
35. B. Efron, R.J. Tibshirani, *An Introduction to the Bootstrap* (Chapman and Hall/CRC, New York, 1994)
36. J. Neyman, E. Pearson, On the problem of the most efficient tests of statistical hypotheses. Phil. Trans. R. Soc. A **231**, 289 (1933)
37. S.E. Maxwell, Sample size and multiple regression analysis. Psychol. Methods **5**(4), 434 (2000)
38. C.E. Bonferroni, Teoria Statistica delle Classi e Calcolo delle Probabilità, in *Pubblicazioni del R Istituto Superiore di Scienze Economiche e Commerciali di Firenze*, vol. 8 (1936), p. 3
39. Y. Benjamini, Y. Hochberg, Controlling the false discovery rate: a practical and powerful approach to multiple testing. J. R. Stat. Soc. Ser. B Methodol. **57**(1), 289 (1995)
40. R.E. Kass, A.E. Raftery, Bayes factors. J. Am. Stat. Assoc. **90**(430), 773 (1995)
41. Z. Dienes, Bayesian versus orthodox statistics: which side are you on?. Perspect. Psychol. Sci. **6**(3), 274 (2011)

Advanced Data Interpretation Strategies

Nataša Kovač, Kruna Ratković, Marko Simeunović, Hojjatollah Farahani, Stevan Kordić, and Peter Watson

1 Multivariate Analysis Interpretation

Multivariate analysis encompasses a suite of sophisticated statistical methods designed to simultaneously analyse multiple dependent variables [1]. These techniques provide detailed insights into complex psychological phenomena that univariate analyses might overlook. Unlike simpler methods that consider each variable separately, multivariate approaches capture the underlying relationships among variables, highlighting their interconnectedness and collective influence on outcomes [2].

Psychological research often addresses multifaceted constructs such as intelligence, personality, mental health, or behavioural attitudes. Such constructs typically cannot be captured adequately by single indicators. Instead, they require multiple measures, leading researchers towards multivariate analytical strategies like *Multivariate Analysis of Variance* (MANOVA), *Discriminant Function Analysis* (DFA), *Canonical Correlation Analysis* (CCA), and *Exploratory and Confirmatory Factor Analyses* (EFA and CFA).

N. Kovač · K. Ratković · M. Simeunović (✉)
Faculty of Applied Sciences, University of Donja Gorica, Podgorica, Montenegro
e-mail: natasa.kovac@udg.edu.me; kruna.ratkovic@udg.edu.me; marko.simeunovic@udg.edu.me

H. Farahani
Department of Psychology, Faculty of Humanities, Tarbiat Modares University, Tehran, Iran
e-mail: h.farahani@modares.ac.ir

S. Kordić
Faculty of Maritime Studies, University of Montenegro, Kotor, Montenegro

P. Watson
MRC Cognition and Brain Sciences Unit, University of Cambridge, Cambridge, UK
e-mail: Peter.Watson@mrc-cbu.cam.ac.uk

N. Kovač et al. (eds.), *Data Science in Psychology*,
https://doi.org/10.1007/978-3-032-18312-5_23

For instance, MANOVA is used extensively to investigate differences across experimental conditions on multiple correlated dependent variables while preserving control over Type I error rates [3]. DFA complements MANOVA by identifying linear combinations of dependent variables that best distinguish between predefined groups, helping researchers pinpoint exactly which factors differentiate groups most effectively [4, 5].

Interpreting results from multivariate tests requires careful attention to the nature of hypotheses tested and the statistical assumptions underlying each method. For example, Wilks' Lambda is one of the most common multivariate test statistics used in MANOVA. It quantifies the proportion of total variance unexplained by group differences, with smaller values indicating greater group differentiation [6]. Relying solely on Wilks' Lambda can be misleading, particularly with unequal group sizes or heterogeneity of variances. Researchers are thus encouraged to consider complementary measures such as *Pillai's Trace*, *Hotelling's Trace*, and *Roy's Largest Root*, each offering distinct insights into multivariate significance [7].

When interpreting MANOVA results, researchers should first examine overall multivariate significance tests. A statistically significant multivariate effect indicates that at least one dependent variable significantly differs between groups. Yet, researchers must delve deeper, utilising discriminant analyses or follow-up univariate ANOVAs to identify which specific variables drive this significance [8].

Importantly, effect size measures like partial eta squared (η_p^2) provide critical insights into practical significance. Effect size interpretation in multivariate contexts assists in distinguishing between statistically significant yet practically trivial effects versus those that are both statistically and practically meaningful [9].

DFA serves as a powerful interpretative companion to MANOVA. It generates discriminant functions, i.e. linear combinations of dependent variables optimised for separating predefined groups. Interpretation focuses on standardised canonical discriminant function coefficients, which indicate the relative importance of each variable to group differentiation [10, 11]. The structure matrix, containing correlations between discriminant functions and dependent variables, aids interpretation by identifying variables most strongly associated with each function.

For example, if psychological well-being, anxiety, and cognitive performance distinguish groups in a therapeutic intervention, DFA might reveal a primary discriminant function heavily weighted towards anxiety and well-being, thereby clarifying that emotional variables contribute more strongly to group differences compared to cognitive measures.

CCA expands the interpretative capacity of multivariate analysis by examining relationships between two sets of variables simultaneously. Unlike MANOVA or DFA, CCA does not categorise variables explicitly into independent and dependent; rather, it assesses the overall correlation between two variable sets [12]. Interpretation involves evaluating canonical loadings, canonical cross-loadings, and redundancy indices. Researchers should interpret canonical variates by identifying patterns that reflect coherent theoretical constructs, thus linking multivariate statistical findings to substantive psychological interpretations. For instance, CCA might identify a strong canonical correlation between one set of psychological distress measures (e.g. anxiety and depression) and another set of coping variables (e.g. resilience and social support), highlighting comprehensive underlying relationships rather than isolated correlations.

Factor analytic approaches further illustrate the interpretative depth of multivariate methods. EFA assists researchers in uncovering latent constructs that explain observed correlations among measured variables without preconceived structure [13]. Conversely, CFA tests predefined hypotheses about underlying factor structures derived from theory or prior research [14]. When factor-derived scores are entered into supervised pipelines, end-to-end reporting of error metrics and explanations is recommended [15].

Interpretation of EFA results involves examining factor loadings, with values above 0.40 typically indicating meaningful association [16]. CFA interpretation focuses on model fit indices (e.g. RMSEA, CFI, and TLI), path coefficients, and residual analyses. Researchers use these metrics to evaluate how well the hypothesised multivariate structures align with observed data patterns.

Despite their interpretative richness, multivariate analyses pose challenges. Violations of assumptions such as multivariate normality, linearity, and homogeneity of covariance matrices significantly affect outcomes and interpretations. Techniques like robust MANOVA methods, bootstrapping, or non-parametric multivariate methods are recommended when assumptions are violated [17, 18].

Multicollinearity among dependent variables can distort interpretations, necessitating strategies such as variable aggregation or dimensionality reduction (e.g. via principal component analysis) before applying multivariate techniques [12].

Visualisation techniques substantially enhance interpretative clarity in multivariate analyses. Applications in interpersonal affect modelling demonstrate how clear plots support communication of risk stratification [19]. Canonical plots, discriminant function plots, and factor loading plots visually depict relationships among variables and group distinctions. For example, canonical discriminant plots can succinctly illustrate group separations in DFA, while heatmaps and dendrograms effectively portray underlying factor structures in EFA or CFA contexts [20, 21].

The proper interpretation of multivariate analyses transcends mere statistical significance; it necessitates a deeper understanding of variable interrelations, statistical assumptions, and theoretical implications. Researchers should integrate statistical rigour with theoretical insight, using these advanced techniques not just to test hypotheses but to enrich psychological understanding profoundly.

2 Interpreting Non-parametric Test Results

In psychological research, it is common to encounter data that violate the assumptions required for parametric statistical tests, such as normality and homogeneity of variances. In such situations, non-parametric tests offer a robust alternative for analysing data without relying on strict distributional assumptions. These methods are particularly well suited for ordinal data, small sample sizes, or when dealing with skewed distributions that are frequently observed in psychological measurements [22]. Interpreting the results of non-parametric tests requires careful consideration of their underlying principles and implications.

Unlike parametric tests that rely on means and variances, non-parametric tests are typically based on ranks or medians. This shift from raw scores to ranks reduces sensitivity to outliers and makes these tests more resilient in non-normal conditions. For example, the Mann-Whitney U test, a non-parametric alternative to the independent sample t-test, compares the distributions of two independent groups by ranking all observations and evaluating whether one group tends to have higher ranks than the other. Importantly, the null hypothesis in a non-parametric test often differs slightly from that of a parametric test, and it typically states that the distributions are equal in shape and location, not just the means.

Interpreting a significant result in a non-parametric test, therefore, implies that there is a difference in the central tendency or distributional shape between the groups. Researchers must be cautious not to overgeneralise the findings. For instance, a significant Mann-Whitney U test does not confirm a difference in medians unless the distributions are similarly shaped. Likewise, in the case of the Wilcoxon signed-rank test for paired samples, the conclusion is based on the ranks of the differences, not the actual values themselves. The Kolmogorov-Smirnov test, which compares the cumulative distributions of two samples, is sensitive to differences in both location and shape, but it does not specify where those differences occur. Therefore, its interpretation must be aligned with an understanding of the underlying distributions and should ideally be complemented with visual inspection or descriptive statistics to guide conclusions.

To illustrate a typical application, consider a simulated example where we compare two groups of psychological scores that are not normally distributed. The Python code below demonstrates how to use the Mann-Whitney U test to compare two samples using *scipy.stats*:

```
import numpy as np
from scipy.stats import mannwhitneyu

# Simulate non-normal data
np.random.seed(42)
group1 = np.random.rand(50)
group2 = np.random.rand(50) + 0.2  # simulate group shift

# Perform Mann-Whitney U test
statistic, p_value = mannwhitneyu(group1, group2,
 ↪  alternative='two-sided')

print(f"U statistic: {statistic:.2f}, p-value: {p_value:.4f}")
```

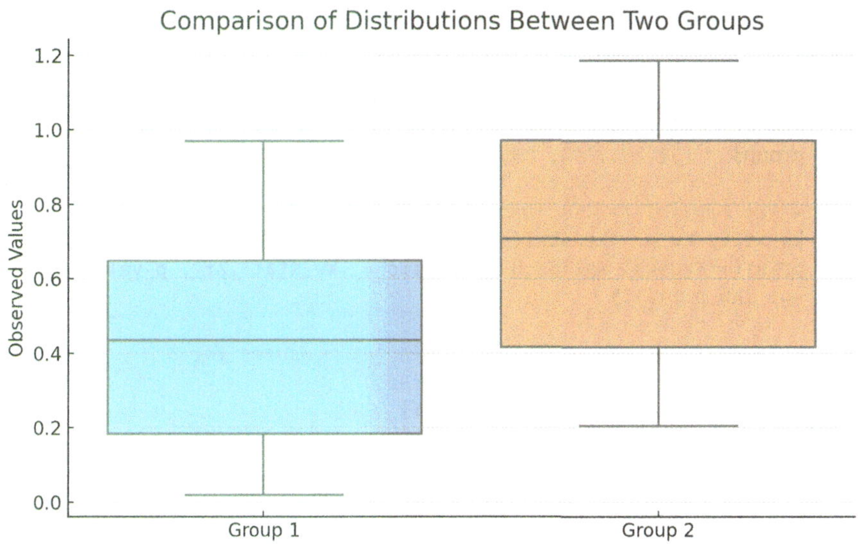

Fig. 1 Boxplot comparing distributions of two independent groups

This example generates two independent groups with a slight distributional shift and applies the Mann-Whitney U test to evaluate whether they differ significantly. If the resulting p-value is below the chosen significance threshold (e.g. 0.05), we can infer that the two groups are likely drawn from different distributions.

The distributional differences between groups can also be visualised using boxplots, which provide insight into medians, variability, and potential outliers. Figure 1 shows a side-by-side comparison of the two groups used in the simulation.

In addition to two-group comparisons, non-parametric methods also extend to repeated measures and multiple groups. The Friedman test serves as a non-parametric alternative to repeated measures ANOVA and is appropriate when the same participants are assessed under multiple conditions. Similarly, the Kruskal-Wallis test generalises the Mann-Whitney U test to compare more than two independent groups and determines whether at least one group distribution differs from the others. Interpretation of these tests also relies on rank-based comparisons and should be supplemented with post hoc pairwise analyses when a significant overall effect is detected [23, 24]. The Python code below illustrates the application of both the Kruskal-Wallis test and the Friedman test using `scipy.stats`:

```python
from scipy.stats import kruskal, friedmanchisquare

# Example data for Kruskal-Wallis (three independent groups)
group1 = [12, 15, 14, 10, 13]
group2 = [22, 25, 19, 23, 21]
group3 = [32, 35, 30, 28, 34]

# Run Kruskal-Wallis test
kw_stat, kw_p = kruskal(group1, group2, group3)
print(f"Kruskal-Wallis H-statistic = {kw_stat:.2f}, p-value =
↪ {kw_p:.4f}")

# Example data for Friedman (repeated measures for 5
↪ participants under 3 conditions)
condition1 = [12, 14, 13, 15, 11]
condition2 = [18, 17, 16, 19, 20]
condition3 = [25, 22, 24, 23, 26]

# Run Friedman test
fr_stat, fr_p = friedmanchisquare(condition1, condition2,
↪ condition3)
print(f"Friedman chi-square = {fr_stat:.2f}, p-value =
↪ {fr_p:.4f}")
```

For analyses involving categorical or nominal data, specialised non-parametric tests are employed. The χ^2 test is one of the most widely used for evaluating associations between two categorical variables in contingency tables. It assesses whether the observed frequencies deviate significantly from expected frequencies under the assumption of independence [25]. When working with paired nominal data, such as pre-test and post-test responses, McNemar's test is appropriate. This test evaluates changes in proportions for dichotomous variables, making it particularly useful for within-subject designs in psychological intervention studies [26]. Both tests provide insights into distributional patterns across categorical groups without requiring assumptions of normality or interval scale measurements. The following Python example demonstrates the use of the χ^2 test and McNemar's test using `scipy.stats` and `statsmodels`:

```
import numpy as np
from scipy.stats import chi2_contingency
from statsmodels.stats.contingency_tables import mcnemar

# Chi-square test: 2x3 contingency table
observed = np.array([[30, 10, 20],
                     [20, 25, 15]])
chi2, p_chi, dof, expected = chi2_contingency(observed)
print(f"Chi-square = {chi2:.2f}, p-value = {p_chi:.4f}")

# McNemar's test: 2x2 table of paired nominal data
#       Post
#       [Yes, No]
# Pre  [[a, b],
#       [c, d]]
table = np.array([[35, 5],
                  [15, 45]])
result = mcnemar(table, exact=True)
print(f"McNemar p-value = {result.pvalue:.4f}")
```

In the example above, the χ^2 test assesses independence between two categorical variables in a 2x3 contingency table, while McNemar's test evaluates changes in binary outcomes for paired observations, such as pre- and post-intervention responses.

A visual summary of commonly used non-parametric tests, organised by data structure and comparison type, is presented in Fig. 2. This diagram helps clarify which tests are appropriate for various psychological data scenarios.

Effect sizes play a crucial role in non-parametric interpretation. While traditional metrics such as Cohen's *d* are designed for parametric tests, alternatives such as the rank-biserial correlation or the common language effect size can provide intuitive interpretations for non-parametric outcomes [27]. For instance, the rank-biserial correlation estimates the probability that a randomly selected observation from one group will exceed a randomly selected observation from the other group, offering a meaningful and robust measure of group differences.

The value of non-parametric tests lies in their flexibility and resistance to violations of assumptions. This robustness should not come at the expense of interpretive precision. Researchers are encouraged to combine non-parametric results with data visualisations, effect size estimates, and contextual knowledge of the psychological constructs under study. When used judiciously, non-parametric methods enable valid statistical inference while maintaining the integrity of the analysis in real-world psychological data.

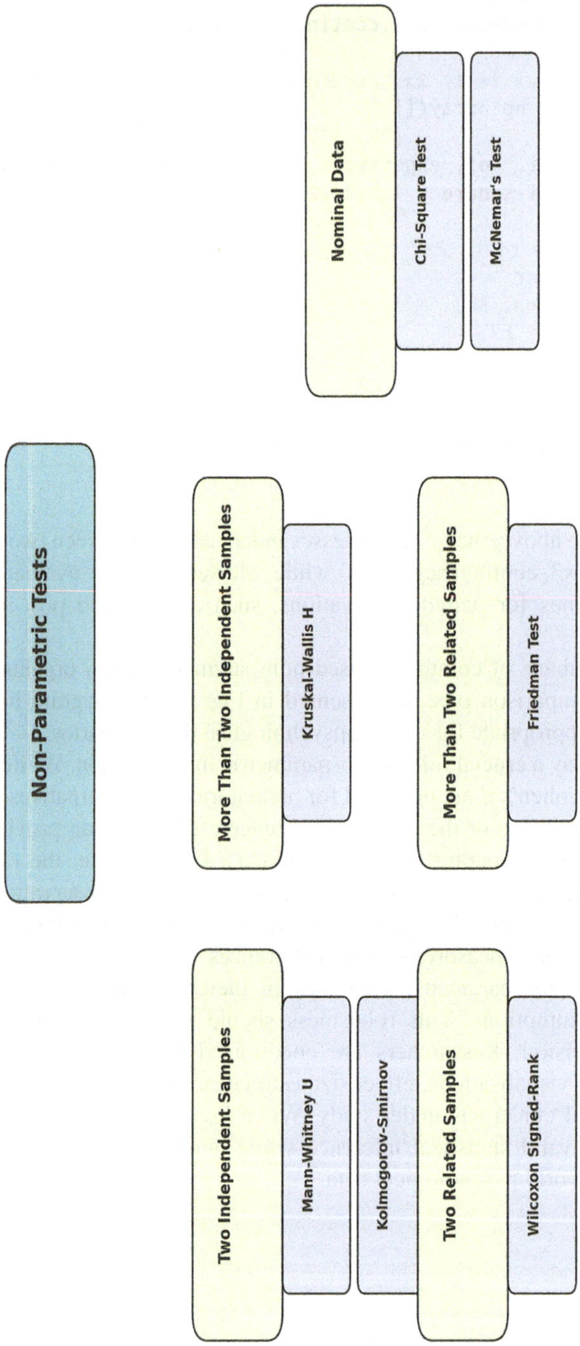

Fig. 2 Overview of non-parametric tests

3 Handling Complex Data Structures

Modern psychological research increasingly relies on data that possess intricate and layered structures. These complexities arise not from the mere volume of data collected but from its inherent organisation, because data are nested, hierarchical, repeated over time, or structured across multiple levels of observation. Handling such complex data structures is vital for extracting meaningful inferences and ensuring the robustness of statistical conclusions.

At the core of this challenge lies the hierarchical nature of psychological phenomena. For example, in educational psychology, students are naturally grouped within classrooms, which are themselves nested within schools. Similarly, in clinical research, patients may be nested within therapists or treatment sites. In such contexts, traditional analytical techniques that assume independence among observations can lead to incorrect standard errors, inflated Type I error rates, and ultimately misleading conclusions [28].

Multilevel models (MLMs), also known as *Hierarchical Linear Models* (HLMs), provide a statistically rigorous approach to modelling such nested structures. By partitioning variance across levels, usually within individuals and between groups, they allow researchers to appropriately account for clustering and explore effects operating at different levels of analysis. For example, in a longitudinal study of stress among adolescents, individual variation in stress trajectories can be modelled at Level 1, while the influence of school-level variables such as student-teacher ratio or campus climate may be assessed at Level 2 [29].

Another layer of complexity arises in longitudinal data, where repeated observations are collected from the same individuals over time. These data structures violate the assumption of independence due to autocorrelation, where observations closer in time are more similar than those further apart. Mixed-effects models, a flexible extension of multilevel modelling, have become a standard tool for analysing longitudinal psychological data. They incorporate both fixed effects, which estimate population-level parameters, and random effects, which capture individual deviations from the group average. This dual modelling of within- and between-subject variation is crucial for understanding developmental trajectories, treatment responses, and cognitive change over time [30].

Psychological research also frequently encounters cross-classified data, where observations are simultaneously nested within two or more non-hierarchical structures. For instance, in studies involving peer assessments, students rate multiple classmates, and each student is both a rater and a ratee. These data do not fit neatly into traditional nested frameworks. Cross-classified multilevel models offer a solution by treating both dimensions of classification as random effects, thereby accommodating the dependencies inherent in the data [31].

A growing area of complexity involves intensive longitudinal data, such as those gathered through *Ecological Momentary Assessment* (EMA), where participants report experiences, emotions, or behaviours multiple times per day over several weeks. These data, rich in temporal resolution, enable researchers to model intra-

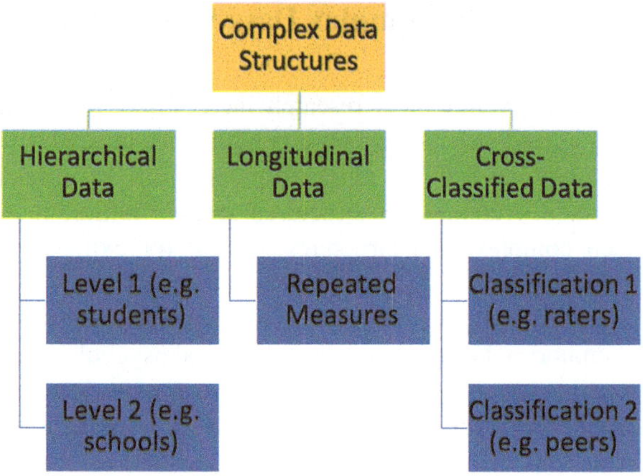

Fig. 3 Complex data structures taxonomy

individual dynamics with unprecedented precision. *Dynamic Structural Equation Modelling* (DSEM), an extension of traditional *Structural Equation Modelling* SEM adapted for time series and multilevel data, has emerged as a powerful framework for capturing both stable trait-like structures and state-based fluctuations in psychological processes [32].

Handling such data requires not only statistical expertise but also thoughtful decisions regarding data pre-processing. For instance, missing data in hierarchical and longitudinal datasets can be particularly problematic if the mechanisms driving the missingness vary across levels. Multiple imputation techniques that respect the data hierarchy or model-based approaches that estimate missing values as part of the likelihood function are commonly employed [33]. Careful model specification is equally critical, especially in determining the random effects structure, selecting appropriate covariance models for time-related dependence, and diagnosing convergence issues in complex estimation routines.

Figure 3 provides a visual taxonomy of the most common complex data structures encountered in psychological studies. This classification is designed to guide analysts in identifying whether their data require multilevel modelling, longitudinal techniques, network-based representations, or non-parametric handling of irregular topologies, thereby serving as a conceptual map for methodological decision-making.

Visualisation plays a key role in understanding complex data structures. Spaghetti plots, which overlay individual trajectories in longitudinal data, help identify patterns, outliers, and potential model misfits. Clustered scatterplots and boxplots stratified by groups or levels offer intuitive insights into group differences and within-group variability. Advances in interactive visualisation tools now enable dynamic exploration of multilevel and longitudinal data structures, supporting both model specification and interpretation.

The computational demands of analysing complex psychological data have driven the development of efficient software tools. In R, packages such as `lme4`, name, and burns offer robust implementations for multilevel and Bayesian multilevel modelling, while lavaan supports structural equation models, including DSEM features. Python-based tools like statsmodels and PyMC are gaining traction as well, especially in interdisciplinary contexts where integration with machine learning pipelines is desired.

Recent developments have also emphasised the importance of simulation studies in evaluating model adequacy. Researchers increasingly use *Monte Carlo Simulations* to examine the performance of multilevel and longitudinal models under various data conditions, including sample size, measurement reliability, and degree of clustering. These simulations not only inform design decisions but also help assess model robustness in the presence of violations of underlying assumptions [34].

In psychological science, where data often mirror the layered nature of cognition, emotion, and behaviour, the ability to handle complex structures is not a luxury but a necessity. Ignoring the multilevel or temporal dimensions of the data risks oversimplifying phenomena and drawing misleading conclusions. When handled appropriately, these structures reveal the richness of psychological processes, from the nested nature of social environments to the evolving patterns of individual behaviour.

Managing complex data structures in psychology requires a multi-faceted approach that combines sound statistical modelling, careful data management, and effective visualisation. The researcher must understand both the theoretical underpinnings of the statistical models and the substantive questions at hand. Only then can the complexity of psychological data be transformed from a methodological challenge into a source of deeper scientific insight.

4 Case Study

To illustrate the practical implementation of advanced data interpretation strategies, we draw upon a comprehensive dataset derived from a longitudinal psychological research study. This dataset encompasses repeated measures collected from 300 participants observed across five therapy sessions, making it suitable for modelling complex structures such as hierarchical, longitudinal, and cross-classified data.

The dataset is structured in a *long format*, where each row represents a single observation per session per participant, enabling the use of mixed models and other multilevel techniques. Participants are nested within psychological clinics while also being independently rated by a set of raters and grouped into peer-based classifications. This combination allows for a full representation of *hierarchical, repeated measures*, and *cross-classified* data patterns.

Each participant is identified by a unique SubjectID and is associated with several static and dynamic attributes:

- Demographic variables include `Age`, `Gender`, and `EducationLevel`, offering context for individual differences.
- Experimental design variables include `TherapyType` (e.g. CBT, Mindfulness, and Control) and `ExperimentalGroup`, which reflect controlled interventions.
- Session-related variables such as `SessionCount` track participant progression over time.
- Psychological scores recorded at each session include:
  - `CognitionScore` and `EmotionScore` are indicators of cognitive and affective functioning.
  - `StressLevel` and `SocialSupportScore` are quantifying perceived stress and received social support.
  - `AnxietyLevel` and `DepressionScore` are reflecting clinical measures of internalising symptoms.
- Performance measures include `TaskPerformance` and `ReactionTime`, providing insight into behavioural outputs and cognitive efficiency.

The dataset also includes `ClinicID`, representing the site of intervention or observation, and `RaterID` and `PeerGroupID`, each forming a separate cross-classification layer. These identifiers allow the modelling of multiple random effects that do not follow a strict nesting hierarchy. They are critical for accounting for non-independent sources of variation, like observer bias or peer group norms.

The breadth of the dataset enables researchers to ask and answer questions at various levels of granularity, whether examining within-subject changes over time, between-subject differences, or institutional and social influences on psychological outcomes. This rich structure presents ideal conditions for applying advanced statistical techniques, from MANOVA and mixed models to Bayesian hierarchical frameworks.

To consolidate the various modelling approaches applied in this chapter, we now present a comparative overview (see Table 1) of the major analytical strategies employed in handling complex psychological datasets. Each of these methods offers unique capabilities in disentangling psychological effects across different structural dimensions of the data. While the previous sections focused on implementing and interpreting each method individually, this table serves as a unifying summary to guide researchers in selecting the most appropriate analytical technique based on their data structure and research question. The comparison includes key aspects such as the nature of the outcome variables, the underlying grouping structure assumed by the model, and representative use cases in psychological research. By organising the insights into a single visual structure, we aim to provide a clear decision-making framework for practitioners navigating complex, multilevel, or longitudinal data.

The MANOVA approach offers a multivariate lens for examining differences across experimental groups but does not account for hierarchical or temporal structure in the data. In contrast, hierarchical models introduce nested random effects, making them suitable for capturing the influence of broader contextual units, such as

Table 1 Comparison of multilevel modelling strategies in psychological data

Method	Main outcome(s)	Grouping structure	Use case in psychology
Hierarchical model	TaskPerformance, Stress, etc.	Subjects nested in clinics	Analyses how higher level contexts (e.g. Clinics) influence individual outcomes
Longitudinal model	TaskPerformance, CognitionScore over time	Repeated sessions within subjects	Captures within-subject changes over time (SessionCount as a time variable)
Cross-classified model	StressLevel	Participants grouped by Clinic and PeerGroup	Explores how overlapping contexts jointly affect outcomes
MANOVA	Multiple continuous outcomes (e.g. stress, anxiety, and depression)	No explicit hierarchy—flat groups like TherapyType	Tests overall group differences across several dependent variables

clinics or schools, on individual-level outcomes. Longitudinal models extend this by emphasising temporal structure, analysing repeated measures within individuals to uncover trends and within-subject variability. Cross-classified models accommodate more intricate data arrangements where individuals are simultaneously embedded in multiple groupings that are not hierarchically ordered, such as peer groups and institutions.

Before examining the hierarchical, longitudinal, or cross-classified models, we first present a classical MANOVA (Table 2) to establish baseline group differences in psychological outcomes. This approach enables a broad-stroke understanding of treatment effects without accounting for individual-level variation, repeated measures, or contextual classification. To preliminarily explore the effects of experimental intervention types on participants' psychological outcomes, we conducted a MANOVA testing for overall group differences in `StressLevel`, `AnxietyLevel`, and `DepressionScore` across `ExperimentalGroup` conditions (CBT, Mindfulness, and Control). This method evaluates whether the mean vectors of the dependent variables differ significantly across the treatment conditions while accounting for their correlations.

The multivariate test results for the *intercept* are highly significant across all multivariate statistics (*Wilks' Lambda* = 0.0546, *Pillai's Trace* = 0.9454, *Hotelling-Lawley Trace* = 17.3061, and *Roy's Greatest Root* = 17.3061; all $p < 0.001$), indicating that the grand means of the outcome variables significantly differ from zero, which is a typical result given centred or non-zero data. The main effect of *ExperimentalGroup* on the combination of outcome variables is also statistically significant across all multivariate tests:

Table 2 Multivariate test statistics for MANOVA (dependent variables: StressLevel, AnxietyLevel, and DepressionScore)

Effect	Test	Value	Num DF	Den DF	F & p
Intercept	Wilks' λ	0.0546	3	1495	$F = 8624.21, p < 0.001$
	Pillai's Trace	0.9454	3	1495	$F = 8624.21, p < 0.001$
	Hotelling-Lawley Trace	17.3061	3	1495	$F = 8624.21, p < 0.001$
	Roy's Largest Root	17.3061	3	1495	$F = 8624.21, p < 0.001$
Experimental Group	Wilks' λ	0.9392	6	2990	$F = 15.87, p < 0.001$
	Pillai's Trace	0.0609	6	2992	$F = 15.67, p < 0.001$
	Hotelling-Lawley Trace	0.0646	6	1991.56	$F = 16.09, p < 0.001$
	Roy's Largest Root	0.0623	3	1496	$F = 31.08, p < 0.001$

- Wilks' Lambda $= 0.9392, F(6, 2990) = 15.87, p < 0.001$
- Pillai's Trace $= 0.0609, F(6, 2992) = 15.67, p < 0.001$
- Hotelling-Lawley Trace $= 0.0646, F(6, 1991.56) = 16.09, p < 0.001$
- Roy's Greatest Root $= 0.0623, F(3, 1496) = 31.08, p < 0.001$

Taken together, these results indicate that the type of psychological intervention had a statistically significant effect on participants' combined psychological states. The consistency of significance across all four test statistics strengthens the robustness of this finding. While MANOVA reveals that group-level differences exist, it does not reveal which dependent variables contribute most strongly to the group separation, nor does it account for individual variability, repeated measurements, or nested structures. For these purposes, more advanced techniques (such as mixed models or multilevel approaches) are better suited and will be introduced in the following sections.

In our dataset, participants are measured repeatedly, and these individuals are also nested within higher level units such as clinics. This hierarchical structure introduces dependencies in the data, as observations from the same participant or clinic may be more similar to each other than to those from other groups. To account for this, we employed a Mixed Linear Model (MLM), which includes random intercepts and slopes for participants, as well as random intercepts for clinics. This model allows us to partition variance across different levels (within-individual, between-individual, and between-clinic) while assessing the effects of predictors like `TherapyType` and `SessionCount` on `CognitionScore`. These results are shown in Table 3.

The hierarchical model evaluates how `CognitionScore` changes with therapy type and number of sessions while accounting for the nested structure of the data. Several findings emerge from this model. The baseline cognitive score is approximately 100.7 when all predictors are at their reference levels (e.g. at Session 0 and in the CBT group). This is statistically significant, reflecting a plausible average baseline. Neither the *Control* group nor the *Mindfulness* group differs significantly from the CBT group in terms of cognition scores. The confidence intervals for both

Table 3 Mixed linear model regression results for CognitionScore

Parameter	Coef.	Std. Err.	z	P > |z|	95% CI
Intercept	100.677	0.870	115.717	<0.001	[98.971, 102.382]
TherapyType: Control	0.394	1.166	0.338	0.736	[− 1.892, 2.679]
TherapyType: Mindfulness	0.749	1.160	0.646	0.518	[− 1.524, 3.022]
SessionCount	− 1.508	0.076	− 19.774	<0.001	[− 1.657, −1.359]
Random effects					
Group variance	56.422				
Group × SessionCount Cov.	0.635 (SE = 0.193)				
SessionCount variance (slope)	0.504				
Clinic variance (intercept)	3.378				

contrast coefficients include zero, and their *p*-values are far above conventional significance thresholds. This suggests that therapy type alone does not explain variance in cognitive scores beyond other modelled factors. The number of therapy sessions shows a *significant negative effect* on cognition score (–1.51 per session), suggesting that as the session count increases, the raw cognition score decreases slightly. This could indicate task fatigue or measurement effects and deserves further exploration, potentially with interaction terms or non-linear trends. The *Group Variance* (56.42) reflects substantial between-subject variation in baseline cognition. The *Group* × SessionCount Covariance (0.635) and *SessionCount Variance* (0.504) indicate that participants differ in how their cognition scores change over sessions. *Clinic Variance* (3.38) suggests that some variability exists between clinics, though it is much smaller than a subject-level variance.

To assess how individuals change over time and whether those changes vary across experimental conditions, we will examine *longitudinal dynamics* (see Table 4). In psychological research, *longitudinal models* are essential for capturing within-subject change trajectories and identifying differential intervention effects over time. In this step, we implement an MLM with *random intercepts and slopes per individual*, allowing for individual baseline differences and session-specific growth patterns. We also introduce *interaction terms* between `SessionCount` and `TherapyType` to assess whether the rate of cognitive change over time differs across intervention types. This model enables us to address key longitudinal questions, such as *do participants in different therapy groups show different learning or recovery trajectories? Are some groups more stable over time?*

The longitudinal model investigates how cognition scores evolve across repeated sessions, taking into account both group-level effects and intra-individual change patterns. The model estimates a baseline cognition score of 100.92, consistent with prior models. This estimate is highly significant and represents the starting point for participants in the reference group (CBT) at Session 0. The coefficients for the `Control` and `Mindfulness` groups (relative to CBT) are again not statistically significant. This suggests that, on average, these therapy types do not produce markedly different cognition scores at baseline. The variable `SessionCount`

Table 4 Mixed linear model results for longitudinal effects on CognitionScore

Parameter	Coef.	Std. err.	z	P > |z|	95% CI
Intercept	100.922	0.916	110.229	<0.001	[99.127, 102.716]
TherapyType: control	0.027	1.241	0.022	0.983	[− 2.406, 2.460]
TherapyType: mindfulness	0.400	1.236	0.324	0.746	[− 2.022, 2.823]
SessionCount	− 1.632	0.139	− 11.717	<0.001	[− 1.904, −1.359]
SessionCount × control	0.174	0.189	0.920	0.358	[− 0.196, 0.544]
SessionCount × mindfulness	0.182	0.188	0.969	0.332	[− 0.186, 0.551]
Random effects					
Group variance	60.483 (SE = 1.520)				
Group × SessionCount covariance	1.011 (SE = 0.179)				
SessionCount slope variance	0.499 (SE = 0.085)				

is strongly negative and significant ($-$ 1.632, $p < 0.001$), implying that cognition scores decline steadily across sessions, independent of therapy type. This decline may reflect cumulative fatigue, adaptation, or increasing task difficulty over time. The interaction terms between `SessionCount` and both `Control` and `Mindfulness` are *not statistically significant*, suggesting that the rate of change over time is *not meaningfully different across therapy groups*. All therapy types follow a similar downward trajectory in cognition scores. *Group variance* remains high (60.48), indicating substantial individual variability in baseline scores. *SessionCount slope variance* (0.499) confirms variability in how cognition changes across individuals. The *positive covariance* between intercept and slope (1.011) suggests that individuals with higher baseline scores tend to experience slightly less decline over time, i.e. indicating a modest buffering effect.

Participants are often simultaneously nested within multiple, non-hierarchical structures. For instance, a subject may belong to a therapeutic clinic (a formal institutional unit) and also be part of a peer group (a social or environmental context). These overlapping influences cannot be modelled accurately using traditional hierarchical approaches, which assume strict nested relationships. *Cross-classified mixed models* (CCMMs) address this by allowing for the simultaneous estimation of random effects across two or more grouping factors that do not nest within each other. Results of CCMM are shown in Table 5.

We model `StressLevel` as the outcome variable while accounting for two crossed random effects: *Clinic* and *PeerGroup*. This approach is ideal for separating the shared variance contributed by each source, providing a clearer understanding of how stress is influenced by both institutional context and social exposure while controlling for participant-level predictors like therapy type and age.

The results of the cross-classified model indicate a baseline estimated stress level of 62.88, which corresponds to the intercept representing individuals in the CBT group with average age and no additional variation attributed to either clinic or peer group membership. When comparing the therapeutic approaches, individuals in the *Control* group exhibit significantly higher stress levels relative to those

Table 5 Cross-classified mixed model for StressLevel with random effects for Clinic and PeerGroup

Parameter	Coef.	Std. err.	z	P > |z|	95% CI
Intercept	62.878	2.277	27.614	<0.001	[58.415, 67.341]
TherapyType: control	1.788	0.764	2.340	0.019	[0.290, 3.287]
TherapyType: mindfulness	1.660	0.755	2.199	0.028	[0.181, 3.140]
Age	0.031	0.031	0.980	0.327	[− 0.031, 0.093]
Random effects					
Clinic variance	37.920				
PeerGroup variance	0.738 (SE = 0.172)				

receiving CBT, with a coefficient of 1.788 and a p-value of 0.019, suggesting that this difference is statistically meaningful. Similarly, participants in the *Mindfulness* group also show elevated stress scores when compared to CBT, with a coefficient of 1.660 and a p-value of 0.028. These outcomes reinforce the interpretation that CBT has a stronger stress-reducing effect than the other two interventions under investigation.

Age was included as a covariate in the model, but the estimated coefficient of 0.031 was not statistically significant (p=0.327). This suggests that, within this dataset, age does not play a meaningful role in predicting variations in stress once therapy type and contextual grouping are accounted for.

The random effects structure offers further insight into how stress varies across institutional and social environments. A substantial portion of the variance in stress levels (37.92) is attributed to differences between clinics. This may be indicative of variations in treatment fidelity, therapist expertise, or broader institutional factors that affect patient experience. In contrast, the variance attributable to *peer groups* is more modest, measured at 0.738, but still noteworthy. This finding implies that peer dynamics, potentially shaped by mutual reinforcement, shared therapeutic engagement, or collective attitudes towards mental health, have a smaller yet still detectable influence on individual stress levels. Altogether, the model confirms the necessity of including both clinical and social grouping structures to accurately interpret stress outcomes in psychologically complex settings.

5 Visualising Advanced Data Interpretation Results

In advanced psychological research, where multilevel structures, longitudinal trajectories, and cross-classified influences intersect, effective visual representation becomes indispensable. To navigate this complexity, visualisations must be tailored to the data's structure and the analytical objectives at hand.

To visualise how psychological scores differ across therapy groups (CBT, Mindfulness, and Control), we start with a pairwise plot (Fig. 4) illustrating the relationship among the key dependent variables: StressLevel, AnxietyLevel, and

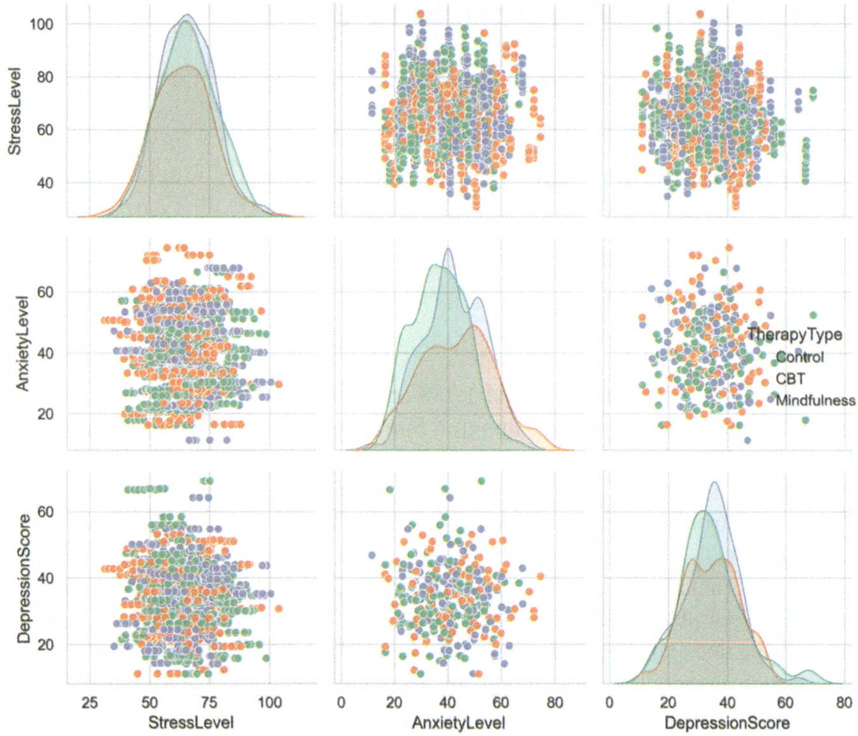

Fig. 4 Pairwise relationships between psychological scores by therapy group (MANOVA analysis)

DepressionScore. This figure presents a pairwise scatterplot matrix and kernel density estimates of three psychological outcomes, StressLevel, AnxietyLevel, and DepressionScore, coloured by therapy group (CBT, Control, and Mindfulness). The diagonal panels show the distribution of each variable for the different groups, while the off-diagonal panels display bivariate relationships between variables. This plot highlights group separation across combinations of variables, revealing potential multivariate group effects even before statistical modelling is applied.

This visualisation offers an initial multivariate overview of emotional states across experimental groups. While the distributions appear generally similar in shape, subtle shifts in central tendency or spread can be noted. For instance, the *Control* group tends to exhibit slightly higher stress levels, while the *CBT* and *Mindfulness* groups show more compact distributions in depression and anxiety scores.

To explore nested data structures, such as individuals within clinics, we apply hierarchical linear modelling. A particularly useful visual tool in this context is the caterpillar plot of random intercepts (Fig. 5), which displays variability across clusters.

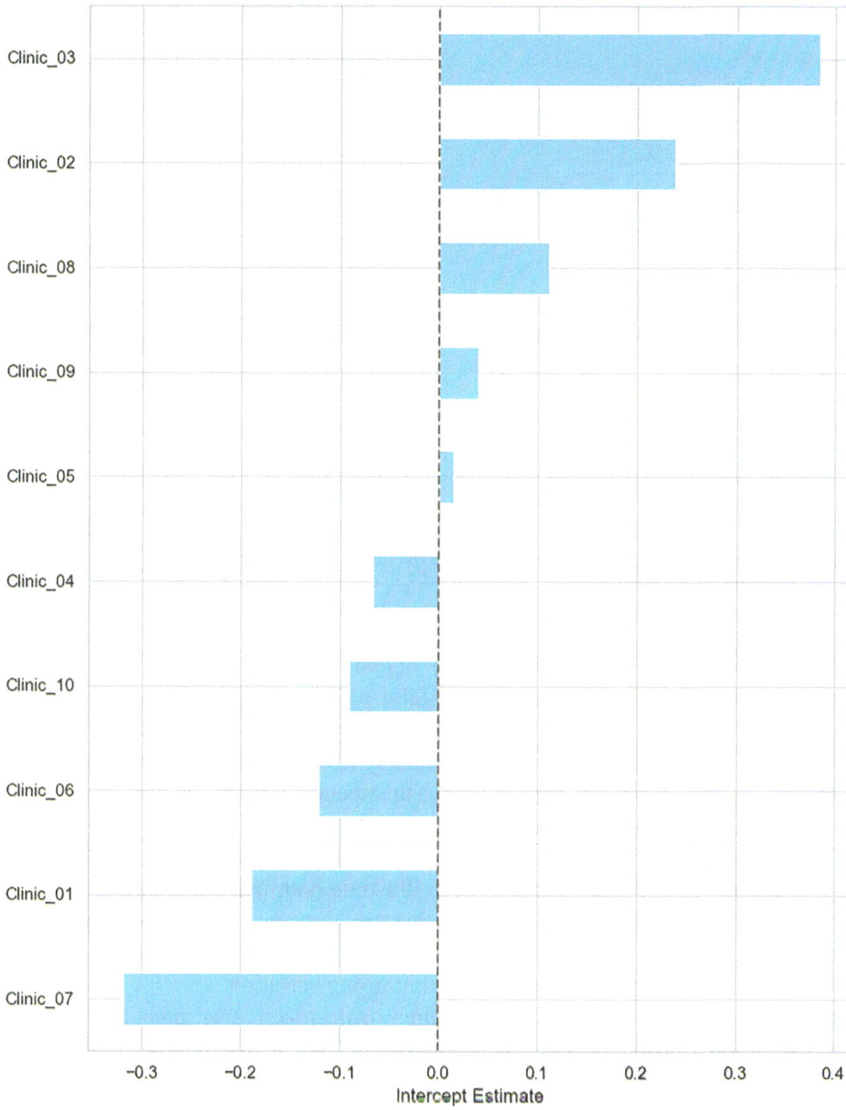

Fig. 5 Caterpillar plot of clinic-level random intercepts in a hierarchical model of cognition

This caterpillar plot illustrates the *random intercept estimates for individual clinics* from the hierarchical model of cognitive performance. Each bar represents how much a specific clinic deviates from the overall average intercept (plotted as the vertical dashed line at zero). Clinics with high positive or negative deviations from the grand mean are visible, offering insight into between-clinic differences in cognitive outcomes. This visualisation helps identify *clinics whose average*

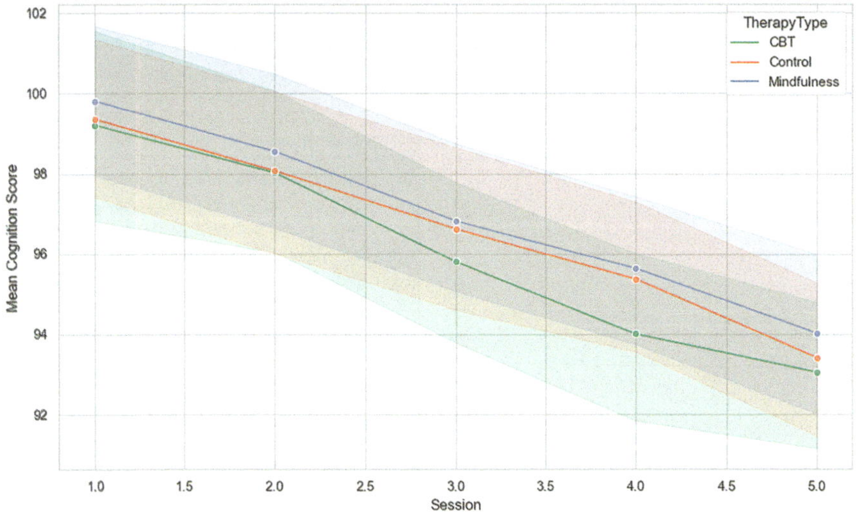

Fig. 6 Line plots showing individual trajectories over time by therapy group with model-predicted means and confidence bands

cognitive performance is systematically higher or lower than the grand mean. For example, *Clinic 03* and *Clinic 02* exhibit positive deviations, suggesting they consistently facilitate better cognitive outcomes, while *Clinic 07* and *Clinic 01* show negative deviations. These insights are valuable for uncovering institutional effects (whether due to resources, staff training, therapeutic fidelity, or other contextual factors) that may not be captured by individual-level predictors.

Understanding how participants' outcomes evolve requires clear longitudinal visualisation. We use line plots (Fig. 6) to illustrate both individual and group-level trends in cognitive performance across therapy sessions. The shaded confidence intervals help convey the average group trend and its uncertainty, while the spaghetti-like lines provide a sense of within-group variation.

Figure 6 presents *cognitive performance trajectories over time*, stratified by therapy group (CBT, Mindfulness, and Control). Each line represents the *mean cognition score across five sessions*, with surrounding shaded regions denoting 95% confidence intervals. The plot reveals a general downward trend in cognitive scores across sessions, which is common in longitudinal studies involving repeated testing or cognitive fatigue. Participants in the CBT group show the steepest decline, whereas the *Mindfulness* group maintains slightly higher scores throughout. The confidence bands allow us to assess the statistical precision of these group differences, suggesting some differentiation between therapy types in preserving cognitive functioning over time. This kind of visualisation is essential for detecting both within-subject changes and between-group effects in longitudinal psychological data.

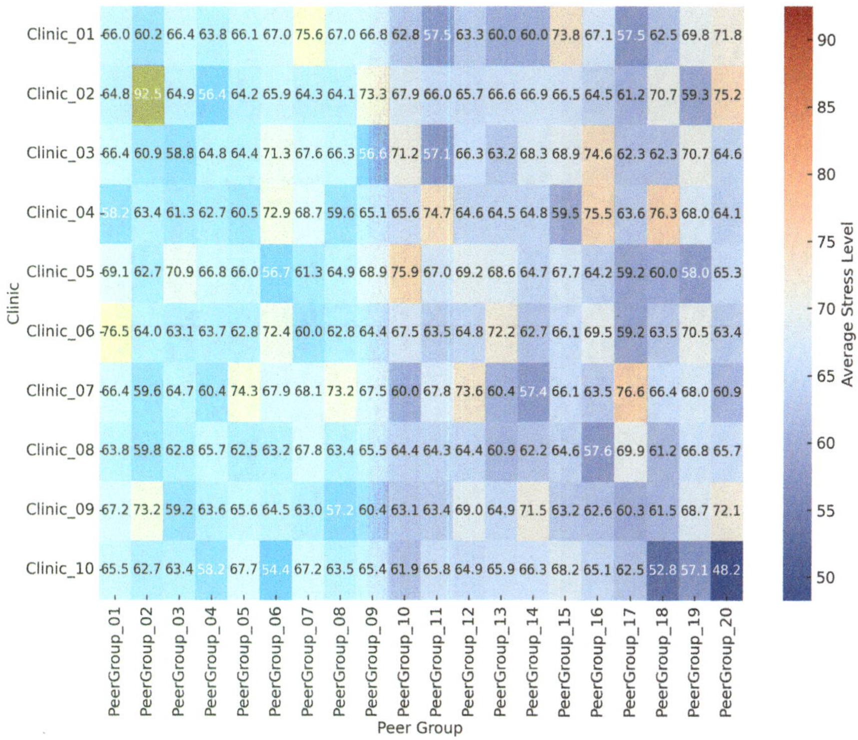

Fig. 7 Heatmap showing clinic-peer interaction effects on stress levels

When participants are simultaneously nested in multiple non-hierarchical groups (e.g. clinics and peer groups), cross-classified visualisations can expose interactions across classifications. The cross-classified heatmap provides a visual representation of the interaction between two grouping factors, clinics and peer groups, in predicting average stress levels. Each cell in the heatmap represents the mean stress score for participants belonging to a particular clinic and peer group combination. Darker shades indicate higher stress levels, while lighter tones reflect lower stress averages.

Figure 7 is particularly useful when examining cross-classified data structures, where units (e.g. individuals) are simultaneously nested within two non-hierarchical categories. Unlike hierarchical data, where one level is nested within another (e.g. students within schools), cross-classification acknowledges the independent contributions of both classification factors. For instance, a participant may be influenced by both the clinic they attend (due to therapeutic setting, staff expertise, or clinical procedures) and the peer group they belong to (which may influence stress through group dynamics, social support, or shared experience).

In the heatmap, some combinations stand out with consistently high or low stress scores, suggesting that certain clinics or peer groups may exert particularly

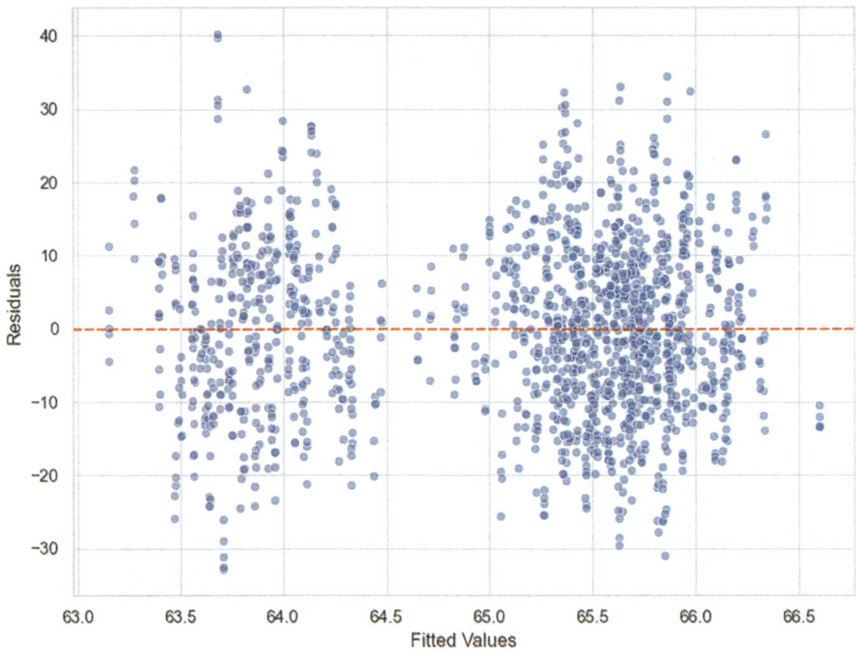

Fig. 8 Residuals vs. fitted values for the cross-classified model of stress

strong effects. For example, a clinic consistently associated with lighter-coloured cells across different peer groups could be interpreted as more effective in stress reduction, regardless of peer context. Conversely, darker rows or columns may reveal problematic peer environments or clinic-level issues that warrant further investigation.

To assess the adequacy of model fit in complex models such as cross-classified random effects, residuals versus fitted values plots are useful for identifying systematic patterns or heteroscedasticity. Figure 8 serves as a diagnostic tool to evaluate the assumptions and quality of the stress-level model fitted in our cross-classified analysis. Each point represents a subject's residual error, i.e. the difference between observed and predicted stress levels, plotted against their predicted (fitted) value.

Ideally, residuals should be evenly scattered around zero, showing no clear pattern. In this plot, we observe clustering and a slight curvature, suggesting potential issues like non-constant variance (heteroscedasticity) or unmodelled structure in the data. These artefacts may indicate that the model could benefit from transformation, interaction terms, or random slopes.

In Bayesian models, uncertainty is central and should be visualised directly. Posterior distributions (Fig. 9) offer insight into the range and shape of plausible values for each parameter. These plots offer a compact summary of parameter

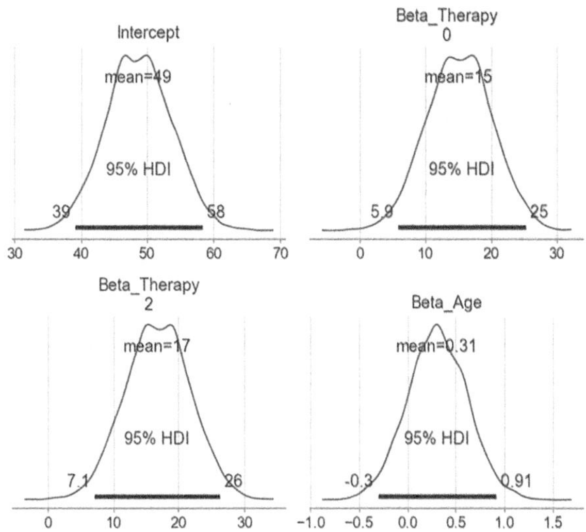

Fig. 9 Posterior distribution plots for selected model parameters with 95% credible intervals

estimates and allow for intuitive probabilistic interpretation, revealing not just point estimates but full distributions of belief.

Figure 9 displays the posterior distributions of regression coefficients derived from a Bayesian model, each annotated with the mean estimate and the 95% *Highest Density Interval* (HDI), which indicates the most credible range of values for each parameter. The plots show that the intercept centres on a mean of 49 with a 95% HDI between 39 and 58, reflecting the baseline stress level. The coefficients for the therapy groups (*Beta Therapy 0*, *1*, and *2*) have means ranging between 15 and 17 with clearly bounded HDIs, providing strong evidence for differences between therapy types in predicting stress. The age coefficient (*Beta Age*) has a narrower and lower displacement posterior centred on 0.31, with its HDI overlapping zero. This suggests that while age may have a small effect, its credibility is weaker compared to therapy effects.

Each visualisation presented plays a unique role in translating complex statistical outputs into actionable insights. From pairwise comparisons and hierarchical shrinkage to time trends and cross-contextual effects, these visuals bridge the gap between model complexity and interpretive clarity.

References

1. H. Farahani, P. Watson, T. Bezan, N. Kovač, L.C. Winter, M. Blagojević, P. Azadfallah, A. Allahyari, S. Masoumian, P. Jiménez, PsAIchology: an intelligent direction in psychological sciences, in *10th International Scientific Conference Technics, Informatics and Education-TIE 2024* (Faculty of Technical Sciences Čačak, University of Kragujevac, 2024)

2. B.G. Tabachnick, L.S. Fidell, *Using Multivariate Statistics*, 7th edn. (Pearson, 2021)
3. R. Warne, A primer on multivariate analysis of variance (MANOVA) for behavioral scientists. Practical Assessm. Res. Eval. **19**(1) (2014)
4. A. Sherry, Discriminant analysis in counseling psychology research. Couns. Psychol. **34**(5), 661 (2006)
5. N. Kovač, K. Ratković, P. Watson, H. Farahani, F. Bagheri Sheykhangafshe, Machine learning classification models for predicting chronic pain. Curr. Psychol. **44**, 15409–15422 (2025)
6. A. Field, Z. Field, J. Miles, *Discovering Statistics Using R* (Sage, New York, 2012)
7. J. Stevens, et al., *Applied Multivariate Statistics for the Social Sciences*, vol. 4 (Lawrence Erlbaum Associates Mahwah, New Jersey, 2002)
8. C.J. Huberty, S. Olejnik, *Applied MANOVA and Discriminant Analysis* (John Wiley & Sons, London, 2007)
9. T. Haslwanter, *An Introduction to Statistics with Python, with Applications in the Life Sciences* (Springer, Switzerland, 2016)
10. W.R. Klecka, *Discriminant Analysis* (Sage, New York, 1980)
11. M.T. Brown, L.R. Wicker, in *Handbook of Applied Multivariate Statistics and Mathematical Modeling* (Elsevier, Amsterdam, 2000), pp. 209–235
12. J.F. Hair, W.C. Black, B.J. Babin, R.E. Anderson, *Multivariate Data Analysis*, 8th edn. (Cengage Learning, 2019)
13. L.R. Fabrigar, D.T. Wegener, R.C. MacCallum, E.J. Strahan, Evaluating the use of exploratory factor analysis in psychological research. Psychol. Methods **4**(3), 272 (1999)
14. T.A. Brown, *Confirmatory Factor Analysis for Applied Research* (Guilford Publications, 2015)
15. N. Kovač, K. Ratković, H. Farahani, P. Watson, A practical applications guide to machine learning regression models in psychology with python. Methods Psychol. **11**, 100156 (2024)
16. A.L. Comrey, H.B. Lee, *A First Course in Factor Analysis* (Psychology Press, 2013)
17. H. Finch, B. French, A Monte Carlo comparison of robust MANOVA test statistics. J. Mod. Appl. Stat. Methods **12**(2), 4 (2013)
18. P. Mair, R. Wilcox, Robust statistical methods in R using the WRS2 package. Behav. Res. Methods **52**, 464 (2020)
19. H. Farahani, P. Watson, N. Kovač, F.B. Sheykhangafshe, P. Azadfallah, A. Allahyari, F. Esrafilian, R.R. Chesli, in *International Handbook of Love: Transcultural and Transdisciplinary Perspectives* (Springer, Berlin, 2025), pp. 1–22
20. M.O. Ward, XmdvTool: integrating multiple methods for visualizing multivariate data, in *Proceedings Visualization'94* (IEEE, Piscataway, 1994), pp. 326–333
21. W.W.Y. Chan, A survey on multivariate data visualization, Department of Computer Science and Engineering. Hong Kong Univ. Sci. Technol. **8**(6), 1 (2006)
22. S. Siegel, N.J. Castellan Jr., *Nonparametric Statistics for the Behavioral Sciences*, 2nd edn. (McGraw-Hill Book Company, New York, 1988)
23. W.J. Conover, *Practical Nonparametric Statistics*, 3rd edn. (Wiley, London, 1999)
24. S. Siegel, *Nonparametric Statistics for the Behavioral Sciences* (McGraw-Hill, New York, 1956)
25. A. Agresti, *Categorical Data Analysis*, 3rd edn. (Wiley, London, 2013)
26. Q. McNemar, Note on the sampling error of the difference between correlated proportions or percentages. Psychometrika **12**(2), 153 (1947)
27. D.S. Kerby, The simple difference formula: an approach to teaching nonparametric correlation. Compr. Psychol. **3**, 11.IT.3.1 (2014)
28. S.W. Raudenbush, A.S. Bryk, *Hierarchical Linear Models: Applications and Data Analysis Methods* (Sage Publications, New York, 2002)
29. T.A.B. Snijders, R.J. Bosker, *Multilevel Analysis: An Introduction to Basic and Advanced Multilevel Modeling* (Sage Publications, New York, 2012)
30. J.D. Singer, J.B. Willett, *Applied Longitudinal Data Analysis: Modeling Change and Event Occurrence* (Oxford University Press, Oxford, 2003)
31. A. Fielding, H. Goldstein, *Multilevel Modelling of Social and Educational Data* (Institute of Education, 2006)

32. T. Asparouhov, E.L. Hamaker, B. Muthén, Dynamic structural equation models. Struct. Equ. Model. Multidiscip. J. **25**(3), 359 (2018)
33. C.K. Enders, *Applied Missing Data Analysis* (Guilford Press, 2010)
34. A. Gelman, J. Hill, *Data Analysis Using Regression and Multilevel/Hierarchical Models* (Cambridge University Press, Cambridge, 2006)

Reporting and Discussing Findings

Nataša Kovač, Kruna Ratković, Marko Simeunović, Hojjatollah Farahani, and Peter Watson

1 Choosing the Right Type of Visualisation

In the vast domain of psychological research and artificial psychology, the act of visualising data is not a cosmetic enhancement, rather it is a scientific commitment to clarity, structure, and epistemological fidelity [1]. When a dataset is reduced to pixels, lines, and shapes, what is being crafted is not just a figure but an *argument*, a representation of structure and meaning [2]. In clinical prediction contexts, clear model comparison visuals (e.g. ROC/PR and SHAP) aid evaluation [3]. As this book draws to a close, the reader must understand that choosing the right visualisation is an act of scientific ethics as much as it is of communication design [4].

Visualisation is a translation process. It transforms statistical summaries, algorithmic outcomes, and raw observational input into cognitive artefacts that others can interpret [5]. But unlike verbal miscommunication, where ambiguity is often evident, visual miscommunication can silently distort insight through poorly selected forms, scale manipulations, or misleading graphical emphasis [6, 7]. Choosing the correct visualisation, therefore, requires thoughtful attention to data type, audience, cognitive ergonomics, and research purpose [8].

The first step in choosing the right type of visualisation is understanding the *structure and semantics* of your data. This requires asking structured questions:

N. Kovač · K. Ratković · M. Simeunović (✉)
Faculty of Applied Sciences, University of Donja Gorica, Podgorica, Montenegro
e-mail: natasa.kovac@udg.edu.me; kruna.ratkovic@udg.edu.me; marko.simeunovic@udg.edu.me

H. Farahani
Department of Psychology, Faculty of Humanities, Tarbiat Modares University, Tehran, Iran
e-mail: h.farahani@modares.ac.ir

P. Watson
MRC Cognition and Brain Sciences Unit, University of Cambridge, Cambridge, UK
e-mail: Peter.Watson@mrc-cbu.cam.ac.uk

N. Kovač et al. (eds.), *Data Science in Psychology*,
https://doi.org/10.1007/978-3-032-18312-5_24

Table 1 Aligning data types to visualisation forms

Data type	Goal	Recommended visuals
Nominal	Compare frequencies	Bar chart, Pie chart, Dot chart
Ordinal	Show progression or ranking	Ordered bar chart, Slopegraph
Interval/ratio	Distribution and central tendency	Histogram, KDE plot, Boxplot
Time series	Show temporal dynamics	Line chart, Ribbon plot, Stream graph
High-dimensional	Pattern recognition	Scatterplot matrix, Heatmap, PCA biplot
Networked data	Connectivity or causality	Force-directed graph, DAG, adjacency matrix

Are the variables discrete (e.g. nominal or ordinal) or continuous? Is missingness present? Are distributions normal or skewed? These data properties directly influence the *graphical grammar* available [9, 10].

For instance, categorical variables with low cardinality lend themselves to bar plots, mosaic diagrams, or spine plots that emphasise frequency and structure [11]. By contrast, continuous variables distributed across time favour line plots or ridge plots, particularly when modelling affective trajectories [12, 13]. More abstract or high-dimensional datasets, such as latent emotion states or attention vectors from neural models, call for complex structures like heatmaps, t-SNE projections, or network visualisations [14, 15]. As shown in Table 1, different types of psychological data demand specific forms of visualisation to achieve clarity, interpretability, and relevance.

The second dimension is *research intent*. Different scientific purposes call for different visualisation strategies [16]. Are you exploring, explaining, or persuading? Exploration requires flexible, interactive visualisations, such as scatterplots with brushing and linked highlighting [17]. Explanatory visualisation is typical in publications. It requires *semantic precision* that can include confidence intervals, regression overlays, or annotated clusters [18].

In psychological modelling, visualisation must also respect construct validity [19]. A heatmap comparing anxiety and curiosity, for instance, should not imply proximity in latent space unless empirically justified. Misusing position, size, or proximity can lead to misinterpreted construct relationships, weakening theoretical precision [20].

Cognitive psychology has long emphasised human limitations in graphical interpretation. Visual encodings like *position and length* are processed more accurately than area, colour saturation, or angle [5, 6]. Therefore, a bar chart communicates more effectively than a pie chart, despite the latter's visual popularity [21].

Aesthetic cues must be aligned with psychological semantics. Colours, for example, must be used carefully in emotion modelling. A deep red bar indicating *anger* may suggest urgency or danger even if the numeric difference is trivial [22]. Designing with *emotive colour palettes*, such as *Plutchik's wheel* or *ColorBrewer schemes*, helps anchor interpretation [23]. Cognitive load can be reduced by using direct labelling, logical ordering, and eliminating chartjunk [2, 24]. A viewer's ability to extract insight from a visualisation depends not just on complexity but on *cognitive accessibility*.

Many modern psychological models involve machine learning techniques such as *support vector machines* (SVMs), bootstrapped exploratory graph analysis (EGA), or *fuzzy cognitive maps* (FCMs) [25–27]. These models often produce outputs that cannot be shown with traditional statistical plots. For example:

- *SVM decision boundaries* are visualised with contour maps overlaid on scatter-plots [28].
- *Attention weights in neural networks* are rendered as dynamic heatmaps or attention rollouts [29].
- *FCMs* require directed graphs with weighted, possibly negative edges, to show activation and inhibition between psychological concepts [30].

These models demand not only technical accuracy but also narrative clarity. Without proper design, visualisations of *artificial intelligence* (AI) cognition can appear as obscure oracles rather than interpretative tools [31]. Visualisation carries ethical weight. In psychological studies, particularly those involving vulnerable populations or mental health inference, poor visualisation can cause harm [4]. For example, misrepresenting small effect sizes through misleading axis scales can encourage false conclusions [32].

It is crucial to visualise *uncertainty* (e.g. confidence bands and bootstrapped error distributions), avoid cherry-picking folds or epochs, and *highlight data limitations* [33]. Visual transparency is a form of scientific integrity. This is particularly important when reporting affect-based or interpersonal-risk classifiers in relational health [34]. In *machine learning* (ML) contexts, consider showing model *disagreement* or *calibration curves*, not just *Area Under Curves* (AUCs) or *confusion matrices* [35]. Visual honesty fosters interpretability, particularly when addressing emotional classification or behavioural forecasting [36].

The core lesson of this section is that *visualisation is not an output, but it is an epistemic commitment*. Choosing the right type of visualisation is selecting a language of interpretation, a tool of reasoning, and a mode of scientific disclosure [37]. Psychological insight cannot emerge from visual noise. Let form follow function, let design serve interpretation, and let every visualisation reflect both *analytical precision and ethical restraint*.

2 Creating Effective Charts and Graphs

Effective visual representation of data is essential for enhancing the interpretability of research findings in psychology. Well-designed charts and graphs not only communicate results more clearly but also highlight patterns, trends, and outliers that may be less apparent in tabular summaries. Visuals serve as cognitive shortcuts that support narrative explanation and facilitate a broader understanding of complex data structures among diverse audiences, including researchers, practitioners, and policymakers. The value of visualisations lies in their clarity and relevance. Poorly chosen or overly complicated graphics can obscure the message, introduce bias, or mislead readers. Therefore, selecting and constructing visuals must be done thoughtfully and in alignment with the study's objectives and audience.

When preparing psychological data for visualisation, the first step is to understand the level of measurement and structure of the data. For example, categorical variables are best displayed using bar plots or mosaic plots, while continuous variables are typically summarised with histograms, boxplots, or density plots. Time-series data or longitudinal measurements benefit from line plots that trace changes across time points. Scatterplots are valuable for illustrating relationships between variables, especially when exploring associations in correlational or regression-based studies [9, 38].

Tools such as `matplotlib`, `seaborn`, and `plotnine` (the Python implementation of the widely used `ggplot2` from R) provide robust and versatile frameworks for creating high-quality visualisations in psychological research. `Matplotlib` serves as the foundational plotting library in Python, offering low-level control for customising virtually every aspect of a figure. Building on this, `seaborn` simplifies the creation of statistically informative plots, such as boxplots, violin plots, and regression plots, with aesthetically pleasing defaults and tight integration with `pandas` data structures. `Plotnine` adopts a grammar-of-graphics approach, allowing users to build complex visualisations by layering elements in a structured and modular way, which is particularly beneficial for researchers familiar with R's visualisation paradigm. Together, these tools enable flexible, transparent, and reproducible data visualisation workflows, ensuring that findings are not only analytically sound but also visually clear and scientifically communicable. Their compatibility with reproducible coding environments like Jupyter notebooks further enhances transparency and supports the principles of open science.

The following Python code demonstrates how to generate three types of commonly used visualisations, bar plots, histograms, and scatterplots, using the `seaborn` library. These plots are shown in Fig. 1, which illustrates how different chart types are applied depending on whether the data are categorical, continuous, or bivariate, thus representing a bar plot for categorical data, a histogram for continuous distributions, and a scatterplot to illustrate bivariate relationships.

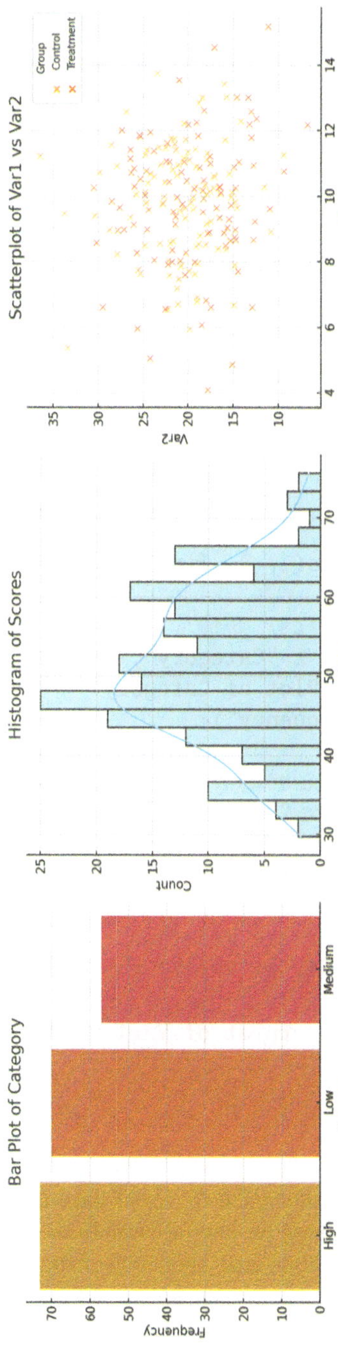

Fig. 1 Examples of common data visualisations

```
import matplotlib.pyplot as plt
import seaborn as sns
import pandas as pd
import numpy as np

# Simulate psychological data for multiple plot types
np.random.seed(7)
df = pd.DataFrame({
    "Group": np.repeat(["Control", "Treatment"], 100),
    "Score": np.concatenate([np.random.normal(48, 8, 100),
                             np.random.normal(55, 10, 100)]),
    "Category": np.random.choice(["Low", "Medium", "High"],
     ↪ size=200),
    "Var1": np.random.normal(10, 2, 200),
    "Var2": np.random.normal(20, 5, 200)
})

# Create a figure with subplots: bar plot, histogram, and
↪ scatterplot
fig, axs = plt.subplots(1, 3, figsize=(18, 5))

# Bar plot for categorical data
sns.countplot(data=df, x="Category", ax=axs[0])
axs[0].set_title("Bar Plot of Category")
axs[0].set_ylabel("Frequency")

# Histogram for a continuous variable
sns.histplot(data=df, x="Score", bins=20, kde=True, ax=axs[1],
↪ color="skyblue")
axs[1].set_title("Histogram of Scores")

# Scatterplot for bivariate relation
sns.scatterplot(data=df, x="Var1", y="Var2", hue=Group",
↪ ax=axs[2])
axs[2].set_title("Scatterplot of Var1 vs Var2")

plt.tight_layout()
plt.show()
```

Equally important is the adherence to visual encoding principles. The effectiveness of a chart is determined by how accurately the graphical elements, such as position, length, angle, colour, and area, reflect the underlying data. Among these, position along a common axis is the most accurate and easiest for viewers to interpret, while area or colour intensity is more prone to misperception. Pie charts, for example, are often discouraged in psychological data reporting because they rely on area and angle to convey proportion, which are cognitively less precise than bar lengths. Whenever possible, the principle of *data-ink maximisation* should be followed, avoiding unnecessary embellishments that do not add information [39].

In the context of experimental psychology or survey research, results are often summarised by means and standard deviations. A common practice is to use bar charts with error bars indicating confidence intervals. This can sometimes hide distributional characteristics of the data. In such cases, violin plots or jittered scatterplots may provide a more honest and detailed view of the variability and shape of the distribution. These choices not only improve transparency but also align with the ongoing movement in psychology toward more open and reproducible science.

The following Python example demonstrates how to generate an effective chart using the `seaborn` library, which is well suited for creating publication-quality visualisations in psychological research. The script simulates psychological test scores for two groups, Control and Treatment, and visualises the data using a combination of boxplots and jittered data points.

```
import seaborn as sns
import matplotlib.pyplot as plt
import pandas as pd
import numpy as np

# Simulate psychological data
np.random.seed(42)
df = pd.DataFrame({
    "Group": np.repeat(["Control", "Treatment"], 100),
    "Score": np.concatenate([np.random.normal(50, 10, 100),
                             np.random.normal(55, 12, 100)])
})

# Boxplot with jittered data points
plt.figure(figsize=(8, 6))
sns.boxplot(x="Group", y="Score", data=df, showfliers=False)
sns.stripplot(x="Group", y="Score", data=df, color='black',
↪  alpha=0.3, jitter=True)
plt.title("Score Distribution by Group")
plt.ylabel("Psychological Test Score")
plt.tight_layout()
plt.show()
```

The resulting visualisation, shown in Fig. 2, combines the interpretability of a boxplot with the transparency of raw data visualisation. Boxplots are effective for summarising central tendency and dispersion; they display the median, interquartile range (IQR), and identify extreme values via whiskers and outliers. Boxplots alone may conceal distributional nuances such as data clustering, skewness, or multimodality.

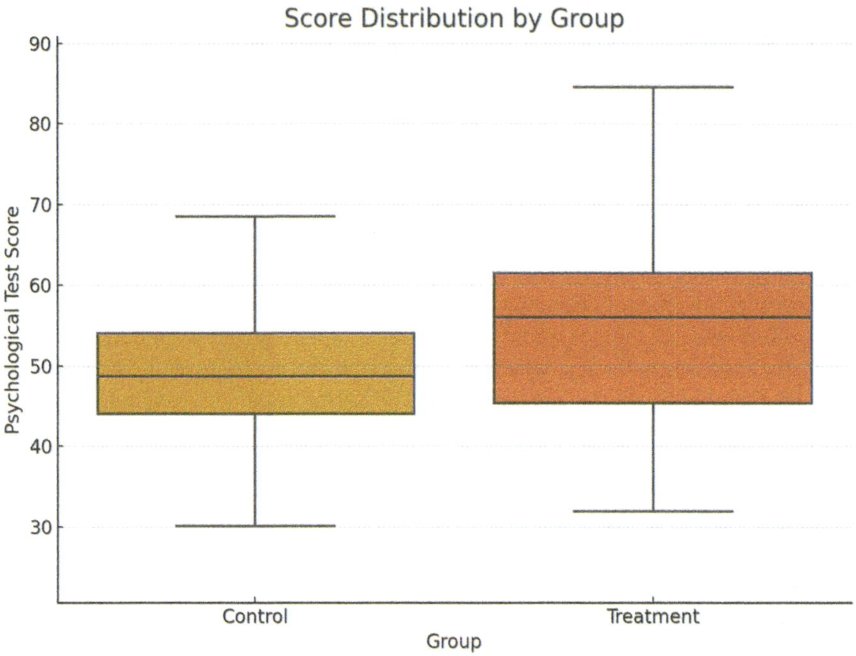

Fig. 2 Boxplot showing the score distributions for Control and Treatment groups

To address this limitation, the stripplot overlays individual data points with slight horizontal jittering. This reveals the density and spread of scores in each group, offering a clearer picture of variability and potential asymmetries. In experimental psychology, where understanding subject-level variability is crucial, this approach enables researchers to present both summary statistics and individual differences in a single, coherent graphic.

This method of visualisation helps avoid the common pitfalls of bar plots with error bars, which often obscure important aspects of the data distribution. For more complex relationships, such as interactions in factorial designs, interaction plots or facet grids can be employed. These allow for side-by-side comparison across levels of multiple independent variables, making interaction effects more interpretable. When dealing with longitudinal data, line plots with confidence ribbons can illustrate trends over time while accounting for individual variability or uncertainty. Figure 3 presents such a visualisation using simulated data from a longitudinal psychological study, illustrating longitudinal score trajectories in Control and Treatment groups, with 95% confidence intervals.

```
import seaborn as sns
import matplotlib.pyplot as plt
import pandas as pd
import numpy as np

# Simulate longitudinal psychological data
np.random.seed(123)
n_subjects = 30
n_timepoints = 5
subject_ids = np.repeat(np.arange(n_subjects), n_timepoints)
time = np.tile(np.arange(1, n_timepoints + 1), n_subjects)
group = np.repeat(np.random.choice(["Control", "Treatment"],
 ↪  size=n_subjects), n_timepoints)
score = 50 + time * np.random.normal(1.5, 0.5, size=n_subjects
 ↪  * n_timepoints)
score += np.where(group == "Treatment", np.random.normal(2, 1,
 ↪  size=n_subjects * n_timepoints), 0)
score += np.random.normal(0, 3, size=n_subjects * n_timepoints)

# Construct DataFrame
df_long = pd.DataFrame({
    "Subject": subject_ids,
    "Time": time,
    "Group": group,
    "Score": score
})

# Plot using seaborn lineplot with confidence ribbon
plt.figure(figsize=(8, 6))
sns.lineplot(data=df_long, x="Time", y="Score", hue="Group",
 ↪  ci=95)
plt.title("Longitudinal Score Trends by Group")
plt.ylabel("Score")
plt.xlabel("Time")
plt.tight_layout()
plt.show()
```

Colour usage should be consistent, accessible, and used only when it adds interpretive value. Redundant coding, such as combining colour with shape or label annotations, can increase accessibility and reduce interpretation errors. All visualisations should include clearly labelled axes, legends, units of measurement, and descriptive captions to ensure the message is fully self-contained and interpretable without reference to surrounding text. In psychological research, graphical displays must adhere to ethical standards, including avoiding distortion and respecting participant confidentiality. Graphs should be used not to persuade but to inform, and

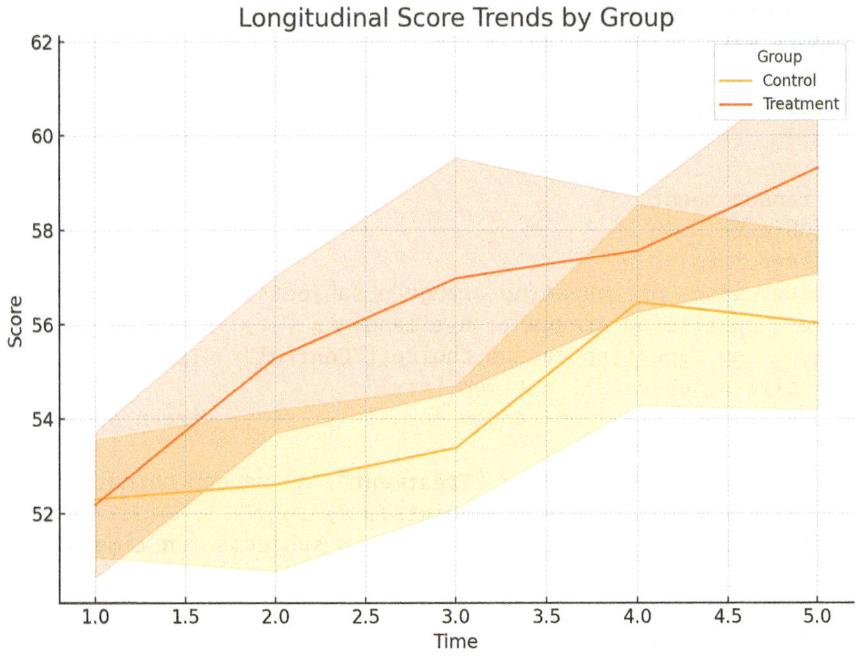

Fig. 3 Line plot with 95% confidence intervals

any smoothing, binning, or transformation applied to the data should be explicitly documented.

Once the appropriate type of visualisation has been selected, the challenge transitions from *what to plot* to *how to plot it effectively*. In psychological science and artificial psychology, effectiveness in data visualisation is not merely a design concern. Visualisation is closely related to epistemological rigour and communication fidelity [2, 8]. A well-chosen graph that is poorly designed can obscure meaning, suggest unintended interpretations, or even mislead viewers [6, 33].

Just as syntax and grammar shape the clarity of language, visual design elements shape the clarity of a chart. Axes, colour, scale, typography, legend placement, and chart layout constitute a *visual grammar* that enables or impedes understanding [9]. Effective chart design must move beyond aesthetic appeal and embrace *functional minimalism*, where every element contributes to comprehension [12, 21].

Edward Tufte's concept of *chartjunk* [2] remains influential: Unnecessary embellishments such as shadows, 3D effects, or overly vibrant gradients reduce signal-to-noise ratio. More recent research indicates that some forms of judicious visual enhancement, such as subtle textures, contextual annotations, and perceptual cues, can improve comprehension and memorability when aligned with cognitive design principles [24, 40]. Therefore, creating effective charts is not about eliminating design, but about designing with purpose.

Axes are often overlooked, yet they frame the interpretation of every visualisation. In psychological datasets where effect sizes are small and variation is high, the integrity of scale is paramount. Charts that truncate the y-axis (e.g. beginning at 90 rather than 0) can exaggerate minimal differences, producing misleading inferences about treatment impact or group differences [32].

When transformations are applied, such as log-scaling reaction time distributions or standardising scores across groups, those transformations must be explicitly labelled. The graphical scale becomes the cognitive anchor for interpreting change, deviation, or magnitude [5, 41].

Effective charts use axis tick marks with *semantically relevant intervals*, limit the number of scale breaks, and align labels clearly with plotted data. Crowded, tilted, or overlapping labels introduce visual friction, discouraging engagement and comprehension [7].

Every chart should be interpretable without excessive narrative support. Legends, axis titles, and in-chart labels must work together to reduce *cognitive load* and minimise extraneous interpretation effort [5, 42]. Direct labelling of lines, bars, or groups, when spatially feasible, has been shown to improve retention and reduce interpretation error [16, 43].

In psychological visualisations, especially those involving emotion, cognition, or behaviour, annotations provide crucial narrative guidance. Arrows that indicate key transitions, shaded confidence regions, or brief textual notes clarifying thresholds (e.g. clinical cut-off scores) help the viewer locate meaning quickly [44]. Annotation should not become clutter. It must serve the visual flow and point to insights, not distract from them [45].

Colour is perhaps the most potent and most misused visual encoding tool. Psychological data often deal with abstract, affective, or ambiguous variables, and colour selections can unconsciously influence interpretation [22, 46]. Effective charts apply:

- Perceptually uniform colour scales (e.g. Viridis and Plasma) for continuous data [47]
- Categorical palettes with clearly distinguishable hues for nominal variables
- Emotionally appropriate tones, especially when visualising affective states or psychological clusters [23]

Importantly, *colourblind-safe palettes* (e.g. ColorBrewer) should be used by default, ensuring accessibility for viewers with red-green colour deficiencies [48]. Dual encoding, which uses both colour and shape or line style, provides redundancy and reduces reliance on hue alone [5]. Colour is never neutral. In artificial psychology, for instance, a *cold* blue may suggest detachment or stability; a *hot* orange might imply risk or urgency. Every shade implies an interpretive tone. Therefore, colour decisions must be grounded in both data semantics and cognitive design.

Modern psychological modelling frequently requires visualising high-dimensional, latent, or temporally complex data. Creating effective charts in such contexts demands hybrid techniques and thoughtful layout. Some key approaches include:

- *Faceted plots* to compare groups or conditions across small multiples [13]
- *Layered visualisations* combining raw data with statistical overlays (e.g. LOESS lines or bootstrapped intervals) [49]
- *Tidy heatmaps* for showing correlation matrices, attention weights, or emotion intensities [50]

In agent-based models or FCMs, node-link diagrams with animated transitions or sequential states can show how cognitive constructs activate or evolve [30]. Complex statistical models benefit from *Bayesian posterior plots*, *uncertainty ribbons*, and *decision curves*, all of which provide a richer view of inference than point estimates alone [51]. An effective visualisation of a complex model often shows its structure, uncertainty, and limits simultaneously. At the same time, it encourages the viewer to reason, not just observe.

Accessibility in chart design is not optional. It is foundational to scientific ethics. In psychology, where visualisations may appear in presentations, journals, apps, or therapy tools, every figure must be readable by the widest possible audience, including individuals with visual, cognitive, or perceptual differences [33]. Basic practices include:

- Ensuring text and background contrast meet *WCAG guidelines*
- Avoiding red/green distinctions without supplemental encoding
- Using sufficient font sizes and logical label placement
- Adding *alt text* or chart summaries in digital platforms

Accessible design also involves reducing clutter and improving legibility, which benefits all users, not just those with disabilities [21, 43]. Clear design is ethical design. Effective charts do not exist in isolation. They are part of a data narrative. They support claims, develop arguments, and reveal stories embedded in the data [40, 52]. Scientific communication must integrate visual structure into the textual and theoretical context.

Consistency across visualisations builds trust. Use the same colour schemes for repeated variables, the same axis scales for comparison plots and the same geometric encoding for related data across a report [44]. Visual harmony supports cognitive fluency and improves comprehension.

An effective chart is not a decoration. It is a carefully shaped artefact of meaning, one that should echo the rigour of your model and the clarity of your question.

3 Drawing Conclusions from the Data

The results of analysis find their broader impact in the way they are communicated. While models compute and charts summarise, it is the narrative, deliberate, structured, and interpretive that brings insight and fosters understanding

[12, 52]. In psychological research and artificial psychology, this task is especially consequential. We visualise data that represent phenomena such as motivation, affect, intention, and belief, which are abstract, multifaceted, and socially situated. Storytelling with data becomes not just a convenience, but a cognitive necessity [20, 53].

Human cognition is intrinsically narrative. From early childhood, we process events, form causality, and derive emotional meaning through story structures [54, 55]. Even in quantitative disciplines, the most memorable and persuasive research follows narrative arcs: introducing a problem, exploring patterns, confronting contradictions, and arriving at insight [56].

Data storytelling leverages this structure by placing figures, statistics, and models into a *temporal and thematic sequence* [57]. In artificial psychology, where complex constructs like belief propagation or emotion dynamics unfold over time or networks, storytelling provides cognitive scaffolding for both researchers and audiences [58]. Visualisations function as story units, each revealing a piece of the argument. A scatterplot shows correlation, a heatmap reveals variation, and a sequence of network graphs shows evolution. When combined with narrative framing, such as through captions, annotations, or slide structure, they become *coherent cognitive artefacts* [33].

Storytelling with data demands deliberate sequencing. Just as literary stories build tension, develop character, and offer resolution, visual storytelling constructs a logical path from question to insight [52]. In practice, a data-driven visual narrative might follow this structure:

- *Framing*: define the context or hypothesis.
- *Exploration*: present initial data structures or anomalies.
- *Tension*: introduce conflicting evidence or unexplained variation.
- *Resolution*: present modelling output or final insight.
- *Implication*: connect the finding to theory, application, or ethical reflection.

This sequence is not arbitrary. Research on *memory and cognition* shows that narrative coherence improves retention, comprehension, and critical engagement [40, 59]. In psychological research, this might involve:

- A bar plot showing initial group differences
- A line graph of longitudinal change
- A structural equation model explaining latent mediation
- An annotated timeline showing emotion shifts
- A concluding figure summarising practical implications

Each figure plays a role. Omitting or misordering them disrupts the logic of the scientific argument.

Visualisation serves different purposes at different stages of analysis. During *Exploratory Data Analysis* (EDA), researchers use interactive plots, scatter matrices, or dimensionality reduction to discover patterns [10, 60]. These plots are flexible, informal, and often internally used. In contrast, *explanatory visualisation* is polished, linear, and communicative [8]. It is designed for publication, presentation, or stakeholder engagement. The same plot used in exploration must be reinterpreted or redesigned for explanation, often simplified, annotated, and structured to emphasise insight [7].

Failing to distinguish these modes risks confusing readers with cluttered or ambiguous visuals. Visual storytelling demands that researchers reshape raw insight into a polished narrative. For example, a *Uniform Manifold Approximation and Projection* (UMAP) of affective embeddings may be used in EDA to explore emotional clusters, but the explanatory version should highlight known categories, label regions, and narrate transitions [15].

Psychological research often deals in metaphors: the *depth* of depression, *balance* of emotion, and *pathways* of cognition. Visualisations, consciously or not, extend these metaphors. We depict emotional states as spatial clusters, belief systems as networks, and motivational change as trajectories [61]. Effective visual storytelling acknowledges and aligns visual form with theoretical meaning. For example:

- Use node-link diagrams to convey *conceptual influence* or causality.
- Use spatial proximity only when justified by semantic or statistical similarity.
- Use colour to represent *affective intensity*, not just categorical separation [23].

Visual metaphor is not only powerful but also risky. A poorly chosen spatial layout or colour scheme can distort the reader's perception of what is latent or uncertain [33, 62]. Storytelling must therefore be both imaginative and grounded. All stories have *frames*, which involve choices of inclusion, exclusion, and emphasis. In psychological visualisation, those frames have ethical stakes. A story about stress reduction may frame intervention success while obscuring variance. A classification model may emphasise accuracy but ignore false negatives that reflect real harm [36]. Ethical storytelling means:

- Representing *uncertainty and disagreement*, not just point estimates [63]
- Avoiding *causal implications* in correlational plots
- Making room for *outliers* and edge cases
- Considering who is *included* and *left out* of the visual narrative

In artificial psychology, where visualisations may represent model cognition or emotion, stories shape how users trust or interpret algorithms. If a visualisation overstates empathy in an agent or hides model drift, it compromises interpretability and user safety [31, 64]. Storytelling with data is not a matter of software or aesthetics. It is a scientific craft rooted in critical thinking, cognitive empathy, and principled design [43]. It requires asking:

- What is the core insight this figure conveys?
- What sequence of visuals best supports it?
- How does each visual relate to audience knowledge and expectation?
- Where is the uncertainty, and is it being shown?
- Who benefits, and who might be misled?

The practice of storytelling with data calls for humility and transparency. No visualisation can say everything, but it can say something clearly, honestly, and memorably, especially if it is shaped with care.

Artificial psychology operates within a domain of constructed states, involving representations that are not directly observable but are instead inferred, modelled, or learned. Unlike structural biology or mechanical systems, psychological models often involve *latent phenomena*: intention, motivation, belief structures, and affective dispositions. These constructs, though theoretically grounded, lack inherent geometry or fixed measurement systems. And yet, to progress in the modelling and communication of artificial minds, we must visualise these abstractions. We must turn the invisible into structured, ethical, and interpretable representations [8, 37].

The role of visualisation in this domain is not merely illustrative. It is epistemic. Through it, we inspect models, communicate uncertainty, track temporal dynamics, and evaluate how artificial agents simulate or internalise psychological mechanisms [65, 66]. Visualisation becomes a medium through which theory, data, and narrative intersect. It becomes a place where meaning is constructed, not merely displayed.

Central to artificial psychology is the notion of latency. These are constructs that are not directly measured but inferred through observed indicators, features, or behaviours [67]. In human psychology, this includes states like anxiety, trust, or cognitive dissonance. In artificial agents, it may refer to internal state vectors, attention distributions, or conceptual activations derived from a neural network's latent layer [31].

What complicates visualisation is that these constructs are not only unobservable, but they are context-dependent and dynamic. Their form may shift depending on the model, the training data, or the task at hand. Thus, visualisation must not reify them, but rather offer transparent proxies [68].

An agent's internal representation of *fear* is not the same as a neuroscientist's measure of amygdala activation. Yet it can be meaningfully explored through:

- *Activation maps* over latent emotion dimensions [69]
- *Trajectory plots* of affective change over time [70] or
- *Attention-weighted word clouds* showing lexical emphasis in response to stimuli [71]

These are not visualisations of the phenomenon itself, but of the model's *interpretive scaffold*. To visualise the invisible, we must first accept that we are rendering conceptual architecture, not physical terrain.

Graphs offer a powerful medium for representing abstract mental architecture, especially in models that simulate causal reasoning, belief propagation, or concept interaction [25, 30]. In FCMs, each node represents a concept, such as attention, arousal, or moral judgment, and edges carry weights indicating the direction and magnitude of influence. These allow both interpretability and mathematical modelling of dynamic reasoning [72]. When visualised:

- Node colour can encode concept category (e.g. emotional and behavioural).
- Edge thickness can reflect the strength of influence.
- And spatial positioning can signal centrality or modularity [26].

Similarly, *Bayesian Networks* and *Directed Acyclic Graphs* (DAGs) are used to model conditional dependencies in psychological inference or agent planning [73, 74]. Their visualisations make explicit the assumptions encoded in the structure, showing how beliefs evolve or how outcomes depend on latent states. But the graph layout is not neutral. A poor spatial arrangement can hide clusters, obscure hierarchy, or imply symmetry where none exists [75]. Visualisation must reflect theoretical interpretability, not just algorithmic elegance.

Artificial psychological models often embed internal states in *high-dimensional latent spaces*. They are represented as vectors that store distributed representations of belief, emotion, or situational awareness [76]. To understand or explain these, researchers frequently apply *dimensionality reduction techniques* like:

- *Principal Component Analysis* (PCA) for variance-based projection
- *t-Distributed Stochastic Neighbour Embedding* (*t*-SNE) for local neighbourhood preservation or
- *UMAP* for topological fidelity [77]

These projections allow internal states, e.g. emotional embeddings of dialogue turns, to be visualised as clusters or trajectories, making it possible to observe convergence, divergence, or periodicity in artificial agents [78]. Dimensionality reduction introduces distortion. t-SNE can be misled by exaggerating cluster separation, while PCA may compress meaningful axes [15]. These methods must be presented with *caveats*, including scale ambiguity, projection randomness, and interpretive uncertainty [79]. A best practice is to overlay *labelled clusters*, *density contours*, or *temporal paths* to reveal structure while acknowledging projection artefacts.

Psychological constructs are not static. They unfold, interact, decay, and transform. Artificial models of mind must reflect this, and so must their visualisations. Effective formats for visualising temporal evolution include:

- *Emotion ribbons* over time series, encoding valence and arousal per turn or episode [80, 81]
- *State transition diagrams*, common in reinforcement learning models of behaviour [82] or
- *Belief shift trajectories*, where agent estimates evolve during dialogue or therapy simulation [83]

In systems trained on conversation or interactive learning, attention weights can be visualised across dialogue turns using *temporal heatmaps*, while *stacked area plots* may reveal shifts in internal confidence or intent [84]. Animation is essential in interactive visualisation tools. Slider-based control or video-like playback can reveal change over model time. Such tools enhance interpretability for clinicians, researchers, or end users. Many artificial psychology models are *multimodal*, since they are processing text, facial expressions, physiological signals, and environmental context simultaneously. To visualise these systems, hybrid formats are needed. Examples include:

- *Sankey diagrams* to show state transitions across modalities
- *Graph-over-time panels* to reveal changes in conceptual weights across interaction phases and
- *Interactive dashboards* integrating graphs, timelines, and embeddings [85]

Visualisation in such contexts is not a single image but a multi-layered interface, designed to explore, interpret, and validate complex internal models. In human-in-the-loop systems or explainable AI contexts, these tools are vital for debugging, evaluating fairness, or inspecting behaviour [86].

Visualising internal psychological representations, especially in artificial systems, raises urgent *ethical questions*. When we draw emotion or belief, we reify it, potentially overstating the certainty or coherence of a construct [87]. In health, education, or justice applications, such visuals may carry persuasive weight without adequate epistemic support. Best practices demand:

- Uncertainty visualisations (e.g. density shading and confidence bands)
- Clear disclaimers when visualising theoretical constructs and
- Avoidance of anthropomorphising agents unless explicitly intended and justified [88]

The most effective visualisations do not claim truth. They offer informed transparency and support dialogue between the model, user, and theorist.

To visualise psychological constructs, real or artificial, is to engage in a scientific and philosophical act. It requires making *structure visible where none is physically evident*, constructing meaning out of computation. In artificial psychology, this act is central to understanding how systems function and how they simulate, support, or extend the human mind. These visualisations are not just reflections of data. They are theorised inscriptions, cognitive mirrors that expose assumptions, relationships, and tensions in our models. Done well, they open a new space for thinking. Done poorly, they obscure or mislead.

As our models grow in complexity and abstraction, the need for thoughtful, ethical, and expressive visualisation becomes not optional, but essential. The visualization of the invisible is not merely a technical challenge; it constitutes the defining challenge of artificial psychology.

4 Case Study

In previous sections, we have emphasised how the effectiveness of data visualisation profoundly shapes the interpretation and communication of psychological research. Here, through a practical and realistic example, we demonstrate how these principles come into play when working with psychological data. This case study utilises a comprehensive psychological dataset encompassing cognitive, emotional, social, behavioural, and demographic variables collected from 800 adult participants. Our

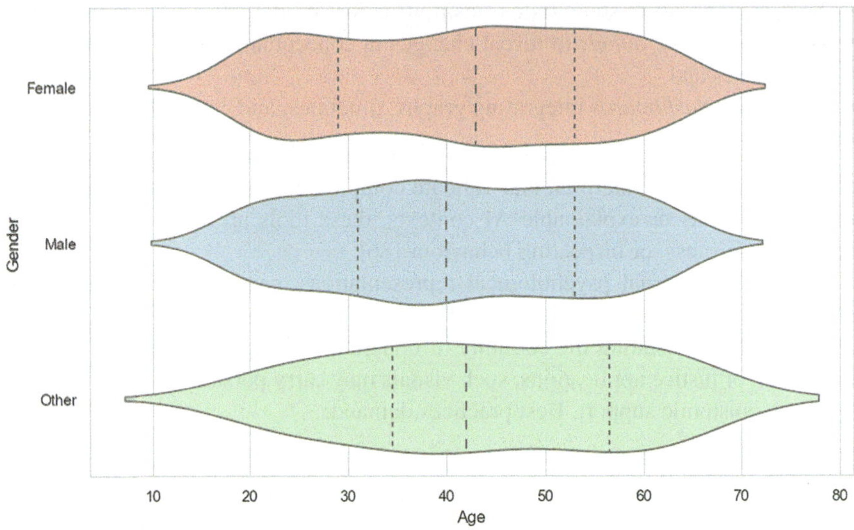

Fig. 4 Age distribution by gender

goal is to apply the best practices discussed previously, demonstrating both strong visualisation strategies and highlighting common pitfalls to avoid.

We begin with demographic characteristics, recognising the critical role demographic factors can play in psychological studies. Figure 4 illustrates these demographic distributions using an enhanced violin plot. Unlike simpler histograms or bar plots, the violin plot provides detailed information about the density of ages across different gender categories, offering insights beyond mere averages or medians. The plot reveals that age distributions are broadly similar across genders, although subtle variations in age dispersion can be observed. Such plots exemplify clarity and depth, directly aligning with widely adopted principles which emphasise careful colour selection, clarity, and detailed density information rather than oversimplified summaries.

Next, we examine the intersection of cognitive abilities and emotional states, which often forms the backbone of psychological analysis. The relationship between `Cognitive Score` and `Anxiety Score` is effectively visualised using a scatterplot enriched with marginal density plots (see Fig. 5). This visualisation elegantly combines the strengths of scatterplots, showing precise relationships, with density plots, which clearly illustrate distributions along each axis. Readers can quickly discern a mild negative correlation, indicating participants with higher cognitive scores typically report lower anxiety levels. The marginal densities reveal detailed distributions, offering a deeper understanding of how each variable individually behaves. This visualisation strategy underscores one of our chapter's central points: Integrating multiple visual elements enhances interpretability and depth, fostering comprehensive insights rather than superficial impressions.

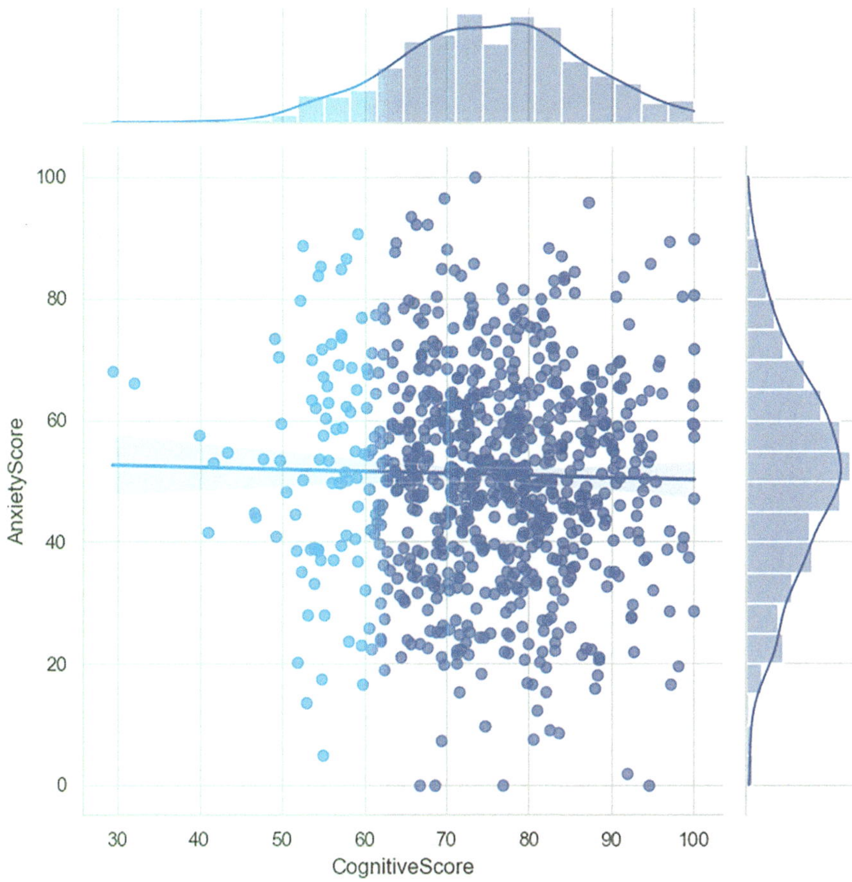

Fig. 5 Cognitive score vs. anxiety score with marginal density

Expanding beyond bivariate analysis, we introduce multidimensional visualisation to explore how `Stress`, `Social Engagement`, and `Physical Activity Level` interrelate. Figure 6 visually communicates three continuous variables simultaneously. Each bubble's position reflects a participant's stress level and social engagement, while bubble size and colour gradient denote physical activity levels. This innovative plot demonstrates a practical application of visual encoding principles, effectively managing complexity without overwhelming readers. It reveals that participants with higher physical activity generally exhibit lower stress and higher social engagement. Such multidimensional plots, when executed thoughtfully, enable researchers to communicate complex interactions intuitively, avoiding confusion or visual clutter.

To illuminate relationships and dependencies across multiple psychological variables, we present Fig. 7. This heatmap succinctly represents interrelations

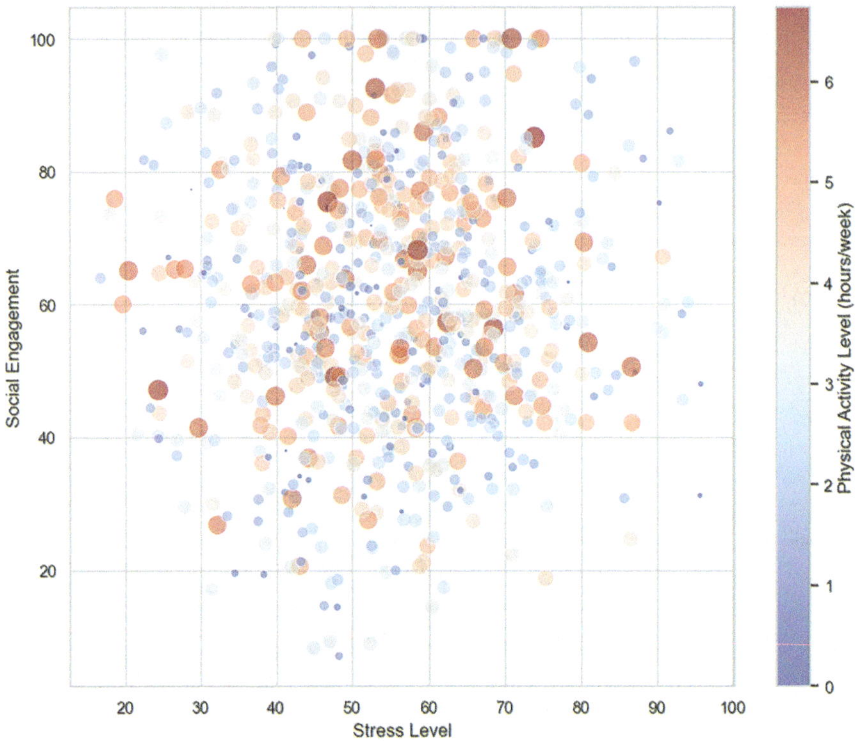

Fig. 6 Bubble plot of stress, societal engagement, and physical activity

between cognitive (`Cognitive Score`), emotional (`Anxiety` and `Stress`), behavioural (`Physical Activity`, `Sleep Quality`, `Screen Time`), and social (`Social Engagement`) variables. Using a carefully selected colour palette, where positive correlations appear in warm hues and negative correlations in cooler tones, this visualisation effectively communicates key psychological insights at a glance. For instance, strong positive relationships between `Anxiety` and `Stress` and negative relationships between `Stress` and `Sleep Quality` emerge clearly. This carefully structured correlation heatmap exemplifies an effective approach to summarising complex relational data, avoiding common pitfalls such as overly granular or confusing presentations that can obscure rather than illuminate insights.

To visualise psychological constructs, especially within artificial cognition, is to operate in a space defined by *translation, abstraction, and ethics*. Unlike plotting a distribution of heights or reaction times, visualising emotion, belief, or intention is a representational act that involves metaphor, inference, and creative approximation [37, 45]. As artificial psychology transitions from academic theory to real-world implementation in clinical support tools, conversational agents, or educational software, the need for reflective and principled visualisation has never been greater.

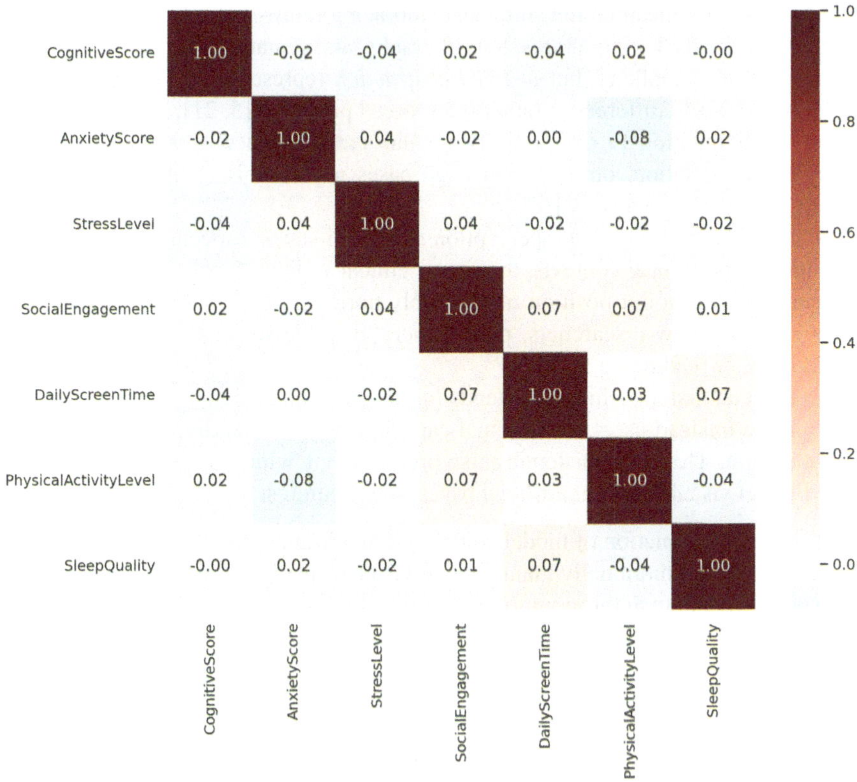

Fig. 7 Correlation heatmap of psychological variables

We often treat charts as answers: end points that communicate a model's performance or a study's findings. But visualisations can also be questions. They can highlight uncertainty, challenge assumptions, reveal anomalies, or provoke new hypotheses [58, 89]. The most powerful figures in psychological modelling often reveal what was not expected. A time-series plot may show a relapse spike after intervention. A confusion matrix may expose a systematic misclassification of neutral states as negative. A UMAP projection may reveal emergent emotion clusters not predicted by theory [15].

To *see beyond the data* is to approach visualisation as epistemic dialogue, not passive output. This shift is especially crucial in modelling artificial psychology, where the internal state of a model is often inaccessible except through its visual traces [65, 79]. Psychological phenomena are rarely reducible to clean dichotomies or Gaussian distributions. Human affect fluctuates, belief changes incrementally, and cognitive dissonance may coexist with behavioural certainty. Artificial systems that attempt to model such complexity must preserve its richness in visual form [62, 90].

This does not mean clutter. It means embracing multi-layered visual narratives: uncertainty bands, temporal arcs, hybrid graphs, and semantic overlays. The clarity we seek is not simplicity, but *justified abstraction* representing a minimalism that reflects real-world differences rather than forced precision [5, 21]. Effective visuals resist the temptation to oversimplify mental states into icons or single metrics. They frame variation, outliers, and edge cases not as noise, but as evidence of psychological heterogeneity [67].

When visualisations shape perception of mental states, especially in vulnerable populations or clinical contexts, they carry ethical weight. A colour gradient might suggest urgency; a dot position might imply normality or deviation. These visual cues influence how researchers, practitioners, or policymakers interpret emotion, motivation, or readiness [33, 36].

In artificial systems, this risk extends further: A visualisation of agent *empathy* or *trust* might mislead users about actual capacity for understanding. Such errors are not aesthetic. They are epistemic misrepresentations with real consequences [64, 88]. Ethical visualisation in artificial psychology requires:

- Transparent depiction of model confidence and limitations
- Avoidance of emotionally manipulative visual tropes
- Reflexivity about anthropomorphism and metaphor
- Accountability for user interpretations

These responsibilities are not optional. They are foundational to scientific integrity and human-centred AI [86, 91]. More than ever, researchers need not just statistical fluency, but *visual intelligence*, a capacity to reason, critique, and create through images. This includes:

- Knowing how to pair visual form with conceptual meaning
- Recognising when a chart misleads by omission, distortion, or overload
- Understanding that a figure is a *scientific argument in graphic form* [20, 45]

Visual intelligence also demands empathy: The ability to anticipate how different audiences, such as students, clinicians, and stakeholders, will interpret what they see. It asks researchers to not only generate insights but to design for understanding. In artificial psychology, where new constructs are constantly being created, this intelligence becomes the interface between algorithmic abstraction and human meaning [68, 87].

As this book concludes, its central premise crystallises: Visualisation is not just about aesthetics, metrics, or communication. It is about understanding. When you choose a colour scheme, you are shaping perception. When you show or hide uncertainty, you are influencing belief. When you draw the internal structure of a model, you are defining how the mind, human or artificial, is imagined. The future of artificial psychology will not be shaped by deeper networks alone. It will be shaped by how we explain those networks, how we interrogate their claims, and how we make their inferences legible to human minds. That future will be *visual*.

Let your plots reveal differences. Let your diagrams respect complexity. Let your stories be transparent. And most of all, let your visualisations serve not just insight, but insightful reflection. Because to see beyond the data is to begin to *see responsibly*.

References

1. N. Kovač, K. Ratković, H. Farahani, P. Watson, A practical applications guide to machine learning regression models in psychology with python. Methods Psychol. **11**, 100156 (2024)
2. E.R. Tufte, P.R. Graves-Morris, *The Visual Display of Quantitative Information*, vol. 2.9 (Graphics Press Cheshire, Connecticut, 1983)
3. N. Kovač, K. Ratković, P. Watson, H. Farahani, F. Bagheri Sheykhangafshe, Machine learning classification models for predicting chronic pain. Curr. Psychol. **44**, 15409–15422 (2025)
4. G.J. McInerny, M. Chen, R. Freeman, D. Gavaghan, M. Meyer, F. Rowland, D.J. Spiegelhalter, M. Stefaner, G. Tessarolo, J. Hortal, Information visualisation for science and policy: engaging users and avoiding bias. Trends Ecol. Evol. **29**(3), 148 (2014)
5. C. Ware, *Information Visualization: Perception for Design* (Morgan Kaufmann, Los Altos, 2019)
6. W.S. Cleveland, R. McGill, Graphical perception and graphical methods for analyzing scientific data. Science **229**(4716), 828 (1985)
7. J. Heer, M. Bostock, V. Ogievetsky, A tour through the visualization zoo. Commun. ACM **53**(6), 59 (2010)
8. T. Munzner, *Visualization Analysis and Design* (CRC Press, Boca Raton, 2014)
9. L. Wilkinson, *The Grammar of Graphics* (Springer, Berlin, 2005)
10. A. Unwin, *Graphical Data Analysis with R* (Chapman and Hall/CRC, 2018)
11. M. Friendly, D.J. Denis, Milestones in the history of thematic cartography. Statistical graphics, and data visualization. http://www.datavis. CA/milestones **32**, 13 (2001)
12. C.N. Knaflic, *Storytelling with Data: A Data Visualization Guide for Business Professionals* (John Wiley & Sons, New York, 2015)
13. H. Wickham, *ggplot2: Elegant Graphics for Data Analysis* (Springer, Berlin, 2016)
14. L. van der Maaten, G. Hinton, Visualizing data using t-SNE. J. Mach. Learn. Res. **9**, 2579 (2008)
15. M. Wattenberg, F. Viégas, I. Johnson, How to use t-SNE effectively. Distill **1**(10), e2 (2016)
16. S. Few, *Now You See It: Simple Visualization Techniques for Quantitative Analysis* (Analytics Press, 2009)
17. J.J. Thomas, *Illuminating the Path: The Research And Development Agenda for Visual Analytics* (IEEE Computer Society, 2005)
18. A. Gelman, J. Hill, *Data Analysis Using Regression and Multilevel/Hierarchical Models* (Cambridge University Press, Cambridge, 2006)
19. L.J. Cronbach, P.E. Meehl, Construct validity in psychological tests. Psychol. Bull. **52**(4), 281 (1955)
20. M. Lima, *Visual Complexity: Mapping Patterns of Information* (Princeton Architectural Press, Princeton, 2011)
21. S. Few, *Show Me the Numbers: Designing Tables and Graphs to Enlighten* (Analytics Press, 2012)
22. C.A. Brewer, et al., Color use guidelines for data representation, in *Proceedings of the Section on Statistical Graphics* (American Statistical Association, 1999), pp. 55–60
23. R. Plutchik, The nature of emotions: human emotions have deep evolutionary roots, a fact that may explain their complexity and provide tools for clinical practice. Am. Sci. **89**(4), 344 (2001)
24. S. Bateman, R.L. Mandryk, C. Gutwin, A. Genest, D. McDine, C. Brooks, Useful junk? The effects of visual embellishment on comprehension and memorability of charts, in *Proceedings of the SIGCHI Conference on Human Factors in Computing Systems* (2010), pp. 2573–2582

25. B. Kosko, Fuzzy cognitive maps. Int. J. Man-Mach. Stud. **24**(1), 65 (1986)
26. A.P. Christensen, H. Golino, On the equivalency of factor and network loadings. Behav. Res. Methods **53**(4), 1563 (2021)
27. H. Farahani, P. Watson, T. Bezan, N. Kovač, L.C. Winter, M. Blagojević, P. Azadfallah, A. Allahyari, S. Masoumian, P. Jiménez, PsAIchology: an intelligent direction in psychological sciences, in *10th International Scientific Conference Technics, Informatics and Education-TIE 2024* (Faculty of Technical Sciences Čačak, University of Kragujevac, 2024)
28. F. Pedregosa, G. Varoquaux, A. Gramfort, V. Michel, B. Thirion, O. Grisel, M. Blondel, P. Prettenhofer, R. Weiss, V. Dubourg, et al., Scikit-learn: machine learning in Python. J. Mach. Learn. Res. **12**, 2825 (2011)
29. A. Vaswani, N. Shazeer, N. Parmar, J. Uszkoreit, L. Jones, A.N. Gomez, L. Kaiser, I. Polosukhin, Attention is all you need, in *Advances in Neural Information Processing Systems (NeurIPS)*, vol. 30 (2017)
30. E.I. Papageorgiou, J.L. Salmeron, A review of fuzzy cognitive maps research during the last decade. IEEE Trans. Fuzzy Syst. **21**(1), 66 (2012)
31. Z.C. Lipton, The mythos of model interpretability: in machine learning, the concept of interpretability is both important and slippery. Queue **16**(3), 31 (2018)
32. A. Gelman, E. Loken, The garden of forking paths: why multiple comparisons can be a problem, even when there is no "fishing expedition" or "p-hacking" and the research hypothesis was posited ahead of time. Dept. Stat. Columbia Univ. **348**(1–17), 3 (2013)
33. J. Hullman, N. Diakopoulos, Visualization rhetoric: framing effects in narrative visualization. IEEE Trans. Vis. Comput. Graph. **17**(12), 2231 (2011)
34. H. Farahani, P. Watson, N. Kovač, F.B. Sheykhangafshe, P. Azadfallah, A. Allahyari, F. Esrafilian, R.R. Chesli, in *International Handbook of Love: Transcultural and Transdisciplinary Perspectives* (Springer, Berlin, 2025), pp. 1–22
35. A. Niculescu-Mizil, R. Caruana, Predicting good probabilities with supervised learning, in *Proceedings of the 22nd International Conference on Machine Learning* (2005), pp. 625–632
36. R. Binns, M. Van Kleek, M. Veale, U. Lyngs, J. Zhao, N. Shadbolt, 'It's reducing a human being to a percentage' perceptions of justice in algorithmic decisions, in *Proceedings of the 2018 CHI Conference on Human Factors in Computing Systems* (2018), pp. 1–14
37. M. Chen, L. Floridi, R. Borgo, What is visualization really for? in *The Philosophy of Information Quality* (2014), pp. 75–93
38. W.S. Cleveland, *Visualizing Data* (Hobart Press, 1993)
39. E.R. Tufte, *The Visual Display of Quantitative Information* (Graphics Press, 2001)
40. M.A. Borkin, A.A. Vo, Z. Bylinskii, P. Isola, S. Sunkavalli, A. Oliva, H. Pfister, What makes a visualization memorable? IEEE Trans. Vis. Comput. Graph. **19**(12), 2306 (2013)
41. H. Wainer, How to display data badly. Am. Stat. **38**(2), 137 (1984)
42. B. Shneiderman, in *The Craft of Information Visualization* (Elsevier, Amsterdam, 2003), pp. 364–371
43. A. Cairo, *The Truthful Art: Data, Charts, and Maps for Communication* (New Riders, 2016)
44. C. Kelleher, T. Wagener, Ten guidelines for effective data visualization in scientific publications. Environ. Model. Softw. **26**(6), 822 (2011)
45. E.R. Tufte, E.R. Tufte, *Beautiful Evidence*, vol. 1 (Graphics Press Cheshire, Cincinnati, 2006)
46. K.B. Schloss, S.E. Palmer, Aesthetic response to color combinations: preference, harmony, and similarity. Attention Percep. Psychophys. **73**, 551 (2011)
47. K.D. Moreland, Why we use bad color maps and what you can do about it. Tech. rep., Sandia National Lab.(SNL-NM), Albuquerque, NM (United States) (2015)
48. R. Bujack, T.L. Turton, F. Samsel, C. Ware, D.H. Rogers, J. Ahrens, The good, the bad, and the ugly: a theoretical framework for the assessment of continuous colormaps. IEEE Trans. Vis. Comput. Graph. **24**(1), 923 (2017)
49. C.O. Wilke, *Fundamentals of Data Visualization: A Primer on Making Informative and Compelling Figures* (O'Reilly Media, 2019)
50. Z. Gu, R. Eils, M. Schlesner, Complex heatmaps reveal patterns and correlations in multidimensional genomic data. Bioinformatics **32**(18), 2847 (2016)

51. A. Gelman, J.B. Carlin, H.S. Stern, D.B. Dunson, A. Vehtari, D.B. Rubin, *Bayesian Data Analysis*, 3rd edn. (Chapman and Hall/CRC, 2013)
52. E. Segel, J. Heer, Narrative visualization: telling stories with data. IEEE Trans. Vis. Comput. Graph. **16**(6), 1139 (2010)
53. J.H. Larkin, H.A. Simon, Why a diagram is (sometimes) worth ten thousand words. Cogn. Sci. **11**(1), 65 (1987)
54. J. Bruner, The narrative construction of reality. Critical Inquiry **18**(1), 1 (1991)
55. H.P. Abbott, *The Cambridge Introduction to Narrative* (Cambridge University Press, Cambridge, 2020)
56. R.C. Schank, R.P. Abelson, in *Knowledge and Memory: The Real Story* (Psychology Press, 2014), pp. 1–85
57. R. Kosara, J. Mackinlay, Storytelling: the next step for visualization. Computer **46**(5), 44 (2013)
58. S.L. Franconeri, L.M. Padilla, P. Shah, J.M. Zacks, J. Hullman, The science of visual data communication: what works. Psychol. Sci. Public Interest **22**(3), 110 (2021)
59. M.C. Green, T.C. Brock, The role of transportation in the persuasiveness of public narratives. J. Pers. Soc. Psychol. **79**(5), 701 (2000)
60. J.W. Tukey, et al., *Exploratory Data Analysis*, vol. 2 (Springer, Berlin, 1977)
61. G. Lakoff, M. Johnson, *Metaphors We Live By* (University of Chicago Press, Chicago, 2008)
62. M. Galesic, R. Garcia-Retamero, Graph literacy: a cross-cultural comparison. Med. Decis. Making **31**(3), 444 (2011)
63. J. Hullman, Why authors don't visualize uncertainty. IEEE Trans. Vis. Comput. Graph. **26**(1), 130 (2019)
64. M.T. Ribeiro, S. Singh, C. Guestrin, Why should I trust you? Explaining the predictions of any classifier, in *Proceedings of the 22nd ACM SIGKDD International Conference on Knowledge Discovery and Data Mining* (ACM, New York, 2016), pp. 1135–1144. https://doi.org/10.1145/2939672.2939778
65. K. Friston, The free-energy principle: a unified brain theory? Nat. Rev. Neurosci. **11**(2), 127 (2010)
66. M. Dastani, L. van der Torre, Programming BOID-Plan Agents deliberating about conflicts among defeasible mental attitudes and plans, in *Proceedings of the Third International Joint Conference on Autonomous Agents and Multiagent Systems, 2004. AAMAS 2004.* (IEEE, Piscataway, 2004), pp. 706–713
67. K.A. Bollen, Latent variables in psychology and the social sciences. Annu. Rev. Psychol. **53**(1), 605 (2002)
68. J. Kleinberg, S. Mullainathan, M. Raghavan, Inherent trade-offs in the fair determination of risk scores (2016). arXiv preprint arXiv:1609.05807
69. B. Zhou, A. Khosla, A. Lapedriza, A. Oliva, A. Torralba, Learning deep features for discriminative localization, in *Proceedings of the IEEE Conference on Computer Vision and Pattern Recognition* (2016), pp. 2921–2929
70. R. Cowie, E. Douglas-Cowie, N. Tsapatsoulis, G. Votsis, S. Kollias, W. Fellenz, J.G. Taylor, Emotion recognition in human-computer interaction. IEEE Signal Process. Mag. **18**(1), 32 (2001)
71. D. Bahdanau, K. Cho, Y. Bengio, Neural machine translation by jointly learning to align and translate (2014). arXiv preprint arXiv:1409.0473
72. C.D. Stylios, P.P. Groumpos, et al., Mathematical formulation of fuzzy cognitive maps, in *Proceedings of the 7th Mediterranean Conference on Control and Automation*, vol. 2014 (Mediterranean Control Association Nicosia, Cyprus, 1999), pp. 2251–2261
73. J. Pearl, et al., Models, reasoning and inference. Cambridge University Press **19**(2), 3 (2000)
74. M.D. Lee, E.J. Wagenmakers, *Bayesian Cognitive Modeling: A Practical Course* (Cambridge University Press, Cambridge, 2014)
75. A. Noack, Energy models for graph clustering. J. Graph Algorithms Appl. **11**(2), 453 (2007)
76. T. Mikolov, K. Chen, G. Corrado, J. Dean, Efficient estimation of word representations in vector space (2013). arXiv preprint arXiv:1301.3781

77. L. McInnes, J. Healy, J. Melville, UMAP: uniform manifold approximation and projection for dimension reduction (2018). arXiv preprint arXiv:1802.03426
78. L. Wang, W. Ouyang, X. Wang, H. Lu, Visual tracking with fully convolutional networks, in *Proceedings of the IEEE International Conference on Computer Vision* (2015), pp. 3119–3127
79. J. Chuang, D. Ramage, C. Manning, J. Heer, Interpretation and trust: designing model-driven visualizations for text analysis, in *Proceedings of the SIGCHI Conference on Human Factors in Computing Systems* (2012), pp. 443–452
80. J.A. Russell, A circumplex model of affect. J. Pers. Soc. Psychol. **39**(6), 1161 (1980)
81. D. McDuff, R. El Kaliouby, R.W. Picard, Crowdsourcing facial responses to online videos. IEEE Trans. Affect. Comput. **3**(4), 456 (2012)
82. R.S. Sutton, A.G. Barto, *Reinforcement Learning: An Introduction*, 2nd edn. (MIT Press, Cambridge, 2018)
83. N. Asghar, P. Poupart, J. Hoey, X. Jiang, L. Mou, Affective neural response generation, in *Advances in Information Retrieval: 40th European Conference on IR Research, ECIR 2018, Grenoble, France, March 26–29, 2018, Proceedings 40* (Springer, Berlin, 2018), pp. 154–166
84. J. Vig, A multiscale visualization of attention in the transformer model (2019). arXiv preprint arXiv:1906.05714
85. J. Heer, B. Shneiderman, Interactive dynamics for visual analysis: a taxonomy of tools that support the fluent and flexible use of visualizations. Queue **10**(2), 30 (2012)
86. L.H. Gilpin, D. Bau, B.Z. Yuan, A. Bajwa, M. Specter, L. Kagal, Explaining explanations: an overview of interpretability of machine learning, in *2018 IEEE 5th International Conference on Data Science and Advanced Analytics (DSAA)* (IEEE, Piscataway, 2018), pp. 80–89
87. Y. Zhang, X. Chen, et al., Explainable recommendation: a survey and new perspectives. Found. Trends® Inform. Retrieval **14**(1), 1 (2020)
88. M.M.A. de Graaf, B.F. Malle, People's judgments of human and robot behaviors: a robust set of behaviors and some discrepancies, in *Companion of the 2018 ACM/IEEE International Conference on Human-Robot Interaction*, HRI '18 (Association for Computing Machinery, New York, 2018), pp. 97–98. https://doi.org/10.1145/3173386.3177051
89. K. Healy, J. Moody, Data visualization in sociology. Annu. Rev. Sociol. **40**(1), 105 (2014)
90. P. Cairns, A.L. Cox, *Research Methods for Human-Computer Interaction*, vol. 10 (Cambridge University Press Cambridge, 2008)
91. B. Mittelstadt, C. Russell, S. Wachter, Explaining explanations in AI, in *Proceedings of the Conference on Fairness, Accountability, and Transparency* (2019), pp. 279–288

Index

A
Agent-based modelling (ABMs), 504, 506, 508, 509, 511, 512, 584
Analytical frameworks, 93, 334, 415, 538
Artificial intelligence (AI), 4, 5, 27, 37, 39, 151, 153–169, 291, 334, 335, 447, 575

B
Bayesian hypothesis testing, 372, 377–379, 540
Bayesian inference, 46, 151, 371, 372, 374–377, 380–382, 506
Behavioural data, 119, 270
Behavioural prediction, 484
Behavioural segmentation, 485
Behavioural simulation, 508, 510, 511, 513
Bootstrapping, 48, 77, 174, 252, 253, 358, 395, 414, 415, 549

C
Chart design, 582, 584
Classification accuracy, 306, 389, 395, 400, 411, 431, 477
Clustering algorithms, 48, 161, 248, 270–276, 285, 477
Cluster validation, 158
Communication analysis, 39, 244, 448, 464, 469
Complex data structures, 270, 330, 555–557
Computational modelling, 46, 153, 156, 467, 504, 508, 556
Conclusion building, 80
Confidence intervals, 26, 46, 54, 187, 257, 372, 376, 511, 527, 530, 531, 534–538, 541, 560, 566, 574, 579, 580, 582
Control flow, 11, 44, 460

D
Data cleaning, 17, 22, 104, 109, 110, 120, 454, 455
Data collection methods, 85, 91, 94–99
Data consistency, 47, 68–70, 73, 85, 127, 134–136, 179, 187, 275, 584
Data inputs, 64–68, 73
Data interpolation, 130–134
Data manipulation, 5, 6, 18, 21, 22, 24, 104–107, 110
Data modelling, 173–200
Data quality, 42, 49, 68, 120, 135, 145, 155, 161, 173, 229
Data science concepts, 8
Dataset representation, 105, 106
Data structures, 14, 16–18, 20, 43, 68, 81, 104, 106, 107, 154, 216, 237, 248, 270–272, 284, 314, 318, 330, 335, 393, 486, 555–558, 564, 567, 576, 585
Data validation, 15, 47–49, 68–73
Data visualization, 7, 22, 24–28, 49, 155, 553, 576, 577, 579, 582, 589
Decision trees, 43, 156, 183, 187, 409–413, 415, 427–429, 431, 433, 436–438, 440, 442, 477, 499

N. Kovač et al. (eds.), *Data Science in Psychology*,
https://doi.org/10.1007/978-3-032-18312-5

Differential item functioning, 229, 233, 237–239
Dimensionality detection, 157
Dynamic processes, 169, 234, 334, 342, 371

E
Effect size, 43, 45, 46, 155, 238, 374, 376, 377, 527, 530–534, 537, 538, 540, 542, 548, 553, 575, 583
Elastic net, 351–369, 394, 485
Estimation methods, 206–208, 251
Exploratory analysis, 153, 250, 464, 485
Exploratory graph analysis, 247–266, 575

F
Factor loadings, 204–206, 209–211, 213, 214, 219, 220, 222, 224, 250, 261, 324, 549
Feature importance, 413, 414, 432

G
Generalised additive models (GAMs), 184, 329–331
Generalized estimating equations (GEEs), 329–332
Genetic algorithms, 393, 396, 477, 485, 488, 490, 496
Graded response model, 228, 233

H
Heuristic search, 496
Hierarchical clustering, 157, 271, 272, 285, 286, 288, 300, 301
Hyperparameter tuning, 129, 179, 182, 353, 357, 360, 389, 390, 396, 399, 412, 437

I
Inference, 27, 44, 46, 62, 91, 103, 131, 151, 153, 230, 239, 371–377, 380, 381, 414, 506–508, 515, 536, 539, 540, 553, 555, 575, 583, 584, 588, 592, 594
Item characteristics, 228, 229, 231–234, 236, 238, 239, 242, 249
Item response theory (IRT), 46, 135, 227–245, 377, 481

K
Kernel functions, 389–393, 395, 399, 400
K-means clustering, 271, 272, 285, 301

L
Latent classes, 295–319
Latent growth models, 327
Latent profiles, 295–319
Latent structure, 151, 244, 247, 249–251, 254, 259, 261, 271, 296, 300, 303–306, 314
Latent traits, 205, 227–239, 242–244, 355, 376, 507
Latent variables, 204, 210–212, 214, 216, 222, 247, 249, 250, 295, 300, 302, 316, 324, 326, 515
Least Absolute Shrinkage and Selection Operator (LASSO), 156, 251, 258, 351–369
Linguistic features, 22, 448, 461
Longitudinal data, 68, 106, 131, 135, 186, 324, 341, 555, 556, 558, 580
Longitudinal interpretation, 556

M
Machine learning (ML), 7, 10, 16, 22–24, 27, 39, 93, 105, 130, 151, 153–169, 174, 270, 353, 392, 397, 398, 409, 413–415, 426, 427, 449, 452, 453, 455, 456, 460, 462, 474, 475, 477, 481, 557, 575
Markov Chain Monte Carlo (MCMC), sampling, 206, 373, 376, 381, 382
Measurement invariance, 205, 210, 231–234, 237, 249
Metaheuristic algorithms, 474, 475, 477–482, 494, 495
Missing data, 47, 49, 69–71, 74, 110, 116, 127–131, 133, 135, 142, 143, 145, 148, 154, 155, 185, 186, 189, 191, 193, 194, 198, 207, 325, 335, 413, 523, 524, 556
Mixture modelling, 303
Model assumptions, 212, 229
Model comparison, 43, 110, 237, 358, 511, 573
Model estimation, 206, 302, 303
Model evaluation, 169, 179, 302, 306, 396, 426, 474
Model fit, 203, 207, 208, 211–214, 220, 221, 231, 232, 241, 253, 254, 299, 301, 305, 306, 324–237, 327–329, 385, 538, 549
Modelling workflow, 10, 119, 305
Model selection, 48, 109, 161, 179, 184, 298, 302, 364, 390, 431, 439, 473
Model tuning, 481
Model validation, 209
Monte Carlo simulations, 504, 505, 507, 509, 511, 518, 519, 521
Multicollinearity, 55, 212, 304, 351–356, 358, 359, 361, 394, 483, 549

Multilevel regression, 154
Multivariate interpretation, 547–549

N
Network stability, 248, 252–256
Neural networks, 39, 42, 156, 159, 161, 162, 180, 183, 184, 186, 187, 260, 392, 416, 418–424, 428, 452, 453, 462, 506, 575, 587
NLP preprocessing, 159
Non-linear model, 331
Non-parametric tests, 47, 77, 154, 549–554
Normality tests, 137, 303

O
Observational data, 45, 98, 103, 104, 135
Outlier detection, 69, 111

P
Particle swarm optimisation (PSO), 396, 477, 478, 480–485
Posterior distribution, 43, 244, 335, 372–376, 379–384, 507, 512, 568, 569
Power analysis, 62, 534, 540
Predictive accuracy, 48, 184, 187, 355, 365, 394, 412, 413, 427, 439, 485, 508
Predictive behaviour modelling, 440
Predictive modelling, 23, 39, 46, 49, 93, 153, 173, 270, 291, 296, 301, 380, 397
Preprocessing pipelines, 460
Prior specification, 373, 376
Probabilistic modelling, 300, 301, 374
Psychological datasets, 26, 27, 68, 70, 71, 73, 104, 106, 128, 136, 139, 155, 157, 250, 255, 258, 259, 271, 274, 354, 357–359, 361, 381, 391, 393–396, 400, 426–428, 437, 458, 482, 518, 519, 558, 583, 589
Psychological heterogeneity, 281, 304, 515, 594
Psychological measurement, 71, 232, 244, 252, 253, 264, 482, 504, 550
Psychological networks, 26
Psychological science, 1, 6, 16, 33–57, 61–82, 87–99, 106, 134–136, 151, 155, 173, 255, 326, 410, 447–469, 482, 501, 510, 535, 538, 557, 582
Psychological statistics, 155
Psychometric modelling, 477, 506
Python basics, 1, 12, 13, 16, 105, 107, 512
Python data handling, 16, 17, 106
Python modules, 21–24

R
Random forests, 43, 110, 137, 156, 162, 183, 186, 187, 253, 390, 410, 413–415, 428, 429, 431, 433–435, 440
Regularization, 156, 251, 352, 354, 355, 357–360, 367, 388, 389, 394, 399, 400, 412, 428, 429, 434, 437, 438
Reporting guidelines, 534
Resampling techniques, 399
Research communication, 10, 27, 346
Research design, 62, 376, 504
Research methods, 291
Research validity, 88, 94, 155, 184, 364
Results evaluation, 164, 275
Ridge regression, 156, 351–369, 485

S
Scale validation, 239
Scientific reporting, 534
Sentiment analysis, 22, 23, 67, 161, 448, 451, 453–457, 459–461, 463, 465, 467, 469
Simulated annealing, 377, 396, 477, 478, 480
Simulation design, 557
Statistical methods, 6, 44, 46, 128, 136, 153, 155, 174, 329, 332, 523, 547
Statistical reasoning, 44
Statistical significance, 43, 45, 155, 213, 527, 529–531, 535, 538
Structural equation modelling (SEM), 203, 300, 329, 340, 556
Support vector machines (SVMs), 156, 161, 162, 183, 387–405, 425, 428, 430, 431, 433–435, 437–440, 575
Surveys and experiments, 85, 93, 103, 104, 127, 377, 511, 579

T
Technology in psychology, 38–40
Text mining, 450
Topic modelling, 67, 448, 451, 453, 457, 458, 461, 463, 467, 469

U
Unsupervised learning, 157, 158, 161, 273

The manufacturer's authorised representative in the EU is Springer Nature Customer Service Centre GmbH, Europaplatz 3, 69115 Heidelberg, Germany. If you have any concerns regarding our products, please contact ProductSafety@springernature.com

Printed and bound by CPI Group (UK) Ltd, Croydon, CR0 4YY
16/09/2026
02217815-0017